Information Systems Applications in the Arab Education Sector

Fayez Ahmad Albadri
Abu Dhabi University, UAE

Managing Director:	Lindsay Johnston
Senior Editorial Director:	Heather A. Probst
Book Production Manager:	Sean Woznicki
Development Manager:	Joel Gamon
Development Editor:	Hannah Abelbeck
Assistant Acquisitions Editor:	Kayla Wolfe
Typesetter:	Adrienne Freeland
Cover Design:	Nick Newcomer

Published in the United States of America by
Information Science Reference (an imprint of IGI Global)
701 E. Chocolate Avenue
Hershey PA 17033
Tel: 717-533-8845
Fax: 717-533-8661
E-mail: cust@igi-global.com
Web site: http://www.igi-global.com

Library of Congress Cataloging-in-Publication Data

Information systems applications in the Arab education sector / Fayez Ahmad Albadri, editor.
     p. cm.
  Includes bibliographical references and index.
  Summary: "This book is a rich source of knowledge about educational reforms through the adoption of information systems applications and technologies in the Arab region, covering current initiatives, approaches, issues, and challenges in the Arab education sector"--Provided by publisher.
  ISBN 978-1-4666-1984-5 (hardcover) -- ISBN 978-1-4666-1985-2 (ebook) -- ISBN 978-1-4666-1986-9 (print & perpetual access) 1. Educational technology--Arab countries. 2. Education--Effect of technological innovations on--Arab countries. 3. Educational change--Arab countries. 4. Information technology--Arab countries. I. Albadri, Fayez.
  LB1028.3.I519349 2012
  371.330917'4927--dc23
                                                      2012009904

British Cataloguing in Publication Data
A Cataloguing in Publication record for this book is available from the British Library.

All work contributed to this book is new, previously-unpublished material. The views expressed in this book are those of the authors, but not necessarily of the publisher.

Table of Contents

Detailed Table of Contents

The first chapter of the book provides an overview of the current status of ICT integration in the Arab higher education sectors. It elaborates on major initiatives that have been implemented by different Arab states It suggests solutions to overcome weaknesses for creative improvements with emphasis on training and infrastructure aspects.

Chapter 2 suggests that effective utilization of technology in UAE schools is highly dependent on teachers' role and ability to address the issue and challenges associated with the change. The chapter provides an overview of the net generation and computer technologies' impact on student performance and draws on aspects of UAE government's efforts to support educational reform and integrate technology into the K-12 classroom.

This chapter presents on how UAE educational system copes with the centralized governance of education in the country, and its impact on the technical architecture. The chapter also reports on the how Information Technology in Educational Management (ITEM) use has developed over the past decade and how it is evolving with the recent modifications towards modernization and decentralization.

This chapter examines the current status and selected aspects of ICT adoption and integration in the Emirate of Abu Dhabi, UAE, to examine the anticipated gains to learning, the problems and challenges hindering the realization of such gains, and the role of educational leaders to utilize technology for enhancing teaching and learning.

Chapter 5 provides educational leaders with a better understanding of the best practices and effective methodologies for proper ERP implementation and utilization in the Arab Education sector. It highlights the main ERP issues and challenges that need special attention to ascertain end-users' acceptance and stakeholders satisfaction.

Chapter 6 discusses the rapid growth in use of multimedia in United Arab Emirates in recent years. The chapter presents to how multimedia is perceived positively by both teachers and students alike. The study is also aimed at increasing educators' awareness of the importance of multimedia technology use in classrooms.

This chapter highlights the importance of admission and registration functions in higher education and discusses the main objectives and benefits from utilizing (ICT) applications to support the automation of admission and registration processes and functions in UAE higher education's institutes.

Chapter 8 examines the role and impact of UAE local culture, which is both conservative multicultural, on the adoption and utilization of new information systems and technologies to enhance core educational functions and enterprise support functions within Arab educational organizations.

Chapter 9 discusses the Jordanian Ministry of Education's reliance on both the local private sector and foreign aids to accelerate its integration of ICT required of the knowledge-based economy, and refers to issues that have risen when international partners and the local private sector were involved in ICT-based education initiatives in Jordan.

This chapter examines issues and challenges that hinder the effective integration of ICT in Arab education. The study suggests that although Arab governments have rapidly established a great number of schools and universities, most programs focus largely on the technology itself, placing little emphasis on the practical implications of the use of ICTs to meet broad educational objectives.

Chapter 11 discusses the issues of security, ethics, and culture, which are considered critical to the success of ICT adoption in the UAE education sector. It is suggested that a proper understanding of these issues in the UAE context is an important input to ICT integration into education sector.

Chapter 12 reflects the findings of a study to investigate the levels and patterns of use of the Internet among secondary school students in Al Ain city, UAE and attempts to assess the levels of parental supervision at home. Majority of respondents seem to use the Internet for communication and leisure rather than for educational purposes.

This chapter documents two case studies in higher education institutions in the Gulf, one in Saudi Arabia and another in the United Arab Emirates. The studies show how the use of computer-assisted language learning (CALL) positively affected Arab students' language skills and their attitudes towards learning English with technology.

This chapter highlights the value of blended learning by combining the advantages of face-to-face instruction and electronic supported learning. The investigation provides an overview of the technology influence supported by evidence from a UAE e-learning University case study.

Chapter 15 discusses a model of understanding student's learning and evaluating a group of adult students learning resulting from using an online discussion board as a social constructivist tool, for sharing and co-constructing knowledge.

Chapter 16 examines the e-learning sphere in the Arab World by exploring the status and quality of e-learning in Arab Universities located in the Middle East, and suggesting solutions for improved adoption of the e-learning technology. The study is supported by the results of a survey of the universities websites in the region and a survey into e-learning courses.

Chapter 17

This chapter describes a framework for building automatic recommendations in e-learning platforms of two modules: an off-line module which preprocesses data to build learner and content models, and an online module which uses these models on-the-fly to recognize the students' needs and goals, and predict a recommendation list.

This chapter proposes an adaptive system of personalized semantic search and recommendation of learning contents on the E-learning Web-based systems, which can help tailor learning content to learners profile ontology.

Chapter 19 describes how Wikis can be used to develop the writing performance of English as Foreign Language (EFL) prospective teachers. Wikis have the potential to provide a collaborative environment which encourages its users to engage effectively in the writing process and to develop their writing performance.

Chapter 20 explores the opportunities and challenges associated with using internet online learning communities to complement and aid conventional classes and enhance learning outcomes in UAE schools.

Chapter 21 reports on a study which invited school teachers and university academics in Egypt, as a developing and Arabic-speaking country, to cooperate in establishing a learning object repository to store, locate, and share quality learning objects for class teaching and e-learning programs.

The final chapter describes how a university in the United Arab Emirates is addressing the evident gap of suitable courses in Enterprise Information Systems that equip graduates with the appropriate competences and skills for the industry.

Foreword

In an era of globalization and a knowledge world economy, this important and authentic research is invaluable to readers in this part of the world and internationally who wish to better understand ICT in the Arab World.

The book includes the valuable contributions of academics, educators and practitioners from different countries, including the United Arab Emirates, The Hashemite Kingdom of Jordan, The Kingdom of Bahrain, The Republic of Egypt, the Sultanate of Oman, and the Kingdom of Saudi Arabia.

The scope of the book includes investigations and case studies related to a rich assortment of topics including; information technology and internet applications, e-learning, social networks for education, ERP for education, ICT education, and strategic information system planning in Arab educational organizations.

Moreover, it tackles the cultural practices, values, and ethics related to this important topic and emphasizes the proven positive correlation between ICT usage and academic achievement.

Schools, colleges and Higher Education have recognized that using technology can enhance the achievement of students by providing creative methods of teaching and flexible ways of assessing their performance. Moreover, examination bodies realized that technology can bring many advantages to increasing efficiency and students' engagement.

Not only does this valuable book list the challenges that technology faces in the Arab world, but it also alludes to the opportunities they present, and to their solutions while also addressing different related issues.

In summary, this research is an excellent literary addition to a unique and important domain, and will certainly be a precious resource for educational decision makers, as well as practitioners, in moving education and other sectors from good to great standing.

Samia Al Farra
Taaleem Management Group, United Arab Emirates

Samia Al Farra *is a prominent educator and a co-founding member of the Middle East International Baccalaureate Association (MEIBA), Samia's role is to lead the Academic and Operational Development of Taaleem, its schools, and initiatives. She is something of a household name on the International Baccalaureate circuit, especially on her home turf in the Arab world. Samia was a member of the IB Council of Foundation, IB Heads Committee and currently she is a member of the IB Regional Council. Samia brings a real depth and breadth of regional experience and understanding to the table. Having notched up over 37 years in the field of international education, she has amassed a huge bank of experience as an educator, as a Principal and through her senior positions on the Jordanian National Education Council, the CIS (Council of International Schools) and NEASC (New England Association of Schools and Colleges) accreditation teams, and the UWC (United World Colleges) national team. Gently spoken yet hard-hitting, Samia's drive and ability to embrace change has made her a pioneer within the Middle East's education arena. She is a firm believer in ICT and in its role in enhancing students' achievement.*

Preface

According to UNESCO, "*Education should be a means to empower children and adults alike to become active participants in the transformation of their societies. Learning should also focus on the values, attitudes and behaviors which enable individuals to learn to live together in a world characterized by diversity and pluralism*" (n.d.).

There is no doubt that only civilizations that had high regard for education, had a far-reaching and lasting influence on the shaping up of the way of life as we know it. As the torch of knowledge and illumination was handed from one civilization to another, and as new milestones and discoveries were achieved, the world was celebrating the intellect and brilliance of mankind in exploring the purpose of their very existence, and in developing and adopting the values of discovery and wisdom to ascertain human dignity and gratification.

What we are witnessing today in the modern world is merely the outcome of the strenuous efforts and the creativity of the unknown soldiers who laid the principles of education and research from all origins and nations and creeds, as no one nation alone can claim the credit for the prosperity, affluence, and technological advancement that we are enjoying the fruition of today. What we enjoy and take for granted is the end result of enormous collaborative efforts, contributed by the Chinese, the Indians, the ancient Egyptian, the Greek, the Romans, the Persians, the Moslem Arabs, and in recent eras the Europeans and Americans.

Today, information and communication technology is continually and creatively introducing new concepts, models, and applications that have a far-reaching impact on individuals, communities, and organizations, and rapidly redefining the way we live, travel, entertain, learn, educate, and do business. The nature of new ICT and Internet Web applications have boosted connectivity and speed, and improved efficiency and performance, leading to substantial cost reduction. These inherent features of the technology have appealed primarily to business organizations as tools to fasten and optimize business processes and integrate business functions as a recipe cost cuts and financial gains.

The rapid acceptance of ICT applications in the industry over the past few decades, coupled with major breakthroughs in both information technology and communication technology, have made it feasible to release new software applications and tools targeting new sectors such as government, transportation, entertainment, health, and education.

No one can deny that technology tools and systems –especially those which were designed specifically based on proper understanding of the education environment and requirements – represent effective solutions to many of the persisting problems in different sectors including education. On this rationale, ICT applications and systems have become key item in the annual budget of organizations of different types and sizes.

As a result of the political situation in the Arab region and the unfortunate waste of local resources, the Arab education system has suffered for many years from aging educational facilities, obsolete curricula, and unproven pedagogical models and instructional techniques. As would be expected, these inadequacies have reflected on students' performance, research status in universities, and the low ranking of Arab educational institutions compared with their international counterparts.

Concerned about this appalling state in their education sectors, different Arab governments – with aid of international organization or local private institutions – embarked on serious and ambitious initiatives to introduce reform and improvement to different aspects of their education systems. Interesting enough, all such initiative have endorsed ICT adoption and utilization as the main vehicle to leverage the positive change and to provide facilitate suitable solutions and emphasized the need for competent resources to manage the technology.

Consistent with its impressive record of investment in both human development and ICT, the United Arab Emirates government announced in 2005 its intent to launch a decade long project for comprehensive reform of the school education system with a budget of around USD 13 Billion. The scope of this major initiative included the following education aspects: curricula, teaching methods, assessment methods, use of ICT, libraries, school culture, facilities, teachers competences, school system, and school budgets. One of the main priorities in the implementation of the reform was to integrate ICT with learning, managing schools, and evaluating the system.

Anticipating the need for competent human resources from within the education sector to participate in this major initiative, Abu Dhabi University has developed a Master's program of Education in Educational Leadership to prepare teachers, administrator and educators with the appropriate skills and competences to take active roles as resources to the reform project. The program offers a number of courses and has included a dedicated course to ICT; (EDT519) Information Systems in Education.

This inception of the idea of this book was in one of the EDT519 classes as the class discussion was indicating the need for a textbook and a reference to be authored by Arab academics, educators, and educational leaders to capture the status of ICT applications in different Arab states and to develop an insight into the issues, challenges, and lessons learned.

With the scholarly contribution of 36 academics, educators, and educational leaders from different Arab countries including; UAE, KSA, Egypt, Oman, Bahrain, and Jordan, this book is excepted to enrich the understanding of the issues faced by many Arab countries in their efforts to adopt new educational technology applications and online learning models. The work will be also useful and stimulating to researchers, practitioners, and consultants from other regions to benefit from the captured experiences.

The textbook is organized in 22 chapters, covering in two parts, ICT applications and issues, and Internet Applications and related issues and challenges. Chapters 1-8 discuss various aspects of ICT applications in different Arab countries.

Chapter 1 draws a representative picture of the current status of ICT integration in the higher education in the Arab region. It presents examples of extensive Arab countries' efforts in terms of adopting ICT in Arabian Gulf countries such as Saudi Arabia, UAE and Qatar, West Asian Arab countries such as Yemen, Jordan, Lebanon and Syria and North African Arab countries such as Egypt, Tunisia and Morocco, highlighting major initiatives and drawing on evident issues and weaknesses to formulate meaningful lessons learnt that can be used to ensure effective and successful integration of new technologies in Arab higher education organizations.

Chapter 2 suggests that effective utilization of technology in UAE schools is highly dependent on teachers' role and ability to address the issue and challenges associated with the change. The chapter provides an overview of the net generation and computer technologies' impact on student performance and draws on aspects of UAE government's efforts to support educational reform and integrate technology into the K-12 classroom.

Chapter 3 presents on how UAE educational system copes with the centralized governance of education in the country and its impact on the centralized technical architecture. The chapter also reports on the how Information Technology in Educational Management (ITEM) use has developed over the past decade and how it is evolving with the recent modifications towards modernization and decentralization.

Chapter 4 examines important aspects of Information and Communication technology adoption and integration in the Emirate of Abu Dhabi, UAE, to examine the anticipated gains to learning, the problems and challenges hindering the realization of such gains and the role of educational leaders to utilize the technology for enhancing teaching and learning. The chapter benefits from previous studies related to the subject and the findings of a survey.

With educational leaders in mind, the main goal of chapter 5 is to develop a better understanding of the best practices and effective methodologies associated with the implementation and utilization of Enterprise Resource Planning (ERP) systems in the Arab Education sector. It also aims to familiarize Arab educational leaders with the key ERP challenges and issues in educational institutions and how to cope with such challenges and issues to ascertain the acceptance and satisfaction of end users and stakeholders.

Chapter 6 discusses the rapid growth in use of multimedia in United Arab Emirates in recent years. The chapter presents to how multimedia is perceived positively by both teachers and students alike for it makes the learning processes more comfortable and more enjoyable that leads to an improved performance. The study is also aimed at increasing educators' awareness of the importance of multimedia technology use in classrooms.

Chapter 7 highlights the importance of admission and registration functions in higher education and discusses the main objectives and sought benefits from utilizing (ICT) applications to support the automation of admission and registration processes and functions in UAE higher education's institutes. The chapter also suggests an effective approach to design and adopt such applications.

The interaction and dependencies between culture and technology has been recognized as an important aspect of the experience of technology adoption and utilization. Chapter 8 examines the role and impact of UAE local culture, which is both conservative multicultural, on the adoption and utilization of new information systems and technologies to enhance core educational functions and 'enterprise' support functions within Arab educational organizations.

Chapters 9- 11 highlight and discuss issues and challenges experienced while attempting to integrate ICT in education in different Arab countries.

Chapter 9 discusses the Jordanian Ministry of Education's reliance on both, local private sector (public-private partnership) and foreign aids, in order to accelerate its integration of ICT to meet the demands of the knowledge-based economy. The study also refers to major issues that have risen when international partners and the local private sector were involved in ICT-based education initiatives in Jordan.

Chapter 10 examines issues and challenges that hinder the effective integration of ICT in Arab education and suggests that most governmental programs focus largely on the technology itself, placing little emphasis on the practical implications of the use of ICTs to meet broad educational objectives.

Chapter 11 discusses some of the most important issues pertaining to information systems' adoption and implementation in the Arab education organizations. The study suggests that a proper attention to security, ethical, and cultural issues is critical to the success of integrating ICT into UAE education sector.

Chapters 12-21 discuss different Internet applications, tools, and social networks such as Wikis, discussion boards and blogs and how they can be used for educational purposes. It highlights new learning models such as online learning, e-learning, and blended learning;

Chapter 12 reflects the findings of a study to investigate the levels and patterns of use of the Internet among secondary school students in Al Ain City, UAE and attempts to assess the levels of parental supervision at home. The study recommends that the use of the Internet be monitored and guided by school authorities and parents, so as to prevent the misuse of this facility and to direct it towards teaching and learning improvement.

Chapter 13 documents two case studies in higher education institutions in the Gulf, one in Saudi Arabia and another in the United Arab Emirates. The studies show how the use of computer-assisted language learning (CALL) positively affected Arab students' language skills and their attitudes towards learning English with technology.

Highlighting the value of blended learning by combining the advantages of technology enhanced face-to-face instruction and electronic supported learning, Chapter 14 offers an overview of the influence of technological development on the post-secondary Distance Education sector, and presents the advantages of the blended learning approach. The study is supported by evidence from a UAE e-learning University case study.

Chapter 15 discusses a model of evaluating a group of adult students learning resulting from using an online social constructivist tool, using a discussion board for sharing and co-constructing knowledge. The case study discusses a model for understanding the students' learning experience and the authors' approach to assess an individual's level of engagement in critical thinking.

Chapter 16 examines the e-learning sphere in the Arab World. The author discusses the status and quality of e-learning in Arab Universities located in the Middle East. The study provides an analytical overview of the use of e-learning and the quality of electronic courses and learning objects in these universities, and draws into solutions for improved adoption of the e-learning technology. The study is supported by the results of a survey of the universities web sites in the region plus a survey into e-learning courses.

To introduce intelligence to e-learning solutions, Chapter 17 describes a framework for building automatic recommendations in e-learning platforms of two modules: an off-line module which preprocesses data to build learner and content models, and an online module which uses these models on-the-fly to recognize the students' needs and goals and predict a recommendation list.

Chapter 18 proposes an adaptive system of personalized semantic search and recommendation of learning contents on the E-learning Web-based systems with a huge potential in the Arab region. Semantic and personalized search of learning contents is based on the expansion of the query keywords by using of semantic relations and reasoning mechanism in the ontology. Personalized recommendation of learning objects is based on the learner's profile ontology to guide what learning contents a learner should study.

Chapter 19 provides a description of how Wikis can be used to develop the writing performance of English as Foreign Language (EFL) prospective teachers. Wikis have gained popularity by educators because of its potential to provide a collaborative environment which encourages its users to engage effectively in the writing process and to develop their writing performance.

Highlighting yet another Internet application, Chapter 20 explores the opportunities and challenges associated with using Internet Online Learning Communities to complement and aid conventional classes and enhance learning outcomes in UAE schools. The study accounts for the use of online forums to support English language classes in Al Foah Primary School, weighing its pros and cons and identifying lessons learned.

Chapter 21 reports on a study which invited school teachers and university academics in Egypt, as a developing and Arabic-speaking country, to cooperate in establishing a learning object repository to store, locate, and share quality learning objects for class teaching and e-learning programs.

The book concludes with a very interesting chapter that discusses how one university in the United Arab Emirates is addressing the evident gap of suitable courses in Enterprise Information Systems that equip graduates with the appropriate competences and skills for the industry, by providing a curriculum and courses that set out to develop local graduates that will be highly valued by organizations seeking to extract full value from their own EIS's.

Fayez Ahmad Albadri
Abu Dhabi University, UAE
Editor

REFERENCE

UNESCO. (n.d.). *Role of education*. Retrieved from http://www.unesco.org/new/en/social-and-human-sciences/themes/fight-against-discrimination/role-of-education/

Acknowledgment

To ensure that this book is unique is in its insight to technology applications in Arab education sector, many hours and a lot of focused efforts were needed by many people. I would like to extend my great appreciation and thanks to everybody who may have contributed in anyway directly or through support and encouragement to successfully complete this fantastic venture. In particular, I would like to thank the respected esteemed members of the editorial advisory board for their important support throughout this undertaking. However, my genuine appreciation is to the great scholarly contributions of the authors of the chapters, who have also helped in the review and proofreading process.

My special thanks are extended to my students of the Master's of *Educational Leadership* at Abu Dhabi University, who I had the honor to lecture (EDT519) *Information Systems in Education* course in 2010 and 2011, for they were my partners in the inception of the book's idea, and they have also participated as chapter authors, reviewers, or supporters. These, students turned friends include: Maryam Al Shamesi, Amena Al Mulla, Eman Al Neyadi, Aisha Al Darmaki, Mouza Salim, Ahmed Ibrahim, Zakieh Al Disi, Salam Omar Ali, Hadia Abboud Abdul Fattah, *Alia Fares* Al Daheri, Nevine El Shoura, Mariam Al Saqer, Maryam Al Belooshi, Ikram Hussain, Imad Maarouf, Mazen Nassar, Ayesha Al Ali, Sameeha Al Ali, Samah Jwaid, Abdulla Al Shamisi, Abdulla Al Ansari, Tariq Al Maskari, Souha Adlouni, Bashaer Al Kilani, Zainab Al Yahyaei, Sara Al Ahbabi, Khalida Saeed, Abbas Naser, Ibtisam Jaber, and Reem Jaber.

I dedicate this work to my beloved parents, brothers and their families, and to my direct family members: Baha, Ahmad, Ayah, Dima, and Omar, and certainly the new addition to the family, my grand daughter Maya – she is just making our life much more enjoyable.

Fayez Ahmad Albadri
Abu Dhabi University, UAE

Chapter 1
Current Aspects and Prospects of ICT in the Arab Higher Education Sector:
Literature Review

Ali Sharaf Al Musawi
Sultan Qaboos University, Oman

ABSTRACT

This chapter offers a brief overview of the current status of formal governmental support for technology integration in the higher education sectors in different countries in the Arab World, in addition to presenting some major initiatives started and implemented in some of the Arab states. Several distinguished initiatives in the Arab countries are reviewed to reflect on the strategies in higher education institutions. The policies and strategies that regulate technology implementation in these countries are described. Analysis of strengths, weaknesses, opportunities, and challenges is conducted. Implications are drawn from the different experiences. The chapter suggests solutions that are required to overcome the weaknesses by presenting thoughts for creative improvements in the future with emphasis on training and infrastructure aspects. Moreover, solutions and recommendations as suggested by the research are summarized in fields of implementation in education.

INTRODUCTION

Information and Communication Technologies (ICT) become an important part of citizens' life in the Arab World where Internet users were put at (28.5) millions in 2007 with the highest growth rate specifically in the Gulf region where income is high enough for computers to become more affordable than in other countries. Despite this, none of the Arab states was among the top (20) countries in the world in terms of users' number (Said, 2007). In addition, the use purposes were humble and are limited to newspaper reading and public services. Mobile technology users, on the other hand, were at (160) millions with little access to Internet due to its high costs and lack of wireless

DOI: 10.4018/978-1-4666-1984-5.ch001

connections. Studies show that impediments such as: lack of infrastructure, content's low quality, lack of legal frameworks, and censorship systems obstruct the optimal use of Internet (Said, 2007).

In this context, Arab higher education (HE) institutions attempt to lead the educational field towards efficient application of ICT both academically and socially. Universities' efforts in this regard show implementation of online education depending on their own resources or by signing deals with partners such as Microsoft and Intel, and local private institutions. For instance, learning management systems such as: WebCT and Moodle are installed in many universities. Training workshops are offered to faculty members and teachers in Arab HE institutions by different foundations and societies including the UNESCO (Guessoum, 2006). Studies show that challenges to ICT the effective implementation in Arab HE can be summarized in the lack of: ICT infrastructure, culture, leadership and e-learning strategy, local content, copyright legalities, awareness among instructors and learners. Regardless of these challenges studies show that there seem to be bright futuristic opportunities into two main categories: business opportunities and the flexible learning environments (Abdelraheem, 2006).

BACKGROUND

In this section, examples of the extensive Arab countries' efforts in terms of adopting ICT will be presented to highlight the current status in this field. The following description focuses on each country's government initiatives establishing ICT in their respective countries and what this looks like for the higher education institutions. The countries are presented in four distinctive regions that include the Gulf, West Asia, and North African countries respectively. It is important to note that the following summary is not comprehensive, but rather offers an overall idea of some of the important aspects in each country.

Gulf Countries

The Gulf countries are made up of the independent countries of Bahrain, Saudi Arabia, Kuwait, the United Arab Emirates, Oman, and Qatar. In all the Gulf countries, the respective governments have organized a variety of approaches to establish ICT in higher education.

In Bahrain, the 2007 issued e-government vision of Bahrain, emphasizes its commitment to provide all government services that are integrated, best-in-class and available to all through their channels of choice helping Bahrain transform as the finest country in GCC to visit, live, work and do business. The vision has five key elements: (1) leadership where the kingdom aspires to maintain and improve upon its position as a regional leader using leading edge technologies; (2) Services focusing on the provisioning of services to customers, and in this respect works towards electronic enablement of all key services; (3) integration by redesigning processes in a customer-centric fashion to interact with one 'government' rather than multiple agencies; (4) availability to all by ensuring effective delivery of applicable government services to all, irrespective of their education, nationality, age and income; and (5) diversity of choices by providing customers multiple channels for availing government services (KOB, 2007). In 2004, the University of Bahrain, in cooperation with a telecommunication company, has established an e-Learning Center to disseminate e-culture among its faculty members and gradually transfer the academic programs and curricula to e-programs. The center initiative is described later in the paper in more detail.

In Saudi Arabia, the Ministry of Communications and Information Technology has prepared a national ICT plan in 2005 that outlines a long-term vision for ICT in the kingdom and a five-year plan to implement the vision. The long-term vision is composed of seven overarching objectives and a set of implementation policies. The main feature of these suggested items is their comprehensive coverage of all aspects of ICT use such as e-government, e-commerce, telecommuting, telemedicine, e-learning, and digital Arabic and Islamic content (ESCWA, 2007b). Most Saudi universities were expected to switch to a system of e-learning by 2010. To achieve this, the Saudi Ministry of Higher Education has established the National Center of E-learning and Distance Learning to organize the change and prepare e-learning material. The Saudi Ministry of Higher Education has set up a repository for e-learning material to help universities adopt the system. E-books for engineering, medical, computer science and humanities courses have been made available. The universities have asked their academics who have agreed to adopt e-learning to be trained by the national center (Re.ViCa, 2011).

In Kuwait, efforts are made to catch up with the rapid changes in the changing world of technology. Kuwait's concept in the ICT field includes four basic principles: establish a clear strategy by the government for information technology and its applications, rehabilitate human resources and develop their capabilities to face the new changes, spread out awareness regarding the electronic information, cooperation between the government and private sector and the civil society (KISR, 2005). In HE institutions, for example, University of Kuwait adopts distance learning approach by linking its three campuses with its distance learning center's facilities. Moreover, Kuwait witnessed the birth of the establishment of the Arab Open University which is a non-profit private Pan-Arab university founded in 2002 for Arabic speaking students; and is affiliated with the UK Open University (Re.ViCa, 2011).

The e-strategy approach in the UAE recognizes that a world-class competitive telecommunication infrastructure is of critical importance to the economic development of the country. The strategy was designed in 2006 to serve as a guideline to all individuals involved in the telecommunications sector, including consumers, service providers, operators, investors and the Government. The policy consists of 5 main objectives (UAE TRA, 2011): establish policies and regulatory framework; promote and develop new technologies; become the regional ICT hub; develop the country's human capital; and encourage research and development. UAE has set the stage for rapid advances in e-learning. Many conferences have been organized in the UAE since 2001 in which participants are trained in creating, managing, and delivering online and Web-enhanced courses. The UAE's national University (UAEU), the largest in the country, has been making significant strides in the adoption and implementation of online learning (Guessoum, 2006).

In Oman, the Information Technology Authority (ITA) was set up to be responsible for implementing national IT infrastructure projects, supervising all projects related to implementation, and providing professional leadership to various other e-Governance initiatives of the Sultanate. The goal includes a significant improvement in the quality of services the government provides to its citizens (e-Oman, 2010). The ministry of higher education has put a particular emphasis on improving the learning methods by developing and implementing a unified e-Learning management system (Moodle) intended to improve the e-learning skills supported by a Learning Resource Center (LRC) that provides IT services for about (1500) students and (150) staff members (Al-Gattoufi, Al-Naabi, and Gattoufi, 2007). Since many HE institutions adopted e-Learning combined with face to face instruction, an increase in the number of online running courses and their users is noticeable (Al Musawi and Abdelraheem, 2004a). At Sultan Qaboos University, the public university, faculty members use the Internet in their instruction, but it was found that web-assisted instruction is equally effective as face to face instruction in students' achievements (Al Musawi and Abelraheem, 2004b). The adoption of e-Learning management systems, and the increase of faculty involvement, marks the beginning of a new era of instructional delivery mode at the Omani HE institutions (Akinyemi, 2002).

In Qatar, Qatar's Supreme Council of ICT (ictQATAR), formed in 2004, holds a clear and authoritative mandate as both a regulator and an enabler of Qatar's ICT sector. In 2005, ictQATAR's vision and mission was announced aiming at creating an advanced information-based society that will improve the life of everyone in Qatar and will enhance the social and economic development of the country. Its main responsibilities include drafting telecommunications-related legislation and regulations as well as designing, maintaining and prosecuting a national ICT vision, strategy and master plan aimed at enabling the socio-economic development of the nation. The national ICT Plan includes four main spheres of action: public service delivery, infrastructure and environment, industry development, and literacy skills and inclusion. At the university level, initiatives to be implemented in the next years (2011-2015) intend to improve the skills of students and support the marketability of ICT graduates by developing intensive ICT educational programs, on-the-job training, internship programs, and international exchange programs (ictQatar, 2010).

West Asia Countries

The West Asia countries are made up of the independent countries of Yeman, Iraq, Jordon, Syria, and Lebanon, and Palestine. As with the Gulf countries, the respective governments of the West Asia countries use different approaches to establish ICT in higher education.

In Yemen, the Ministry of Education has taken measures to secure sustainability of all ICT resources in the HE sector by establishing the foundation of information technology in higher education to manage and maintain all common ICT assets, information resources, and other ICT related services such as training and end-user support. The development of ICT management and support services staff continues and recently has been facilitated by establishing training programs and facilities. A project, completed in 2006, to de-velop ICT policy for the Yemen higher education system with Dutch and Tanzania partners continues to guide the process for other higher education institutions in the country (Re.Vica, 2011).

In Iraq, little ICT policies and procedures have been established by the government. The ICT situation has been characterized by poor use of applications in government, weakness or absence of e-commerce and related legislation, limited usage of ICT in education, inferior usage of ICT in health care, and barely perceptible use in the employment sector (Elameer, Idrus, and Jasim, 2011). The Iraqi higher education system is in need of an e-learning system that may help solve problems of brain drain, shortage of educational materials and equipment, outdated traditional teaching methods, and the knowledge gap between Iraqi universities and others abroad (Elameer, Idrus, and Jasim, 2011).

In Jordan, the National ICT Strategy, designed by Information Technology Association in 2007, guides the ICT approach for the country. The ITA serves two basic goals. First, it identifies the subsectors that national ICT sector leadership will be best-suited for growth given the environment in Jordan. Second, it defines actions that Government must take to do its part to facilitate ICT sector growth. The strategy emphasizes the role of higher educational institutions in fostering research and development. However, the strategy states that the existing university regulations fail to encourage professors to initiate research and development activities that meet market needs. It also mentions that few coordination efforts exist for communication between universities and with industry. In addition, the Ministry of Higher Education and Scientific Research has been too focused on universities rather than encompassing country-wide cross-body coordination (int@j, 2007).

In Syria, a national strategy was written in 2004 focusing on: increasing the Grand National Product (GNP) and retaining economic balances, providing high-quality information and communication services with affordable prices for individuals and institutions, providing required computer and information processing systems for all institutions and activities, building an economic and industrial sector with focus on ICT, disseminating and producing knowledge through application of ICT with emphasis on the significance of the cultural and linguistic contents, and providing the legislative framework necessary for the development, application and organization of ICT (UNDP and MCT, 2004). The most prominent project at the higher education level is the Syrian Virtual University, which was inaugurated in 2002 by the Ministry of Higher Education. It provides virtual education to local and international students with goals of offering education to those who want to learn but cannot afford to do so by going to a traditional university (SVU, 2011). In addition to this pioneering project, there are a number of initiatives for direct e-education in universities and private schools and indirect life-long education and training (Re.Vica, 2011).

In Lebanon, a national e-strategy was adopted by the Council of Ministers in 2004. It constitutes a plan providing a coherent vision for the future and across sectors, including specific projects that enable a conducive environment for ICT and e-government throughout the country (Haddara, 2004). Beirut University Online; a private institution, starting in 1998, states that their mission is "to bring quality education to the Arab World". It covers the areas of business administration, computer sciences, health sciences and environment studies in a fully online, computer-driven, internet-hosted instructional format. In addition, periodic residency sessions are held for all registered students (Re.Vica, 2011).

In Palestine, the approval and endorsement of the national ICT strategy took place by the Palestinian National Authority in 2004. The Ministry of Telecommunications and Information Technology adopted the development of the ICT sector by establishing a telecommunication regulatory authority and e-government committee, allocating a more generous budget for the ICT sector and

establishing the licensing of mobile phone operators (ESCWA, 2007a). Al-Quds Open University (QOU) opening in the Palestinian territories in 1991, is one of the first open and distance education universities in the Arab World. It has over (60,000) students studying in (24) educational and regional centers (Re.Vica, 2011).

North African Countries

The West Asia countries are made up of the independent countries of Egypt, Tunisia, Morocco, Mauritania, and Algeria. As with the Gulf and West Asia countries, the respective governments of the North African countries use different approaches to establish ICT in higher education.

In Egypt, ICT is considered as a national development priority establishing a new ministry for that purpose in 1999 to achieve the information society which aims to offer individuals, businesses and communities the opportunity to harness the benefits of ICT within the boundaries of national priorities and issues (Re.Vica, 2011). "In the course of the ICT Strategy 2007-10, Egypt has become a global destination for information technology outsourcing and business process outsourcing" (MCIT, 2010, p. 126). Within this scope, HE sector plans its policies in ICT field. "Research revealed large disparities between institutions regarding ICT resources and use of e-learning, with some universities having established e-learning centers, while others did not provide any e-learning facility. In addition, reports on challenges facing the higher education sector point to the need to focus on e-learning as an area of priority" (Re. Vica, 2011).

In Tunisia, the main government focus of ICT strategy, encompasses information technology, and more particularly, software industry technologies, services and multimedia. International organizations (e.g., the World Bank, Microsoft, and Apple) provide support to incorporating ICT at all levels of education. These organizations provide support to the government in implementing ICT staff training programs, supporting professional development, providing networking opportunities; researching, developing and evaluating new policy approaches in setting up ICT infrastructure in the country. Tunisia also hosted the second phase of the world summit on information systems. All HE institutions are connected to the internet by El-Khawarizmi Calculus Center, which is the official public internet service provider to higher education institutions. The integration of ICT in education is further reinforced by the establishment of the Tunisian Virtual University (Re.ViCa, 2011).

In Morocco, the government focused on five key themes that are important for facilitating the role of knowledge in development and for the effective use of ICTs: education, governance, private sector development, e-commerce, and access. These themes formed the basis for the national strategy for ICT development and together were called the e-Maroc Plan. Since 2006, Ibn Zohr University led a project to create a virtual Moroccan campus that aims to pool the resources of e-learning programs throughout the university system, with the ultimate goal of developing full remotely-provided courses of study at the vocational, undergraduate, and graduate degree levels (Re.ViCa, 2011).

In other North African countries, some universities and agencies are interested in initiating distance education. For example, an e-learning center was opened in Mauritania in collaboration with the University of Nouakchott. The center offers computer training, and teaches electronic skills to university students for them to be competitive in the job market (Telba, 2010). Algeria is encouraging the use of ICT in education by preparing an ICT policy framework along with an implementation strategy. The government has set up a special committee to synergies different sectors in the area of ICT (Re.ViCa, 2011).

To this, it can be concluded that most Arab countries have adopted ICT strategies and higher education institutions play a central role in realizing these strategies by: incorporating them, preparing human resources to contribute to operationalize these strategies after graduation, and researching/developing methods to localize these technologies. These roles have yet to become more effective when the strategies are implemented in reality by providing prototypes, projects and initiatives. The next section will focus on distinguished initiatives and approaches taken place by some Arab countries and HE institutions.

INITIATIVES AND APPROACHES

This section purpose is to describe five distinguished initiatives in some Arab countries mentioned above to reflect on these countries' ICT strategies in HE level. Certainly, there are other important initiatives in the Arab World but the selected ones have been either thoroughly investigated through research or literature. In addition, they present combination of initiatives that tackle important issues such as: Arabic content, open learning, and collaboration with the public sector. Therefore, the section will show these cases' strengths, weaknesses, and obstacles that impede their implementation. This will pave the way to derive implications for future improvements which will be discussed later in the chapter.

General Organization for Technical Education and Vocational Training e-Learning Initiative, Saudi Arabia

This e-Learning initiative was conducted by the General Organization for Technical Education and Vocational Training (GOTEVT) in 2001 in order to institute an e-Learning system and its human, technical, and administrative resources and requirement. Alherbish (2005) states that this initiative has many tracks as follows:

- **Track 1:** Establishment of the e-Learning and training center in 2002 to act as the technical leader of the initiative. It has developed some e-Learning materials.

- **Track 2:** Adoption of an e-Learning system to train students on basic computer skills. In this track, GOTEVT has been in a strategic alliance with an international e-Learning company to deliver an online Arabic computer skills training. Such training has been conducted in (10) GOTEVT technical colleges in Saudi Arabia.

- **Track 3:** Production of e-Learning courses for GOTEVT colleges: In this track a sample of (6) academic courses have been chosen. A project was conducted to produce e-courses to be published on a suitable Learning Management System. These courses were developed to comply with the SCORM standards as a method to ensure quality and portability of developed models. All produced courses are in Arabic.

- **Track 4:** Production of self-learning electronic materials. In this track, more than (300) training videos owned by GOTEVT were transformed into e-Learning packages where each package contained a topic in technology. Each package contained an illustrative video clip about a certain technology topic accompanied with needed text and interactive assessment tool.

- **Track 5:** Establishment of self-learning centers: to serve as an attraction center for both students and teachers in each college. In 2003, a module center was established in one of the colleges. The center contained a network of (12) powerful PCs connected to a server where more than (100) self-learning CDs and programs are stored for the public use in each campus.

- **Track 6:** Design of the e-learning strategic plan: Given the above tracks, GOTEVT is in a need for long term e-Learning strategic plan. A main task force has been formed to design that plan which will include the above (5) tracks as well as long term schedule to apply them.

- **Obstacles to complete this project were:** high-initial costs and indirect costs, Internet speed and availability, resistance of change by different organizational levels, the language barrier (Arabic content is needed), and shortage of qualified e-learning staff (Alherbish, 2005).

King Saud University Smart University Town Project, Saudi Arabia

This project was initiated by King Saud University (KSU) administration to set the stage for a transformation towards an on-campus culture of e-Learning. It seems to be comprehensive and involved all the KSU community to achieve its goals. The following points show how the initiative was planned and implemented:

- This Project aims to (Alsalloum, 2011): develop the infrastructure for e-learning systems in all KSU facilities; achieve full integration between all administrative and educational systems in the university; automate all classrooms at the university, train all faculty members to enable them from the best use of these technologies; adopt standardized, modern and technical specifications for all technologies to ensure their maximum utilization; establish a center to operate and support these technologies with a (Help Desk) and remote control systems; and build a gateway for e-learning to be a unified interface to provide all the services provided.

- It is worth mentioning that this project is the largest in the region/world in the application of these technologies and use them.

- It can be divided into three main components: (1) educational technologies;

(2) control and support systems; and (3) training.

- Educational technologies that include: halls, smart classrooms, teaching studios, visual communication devices, video broadcast system classrooms, participation system, digital studio, educational auditoriums.
- Control and support systems that regulate the above technologies work and facilitate the process of managing and maintaining them such as protection and surveillance system to prevent theft. They include: electronic display system, information kiosks, electronic safes, remote management system for classrooms. All this through a sophisticated data center.
- Training: Despite the importance of technologies that have been installed and their great usefulness of the university, they become worthless if not used by employees of the university and especially the faculty members. Therefore, it was one of the basic strategies to provide training for faculty members to optimally utilize these systems. A training plan was prepared for the entire faculty on the use of different e-learning technologies. Based on this plan, training on the use of systems and smart classrooms has been provided to faculty in all colleges, whether through training or independent courses (Alsalloum, 2011).

King Abdullah Arabic Content Initiative, Saudi Arabia

There is an obvious scarcity in the Arabic content on the Internet. The following project was carried out to look into the methods to solve this problem. It was adopted in 2008 by King Abdul Aziz city for Science and Technology in Saudi Arabia. The following is a description of this initiative:

- Noting the weakness of the online Arabic content, as the statistics indicate that the proportion of Arabic digital content is scarce, so much so that the rate does not exceed (0.3%) of global content for other languages.
- This initiative to enrich Arabic content came as a response to this need.
- King Abdulaziz City for Science and Technology supervises the implementation of this initiative in coordination with the relevant authorities within and outside the Kingdom to promote Arabic content quantity and quality.
- The initiative vision: "Promote digital Arabic content in terms of production and use to support development and transition to a knowledge society and to preserve Arab and Islamic identity".
- The main objectives of the initiative are as follows:
  1. Harness the digital content to support development and transition to a knowledge society.
  2. Ensure that all segments of society can access information and electronic opportunities.
  3. Preserve the Arab and Islamic identity of the community and promote cultural and civilizational digital stock.
  4. Enable the production of rich electronic content Arab to serve Arab and Islamic societies.
- Main projects of the initiative: there are several projects such as:
  1. Strategy for the enrichment of local and Arabic content,
  2. Wiki Forum- a project to enrich the Arab Wikipedia,
  3. Arab Blog, interactive computer dictionary, and;
  4. Strategic technologies books (KAACI, 2011).

Zain e-Learning Center at the University of Bahrain, Kingdom of Bahrain

As mentioned before, this center was instituted in 2004 by the University of Bahrain, in cooperation with the telecommunication company 'Zain', for a comprehensive but gradual transformation of the university teaching and learning processes to e-Learning format.

- The e-Learning center was established in 2004 to cope with the latest developments in ICT and to employ this technology in teaching and learning processes at the university and academic institutes.
- The center aims at providing qualitative development in learning and to qualify learning to a better educational output in order to create graduates capable of coping with continuous changes to serve their country. Its vision is: accessing knowledge and methodological scientific research through use of ICT in a flexible manner to create interactive learning mode, enhancing creative thinking enrichment and supplementary materials. Its mission is: providing means to use technology in learning and teaching situations via offering self-learning pattern by employing multi-media to allow the learner is the center of the educational process and to create academic creative environment to achieve quality learning.
- Objectives of the center are to:
  1. Disseminate e-culture through awareness and media campaigns to prepare the community to accept and interact with e-learning.
  2. Gradual transfer of fully or partially current academic programs and curricula to e-courses and programs in accordance with tailored designs for each, and the design and the adminis-

tration of e-courses using educational technologies according to the nature of the course to be offered.
  3. Establish principles of self and long life learning and training and enhancing the e-learning skills for UOB staff and students to employ them for long life learning.
  4. Create open channels for international and regional cooperation in e-learning to cope with the latest in the field, in order to utilize it in the development of knowledge and scientific research.
  5. Create community partnership and communication.
  6. Support academic and scientific programs through providing services and alternative or assisting technologies, in accordance with the nature or type of these courses and programs.
- The center adopts a strategy that depends on the gradual offering of electronic courses and academic programs with the aim to allow the university and educational community outside to recognize and accept the e-learning mode.
- The following stages have been considered in order to make the move to e-Learning smooth and gradual.
  1. **Stage I:** offering university requirements to all students in all colleges on line.
  2. **Stage II:** offering selected courses from all academic programs with the approval of each concerned department.
  3. **Stage III:** offering academic programs with the approval of the concerned departments.
  4. **Stage IV:** the gradual transformation to the virtual university and the offering of full academic programs on line. During this stage the center will carry out research activities and quality assure all courses.

- Services and Activities: The services and activities of the center can be classified as:
  1. Academic and Technical Services: transformation of regular textual courses into electronic courses; offering some courses online; drafting a framework and laying out some conditions in accordance with the quality control and academic accreditation criteria; e-testing.
  2. Training and Workshops: The e-Learning center has organized a number of training courses and workshops to prepare the academic community at the University to interact with e-Learning and to equip them with necessary skills. The center offered these courses: course instructional design; courses on using LMS; using multimedia in course design; transformation of textual courses into online courses
  3. Awareness Campaign: The center started an awareness campaign on e-Learning in higher education and observes impact of such education on society. A number of lectures, seminars and conferences are organized with participants from specialists in this field at the local, regional and international levels. For example, the center organizes the 4th international symposium on "Best Practices in Management, Design and Development of e-Courses: standards of excellence and creativity" from 17-19 April 2012.
  4. Consultation Services: The center provides consultation services for all departments and colleges regarding the transformation of textual and traditional courses into electronic courses and all related issues (Zain e-Learning Center, 2011).

Arab Open University

Open learning remains new to the Arabic context as no typical application has been made available to Arab learners before launching the Arab Open University (AOU) in 2002. However, AOU sets the rules and regulations and provide the example for open learning at HE in the Arab World. Below is a description of steps taken by this university to plan and implement open leaning:

- AOU has campuses in Kuwait, Jordan, and Lebanon, Bahrain, Saudi Arabia, Egypt and Oman.
- AOU open learning platform relies heavily on the tutoring process that aims, in turn, at promoting a proactive environment of learning. In addition, course lectures are laid out in a programmed and progressive mode via well-prepared textbooks and supporting notes, besides other supporting forms of delivery media based on audio and video cassettes, CD-ROMs and on-line websites (Internet-based). Intertwined together, these various components aim to offer an environment of supported open learning.
- Library and computer-based resources are also deployed throughout AOU's various regional branches that are augmented by a number of learning centers in the subscribing countries.
- Perhaps, the main paradigm upon which the pillars of an open system of education stand lies in its flexibility to accommodate a wide base of HE seekers, thereby offering open opportunities of education to many qualified applicants.
- While there are no preconceived limitations on admission numbers, practical realities may limit numbers according to available logistic and human resources. Nevertheless, constraints of admission are,

by far, less stringent than those prevailing in comparable traditional institutions.

- For the AOU, students wishing to enroll in the undergraduate program of study must have successfully completed their high school studies that usually culminate in a state-sponsored general secondary school certificate. In addition, the AOU considers for admission community college graduates with the privilege of earning some credits for the successful completion of certain appropriate courses at the CC level. The AOU also considers students who have successfully completed "relevant" courses at a recognized Institution of Higher Learning.

- In principle, for every 20 students, a course-specialized tutor is assigned. The time schedule of the tutorial sessions will be arranged completely prior to the commencement of a term of study. While these sessions make it possible for fruitful interaction between students and tutors, they can also entice students to explore other logistic support resources available at the Learning Centers. In addition, the learning centers, in the different Arab countries, will be connected by an integrated satellite network supported by a host of VSATs at the learning centers.

- Computer and multimedia laboratories are also intended to play an important role in enhancing the learning experience. These laboratories will be deployed at the LCs as integral components of logistic support for the learning process. Plans for utilizing various forms of ICT resources including the Internet as a medium of course delivery and support, in whole or in part, form integral components of the AOU's strategic planning (Hammad, Al-Ayyoub, and Sarie, 2004).

CURRENT ISSUES OF IMPLEMENTATION

After the above review, ICT issues will be discussed in this section to analyze their strengths, weaknesses, opportunities, and challenges; and to glean from the different experiences. The issues are categorized into subsections representing these main issues.

Human Resources Development

Implementing ICT in education and e-Learning requires training. However, traditional training needs physical attendance, accommodation, facilities, and other costly requirements. Further, it seems that there is a need in certain instances for structured form of program or plan that has a clear vision, goals, and strategies for faculty development (Al-Washahi, 2007). E- Training is an optional approach to offer various types of self-learning through online workshops/programs to the institution staff, student and faculty members regardless of the place and time. This entails building the capacity and culture among the institution staff to accept this approach. Systematic and careful planning through needs assessment and long-term strategies should be considered to implement e-Training in the Arab context (Al Musawi, 2010). E- Training provides trainees with the latest information on training programs conducted by numerous training providers. It enables them to process their registration of training programs online. It enables the institution from publishing its profile, training facilities, trainers' profiles, course outlines, course schedules, cost prices, and training venues in the portal (QOU, 2007). Studies notice a shortage of qualified e-learning Staff (Alherbish, 2005).

Use in Teaching/Learning

The faculty members at the Arab HE institutions overall used ICT where the most frequently used and skillful ICT functional areas are: website browsing, Internet search engine, and word processing (Al Senaidi, 2009). These faculty's frequency use of the Internet is ranged between (2-3 times a week) to (daily) and that e-mail is the most often used e-tool on a daily basis, followed by the World Wide Web, then electronic journals. The assistant professors followed by instructors/lecturers are more satisfied with their Internet use for academic purposes than associate professors and professors (Aldojan, 2007).

The CGPAs of the online students were higher than their face to face CGPAs. This may be attributed to the students' ability, the lab component in the online offerings, the increased number of quizzes and homework assignments in the online offerings or attributed to a synergy of all these (Junaidu and AlGhamdi, 2004). In terms of attitudes, it seems that Arab students who were exposed to the online learning environment, had positive attitudes toward this type of learning and in turn had better learning and understanding of the course material (Naqvi, 2008). Online special needs students should be dealt with using assistive technologies and provided with guidance and initial evaluation of their needs and learning difficulties (Bakerman, 2002).

Factors that limit faculty use of the Internet in the academic work are: access to the Internet, Internet content, administration-related limitations, and lack of time, affordability-related issues (Aldojan, 2007). Factors that, in general, challenge higher education institutions in relation to the offering and delivery of educational programs include: ensuring there is a quality curriculum, there is appropriate infrastructure and resourcing, ensuring the programs are well administered and that there are processes in place to ensure quality assurance (Oliver, 2011).

Management and Technology

Although broadband internet has become popular, there is some time needed to move the country from low-bandwidth internet to broadband and higher. Possible alternatives are providing internet through satellite which is about to be legalized by the government (Alherbish, 2005). In addition, technologies such as e-library could support e-learning courses with a bundle of networked e-information services such as development of course-related electronic collections, virtual reference help, and online document delivery (Taha, 2007).

Like any place in the world, the desire for change is there but few know how to implement change. In addition, resistance of change exists by different organizational Levels (Alherbish, 2005). In addition, the educational leader has a huge quantity of information and needs to acquire and use technology skills in filtering, employing, organizing and indexing it effectively to take a decision (Kaaki, 2002).

Opportunities of e-Learning industry in the Arab World involve: the governments' awareness of the need to illuminate the digital divide, funding and sponsorship of e-Learning dissemination initiative, promising market of more than (150) million people, the social aspiration for better future, and the cultural specificity. However, this industry is passively affected by several factors: lack of institutional cooperation, fragmented efforts, duplication of nonstandard products, projects with no return on investment, lack of specialists, and lack of financial support. Financial factors play important part in establishing and maintaining effective ICT implementation in education. It also can be helpful in generating revenue and profitability for the institutions that intend to sell their e-Learning and m-Learning products. However, in this case, institutions should acquire new customers and take care of their customer satisfaction. In addition, product and service quality and development are of great importance to sustain commercial online delivery (eLabs, 2006). E-learning is an activity that has many costs and makes many demands on institutions, students and teachers. It is important to be able to satisfy stakeholders that the activity is providing the maximum possible return on the investment and that the demands are warranted (Oliver, 2011). A UNESCO report indicates that using ICT in education can be of high initial and indirect costs depending on two factors: the size of the curriculum and the number of years over which courses are offered without change. This is because the broader and more changing the curriculum on offer, the more courses will need to be offered and changed, and the greater the volume of course materials that will need to be developed. However, these reports show the trend in higher education towards the blended format since the marginal costs of adding a flexible learning capability to traditional higher education is not only a cheaper option than setting up a new distance learning system, but delivers a wider curriculum choice (UNESCO, 2002).

Ethical and Cultural Issue

A list of ethical standards for the use of computers and the Internet by faculty members in the Arab higher educational institution is proposed referring to the importance of these standards and to the ability of faculty members for coping with such standards and develops an integrated framework of standards and how to teach and adopt it in the curriculum (Amer and Al Musawi, 2009).

Studies reveal that the interactivity factor in web based learning poses an obvious threat to the Arab culture. In view of some of the foregoing learner reactions and the uncontrollable, inevitable potential of virtual learning to interfere with cultures in coeducational institutions and settings, there is need for an action plan to control and contain the situation (Akinyemi, 2003). Studies explain that some cultural alternatives produced

by technological tools can be useful but perhaps, at the same time, harmful and then the HE institutions must be careful and cautious before introducing such tools to the academic community in Arab World. They should train them on how to use the tools to avoid any cultural friction. There is no doubt that ICT can play an influential role in raising awareness of Arabic adults to achieve the highest benefit from them (Haikal, 2002).

Another cultural issue is that most courses and training packages are in Arabic. Thus, localization of both contents and LMSs (which are usually in English) is a must (Alherbish, 2005). However, in Lebanon for example, most HE institutions use English as a medium of instruction and the Arabic language resources does not pose a problem.

Studies seek to identify the policies pursued by universities to protect the intellectual property of faculty members and researchers who are considered the owners of intellectual creativity and scientific innovations. As well as exploring the universities' approaches for maintaining e-content submitted either to serve the e-learning programs or to build a digital repository, digital library, electronic memory or other forms of conservation and management of the institution history. An open textbook initiative is recommended in this regard (Shaheen, 2011).

However, it should be said that the above revision talks about a large number of countries that include a large variety in their cultural orientations. The author does not intend to generalize results and/or provide a uni-picture that does not take such variability into considerations; and thus, the review or issues addressed, specifically from the cultural aspects, are not representative of all the cases and Arab countries.

Quality Assurance

Evaluations provide important information to university administrators and instructors: information that can prevent programs or courses from floundering or failing to meet the needs and goals of students. However, traditional courses and distance education courses are dissimilar enough to warrant different student and administrative evaluation procedures (Alzind, 2011). An important focus in all higher education institutions employing technology-supported learning in e-Learning and distance education is ensuring that learning is effective and processes are efficient. There are many factors in the use of learning technologies that can limit and impede the quality of program delivery and learning outcomes (Oliver, 2011). Studies show that in order to meet the needs of education and training market today, more and more educational institutions in the Arab world are likely to take advantage of ICTs to offer virtual education. In addition, educational institutions from abroad may offer courses and degrees to education market in the Arab world. These institutions need policies and standards to participate in virtual education in the Arab world. To exploit the full potential of virtual education, there is a tremendous need for the development of virtual education plan (or e-Learning plan) at the various levels (i.e., national and institutional) (Khan, 2003). The need for objective measures of quality will grow.

Prospects of Creativity and Improvement

Based on the above literature and experiential evidence, thoughts for creative improvements in the future are posed below with emphasis on training and infrastructure aspects.

- There is a need to establish e-Learning portals and virtual centers for higher education institutions. In addition, quality measures should be adapted to enable these institution developing learning materials which are complaint with international industry standards.

- Flexible and efficient training programs in e-Learning should be designed and conducted in the Arab HE institutions to empower new generation of implementing and running e-Learning systems (Alherbish, 2005).
- Arab universities have to utilize a blend of self-instructional text, video conferencing learning environment, and an electronic portal with a learning activity management system (Elameer, Idrus, and Jasim 2011).
- The limited publication of empirical research is clearly noticed in both the Arabic and international literature. There seems to be a need to conduct more experimental research on e-learning and its effects on the educational process in the Arab HE institutions.
- HE institutions need to continue training the faculty members, contract and cooperate with international and regional communities in the field of e-learning, place a strategic plan for course delivery methods, from face-to-face courses in hybrid e-learning to totally online courses for distance learning, schedule courses to meet degree requirements for distance and off-campus learners, and create a distance learning program and associated courses.
- When designing e-Learning materials, proper learning principles must be followed so that learners' experience quality learning and the instruction caters for students' individual needs. Also, best practices and standards must be followed when delivering E-learning to students (Ally, 2011).
- Blended learning has a great potential for the development of Arab higher education. But careful consideration of the concept of blended learning and pedagogy strategies is essential for promised outcomes (Alebaikan, 2011).

SOLUTIONS AND RECOMMENDATIONS

Solutions and recommendations as suggested by the research are summarized below in fields of ICT implementation in education.

In the field of human resources development, the need to develop faculty technological pedagogical content knowledge (TPACK) is crucial for the purpose of appropriate technology integration in higher education institutions. A model comprises of synchronous expository experience (webinar sessions) and asynchronous active experience (interactive web-based modules) can be selected to reduce instructional time, facilitate social interaction and support self-paced learning that in turn can promote faculty TPACK. This model can be used by Arab higher education institutions as well in their initiatives to develop faculty members (Alsofyani, Aris, and Alshareef, 2011). Further, it was proposed that higher education institutions can be linked together through e-Connect, a center that promotes projects and mechanisms and facilitates the continuous exchange and smooth flow of information, expertise, and educational, training and research resources using the powers of ICT (Al Khayyat and Al Musawi, 2004). This is substantiated by research which states that Arab countries with large spatial extension a common language as well seem to be ideal candidates for web based education. Virtual systems should start at national level not with international projects. They should link existing institutions preferably already to those engaged in electronic delivery formats (Laaser, 2006). Human resources in the Arab World can be also developed by establishing specialized educational technology departments in addition to those already exist to prepare e-Learning graduates and support the higher education sector's role in this field. In addition, Arabs are in need for more professional organization to carry out training tasks among young Arab educational technologists. Some professional organizations have been instituted in Egypt and other Arab states but they suffer from shortages in membership and active participation in their parent societies.

In the field of ICT use in teaching/learning, the outcomes of studies show that applying computer-supported collaboration learning environments in the university context outweigh its barriers to adoption. These outcomes include enhanced course content knowledge, increased confidence in applying course knowledge and skills, stronger collaboration skills (arguing ideas, making decisions, providing solutions), more ability to create instead of simply consume knowledge, as well as the added benefits of leadership and presentation skills. In this way, students in the Middle East can be better prepared for the careers of the future, and for collaboratively creating solutions to many of the region's most pressing problems (Porcaro and Al Musawi, in press).

In the field of e-Learning management and technology, higher education institutions should develop a comprehensive plan of ICT faculty development in which it defines the vision, goals, and strategies by conducting needs assessment, offering different types of delivery strategy, providing follow-up, and conducting continuous evaluation to ensure application (Al-Washahi, 2007).

In the ethical and cultural field, the effect of cultural values and preferences in e-Learning must be considered in the way that learning is designed. However, studies found that culture in the Arab World does impact learning significantly, and this emphasizes the necessity of using design principles that account for culture and enable the challenges of quality and access to be met more effectively (Hall, 2009).

In the field of quality assurance, attempts to seek application of governance in e-learning and distance education through a variety of strategies applied to develop e-learning and distance education to meet the challenges of current and future opportunities for growth and development through will help to achieve sustainable development for the Arab community (Abdelbaqi and Abdelaziz,

2011). There is a need to discover and document best practice models that institutions can use to grow their capabilities and performances and also as benchmarks against quality can be demonstrated (Oliver, 2011).

FUTURE RESEARCH DIRECTIONS

In the HE institution of the Arab World, there are many areas that need to be thoroughly investigated. For example, the above mentioned initiatives should be evaluated to measure their impact on the faculty member and the society. In addition, other area of research may include the followings:

1. Most of the previous published works in e-learning showed that little has been carried out to examine empirically e-learning effectiveness within higher-education institutions. This reveals the need to conduct field research on the effectiveness of e-Learning on the learners, educational contexts, and the attitudes towards it.
2. More research is required on cultural issues to set ethical netiquette standards in terms of internet ethic codes, copyright use, digital divide, and other related issues. These issues are important to be investigated when e-Learning is adopted because they affect its implementation.
3. Moreover, past studies show that there is still a gap in evaluation of e-learning environment's effectiveness in between theoretical level and application level, and much of the literature has undocumented student' experiences (Alherbish, 2005; Ahmed, 2011). This means that there is a need for research to determine the standards of quality ICT environments in the Arab HE systems and their effectiveness on learner's studies, achievement, and attitudes.

CONCLUSION

This chapter focused on reviewing the ICT initiatives of some Arab countries and their HE institutions. In addition, it described the policies and strategies that regulate the ICT implementation in these countries. The chapter then reviewed the main issues and impediments and suggested solutions that are required to overcome the weaknesses.

In general, it seems that HE institutions in the Arab World are in need to:

*   Initiate projects in cooperation with the governmental and private sectors' institutions.
*   Conduct research to measure the impact of ICT initiatives/projects on education and students achievement.
*   Use these initiatives to increase the efforts in terms of: training faculty, building infrastructure, promoting innovations, and strategizing for technology adoption.
*   Take advantages of these initiatives to collaborate with external agencies to generate fund and financial resources for technology, software development, and training.

REFERENCES

Abdelbaqi, W., & Abdelaziz, W. (2011, February). *Governance in e-learning*. Paper presented at 2nd International Conference on e-Learning and Distance Learning, Riyadh, Saudi Arabia.

Abdelraheem, A. (2006, November). *The implementation of e-learning in the Arab universities: Challenges and opportunities*. Paper presented at DLI 2006, Tokyo, Japan.

Abouchedid, K., & Eid, G. (2004). E-learning challenges in the Arab world: Revelations from a case study profile. *Quality Assurance in Education, 12*(1), 15–27. doi:10.1108/09684880410517405

Ahmed, T. (2011, February). *Evaluating e-learning effectiveness in higher-education institutions at developing countries: An empirical study and proposed model*. Paper presented at 2nd International Conference on e-Learning and Distance Learning, Riyadh, Saudi Arabia.

Akinyemi, A. (2002). E-learning: A reality in Sultan Qaboos University. In G. Richards (Ed.), *Proceedings of World Conference on E-Learning in Corporate, Government, Healthcare, and Higher Education 2002* (pp. 1113-1115). Chesapeake, VA: AACE.

Al-Gattoufi, S., Al-Naabi, S., & Gattoufi, B. (2007). Readiness for shifting from a traditional higher education learning system to an e-learning system: A case study from the Sultanate of Oman. *Journal of College Teaching and Learning, 4*(11), 55–60.

Al Khayyat, I., & Al Musawi, A. (2004, April). *E-connect, electronic linking among higher education institutions in the Gulf cooperation council states*. Paper presented at 2nd Meeting on Implementing Higher Council's Decisions in HE Field, Riyadh, Saudi Arabia.

Al Musawi, A. (2010, April). *E-training and its HRD applications in education sector of the GCC countries* (Invited Paper). Paper presented at 1st Symposium on ICT Applications in Education and Training Proceedings, King Saud University, Riyadh.

Al Musawi, A., & Abelraheem, A. (2004a). E-learning at Sultan Qaboos University: Status and future. *British Journal of Educational Technology, 35*(3), 363–367. doi:10.1111/j.0007-1013.2004.00394.x

Al Musawi, A., & Abelraheem, A. (2004b). The effect of using on-line instruction on Sultan Qaboos University Students' achievement and their attitudes towards it. *Education Journal, 18*(70), 11–26.

Al Senaidi, S. (2009). *An investigation of factors affecting Omani faculty members' adoption of information and computing technology*. Unpublished doctoral dissertation, University of North Texas, USA.

Al-Washahi, M. (2007). *The perceived effectiveness and impact of educational technology faculty development activities in the College of Education at Sultan Qaboos University*. Unpublished doctoral dissertation, Ohio University, USA.

Aldojan, M. (2007). *An exploratory study about internet use among education faculty members in Jordanian public universities*. Unpublished doctoral dissertation, Ohio University, USA.

Alebaikan, R. (2011, February). *A blended learning framework for Saudi higher education*. Paper presented at 2nd International Conference on e-Learning and Distance Learning, Riyadh, Saudi Arabia.

Alherbish, J. (2005, November). *GOTEVT e-learning initiative*. Paper presented at 4th e-Merging e-Learning Conference, Abu Dhabi, United Arab Emirates.

Ally, M. (2011, February). *Best practices and standards for e-learning*. Paper presented at 2nd International Conference on e-Learning and Distance Learning, Riyadh, Saudi Arabia.

Alsalloum, O. (2011, February). *E-learning and UN award: King Saud University case study*. Paper presented at 2nd International Conference on e-Learning and Distance Learning, Riyadh, Saudi Arabia.

Alsofyani, M., Aris, B., & Alshareef, M. (2011, February). *A blended online training model for TPACK development in Saudi higher education institutions*. Paper presented at 2nd International Conference on e-Learning and Distance Learning, Riyadh, Saudi Arabia.

Alzind, W. (2011, February). *Distance learning programs evaluation.* Paper presented at 2nd International Conference on e-Learning and Distance Learning, Riyadh, Saudi Arabia.

Amer, T., & Al Musawi, A. (2009). *Ethical standards for the use of computers and the Internet by faculty members in the Arab World. International Council on Education for Teaching (ICET) World Assembly 2009.* Oman: Sultan Qaboos University.

Bakerman, M. (2002, October). *Children with learning difficulties at future school.* Paper presented at KSU's Future School Seminar, Riyadh, Saudi Arabia. eLabs- eLearning and Business Solutions (2006). *Towards an Arabic elearning strategy: Future prospect, eLabs Portal.* Retrieved August 11, 2011, from http://www.elabs.org.eg/index.html

Elameer, A., Idrus, R., & Jasim, F. (2011, February). *ICT capacity building plan for The University of Mustansiriyah, Iraq Blended learning project.* Paper presented at 2nd International Conference on e-Learning and Distance Learning, Riyadh, Saudi Arabia. ESCWA- Economic and Social Commission For Western Asia. (2007). *National profile of the information society in Palestine.* New York, NY: United Nations.

Guessoum, N. (2006). Online learning in the Arab world. *E-Learn, 10.* Retrieved August 11, 2011, from http://dl.acm.org/citation.cfm?id=1190058&CFID=35185063&CFTOKEN=66842558

Haddara, Z. (2004, Sept.). *Launching the national e-strategy.* Paper presented at The Arab Technology for Development Conference, Beirut, Lebanon.

Haikal, S. (2002, October). *Education and upbringing of the individual in a balanced context between his society and interaction with other communities' cultures: Conceptual analytical study.* Paper presented at KSU's Future School Seminar, Riyadh, Saudi Arabia. ictQatar- Supreme Council of Information and Communication Technology. (2010). *Annual report 2010.* ictQatar, Doha, Qatar.

Hall, A. (2009). *Designing online learning environments for local contexts, as exemplified in the Sultanate of Oman.* Unpublished EdD dissertation, University of Wollongong, Australia. Retrieved August 11, 2011, from http://ro.uow.edu.au/theses/272

Hammad, S., Al-Ayyoub, A., & Sarie, T. (2004). *Combining existing e-learning components: Towards an IVLE: The Medforist knowledge base.* Europe Aid Cooperation Office. Retrieved from http://medforist.grenoble-em.com/Contenus/Conference%20Amman%20EBEL%2005/pdf/15.pdf

(2011). *Information Technology Association-int@j. (2007). National ICT strategy of Jordan 2007.* Amman, Jordan: Author.

Information Technology Authority- e-Oman. (2010). *Annual report 2010.* Muscat, Oman: Author.

Junaidu, S., & AlGhamdi, J. (2004). Comparative analysis of face-to-face and online course offerings: King Fahd University of Petroleum and Minerals experience. *International Journal of Instructional Technology, 1*(4), Retrieved August 11, 2011, from http://www.itdl.org/Journal/Apr_04/article03.htm

KAACI- King Abdullah Arabic Content Initiative. (2011). *About the initiative.* Retrieved August 11, 2011, from http://www.econtent.org.sa/AboutInitiative/Pages/AboutInitiative.aspx

Kaaki, S. (2002, October). *Future school manage-ment*. Paper presented at KSU's Future School Seminar, Riyadh, Saudi Arabia.

Khan, B. (2003). National virtual education plan: Enhancing education through e-learning in developing countries. *Educomm Asia, 9*(1), 2–5.

KISR- Kuwait Institute of Scientific Research. (2005). *State of Kuwait working paper to the World Summit on Information Society*. Retrieved August 11, 2011, from http://www.kisr.edu.kw/webpages/summit/summit.htm#A.%20%20Kuwaits%20Vision%20towards%20the%20Development%20of%20an%20Information%20Society

KOB- Kingdom of Bahrain. (2007). *E-govern-ment strategy: Summary*. Retrieved August 11, 2011, from http://www.ega.gov.bh/downloads/resources/Strategy-English.pdf

Laaser, W. (2006). Virtual universities for African and Arab countries. *Turkish Online Journal of Distance Education (TOJDE), 7*(4).

MCIT- Ministry of Communication and Infor-mation Technology. (2010). *Yearbook 2010, MCIT- Arab Republic of Egypt*. Retrieved August 11, 2011, from http://www.mcit.gov.eg/Upcont/Documents/MCITYearbook2010.pdf

Naqvi, S. (2005). Impact of WebCT on learning: An Oman experience. *International Journal of Education and Development using Information and Communication Technology, 2*(4), 18-27.

Naqvi, S. (2008). WebCT and learning (an Oman experience). *International Journal of Computer Science, 35*(4), 4–11.

Oliver, O. (2011, February). *Achieving quality in technology-supported learning: The challenges for e-learning and distance education*. Paper presented at 2nd International Conference on e-Learning and Distance Learning, Riyadh, Saudi Arabia.

Porcaro, D., & Al Musawi, A. (in press). CSCL in higher education in Oman. *EDUCAUSE Quarterly*.

QOU- Al Quds Open University. (2007, No-vember). *The future of e-training technologies at Al-Quds Open University*. Paper presented at 13th International Conference on Technology Supported Learning and Training- Online Educa Berlin, Berlin, Germany.

Re.ViCa. (2011). *Researching virtual initiatives in education*. The European Commission. Retrieved August 11, 2011, from http://www.virtualcam-puses.eu/index.php/

Said, K. (2007). Arab states strive to bridge the digital divide with the developed world. *Al-Arabiya for Journalism*. Retrieved August 11, 2011, from http://www.al-arabeya.net/index.asp?serial=&f=3392581820

Shaheen, S. (2011, February*). Intellectual copy-right in an e-learning environment: Towards open textbooks initiative in the Egyptian universities*. Paper presented at 2nd International Conference on e-Learning and Distance Learning, Riyadh, Saudi Arabia.

SVU- Syrian Virtual University. (2011). *Syrian Virtual University prospectus*. Retrieved August 11, 2011, from http://www.svuonline.org/images/upload/File/Prospectus.pdf

Taha, A. (2007). Networked e-information services to support the e-learning process at UAE Univer-sity. *The Electronic Library, 25*(3), 349–362. doi:10.1108/02640470710754850

Telba, E. (2010). *E-learning and potential change and development in the Arab Maghreb countries*. Retrieved August 11, 2011, from http://zawaya.magharebia.com/en_GB/zawaya/opinion/257

UAE TRA. (2011). *ICT initiatives*. Retrieved August 11, 2011, from http://www.tra.gov.ae/tra_initiatives.php

UNDP- United Nation Development Program and MCT- Ministry of Communications and Technology. (2004). *National ICT strategy for socio-economic development in Syria.* Damascus, Syrian Arab Republic.

UNESCO- United Nations Education, Science, and Culture Organization. (2002). *Open and distance learning: Trends, policy and strategy considerations.* UNESCO, France.

Zain e-Learning Center. (2011). *Welcome to Zain e-learning center.* Retrieved August 11, 2011, from http://www.elearning.uob.edu.bh/

ADDITIONAL READING

Ahmad, A. A., & Zink, S. D. (1998). Information technology adoption in Jordanian public sector or organizations. *Journal of Government Information, 25*(2), 117–134. doi:10.1016/S1352-0237(97)00094-4

Akinyemi, A. (2003). Web-based learning and cultural interference: Perspectives of Arab students. In G. Richards (Ed.), *World Conference on E-Learning in Corporate, Government, Healthcare and Higher Education*, (pp. 1858-1862). Chesapeake, VA: AACE.

Al-Asmari, A. M. (2005). *The use of the Internet among EFL teachers at the Colleges of Technology in Saudi Arabia.* (Doctoral dissertation, The Ohio State University, 2005). Abstract from: ProQuest File 932375011: Dissertation Abstracts International, AAT 3177167.

Al Balushi, F. (2001). Creating e-learning communities: Effective strategies for the Arab world. In A. Al Musawi (Ed.), *Educational Technology Symposium & Exhibition ETEX2001*, (pp. 42-60). Muscat, Sultanate of Oman: Sultan Qaboos University.

Al-Fulih, K. (2003). *Attributes of the Internet perceived by Saudi Arabian faculty as predictors for their Internet adoption for academic purposes.* Dissertation Abstracts International, 63(08), 2842A. (UMI No. 3062771)

Al-Furaih, I. S. (2002). Internet regulations: The Saudi Arabian experience. In *Proceedings of the Internet Society's 12th Annual INET Conference*, June 18-21, Washington, D.C. USA

Al-Harthi, A. S. (2005). Distance higher education experiences of Arab Gulf students in the United States: A cultural perspective. *The International Review of Research in Open and Distance Learning, 6.* Retrieved October 16, 2006 from http://www.irrodl.org/index.php/irrodl/article/view/263/406.

Al-Jarf, R. (2007). Online instruction and creative writing by Saudi EFL freshman students. *Teaching Articles for the Profession, 22.*

Al-Khalidi, S. (2002). The Internet in Jordan is surely becoming part of our everyday lives. *The Star, 103*, 18–24.

Al-Khanjari, Z. A., Kutti, N. S., & Ramadan, H. A. (2005). E-learning under WebCT. *Journal of Computer Sciences, 1*, 488–494. doi:10.3844/jcssp.2005.488.494

Al Kindi, M., Al Musawi, A., Eltahir, M., & Al Naamany, A. (2006). Analyzing theoretical approaches and their implications to the development of distance learning courses research project at Sultan Qaboos University. *Malaysian Journal of Distance Learning, 8*(1), 15–29.

Al-Mashagbeh, W., & Gannon, B. (2001, June 1). Expanding the usage of the Internet and bridging the digital divide. *Jordan Times, 167.*

Al Musawi, A. (2007). *Current status of educational technologies at Omani higher education institutions and their future prospective.* Educational Technology Research and Development (ETR&D), 55(4), 395-410, Association of Educational Communication and Technology, DOI: 10.1007/s11423-007-9041-x, USA.

Al Musawi, A. (2010). E-learning from an Omani perspective. In U. Demiray, *et al.,* (Eds.), *Cases on challenges facing e-learning and national development: Institutional studies and practices,* (pp. 603-626). Retrievedf from http://www.midasebook.com/dosyalar/FINAL_ELEARN_EBOOK_VOL2.pdf

Al-Omari, K. (2002). The situation of using the Internet by faculty members and students at Jordan University of Science and Technology. *Journal of the Association of Arab Universities, 40*(July).

Al Rawaf, H. S., & Simmons, C. (1992). Distance higher education for women in Saudi Arabia: Present and proposed. *Distance Education, 13,* 65–80. doi:10.1080/0158791920130106

Al Rawas, A. (2001) The challenges of new learning technologies for higher education in Oman. In *The Proceedings of the International Conference on the University of the 21 Century, Ministry of Higher Education,* Muscat, Sultanate of Oman.

Al-Shaibany, S. (2008). *Oman places ban on foreign workers.* Retrieved December, 7, 2008, from http://www.arabianbusiness.com/525975?tmpl=print&page=

Al-Suqri, M. N. (2008). *Information needs and seeking behavior of social science scholars at Sultan Qaboos University in Oman: A mixed-method approach.* Dissertation Abstracts International, 68(12), 4905A. (UMI No. 3294687)

Allehaibi, M. M. (2001). *Faculty adoption of Internet technology in Saudi Arabian universities.* (Doctoral dissertation, The Florida State University, 2001). Abstract from: ProQuest File 728889121: Dissertation Abstracts International, AAT 3011877.

Almobarraz, A. (2007). *Perceived attributes of diffusion of innovation theory as predictors of Internet adoption among the faculty members of Imam Mohammed Bin Saud University.* Dissertation Abstracts International, 68(08), 3190A. (UMI No. 3276419)

Almusalam, S. N. (2001). *Factors related to the use of computer technologies for professional tasks by business and administration teachers at Saudi technical colleges.* Dissertation Abstracts International, 62(04), 1382A. (UMI No. 3011019)

Alshawi, A. M. (2002). *Investigating predictors of faculty Internet usage.* (Doctoral dissertation, George Mason University, 2002). Abstract from: ProQuest File 764978461: Dissertation Abstract International, AAT 3066271.

El Kosheiry, A., & Elazhary, M. (2001). E-learning versus traditional education for adults. Information technology in Egypt: Challenges & impact. *Proceedings of the BITWorld Conference,* Cairo, Egypt 4-6 June.

Ibrahim, M., & Kamel, S. (2002). Effectiveness and applicability of internet-based training in the corporation – Case of Egypt. *Proceedings of the 36th Hawaii International Conference on System Sciences.* Retrieved from http://ieeexplore.ieee.org/iel5/8360/26341/01174344.pdf?arnumber=1174344

KEY TERMS AND DEFINITIONS

Distance Learning: An instructional approach that connects learners to the learning resources at a distance from the between instructor in terms of place and/or time using media technologies.

E-Learning: An online interactive learning approach that provides e-content, activities, tests, and feedback directly to the student supported by various communication technologies.

E-Training: Offering various types of self-learning through online workshops/programs to the institution staff, student and faculty members regardless of the place and/or time.

Information and Communication Technology (ICT): Technologies, through which a person can collect, store, recover, process, analyze and transfer information.

Learning Management System (LMS): A computer application, by which e-Learning can be administered, tracked, evaluated, and documented using online tools: e-mail, discussion board, quizzes, and programs.

Sharable Content Object Reference Model (SCORM): Group of common standards and specifications for e-learning content through which learning management systems can easily communicate, support, and adapt the e-materials.

Chapter 2
Technology Integration in UAE Schools:
Current Status and Way Forward

Rana Tamim
Zayed University, UAE

ABSTRACT

Research has supported the assumption that computer technology is beneficial for students' performance. Nevertheless, knowing that technology is beneficial is not sufficient on its own where teachers remain the key stakeholders in the success of the process. Teachers need to be aware of various issues, challenges, and ethical aspects when using technology for teaching, with such aspects being alleviated further in a young country with a conservative society such as the UAE. The chapter offers an overview of the Net Generation and computer technologies' impact on student performance. It provides a briefing about the United Arab Emirates (UAE) and its educational system while highlighting formal initiatives launched by the government to support the educational reform and introduction of technology into the K-12 classroom. Finally, the chapter presents preliminary findings from a research study that investigates teachers' perceptions about technology integration and their current practices in a UAE private school.

INTRODUCTION

No one can deny the current importance of computer technology and the level to which it has pervaded our daily lives. Its impact on different aspects of our communities is escalating on a daily bases and is being sensed more than ever before. The domains in which technology is getting to be significant and fundamental are highly varied and include entertainment, knowledge retrieval, governmental services, transmission of information, business transactions, health services, and communication across various areas around the globe.

Within the educational context, computer technologies' impact is increasing on a continuous basis. Research has supported the hypothesis that computer technology is beneficial for students' performance. However, the naïve assumption that introducing computers into the classroom and

DOI: 10.4018/978-1-4666-1984-5.ch002

providing the technological infrastructure will lead to the successful integration of technological tools into the teaching and learning process has not been reflected in reality. While the actual impact of the teachers' role is not fully understood, the plethora of research conducted worldwide indicates that the actual success of technology integration is highly dependent on the teachers' perceptions, skills, and ability to utilise technology within pedagogically adequate frameworks. After all there are various issues, challenges, and ethical aspects that are to be considered when the decision is taken to introduce technology into the K-12 classroom. Such aspects are augmented further in a young country with a conservative society such as the UAE.

This chapter will offer an overview of the net generation and computer technologies' impact on student performance. In addition, it will provide a briefing about the United Arab Emirates (UAE) and its educational system while highlighting formal initiatives launched by the government to support the educational reform and introduction of technology into the K-12 classroom. Finally, the chapter will present preliminary findings from a research study that investigates teachers' perceptions about technology integration and their current practices in a UAE private school.

Technology and the Net Generation

At the beginning of the 21st century, many individuals may have brushed off the notion that in less than a decade two-year-old children from middle socio-economic classes will be solving electronic jigsaw puzzles in addition to many other games on iPhones and iPads. Clearly, time has proven otherwise. One decade after the start of the 21st century and our children's relationship with technology is accurately depicted by the quote "they say one of a baby's first non-verbal forms of communication is pointing. Clicking must be somewhere just after that" (Computer Quotes, 2008). According to Oblinger and Oblinger (2005)

students currently going to high schools and colleges were born and have grown up in a digital supported environment with at least 20% of them having started using computers by the age of five and eight. After six years, and in the fast paced technological changes we are witnessing, it would be reasonable to assume that the percentage has at least doubled.

In the spring of 2003 an extensive survey was conducted in the USA with more than 1000 parents of children younger than six years. Results unsurprisingly revealed that USA children are growing immersed in technology (Rideout, Vandewater, & Wartella, 2003). Based on the results, more than half the children start working with the computer at the age of four and almost 30% of them spend more than one hour a day working at the keyboard. Findings related to other forms of technology use such as the TV, video, and video games reveal a higher level of usage by the children. A more recent Kaiser Family Foundation study revealed that the years from 2005 to 2010 witnessed an extensive increase in different forms of media usage including mobile and online media (Rideout, Roberts, & Foehr, 2005). Specifically findings revealed that young people aged between eight and eighteen years spend more than seven hours daily working with electronic media.

While there are no formal research findings that provide concrete evidence or information about children's use of technology and media in Middle East countries, it is safe to say that the situation is not very different from that in the USA. On the contrary, it would not be misleading to assume that the availability of technological tools and children's connectivity may be higher in certain Middle Eastern countries such as the United Arab Emirates due to the economic situation. In addition to the TVs, computers, and laptops, children in the UAE have access to the newest releases of the different technological tools including iPads, iPods, and smart phones.

Numbers and statistics pertaining to the ownership and use of computer and computer related communication tools around the world reveals the level of dependency, and the amount to which computers are becoming a central part of our lives and environments. According to a report published by the Pew Research Center, 82% of Swedes, 81% of South Koreans, 80% of Americans, and 76% of Canadians were computer users in the year 2007 (Kohut, Wike, & Horowitz, 2007). According to the same report, although there still is a digital divide between developed and developing countries, the overall use of computers in many poor or middle income countries has witnessed an increase over the five year period from 2002 to 2007. For example, computer usage in India has increased from 22% to 28% while usage in Peru increased from 26% to 39%.

According to the Internet World Stats, the world total of Internet users has increased from 360,985,492 individuals in the year 2000 to 2,095,006,005 in the year 2011 indicating a 480.4% growth over an eleven-year period (Internet World Stats, 2011). This high level of pervasiveness of computer technology in the different aspects of society has influenced many facets of our lives including language to the point that the noun "mouse potato" and the verb "Google" have found their way to the Merriam-Webster's Collegiate Dictionary (USA Today, July, 2006). Further and beyond, online connectivity and communication have resulted in the emergence of abbreviations that cross the boundaries of language, age, culture, and geography such as LOL for "laughing out loud", and TFTF for "thanks for the follow" on Twitter. Interestingly, the utilization of this online language has crossed over to everyday use to the point where some are formally added to the Oxford English Dictionary, namely OMG for "oh my God", BFF for "best friends forever", and the famous LOL (USA Today, March, 2011).

A major outcome of the quick advancement and change in technological innovations has also resulted in the need for a higher level of adaptability and capability to learn new skills and expertise, giving rise to the higher attention to life-long learning. Particularly speaking, the flexibility, access to information, and opportunities offered by Internet-based technologies have played a role in changing the students' profile (Moore & Kearsley, 2005; Naidu, 2003), in addition to changing the workplace and how people locate and retrieve information (Bernard, De Rubalcava, & St. Pierre, 2000). More importantly is the impact on the skills required for success in the job market. According to the job outlook 2002 report published by the National Association of Colleges and Employers, the top ten personal qualities and skills that are sought by employers are communication skills; honesty/integrity; teamwork skills; interpersonal skills; strong work ethics; motivation/initiative; flexibility/adaptability; analytical skills; computer skills; and organizational skills, with performance as reflected by GPA being 17th on the list.

Computer Technology in the Educational Context

Throughout the years, computer technology has been used to enhance instruction through a variety of approaches or strategies. Some of the technological approaches are clearly understood and defined such as drill and practice which refers to software programs that offer the students the chance to work on structured problems or exercises while providing immediate feedback. Another example is computer-mediated communication that refers to "communication between two or more individuals with text-based tools such as e-mail, instant messaging, or computer-based conferencing systems" (Spector, Merrill, Van Merrienboer, & Driscoll, 2008, p. 819)

Other technological applications have more than one definition such as a simulation which may refer to any of the following "a working representation of reality; used in training to represent devices and process and may be low or high in terms of physical or functional fidelity........ an executable (runnable) model; computer software that allows a learner to manipulate variables and processes and observe results…….. a computer-based model of a natural process or phenomenon that reacts to changes in the values of input variables by displaying the resulting values of output variables." (Spector, et al., 2008, p. 826).

Alternately, some educational technology terms are not clearly defined in the literature such as computer-assisted instruction. It may be used as a general term to represent a variety of technology uses for the enhancement of instruction such as drill and practice and tutorials, or as a specific approach to technology such as computer-based programmed instruction (Schenker, 2007). Finally, some terms are used flexibly and interchangeably such as computer-based instruction that is considered to be the newer version of computer-assisted instruction (Computer-assisted instruction, 2008).

Despite the ambiguity of terms in the field, one thing is absolutely clear; computer technology is unquestionably a central element in the 21st century classroom. The pervasiveness of computer technologies has reached a degree where it is almost hard to find an educational institution in the developed countries that is computer and Internet free. For example, it was reported that in 2003 more than 91% of American students in K-12 formal education with 59% being Internet users (DeBell & Chapman, 2006). In Canada, over 90% of elementary and secondary schools were connected to the internet in 2003-2004, and 99% of the schools had computers amounting to students and teachers having access to more than a million computers (Plante & Beattie, 2004). As for the UAE, a 2003 ESCWA report noted that all boys and girls public schools are equipped with IT labs and are connected to the Internet (Karake-Shalhoub, 2003).

Computer Technology and Learning

Ever since its introduction to the classroom the argument over technology's impact on the learning process has taken center stage in the educational arena. It has been long stressed that technology has proved to be cost effective from an administrative point of view, and has instigated new ways of looking at teaching and learning (Van Dusen, 2000). Major uses of computer technology in the educational context include: a) gathering information; b) keeping records; c) creating proposals; d) constructing knowledge; e) performing simulations to develop skills; f) distance learning; and g) global collaboration for lifelong learning and work (Jacobson, 1998; Kimble, 1999).

However, the effect of computer technology on the learning process per se has been arguable for a long time with the most prominent debate being the one between Richard Clark and Robert Kozma. Clark (1983) started the argument with the stand that computer technology has no impact on learning, and that media is a mere vehicle that delivers goods (knowledge) to the learner. This led Kozma (1991) to retaliate by arguing that computer technology is much more than a mere truck, and that it has an actual impact on the learning process. At that time, no main findings were reported by researchers to back up Kozma's argument (Clark, 1994). A subsequent call by Kozma was to restructure the debate to will media influence learning (Kozma, 1994). Clark (1994) responded by noting that media will never influence learning, and the active ingredient in the learning process is the learning strategy confounded with the use of a certain medium. This brought a third party to the debate, where Jonassen, Campbell, and Davidson (Jacobson, 1998) argued that there is no use in going on with an instruction/media centered debate. In their opinion, the focus should be on a learner-centered debate where the main attention should be on how to use computer technology most effectively to support a learner-centered environment.

While the debate was running on, research findings offered a variety of contradictory results regarding the impact of computer technology on student achievement that only added to the controversial issue. However, a recent second-order meta-analysis synthesized findings from different meta-analyses comparing technology enhanced settings with traditional contexts (Tamim, Bernard, Borokhovski, Abrami, & Schmid, 2011). The extensive literature search and systematic review process resulted in the inclusion of 25 meta-analyses with minimal overlap in primary literature. In total the synthesis encompassed 1,055 primary studies and resulted in an effect size of 0.35 in favour of the technology enhanced contexts. An effect size of this strength indicates that an average student in the experimental condition where technology is used will perform 12 percentile points higher than the average student in the control group with the traditional setting that does not use technology to enhance the learning process. In addition, the results of the second-order meta-analysis revealed that the main purpose of technology use was a significant moderator. Particularly speaking, the impact of technology use tends to be significantly higher when it is used to support instruction rather than for direct instruction or delivery of material.

Findings of Tamim et al. with regards to computer use were in agreement with a previously published Stage I meta-analysis that investigated the effect of computer-based technology use on student achievement (Schmid, Bernard, Borokhovski, Tamim, Abrami, Wade, et al., 2009). The preliminary synthesis of a representative sample of 541 effect sizes (from a total of more than 1000) addressing achievement outcomes resulted in an average effect size of 0.28 with the type of technology use being a significant moderator variable. Particularly, technology used for cognitive support resulted in a significantly larger effect size in comparison with presentational technology use. Such findings offer solid support for previous calls for the use of computer technology as cognitive tools (Jonassen & Reeves, 1996). Jonassen and Reeves have long argued that the use of computer technologies as cognitive tools will support reflective thinking; help in learning through designing; and assist in off-loading some of the demanding yet unproductive tasks thus helping the learner in thinking more productively.

As such, the above research findings offer justification for academicians' calls for active and student-centered use of technology in the K-12 classroom. One of the most prominent calls is by Laurillard (2002) who advocates that the effectiveness of computer technology use is influenced by instructional design, learner characteristics, and nature of the learning task and that the benefits of technology cannot be separated from these pedagogical approaches in the larger instructional context. Many researchers have advocated for the use of adequate instructional design with appropriate pedagogical approaches for the enhancement of the learning process. Johnson and Johnson (2004) propose cooperative learning as a potentially promising approach to making the best out of computer technology. Similarly, Bernard, De Rubalcava, and St. Pierre (2000) recommend collaborative online learning as an advantageous approach. On a different note, Grabowski (2004) recommends the generative learning approach while integrating technology with instructional design.

With a more general approach, the American Psychological Association (APA) learner-centred principles are presented as a framework within which computer technologies have the greatest utility and effect (McCombs, 2000; McCombs & Vakili, 2005). The APA learner-centred approach consists of 14 principles that focus on the psychological factors under the learner's control that include: cognitive and meta-cognitive factors; motivational and affective factors; developmental and social factors; and individual differences (APA, 1997).

Overall, research findings and academicians' calls are in agreement with regards to the need to make use of technology. Even the most adamant critics do not refute the positive research findings, but mainly criticize the way it is being used in classrooms, the teacher preparedness, and the relative cost to acquiring technology in the academic context (Kimble, 1999). One of the most important points is the consensus that technology use as a delivery or presentation tool is not the most advantageous approach.

Since the year 2004, the New Media Consortium and the Educause Learning Initiative has conducted extensive annual reviews to identify key emerging technologies expected to enter mainstream educational contexts in the few years to come. The computer innovations or tools reported in each of the eight editions are listed in Table 1 to offer an idea about the variety of tools available for teachers and instructional designers.

Teachers and Technology Use

With all the technological advancements and widespread use of the latest tools and gadgets in almost all aspects of our daily lives, and in light of the supportive research findings, technology integration is becoming a central part of K-12 teachers' roles. However, while technology integration is part of the expectations, teachers' beliefs about the advantages of technology use

and their willingness to put the extra effort needed for successful integration is still under question. This is of utmost importance since research has long indicated that teachers' beliefs and attitudes regarding the learning process highly influence their practices in the classroom (Tobin, Tippins, & Gallard, 1994). This is also true for the effective implementation of technology in educational contexts (Wozney, Venkatesh, & Abrami, 2006) where the literature supports the assumption that if teachers are not aware of technology's benefits or are not willing to invest the time and effort in its integration, introducing computers into the classroom will only support existing practices and strategies rather than alter them (Cuban, Kirkpatrick, & Peck, 2001).

Particularly in the UAE, Al-Mekhlafi conducted a research study with 250 English Language teachers, with results indicating that most teachers are familiar with the modern technologies, and despite their understanding of the advantages of technology use, their classroom practices are not

Table 1. List of emerging technologies listed in the Horizon reports

Time for Adoption			
Year	One year or less	Two to three years	Four to five years
2004	Learning objects	Rapid proto-typing	Context aware computing
	Scalable vector Graphics	Multimodal interfaces	Knowledge webs
2005	Extended learning	Intelligent searching	Social networks and knowledge webs
	Ubiquitous wireless	Educational gaming	Context aware computing/ augmented reality
2006	Social computing	Cellphones	Augmented reality and enhanced visualization
	Personal broadcasting	Educational gaming	Context aware environments and devices
2007	User created content	Mobile phones	New scholarship and emerging forms of publication
	Social networking	Virtual worlds	Massively multiplayer educational gaming
2008	Grassroots video	Mobile broadband	Collective intelligence
	Collaboration webs	Data mashups	Social operating systems
2009	Mobiles	Geo-everything	Sematic-aware applications
	Cloud computing	The personal web	Smart objects
2010	Mobile computing	Electronic books	Gesture-based computing
	Open content	Simple augmented reality	Visual data analysis
2011	Electronic books	Augmented reality	Gesture-based computing
	Mobiles	Game-based learning	Learning analytics

yet reflective of their self-reported willingness to use it (2004). A more drastic image is reflected by some research that indicates teachers' negative attitudes towards computer technology integration with a high level of resistance to incorporating them in their teaching techniques (Romiszowski & Mason, 2004).

Reasons for teachers' reluctance to integrate technology use are varied and obstacles hindering teachers' successful integration of technology in the classroom may be categorized into four main types: resources, institutional and administrative support, training and experience, and attitudinal or personality factors (Brinkerhof, 2006). The introduction of computers imposed an extra burden on K-12 teachers who in many instances are not trained or prepared to do, and which on many occasions comes with no extra value or benefit (Gunawardena & McIsaac, 2004; Naidu, 2003). The problem is further augmented by the absence of proper training and support (Romiszowski & Mason, 2004). As such, teachers' readiness and ability to successfully utilize technological tools to enhance the learning process is still under question in many countries around the world including the Middle East. This is particularly true in the relatively new UAE educational system since technology integration is not as straight forward as some may believe it to be with various issues that need to be addressed including pedagogical, ethical, and cultural concerns. Moreover, it is important to keep in mind that many teachers join the task force without formal professional teacher training and few pre-service teacher-training programs focus on technology integration across the curriculum.

Overview of the United Arab Emirates and its Development

The United Arab Emirates is a young country comprising of seven emirates, namely Abu Dhabi, Ajman, Dubai, Fujairah, Ras al-Khaimah, Sharjah, and Umm al-Quwain, with Abu Dhabi being the capital. Located on the shores of the Arabian Gulf in the Middle East, it was known as the Trucial States and became a federation in 1971 (Morris, 2005). Prior to the Federation, the UAE was among the less developed countries in the world with its economy depending on agriculture, nomadic animal farming, fishing, seafaring, and the pearling industry and trade. The formation of the Federation overlapped with the increase in oil production and export which provided the economical support enabling the country to achieve developments comparable to industrialized nations without having to go through the development "stages" that other countries tend to traverse (De, Ahmad, & Somashekar, 2004; Shihab, 2001).

The UAE has achieved impressive developments in various social and economic sectors leading to high human development indicators at the national and international levels. Particularly within the Information Communication Technology (ICT) sector, the UAE government has invested extensively allowing for the country to become a regional hub for ICT services and manufacturing (Karake-Shalhoub, 2003). The government's ICT initiatives in the government and private sectors are numerous and varied including the Abu Dhabi Innovation Center, Dubai Internet City, and Silicon Oasis. With regards to Internet connectivity, the UAE is the most wired country in the Arab region, and in the year 2000 was ranked in an Economist report as the 18th country in the world with regards to its Internet infrastructure (Karake-Shalhoub, 2003).

The success of the UAE's efforts and investments in the advancement of the ICT infrastructure and utilization is reflected by its Networked Readiness Index (NRI) ranking on the tenth Global Information Technology Report produced by the World Economic Forum in collaboration with INSEAD. The NRI is a measure of the degree to which developed and developing countries around the world leverage ICT for enhanced competitiveness and is based on three subindexes, namely the environment, readiness, and usage. The environment subindex addresses the market environment, the political and regulatory environment, and the infrastructure environment. The readiness subindex targets individual, business, and government readiness. Similarly, the usage subindex addresses the individual, business, and government usage. According to the Global Information Technology Report (2010-2011), the UAE ranked 24th among the 138 countries with its and took first position among the Arab countries reflecting the success of the governments' efforts in this area (Dutta & Mia, 2011).

Education and Technology in the United Arab Emirates

Before offering an overview about technology within the educational sector in the UAE, an understanding about the educational system is warranted. Relative to other countries in the region, the UAE's educational system is a new one (Gaad, Arif, & Scott, 2006) with the first government-funded public school being established in 1953 in Sharjah (Abu-Samaha & Shishakly, 2008). The educational system is divided into public and private sectors, with the government funding the public schools that follow a single gender model and are limited to national students only. Compared to other developed nations, the UAE is among the most progressive with regards to female student education (Tubaishat, Bhatti, & El-Qawasmeh, 2006). The private sector caters mainly for expatriate students and with a growing body that targets national students while having a more diverse teacher profile that incudes expatriate teachers mainly from the Middle East.

The educational system is consistent across the seven Emirates (Abu-Samaha & Shishakly, 2008) and is a four-tier system that covers 14 years of education with the first level being the kindergarten which students join at the age of four before moving to the primary grades at the age of six (Gaad, et al., 2006). The primary school level includes five years (levels 1-5) which is

compulsory for all national students, after which the students join the middle school that includes four years (levels 6-9) after which the students progress to the secondary school that has three levels (levels 10-12) (Abu-Samaha & Shishakly, 2008) leading to their graduation at an average age of 18 years (Gaad, et al., 2006).

Overall, the educational system in the UAE, particularly in the public sector, depends on a more teacher centered approach where higher importance is given to rote learning and the traditional model of curriculum design and implementation (Farhat, 2008; Tubaishat, et al., 2006). However, the Ministry of Education is attempting the implementation of newer approaches, with a number of initiatives, with the most prominent being the "Vision 2020" launched in the year 2000 (Farhat, 2008). The strategic plan aims at restructuring the teaching and administrative aspects in order to enhance the learning process to enable schools to survive and flourish in the "Information Age" (Farhat, 2008). Vision 2020 "aspires to achieve high quality education in all schools to produce a generation equipped with basic skills in work, production, communication and citizenship, to prepare professionals equipped with creative thinking and continuing self-learning skills and able to adapt with changes and deal confidently and efficiently with the future" (official document of Ministry of Education and Youth (2000) Education Vision 2020, pp 188).

On the technology integration front, the Ministry of Education is highly supportive of utilizing the power of technology within the educational system and the overall technological advancement in the country provides good ground for that. A number of initiatives are underway, however, the majority focus on using computers for organizational and administrative purposes. One example is the National Project for Statistical System (NA- SAP), which is an online system that will enable the ministry to collect student and teacher data for overall analytical and reporting purposes (Abu-Samaha & Shishakly, 2008). In her report, Karake-Shalhoub (2003) stresses that the Sheikh Mohammed IT education project has been successful in offering benefits to administrators, teachers, and parents with regards to facilitating student supervision and monitoring. Similarly, Tubaishat and his colleagues (2006) argue that the higher accessibility to technology in UAE public schools is not necessarily translated into adequate and more effective technology use for a variety of reasons. Nevertheless, there is a growing awareness for the need to enhance the curriculum with the objective of utilising technology to provide students with a better learning environment. One of the resulting initiatives by the Ministry of Education is the change in its future strategy that now includes technology integration in the curriculum through teaching and learning (Abu-Samaha & Shishakly, 2008).

With the technological readiness of the UAE and the various curricular reforms and program development initiatives launched to support technology-enhanced teaching, the key variable for technology integration in the UAE's K-12 classrooms is still the teacher. As such, understanding teachers' perceptions and beliefs in addition to assessing their technical abilities and teaching practices becomes very pressing. This is further augmented by the shortage in empirical studies addressing the issue in the region. In the following section, preliminary findings from an exploratory investigation addressing K-12 teachers' readiness for technology integration, perceptions about its advantages, and prevalent practices are presented.

Teachers' Practices, Perceptions and Beliefs: Preliminary Investigation

The study was conducted at a private school located in Dubai, UAE, which caters mainly for Emirati students in addition to Arab expatriates. Data were collected in the academic year 2010/2011 after contacting administrators and obtaining teachers' informed consent, with a total of 62 teachers providing consent for participation.

Research Instrument

The instrument used was the Technology Implementation Questionnaire (TIQ) developed by the research team at the Center for the Study of Learning and Performance at Concordia University (Wozney, et al., 2006) based on the expectancy-value theory. The questionnaire addressed teacher demographics, current technology use, and the availability of resources. It also included 33 belief items addressing three motivational categories: perceived expectancy of success, perceived value of technology use, and perceived cost of technology use.

In order to clearly attest to how the teachers are using the technology in their classroom, and avoid biased self reported responses on the questionnaire, participants were asked to respond to another survey with open ended questions and describe their actual use of YouTube in their teaching practices, while specifying the major advantages and disadvantages of the website, in addition to the major challenges they are facing. YouTube was selected as a specific example due to the fact that it is free, accessible, widely popular, and has multiple usages ranging from a pure presentational tool to a high level collaborative problem based tool where students may participate in designing and developing a particular video (Tamim, 2009; Tamim, Shaikh, & Bethel., 2007).

Findings and Discussion

Within the overall sample, the gender distribution was relatively balanced with a slightly higher male percentage where 54% were males. With regards to grade level, the majority were secondary level teachers (43%) followed by elementary level teachers (33%) and finally middle school-teachers (33%). As for subject matter, English and Science teachers comprised the largest categories with each group representing 27% of the sample. These frequencies were followed by the Math and IT teachers' groups reflecting 18% and 15% of the participants respectively, with social studies and other subject matter being less represented in the sample. The average years of teaching experience for the overall sample was 6.8 years (SD=5.5) reflecting a relatively young teacher profile. An important finding is related to the shortage of training on technology use for educational purposes where the majority of teachers reported very limited prior training (32% reported no training and 21% reported one day or less).

In general, teachers preferred a balanced approach to teaching with 45% selecting the balanced option over full teacher centered or student centred approaches. Participants rated themselves highly with regards to technological skills (46% advanced/expert, 50% beginner/average, 4% unfamiliar/newcomer) reporting relatively high usage of technology at a personal level (70% 5 hours or more/week, 15% 1 to 5 hours/week, 5% less than 1 hour/week). Results reflect that teachers seem to be proficient with technology use and do not feel intimidated by its introduction into the classroom.

Teachers' feedback was positive pertaining to students' access to technology with 70% of the teachers noting that their students' access to technology at the school ranges between good and excellent with less than 3% noting that access was poor. Such findings are promising with regards to the availability of technology in the

school, and is a good reflection of the overall attention given to technology in the country. As for the frequency of technology integration, most of the teachers reported using it on a frequent to very frequent bases (70%) with specific results for each type of technology usage summarized in Table 2. Percentages represent teachers who reported fairly often to almost always usage of a particular integration process.

Concerning perceptions about technology use, participants' responses to items addressing the value and benefit of technology's integration with teaching practices revealed overall positive attitudes. The most positive responses were for: "technology use increases academic achievement", "technology use is effective because I can implement it", "technology is a valuable instructional tool", " technology integration is successful with regular maintenance", and "with technology, teacher becomes a facilitator"

Teachers' Perceptions Regarding Technology Use

While data from the questionnaire seemed to draw a very positive picture about the current status of technology integration at the given school, the open-ended questionnaire did not offer such a bright image. On the positive side,

Table 2. Percentage of teachers' frequency of different usage of technology

Use	Example	UAE
Instructional	Drill, practice, tutorials, remediation	62%
Communicative	e-mail, computer conferencing	78%
Organizational	Database, spreadsheets, record keeping, lesson plans	87%
Analytical/Programming	Statistics, charting, graphing, drafting, robotics	65%
Recreational	Games	35%
Expansive	Simulations, experiments, brainstorming	49%
Creative	Desktop publishing, digital video/camera, graphics	49%
Expressive	Word processing, on-line journal	48%
Evaluative	Assignments, portfolio, testing	49%
Informative	Internet websites, CD-ROM	89%

teachers' responses reflected their awareness to the advantages of YouTube especially with regards to student motivation and minimizing boredom. They also noted that its major positive points are the free accessibility and large variety of available topics. Responses also reflected that the majority of the teachers use YouTube movies in their teaching. However, the overwhelming use was for presentation and motivational purposes with minimal or practically no implementation with a collaborative or learner centered approach. The most prominent usage approaches were for: a) presentation and illustration of related topics; b) visual demonstration of some aspects that are not easy otherwise, especially in science; c) in support of topics covered; and d) to present fun and interesting songs and animations. From the sixty participants, only five mentioned using YouTube movies to start in-depth and critical analysis of issues presented in the movies, and only one teacher noted using it to upload English plays by students.

Moving to challenges, teachers' responses revealed that the major obstacles include: a) technical issues; b) administrative consent to use the website; c) inappropriateness of some scenes in some movies; and d) relevance of material to the subject matter covered in class. Only two teachers mentioned the issue of quality and correctness of the presented material where they noted that there are some misconceptions incorporated in some of the movies.

Overall findings indicate that there is no shortage in the availability of technology in the classroom or in teachers' personal technological skills and expertise. It is also clear that teachers are highly aware of the advantage of technological integration and they seem to be willing to work on making use of technological tools in their teaching practices. What is interesting is that the teachers perceive themselves as successful technology integrators. However, when asked specifically about how they are making use of technology, responses revealed that their utilization is still at the presentation level with a teacher-centered orientation. Findings indicate that teachers do not have a deep understanding of various pedagogical approaches of technological usage, especially with regards to learner-centered principals. While they are confident about the fact that they are utilizing technology, they are not aware of the various methods and techniques with which technology needs to be incorporated to support the development of meaningful and successful learning environments. This is definitely reflective of the shortage in pre-service and in-service training.

CONCLUSION

In conclusion, it is no secret that the prevalence and importance of computer technologies in our lives is remarkable, while its impact on students' performance in the educational context is undeniable. Although the UAE is a young country, it has achieved notable progress on all fronts, including the technological and educational ones. The literature, as well as the preliminary findings of the reported study indicates that UAE teachers have positive perceptions about the importance of technological integration for the enhancement of the learning process. They also reveal that there is no major shortage in teachers' technological expertise or willingness to make use of technology in their teaching practices. However, it is evident that there is a shortage in the knowledge and expertise of how to adequately utilize technology with a learner centered approach in order to make the best of what technology has to offer.

With the availability of technology in the school, and the participating teachers' current technical expertise, their awareness to technology's advantages, and their willingness to put the effort needed to succeed in technology integration, the situation seems to be very promising. What is still needed is an adequate and an appropriate level of training about how to utilize technology for the enhancement of the learning process rather than just how to use technology. More attention needs to be given by policy makers and academic administrators to the importance of professional development with regards to successful implementation of technology in the K-12 classroom. After all, and as research has proven over and over again, it is not enough to have a computer in the classroom with a teacher who knows how to run it, if we want o help our students in building the needed skills for them to excel in the future.

REFERENCES

Abu-Samaha, A. M., & Shishakly, R. (2008). Assessment of school information system utilization in the UAE primary schools. *Issues in Informing Science and Information Technology, 5*, 525–542.

Al-Mekhlafi, A. (2004). The Internet and EFL teaching: The reaction of UAE secondary school English language teachers. *Journal of Language and Learning, 2*(2), 88–113.

APA. (1997). *Learner-centered psychology principles: A framework for school redesign and reform.*

Bernard, R. M., De Rubalcava, B., & St. Pierre, D. (2000). Collaborative online distance learning: Issues for future practice and research. *Distance Education, 21*(2), 260–277. doi:10.1080/0158791000210205

Brinkerhof, J. (2006). Effects of long-duration, professional development academy on technological skills, computer self-efficacy, and technology integration beliefs and practices. *Journal of Research on Technology in Education, 39*(1), 22–44.

Clark, R. E. (1983). Reconsidering research on learning from media. *Review of Educational Research, 53*(4), 445–449.

Clark, R. E. (1994). Media will never influence learning. *Educational Technology Research and Development, 42*(2), 21–29. doi:10.1007/BF02299088

Computer-assisted instruction. (2008). In *CSharpOnline.NET*. Retrieved December 10, 2008, from http://en.csharp-online.net/Glossary:Definition_-_Computer-Assisted_Instruction

Computer Quotes. (2008). Retrieved December 22, 2008, from http://www.gdargaud.net/Humor/QuotesComputer.html

Cuban, L., Kirkpatrick, H., & Peck, C. (2001). High access and low use of technologies in high school classrooms: Explaining an apparent paradox. *American Educational Research Journal, 38*, 813–834. doi:10.3102/00028312038004813

De, P. K., Ahmad, S., & Somashekar, M. A. (2004). *Impediments to technology transfer and technology absorption in United Arab Emirates.* Paper presented at the International Association for Management of Technology, Washington.

DeBell, M., & Chapman, C. (2006). *Computer and internet use by students in 2003.* National Center for Education Statistics.

Dutta, S., & Mia, I. (2011). *The global information technology report 2010-2011.* INSEAD.

Education Vision 2020. (2000). *Pillars, strategic objectives, projects and implementation programs for UAE education development.*

Farhat, N. (2008). *The impact of technology on teaching and learning in high schools in the United Arab Emirates.* University of Leicester Doctor of Education.

Gaad, E., Arif, M., & Scott, F. (2006). Systems analysis of the UAE education system. *International Journal of Educational Management, 20*(4), 291–303. doi:10.1108/09513540610665405

Grabowski, B. L. (2004). Generative learning contributions to the design of instruction and learning. In Jonassen, D. (Ed.), *Handbook of research on educational communications and technology.* New York, NY: Simon &Shuster Macmillan.

Gunawardena, C. N., & McIsaac, M. S. (2004). Distance education. In Jonassen, D. (Ed.), *Handbook of research on educational communications and technology*. New York, NY: Simon &Shuster Macmillan.

Internet World Stats. (2011). *World internet users and population stats*. Retrieved 12 July, 2011, from http://www.internetworldstats.com/stats.htm

Jacobson, M. (1998). *Adoption patterns of faculty who integrate computer technology for teaching and learning in higher education*. Retrieved 15 March, 2005, from http://www.ucalgary.ca/~dmjacobs/phd/phd-results.html

Johnson, D. W., & Johnson, R. T. (2004). Cooperation and the use of technology. In Jonassen, D. (Ed.), *Handbook of research on educational communications and technology*. New York, NY: Simon & Shuster Macmillan.

Jonassen, D., & Reeves, T. C. (1996). Learning with technology: Using computers as cognitive tools. In Jonassen, D. (Ed.), *Handbook of research for educational communications and technology*. McMillan.

Karake-Shalhoub, Z. (2003). *Profile of the information society in the United Arab Emirates*. ESCWA.

Kimble, C. (1999). *The impact of technology on learning: Making sense of the research*. Retrieved 25 March, 2005, from http://www.mcrel.org/PDF/PolicyBriefs/5983PI_PBImpactTechnology.pdf

Kohut, A., Wike, R., & Horowitz, J. M. (2007). *World publics welcome global trade - But not immigration*. Washington, DC: Pew Research Center.

Kozma, R. (1991). Learning with media. *Review of Educational Research*, *61*(2), 179–221.

Kozma, R. (1994). Will media influence learning: Reframing the debate. *Educational Technology Research and Development*, *42*(2), 7–19. doi:10.1007/BF02299087

Laurillard, D. (2002). *Rethinking university teaching: A framework for the effective use of educational technology* (2nd ed.). London, UK: Routledge. doi:10.4324/9780203304846

McCombs, B. L. (2000). *Assessing the role of educational technology in the teaching and learning process: A learner-centered perspective*. Retrieved September, 2005, from http://www.ed.gov/rschstat/eval/tech/techconf00/mccombs_paper.html

McCombs, B. L., & Vakili, D. (2005). A learner-centered framework for e-learning. *Teachers College Record*, *107*(8), 1582–1600. doi:10.1111/j.1467-9620.2005.00534.x

Moore, M. G., & Kearsley, G. P. (2005). *Distance education: A systems view*. Belmont, CA: Wadsworth.

Morris, M. (2005, October). *Organisation, social change and the United Arab Emirates*. Paper presented at the Social Change in the 21st Century Conference, Queensland.

Naidu, S. (2003). Designing instruction for e-learning environments. In Moore, M. G., & Anderson, W. G. (Eds.), *Handbook of distance education*. Mahwah, NJ: Lawrence Erlbaum associates.

Oblinger, D. G., & Oblinger, J. L. (Eds.). (2005). *Educating the net generation*. EDUCAUSE.

Plante, J., & Beattie, J. (2004). *Connectivity and ICT integration in Canadian elementary and secondary schools: First results from the information and communications technologies in schools survey*. Retrieved September 19, 2006, from http://www.statscan.ca/english/freepub/81-004-XIE/200409/ict.htm

Rideout, V., Roberts, D. F., & Foehr (2005). *Generation M: Media in the lives of 8-18 year-olds*. Washington, DC: Kaiser Family Foundation.

Rideout, V. J., Vandewater, E., & Wartella, E. A. (2003). *Zero to six: Electronic media in the lives of infants, toddlers and preschoolers*. Kaiser Family Foundation.

Romiszowski, A., & Mason, R. (2004). Computer-mediated communication. In Jonassen, D. (Ed.), *Handbook of research on educational communications and technology*. New York, NY: Simon & Shuster Macmillan.

Schenker, J. D. (2007). *The effectiveness of technology use in statistics instruction in higher education: A meta-analysis using heirarchical linear modeling*. Ohio: Kent State University.

Schmid, R. F., Bernard, R. M., Borokhovski, E., Tamim, R. M., Abrami, P. C., & Wade, A. (2009). Technology's effect on achievement in higher education: A stage I meta-analysis of classroom applications. *Journal of Computing in Higher Education, 21*, 95–109. doi:10.1007/s12528-009-9021-8

Shihab, M. (2001). Economic development in the UAE. In Al Abed, I., & Hellyer, P. (Eds.), *United Arab Emirates: A new perspective*. London, UK: Trident Publishing.

Spector, J. M., Merrill, M. D., Van Merrienboer, J., & Driscoll, M. P. E. (Eds.). (2008). *Handbook of research on educational communications and technology* (3rd ed. ed.). London, UK: Lawrence Erlbaum Associates.

Tamim, R. M. (2009). *YouTube in learner centered classrooms*. Paper presented at the Designing and Delivering Blended Learning in Second Language Context Symposium.

Tamim, R. M., Bernard, R. M., Borokhovski, E., Abrami, P. C., & Schmid, R. F. (2011). What forty years of research says about the impact of technology on learning: A second-order meta-analysis and validation study. *Review of Educational Research, 81*(3), 4–28. doi:10.3102/0034654310393361

Tamim, R. M., Shaikh, K., & Bethel, E. C. (2007, October). *EDyoutube: Why not*. Paper presented at the AACE E-Learn Conference, Quebec.

The New Media Consortium & Educause Learning Initiative (2004). *The Horizon report*.

The New Media Consortium & Educause Learning Initiative (2005). *The Horizon report*.

The New Media Consortium & Educause Learning Initiative (2006). *The Horizon report*.

The New Media Consortium & Educause Learning Initiative (2007). *The Horizon report*.

The New Media Consortium & Educause Learning Initiative (2008). *The Horizon report*.

The New Media Consortium & Educause Learning Initiative (2009). *The Horizon report*.

The New Media Consortium & Educause Learning Initiative (2010). *The Horizon report*.

The New Media Consortium & Educause Learning Initiative (2011). *The Horizon report*.

Tobin, K., Tippins, D. J., & Gallard, A. J. (1994). Research on instructional strategies for teaching science. In Gabel, D. L. (Ed.), *Handbook of research on science teaching and learning*. New York, NY: Macmillan Publishing Company.

Tubaishat, A., Bhatti, A., & El-Qawasmeh, E. (2006). ICT experiences in two different Middle Eastern universities. *Issues in Informing Science and Information Technology, 3*, 668–678.

USA Today. (2006). *'Google,' 'unibrow' added to dictionary*. Retrieved 25 September, 2006, from http://www.usatoday.com/news/offbeat/2006-07-06-new-words_x.htm

USA Today. (2011). *OMG! Online abbreviations make dictionary*. Retrieved 15 April, 2011, from http://www.usatoday.com/tech/news/2011-03-25-online-dictionary_N.htm

Van Dusen, G. (2000). Digital dilemma: Issues of access, cost, and quality in media—enhanced and distance education. *ASHE-ERIC Higher Education Report*, *27*(5), 1–120.

Wozney, L., Venkatesh, V., & Abrami, P. (2006). Implementing computer technologies: Teachers' perceptions and practices. *Journal of Technology and Teacher Education*, *14*(1), 173–207.

ADDITIONAL READING

Alessi, S. M., & Trollip, S. R. (2000). *Multimedia for learning: Methods and development* (3rd ed.). New York, NY: Allyn & Bacon.

Anderson, T. (Ed.). (2008). *The theory and practice of online learning*. Edmonton, Canada: Athabasca University Press.

Bauer, J., & Kenton, J. (2005). Toward technology integration in the schools: Why it isn't happening. *Journal of Teacher Education*, *13*(4), 519–546.

Baylor, A. L., & Ritchie, D. (2002). What factors facilitate teacher skill, teacher morale, and percieved student learning in technology-using classrooms? *Computers & Education*, *39*, 395–414. doi:10.1016/S0360-1315(02)00075-1

Bitner, N., & Bitner, J. (2002). Integrating technology into the classroom: Eight keys to success. *Journal of Technology and Teacher Education*, *10*(1), 95–100.

Bleed, R. (2006). The IT leader as alchemist: Finding the true gold. *EDUCAUSE Review*, *41*(1), 32–42.

Bonk, C. (2008, March, 2008). *YouTube anchors and enders: The use of shared online video content as a macrocontext for learning*. Paper presented at the American Educational Research Association New York.

Bransford, J. D., Vye, N. J., & Bateman, H. (2002). Creating high-quality learning environments: Guidelines from research on how people learn. In Graham, P. A., & Stacey, N. G. (Eds.), *The Knowledge Economy and Post Secondary Education: Report of a Workshop*. Washington, DC: National Academy Press.

Chuang, H. H., & Thompson, A. (2006). Students teaching teachers. *Educational Leadership*, *63*(4), 70–71.

Cochran-Smith, M. (2005). The new teacher education: For better or for worse? *Educational Researcher*, *34*(7), 3–17. doi:10.3102/0013189X034007003

Cuban, L. (2003). *Oversold and underused: Computers in the classroom*. Harvard University Press.

Dale, R., & Shortis, S. R. (2004). You can't not go with the technological flow, can you? Constructing "ICT" and "teaching and learning". *Journal of Computer Assisted Learning*, *20*, 456–470. doi:10.1111/j.1365-2729.2004.00103.x

Dutta, S., & Mia, I. (2011). *The global information technology report 2010-2011*. INSEAD.

Ertmer, P. (2005). Teacher pedagogical beliefs: The final frontier in our quest for technology integration? *Educational Technology Research and Development*, *53*(4), 25–39. doi:10.1007/BF02504683

Franklin, C. (2007). Factors that influence elementary teachers use of computers. *Journal of Technology and Teacher Education*, *15*(2), 267–293.

Johnson, D. W., & Johnson, R. T. (2008). Cooperation and the use of technology. In Spector, J. M., Merrill, M. D., Merrienboer, J. V., & Driscoll, M. P. (Eds.), *Handook of research on educational communication and technology* (3rd ed.). New York, NY: Lawrence Erlbaum Associsates.

Jonassen, D. (Ed.). (2004). *Handbook of research on educational communications and technology*. New York, NY: Simon & Shuster Macmillan.

Kadel, R. (2005). How teacher attitudes affect technology integration. *Learning and Leading with Technology, 32*(5), 34–35.

Kiboss, J. K., Ndirangu, M., & Wekesa, E. W. (2004). Effectiveness of a computer-mediated simulations program in school biology on pupil's learning outcomes in cell theory. *Journal of Science Education and Technology, 13*(2), 207–213. doi:10.1023/B:JOST.0000031259.76872.f1

Liao, Y.-K., Chang, H. W., & Chen, Y. W. (2008). Effects of computer applications on elementary school students' achievement: A meta-analysis of students in Taiwan. *Computers in the Schools, 24*(3), 43–64. doi:10.1300/J025v24n03_04

Mayer, R. (2011). Towards a science of motivated learning in technology-supported environments. *Educational Technology Research and Development, 59*, 301–308. doi:10.1007/s11423-011-9188-3

Swain, C. (2006). Preservice teachers self-assessment using technology: Determining what is worthwhile and looking for changes in daily teaching and learning practices. *Journal of Technology and Teacher Education, 14*(1), 29–59.

Vannatta, R. A., & Fordham, N. (2004). Teacher dispositions as predictors of classroom technology use. *Journal of Research on Technology in Education, 36*(3), 253–271.

Whale, D. (2006). Technology skills as a criterion in teacher evaluation. *Journal of Technology and Teacher Education, 14*(1), 61–71.

Zimmerman, J. (2006). Why some teachers resist change and what principals can do about it. *National Association of Secondary School Principals Bulletin, 90*(1), 238–249.

KEY TERMS AND DEFINITIONS

Computer Assisted Instruction: A term that encompasses various teaching and instructional strategies that make use of computer technology in the delivery and presentation of the content.

Computer-Mediated Communication: Refers to any communication that takes place with the help two or more networked computers.

Information Communication Technology: A broad term that is used in reference to contemporary technologies that provide access to information and enable higher levels of communication, mostly these are computer-based and internet enabled.

Internet-Based Technologies: A term used to refer to the communications infrastructure of the Internet, and any tools that are dependent on it for its functioning.

K-12 Education: Refers to the school years spanning from preschool, elementary, middle and secondary years.

Learner-Centred Principles: A set of principles advocated by the American Psychological Association to be required for the advancement of the educational context and the positive involvement of the students in the learning process. The principles focus on cognitive and meta-cognitive factors; motivational and affective factors; developmental and social factors; and individual differences.

Net Generation: A term used to describe the generation of individuals who were born and are growing in the wired 21st century.

Chapter 3
Computer Assisted School Administration in the United Arab Emirates

Rima Shishakly
Ajman University of Science and Technology, UAE

ABSTRACT

The United Arab Emirates (UAE) is a country in which the governance of education has been centralized. The use of computers for administrative applications in education reflects the approach of centralization. As an evolution, most development work is done in a centrally located computer center at the Ministry of Education. School administration in the UAE educational system has experienced a rapid computerization process. The chapter presents the ways in which the Emirates educational system is coping with this issue. A brief overview of the structure of the educational system in UAE will be presented. Subsequently, the chapter will study how Information Technology in Educational Management (ITEM) use has developed over a decade. Recently, there have been various modifications within the educational system in the UAE, specifically towards modernization and decentralization. Nonetheless, a certain maturity has been reached in using ITEM. Therefore, the chapter will attempt to monitor the significance of this alternation on the system's implementation and use of technology.

INTRODUCTION

This chapter gives an outline of the developments in School Information system (SIS) in UAE over the last twelve years and gives a more detailed description of the current Enterprise School Information System (eSIS). After a general overview of the historical context of Information Technology in Educational Management (ITEM) in UAE, the details of the educational system innovation and the eSIS development will be described.

The Context and History of ITEM in the UAE

The UAE is considered to be a young state compared to other countries in the region and worldwide. The United Arab Emirates, as a political

DOI: 10.4018/978-1-4666-1984-5.ch003

union came to life in the year 1971, between the seven Emirates (Abu-Dhabi, Dubai, Al-Sharjah, Ajman, Ras-Al-Khaima, Al-Fujira and Um- Al-Quwain)

The Educational System as a structure is not complex; it consists of basic schools and secondary schools. The basic public schools start at 6 years of age and the student spends five years at the first unit (level 1-5), four years at the second unit of the basic school (level 6-9) and three years at secondary school (level 10-12). Schools are funded, staffed and facilitated by the government of the UAE. Basic public education in the UAE is free and compulsory at the first unit between the ages of 6 and 12.

The basic public schools' structure and characteristics in the seven Emirates are similar. The UAE, as a young nation having adequate resources, is willing to invest in this area in order to improve its educational infrastructure. The Ministry of Education (MOE) intends to devolve some of its authorities to the nine educational zones (Abu Dhabi educational zone, Al-Ain educational zone, Al-Gharbia educational zone, Dubai educational zone, Sharjah educational zone, Ajman educational zone, Ras Al-khaimah educational zone, Al-Fujira educational zone and Um Al-Quwain educational zone) in line with its centralization of decision making and kind of decentralized managements. Under the proposed Act of Authorisation, schools, both public and private, will report directly to their own educational zones. (MOE, 1998)

The United Arab Emirates is a country in which the governance of education has been centralized since the early attempts to computerize school management in 1999. The Ministry of Education strategy for ITEM reflects centralizing school management in certain areas and de-centralizing school management in other areas. The centralization strategy of the Ministry aims to install a countrywide network of computers and servers to connect all schools (basic and secondary) in each educational zone to the Ministry of Education by the year 2020.

The decentralized strategy in school management which starts at the primary and secondary school level gave school management the opportunity to use commercial companies to develop computer based finance packages due to the business-oriented nature and the size of such schools.

In order to achieve the strategic aims and operational targets of the Ministry of Education's 2020 vision; a number of investments in Information Technology and Information Systems were started in the year 1998. These investments targeted the automation of the Ministry's activities relating to school management. These investments in Technology and Systems came as an integral part of the UAE's government strategy to automate all ministerial activities, banks, hospitals and many other organisations to create the region's first electronic government (e-Government). Three major investments can be identified so far in the UAE's educational sector:

1. High School Certificate Control System and Infrastructure
2. Student and Staff Registration Systems
3. e-learning (Curricula delivered via technology)

As an early experiment, the MOE commissioned a High School Certificate Control System (HSCCS) to be developed by a third party system provider in 1998. This system mainly provided high school students' enrolment, exams and results for the Science and Art streams and was enhanced two years later to include the technical stream of the high school certificate. The system facilitates the use of data related to student registration, examination timetables, examination scores and certificate printouts. In the year 2000, the Ministry of Education added three more systems to the existing HSCCS; Student Registration, Staff Registration and Inventory Management System. Figure 1 represents the different activities programmed though the Student and Staff Registration systems.

MOE has mounted a great effort to enter student enrolment data, tests, final examination scores and school reports of more than 200,000 students in 451 schools in the seven educational zones while student data from approximately 209 schools (mainly in Abu Dhabi and Al-Ain educational zones) are yet to be entered in such a system.

Despite the fact that the staff registration system has been functioning for one year only, it provides an accurate record of all employees and personnel in the Ministry and its schools countrywide. Provided by the Emirates Institution for Computers and used in Abu Dhabi and Dubai emirates so far. Regarding the Inventory Management System is a precise record keeping system of inventory data to control the daily, monthly and yearly movement, distribution and storing of the Ministry and its physical asset, and the Educational institutions (MOE, 2005). It is evident from the Ministry's documents that the system is yet to cover the other five emirates and suffers from a number of technical problems and lacks appropriate user training (Shishakly, 2006). Figure 2 provides a description of the modules/subsystems that cover the different activities of the High School Certificate Control System and Inventory Management System.

The Ministry's next strategic investment is in the National Project for Statistical System (NASAP), which will gather and analyse data for student and educational staff from all schools countrywide. This system will be available on the Internet and will enable the Ministry to publish such data analysis through a dynamic Website infrastructure. In addition to (NASAP) and as part of the MOE's future strategy, Information Technology will be integrated into curriculum delivery in terms of teaching and learning, teacher training and monitoring and evaluation.

Current Status and Future View

Since the project started in 1999, and was internally developed to aid schools in administrative tasks, terminals were provided to a few users in the schools (mostly administration staff). Their task was to enter students' data, and tests scores.

Figure 1. The available applications for student and staff registration systems and their use

STUDENT REGISTRATION SUBSYSTEMS	STAFF REGISTRATION SUBSYSTEMS
General School Administration	General Staff Registration
Administration of Pupil Data	Administration of Staff Data
Enrollment Registration	Staff Returns
Examination Registration	Maintenance of Staff Absence Details
Test Score Registration	
Final Examination Registration	

Figure 2. High school certificate and Inventory systems' uses

HIGH SCHOOL CERTIFICATE CONTROL SYSTEM	INVENTORY SYSTEM
Student's Registration Number	Inventory Listing Data
Student's Examination Timetable	Inventory Distributing Data
Student's Score Results	Inventory Journal
Student's Certificate Control	Inventory Control

Most of the Software for administrative applications in the MOE has been developed in-house. Furthermore, microcomputers have been installed in several layers of the educational system, network to connect schools, the educational zones and MOE. Therefore, there was a growing use of commercial packages such as word processors, database managers, drawing packages and communications software in school offices. At this level the MOE's goal was to computerize students' recorders as an initial stage of using technology effectively in educational management.

Through study conducted prior to the low levels of school information system (SIS) used to assist school management and administrative tasks, in the UAE government (public) schools. Reasons for this deficiency in computer-assisted administration use were related to the lack of clear strategic goals, lack of system implementation framework, system quality, system implementation process and quality training (Shishakly, 2006, 2008).

System Development

A rapid rise in population produce a rise in government (public) school, there were 723 government schools in the UAE in 2009. 303 schools in Abu Dhabi (the capital), 79 schools in Dubai, 124 schools in Sharjah, 90 schools in Ras al-Khaimah, 41 schools in Ajman, 61 schools in Al-Fujairah and 25 in Umm- al Quwain (MOE,2010) (Figure 3). The students' number is raised from 200,000 students to 262,373 students; these students are educated by 22,732 teachers and 4,737 administrators (MOE, 2009).

In 2005 the trend in UAE was towards decentralizing the education. Education decentralization seems to be a global trend in the past decade. (Astiz et al, 2002, p.1) mention that "over the past several decades, there has been a preoccupation with decentralization in the policy discourse about education, particularly among the developing nations of Latin America, South Asia, and Eastern

Figure 3. The government (public) schools in the UAE

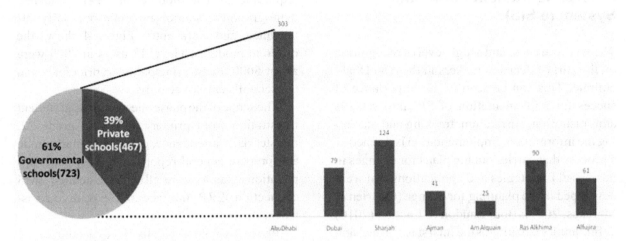

Europe and among international developing agencies." The decentralization processes are being required more and more for the future schools worldwide. And Abu-Duhou (1999) supports the statement that the interest in decentralization of education is a worldwide phenomenon.

In general public education is bureaucratic. Bureaucracy discourages creativity and innovation and encourages focus on fulfillment with the rules. Decentralization could provide authorization in decision making within the school management. According to Paqueo & Lammert (2000) decentralization involves shifting management responsibilities from the central to regional or lower levels so that the center retains control the decision. Hanson (1998) defines decentralization as "the transfer" of decision-making authority, responsibility, and tasks from higher to lower levels or between organizations. (Behrman et al, 2002, p.8) mention that "decentralization of education includes devolution of authority and responsibility for schools from central to local levels, increased local financing of schools, decentralization of school functions, and reforms to be incentive structure of schools and their teachers ".

The emirates of Abu Dhabi, Dubai, Sharjah and Fujairah moved towards the decentralization of the educational system by creating education councils in 2005 in those four emirates; Abu Dhabi Education Council (ADEC), Sharjah Education Council, Fujairah Educational Council and the knowledge and Humanities Authority in Dubai (ESCCR, 2011). In particular, ADEC involves decentralized decision making as close as possible to the MOE's general vision in 2005. For examples, in order to increase efficiency and effectiveness in the school organization, ADEC started the project of Enterprise Student Information Systems (eSIS) in 2008. School information systems are intended to support principals, vice principals, administrative staff, teachers, students and parents. The strategy started at the level above the individual schools but it covers three hundred schools in three regions of Abu Dhabi. The strategic vision was to use technology to facilitate change in all the schools in the Abu Dhabi region and to provide school information systems assist in school teaching and management. The vision of ADEC was to implement systems well designed to satisfy all the stockholders and decision makers within the educational system and to carry the innovation to the management systems from its current state to one of high quality standard is using ITEM (ADEC, 2009).

Enterprise Student Information System (e SIS)

There is awareness and a high level of recognition on the part of decision makers in the Abu Dhabi emirate. This can be seen in the importance of successful implementation of SIS into schools administration, curriculum, tracking and managing the information. Implementation is defined as a process that carries out the plans for changes in business/IT strategies and applications that were developed in the planning for change (O'Brien & Marakas, 2009). Both Laudon & Laudon (2010) define implementation as the final stage of decision making, when the individual puts the decision into effect and reports on the process of the solution. Telem (1996) mentions that implementation of a school management information system (SMIS) constitutes a big challenge for schools and decision makers as well. Successful implementation according to Fung's (1995) explanation is in effect the facilitation of an integration process of the school information system by the school.

Enterprise Student Information Systems (eSIS) has two computerization phases that are urbanized for the development and system implementation in 2008. Figure 3 shows the different assistant subsystems. The eSIS are being designed for the education authority in the Abu Dhabi emirate and the Abu Dhabi region. eSIS was designed and integrated across a range of levels and functions to fit the requirement of large numbers of the users. Furthermore the design goal was to make the system easy to use and easy to navigate. eSIS system other perspective goal was to support decision makers, student services, health and wealth tracking, curriculum tracking, and eSIS wireless. The eSIS can track the student from kindergarten till the final year of school and assist teachers, student and parents to communicate and follow the educational operation.

The eSIS system consists of two phases. Phase one: Implemented in 2009 and defined with four major modules customized to meet Abu Dhabi's requirements. The modules are: P-12 students' demographics, school information, daily attendance, and mark entry. Figure 4 shows the different modules. The eSIS users in 2009 were about 5000 users; principal, vice principals and the school's employee only.

The scope of the phase one was to assist student registration from primary school to grade 12, register daily attendance, enter class mark/grade and prepare general reporting. The systems applications was to store all teacher details, SMS connection, ERP interface and executive assistance.

Phase two strategically is expected to be implemented in September 2011. The scope of this phase is to assist teacher and parent, provide wireless access to eSIS from any wireless, automated school time tables, student suspensions/ discipline, selecting gifted students and transportation. And this will raise the number of users from 5000 to 12000 users.

The system is going to provide a vision to be shared by all the school stakeholders. Fung (2001) states that the role of SIS is to support the development of a professional learning community both within and across the schools, staff development online, global collaborations on the internet and cross-cultural exchange will all become commonplace.

eSIS Evaluation

One of the major challenges that ADEC faces was evaluating eSIS first phase, regarding the systems functioning and user satisfaction. User acceptability to the system is a key cause of successful system implementation and Wild et al. (1992) mention that user acceptability is one instrument that incorporates system evaluation. Griffiths et al. (2007) state that information retrieval and information systems literature is important in attempting to understand what user satisfaction is.

Training is undoubtedly a crucial factor affecting the implementation and use of eSIS. Nolan

Figure 4. eSIS modules and functionalities

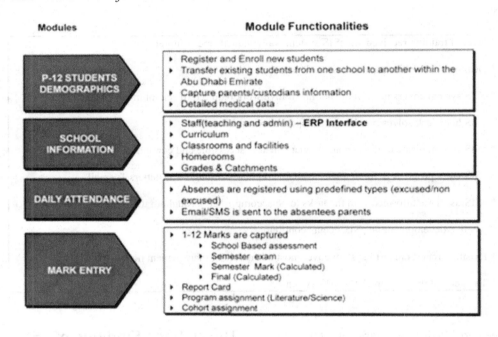

et al. (2001) mention that the suitability and appropriateness of professional development and training must in the first instance be linked to user concerns and provided in response to them. In 2010-2011 ADEC strategy was to expand the numbers of the trained users such as teachers. There are now 12000 users trained to use the first phase and to be continuing training for the second phase (ADEC, 2009). The major challenge faced in eSIS is training the large numbers of users. Tatnall (2001) mentions that users in the school must be regarded as the most important consideration in the systems implementation. O'Mahony (1997) states that problems with ITEM include use and usability, staff training, staff awareness and reSIStance to change.

ADEC found that the solution for providing training for the big numbers of the system users is to provide peer training between the staff members, on line training and video training. ADEC prepared an online survey to get feedback concerning users' satisfaction and system functioning. The survey was distributed to the three hundred schools in the regions of Abu Dhabi. The analysis of the survey is enumerated below. Figure 5 shows the questions that were asked in the survey to measure the user's satisfaction towards eSIS regarding the level of training, problem solving, communication and general impression about eSIS system. The survey was distributed online. The survey showed that: 13% strongly agreed, 60% agreed, 10% were hesitant, and 11% do not agree and 6% do not agree at all that the level of training received on eSIS system use was adequate. 32% strongly agree 53% agree, 8% hesitant, 7% do not agree and 1% only does not agree at all that dealing with eSIS system is easy and simple. Concerning eSIS system covering most of the administrative work required of school management the percentage showed 17% strongly agree, 47% agree, 19% were hesitant, 15% do not agree and 2% do not agree at all.

Additionally, 34% strongly agree, 47% agree, 10% were hesitant, 7% do not agree and 2% do not agree at all that the way to communicate with the eSIS team and management is accessible and continuously available. On the other hand, 43% strongly agree, 45% agree, 9% were hesitant, 2%

Figure 5. The questions that were available in the survey carried out by ADEC in order to get feedback about eSIS

---

* level of training received on eSIS system was adequate and comprehensive

* Dealing with eSIS system is easy and simple

* eSIS system covers most of the administrative work required of school management

* eSIS help desk solves problem and responds to inquiries

* eSIS communicate eSIS team and management is accessible and continuously

* eSIS work progress & future plans available regularly through newsletters & email

* eSIS users are informed with the tasks to be accomplished throughout the year

* positive development on eSIS occurs continuously

* Exisiting reports in eSIS system cover most of the school management needs

* The general impression about eSIS system

---

do not agree and 1% does not agree at all that the eSIS help desk solves problems and responds to inquiries. 33% strongly agree, 55% agree and 8% hesitant, 2% do not agree, and 2% do not agree at all that eSIS users are informed with tasks to be accomplished throughout the year.

Concerning the existing reports in eSIS that cover most of the school management needs the percentages showed 13% strongly agree, 50% agree, 7% hesitant, 15% do not agree and 5% do not agree at all. 30% strongly agree, 55% agree, 11% were hesitant, 4% do not agree, 1% does not agree at all that positive development on eSIS system occurs continuously. 32% strongly agree, 57% agree, 7% hesitant, 3% do not agree and 1% does not agree at all. The last question's aim was to examine the general impression and satisfaction regarding the eSIS system, the results indicated that 21% were strongly satisfied, 67% were satisfied, 6% were hesitant, 4% were dissatisfied and 1% were not satisfied at all.

Through the Findings of eSIS

The survey results are displayed in figure 6 and figure 7. The survey shows that in general the users' satisfaction and acceptability toward phase one of the system is around 50%. In response to the training provided by ADEC, 60% agreed that the level of training receive on eSIS training was adequate and comprehensive. This result not only stresses the importance of the training, but also gives some indications to the contents of training. Training is a crucial factor affecting the implementation and use of any system. Visscher & Bolemen (2001) mention that there is strong empirical evidence that user training strongly influences the degree of information system usage. Without training, the systems implementation will take longer, adaptation will be more problematic and frustration will be higher. The major challenge for ADEC's system is how to provide training for the big number of users. Especially that the number is raised from 5000 to 12000 including the arrangement of appropriate timing for all those stakeholders and coordinating between users' technological levels and systems used. The goal of the project is designed to provide complete training courses to accomplish full utilization of the system. A training plan should be developed to the three primary stakeholders; teacher, principals and employees and everyone who will either support or use eSIS.

ADEC's strategic plan was to provide online training. Computer based training and website training are virtually similar. With this type of training, content is delivered through the computer, using any combination of text, video, audio, chat rooms, or interactive assessment. Blanchard (2008) mentioned that all types of training are effective at developing declarative and, in particular, procedural knowledge.

The major question is if the online training course is enough to help to reach ADEC's training target? It is important to keep in mind that this can only be answered based on effective training, the users' levels of eSIS utility and experience of stakeholders. Baldwin and Ford (1988) defined 'positive transfer' as the degree to which trainees effectively apply knowledge, skills and attitudes gained in training context to their job. A large number of organizations all over the world are now using low cost solutions like online training programs. Web-based training is one of the methods which help a company's employees to use the same program; materials are also easy to update and online programs are effective for training across multiple locations and large numbers of trainees. Delahoussaye et al. (2002) say that organizations that make large investments in people typically have lower employee turnover, which is associated with higher customer satisfaction and this in turn, is influenced by training and development.

Figure 6. Survey results derived from the ADEC eSIS survey

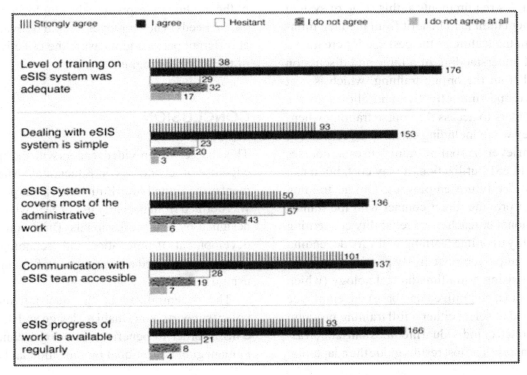

Figure 7. Survey results derived from the ADEC eSIS survey

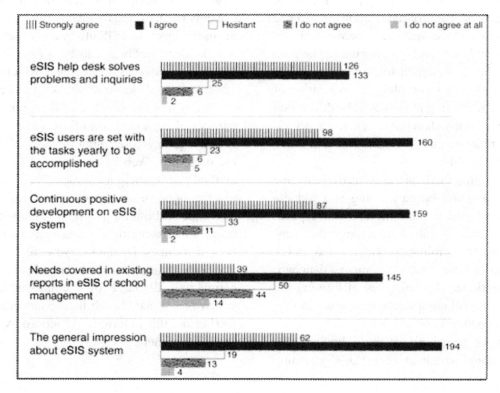

ADEC's requirements at this stage of system implementation is to benefit from blended training from the lecture as the best use for creating a general understanding of a topic and discussion method from the online training, which is cost effective and time effective and allows all the stakeholders to access the course training whenever they want; including catch-up on all training program levels. As online training uses set courses related to eSIS utilization, it may cost, but it can be used for future employees. Online training does not provide direct contact with the trainee professional or teachers so reliability concerning the quality of online learning will vary depending on each employee's needs. By providing training contents using a multimedia technology (which is stored in a centralized database) the employee is allowed to select either a full training program from scratch or individual modules and take an assessment test. The test results guide the adaptation

of the module to respond to the employee's individual needs. The employee should be evaluated at different periods to measure the effectiveness of the training program.

CONCLUSION

This chapter has provided readers with the knowledge use of technology in Educational Management in the United Arab Emirates. This experience was defined from the early use of SIS, which was designed by non-professionals. But through the development of innovation and technology the experience reached a certain level of maturity in using ITEM.

The decentralized of the decision making policy supports Abu Dhabi to design and develop eSIS in order to benefit from using technology in managing educational organization and assist educational managers in planning, organizing, controlling, reviewing, monitoring, and evaluating the operation of their schools.

The success or the failure of eSIS is reflected by the degree of system usage and user participant, acceptance and satisfaction. User training is vital in system implementation and it is a major challenge for ADEC. The training is clearly an issue that requires an ambitious training plan in order to have successful system implementation.

REFERENCES

Abu Dhabi Education Council (ADEC). (2009). *Enterprise school information system eSIS*. Official Documents.

Abu-Duhou, I. (1999). *School-based management. Fundamental of Education Planning, 62*. Paris, France: UNESCO.

Astiz, M. F., Wiseman, A. W., & Baker, D. P. (2002). Schooling towards decentralization: Consequences of globalization for curricular control in national education systems. *Comparative Education Review, 1*(1), 66–86. doi:10.1086/324050

Baldwin, T. T., & Ford, J. K. (1988). Transfer of training: A review and directions for future research. *Personnel Psychology, 41*, 63–105. doi:10.1111/j.1744-6570.1988.tb00632.x

Behrman, J. R., Deolakira, A. B., & Soon, L. Y. (2002). *Conceptual issue in the role of education decentralization in promoting effective schooling in Asian developing countries*. ERD working paper series No 22. Economic and Research Department.

Blanchard, P. N. (2008). *Training delivery method-organization levels: Advantages, manager, model, type, company, disadvantages, workplace, business*. Retrieved at http://www.refernceforbusiness.com/management/Tr-Z/Training-Delivery-Methods

Deetz, S., Sarah, J. T., & Simpson, J. L. (2000). *Leading organization through transition*. Thousand Oaks, CA: Sage Publication Inc.

Delahoussaye, M., Ellis, K., & Bolch, M. (2002, August). Measuring corporate smarts. *Training Magazine*, 20-35.

Fung, A. C. W. (1995). Managing change in ITEM. In Barta, B., Telem, M., & Gev, Y. (Eds.), *Information technology in educational management* (pp. 37–45). London, UK: Chapman and Hall.

Griffiths, J. R., Johnson, F., & Hartely, R. J. (2007). Satisfaction as a measure of system performance. *Journal of Librarianship and Information Science, 39*(3), 142–152. doi:10.1177/0961000607080417

Hanson, E. M. (1998). Strategies of educational decentralization: Key questions and core issues. *Journal of Educational Administration, 36*(2), 111–128. doi:10.1108/09578239810204345

Laudon, C. K., & Laudon, J. P. (2010). *Management information systems: Managing the digital firm* (11th ed.). Pearson.

Ministry of Education. (1998). *The development of the education system in The United Arab Emirates* (pp. 33–40).

Ministry of Education. (2005). *Research and development document / IT and MIS department*.

Ministry of Education. (2009). *Students and schools numbers/ academic year 2008-2009*. Official document.

Ministry of Education. (2010). *The strategic vision 2010*. Official Documents, the Ministry of Education in United Arab Emirates.

Nolan, C. J. P., & Lambert, M. (2001). Information system for leading and managing schools: Changing the paradigm. In Nolan, C. J. P., Fung, A. C. W., & Brown, M. A. (Eds.), *Pathways to institutional improvement with information technology in educational management*. London, UK: Kluwer. doi:10.1007/0-306-47006-3_7

O'Brien, J. A., & Marakas, G. M. (2009). *Management information systems* (9th ed.). Mac Graw-Hill.

O'Mahony, C. D., Wild, P., Selwood, I. D., Kraidej, L., & Reyes, M. G. (1997). Evaluation strategy for ITEM quality. In Fung, A. C. W. (Ed.), *Information technology in educational management for the school of the future*. Kluwer Academic Publisher.

Paqueo, V., & Lammert, J. (2000). *Decentralization and school-based management resource kit*. World Bank.

Shishakly, R. (2006). *Information technology in education management: Zayed School Information System (ZSIS) implementation model: United Arab Emirates*. Unpublished doctoral dissertation, University of Manchester, Manchester.

Shishakly, R. (2008). Assessment of school information system utilisation in UAE primary school. *Journal of Informing Science and Information Technology*, *5*(1), 525–542.

Tatnall, A. (2001). Information technology in educational management: Synthesis of experience. In Visscher, A., Wild, P., & Fung, A. C. W. (Eds.), *Research and future perspectives on computer-assisted school information systems*. Kluwer Academic Publisher.

Telem, M. (1996). Recently MIS implementation in school: A system socio-technical framework. *Computers & Education*, *27*(2), 85–93. doi:10.1016/0360-1315(96)00021-8

The Emirates Center for Strategic Studies and Research (ECSSR). (2011). *Education in the UAE current status and future developments*. Abu Dhabi, UAE: ECSSR.

Training Today. (n.d.). *How-to-choose the most effective training techniques*. Retrieved at Http://training.blr.com/employee-training-resources/

Visscher, A. J., & Bloemen, P. P. M. (2001). School managerial usage of computer-assisted school information systems: A comparison of good practice and bad practice school. In Nolan, P., & Fung, A. (Eds.), *Institutional improvement through information technology in educational management*. London, UK: Kluwer.

Wild, P., & Fung, A. C. W. (1996). Evaluation of ITEM for proactive development. In *Proceedings of the 2nd IFIP International Working Conference on ITEM*, July, 1996, Hong Kong Baptist University, Hong Kong.

ADDITIONAL READING

Barta, B. Z., Gev, Y., & Telem, G. (1994). *Information technology in educational management*. Chapman & Hall.

Davis, G. B., & Olson, M. H. (1984). *Management information systems: Conceptual foundation, structure and development* (International Edition). McGraw-Hill.

Fung, A. C. W., Visscher, A. J., Barta, B. Z., & Teather, D. (1997). *Information technology in educational management for the schools of the future*. Kluwer Academic Publishers.

Kallick, B., Wilson, J., & James, M. (2000). *Information technology for schools: Creating practical knowledge to improve student performance*. Jossey-Bass.

Nolan, P. C. J., Fung, A. C. W., & Brown, M. A. (2000). *Pathways to institutional improvement with information technology in educational management*. IFIP TC3/WG3.7 Fourth International Working Conference on Information Technology in Educational Management, July 27-31, 2000, Auckland, New Zealand. Kluwer Academic Publishers.

Tatnall, A., Kereteletswe, O. C., & Visscher, A. (2011). *Information technology and managing quality education.* 9th IFIP WG 3.7 Conference on Information Technology in Educational Management, ITEM (2010). Springer.

Tatnall, A., Okamoto, T., & Visscher, A. J. (2006). Knowledge management for educational innovation. *IFIP WG 3.7 7th Conference on Information Technology in Educational Management (ITEM)*, Hamamatsu, Japan, July 23-26, 2006. Springer

Tatnall, A., Osorio, J., & Visscher, A. (2010). *Information technology and educational management in the knowledge society.* IFIP TC3 WG3.7, 6th International Working Conference on Information... in Information and Communication Technology. Springer

Tatnall, A., Visscher, A. J., Finegan, A., & O'Mahony, C. (2009). *Evolution of information technology in educational management.* Springer.

Visscher, A. J. (2009). *Improving quality assurance in European vocational education and training factors influencing the use of quality assurance finding.* Springer. doi:10.1007/978-1-4020-9527-6

Visscher, A. J., Barta, B. Z., & Teather, D. C. B. (1997). *Information technology in educational management for the schools of the future. IFIP Advances in Information and Communication Technology.* Chapman & Hall.

Visscher, A. J., Osorio, J., & Tanall, A. (2004). *Information technology and educational management in the knowledge society.* IFIP TC3 WG3.7, 6th International Working Conference on Information Technology in Educational Management. Springer

KEY TERMS AND DEFINITIONS

ADEC: Abu Dhabi Education Council.

eSIS: (Enterprise Student Information Systems): an information system designed to organize, manage, facilitate and communicate all the government schools in Abu Dhabi Emirates in the United Arab Emirates.

HSCCS: High School Certificate Control System.

ITEM (Information Technology in Educational Management): The use of technology to automate all school activities and functioning to support school management, administrative and teacher in their daily activities and in decisions making and to assist the school to be more efficient and effective organization.

MOE: Ministry of Education.

NASAP: National Project for Statistical System.

SIS (School Information Systems): The combination of hardware, software, infrastructure and trained personnel organized to facilitate, control and provide better school daily office work.

UAE: United Arab Emirates.

Chapter 4
ICT in the UAE Educational Setting:
The Case in the Schools of Abu Dhabi Emirate

Ahmed Ibrahim
Al Ain Model School, UAE

ABSTRACT

Compared to the other Arab countries, the United Arab Emirates is in an advanced position regarding ICT in the educational setting. Yet, more efforts are still needed to put the UAE in a global competitive status. This chapter is meant to investigate the current educational situation in the Emirate of Abu Dhabi, United Arab Emirates to: a) discuss the impact of technology integration and the precise roles ICT plays in fostering learning, b) explore the most various problems and challenges teachers face in implementing ICT in teaching, and c) shed light on the role of educational leaders in enhancing teaching and learning through integrating ICT. This research-based chapter tackles the above-mentioned issues relying on the previous studies in the same field (literature review) and conducting a qualitative and a quantitative study- using surveys and interviews-to gather authentic data to assess the current situation of ICT in Abu Dhabi Emirate.

INTRODUCTION

ADEC's ICT efforts are endless. On one hand, at the hardware level, schools are provided with well-equipped computer labs, over head projectors, plasma LCDs, Internet, and other technological devices that enhance communication among students. On the other hand, ADEC provides schools with all the needed software programs to facilitate teaching and learning at schools. Furthermore, at the educational programs and curriculum level, IT, as subject matter, has replaced ICT. Being an English teacher/coordinator and witnessing two eras of education in the United Arab Emirates-the previous era of time when the chalkboard was used, and the current era when ICT is part of the teaching and learning process-I can strongly value the impact of ICT on the students' achievements.

DOI: 10.4018/978-1-4666-1984-5.ch004

Perhaps the biggest the challenge for any education organization in the 21st century is to prepare generations who are able to play their part in the present day knowledge-based economy and yet, at the same time, remain imbued with strong state values. To meet this challenge, Abu Dhabi Education Council (ADEC) was formed in 2005 with the aim to produce citizens who are able to participate fully in the knowledge-based economy of the twenty-first century, who are also technologically literate; there is a need for paradigm shift in education. ICT, primarily computers, is one of the major tools that can be used to achieve this goal. In this respect, Abu Dhabi Education Council has a very important role to play such as providing the ICT infrastructure and training needed in schools.

In fact, ADEC's ICT efforts are endless. On one hand, at the hardware level, schools are provided with well-equipped computer labs, over head projectors, plasma LCDs, Internet, and other technological devices that enhance communication among students. On the other hand ADEC provides schools with all the needed software programs to facilitate teaching and learning Furthermore, at the educational programs and curriculum level, IT, as subject matter, has replaced ICT. Being an English teacher/coordinator and witnessing two eras of education in the United Arab Emirates-the previous era when the chalkboard was used, and the current era where ICT is part of the teaching and learning process-I can strongly value the impact of ICT on the students' achievements.

BACKGROUND

To start with, let's begin with looking at the word ICT. ICT (information and communications technology) is a common term that includes any communication device or application, including: radios, televisions, cell phones, computers and networks hardware and software, satellite systems and so on, as well as the various services and applications associated with them, such as videoconferences and distance learning. ICT is also defined as the study or business of developing and using technology to process information and help communications. With these in mind, ICT integration should neither be restricted to computers only nor should it be confronted to certain subject matter. It should include all other communication devices and it can be used in teaching any subject matter.

According to Pisapia, (1993) integrating technology with teaching means the use of learning technologies to introduce, reinforce, supplement, and extend skills. For example, if students are being instructed to read reading comprehension passage and they are provided with a computer follow up activities, this is integration. If they are just provided with computers to watch or play games or surf the Internet without any follow-up activities that leads to mastering certain skills, there is no ICT integration.

Breuleux, (2001) states that providing ICT facilities and related programs is not enough to enable students to master the skills and proficiencies. He argues that ICT can, in fact, support more powerful and complete knowledge-building experiences for learners "if we integrate well-designed technologies in the context of meaningful, mindful inquiry projects, non-presentational pedagogies, access to resources and tools, and adequate support for technological maintenance and pedagogical renewal" (Breuleux, 2001, p. 3).

Also, Roblyer (1997) states that the most important and the most difficult challenge in ICT is how teachers can help to improve existing conditions or to create important educational opportunities that did not exist without ICT. As part of this process, teachers decide what they need to make these changes occur. This process of determining where and how technology fits is known among educators of educational technology as integration.

ICT Empowers Teaching and Foster Learning

It should be assured that only effective Integration of ICT can result in what we call meaningful learning. Meaningful learning experiences that leads to a sense of understanding and is connected to the personal experience or other knowledge which learners' posses. Meaningful learning is viewed as necessary for academic achievement, for making one's way in a complex world, and for engaging in problem solving. It creates the opportunity to interact with other learners in sharing, discussing, constructing, and negotiating meaning leads to knowledge construction. This is contrasting with traditional learning environment where learning was happening in classrooms without integration of technologies. Nowadays, teachers have the opportunity to use technology in different ways: drill and practice (i.e. learning new English language vocabulary), tutorials, simulations, problem-solving and productivity tools.

In summary, effective use of ICT in classrooms enhances learning process in many ways: motivate learners, promotes active learning, provide practice required to master basic skills, help learners investigate reality and build up knowledge, it provides tools to increase student productivity, promote higher thinking skills, help learners work at their own pace, it gives learners more control over their own learning, it facilitates collaborative and cooperative learning, it promotes independent learning and offer an opportunity to accommodate different learning styles and give learners instant feedback to their responses.

Computer Assisted Language Learning and Interactive Multimedia

Iheanacho (1997) investigated the effectiveness of two multimedia programs - one with motion graphics and text and the other with still graphics and text- on students' vocabulary acquisition of ESL. The two programs were effective in learn-

ing vocabulary but the experimental study did not show significant difference between the achievements of the two groups. However, in a delayed posttest, the recall test, significant difference between the two groups is traced in favor of the group that used the program with motion graphics. In addition, the two groups revealed positive effects towards the programs. One can also guess from this study that video can be more effective than pictures when integrating ICT tools with the intention of enhancing students' retention.

In another study, Almekhlafi (2006a) investigated the effects of interactive multimedia on students' achievements in English as a foreign language in an experimental study. Although the experimental study did not show significant differences between the achievements of the control group (paper-based learning) and the experimental group (Interactive Multimedia users), significant difference within the experimental group is traced depending on the students' different cognitive learning styles. Field-independent students seemed to benefit more from the treatment than field dependent. This important discovery bears a significant orientation that should be taken in account when tailoring ICT tools to meet the different cognitive styles of the students to achieve effective technology integration.

Moreover, Almekhlafi (2006b) explored the effects of computer assisted language learning - in the form of an interactive CD-Rom that includes video, sound, pictures, and other interactive features- on students' achievement of English as a Foreign Language. Five important results were reached in that study; a) the effectiveness of technology integration in teaching EFL, b) necessity of encouraging teachers to make use of technology, c) inevitability of integrating technology in all stages to improve learning English since the UAE became an international economic center, d) ability of technology integration to adapt to various learning styles and e) technology integration can enhance student- centeredness alleviating the role of the teacher. It can also, create an attractive learning environment for students whether they are young or old graders. Learners usually tend to break the routine in their learning. They love motivating learning atmosphere. An interview with some students from different schools in Abu Dhabi schools revealed that they greatly prefer to learn English through the ICT. Some students reported that English vocabularies are easier when presented on computer and are animated. Others stated that they use their iPhones and Blackberries to communicate in classes. Universities students valued the use of blackboards on websites in discussing and exchanging their assignments. When I was an MA student in Abu Dhabi University, the video conference was used by students in Al Ain and Abu Dhabi (two separated cities) to discuss issues related to courses.

PowerPoint and Video

From the previously mentioned conclusion derived from Iheanacho (1997), video seemed to be superior to PowerPoint. However animated pictures or integrating flash animation can assist PowerPoint to enhance students' vocabulary retention. In addition, PowerPoint is a very effective ICT tool in many learning contexts. Clovis (1997) conducted a study in the US that investigated the usefulness of video in teaching English to foreign children. She found that video has positive impact on the students' learning and success.

Concerning PowerPoint, Susskind (2005) argued that PowerPoint is more efficient time management strategy than writing on a whiteboard or using transparencies. The major finding of his study is; students who were taught in classrooms with PowerPoint presentation display more positive attitudes for PowerPoint presentations. Further, students were more confident for the exam that covered PowerPoint presentations.

Bahrani (2011) explored the effects of exposure to authentic video materials recorded from mass media as a source of language input on speaking English fluency. Two different groups partici-

pated in this experimental study that had Pre-test/post-test design. The first group was EFL Iranian students who were exposed to the video materials. The second group was ESL Malaysian students who were exposed to traditional social interaction. Analysis of results showed that exposure to video materials improved speaking performance for EFL students more than the social interaction for ESL students.

Virtual Learning Environments and Online Learning

Rush (2008) emphasized there seems to be an obvious increase in the use of technology and online learning in the world. There are several initiatives report case studies of e-leaning deployment and management in education. For example, Browne, Jenkins & Walker (2006) state that online learning have been adopted by many UK higher education institutions. Based on two surveys (UCISA, 2001 and MLE landscape report 2003) cited in Britain & Liber (1999), there was an increase of online learning use in higher education institutions (from 7% to 40%) in about four years prior to 2001. In their report, the responses collected from 358 different institutions in the second survey shows a domination of online learning adoption of about (85% - 97%) by all types of institutions surveyed in 2003.

In the US, online learning education provides nearly all or a portion of formal schooling for nearly one in every 50 students according to Glass (2009). Glass (2009) adds that almost 3 out of every 4 public K-12 schools provide full, partial or 'hybrid' online courses to their students. Glass (2009) also states that there is no accurate data so far to estimate the percent of virtual schooling in the US. With more national educational centers working on national reports of this type, this situation may change soon to give more accurate data on the spread of use of virtual courses and other related online learning. Another report by Allen & Seaman (2004) cited in Albion & Weaver

(2006) reveals that "Over 2 million higher education students took at least one online course that is around 90% of public institutions offered online courses in 200" (Allen & Seaman as cited in Albion & Weaver, 2006, p. 2541). Because online education nowadays seems to provide more access and affordability, Clark (2009) states that the number of Americans enrolled in at least one online course increased from 2 million in 2003 to over 4 million in 2009. One of the reasons she mentioned in her report for that increase relates to the current economic recession. Therefore, learners seem to find it cheaper to access educational courses and programs. It also eliminates the cost of transportation, childcare, time off from work and other miscellaneous costs common to most Americans.

Webster & Murphy (2008) refer to the socio-political and technical reasons as the main challenges facing the adoption of innovations related to educational technologies in some parts of the world. Additionally, MCPherson (2008) clarifies the role of the IT administrator/ instructor in 'articulating and re-articulating' the educational managers or decision makers of what is happening in the field of educational technology (MCPherson, 2008, p. 98). This could be widely debated in certain contexts where educators' voices and other research-based educational recommendations are not well handled by non-specialized managers. In other words, it is a common shared relationship between educators, technology specialists, and decision makers to first share their knowledge and recommendations in order to raise awareness and understanding of these technologies and their potentials. This is normally followed by more maturity and understanding from the decision-makers who would be able to sensibly apply these new technologies and methods in their educational institutions.

Browne et al. (2006) explore the differences in practice among universities deploying online learning in the period between 2001 and 2005 in the UK as a country with a high percentage of adoption and implementation of online learning. Using two different surveys that were conducted in 2001 and 2005, their study shows that 80% of the institutions that participated in the survey used commercial online learning. The authors see an increasing interest in open source online learning as they become 'more reliable' and 'more recognized' in both the educational and academic levels. They conclude by stating that in order to witness a real change in online learning' adoption, we need to first witness a real change in instructional methods and students active participation in these types of courses.

These reasons may vary in higher education from those in other educational sectors as discussed by Albion & Weaver, (2006). They refer to the overall quality and other crucial aspects that will support education in general, "In the tertiary sector they may include providing more flexible access to courses, raising the quality of pedagogy, developing faculty and student IT literacy, reducing distribution costs, and keeping up with the competition" (Albion & Weaver, 2006, p. 2).

In general, some of the key benefits of Online learning in HE according to Britain & Liber (1999) are:" Flexibility of time and place, Coping with increased student numbers, Sharing and re-use of resources, Collaborative work, Student-centered learning, Reducing the administrative burden, Staff Development" (Milligan, 1998, p. 9).

Al- Jarf (2005) reports her use of three online learning systems with a controlled group of learners who study the same course at King Saud University. She comes to a conclusion that careful course design could be crucial in achieving success in online learning or an online course. Kalay (2004) goes one step further in exploring more advanced forms of online learning as in the case of some social-networking environments (e.g. micro-blended bogging websites or avatar worlds). In a reported study on the use of online learning in an architecture course at the University of California, he explains the advantages of using this environment to provide ideal learning opportunities for his students due to the nature of the course. In such a course learners are supported in knowledge, social, and behavioral aspects.

He adds that in these environments time and space are 'malleable constructs' where it is possible to create certain virtual worlds or contexts for the learners to make a context 'more appropriate' as a 'constructive' learning environment. This could be done through both the revolutionary social actions and cultural settings provided in these new online learning environments. It is obvious that using online learning requires the existence of computers, internet connectivity, and appropriate online materials to be used in a course. In many contexts, none of these aspects may represent crucial obstacles as there is an increasing use of computers and the Internet both at home or in school all over the world. Because of the popularity and increase of interest in technology around the world, there also seems to be an interest in investing in ICT and educational technology, although it might not be fully understood by decision makers in some countries or regions.

In their review of published research in ICT in education, Fox & Pearson (2008) describe most of these studies as representing the 'early stages of technology adoption' where the focus is on raising awareness, learning new processes, understanding and applying, building confidence, and or the adaptation of outcomes to other contexts". They also add that a high proportion of work on this field (around 16% of a total 461 publications) highlighted 'second language acquisition in autonomous, self-accessed or distance education programs and on the analysis of computer conferencing and guided self-study' (Fox & Pearson, 2008, p. 177).

Many studies that relate to the use of online learning tend to discuss the features and choice of online learning. Others may relate to the free open sources versus other commercial environments. They may also discuss, in one way or another, the potentials of using third-party plug-ins or extra scripts to enrich online courses or discuss the fac-tors that may lead to its spread in an educational institution. A more important discussion, however, should address how these online learning are integrated to facilitate learning.

Blended Language Learning

Kumar & Maija (2008) pointed to the modern trend of turning language learning classroom to blended learning environment. Blended learning environment is defined as the learning environment that "uses multiple teaching and guiding methods by combining face-to-face sessions with online activities and utilizing a mix of technology-based materials" (Kumar & Maija, 2008, P. 5). In fact blended learning opens lots of closed doors for teachers and learners. Even in the best classroom settings, there are always limitations related to the classroom environment, size, number of students, number of weekly sessions or their duration, and the available blended learning resources and technologies. Blended learning in that case looks like an ideal extension of the classroom experience so it is not a 'one-time experience' (Singh & Reed, 2001, p. 1). The learners can then enrich their work, review lessons, interact and inquire about learning concepts and other social topics. Many technologies could support this enrichment process (e.g. videos, flash and other animated objects, recorded lessons, audio conversations, discussion forums, emails, and PowerPoint slides). Virtual learning environments may open doors for better implementation of blended learning through the use of consistent and secure learning environments with controlled access and organized management and communication systems. Steward (2002) emphasized that blended learning could motivate learners where they value this mixed mode approach than a traditional single-mode learning approach.

Other researchers such as Ennew and Fernandez-Young (2005) see that blended learning delivery has been limited so far due to a failure to 'understand the market' and what the learners or 'customers' need not what is 'technologically' appropriate. Technology, particularly web-based learning, seems to require a 're-conceptualization of the learning paradigm' as Dziuban, Hartman & Brophy-Ellison (2004) suggest. This change as may lead to a development in the 'quality, effectiveness, convenience and cost of learning' (Singh & Reed, 2001, p. 2).

In a study on the use of virtual learning environments and other online tools in a number of courses run for Scottish HE Institutions' teachers at the University of Heriot-Watt, Milligan (1998) experimented several roles through these courses. The courses offered students a dual role by providing access to course content as well as investigating the 'quality' of course structures. Over a period of two years in this project, a range of approaches were used for materials delivery, (e.g. task based, self-paced, and discussions). This type of teaching requires careful planning and awareness of its nature as different from traditional f-2-f instructions. In many instances the material design and the instructional technologies that are applied in a blended learning will vary relatively from those directly applied to a traditional teaching program.

Blended learning is always characterized as a remedy for problems in many contexts. It can help individual teachers adopting a virtual learning environment or the more organized institutions offering online learning solutions as a main learning component. Carman (2002) introduces five key characteristics or 'ingredients' for blended learning modes of teaching and interaction as follows;

- Live events: with attention, relevance, confidence, and satisfaction
- Self-Paced learning: with appropriate and modern multimedia and reusable learning objects
- Collaboration
- Assessment
- Performance support materials: as (the most important' element in all the above ingredients).

A lot of documented literature has shown that the quality of learning can be significantly enhanced when ICT is approached and utilized as an intellectual 'multi-tool', adaptable to learners' needs (Davis et al., 1997). Also, Bransford et al, (1999) shows that ICT can enhance:

- Critical thinking;
- Information handling skills
- Higher level conceptualization
- Problem solving.

Rather than this, the literature shows that (Leach 2000, Leach et al., 2002) ICT can facilitate:

- The refining of understanding;
- The giving and receiving of feedback;
- Collaborative tasks;
- Joint decision making and reflection;
- Complex group interactions.

All in all, ICT should not be viewed as the "vitamin" which can produce better educational outcomes. The concept of ICT in the field of education should include many systems that can enable information gathering, management, manipulation, access, and communication in various forms. ICT should be used as an enabler to reduce the digital gap amongst students within the school and between schools as an effort to narrow the gap of digital divide. Abu Dhabi Education Council (ADEC) has already realized this truth and many information systems are working under ADEC to enhance the teaching and learning process. The following list shows these information systems:

- eSIS
- Internet
- Exchange email
- Phone Services
- Enterprise Right Fax
- Enterprise Blackberry
- SharePoint Portal

- Database & Planning
- GIS
- Library Management System
- Scholarship Management System
- Public Web Site
- SMS Gateway
- Audit Authority System
- Video Conferencing
- Access Control System

It should be assured that only effective Integration of ICT can result in what we call meaningful learning. Meaningful learning that leads to a sense of understanding and is connected to the personal experience or other knowledge which learners' posses. Meaningful learning is viewed as necessary for academic achievement, for making one's way in a complex world, and for engaging in problem solving. It creates the opportunity to interact with other learners in sharing, discussing, constructing, and negotiating meaning leads to knowledge construction. This is contrasting with traditional learning environment where learning was happening in classrooms without integration of technologies. Nowadays, teachers have the opportunity to use technology in different ways: drill and practice (i.e. learning new English language vocabulary), tutorials, simulations, problem-solving and productivity tools.

How Can ICT Enhance Learning?

This is a very crucial question that needs a convincing answer. In summary, and based on students' outcomes, effective use of ICT in classrooms enhances learning process in the many ways. It can motivate learners, promote active learning, provide learners with unlimited practice required to master basic skills, help learners to investigate reality and build up knowledge, and provide tools to increase student productivity. Moreover, it promotes higher thinking skills, help learners the opportunity to work at their own pace, help learn-

ers more control of their own learning, facilitate collaborative and cooperative learning, promote independent learning ICT offers an opportunity to accommodate differing learning styles, and give learners instant feedback to their responses.

Big Challenges

Although it cannot be denied that ICT plays a big role in teaching and learning nowadays in the schools of Abu Dhabi Emirate, still many drawbacks and challenges stand as barriers on the way. These drawbacks and challenges can be outlined as follows;

First of all, ICT infrastructure in classrooms, teachers' training programs and attitudes, and e-awareness campaigns have become of great need. Second, students' ICT skills, curriculum, resources, are essentials to successful integration of ICT in education. Third, hardware maintenance, more support from government and private agencies, broadband access, network access, and cost of service are crucial.

SOLUTIONS AND RECOMMENDATIONS

I think all the drawbacks related to integrating ICT into teaching and learning in Abu Dhabi schools are not so difficult to be solved. The following recommendations can help in tackling the issue.

- More training programs are needed to help teachers use ICT effectively in teaching.
- Educational leaders-principals, vice principals, faculty heads, coordinators, social workers, and academic advisors- need to well understand the ICT concept.
- Parents should understand the beneficial role of ICT in fostering their children's learning.

- More involvement of local community organizations. IT Companies should have a hand in supporting and sponsoring ICT events at schools.

CONCLUSION

No one can deny that the 21st century students need to develop their learning skills to be able to think critically and analytically, to communicate, and to collaborate and problem-solve in today's knowledge-based society. In order to reach the international standards in education, ADEC does all the possible means to provide schools with the infrastructure necessary for integration of ICT in teaching and learning. But, effective ICT integration must also be supported by a shared vision of learning through technology, equitable access and use of technology by students, ICT integrated curriculum, ongoing professional development and technical support.

Now since this is the current situation, so what? What should be done? Something should be by school leaders to develop a shared vision and a work plan to make use of the allocated budget of each school to improve teaching and learning. Schools need to follow ADEC's plans of ICT and organize schedule access to technology to provide equitable opportunities to students to use technology in meaningful, authentic tasks that develop higher- order thinking skills.

Successful integration of ICT depends mainly on teachers' support for innovation. It is therefore important to provide professional development and ICT training to teachers to help them choose the most appropriate technologies, instructional strategies, and information systems that enable students to benefit from technology. Adequate infrastructure and technical support is crucial to foster ICT integration. Teachers must have access to on-site technical support personnel who are responsible for troubleshooting and assistance after the technology and lessons are in place.

If teachers are working with a technology infrastructure that really cannot support the work they are trying to do, they will become frustrated.

All in all, to facilitate ICT integration, it is important to integrate ICT component in the national curriculum which will not only enhance the use of technologies by teachers but also will be beneficial for student learning.

REFERENCES

Abu Dhabi Education Council. (2009). *Strategic plan for P-12 education*. Retrieved from http://www.adec.ac.ae/ADEC%20Shared%20Documents/attachments/Public%20schools/Strategic%20Plans/P12-Summary-June-2009-D.pdf

Al-Jarf, R. S. (2005). *Using three online course management systems in EFL instruction*. The Annual Meeting of the Asia Association of Computer Assisted Language Learning (AsiaCALL). Geongju, South Korea: Sorabol College.

Almekhlafi, A. G. (2006a). Effectiveness of interactive multimedia environment on language acquisition skills of 6th grade students in the United Arab Emirates. *International Journal of Instructional Media, 33*(4), 427–441.

Almekhlafi, A. G. (2006b). The effect of computer assisted language learning (CALL) on United Arab Emirates English as a foreign language (EFL) school students achievement and attitude. *Journal of Interactive Learning Research, 17*(2), 121–142.

Bahrani, T. (2011). Speaking fluency: Technology in EFL context or social interaction in ESL context? *Studies in Literature and Language, 2*(2), 162–168.

Breuleux, A. (2001). Imagining the present, interpreting the possible, cultivating the future: Technology and the renewal of teaching and learning. *Education Canada, 41*(3), 1–8.

Britain, S., & Liber, O. (1999). *A framework for pedagogical evaluation of virtual learning environments*. Bangor, ME: JISC Technology Applications Programme.

Carman, J. M. (2002). Blended learning design: Five key ingredients. *Knowledge Net*. Retrieved from http://www.agilantlearning.com/pdf/Blended%20Learning%20Design.pdf

Ennew, C. T., & Fernandez-Young, A. (2005). Weapons of mass instruction? The rhetoric and reality of online learning. *Marketing Intelligence & Planning*, *24*(2), 148–157. doi:10.1108/02634500610654008

Fox, R., & Pearson, J. (2008). Reviewing ICT research publications in Hong Kong post-secondary education. In Kwan, R., Fox, R., Tsang, P., & Chan, F. T. (Eds.), *Enhancing learning through technology*. Singapore: World Scientific Publishing Co. Pte. Ltd. doi:10.1142/9789812799456_0011

Glass, G. V. (2009). *The realities of K-12 virtual education*. Boulder, CO: Education and the Public Interest Center & Education Policy Research Unit. http://www.cscanada.net/index.php/sll/article/download/1758/2092

Iheanacho, C. (1997). *Effects of two multimedia computer-assisted language learning programs on vocabulary acquisition of intermediate level ESL students*. (Ph.D) Dissertation: The Virginia Polytechnic Institute and State University. Retrieved from http://scholar.lib.vt.edu/theses/availablended learninge/etd-11397-193839/unrestricted/Clems.pdf

Kalay, Y. E. (2004). Virtual learning environments. *ICT Supported Learning in Architecture and Civil Engineering*, *9*, 195–207.

Kumar, S., & Maija, T. (2008). *Integrating ICT into language learning and teaching: Guide for institution*. New Delhi, India: ODLAC Press.

Milligan, C. (1998). *The role of VLEs in the online delivery of staff development. JTAP Report 573 Riccarton*. Edinburgh: Heriot-Watt University.

Singh, H., & Reed, C. (2001). *A white paper: Achieving success with blended learning*. Retrieved from http://www.chriscollieassociates.com/BlendedLearning.pdf

Webster, L., & Murphy, D. (2008). Enhancing Learning through technology: Challenges and responses. In Kwan, R., Fox, R., Tsang, P., & Chan, F. T. (Eds.), *Enhancing learning through technology*. Singapore: World Scientific Publishing Co. Pte. Ltd. doi:10.1142/9789812799456_0001

ADDITIONAL READING

Assude, T., Bessieres, D., Combrouze, D., & Loisy, C. (2010). Conditions des genèses d'usage des technologies numériques dans l'éducation. *Revue STICEF, 17*. ISSN: 1764-7223

Brown, J. S., & Duguid, P. (2000). *The social life of information*. Boston, MA: Harvard Business School Press.

Carlson, S., & Gadio, C. T. (2002). Teacher professional development in the use of technology. *Computer Review*, *16*(1), 15–28.

Counsell, C. (2000). Editorial. *Teaching History*, *101*(2).

Cuban, L. (2002). *Oversold and underused: Computers in the classroom*. Cambridge, MA: Harvard.

Daniel, J. (1996). *Mega universities and knowledge media: Technology strategies for higher education*. Department for Education and Employment. (2000). *Survey of information and communications.*

Haddad, W. (1994). *The dynamics of education policymaking: Case studies of Burkina Faso, Jordan, Peru.*

Janet, M., Lee, G. C., & Chen, H.-Y. (2003). Exploring potential uses of ICT in Chinese language arts instruction: Eight teachers' perspectives. *Computers & Education, 42*(2).

Steffe, L. P., & Gale, J. (1995). *Constructivism in education*. Hillsdale, NJ: Lawrence Erlbaum.

Strommen, E. (2000). *Constructivism, technology and the future of classroom learning.*

Taiwan Ministry of Education. (2002). *The nine year joint curriculum and instruction web*. Taipei, Taiwan: Author. (in Chinese)

Warschauer, M., & Healey, D. (1998). Computers and language learning: An overview. *Language Teaching, 31*, 57–71. doi:10.1017/S0261444800012970

Wishart, J., McFarlane, A., & Ramsden, A. (2005). *Using personal digital assistants (PDAs) with Internet access to support initial teacher training in the UK*. mLearn 2005, 4th World conference on mLearning, Cape Town, South Africa, 25 –28 October 2005. Retrieved from http://www.mlearn.org.za/CD/papers/Wishart.pdf

KEY TERMS AND DEFINITIONS

ADEC: Abu Dhabi Education Council.

ERP: Enterprise Resource Planning.

eSIS: Electronic Student Information System.

GIS: Geographic Information Systems.

Hardware: All tools and devices used in teaching.

ICT Integration: Combining ICT in teaching to facilitate learning.

ICT: Any technological device that help students communicate while learning.

Learning Environment: All the surroundings around the learning during the learning situation.

Software: All programs used in teaching.

Chapter 5
ERP Systems in Arab Education Sector:
Towards Improved Implementation and Utilization

Bashaer Al Kilani
Institute of Applied Technology, UAE

Sara Al Ahbabi
Abu Dhabi Education Council, UAE

Souha Adlouni
Al Rowdah Academy, UAE

Zainab Al Yahyaei
Abu Dhabi Education Council, UAE

ABSTRACT

Education leaders are challenged with maintaining high level information systems that are capable of generating real time complex reports which help in planning an institute's resources and take the risk of decision making. To meet this challenge, an effective ERP system could help schools manage their resources and time. The main goal of this chapter is to develop a better understanding of the best practices and effective methodologies associated with the implementation and utilization of Enterprise Resource Planning (ERP) systems in the Arab Education sector. The chapter is also intended to familiarize Arab educational leaders with the key challenges and issues that could be encountered while implementing ERP systems in their educational institutions, and how to adequately cope with such challenges and issues to ascertain the acceptance and satisfaction of end users and stakeholders. It also tries to potentially contribute to enhancing the institutions' performance and quality of education and learning as well as promoting organizational efficiency, institutional transparency, flexibility and mobility for students and staff access to services, and data anytime and anywhere.

INTRODUCTION

The majority of educational institutions of different levels and sizes, both public and private are increasingly in need of new information technology applications and systems to cope with a new complex and competitive environment. The need to acquire such technology solutions arises from the inadequacy of the conventional way of managing institutions' data, operations and resources, which resembles isolated islands as a result of using separate software and applications

DOI: 10.4018/978-1-4666-1984-5.ch005

to support different functions such as finance and accounting, human resources and administration. The lack of integration of applications supporting these functions leads to asynchronies in the databases, work duplications, ineffective management of resources, and excessive loss of time and cost on searching for relevant information to produce meaningful reports to support forward planning and decision making. Nowadays, the rapid development of information and communication technologies (ICT) that are affordable and easy-to-use encourage educational institutions to consider replacing their disparate function-supporting software by an integrated system that uses a single data repository accessible by end users from all areas and automates processes across different functions connecting and all concerned parties as well as providing the tools for standard and analytical reporting that can help educational institutions develop and improve their performance and attain the satisfaction of all stakeholders.

In their search for a suitable integrated system, educational institutions are prompted to consider the acquisition and implementation of ERP systems which have been proven popular and widely accepted by business organizations.

ERP systems are the front runners among other systems and they appeal to educational institutions as a suitable technology solution due to their integrated modular nature, embedding best practices, their configurability to match specific requirements of different organizations, their workflow process-automation and the capabilities of their searching and reporting tools. So what is ERP system? And what are the main impacts of ERP systems on the institution's performance?

(ERP) Enterprise Resource Planning is a category of information systems that enables business organization and educational institutions to manage and control all of their functions and processes through deployment of ERP software. ERP systems support different functions and processes including but not limited to those pertinent

to financials, human resources and operating functions.

For example, if we consider the ERP Human Resources (HR) module that is used by ADEC (Abu Dhabi Education Council, UAE), we find that it comprises the following functions / processes; the personal information, leave management, payroll information, HR letter request (To whom it may Concern), creating and updating bank account number, duty resumption and alerts, education and professional qualification details, emergency contact details, and employee resume upload (Balooshi, 2010).

Even though, that part of the ERP system focused on and intended for ADEC's staff, ADEC also uses another set of applications of the ERP system (eSIS) for student's data. eSIS system is planned in the first stage to allow schools to manage their students' data that is related to registration, daily attendance, students' marks and grades and generating students result reports. Moreover it helps in transferring students between schools. However, the second stage will include more functions such as allowing the parent to communicate effectively with their children's schools and teachers (ADEC, 2011).

The experience of implementing ERP systems in different organizations have indicated that the rosy picture drawn by vendors prior to the implementation about the anticipated benefits of integration and the realization of the organizational improvements is not that rosy. In fact many ERP implementation projects have ended in complete or partial failures with huge losses incurred by the implementing organization. This supports the notion that ERP success in educational institutions is not only a function of selecting a suitable ERP system but also of adopting a suitable approach (methodology) to guide the implementation.

The following are some steps that are viewed as important to help plan and implement ERP system successfully and which can be considered as components in a proven ERP methodology: (Cornelius, 2007)

1. Strategic planning, where the institution decides to look for a suitable ERP system that supports the institution's aims and objectives.
2. Feasibility/Business case investigation, to justify and validate ERP as the appropriate option by addressing and analyzing strengths and weaknesses of the current institution's system and analyze it in order to select an ERP system that could enhance the institution's performance.
3. Needs Analysis that includes identifying and consolidating the institution's needs and requirements. These can be used as basis for the selection of a suitable ERP system and implementation vendor capable of providing effective and timely support to the ERP system and end-users within the organization.
4. Selection of the most suitable ERP system and capable vendor to provide both technical and functional consulting and training services as well as licenses to the ERP system software. Also the selected provider has to provide a training strategic plan that meets the end users' requirements and the organization's quality standards. Also the selection of the ERP system could be based on the size of the organization and the available budget.
5. Planning for the implementation of the system by developing a plan and schedule to manage the implementation of the ERP system on time to budget, delivering a working solution matching the institutions needs and requirements.
6. Implementation of the ERP system using suitable implementation methodology and project management approach with competent resources from both the implementation vendor and the organization. The implementation could be carried out in stages to test each part of the system and give the users enough time to practice with it.
7. Post implementation assessment and audit review to decide if it meets the institution's objectives and goals and to examine the system functionality. This post implementation assessment and review will help the leader to go back and make changes regarding the selection or training to make sure the implementation really serves the organization's needs.

As a result this chapter aims to explore and discuss the challenges and issues facing the implementation of ERP systems in the Arab education sector, especially in UAE, and how they could be addressed and managed.

The first section of this chapter provides a review of some of the literature related to the use and implementation of ERP in educational institutions with a comparison of the status before and after implementing ERP system. In this section the authors will discuss some ERP definitions, examples of successful ERP implementations in some educational institutes and presenting some ERP system providers. The authors will also present some common causes of ERP failures and the challenges faced when implementing the ERP system in some educational institutes. Also in this section the authors discuss the cost of implementing the ERP in small schools versus large schools and the factors that could help to make the implementation of ERP system successful. Moreover, it discusses the benefits of implementing the ERP system in schools.

The second section presents and analyzes the data collected using a survey that was distributed to a number of different educational institutes, including schools and higher education institutions. The survey was used to investigate the implementation, utilization and benefits of ERP in eight UAE education institutes, five of which are schools and three higher education institutes. Also the survey seeks to provide the end users recommendations to enhance the use of the ERP system.

The third section discusses the findings and challenges facing the end users in terms of technical problems, data availability, end-user training, system integration and the return on investment (ROI). The chapter is concluded with the presentation of the investigations' findings, results' analysis and a recommendation for optimizing the benefits of ERP system in educational institutes.

LITERATURE REVIEW

ERP Definition

The term 'Enterprise Resource Planning', abbreviated as 'ERP' was used for the first time in the early 1990s.ERP is a term that represents computer and software systems which incorporate and integrate the chief enterprise processes, and allow end users to manage all key business functions in that enterprise (Swartz & Orgill, 2001).

One of the comprehensive definitions of the concept of ERP was offered by Razmi, Sangari, and Ghodsi in 2009. It states that "ERP systems are integrated and corporate-wide systems that automate core activities such as manufacturing, human resources, finance and supply chain management. In such systems the fragmented information is integrated to support the decision making process." As companies implement such integrated information solutions, it is expected that their productivity, efficiency and profitability will increase.

ERP Success

Literature reveals that there are some examples of successful ERP implementations in educational organizations. Georgetown University was able to successfully automate financial aid and admissions for more than 30,000 students with PeopleSoft (Blitzblau & Hanson, 2001); Louisiana State University succeeded in implementing course listings, libraries, human resources, e-mail, campus information, public relations, registration, and admissions using Lotus Domino Notes (Ethridge, Hadden, & Smith, 2000). The University

of Nebraska-Lincoln successfully implemented an ERP system for recruiting and admissions for it's more than 22,000 students using Talisma (Gaska, 2003).

ERP Failures

Although the implementation of ERP system promised institutes a positive picture of their productivity and profitability, a lot of ERP projects ended up in complete or partial failure. The literature divulges a number of cases where ERP projects were started by British higher education institutes but never completed, as reported by Ferrell (2003).

According to Umble and Umble, the common causes of ERP failures could be summarized by the following:

- The organization's management did not put specific, clear, strategic goals for implementing the ERP system, as well as not having the needed skills to participate themselves in the implementation process.
- The organization is not ready for the implementation of systems like ERP due to lack of resources (IT infrastructure) or teachers' knowledge and skills in the field of IT.
- The employees did not have sufficient training to run the system.
- Data entered into the system was inaccurate.
- Expectations of the organization are not reasonable.
- Lack of available technicians to answer teachers' questions and solve possible technical problems (2002).

ERP Project Life-Cycle

Any ERP project should go through a serious of events (Swartz &Orgill, 2001) as follows:

- Need Assessment
- Software Selection

- Process Reengineering
- Conference Room Pilot
- Training
- Phased Implementation

The first stage in the cycle is a needs assessment and requirements analysis, and it ends in training and a phased implementation. The continuous circle of development suggests that directly after completing the first cycle of an ERP project, the cycle reverts back to planning the next phase. Each consecutive round of development arises from the need to add functionality and the rapidity of upgrades to ERP software (Swartz & Orgill, 2001). Consequently, if any of the stages in the cycle are not fulfilled, the successful implementation of the ERP system will not be successful.

Challenges in Implementing ERP Systems

According to a study done in Egypt by Abdelghaffar & AbdelAzim in 2010, one of the challenges that could face international companies in implementing ERP systems is the place in which the organization is implementing its ERP system; in a developed country or a developing country. This difference has to do with the economic and technological condition of each country.

The same thing could apply to educational institutes, if the educational institute has an IT infrastructure that is capable of meeting the demands of ERP, this will help in the success of implementing ERP.

Adopting ERP systems as integrating programs is not restricted to large scale companies; many small and medium companies have tried to implement it in order to have a competitive advantage in the market. It is important for both large scale and small scale organizations to adopt information integrating systems; however, small organizations face more challenges in terms of resources and lack of appropriate infrastructure (Seethamraju & Seethamraju, 2008). As we will see in the next

section, the same situation applies to ERP being adopted by small schools or large schools.

Another barrier or challenge for ERP implementation is the IT maturity knowledge level of employees of IT skills, at both the organizational and national level (Seethamraju & Seethamraju, 2008).

ERP systems could not be implemented in any organization, whether it is educational or business, oriented in isolation from the external world of the organization. The Information and Communications Technology (ICT) infrastructure of the country affects the adoption and implementation of ERP systems (Abdelghaffar & AbdelAzim, 2010).

ERP Cost

The extreme cost of an ERP system is considered one of the main obstacles for implementing ERP systems especially for Small and Medium Enterprises (SMEs) and educational organizations. A deep and thorough study should be done at any organization before implementing any ERP system as its cost is enormous. According to some authors, expenses for the implementation of integral information solution for a medium-sized enterprise or educational institute may range between $2m to $4m. On the other hand, the expenses for the implementation of ERP systems in a large enterprise can exceed $100m (Umble & Umble, 2002).

The importance of the cost factor is supported by the reported cases of unsuccessful ERP implementation in higher education, where the designed cost of the implementation of ERP systems surpassed $15m (Parth & Gumz, 2003).

Small vs. Large School Implementation

Knowing the high costs of implementing ERP systems; how could small and medium schools afford them? Literature reveals that it is doable if small and medium schools modified their approaches in dealing with ERP implementation and post implementation costs.

The first and most important factor to control cost is the number of custom modifications for the project (Swartz &Orgill, 2001). Another way by which small schools can save some costs in implementing ERP projects is outsourcing. They do not have to employ experts in the area of Database and System Administration because they are not needed continually. A rational solution could be a conglomerate, where several smaller schools can share a Database Administrator (DBA) or System Administrator (SA), (Swartz &Orgill, 2001). Other ways to reduce cost that could be adopted by small schools could be to use internal resources like teachers and administration officers for data entry. Also, computer technology teachers could be trained to provide other employees with technical support whenever it is needed (Swartz &Orgill, 2001).

ERP Success Factors

The high frequency of ERP failures led many universities to launch many studies on ERP success factors. In the introduction of the literature review, it was mentioned that an ERP system "incorporates the chief enterprise processes" so it does not involve one section or area of an organization. As a result, if we want to discuss the success of ERP systems we have to discuss many factors.

According to Bingi, Sharma, & Godla, the key success factors of any ERP system could be summarized by:

- The extent to which management participates in the implementation of ERP systems and professional development for teachers.
- The continuous upgrading/ innovation of the business process at a certain organization.
- A collegial cooperative relationship should be prevalent among employees, management and advisors.

- Providing all possible end users with the needed training.
- There should be an option in the integrating information system used to connect with other business information systems (1999).

In their investigation of ERP implementations in Egypt, Abdelghaffar & AbdelAzim suggested that "different Critical Success Factors (CSFs) would certainly have different weights of influence over organizations functioning in developing countries" (2010). Furthermore, Fawaz, Salti & Eldabi have stressed in their study that top management's support and choosing the appropriate ERP system are two of the most important success factors for the implementation of successful ERP systems (2008). So, it is not enough to purchase an ERP system from a well-known vendor and install it in the organization's hardware, it is the involvement of managers in the training and implementation process, as well as selecting the most appropriate ERP system, that will provide the organization with its competitive advantage.

Koh, Simpson, Padmore, Dimitriadis, and Misopoulos point out that there are two main drivers for ERP implementation in an organization; the first one is increased demand for real-time information and the second is the need of information for decision making.

ERP Benefits

According to Educause Center for Applied Research (ECAR) organization, the main advantages of ERP for higher education institutions include the following:

- Improved access to timely and accurate information that is needed for planning and managing the institution.
- Improved communication among students and faculty.

- Improved services for the faculty, students and employees.
- Increased income due to ability of adopting best business practices.
- Decreased expenses due to improved efficiency and reduction in usage of stationary (King, 2002).

In a higher education environment there is more than one business function, some are related to students, others to faculty and Human Resources Department. If each business function has its own information system that is incompatible with the others, it will create a set of islands working in isolation without any kind of integration. When one integrating system is used for all business functions, then the database could be shared by everybody with the same accuracy. So, *"data can be transferred between individual processes and accessible by various users in real time"* (Zornada & Velkavrh, 2005).

An interesting statement that summarizes the benefits of ERP is mentioned by Swartz & Orgill *"The ERP project often prompts significant process reengineering and can breathe new life into ineffective and inefficient departments or processes. During an ERP project you have an opportunity to correct broken processes and replace them with modern, system-enabled, state-of-the-art business — you don't just want to pave cow paths!"* (2001).

CHAPTER STUDY

ERP systems, though widely implemented, and rapidly spreading to be actionable in education sector, still lack evaluation of pros and cons of such systems. It is perceived that variation of implementation and utilization of ERPs may have significant impacts on how successful they are in such context. The study made by the authors of this chapter investigated the implementation and utilization of ERP systems in education sector in UAE. It examined how the sector captures ERP's

benefits and sought recommendations by end users to enhance the use of such systems. The study attempted to answer the question stated by this chapter: How can ERP systems in Arab education sector be improved in terms of implementation and utilization?

Methodology

End-users perspectives and attitudes towards ERPs were surveyed by a questionnaire. This method was chosen to allow the authors to collect data from a wide number of organizations. The questionnaire was sent to a number of education sector organizations which are represented by schools and higher education facilities. As this study is not intended to serve as research and generalization inferences about the targeted population is not its aim, identifying the populations and deciding on sample size and sampling techniques were not followed. A random sample of end users was drawn to provide a quick feedback on ERP systems usage. Schools and higher education organizations selection were based on the fact that they are implementing and relying on ERP systems to fully function.

The number of education parties covered was eight, three of which are higher education organizations and five are schools; all of which had ERP systems implemented and rolled out for a period between 1 to 3 years. The number of respondents to the questionnaire was forty five. The sample subjects varied in gender, affiliation, years of experience in education field and educational level as follows: The ratio representing male to female interviewed was 1:4. Their affiliation diversity included: Teacher, Vice Principal, Senior IT officer technician, secretary, education advisor, and postgraduate students. Their years of experience ranged between 1.5 years to 20 years in the field of education and the subjects' educational level varied as follows: 15 have a postgraduate degree while the rest hold Bachelor degrees.

The survey was administered using face to face approach. The person in charge of distributing the questionnaire emphasized to the participant that it is an anonymous questionnaire where organization evaluation was not the purpose behind the study and that it was mainly conducted as a general study on ERPs. Explanations of questions and clarification of terminology used in survey were communicated to participants to ensure integrity of the process.

The survey used both closed and open ended questions. The latter was used to provide the participants with an opportunity to express and reflect on their experience and to understand the rationale behind their responds to the questionnaire items.

Likert scale was used with 15 different items of the questionnaire. These items were divided into 3 main indexes: Implementation – Utilization and Benefits. While the open ended questions investigated: recommendations for improvement and the return on investment of the ERP system which as might imply confidential data, left optional to answer.

Results and Discussion

Analysis of data collected upon the responses of participants to different questionnaire items was made. Results of index (1)-(Implementation) are illustrated in Table 1.

The rating of approval is measured by collating (strongly agree) and (agree) rating scale percentage, while disapproval is measured by collating (strongly disagree) and (disagree). Analysis shows that majority of participants are neutral towards different items of this index which reflects a foggy vision of the end user towards the implementation of ERP systems. However when collating rating scales results, it was evident that a majority of 42% believe in adequacy of IT infrastructure for implementing the system. In terms of employees' readiness to use the ERP item, the majority are neutral about it (43%) which again implies a blur vision. While second highly rated result was disapproval on employees' readiness (35%). The results for choosing the suitable ERP system that meets organization needs is almost equally distributed for the different rating scales 33% agree, 38% are neutral while the

Table 1. Results of implementation index

		1	2	3	4	5
		Strongly Agree	**Agree**	**Neutral**	**Disagree**	**Strongly Disagree**
Implementation						
1.1	The Infrastructure of IT in my school helps in the implementation of ERP.	14%	28%	37%	12%	9%
1.2	Employees at my institute show great readiness to apply new systems like ERP.	7%	15%	43%	20%	15%
1.3	My institute uses the most suitable type of ERP systems that serves its needs.	5%	28%	38%	25%	4%
1.4	Objectives behind adopting an ERP system at my institute were clear to me.	5%	27%	38%	20%	10%
1.5	I received enough training on ERP usage before it was implemented.	2%	5%	31%	33%	29%
1.6	ERP system in my institute has replaced paper work by more than 80%	22%	18%	31%	16%	13%

least disagree with 29%. Same analysis implies for clarity of objectives behind ERP implementation. More than half of respondents disagree on having enough training prior to system implementation (62%) which is a high percentage.40% believe that ERPs replaced the paper work by more than 80%. Figure 1 illustrates the results of Table 1 after data collation.

Results of index (2)-(Utilization) are illustrated in Table 2. Same collation of results is made. Analysis shows the highest percentage of approval (40%) on continuity of ERP development followed by (34%) of disapproval. Majority agrees on lack of dedicated team to manage the system (48%). Perspective of end user towards real time data availability is neutral (39%) followed by close results of agreement (32%) and disagreement (29%). The highest percentage of results reflects that the ERP system was introduced as an integrated solution (47%). Figure 2 illustrates the results of Table 2 after data collation.

Results of index(3)-(Benefits) are illustrated in Table 3. Analysis shows that majority of participants agrees that ERP implementation speed up transactions in the organization (46%), though a considerable ratio disagree (37%). Disapproval for ERP enhancing quality of service stands at

(39%) followed by (32%) and (29%) of agreement and neutrality respectively.

In regards to the questionnaire item "decreasing workload of the organization", agreement and disagreement are nearly equal at (43%) and (47%) respectively. It shows clearly that most participants believe that their organization productivity is improved through implementing ERP system (54%). The same is reflected in the respond to "I believe our ERP system helps to raise the stakeholders' confidence in our school/institution" at (47%). Figure 3 illustrates the results of Table 3 after data collation. As per the open ended questions responses, recommendations by end users on how to improve the ERP systems implementation and utilization are summed up as follows:

- The implementation of an ERP system is a substantial undertaking that needs to be monitored and updated continuously. This could be achieved by allocating specialized people to maintain the system.
- Technical issues rise all the time and sometimes the user is trapped, consuming time and effort with no output in return. Some malfunctioning features of the system seem to be due to faults in tailoring the system

Figure 1. Results of (implementation index)

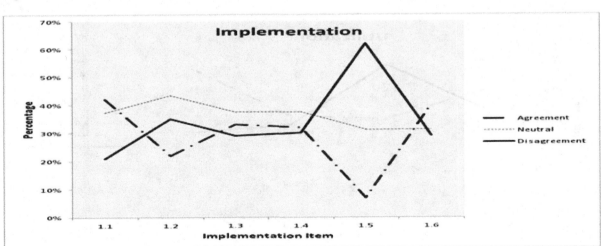

Table 2. Results of utilization index

		1 Strongly Agree	2 Agree	3 Neutral	4 Disagree	5 Strongly Disagree
Utilization						
2.1	The ERP system at my institute is continuously developed.	16%	24%	26%	24%	10%
2.2	There is a team at my institute that manages the ERP project.	14%	17%	21%	21%	27%
2.3	Real time data is always available	14%	18%	39%	18%	11%
2.4	ERP has replaced other fragmented Solution to have an integrated one	21%	26%	26%	14%	13%

to fit to the organization requirements. The system in some organizations could not be accessed at home.

• ERP system as used extensively by end users is expected to have more user friendly interface to be perceived in a positive manner.

• The ERP system implementation is a comprehensive undertaking that requires more than average IT skills to deal with it. The implementation should be preceded by holistic training and orientation.

• The system should go through a developmental cycle where feedback and input from the user is taken into consideration.

• Data fed into the ERP system should be updated.

• ERP when fully functioning should replace the paperwork.

Figure 2. Results of utilization index

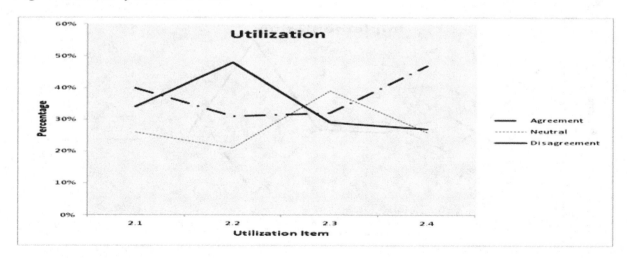

Table 3. Results of benefits index

Benefits		1 Strongly Agree	2 Agree	3 Neutral	4 Disagree	5 Strongly Disagree
3.1	The ERP system we have improves speed of transaction/process.	20%	26%	17%	11%	26%
3.2	The ERP system in my institute improves services that is provided to students and staff	6%	26%	29%	16%	23%
3.3	The ERP system decreases the workload of school / institute / staff	23%	20%	10%	17%	30%
3.4	The ERP system helps in improving the productivity of the school/ institute	30%	24%	12%	12%	22%
3.5	I think our ERP system helps to raise the stakeholders' (students , parents) confidence in our school / institution.	32%	15%	21%	11%	21%

- It is mystifying when partial ERP solutions are implemented instead of an integrated one.

While the question: Do you think that your institute has enough return on investment on ERP system implied? Was simply answered by few users as quoted below:

No because it did not facilitate processes. It just made it more complicated

No, because still all the processes are done in both ways ERP and hardcopy, it needs time to manage these things perfectly.

Findings of the survey are presented in the tabular form below where the rating of approval is measured by collating (strongly agree) and (agree) rating scale percentage, while disapproval is measured by collating (strongly disagree) and (disagree).

RECOMMENDATIONS

- ERP systems requirements should be clearly defined. Ambiguous implementation will definitely lead to a waste of time and resources.
- Plan for organizational change when implementing new ERP system, particularly for change which may drastically impact business processes and organizational configuration. Investing in organizational change in this case is well justified.
- ERP system should provide an integrated solution across different business requests.
- ERP system should be focalized to resolve organization key problems.
- Always select a strong project management team.
- Avoid imposing simulated deadlines on the project because these unnecessary deadlines may increase organizational and project team stress and affect their efficiency.
- Your project management team should have the ability to manage scope and bud-

Figure 3. Results of benefits index

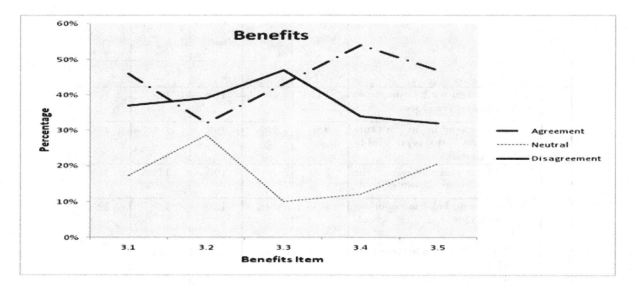

get. Increasing the scope without increasing budget and timeline increase the risk of failure.

• After installation you need to test the system properly on daily basis to avoid any problems.

• To get the best results from your ERP system it is important to train the employee properly and to train them ahead.

• Clarify objectives of ERP system to your employees. Present your inclusive de-

Table 4. Survey findings (implementation)

		Strongly Agree/Agree	Neutral	Strongly Disagree/Disagree
Implementation				
4.1	The Infrastructure of IT in my school helps in the implementation of ERP.	42%	37%	21%
4.2	Employees at my institute show great readiness to apply new systems like ERP.	22%	43%	35%
4.3	My institute uses the most suitable type of ERP systems that serves its needs.	33%	38%	29%
4.4	Objectives behind adopting an ERP system at my institute were clear to me.	33%	38%	30%
4.5	I received enough training on ERP usage before it was implemented.	7%	31%	62%
4.6	ERP system in my institute has replaced paper work by more than 80%	40%	31%	29%
	Average Implementations	**30%**	**36%**	**34%**

Table 5. Survey findings (utilization)

		Strongly Agree/Agree	Neutral	Strongly Disagree/Disagree
Utilization				
5.1	The ERP system at my institute is continuously developed.	40%	26%	34%
5.2	There is a team at my institute that manages the ERP project.	31%	21%	48%
5.3	Real time data is always available	32%	39%	29%
5.4	ERP has replaced other fragmented Solution to have an integrated one	47%	26%	27%
	Average Utilization	**38%**	**27.5%**	**34.5%**

sign in the form of a conference room presentation.

- The project manager should also get all historical data of the company. This will help him to identify the key problem.

- 'Effective' support from the upper management of the company is significant to the overall success of the implementation of ERP systems.

- Do all financial analysis against the ERP system which includes Return on

Table 6. Survey findings (benefits)

		Strongly Agree/Agree	Neutral	Strongly Disagree/Disagree
Benefits				
6.1	The ERP system we have, improves speed of transaction/process.	46%	17%	37%
6.2	The ERP system in my institute improves services that is provided to students and staff	32%	29%	39%
6.3	The ERP system decreases the workload of school / institute / staff	43%	10%	47%
6.4	The ERP system helps in improving the productivity of the school/ institute	54%	12%	34%
6.5	I think our ERP system helps to raise the stakeholders' (Students, parents) confidence in our school / institution.	47%	21%	32%
	Average Benefits	**44%**	**18%**	**38%**

Investment (ROI) analysis of direct and indirect cost. It may be possible that your payback period is long but at the same time you will get profit in shape of goodwill and improvement in services.

- ERP changes the business processes which may change the job nature of employees. Change is a natural part of the ERP usage therefore we should plan accordingly.

CONCLUSION

To conclude this study, implementation of ERP system relies on the grasp of critical success factors mentioned in the literature review. These factors affect the implementation of ERP system which ultimately affects the utilization of ERP in an organization. As leading to a core change in the business processes flow and mechanism, pavement should precede ERP implementation. This could be accomplished by illuminating goals behind ERPs implementation to organization employees and by training which resembles the backbone of running an ERP system successfully. Allocating a team to maintain the ERP system is crucial, specially to treat technical issues that will arise. Tailored solutions to specific needs and requirements of an organization are a cut off between success and failure. Lastly, this solution should be unified among all business processes. Integration is a key word that guarantees comprehensive solution for all needs.

REFERENCES

Abdelghaffar, H., & AbdelAzim, R. H. (2010). *Significant factors influencing ERP implementaion in large organizations: Evidence from Egypt.* European, Mediterranean & Middle Eastern Conference On Information systems. Abu Dhabi, UAE.

ADEC. (2011, June 27). *AL Khaili: 400 public & private schools have benefitted from eSIS.* Retrieved December 13, 2011, from http://www.adec.ac.ae/English/Pages/NewsDisplay.aspx?ItemID=395

Balooshi, A. A. (2010, March 15). *News catalog: ERM in institutions.* Retrieved December 13, 2011, from http://www.adec.ac.ae/NewsCatalog/Forms/DispForm.aspx?ID=115

Bingi, P., Sharma, M. K., & Godla, J. K. (1999). Critical issues affecting an ERP implementation. *Information Systems Management, 99*(16).

Blitzblau, R., & Hanson, M. (2001). Transforming Georgetown through technology. *EDUCAUSE Quarterly, 2.*

Cornelius, E. T. (2007). *Seven steps in the ERP process: An overview of the higher ed ERP journey.* Retrieved December 13, 2011, from www.collegiateproject.com

Ethridge, R. R., Hadden, C. M., & Smith, M. P. (2000). Building a personalized education portal: Get a behind-the-scenes look at LSU's award-winning system. *Educause Quaterly, 23*(3).

Fawaz, K. A., Salti, Z. A., & Eldabi, T. (2008). *Critical success factors in ERP implementation: A review.* European and Mediterranean Conference on Information Systems, Dubai.

Ferrell, G. (2003). *Enterprise systems in universities: Panacea or can of worms?* Northumbia University, JISC info Net Publication. Retrieved from http://www.jiscinfonet.ac.uk/InfoKits/infokit-related-files/erp-in-univs.pdf

Gaska, C. L. (2003). CRM hits the campus. *University Business, 6*(11).

King, P. (2002). *The promise and performance of enterprise systems in higher education.* Respondent Summary. ECAR Respondent Summary.

Koh, S., Simpson, M., Padmore, J., Dimitriadis, N., & Misopoulos, F. (2006). An exploratory study of enterprise resource planning adoption in Greek companies. *Industrial Management & Data Systems, 106*(7). doi:10.1108/02635570610688913

Parth, F. R., & Gumz, J. (2003). *Getting your ERP implementation back on track.*

Razmi, J., Sangari, M. S., & Ghodsi, R. (2009, November). Developing a practical framework for ERP Readiness assessment using fuzzy analytic network process. *Advances in Engineering Software.*

Seethamraju, R., & Seethamraju, J. (2008). *Adoption of ERPs in a medium-sized-enterprise-A case study.* The 19th Australian Conference on Information Systems. Sydney.

Swartz, D., & Orgill, K. (2001). Higher education ERP: Lessons learned. *Educause Quarterly.*

Umble, E. J., & Umble, M. M. (2002, January). Avoiding ERP implementation failure. *Industrial Management.* http://findarticles.com/p/articles/mi_hb3081/is_1_44/ai_n28902999/

Zornada, L., & Velkavrh, T. B. (2005). *Implementing ERP systems in higher education institutions.* 27th International Conference on Information Technology Interfaces ITI 2005, Cavat, Croatia.

ADDITIONAL READING

Al-Mashari, M. (2003). Enterprise resource planning (ERP) systems: A research agenda. *Industrial Management & Data Systems, 103*(1). doi:10.1108/02635570310456869

Al-Sehali, S. (2000). *The factors that affect the implementation of enterprise resource planning (ERP) in the international Arab Gulf States and United States companies with special emphasis on SAP software.* Saudi Arabia: University of Northern Iowa.

Albadri, F. A., & Abdallah, S. (2009). ERP training and evaluation: ERP life-cycle approach to end-users characterization and competency building in the context of an oil & gas company. *IBIMA Business Review, 3.*

Anderegg, T. (2000). *ERP: A-z implementer's guide for success.* Resource Pub.

Boyle, T. A. (2007). Technical-oriented enterprise resource planning (ERP) body of knowledge for information systems programs: Content and implementation. *Journal of Education for Business, 82*(5), 267–275. doi:10.3200/JOEB.82.5.267-275

Bradford, M. (2010). *Modern ERP: Select, implement & use today's advanced business systems.* Retrieved from LuLu.com.

Cheng, D., Deng, F., & Li, H. (2006). *Critical factors for successful implementation of ERP in China.* IEEE International Conference on e-Business Engineering (ICEBE'06).

Grabot, B., Mayere, A., & Bazet, I. (2008). *ERP systems and organizational change: A socio-technical insight.* Springer. doi:10.1007/978-1-84800-183-1

Haab, M. (2009). *Implementation of ERP systems in higher education: Relationship between modes of participation and satisfaction with implementation of enterprise resource planning system in higher education.* VDM Verlag.

Hellens, L. V., Nielsen, S., & Beekhuyzen, J. (2005). *Qualitative case studies on implementation of enterprise wide systems.* Idea Group Publishing.

Holsapple, C. W., & Sena, M. P. (2003). The decision-support characteristics of ERP systems. *International Journal of Human-Computer Interaction, 16*(1), 101–123. doi:10.1207/S15327590IJHC1601_7

Kapp, K. M. (2001). *Integrated learning for ERP success: A learning requirements planning approach.* CRC Press.

Karaarslan, N., & Gundogar, E. (2009). An application for modular capability-based ERP software selection using AHP method. *International Journal of Advanced Manufacturing Technology, 42*(9/10), 1025–1033. doi:10.1007/s00170-008-1522-5

Klee, A. (2010). *The ERP training life cycle*. Klee Associates, Inc.

Kumar, K., & Van Hillegersberg, J. (2000). ERP experiences and evolution. *Communications of the ACM, 43*(4), 22–26. doi:10.1145/332051.332063

Kvavik, R. B., Katz, R. N., Beecher, K., Caruso, J., King, P., Voludakis, J., & Williams, L. A. (2002). *The promise and performance of enterprise systems for higher education* (ERS0204). Boulder, CO: EDUCAUSE Center for Applied Research (ECAR).

Rothenberger, M. A., & Srite, M. (2009). An investigation of customization in ERP system implementations. *IEEE Transactions on Engineering Management, 56*(4), 663–676. doi:10.1109/TEM.2009.2028319

Simon, P. (2010). *Why new systems fail: An insider's guide to successful IT projects*. Course Technology PTR.

Steen, M. (1998). ERP professionals. *InfoWorld, 20*(45), 103.

Sullivan, L., & Bozeman, W. (2010). Post-implementation success factors for enterprise resource planning student administration systems in higher education institutions. *College and University, 86*(2), 22–31.

Swartz, D., & Orgill, K. (2001). Higher education ERP: Lessons learned. *EDUCAUSE Quarterly, 24*(2), 20–27.

Vaman, J. N. (2008). *ERP in practice: ERP strategies for steering organizational competence and competitive advantage*. Tat McGraw-Hill Publishing Company Limited.

Wallace, T. F. (2001). *ERP: Making it happen: The implementers' guide to success with enterprise resource planning*. Wiley.

Wei, C. (2008). Evaluating the performance of an ERP system based on the knowledge of ERP implementation objectives. *International Journal of Advanced Manufacturing Technology, 39*(1/2), 168–181. doi:10.1007/s00170-007-1189-3

Wen-Hsien, T., Yi-Wen, F., Jun-Der, L., Li-Wen, C., & Ching-Chien, Y. (2007). The relationship between implementation variables and performance improvement of ERP systems. *International Journal of Technology Management, 38*(4), 350–373. doi:10.1504/IJTM.2007.013406

Wu, W. (2011). Segmenting and mining the ERP users' perceived benefits using the rough set approach. *Expert Systems with Applications, 38*(6), 6940–6948. doi:10.1016/j.eswa.2010.12.030

KEY TERMS AND DEFINITIONS

ADEC: Abu Dhabi Education Council that established to develop and improve the educational outcomes quality in the Emirate of Abu Dhabi, implement educational policies, plans and programs to achieve the objectives of national development in accordance with the highest international standards.

End User: Is the individual who uses the product after it has been fully developed and marketed.

ERP: Enterprise Resource Planning is a category of information systems that enables business organization and educational institutions to manage and control all of their functions and processes through deployment of ERP software.

eSIS: Eenterprise students' information system is an application of the ERP system for student's data used from ADEC's schools to manage their students' data and records.

Information System: A combination of hardware, software, infrastructure and trained personnel organized to facilitate planning, control, coordination, and decision making in an organization.

System Implementation: System implementation is the practice of creating or modifying a system to create a new business process or replace an existing business process.

Utilization: The proportion of the available time (expressed usually as a percentage) that a piece of equipment or a system is operating.

Chapter 6
Multimedia Use in UAE Education Context

Salam Omar Ali
Al-Ain English Speaking School, UAE

Fayez Ahmad Albadri
Abu Dhabi University, UAE

ABSTRACT

The growth in use of multimedia in United Arab Emirates schools has accelerated in recent years. Multimedia can be useful for both teachers and students alike. For example, multimedia is viewed as an important source of educational aids and a generator of resources that can add a lot to their performance. On the other hand, multimedia is positively perceived, for it makes the learning processes more comfortable and more enjoyable that leads to an improved performance. Generally, children are excited and fascinated by technology, and they are more receptive to lessons that are aided by multimedia. This is perhaps why many teachers are using multimedia in their classes to accomplish their learning objectives by creating a more interesting learning environment. For educators, multimedia provides a golden opportunity to promote interactive, technology-based collaborative learning that is perceived positively by all parties involved. This chapter investigated the role of the multimedia technologies in enhancing students' performance as many studies showed that technology has a great effect on improving students' reading, writing, and other skills. The study is also aimed at increasing educators' awareness of the importance of multimedia technology use in classrooms.

INTRODUCTION

Using multimedia in teaching can be an effective tool in enriching students' learning; though, it is of a great importance to integrate different kinds of technology into the curriculum to get the desired benefits. In order to reach this important result, cooperation should be established among teachers, parents, students, administrators, specialists of curriculum, and researchers to be able to produce a successful integration of technology for the sake of the students' performance.

As part of the "Teachers for the 21st Century' initiative," the United Arab Emirates (UAE) plans to earmark up to $55 million for a professional development program for teachers. International

DOI: 10.4018/978-1-4666-1984-5.ch006

experts will advise UAE educators on ways to introduce modern educational methods in their classrooms (Middle East Educator, 2009).

According to Hofstetter (2001), stated that multimedia is the use of computer to present and combine text, graphics, audio and video with links and tools that let the user navigate, interact, create and communicate. Multimedia combines five basic types of media into the learning environment: text, video, sound, graphics and animation, thus providing a powerful new tool for education. Providing teachers with the tools they need to negotiate the changes is crucial to their success (Muir-Herzic, 2004).

This chapter provides an over view of different kinds of educational multimedia and their effective use as they pertain to the United Arab Emirates context; it provides an account of multimedia types, uses, and policies in the UAE with a critical analysis of its effective use with educators and academics in the educational fields. There is an increasing belief that Information and Communication Technologies (ICT) have been gaining importance in education and that its pedagogy has generated the need to preparing proficient ICT teachers who can effectively utilize it in different subjects. Even though the number of computers installed in schools significantly increased during the last several decades (Kleiner & Lewis, 2003), the way we teach in schools has changed little, and computers have not been fully integrated into school curricula (Collins & Halverson, 2009).

Generally, many multimedia types are used for different purposes in the UAE such as for presentations, online and print advertising, Email & viral marketing, e-cards, website development, database software creation, projects, development and production of CD ROMs & 3Ds, audio-visual shows, immersive media & high-end photography…etc. However, their uses in education have been limited to administrative and instructional uses by school staff and teachers. As indicated by many researchers (Forawi, Almekhlafi & Almekhlafy, 2011; Muir-Herzic, 2004) multimedia

activities can advance student learning of various subjects. Recently, Wu-Yuin, Rustam, and Szu-Min (2011) found that the designed learning activities supported by the VPen system, a multimedia program developed for students, could facilitate students' writing and speaking performance and therefore improve their learning achievement.

This chapter focuses on the multimedia and computer technology applications that are used in the UAE educational contexts and their effectiveness in advancing student learning. In particular, types of multimedia will be identified, schools' use of multimedia, and the UAE school experience with multimedia and computer technology.

BACKGROUND

It is believed that using multimedia and computer technology does not mean using computers only. When using any kind of technology in the classroom, it should open an endless access to different resources of knowledge. It should help in adding excitement and joy while learning. On the other hand, it should strengthen the idea of individual work as well as the group one for greater constructivist learning experiences. The importance of technology comes from the fact that it not only gives learners the opportunity to control their own learning process, but also provides them with ready access to a vast amount of information over which the teacher has no control (Lam & Lawrence, 2002).

Many studies showed that technology in general has a great effect on improving students' performance. On the other hand, using the internet in the class, as an example, can be fun. Internet is a whole world of information where students can benefit in an enjoyable way. Technology can provide teachers with the ability to convey concepts in new ways that cannot be achieved using other traditional instructional practices.

Since the secret of our success is our young generations who will be forming our future, so it is very important to prepare them to face the challenges of our life. The need to introduce technology at an early age in life is very vital for them. For example, we should make sure that students are familiar with the basic skills of using computers which will enable them to use the latest tool for getting knowledge. More importantly, the world in which we live is progressing in a fast way, and so, the education is also expected to change too. We can never forget the old days when the audio-visual lab is isolated from the whole schools, while nowadays, it is important for every teacher to integrate technology in a way or another in teaching. The use of multimedia in schools has accelerated in recent years. Multimedia can be useful for both teachers and students as well. For example, teachers can have great resources that can add a lot to their performance. Students also can work on their learning by using multimedia in different ways. Children do care about technology, that's why teachers should present their lessons in a way that suits their way of thinking. Nothing can be better than multimedia to give children the right motivation to learn. We can realize that most schools have a certain kind of technology already, but lots of them aren't integrating or utilizing it into classroom practice.

METHODOLOGY

This chapter used different qualitative methods to support topics and issues presented in the chapter. Mainly descriptive and analytical approach was used with related data and literature review and information gathered for this chapter. Also interviews were conducted with a sample of teachers and principals in Al Ain Educational Zone. This methodology is followed the rationale of many similar chapters. Critical analyses are provided to come up with findings that are followed by utter discussions and recommendations. As this is an exploratory study, results and recommendations need to be taken carefully.

Educational Technology in the UAE

Let us have a look at what we call model schools in UAE which provide a comprehensive educational program in an ideally prepared humanistic developmental learning environment. It is worth mentioning that when these schools were inaugurated more than a decade ago, they had advantages over typical schools, particularly in their infrastructure and teacher professional development activities. Due to the success of these schools, most public schools around the country started to follow their path. As a result, these days the gap between model schools and public schools almost vanished when it comes to technology availability and teacher professional development (Almekhlafi & Almegdadi, 2010, 173).

To talk about ways and methods of teaching in the past, one should mention that, in the past, more emphasis was given to teaching theory without any practical and real life time situations. Memorization was more important than understanding. Referring to different kinds of educational theories and approaches in that time, educators used to believe and apply what we call behaviorism. According to that theory, behavior can be studied in a systematic and observable manner with no consideration of internal mental states. Furthermore, it implies the dominance of the teacher; the teacher is the main important element in the educational process and he acts like a model to be followed by his students. Unlike behaviorism which is not as dominant today as it was during the middle of the 20th-century, constructivism is very reasonable and applicable educational approach nowadays. It is a philosophy that views knowledge as the outcome of experience. Constructivism learning theories are, essentially, a branch of philosophy that tries to understand how we construct knowledge. Constructivism theorists ask the following questions (Hofer & Pintrch, 1997; Jonasson, 1996):

What does it mean to know something? How do we come to know it? How does this knowledge influence our thinking processes? In this case, we construct knowledge based on our environment and experiences (Clancy, 1986; Winograd & Flores, 1986). Constructionism is built on the fact that children will achieve the best if they find a specific knowledge they look for on their own.

To relate what has been mentioned above, one should say that life has been changed and so, students need a much broader set of skills and abilities to be able to analyze, investigate, collaborate and relate to what they know. Consequently, computer technology and multimedia can be very efficient tool in fulfilling students' needs of constructing their own knowledge and experiences if teachers integrate them properly into the curriculum in suitable ways. They add life to the subject as well as enhance and support learning and understanding because of their visual and sound impact on the students' thinking processes.

EDUCATIONAL MULTIMEDIA

To integrate technology in teaching is very important; for instance, computer can act as a tutor. Teachers' contribution in this case is so little. A report entitled *Computer Advantages: Tutoring Individuals*, states "with computers as tutors, no student will be overwhelmed because he or she is missing fundamentals the computer will repeat material until each lesson has been sufficiently mastered" (Bennett, 1999, p. 3).

The use of computers and other kinds of technology help students to achieve their full potentials. Technology allows participants in the two-way learning process to communicate and interact adding a variety of audio-visual tools that help to enhance learning which becomes easier and faster with the help of different kinds of technology. Dwyer et al. (1991) indicates that computers can be used in collaboration for all subject areas, but, at the same time, teachers should be aware of styles of teaching and how to get the students involved in learning.

One of the advantages of using multimedia is to convey information quickly and effectively to all students and keep them interested in learning, (Zimmer, 2003 taken from Savage & Vogel, 1996).

No one can deny the fact that technology at schools can save time and keep information easily accessible to all and reduce the amount of paper we use. Using technology in presenting the curriculum can be powerful tools in helping students achieve higher levels of expertise. It extends depth of existing curriculum beyond what can be gained with traditional ways of teaching.

There are many great programs which claim to have some kind of pedagogic value. These claims may, of course, not be well founded. Educational software has often been very grey and boring and quite unattractive. Nonetheless, teachers have often found that children are more motivated to learn their times tables with the help of a program than otherwise. Multimedia technology can be used to make the programs more interesting with the addition of color, advanced graphics, animation and sound (Cunningham & Andersson, 1999). Currently, we can find different types of educational software; tutorial programs, simulation programs, drill and practice, problem-solving programs and game programs. Using computer technology for students has many advantages as it provides them with immediate feedback; on the other hand, it keeps on motivating and challenging them and so, enriching their concepts and knowledge.

An increase in factual information exchanges and task conceptualization, interactions between teachers and students when teaching occurred across computers (Karasivvidis, 2004). Using technologies in education, has the potential to improve access to information; it helps in getting tasks done better or more quickly, and moreover, facilitating communication (National Research Council 1999).

Undoubtedly, without these recent technologies in the classroom, strong lessons can still be achieved, but there's a sharp disconnect between the way students are taught in school and the way the outside world approaches socialization, meaning-making, and accomplishment. It is critical that education not only seek to mitigate this disconnect in order to make these two "worlds" more seamless, but of course also to leverage the power of these emerging technologies for instructional gain (Kloper, Osterweil, Groff, & Hass, 2009)

Using technology nowadays is becoming so widely used. It is obvious that many students spend countless hours using popular technologies in their houses and so, why can't they continue using them as means of education? Applying technology in education, is interactive and easier to individualize for specific student needs and it can be used in a variety of settings, including on a computer at home or school, a web-enabled or smart phone, or portable device such as a laptop, notebook, or I pad, (Andrew: 2011). It is a very important issue to make sure that the teachers themselves are aware of using technology to present their lessons in an enjoyable and beneficial way. A critical element is for teachers to be familiar with multimedia technologies in order for them to know how to use them within their curriculum areas. Both Initial Teacher Training and Continuous Professional Development in the area of multimedia in education need to be improved, (European Parliament STOA: 1997). For that reason, schools should take into consideration the issue of teachers' training on the use of technology to keep them up to date with all technology development and changes taking place around the world. Having the latest news and information about technology that are available to be used in schools, can be invaluable for all teachers who work on their professional development basically to raise up their performance that affects their students' performance positively.

UAE Teachers' Perceptions of Technology Multimedia

Almekhlafi and Almegdadi (2010) stated major perceptions regarding UAE teacher's percep-

tions about the use of technology multimedia in schools. The following data is partially taken from Almekhlafi and Almeqdadi. Participants were 100 teachers from two middle model schools, grades 6 to 9, in Al-Ain educational zone, in the United Arab Emirates. Participating teachers were sixty male and forty female. All teachers in both schools had between 5 and 15 years of teaching experience. All had experience using technology in their classes as it is mandated by the model schools. Both schools have good technology infrastructures available for teachers. This situation is similar to model and 'future' schools in the UAE and with less emphasis on technology and its infrastructure to private and public schools, respectively. Therefore results of teachers' perceptions regarding the multimedia portion seemed applicable. It shows that the majority of the teachers are capable of using technology and dealing with issues related to it. Table 1 is partially taken from Almekhlafi and Almeqdadi (mean out of 5 point scale).

UAE and Electronic Portfolios

Electronic portfolios have been used for program evaluation in the UAE. There is, however, a limited use of them in advancing learning and assessment. In another study conducted by Forawi, Almekhlafi, and Almekhlafy (2011), 'Development and validation of electronic portfolios: The UAE pre-service teachers' experiences,' it was concluded that senior college of education students held certain perceptions regarding development and use of electronic portfolios in the UAE universities. This study had threefold purposes, (1) describe the process of developing an electronic portfolio for the UAE teacher education programs, (2) find out relationships of the use of portfolio with the other program variables, and (3) examine the UAE pre-service science teachers' perceptions regarding their performance through the use of electronic portfolios. The assumption is that if electronic portfolios were to be used with pre-service teachers, they need to be successful

Table 1. Teachers' perceptions regarding multimedia

1.	I can use technology in the development of strategies for solving problems in the real world.	4.0
2.	I have knowledge to discuss health and ethical issues related to technology	4.0
3.	I can use technology tools and resources for managing and communicating information (e.g., finances, schedules, addresses, purchases, correspondence).	4.0
4.	I can discuss diversity issues related to electronic media.	4.5
5.	I can evaluate and select new information resources and technological innovations based on their appropriateness to specific tasks.	4.0

in accomplishing their goals, worth the time spent in creating them, and advance learning and completion of programs. Participants were 67 female pre-service teachers at a national UAE university who were enrolled in their last course in the program, Capstone Experiences. Among the 67 pre-service, 37 were in the Arabic section, 10 were in the Early Childhood section, and 9 were in the Science section, and 11 were in the other sections namely Islamic Education, Math, and English. A survey was developed by researchers to include aspects related to the electronic portfolio development, usefulness, and experience gained to adequately provide insight into participating pre-services' perceptions. Twenty items were included, in additional to 11 sub-items that were purposefully presented to reflect good practice and theory in a 5-point Likert scale.

A major result indicated that the use of electronic portfolio is considered a pragmatic vehicle to assess pre-service teachers' performance and evaluate teacher's education programs. In using new multimedia technologies such as the portfolio, the assumption seems to be that we can substitute one medium for another—keeping the benefits of traditional print formats while adding a host of new conveniences. In a previous research study (Forawi & Wonderwell, 2003), it was found that pre-service teachers' learning and teaching skills have been impacted by use of electronic portfolios. Participants of that study developed understanding of learned materials and technology use through their portfolio's reflective narratives. They were able to show a progress in their learn-

ing and readiness to become teachers. There is a great need to address whether the experience of creating an electronic portfolio contributes to the development of reflection and overall teaching excellence and, if so, how this improvement occurs. Research indicated that electronic portfolios are robust with many purposes which can be for learning, assessment, and employment.

We need also to meet the needs of the infrastructure needs of the schools by preparing and equipping our schools with different kinds of technology including computers so as not to be isolated from what is happening around. Using computers is very important as it helps students to play an active role rather than being recipients of information transmitted by a teacher.

The use of instructional multimedia in classrooms is unequivocally important in advancing student learning and understanding of materials. Various software, internet sources and the web appear to offer some advantages. First, once resources are posted on the web, they are available at low cost to any school that has a connected computer and data projector. Second, multimedia can be used to provide learning materials that can reduce the demands on the time of teachers. Technology brings about changes to the classroom roles and organization. It allows the students to become more self-reliant. Students may use peer coaching, and teachers may function more as facilitators than lecturers (Means, 1997). Universities have been using web resources to support students learning and consequently personal use after graduation, but with less effective use after at workplace. The UAE experience seems to fit this profile. Few teachers incorporate use of website into instruction, such as science-chemistry, physics, math and languages. In a study conducted by Forawi and balfakih (2009), students were able to incorporate Vernier multimedia and sensor probe ware to conduct science activities related to water quality testing in summer camp.

UAE SCHOOL EXPERIENCE WITH MULTI MEDIA

To start talking about the huge development in the use of multimedia in classrooms specifically in UAE, let us give an example about what is taking place in Dubai when integrating new technology in the schools. In 1998 Dubai started a new experience starting with English language teaching. Teachers got training on the multiple uses of multimedia interactive DVD that include the use of electronic boards, group work, and individual work. Lesson procedures were thought out in advance, and post lesson discussions of different topics took place to ensure a high level of performance. This experience was evaluated and it showed that the results were amazing in the sense of the results of students' performance. To show the great positive effect of this experience, I am going to shed light on the report that is taken from (UAE Dubai Modern Education School, Multimedia English Lab Final Report, (2002). The figure below is giving us percentages of the responses of the students in grade2, 3, 4 and 5 towards using a certain type of technology in their education.

From using the figures in table 2, one can conclude that, students are so excited and happy when using technology in learning as 90% of them were so excited to use to the lab; they even think that using a CD-I is an easy task. More importantly, 82% found the sound and pictures were very clear and they did not face any difficulty in hearing or seeing. 70% of the students preferred to have more

than one lesson a week; this percentage can be an indicator of how much students get interested in such kinds of lessons. On the other hand, 89% thought that leaning using such technology is more interesting and fun than the traditional and classical techniques of teaching. A percentage of 84% of the students told their parents about it which reflects their interest in it and finally 99% would like to use the same method for next year as well.

Reflecting on my own experience with multimedia technologies as a teacher in one of the private schools in Al-Ain, I searched for an answer to the question of the present situation of multimedia and computer technology in teaching and learning in private schools and whether the teachers are getting enough training on the usage of technology or not. To collect data about private schools in Al-Ain, thirty-five female teachers of different subjects; Math, Geography, Islamic Studies, English and Arabic and five principals; 3 female principal and 2 male principal were interviewed. The schools I chose consist of large number of students from K-10. Teachers and principals were chosen randomly. There were four questions to be answered by the teachers. The first question is about how often they use the computer lab for their lessons. The second one is to mention the obstacles that prevent teachers

Table 2. Consolidated figures for grades 2, 3, 4 and 5 (total no. of students 74)

82% of students believe that CD-1is easy to use
95% of students were happy going to the lab
82% of students didn't have any hearing or vision problems
24% of students sometimes watched where their friends were doing
85% of students read what is on the screen
70% of students wanted more than one lesson per week
89% of students thought that learning with CD-1 is more interesting
84% of students told their parents about it
99% of students would like to use CD-1 next year

from regular use of technology in their lessons, and the other one is about the teachers themselves if they get any planned training to use technology available in their school. Also, finally they can add any additional comment if they like to.

From these interviews, six teachers of English language, said that they are glad to have computer labs as before they used to teach without using any kinds of technology, so lessons were very boring and teachers were the center of the teaching process unlike nowadays after using technology where students are the main element in the whole process, consequently, lessons become interesting and enjoyable. On the other hand, it is so pleasing that students are able to write and produce neat and correctly spelled work. The teachers added that they used to feel very tired when explaining any lesson without having any technology helping them to demonstrate the lesson and so, lecturing the students in the traditional, classical, boring way was the only alternative. They also commented that after having computer labs, it is now possible for the teachers to use them once or twice a week only, which is not enough to meet all the students' needs and this is the main obstacle they really face; they need to have adequate time to use the lab whenever they need.

When I asked them about their own comments if they would like to add, they said," we would like to have at least one computer and a projector in every classroom so it will be possible for all teachers to change their methods and techniques and use the most updated information in the most likable way to all students at any time". For English teachers in specific, they feel that it is a must to use the internet as they are plenty of wonderful activities that can enhance students' learning. I can also add that there are plenty of activities for students as well as for the teachers in all subjects and not only for English.

The second part of the interviews was interviewing twelve teachers of Math. The same five questions were asked. The results of these interviews were amazing as all of the teachers gave the same answer but in a different way. They said that they feel that using computers changed students' opinions in this subject. Others said that when taking their students to the lab once a week or every other week as it is not allowed to use the lab at any time they need, students start showing enthusiasm in solving problems using computers instead of papers and pencils. More importantly, they like to prepare their own worksheets which is as beneficial for them as they feel responsible to show the best design and content. One of the teacher added that using the internet makes it possible for my students to participate in some on - line international competition of math. They wish that they can use the lab in all math lessons as their problem is that they cannot use the lab whenever they need; they should book it in advance as the other teachers will be waiting for their turns to come.

The third part of the interviews was with eight Arabic teachers. They said," It is wonderful that we can use different kinds of technology to help our students learn in an effective and a fun way. Using Computers adds a lot to education as it is continuation of the life style of the present generation. As all know most children use computers in their homes for hours and they like using it especially at school so as teachers, we have to take advantages of this situation and make computers available for them for the sake of their learning. One of the teachers said," usually I ask my students to prepare power point presentations especially for grammar lessons; no one can imagine how successful these lessons are". Other teachers added," Some students try to misuse computers in the searching for games or different stuff while doing the task they are asked to do so I need to keep them focused all the time. Other teachers stated," Our school keeps on forgetting the importance of providing us with special training to enable us as teachers to use technology in the right way and to work on improving our skills and abilities in teaching our students.

The fourth part was the interview of a group of four teachers of Islamic Studies. They focused on the importance of using computers to find some stories or articles related to their subjects. They said that students always get excited to choose their best readers of the Holy Quran to listen to which is very useful for students who try to copy these great people. And as a result, improve their recitation in return. To ask students to find stories from the internet for the Prophet's Sirah is their favorite job. In general, using technology helps us as teachers in presenting lessons in the best way adding a flavor of fun and life to it. They added, we have never got any training on the use of technology or even nobody asked us if I am able to use technology in classrooms or not. Furthermore, to adapt new learning technologies, the school should place a strong emphasis on the training and skill development of its teachers.

The last part of the interview was with five Geography teachers; they were very enthusiastic about using technology in their classrooms. They said," Finally, with the new lab we can add life to Geography lessons. Within a minute student can use the computer to find maps, live pictures about different places and even essays and articles about different topics in Geography. Using technology allows students for more variety of resources that they can learn from.

The last question was for all teachers was whether there are any disadvantages for using computers and multimedia in the UAE context; the majority of them said that it is just the misuse of the Internet, gaming, and other distractions that can make it a challenge to keep students on-task, but an experienced teacher could keep his students on the right track all the time. Other five teachers said that it is not an easy task to integrate technology in all subjects or topics. Sometimes, it is a real challenge for us to deal with technology as we are not specialized in this area and so we keep on asking for help. We've never got any real training; we just rely on our peers' help.

Finally, after interviewing the five principals, I found out that all of them realized that teachers' performance has been improved since they have started integrating computer's technology in demonstrating their lessons. For example, teachers can organize their students to search for educationally useful material on topics which were of interest to their lessons. They added that not only the teachers' performance was clearly influenced, but also, students' performance has been positively affected in return. Students start getting excited and their interaction has been increased when having their lessons in the computer's lab using computers as means of acquiring knowledge and information. The only point they are unhappy about is that there is not enough computers to be used by teachers at any time they need to use as they have either one or two labs for the whole school which is not fair for teachers whom we always ask to use technology in teaching in their classrooms. They added, there is no specific educational pattern associated with success, but, of course, there are many other factors which influence success; technology is one of these important factors. They think that teachers should embed technology into teaching and learning processes and of course, schools must adjust its system and practices to be successful in its adoption of the new technology.

CONCLUSION

Using Multimedia and computer technology in classrooms is very vital in enhancing and raising up students' progress. It can add joy and fun to our schools. It provides teachers with a variety of activities as well as new ways to present and demonstrate lessons in. On the other hand, it is obvious that some teachers resist the use of technology neglecting the fact that using computers nowadays is the same as opening a huge gate to knowledge. In such a case, teachers' awareness of the importance of using technology in stimulating students' learning is highly needed. They should have dedicated instructional advisers who help them to integrate technology into their lesson's plans.

Obviously, there are several barriers facing education when implementing any kind of technology. Some of these barriers are related to the teachers themselves and lack of training on the use of the technology. Consequently, it is very important for teachers to get training that meet their needs to enable them to utilize available technology. On the other hand, one should realize that sometimes, the main reason of teachers' resistance to use technology is their ignorance of using any technological device. So providing them with the needed training will help them to accept the change. Furthermore, teachers' training should be on-going and offered at different levels, such as basic, moderate, and expert according to their needs. The other barrier is the technology itself whether it is available in schools or not; as we realized, some private schools have only one lab to be used by all teachers for all subjects so we can expect the amount of each teacher's share. And finally, students themselves who may cause some troubles when using technology especially the internet and so, teachers should keep their students on the right track all the time.

With public schools, the situation is completely different; UAE has good commitment from the principals as well as teachers and all of the stakeholders of education to work on and support students' progress and attainment by applying the most recent and modern methods of technology in classrooms, however, as it is highly believed that even the use of computers was not fully exploited as a teaching and learning method in all schools of the UAE. It has been announced at the beginning of the year 2011 that five initiatives for information technology in the schools of Abu Dhabi and that is really promising of a good future for our schools in the region.

More importantly, UAE has many future plans to well equip all public and private schools with all kinds of modern technology to keep the education system at the top of all countries and to meet the explosion of information revolution in the whole world as it realizes that using technology in education can add various media and different delivery methods that allow better learn ability that suites all learners' needs and interests. Many training workshops have been held in different areas especially in the government sector to train teachers of how to use the latest technological teaching tools as we all know that interactive teaching can be more effective than lecturing.

Universities need to take responsibility in preparing students for lifelong learning. While engineering and science degrees traditionally do not emphasize the importance of lifelong learning skills new programs of study are now being introduced, often using electronic portfolios to support engagement with learning objectives and reflection. As the literature shows, portfolios are often used in conjunction with assessment. However, their roles in improving learning and developing reflection are important areas note emphasizing. As indicated by similar UAE studies in this chapter, use of multimedia and electronic portfolio has opened new ways to incorporate such powerful tools to enhance learning at grade and university levels and therefore support self learning and reflection. Despite the challenges of motivating students to develop the electronic portfolios and accommodating time spend in creating them within courses and school work (Heinrich, Bhattacharya, & Rayudu, 2007), these tools can still be effective to use in education in developing countries. In particular, students' experiences in developing the 'programatic' e-portfolio at the United Arab Emirates University are recognized and they promise improvement in student achievement at higher education in the country.

Educational institutions need to change their organizational structure and processes if they want to succeed in adapting and utilizing available technology in the educational field as they are the basic requirement for integrating learning technologies. It is found that to incorporate new technology will be almost impossible with same traditional structure of educational organizations

Technology concerns knowledge not merely artifacts. To transfer it effectively requires prepared minds on the part of the receivers and some measure of shared cognitive frameworks. The culture has to change as well to make any necessary changes a reality. It also requires coordinated policies on investment, education and training, employment, the economy and development. Thus, technology is the need of today and the future, and the application of this technology means a leap towards success. Consequently, an attention should be paid to introduce technology to our students at an early age in schools to have a shortcut from present into future progress. Finally, it is so important to mention that the UAE is keen to create equal educational chances for our students to get their full rights just like other students in other countries (Shaw, 2002).

REFERENCES

Almekhlafi, A. G., & Almeqdadi, F. A. (2010). Teachers' perceptions of technology integration in the United Arab Emirates school classrooms. *Journal of Educational Technology & Society*, *13*(1), 165–175.

Bennett, F. (1999). *Computers as tutors: Solving the crisis in education. Publishers Middle East Educator, 11*. Sarasota, FL: Faben Inc.

Collins, A., & Halverson, R. (2009). *Rethinking education in the age of technology*. New York, NY: Teachers College Press.

Cunnington, U., & Andersson, S. (1999). *Teachers, pupils and the internet*. Nelson Thomas.

Dwyer, D., Ringstaff, C., & Sandholtz, J. (1991). Changes in teachers' beliefs and practices in technology-rich classrooms. *Educational Leadership*, *48*(8).

Forawi, S., Almekhlafi, A., & Almekhlafy, M. (2011-in press). Development and validation of electronic portfolios: The UAE pre-service teachers' experiences. *US-China Education Review Journal.*

Forawi, S., & Wonderwell, S. (2003). Examining electronic portfolio reflective narratives. *Proceedings of Society of Information Technology and Teacher Education,* Albuquerque, New Mexico, (pp. 2101- 2117).

Heinrich, E., Bhattacharya, M., & Rayudu, R. (2007). Preparation of lifelong learning using e-portfolios. *European Journal of Engineering Education*, *32*(6), 653–663. doi:10.1080/03043790701520602

Hofer, B. K., & Pintrich, P. R. (1997). Development of epistemological theories: Beliefs about knowledge and knowing and their relation to knowing. *Review of Educational Research*, *67*(1), 88–140.

Hofstetter, J. S., & Corsten, D. (2001). *Collaborative new product development - First insights.* Presented at the First International ECR Research Symposium, November 1, 2001, Cambridge.

Hwang, W.-Y., Shadiev, R., & Huang, S.-M. (2011, May). A study of multimedia web annotation system and its effect on the EFL writing and speaking performance of junior high school students. *ReCALL*, *23*(2), 160–180. doi:10.1017/S0958344011000061

Klopfer, E., Osterweil, S., Groff, J., & Haas, J. (2009). *Using technology of today in the classroom of today*. The Education Arcade Massachusetts Institute of Technology.

Lam, Y., & Lawrence, G. (2002). Teacher-student role redefinition during a computer-based second language project: Are computers catalysts for empowering change? *Computer Assisted Language Learning*, *15*(3), 295–315. doi:10.1076/call.15.3.295.8185

Means, B. (1997). *Critical issue: Using technology to enhance engaged learning for at-risk students.* Retrieved on 21 November, 1999, from www.ncrel.org/sdrs/areas/issues/students/atrisk/400

Muir-Herzig, R. M. (2004). Technology and its impact in the classroom. *Computers & Education, 42,* 111–131. doi:10.1016/S0360-1315(03)00067-8

Multimedia in Education - European Parliament STOA. (1997). *The transition from primary school to secondary school.*

Savage, T. M., & Vogel, K. E. (1996). Multimedia. *College Teaching, 44*(4), 127–132. doi:10.1080/87567555.1996.9932339

Shaw, E. (2002). Education and technological capability building in the Gulf. *International Journal of Technology and Design Education, 12,* 77–91. doi:10.1023/A:1013002828605

UAE Dubai Modern Education School. (2002). *Multimedia English lab final report.*

Winograd, T., & Flores, F. (1986). *Understanding computers and cognition: A new foundation for design.* Norwood, NJ: Ablex Publishing Co.

ADDITIONAL READING

Barker, J., & Tucker, R. N. (Eds.). (1990). *The interactive learning revolution: Multimedia in education and training.* London.

Bransford, J., Brown, A., & Cocking, R. (2000). *How people learn. Brain, mind, experience, and school, expanded version.* Washington, DC: National Academy Press.

Brooks, R. M. (1993). Principles for effective hypermedia design. *Technical Communication, 40*(3).

Burbules, N. C., & Callister, T. A. (2000). *Watch IT: The risks and promises of information technologies for education.* Boulder, CO: Westview.

Chandler, P., & Sweller, J. (1996). Cognitive load while learning to use a computer program. *Applied Cognitive Psychology, 10*(2). doi:10.1002/(SICI)1099-0720(199604)10:2<151::AID-ACP380>3.0.CO;2-U

Clariana, R. B., Ross, S. M., & Morrison, G. R. (1991). The effect of different feedback strategies using computer administer multiple choice questions as instruction. *Educational Technology, 39*(2).

De Westelinck, K., Valcke, M., De Craene, B., & Kirschner, P. (2005). Multimedia learning in social sciences: Limitations of external graphical representations. *Computers in Human Behavior, 21*(4).

Kalyuga, S., Chandler, P., & Sweller, J. (2004). *When redundant on-screen text in multimedia technical instruction can interfere with learning.*

Kellner, D. (2000). New technologies/new literacies: Reconstructing education for the new millennium. *Teaching Education, 4*(2).

Mayer, R. E., & Moreno, R. (1998). A split-attention effect in multimedia learning: Evidence for dual processing systems in working memory. *Journal of Educational Psychology, 90*(2). doi:10.1037/0022-0663.90.2.312

Plass, J. L., & Salisbury, M. W. (in press). A living systems design model for web-based knowledge management systems. *Educational Technology Research and Development, 50*(1).

Reddi, U. V. (2003). Multimedia as an educational tool. In Reddi, U. V., & Mishra, S. (Eds.), *Educational multimedia: A handbook for teacher-developer.* New Delhi, India: CEMCA.

Rosen, Y., & Salomon, G. (2007). The differential learning achievements of constructivist technology-intensive learning environments as compared with traditional ones: A meta-analysis. *Journal of Educational Computing Research, 36*(1). doi:10.2190/R8M4-7762-282U-554J

KEY TERMS AND DEFINITIONS

Communication Technologies: Use of advanced technologies, such as mobiles, digital videos, HD, 3Ds, in communication for greater benefits.

Constructivist Learning: A learning that is based on constructivist theory where students are independent in their attainment of knowledge, skills and dispositions for meaningful understanding.

Educational Technology: Educational technology is the use of technology to improve education. It is a systematic, iterative process for designing instruction or training used to improve performance.

Educational Theories: The theories that explain teaching and learning such as behaviorism, positivism, and neuropsychology.

Electronic Portfolios: According to Forawi & Liang (2005), electronic portfolios are containers of students' best learning experiences that supported by their reflective narratives for authentic experiences that are done with use of electronic medium, such as use of FrontPage, Webs,..etc.

Integration of Technology: It is the process that utilizes technology tools into various school subjects to maximize student learning.

Interactive Teaching: It is the use of different methods that allow students to be active learners and provide them with opportunities to share and participate in.

Multimedia Technology: The use of computers to present text, graphics, video, animation, and sound in an integrated way through the advancement of technology. This is an exciting new area for those interested in the use of computers and technology.

Chapter 7
Automated Enrollment in Higher Education in the UAE Universities

Zeinab Al Husari
Federal Authority for Nuclear Regulation (FANR), UAE

ABSTRACT

Information and Communication Technology (ICT) has a far reaching impact on both organizations and individuals. ICT solutions are indispensable for schools, colleges, and organizations. Educational organizations are specifically interested in ICT solutions to support their primary teaching and learning functions as well as supporting functions such as human resources, logistics, finance, and accounting.

This chapter highlights the importance of admission and registration functions in higher education and discusses the main objectives and sought benefits from utilizing Information and Communication Technology (ICT) applications to support the automation of admission and registration processes and functions in UAE higher education's institutes. The chapter also suggests an effective approach to design and adopt such applications to ensure the realization of benefits to both students and universities. Of particular interest to this investigation is how can universities successfully and effectively apply the e-admission and e-registration system. The chapter concludes with a positive outlook of future Internet and e-applications to improve admission and registration in terms process streamlining, ease of use, easy access, and connectivity. It also points out some challenges that normally occur when some ICT solution is applied at a number of higher educational institutes.

INTRODUCTION

Today, admission and registration processes in most universities and higher educational institutes continue to be manually processed and using a variety of forms and applications and paperwork.

Only a small number of institutions have opted to use technology to partially automate admission and registration functions. Unfortunately, when ICT has provided many applications to support business applications and automate business processes, education had only small share of the

DOI: 10.4018/978-1-4666-1984-5.ch007

technology application and have missed out on its benefits.

The potential gains that higher education can realize from automated admission registration system, justifies the need to design and implement a Computerized Automated Student Admission and Registration System. The need for such automated registration and admission system in today's universities will speed up the admission and registration process, attract national and international students, save lots of time and efforts that usually needed from both universities and students, give the higher educational institutes opportunity to grow rapidly locally and globally and compete effectively in education industry.

At Newcastle University in England "The decision was also made to decentralize the registration process so that the end users of the course data, the various University departments, would have more control over the accuracy of the data entered. It was also expected that the delay before the final data could be delivered back to the departments would be considerably reduced. Although the same registration forms were issued to students, available data concerning each student had already been entered in the system database. At the registration, using unique student number as a key, student data was retrieved from the database and updated as necessary" (Little M. C & et al, 1999).

The main objectives of this chapter are to review the following issues:

- To introduce the importance of automated admission and registration system in higher education.
- To explore how can universities apply the e-admission and e- registration system.
- To review the potential gains and the anticipated impact of applying automated system in higher education field on the universities and students.
- To endorse a paperless environment in conjunction with automating universities admission and registration.

- To highlight how automated system can be applied in education field and the benefits and need of applying it in today's universities.
- To explore ideas for future Internet and e-application and how they can be utilized to improve admission, registration and enrolment in UAE educational institutes.

BACKGROUND

A typical Arab university would have a dedicated office for admission and registration within the university campus, where new students are expected to report to in order to complete their admission and registration procedures. Normally, a new student would be asked to fill out an admission form and to have the completed form submitted with supporting legal and academic documents to the admission office. A current student would fill out a registration form for selected courses in the upcoming academic semester.

Likewise, in the United Arab Emirates (UAE) all universities and colleges have physical or traditional admission and registration systems in addition to some partially automated systems like course registration, where current students have to login and electronically enroll in courses of interest, while some major admission process is still not fully automated.

Admission and Registration processes are extremely important to both students and universities. Universities can't create full admission records of new and current students without proper admission and registration system. Such a system is also essential and convenient to students because it provides them with a faster and less cumbersome procedure and easy to use tools to register and enroll in selected courses.

The scale and the persisting nature of students' admission and courses registration issues in many universities in the Middle East, warrant the need for a sophisticated and advanced automated system to manage student application admission and registration process.

Currently many governmental universities in the UAE have adopted fully e-registration system for academic courses. However, admission process is still not fully automated due to many rezones such some private universities are newly established, high cost of secured automated admission system, and the risk involved in transferring the hard copy information and students' records to fully automated system.

Higher Education System in the UAE

The UAE is emerging as a significant site of private and foreign education. This is clearly manifested by the level of expansion in state and private universities of indigenous and overseas origin. UAE government sought the support of many agencies, such as UNDP (United Nations Development Programme) and the World Bank for sitting up and running higher education institutions. Such international agencies provided invaluable technical assistance and consultation to streamline processes, and utilize network communications (UNESCO, 2008).

The United Arab Emirates University, the first government university in the country was established in 1976 with the aim of welding the new nation. Whilst, UAE University had an important contribution to cope with the increasing numbers of school leavers entry to university education, it was evident there was additional need for higher education provision, which was answered by establishing the Higher Collage of Technology (HCT) Group in 1988 and Zayed University (for women) in 1998.

Later, over thirty private and semi-private educational institutions have been established through the UAE, enabling the rapid increasing numbers of university student to study near their homes. Some of the private universities that have grown in popularity including; Ajman University of Science & Technology Network, American Universities of Sharjah, American University in

Dubai, Etisalat College of engineering and Abu Dhabi University. There is also one leading accredited and licensed electronic university in the Middle East region which is called Sheikh Hamdan bin Mohamed e-university and it is located in the emirate of Dubai.

Both governmental and private universities believe in the importance of enrolment of ICT solutions in education field and how IT (Information Technology) applications sorted out many issues for the universities and students. All universities have the basic ICT solutions like TV broadcasting, and teleconferencing beside partially advanced admission and registration ICT solutions.

Yet the UAE government strongly push higher educational sector to apply ICT solutions in all admission and educational processes in effective way in order to catch up with global electronic development to enhance efficiency in admission, registration, academic e-transactions.

Existing Situation (Scenario)

A typical registration day at students admission and registration section in most universities in the UAE may be described by the following scenario:

- **8.30 am:** Average of three Administration Officers enter their offices and before they have their own cusp of coffee their phones are already ringing.
- **8.45 am:** After settling, turning on their computers each Administration Officer will find more than 40- 60 emails in his/her mail inboxes. At least one the two phones keep on ringing, distracting officers from reading their emails. Since coming into office, Administration Officers have great difficulty to take pick up a phone and properly attend to the query at the other end.. The Officers know with high certainty that there are might at the other end a worried parent or a student who wants to inquire about an application status.

- **10.45 am:** Most Administration Officers have managed to either directly respond to more than half of their emails, or else have forwarded other emails to the respective departments or faculties within the universities. From time to time two of the Officers would actually pick up the phone to respond to a worried parent or student, spending time to either search through some hard-copy papers on stacks on the desk, or across soft-copy files on the Officer's individual computer. A call lasts between five and twenty five minutes. Every time one of the Officer's has actually completed a call and put down the receiver once again he/she takes a deep breath- only to find the phone ringing once again nearly simultaneously.

Apart from the ongoing phone inquiries a total of around 10- 15 worried parents or students have gathered in the Administration Office, each of them aiming to follow up on an individual's application status. The Administration Officers attempt to stay polite and calm, most of the time it works, yet from time to time the frustration in this constant demand on them is visible.

The day for the Administration and Registration Officers proceeds in a similar manner until 5:00 pm when the working day for the Administration Officers is normally finished, yet none officers makes an attempt to leave. Apart from serving worried parents or students face-to-face on their respective application status, they have managed to respond to numerous emails and some phone calls- all on the same matter. The number of physical parents/ students arriving has declined after 5.30 pm and the most Officers know that finally they can work on some of their pending tasks. In the ideal case these tasks are done within their normal working hours, yet with the constant demand on them from parent or student side it is unthinkable.

Students at Today's Universities

Today, a potential student for UAE Universities can apply either in person or via mail. The application process is described on the University Website; Application Forms for both undergraduate and postgraduate studies are available on the website for retrieval and download and can be obtained from the Office of Admission and Registration.

No matter whether a student applies online or physically, there are two to three times of the year that applications can be processed, for fall, spring or summer semesters. Deadlines for any admission are announced by the Admission Office and Registration.

In case a student prefers to physically visit the university he/she can obtain an admission package for registration, complete it and provide all required documents to the Admission Office. On the other hand, a student can also apply electronically by visiting the website of the selected university, download the respective application form, and then go to university building to summit his/her admission application. Alternatively, a student can download the application form, complete it and send all required papers, together with the Application Fee by email. Thereafter, a student can follow up the application status by calling the university by phone, sending an email or by physically visiting the university.

Thus, with this partially automated admission and registration system or physical registration system, it can be concluded that presently most of the universities receive student information from the hardcopy applications or through e-mail. There is a delay in getting data from some colleges or students and this will delay registration and admission process. High workload on the admission and registration officers. Complains and frustration from some students due to delay in getting the accurate information of admission.

From above explained situation, it can be noticed that all higher educational institutes in the

UAE needs to adopt fully automated admission and registration solutions for the benefits of both parties the students and university.

FROM TRADITIONAL ADMISSION AND REGISTRATION TO E-ADMISSION AND E-REGISTRATION

The Problem and Solution

A good understanding of admission and registration processes and the preceding description of the chaotic environment in a typical university administration and registration office, one can identify issues and problems that contribute to a complex, lengthy, costly, unclear, slow, ineffective, unorganized practices that troublesome to both university officers as well as students and parents.

Furthermore, if we think of the education institute as a business organization and that the students and parents represent the category of customers, one additional problem that characterize such practices is 'customer dis-satisfaction' one of the most important success indicators in any business.

A feasible solution to the above situation must address the specific persisting problems. The value chain model associated with using technology solutions confirms that technology is more effective in addressing certain issues than others in any process. Accordingly, it is suggested that a suitable web-based information system solution with dedicated functionality to support admission and registrations function and processes would be an effective platform to transform the cumbersome manual or traditional admission and registration practice into a simpler, shorter, less costly, clear, faster, effective and organized practices that will improve performance, productivity and customer satisfaction.

Implementation Methodology

In this section the author explains the workflow of fully automated admission and registration system and how it should be implemented.

The student that interested to apply at a university that adopts the automated admission and registration system needs to follow certain steps to complete the e- admission process as illustrated below:

The student needs to create online profile and has user name and password:

1. Once student profile is created, the student will received confirmation email from the university.
2. From the time that the student received the conformation email, he/she can login via the university website and fill out the e- application form along with the required admission documents and certificates.
3. If all needed documents are fulfill the university admission requirements the registered student should receive an e-mail of completed and submission of the e-application along with a student tracking number.
4. The student can login the university web page and check the status of the application.
5. With two to three weeks the university admission team will check the validation and accreditation of all applied students' certificates and legal documents that were requested in the earlier registration step. To ensure the creditability of the certificates, the university needs to have database linked with Ministry of Education (MOE) and Ministry of Higher Education (MOHE) to verify the accreditation of the submitted certificates and documents.
6. If all submitted certificates and documents are fulfill the university requirements and in addition to MOE and MOHE the student will receive confirmation letter of registration and admission and he/ she can start to register courses for the first academic semester.

E-Registration Process

Students who are admitted can use the university e-registration system once they have the university Identification Number (ID) and password. Every academic semester the university offers some mandatory and optional courses for every specialization. Once student login process is completed, the offered courses will show up. Then the student can select the desired course the he/ she needs to register at and finalized registration.

During course registration time, the university admission and registration team will be available 24/7 to provide student with instant assistance to resolve any e-registration problem that the students might face and to answer students inquires (Figure 1, Figure 2, and Figure 3).

POTENTIAL GAINS OF AUTOMATED ADMISSION AND REGISTRATION SYSTEM

There is no doubt that a partial or full automation of higher education admission and registration functions have anticipated gains to both students and the organization. Considering the scenario that was described earlier and the problems associated with that, one would expect that having an information system could contribute to a smoother faster processing of students applications especially with online access to all concerned parties. (Akken, 2008). The acquisition and implementation of a fully automated admission and registration system by higher education institutes can be justified by any of the following reasons and anticipated gains:

- Facilitation of Time and Costs for Students
- Now a day internet accesses it available everywhere. Introducing e-application and e-registration will facilitates registration process for undergraduate and postgraduate students, through saving their time and travelling costs.

- Reason 2: Ease of Use of Application Handling for university admission and registration staff
- It is an easy to use e-service since it does not require the help of IT department.
- Reason 3: Cut Registration and Administration Costs at universities
- It helps universities to cut huge registration and admin costs by speeding up application process with a secure e-solution.
- Reason 4: Instant Return on Investment for semi-governmental and private universities:
- It is an affordable service that allows universities to increase productivity. Costs range at around 100 USD or approximately 500AED per month for unlimited access, beyond this the authors of this paper expect a one-off installation fee of less than 10 000 USD or approximately 50 000 AED.
- Reason 5: Automation of Admission Services saves time for universities Staff
- The requirement for verbal communication between Admission Office and students can be greatly reduced. The e-admission and registration solution can display a student application status in real time and thus, allows students to check their application and registration at any time. For that reason the system reduces the time employees and students spent on the phone (as well as the respective costs of these calls).

In summary, while the author of this chapter is aware that there are several more reasons beyond aforementioned ones in this chapter, the author is confident that all five of the aforementioned reasons do in fact justify the need for a sophisticated online admission and registration system.

Value-Adds for Universities

This section highlights in brief the value-adds for the University that derive from the implementation

Figure 1. Part one of workflow of automated enrollment and registration process

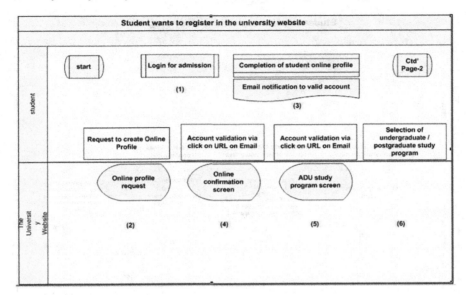

of the new and sophisticated online admission and registration system that has been illustrated in the previous sections (Turban E.2008).

- **Value-added 1:** Increase Work Effectiveness of the university Administration and increase Productivity. As a consequence of not being continuously called or contacted by email about a student's application status, the author of this project claim that the university Administration might be able to work more undisturbed and focus more on given tasks, which in turn might speed up task completion within their scope of work, as well as increase the overall productivity of the university Administration staff.
- **Value-added 2:** Increase Competitiveness - The adoption of the highly sophisticated e- admission and e-registration system is a highly innovative and western-based system that is likely to facilitate the improvement of the University's reputation across the United Arab Emirates and beyond. With means of marketing, including arti-

cles in the "Gulf News", IT and Education related magazines or journals where the system is announced and highlighted.
- **Value-added 3:** Increase in number of received Student Applications - An additional effect might also be the improvement in the related value perception of the University, and as a consequence this is likely to raise the number of student applications, making the university more popular than competitive tertiary institutions across the United Arab Emirates.
- **Value-added 4:** Attract additional highly educated/skilled lecturers and professors - Coming along with the improved external value perception might also be the attraction of additional highly educated and skilled lecturers and professors to the university or educational institute, which in turn is again likely to positively affect on the number of student applications, especially when word of mouth about the quality of lecturers and professors spreads.
- **Value-added 5:** Increase in Profit and Revenue - The author of this project claim

Figure 2. Part two of workflow of automated enrollment and registration process

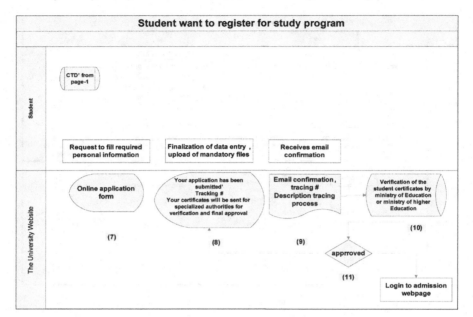

that all the aforementioned value-added contributes positively on an increasing profit and revenue flow for the University that adopts such electronic system.

- **Value-added 6:** Improve the university Infrastructure - The author of this chapter claims that with an increased profit deriving from larger numbers of students at the tertiary facility, the additional monetary flow can be used to improve the infrastructure of the University. This could possibly affect in providing online databases of educational magazines, journals and market research institutes in the university's library, the provision of sports facilities both indoor and outdoor, which might include sports teams that compete with sports teams of other universities across the entire United Arab Emirates (which in turn puts the name of the University in international context, with additional effect on the university's reputation).

- **Value added 7:** Increase Customer Satisfaction = Providing the Online admission system together with the sophisticated registration system is likely to make the universities customers/ stakeholders (students/parents) more satisfied since the live electronic data system provides flexibility, transparency as well as increases the user-friendliness of the university website.

- **Value added 8:** Go for paperless solution - Applying fully e-admission and e-registration solution will help to go paperless. Thus, decrease the use of papers and reduce the needed storage area for student applications and records.

While the author of this chapter is aware that there are several more reasons beyond the aforementioned ones in this chapter, the author is confident that all eight of the aforementioned reasons do in fact justify the need and respective investment for an advanced online admission and registration system

Figure 3. Student application reaches the university via IT system

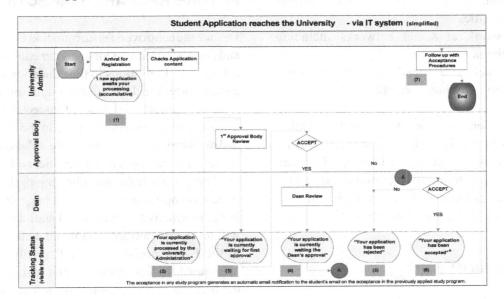

Challenges and Critical Success Factors

- **Security:** The university website and database might be targeted by hacker attacks.
- **Loss of Backup Information:** The information that has been backed up might be damaged or destroyed due to several reasons such as: fire, thrift and natural disaster.
- **Service Down:** Every ICT application might get down due to unpredictable response this will slow the admission and registration possess until problem is resolved.
- **Spirit Conservation to ICT Changes:** Some admission and registration officer's prefer to deal with physical applications and records rather than electronic system. This may delay the processing.
- **Cost involved in ICT Solutions:** High cost likely to be associated with IT solutions for their implementation and maintenance (Vargas, 2009).

Suggested E-Business Strategy

The author of this paper advises universities towards a clicks and mortar strategy, with the particular e-business strategy targeted towards becoming an e-enabled University that increases the richness and reach of different Universities in the Middle East. By e-enabled the author means the provision of an extended lot of e-services that facilitates the life of all universities stakeholders. These e-services may include, but are not limited to the following:

- e-library facilities and access to online databases for students and lecturers
- e-booking of working rooms for students and lecturers
- e-student support with an e-board for asking critical study questions
- secure online chat facilities for the university students only
- e-conferences for staff (considering travel needs of some lecturers at times)

- e-collaborations with other partner universities
- e-network at social networks including facebook and twitter
- e-marketing at social networks including facebook, twitter and others

An efficient implementation and execution of this e-strategy, is likely to improve the quality of higher educational service in the UAE, which in turn is likely to improve customer (student + parents) satisfaction and consequently its competitive standing and external perception.

CONCLUSION

It can be concluded that ICT use in higher education can be expected to increase dramatically due to access to digital tools, applications, and networks continue to grow worldwide and media are increasingly available in digital form.

Thus, every higher educational institute will have a huge demanded to adopt and implement at least full e-admission and e-registration to survive and compete effectively in the education industry with the current internal and external challenges which are facing all educational institutes due the explosion of the information technology solutions worldwide

Adopting this ICT approach has provided the UAE universities with the competitive advantage and has allowed the universities that applied e-admission and e-registration to capture the result of being the first movers to the new technology; the universities will benefit from cost advantage and will be able to pick and focus on the most attractive student/customers segment.

Yet, most of higher educational institutes initiatives are technology dependent. Any initiative requires technology, the more innovative technology acquired, the more creative, developed and attractive are the universities to the current and future local and international students.

FUTURE RESEARCH DIRECTIONS

Despite the controversies surrounding e-admission and e-registration system in higher education, the future of ICT solutions in the education industry appears bright as the industry counties to flourish with the applications number of student enrolment. The flexibility and convenience in the admission and registration processes makes e-solutions a very attractive option to many universities and students.

Apply ICT solutions are challenging. However, once it is applied and activated a huge difference in the productivity, student and staff satisfaction will be clearly noticed. Higher education system in the UAE should go for full involvement of automated student admission and registration for the benefits of parties, students and universities.

The author suggests that the UAE universities can look for linking the university student database with the UAE Identification Authority to ensure that the received legal documents of the applied students are acceptable and to eases the verification process of the students identity. This way the local universities' students can get quicker e-admission permission and admission section in the university can process more e- applications within short time.

E-payment: once e-admission and registration system is fully applied, the university has to adopt e-payment. The admission and registration fee could be paid either online by visa cards or by mobile banking (m-banking) services.

For future development the student also will need to get their text books, needed study materials for the registered courses thru the e-payment system. Having this feature will enable the students to view their current financial status from anywhere and anytime and will save their time and add unique value to the university that adopted ICT solutions.

REFERENCES

Akken. (2008). *Application price and online e-works*. Retrieved April 14, 2012, from http://www.akken.com/pricing.php

Clancy, D. (2009). *Property registration authority*. Retrieved April 13, 2012, from www.eregistration.ie/termsAndConditions.aspx

Economy Watch. (2009). *E-business strategy*. Retrieved April 13, 2012 from http://www.economywatch.com/business/e-business-strategy.html

Farlex Free Dictionary. (2012). *Admission*. Retrieved April 14, 2012, from http://www.thefreedictionary.com/admission

Interact, U. A. E. (2008). *International Association of Universities UNESCO*. Retrieved 12 April, 2012, from http://www.uaeinteract.com/education

Interactive Education. (2007). Retrieved 12 April, 2012 from http://ict-solutions-provider.blogspot.com

Izquierdo, L. O., & Manuel, J. (2007). Information technology and communications (ICT) in academic management of the educational process in higher education. *Pedagogical University Magazine, 12*(1).

Jelassi, T., & Enders, A. (2008). *Strategies for e-business: Creating value through electronic and mobile commerce* (2nd ed.). Prentice Hall.

Little, M. C., Wheater, S. M., Ingham, D. B., Snow, C. R., Whitfield, H., & Shrivastava, S. K. (1996). *The university student registration system. A case study in building a high-availability distributed application using general purpose components*. Department of Computing Science, Newcastle University.

Turban, E., King, D., McKay, J., Marshall, P., Lee, J., & Viehland, D. (2008). *Electronic commerce: A managerial perspective* (International Edition). Pearson.

United Nations Development Programme (UNDP). (2008). *Website*. Retrieved April 13, 2012, from http://www.undp.org.ae/

VandenBos, G., Knapp, S., & Doe, J. (2001). Role of reference elements in the selection of resources by psychology undergraduates. *Journal of Bibliographic Research, 5*, 117–123. Retrieved October 13, 2001

Vargas, O. B. (2009). *Online education*. Retrieved April 14, 2012, from http://www.centrorisorse.org/proposed-ict-solution-to-educational-problems.html

ADDITIONAL READING

Al Shaiba, A. (2007). *Higher education strategy takes new turn*. Retrieved from http://gulfnews.com/about-gulf-news/al-nisr-portfolio/notes/articles/higher-education-strategy-takes-new-turn-1.195993\

KEY TERMS AND DEFINITIONS

E-Admission: Electronic admission where process of permission to enter or register at certain educational institute is occur electronically there might be charges required for entrance of the selected educational institute (Farlex. 2012).

E-Business Strategy: A 'strategy that (can) govern an e-business through calculated information dissemination'. (Economy Watch, 2009).

E-Registration: Is electronic registration where group of documents or instructions occurs in electronic format only and all registration processes are made on an electronic register. The e-registration system is only permitted for the purposes of transactions in all respects lawfully carried out (Clancy, 2009).

ICT Solution: Is any product or service through which information can be digitally stored, retrieved or manipulated. (Interactive education, 2007).

Physical or Traditional Admission: A place where a new or current student visits to apply for certain colleges in the university and a hard copy of the academic and legal document are needed to complete the first stage of admission. Once needed documents are fulfilled the university admission required, the student receive a call or Letter of admission from the university office (Husari, 2010).

UNDP: Is standing United Nations Development Programme. It is a global development network, dedicating for change and connecting countries to knowledge, experience and resources to help people build a better life. UNDP is on the ground in 166 countries. They are working with them on their own solutions to global and national development challenges. UNDP develops local capacity and progress towards the achievements, by 2015 of Melamine Development Goals (UNDP, 2008).

Chapter 8
ICT Applications in Arab Education Sector:
A Cultural Perspective

Hadia Abboud Abdul Fattah
Fatima College for Health Services, UAE

Fayez Ahmad Albadri
Abu Dhabi University, UAE

ABSTRACT

The far-reaching impact of the emergence of new applications in the field of Information and Communications Technology (ICT) has been evident in individuals, society, and business over the past two decades. However, educational organizations have only marginally gained benefits from such technologies until new information system and applications were designed and developed specifically to meet the needs of such organizations. This novice system has assisted both primary education functions and supporting enterprise functions such as finance, human resources (HR), and procurement.

Although technology adoption in education is generally viewed positively by educators, the shift in technology adoption by educational organizations, from simple class-resources and learning aids to a much more complex and sophisticated information systems, represent a major challenge to cope with, especially to many educational organizations in the Arab region, while the role and impact of culture on the outcomes is yet to be verified. Thus, this chapter examines the role and impact of local culture on the adoption and utilization of new information systems and technologies to enhance core educational functions and enterprise support functions within Arab educational organizations.

INTRODUCTION

The increasing interest in Information and Communications Technology (ICT) applications in the Arab education sector is thought to be linked to, as well as resulting from, a general trend of openness, transparency and reforms which are all associated with 'globalization'. From an earlier perspective, Held, McGrew, Goldblatt, and Parraton (1999) defined globalization as, " a process fueled by, and resulting in, increasing cross-border flows of goods, services, money,

DOI: 10.4018/978-1-4666-1984-5.ch008

people, information, and culture" (p.16). Later, the concept was perceived as an umbrella term for a complex series of economic, social, technological and political changes which are seen as increasing interdependence and interaction between people, cultures, states and companies in disparate locations (Ssenyonga, 2007). Both definitions advocate that the Arab nations are no exception to others in terms of impact of the massive world effect and global change associated with globalization. Globalization, together with new Information systems and technologies provided the leverage for improving higher levels of efficiency and productivity, proved that selling products on an international scale would reach a greater market, and showed that production has achieved extraordinary savings in labor costs on a global scale.

The main objective of this chapter is to examine the impact of culture on the outcomes of technology adoption in the Arab educational organizations. In addition, the chapter aims to identify the problems and other issues encountered with the emergence of new ICT Applications in the Arab Education sector to aid teaching and learning, and support functions in the Arabic schools with multicultural environment. In fact, the basic interest in technology solutions and systems is attributed to the evidence that using technology as an instructional tool in the classrooms would improve the student learning and educational outcomes, (Hanna & de Nooy, 2003). However, the key challenge that faced the author in searching for Information and Communications Technology (ICT) applications in the Arab education sector was the scarcity of reliable and accurate information, from simple case studies to investigations pertinent to the effectiveness of ICT application in education in the Arab world. Therefore, the literature review part focused on locating information that can help in drawing a realistic picture of the current status of technology adoption in the education sector in the region as well as exploring evidence of any positive or

negative cultural impact on the successful utilization of such technology applications, taking into consideration the interest in educators' role, the required techniques, and special teaching skills that are needed for multicultural teachers in the Arabic schools.

The chapter begins with a presentation of some excerpts and insights from the existing literature on ICT application in the Arabic schools from both cultural and globalization perspectives, highlighting and critically analyzing some concurrent teaching and learning problems that might occur in a multicultural environment. A special emphasis in this area will be given to the problem of inequalities with suggestions for some strategies for further inclusion of marginalized groups. Towards the end of the chapter, the main findings and observations will be presented and discussed with reference to possible teaching and organizational implications and will be concluded with recommendations for future improvement.

The investigation is expected to be of value to Arab education leaders with vision and interest in reforming their educational institutions through technology adoption. It can also help information systems developers to have a better insight to the specific needs of the Arab education sector, including new ICT educational applications and software tools.

LITERATURE REVIEW

Shana (2009) investigated rationalizing learning with technology by using the discussion forums in the classrooms to increase and develop the traditional teaching style. Using this technology is not new or recent in the highly developed and technically sophisticated countries. However, the use of such technologies as tools for instruction in education in many developing countries is relatively new and not yet well spread in all the schools. In a teacher-centered, traditional behaviorist stimulus response learning model adopted in these countries, both the school education and the students preparation to enter universities was heavily based on rote learning and memorization-based assessment methods which lead to less creativity, less individuality and narrow mindedness among students The main problem with such traditional models is that they present the students of the current generation with a very small fraction of quality education which they could achieve in the informational age. Therefore, the onus is on the higher educational institutions not only to select and utilize suitable and effective information but also to take up the challenge of preparing students to benefit from such information and communication technology applications.

Commenting on the initiative by Ajman University of Science and Technology (AUST) to adopt such new technologies and to educate students to meet the requirements of the telecommunications information technology revolution age, Shana (2009) reports that an electronic, ready-made Learning management systems was in a trial period and on the university's Local Area Network (intranet) rather than the internet. (P1). It is necessary then to believe that today, students have to develop their skills and competencies if they need to live, learn and work successfully in a rapidly changing society. Therefore, this requires a huge shift to the constructivist information processing model as a replacement or as a support to the previous old traditional learning teaching style and model.

In addition, Martin (2003) guarantees that "as theories of learning have developed, so has the model of the learner, from a model of an empty pot to be filled with knowledge through a behaviorist one of the learner as enthusiastic rat to be rewarded for displaying remembered behavior or knowledge, to a constructivist model of an individual creating and re-creating his/her map of existence and planning/re-planning the way through it." (p. 5)

Changes on how the student's role is perceived have deeply influenced that of teachers'.

Research findings showed that the teacher's main role is to create the best learning environment for the students in the classroom to ensure good students' performance and learning outcomes in the constructivist learning. According to Dewald (2003), "…the teacher, as a facilitator, is responsible for process design, creating the climate for learning and making resources available" (p.48). Alternatively, in the traditional approach and the old teaching model, the roles of an authoritarian teacher and passive learners still persist. This model maintains the teacher's authority and influence on the students and emphasizes that it is the teachers' responsibility to do all the work and prepare for the class activities and analyze and explain the lesson tasks through a well planned and structured sequenced lesson plan as the leading vehicle for learning (Tam, 2000).

Keivani, Parsa, and Younis (2003) stated that "Urban competitiveness is at the same time directly related to the effectiveness and efficiency of its urban governance structure in providing a supportive business environment both in terms of strategic policy development and service delivery. Here again, Information and Communication Technologies (ICTs) can play a significant role in enhancing local government capabilities through the e-government concept." (p.20). At the same time, the society vision usually changes and improve as an effect of the ICT application, as evident in the case of Dubai which is described to be "promoting a vision of the networked knowledge society through public awareness programs and practical measures for engaging ordinary citizens, including e-government initiatives and innovative –based interaction programs encompassing public, community, and private spheres." (Keivani et al, 2003, p 22)

Dubai is one of seven emirates of the United Arab Emirates (UAE). The country had an estimated population of 3.5 million in 2001 with a considerable and obvious autonomy in its economic growth and objectives development. Accordingly, they have considered some functions, like telecommunications, to be primarily a federal responsibility. Similar to the majority of governments in the Arabian Gulf region in achieving its vision and objectives of moving to a society of knowledge, with the help of ICT, the UAE has overcome its shortage of local human resources by attracting ICT skilled resources and other key knowledge-based sectors of the country economy from all over the world, Over a decade it is estimated that the contribution of foreign workers in the economy of Dubai amounts to around 36.9 percent of the GDP, reflecting on their strong and important role in the country economy during that period. This major gain can be attributed among other things to the free open environment that benefited from globalization to in favor of economy and prosperity (Keivani et al, 2003).

The impact of the globalization on education sectors, which is the most recent factor on societies reforming, is emphasized further in multicultural environments. Considering that 'globalization' is a process that has widely influenced the whole world, and the fact that there are nationals and expatriates from multiple cultures and different languages, norms and values live side by side in the UAE, represents a major challenge for the government and people alike to capitalize on the positive aspects of diversity and to cope with the social and educational challenges of multiculturalism in society. According to Paul Gorski (2000), "It is equally critical that the children recognize and appreciate their own ethnicity and learn to appreciate those of the other children in the class." As globalization challenges, it also offers powerful opportunities for the higher education community to play a key role in shaping the future (McBurnie, 2001).

Globalization refers to the formation of the world systems and its internationalization, including finance, trade, linguistic, cultural communications and information technologies, migration and tourism, global societies. World-widely, the government structure forms and the education system continue to be widely national, while the issues of identity and differences have become more important in the politics of education (Currie, & Vidovich, 1998; Edelson, 2003; Marginson, 1999; and Cornwell, 2001). At the same time, globalization in this term is viewed as a system and a network for the exchange of power, which encourages the public to form a developmental model that is comprised of shared common habits, forms or photos of production, life styles, social organization and success criteria. It consists of ideologies, cultural references and even forms of political organization. (Komilian, 1997)

This perception indicates that the learning and teaching processes which are carried out in the classrooms are becoming more complicated and more difficult than anywhere else in the world, due to the diversified backgrounds of students in the same classroom. Nonetheless, the educational markets which have become more and more internationalized have evident impacts on the national education within countries and are viewed as strong competitions. Nowadays, the UAE institutions of education compete intensively trying to attract young people from the whole UAE areas and also from more distinct regions. Held et al. (2003) argues that globalization is a historically rooted phenomenon and that the early phase between 1859 and 1945 was characterized by the expansion of economic relationships, through trade colloquially known as the colonial period. Unlike most of the other educational systems around the world, the UAE education system is distinctive in nature by establishing equity in the society through the universal education for all. The UAE school system is implementing the equal educational access and opportunities for all citizens because they understand those feelings about people of different races and ethnicities and how it will affect the classroom teaching and learning process.

Globalization has a homogeneous effect on the people moderation and the possibility to change the structure of the countries around the world. So, the demand on changing the nation building and its democratization will affect the educational system. One of the greatest challenges currently facing the new educational organizations is the educational reform, is expected to be much more responsive to consumer demands and looking for further individual talent (Janmaat 2008).

Murphy (2006) said that "The past 20 years have witnessed a revolution in technology which is transforming the global economy, and the place of national economies within it. National development strategies around the world increasingly assume Information and Communication Technologies to be the new engine of growth. The Gulf Arab states have not been immune from this trend; indeed their national development strategies are increasingly predicated upon integration of ICTs." (1060).

Accordingly, the multicultural education has become a major challenge for the UAE schools as an educational alternative which aimed to critically analyze inequalities within the UAE school systems. It has also suggested new strategies for further inclusion of marginalized groups in the society. The majority of the UAE schools followed international schools models in implementing some ICT tools to facilitate their education system, allowing them to enter the real multicultural environment which may be treated as a source of both opportunities and threats. New multicultural curriculum is being introduced into classrooms all the time but there is some arguments like that it "does not successfully address racism and ethnocentrism," (Pedelty, 2001, p1).

UAE POPULATION DIVERSITY

The demography of the UAE has changed dramatically since the independence, with an obvious rapid transformation from a traditional old culture to a modern developed country. It has offered world class infrastructure and attractions, and has made dramatic developments in education, healthcare and the institutions of government and justice.

Therefore, it has become one of the most diverse countries in the world population: 4,798,491 (CIA World Factbook, 2009), most of whom are non nationals from many different countries.

The global rapid emergence and wide spread acceptance of information and communication technologies over the past two decades was positively received by the UAE authoritarians who linked it to the development revolution in the country. Thus, a lot of investments in ICT infrastructure and applications have been carried out, and residents have been provided with uncomplicated accessibility to the Internet, encouraging government and non-government organizations to benefit from all aspects of ICT to serve the economy and the quality of life for all communities.

A global information system supports the operations and decision making of an enterprise's multi country strategy. Contrary to what many believe, the global integration of ICT networks has not emerged all of a sudden; rather it was supported through the institutional and ideological work of governments, industry associations, and professional organizations. On the other hand, the development of the Internet and its diffusion with a high spread and the affordable prices of the personal computer have all increased the access and the use of a lot of information, giving increase to visions of the democratization of knowledge, education, and economic opportunity for everybody. The realization of such a vision is conditional to the availability of high quality equipment, high speed net work connections, and good follow up and maintenance services. (Reinout Kuiper, Nijmegen, 2005).

Almekhlafi and Almeqdadi (2010) studied the teachers' perceptions of technology integration in the United Arab Emirates school classrooms. The study participants were made of 100 grades 6-9 male and female teachers from two model schools in Al-Ain educational zone, in the emirate of Abu Dhabi.

Each of the participating teachers had (5-15) years teaching experience with a good experience of using technology in their classrooms. All schools had good technology infrastructure available and accessible by teachers at any time. Generally, teachers were encouraged to use and utilize such technologies in the classroom as they were perceived as vehicles for the delivery of successful teaching, allowing students to learn more with minimal time, and at the same time allowing schools to focus on global learning environments with ready access to a large amount of information.

A positive impact on the outcomes of the teaching and learning has been reported by the teachers who used aspects of the technology such as computers and the Internet to support conventional classes, to create instructional material and to achieve teaching objectives. The results of the study indicated that 34% of technology was used for administrative record keeping and less than 10% reported to access model lesson plans or to access research. The teachers' high perception recorded was due to the fact that technology integration, capability to use hardware and software, using technology to locate, evaluate, and collect information from a variety of resources constitute one main part of the teacher's annual evaluation at model schools. Most of the teachers were willing to use technology and showed a positive attitude towards technology integration training, and creative technology use in the classrooms.

Interestingly, Gulbahar's, (2007) findings in this regard showed that although the teachers and administrative staff were more competent in using ICT available at their school, and believed that technologies are essential for the process of education, they lacked guidelines, time, support, resources, and training that would lead them to more successful integration. Alternatively, he found that the students reported that ICT is not utilized sufficiently in their classes.

BACKGROUND

Culture

Culture consists of the totality of socially transmitted knowledge of values, beliefs, norms, and life ways of a particular group that guides their thoughts and behaviors. (Griswold, 2008) Culture evolves as a way of life by a group of people who deal with similar issues of survival over a period of time in their environment. Any Culture has both visible and invisible components. It would be easy to identify a culture bound Arab from his traditional costume (visible), but it is hard to tell to what extent this Arab is holding tight to the culture. Accordingly, in any society there is a dominant culture that exists along with other variant cultural patterns. These variant patterns may be referred to as diverse cultures, subcultures, or minority cultures. For example, In the UAE, the dominant culture has its origins from Islamic beliefs. Being a country of diverse nationalities, subcultures exist on a large scale. (Purnell and Paulanka, 1998; Leininger, 2002a).

Arabic Culture

Murphy (2006), during examining how the range of agents of ICT production and diffusion in the region have changed the actual impact upon political space, said that " recent political reforms in the Gulf Arab countries have been variously understood as regime survival strategies, correlates of economic globalization, and even the end result of US pressure to democratize states.. To the surprise of many, the past few years have witnessed significant political reforms in the Arabian Peninsula. The regimes of Qatar, Bahrain, Kuwait, Oman and even Saudi Arabia have been introducing constitutional reforms and new electoral practices which appear to have substantively altered the dynamics of political space in countries previously thought to be perhaps uniquely impervious to pressures for democratic change." p (1059).

Moreover, Nagel and Staeheli (2010) stated that "We use the example of al-Awda and the complexities surrounding it as an entry point to our analysis of the spatiality of immigrant activism and the use of information and communication technology (ICT) in it. Scholars in recent years have paid increasing attention to migrants' use of ICT to sustain transnational ties and to create diasporic communities."(p 2). This study was about ICT and geographies of British Arab and Arab American activism. Al-Awda is an organization devoted to securing the right of Palestinians to return to land and homes lost during the establishment of the Israeli state. It organizes demonstrations and other online and offline activities in European and North American cities that allow thousands of people to show their support for Palestine. Murphy, (2006), on the other hand, used Egypt as an example for services such as the main program and voice of the Arabs which targeted specific audiences and joined it with other programming designed to prop up the nationalist feelings and to secure and keep on the full support for the ongoing contend and compete with Israel.

Three years later, Murphy, (2009) discussed the ICT at the Arab region from a historical perspective and found that the Arab countries did not follow a comparable capitalist developmental route like the Europeans democracy with no clear equal experience which can be considered as a public sphere. While a new research on the Arab world suggested a starting point for examining the impact of modern information and communications technologies (ICTs) on the politics of the region especially the media following the critical theory, and sociological theory to explain and evaluate the emergence of a contemporary, ICT-based public sphere, critical rational values, truth value regardless of the status of the speaker, and financial disinterest in engagement.

Today, the public sphere has played a critical role in establishing the role of public opinion in holding the government accountability and the complexities of civil status, society relations, politics and culture, and the role of modern communications media, the social construction of identities and norms, and carrying out of international relations (Murphy, 2009).

Furthermore, Murphy, (2009) found that after World War One (WWI), Arab audiences were affected by newsprint, radios, and cinema, and interpreted at the local level the mediation of local intellectuals and professional classes. At the same time, Arabs were influenced by the mosque, the party, the trade union, and the military structures, to have a clear progress in media freedom which was manifested by the Islamic roles formally and informally.

Murphy,(2009) said "When contemporary ICTs began to make their mark, however, a new body of research on the Arab countries began to suggest that the society was now able to evade the censorial controls of the state and could begin to engage in reasoned, oppositional, and critical debates via the Internet, mobile telephone technologies, and satellite television. Early indicators of this possibility might perhaps be considered to have been the use in the 1980s and 1990s of visual and audio tape recordings and fax machines to spread Islamist critiques of authoritarian government following the trend set by Ayatollah Khomeini and his adherents in the 1970s."(p1134).

However, with the new technologies like satellite television and the Internet, a much broader range of voices could be heard and allowed Arabs to talk and show their identity to the whole world., that was fostered by state policy in the post colonial era through the lively comitial debates and "Arabized" news coverage of satellite television channels like AlJazeera. (Al- Jazeera, 2007)

Elnaggar. (2008). Presented the sensitive current situation of the ICT sector in Oman with a focus on the gender dimension and he found that, women in the Arab Gulf region, in general, and in Oman, in particular, are at a higher risk of being marginalized from today's knowledge based economy, due to a traditionally male dominated ICT sector, unequal access to training, the lack of Arabized Internet content and training, and the lack of awareness and policy advocacy.

The results of the survey conducted by Elnaggar (2008) showed that socio-cultural norms, the innate character issues of Omani females, access and training, and career counseling are mostly the factors that inhibit or stop them from entering and adopting a career in ICT. This research explained that with exception of Gulf Cooperation Council (GCC) States; Kuwait, Saudi Arabia, Qatar, Bahrain, UAE, & Oman, most of the Arab countries suffer from a very low Internet population (Elnaggar, 2008). The findings of the previous survey also revealed that internet access is particularly difficult for women in poorer and less urbanized areas where telecommunications infrastructure is poor, and that was not due to the lack of reachable computers, telephones, and other resources, but also a severe absence of training and application opportunities for women and girls. The socio-cultural norms in the GCC, for instance, are limiting the women's thinking ability and mobility whether they are living in urban center or at remote rural village. Most of the social and cultural values are based on high segregation between genders, and they don't allow the free mixing and interaction of members from both genders at work, education, and transportation. For example, cultural norms discourage interaction between women and men outside the family, and women, might feel agitated in situations where men are present either as trainers or as peers (Elnaggar, 2008).

The Purpose of ICT in Education

In general, the implementation of ICT applications in education is about teachers using and utilizing different technology hardware and software to aid the teaching and learning processes. For instance,

teachers would use technology as part of education methodology and as a creative media, to train the students on how to use, and deal with the computers and their social and ethical issues (Watson, 2005). Active learning in the modern teaching done through all senses conveniently uses one of the most popular ICT applications (Computer games) for teaching and learning purposes.

Some suggest that it all started back in 1998 when technology was to be used in the classroom on the teacher's desk and not in a separate lab. The challenge and the difficulty were not about improving the handling technology in schools, but rather related to coping with the changes in the teaching methodology to a non-conventional approach and also by training and preparing teachers with the skills needed to use such technologies in class activities. Therefore, training courses were offered for users to improve their capabilities, skills, technology, knowledge and experiences with good understanding of all stakeholders, communities and partners that can be involved in the project to promote the community by taking their agreement and acceptance.

Educational history teaches us to learn from others' mistakes. Understanding what is still happening today, as a result of that history, it is important for our school leaders to create our autonomy and social justice. (Watson, 2005)

There is no doubt that new inventions and new technologies have always had their impact on people and their living patterns. At the beginning, new technologies kept people at home for long time to listen to radio or watch television. With the advent of technology and the ability to access television through the Internet from anywhere, and at any time, information technology today has a huge cultural impact and presents great influence on the way people live and how they entertain themselves.

In the 20th century, inexpensive personal computers diffusion, with the beginning of data exchange protocols, the users around the world had a direct access to an increasing mass of data, texts, and multimedia documents with the power to create and spread their own documents. This massive cultural exchange influenced and supported the transnational investment, production, and trade in both goods and services. New markets opened and that improved the countries' economic status and the people's productivity and efficiency. (Watson, 2005).

According to the National Association for Multicultural Education (2003), multicultural education "prepares all students to work actively toward structural equality in organizations and institutions by providing the knowledge, dispositions, and skills for the redistribution of power and income among diverse groups." The main important goal of multicultural education is making the education more equitable for minority multicultural student groups by working towards filling the educational gap between them and promoting social justice. Araujo and Strasser (2003) reflected on this notion by notifying that, "Education in a democratic society should help students acquire the knowledge, attitudes, and skills they will need to participate in civic actions to make society more equitable and just." All the students need to be taught that they have to be proud of their cultural beliefs, and that they can stand up for what they believe in and make positive changes in the world. They need to realize that no one race, ethnicity, or culture is better than any other. Everyone should respect and validate all people no matter how much they differ from what society says is normal.

Using pictures is another good way to teach children about the experiences of other people. Araujo and Strasser (2003) said that "the use of picture books, with discussions and related activities, can be a first step in creating within the early childhood classroom as anti-bias environment." Role-playing is an additional effective method to teach children what life is like for minority people and what it feels like to be discriminated against based on their outer appearance. However, No matter what resources teachers use to teach multicultural education, it is important to remember

that teaching respect of other races, ethnicities, and cultures is not enough. We must also teach children that racism, ethnocentrism, and privilege still exist in our society. It is important to teach them that they can do something to fight to change and make it better as they are the coming future leaders.

Moreover, Duren (2000) remarks that, "books, as written narratives, provide a way for us to conceptualize the word and locate ourselves in context of the experience of others." She goes on to say that, "reading aloud to students introduces them to books that they might read on their own and allows them to use their imaginations" (p 2). By that, it will enhance the students' critical thinking skills which are, e maintaining doubt and suspending judgment, being aware of different perspectives, testing alternatives and letting experience guide, and being aware of organizational and personal limitations. From here the ICT becomes an additional tool to improve the teaching and learning process. Brunello (2010) highlighted that the natural perception prefers things over processes. Things like computer can be pictured and shown and these could hardly be questioned. However, in processes such as learning, it might take longer time because they are inherently harder to capture and therefore much more questionable. Thus, there is a great effect of the inherently and the natural insight of people that would make r preferences like using computers not on the top of their priorities which will lead the learning process to take longer time if the person is not interested.

Physical technological infrastructure has bias over the educational use. It is due to the nature of cooperation and development project management practices, as the whole system revolves around quantitative controls and standards. In his approach, Brunello (2010) suggests three important side-effects. the first is that it negatively affects the project management commitment for the best use of technology in everyday teaching practices that second is that it, enhances the use of simplistic objective indicators (i.e. ratio computer to pupils, number of hours the school's computer room is open); that last is that, it treats technology use as a subject in itself, rather than as a teaching and learning aid to serve other disciplines.

To find out what is going on in the Arab countries, as part of the developing countries, Brunello (2010) asked about the number of teachers who use the computer labs to creatively enhance the teaching of their specific subject. He also discussed that the industrialism burden technologically intensive projects are still developing, and invested Avgerou's quotation of, it is mainly "rooted on the assumption that Information Systems innovation in developing countries is mainly concerned with catching up with the technologically advanced rich economies through transferring their technologies and emulating their institutions" (Avgerou, 2008, p. 135).

On the other hand, Brunello argued that, this top-down approach is embedded in the industrial revolution, which leads to the whole project management cycle. To apply this in education, this dominant model proposes and imposes a mechanistic idea of education and learning that leads to limit teachers' and students' creativity in order to have a unified set of minimal skills as an output (Robinson, 2009a, 2009b).

Shana. (2009) in his study on the effects of using discussion forums on the achievement of students stressed on the fact that, if used effectively and widely provided, utilizing technologies in the teaching process and resource facilitation will promote lifelong learning, and support learner centered approaches. The information system improves the quality, simplifies the product, and the production process benchmarking, uses customer demand to improve products and services, reduces the cycle time, improves design quality and precision, improves production precision and tightens production tolerances. Information systems tie together disparate units so they act as a whole, enhancing core competencies.

SOLUTIONS AND RECOMMENDATIONS

Educators may include ICT in education within the curriculum in all Arab schools because they understand that the nation notion of mass communication is used to improve and foster individualized moderation, and teach students that all cultures are related and respectful. Still, it seems that not enough teaching is provided to students on what life in the society is like for students who come from those diverse cultures. Then, educational team members need to consider the role of students' culture, values, believes, and practices. After that, they need to implement the culturally competent care, which is the ability of the practitioner to bridge cultural gaps in caring, work with cultural differences, and enable the students and families to achieve meaningful and supportive caring. Culturally Competent Care requires specific knowledge, skills, and attitudes in the delivery of culturally congruent care. Such competency should be evident at the practitioner, organizational, and societal levels. (Germov, 2009)

For instance, Chanlin and colleagues. (2006) supported the idea of teachers' perceptions about using technology in order to find out which factors influence their use of technology in the teaching and learning process. The researchers tackled two major issues. The first focused on how the teachers are using technology in creative teaching, and the second is identifying the factors that would affect using technology in teaching.

Chanlin and colleagues, (2006) classified the factors into four categories: environmental, personal, social and curricular issues. Other barriers were found after deep studying to the focus group interviews one of which was that male teachers lack training on how to integrate the technology effectively and instead they depend on their own professional development and training. Teachers in general expressed their desire to be involved in decisions related to their needs in order to be able to utilize technology techniques and strategies effectively in their classrooms.

Another barrier was the negative attitudes of both parents and teachers toward the importance and benefits of using technology in the educational process.. Yet, female teachers felt that a large number of students, technical problems, and expensive tools are the common problems that might negatively influence the effectiveness of technology employment.

In consolidation to what has previously mentioned, Brunello (2010) clarified that "Teachers who "dare" to use technology in class tend to be very afraid of the slightest technological breakdown, as not only can it easily compromise a whole lecture, but more importantly, it exposes them to the risk of feeling incompetent while facing their pupils, thus inhibiting further attempts to use the computer room in the future" (p. 237).

In a study conducted by Zamani, Reza, Isfahani & Shahbaz, (2010), on the use of computers in Iranian educational system h,, they found that the amount of ICT utilization in educational field and communicative fields were not at competent level and the obtained averages were far from the assumptive average of 3. In addition, the least use of computers was for communication purposes (Zamani, Reza, Isfahani & Shahbaz, 2010).In interviews done, teachers stressed the importance of the professional training sessions to promote students' learning. The training programs should be related to the educational and teaching curriculum. Furthermore, sufficient technological and administrative support for teachers should be provided (Zamani, Reza, Isfahani & Shahbaz, 2010).

It is also vital to mention that the United Nations has developed its successful Millennium Goals based on minimizing the inequalities of access to ICTs resources and they established a UN (ICT) agency in 2006 to foster stakeholder participation and management to create a Global e-policy Resource Network. (Murphy, 2006) The United Nations Development Program (UNDP)

has classified five developmental areas for (ICTD) interventions, funded by a dedicated ICTD Trust Fund to support its projects in the developing countries. The aim of such projects is to promote access to ICTs in the needed countries projects and to maximize the economical developmental benifits and minimize the political developmental impact. Additionally, it would provide new opportunities of information exchange to empower individuals to share knowledge with their partners everywhere else in the world and not to isolate them away from others. (Murphy, 2006)

Such programs would assist teachers, policymakers and stakeholders who are committed to reorient ICT policy to take into account the needs to empower everybody in the society in the Arabic educational sector, and develop a model of gender sensitive indicators that may be adopted by the government and policy makers to evaluate the gender stigmatism by other countries, and more important, to establish better ICT policies, programs, and project and promote gender equity to ICT.

CONCLUSION

One of the greatest challenges currently facing the Arabic educational system in specific and the world in general is the educational system reform. Tikly (2001) suggests that there is a strong and a close relationship between any education system and the people who are educated through it, and the education leaders and teachers who organize and lead the global education domain. That means that the learning and teaching process which is carried out in the classrooms is becoming more complicated and more difficult than before, but also the educational market, which has become more and more international base, has been affected in the Arab countries as well.

ICTs freedom, equal opportunity and easy access for women and men in any society, are important steps towards bridging and filling the gaps in the gender digital equity and opportunity especially at the decision making level. However, being aware of the socio cultural and institutional barriers is essential if decision makers are to shape remedial programs, prepare working environments, and design facilities that encourage women's participation. Accordingly, women's empowerment with equitable access to IT and autonomy to receive and produce information relevant to men's and women's needs and concerns are major points of an information society for all.

REFERENCES

Al-Jazeera. (2007). *Al-Jazeera TV Viewer Demographic*. Retrieved November 27, 2007, from http://www.allied-media.com/aljazeera/JAZdemog.html

Brunello, P. (2010). ICT for education projects: a look from behind the scenes. *Information Technology for Development, 16*(3), 232–239. doi:10.1080/02681102.2010.497275

Central Intelligence Agency. (2010). *CIA- The world factbook*. Retrieved September 12, 2011, from https://www.cia.gov/library/publications

Dewald, N. H. (2003). Pedagogy and andragogy. In Dupuis, A. E. (Ed.), *Developing web-based instruction: Planning, designing, managing, and evaluating results* (pp. 47–68). London, UK: Facet.

Elnaggar, A. (2008). Towards gender equal access to ICT. *Information Technology for Development, 14*(4), 280–293. doi:10.1002/itdj.20100

Germov, J. (2009). *Second opinion: An introduction to health sociology* (4th ed.). Oxford, UK: Oxford University Press.

Griswold, W. (2008). *Cultures and societies in a changing world* (3rd ed.). California: Pine Forge Press.

Hanna, B. E., & de Nooy, J. (2003). A funny thing happened on the way to the forum: Electronic discussion and foreign language learning. *Language Learning & Technology, 7*(1), 71–85. Retrieved September 15, 2010

Held, D., McGrew, A., Goldblatt, D., & Perraton, J. (1999). *Global transformations*. Stanford, CA: Stanford University Press.

Janmaat, J. G. (2008). Nation building, democratization and globalization as competing priorities in Ukraine's education system. *Nationalities Papers, 36*(1), 1–23. doi:10.1080/00905990701848317

Keivani, R., Parsa, A., & Younis, B. (2003). Development of the ICT sector and urban competitiveness: The case of Dubai. *Journal of Urban Technology, 10*(2), 19–46. doi:10.1080/1063073032000139688

Komilian, K. (1997). The challenges of globalization. *Journal of Futures Markets, 1*.

Kuiper, R. (2005). *ICT and culture*. Retrieved from http://www.cs.ru.nl/mtl/scripties/ 2005/ReinoutKuiperScriptie.pdf

Martin, A. (2003). Towards e-literacy. In Martin, A., & Rader, H. (Eds.), *Information and IT literacy: Enabling learning in the 21st century* (pp. 3–23). London, UK: Facet.

Murphy, E. (2006). Agency and space: the political impact of information technologies in the Gulf Arab states. *Third World Quarterly, 27*(6), 1059–1083. doi:10.1080/01436590600850376

Murphy, E. (2009). Theorizing ICTs in the Arab World: Informational capitalism and the public sphere. *International Studies Quarterly, 53*(4), 1131–1153. doi: 10. 1111/ j.1468-2478.2009.00571.x

Nagel, C., & Staeheli, L. (2010). ICT and geographies of British Arab and Arab American activism. *Global Networks, 10*(2), 262–281. doi:10.1111/j.1471-0374.2010.00285.x

Purnell, L. D., & Paulanka, B. J. (2005). *Guide to culturally competent health care*. Philadelphia, PA: F.A. Davis.

Shana, Z. (2009). Learning with technology: Using discussion forums to augment a traditional-style class. *Journal of Educational Technology & Society, 12*(3), 214–228. Retrieved from http://www.ifets.info/journals/12_3/19.pdf

Ssenyonga, A. B. (2007). Americanization or globalization. *Global Envision.* Retrieved from, http://www.globalenvision.org/library/33/1273/

Tam, M. (2000). Constructivism, instructional design, and technology: Implications for transforming distance learning. *Journal of Educational Technology & Society, 3*(2), 50–60. Retrieved from http://www.ifets.info/journals/3_2/tam.html

Tikly, L. (2001). Globalisation and education in the postcolonial world: Towards a conceptual framework. *Comparative Education, 37*(2), 151–171. doi:10.1080/03050060124481

Zamani, B. E., Reza, A., Isfahani, N., & Shahbaz, S. (2010). Isfahan high schools teachers' utilization of ICT. *British Journal of Educational Technology, 41*(5), 92–95. doi:10.1111/j.1467-8535.2009.01000.x

ADDITIONAL READING

Abbit, J. T., & Klett, M. D. (2007). Identifying influences on attitudes and self –efficacy beliefs towards technology integration among pre-service educators. *Electronic Journal for the Integration of Technology in Education, 6,* 28–42.

Abu Dhabi University. (2006). *Professional development policy and procedures.* Abu Dhabi, UAE: ADU.

Abu Dhabi University. (2006). *Faculty promotion in rank - Policy and procedures.* Abu Dhabi, UAE: ADU.

Almekhlafi, A. G. (2006a). The effect of computer assisted language learning (CALL) on United Arab Emirates English as a foreign language (EFL) school students achievement and attitude. *Journal of Interactive Learning Research, 17*(2), 121–142.

Almekhlafi, A. G. (2006b). Effectiveness of interactive multimedia environment on language acquisition skills of 6th grade students in the United Arab Emirates. *International Journal of Instructional Media, 33*(4), 427, 241.

Anderson, S., & Maninger, R. (2007). Preservice teachers' abilities, beliefs, and intentions regarding technology integration. *Journal of Educational Computing Research, 37*(2), 151–172. doi:10.2190/H1M8-562W-18J1-634P

Anon. (19 November 2005). Problems face education: Unsuitability of curricula, collapsing school buildings, and low salaries. *Al Ittihad,* (translated from Arabic), pp. 8-9.

Anon. (20 November 2005). 46 billion dirhams will be spent developing the education system in the next ten years. *Al Ittihad,* (translated from Arabic), p. 8.

Anon. (21 November 2005) Spending on education is 60% less than international standards. *Al Ittihad,* (translated from Arabic), p. 9.

Bottery, M. (2006). Educational leaders in a globalising world: A new set of priorities? *School Leadership & Management, 26*(1), 5–22. doi:10.1080/13634230500492822

Godwin, S. M. (2006). Globalizaton, education and emiratization: A study of the United Arab Emirates. *Electronic Journal on Information Systems in Developing Countries, 27*(1), 1–14.

Murphy, J. (2005). Unpacking the foundations of the ISLLC standards and addressing concerns in the academic community. *Educational Administration Quarterly, 41*(10), 154–191. doi:10.1177/0013161X04269580

KEY TERMS AND DEFINITIONS

Culture: The totality of socially transmitted knowledge of values, beliefs, norms, and life ways of a particular group that guides their thoughts and behaviors. (Griswold, 2008). Culture evolves as way of life by a group of people who deal with similar issues of survival over a period of time in their environment.(Purnell and Paulanka, 1998; Leininger, 2002a).

Dominant Culture: A culture that exists along with other variant cultural patterns. These variant patterns may be referred to as diverse cultures, subcultures, or minority cultures.

Educational Inequality: The lack of equal opportunities that people have the result of disparities in quality education and factors.

Ethnicity: Refers to a shared identity related to social and cultural heritage such as values, language, geographical space, and racial characteristics (Turkish, Irish…).

Globalization: A system and network for the exchange of power, which encourages the public to form the developmental model of shared common habits, forms or photos of production, life styles, social organizations and success criteria. It also consists of ideologies, cultural references and even forms of political organization. (Komilian (1997).

Information and Communication Technology (ICT): Technologies that can be used to store, retrieve, manipulate, transmit or receive information electronically in a digital form. The term ICT is used interchangeably with information technology (IT). The expression was first used in 1997 in a report by Dennis Stevenson to the UK government and promoted by the new National Curriculum documents for the UK in 2000. (Wikipedia, 2005).

Multicultural Education: Multicultural education is a philosophical concept built on the ideals of freedom, justice, equality, equity, and human dignity as acknowledged in various documents. Multicultural education is a process that permeates all aspects of school practices, policies and organization as a means to ensure the highest levels of academic achievement for all students.

Multiculturalism: An ideology that promotes the institutionalization of communities containing multiple cultures. It is generally applied to the demographic make-up of a specific place, usually at the organizational level, e.g. schools, businesses, neighborhoods, cities, or nations.

Chapter 9
ICT for Educational Excellence in Jordan:
An Elusive Objective

Atef Abuhmaid
Middle East University, Jordan

ABSTRACT

This chapter discusses the Jordanian Ministry of Education's reliance on both the local private sector (public-private partnership) and foreign aids in order to accelerate its integration of ICT to meet the needs and demands of the knowledge-based economy. The discussion sheds light on strings attached to the role played by the Ministry of Education, as the central educational authority, in the diffusion of ICT across the education system. Understandably, in the Jordanian context, likewise other countries in the Middle East and North Africa region, the education system has to deal with a great deal of complexities in which, internal and external issues can impede reform efforts. Partnership with local and international partners might be needed in the Jordanian context in order to initiate reform especially the large-scale and costly ones. ICT-related reform initiatives are expensive and require expertise in various areas which might justify seeking external assistance by the educational system. However, external involvement can impact the integrity of the educational reform when it is left with inadequate coordination and efforts in order to keep them in line with national interests and agendas. Furthermore, the impact of these issues can be severer when they are not taken into account during the planning stage of the reform. Thus, this chapter discusses major issues arose when international partners and the local private sector were involved in ICT-based education initiatives in Jordan.

COMPLEXITY: EDUCATION REFORM

In development, education can be viewed in two perspectives: education as a main standard for development on one hand, and as leverage for prosperity and development in society at large on the other. The former can be linked to the definition of economic development which is, according to Devlin (2010), the sustainable increase in living standards including education, health, environmental protection, and material consumption. Therefore, although the relationship between

DOI: 10.4018/978-1-4666-1984-5.ch009

education and prosperity is not necessarily a cause-and-effect; there are indications that the 77 Million children who do not have education are poor (Devlin, 2010). Regarding the latter, education as leverage for prosperity, investing in education is often perceived as investment in the future with countries having large proportions of their citizens as students at some stage or another. Fullan (2005) argued that a strong public school system is the key to social, political and economic renewal in society making education, according to Leithwood et al., (2002), a key for large social and economic transformations. Thus, Fullan (1993) stressed that among all other societal organizations, education is the only "one that *potentially* has the promise of fundamentally contributing to this goal [large social and economic transformations]" (p.4, italic in source). In addition, societies rely extensively on education to maintain its values and to prepare its citizens to be part of flexible, dynamic, and skilled workforce.

Governments and education authorities as well as the public are concerned with effective education reforms that hold the promise of improving education outcomes in order to meet the demands and expectations of the 21st century for which there is no more promising initiative to improve education than information and communication technology initiatives.

ICT IN EDUCATION

There is a strong consensus around the central role of information and communication technology (ICT) in education. Previous studies have identified several rationales for integrating ICT into education including social, vocational, and pedagogical (Castells, 1999a; Hawkridge, 1989; Logan, 1995; MacDonald, 2008; Maddux et al., 2001; Means, 1994; Reeves, 1998; Subhi, 1999). Fullan (1993) also asserted the "moral purpose" of education as its potential for making a difference in the lives of students and for helping to produce citizens who can "live and work productively in increasingly dynamically complex societies" (Fullan, 1993, p.4). The pervasive role of ICT in all aspects of life makes students' ICT proficiency a necessity for them to compete in increasingly competitive era. Thus, in order to prepare students for the future education systems have little choice but to adopt ICT (Abuhmaid, 2010).

The pedagogical rationale is a key driver for the education systems to adopt ICT, as it emphasizes the ICT role in enhancing the contemporary students' learning and skills they will be developed during their schooling (Hawkridge, 1989; Subhi, 1999). This stems from the work of scholars such as Vygotsky and Dewey, whose works have motivated a range of educational theorists who wish to make the education environment more effective, and change schooling from a place where 'knowledge' is 'transmitted' to a place where students become active and dynamic participants in learning (Cuban, 1993). Certainly, ICT, with the more sophisticated visual and processing power of today's personal computers, has the power to do just that. Moreover, it is widely believed that ICT can scaffold learning and teaching in addition to providing interactivity for teachers and students (Kozma, 2003).

However, despite the growing recognition of the key role of ICT in improving the quality of education, its integration within the educational sector is still shadowy in developing countries. Fullan (1993) also warned that rationales for ICT integration into education have become clichés used by policy-makers, which might explain why ICT plans in developing countries are generally detached from national educational strategies (Kozma & Wagner, 2006). Additionally, education is increasingly more attractive to the private sector as countries worldwide are becoming more willing to invest in e-learning, hardware, software, networks and training. Thus, education itself has become part of a huge global market with increasing competitiveness between international businesses (Hawkridge, 1989).

DEVELOPMENT FOR THE KNOWLEDGE-BASED ECONOMY

Overall, education reform falls under the notion of "development". ICT adoption by education systems is perceived as a key path to improving educational processes and outcomes and eventually economic, social and standards of living for citizens. The discourse regarding the ways in which nations are classified may represent a notion of 'underdevelopment' in a way that suggests deficiency in particular contexts requiring remedy. Usually, the remedy for developing and poor countries is prescribed based on the experiences and standards of developed nations and delivered by foreign aid (Appleby, 2005). That is, the aid provided by developed countries to developing contexts usually has strings attached, they are uTherefore, the intervention of international aid agencies and other countries has been promoted as an attempt to helping developing countries to draw alongside the more developed nations by providing them with financial assistance and expertise. However, after decades of international aid programs, the gap between developed and developing nations has not diminished; rather, economic disparity has increased (Castells, 2010a).

The information technology revolution has added new elements to the discourse over 'underdevelopment', as the 'digital divide' has added another dimension to the classification of nations. Advancements in information and communication technologies has paved the way for the "network society" in which countries strive to stay connected to the global network, where valuable people and territories are switched on, and devalued ones are switched off the global network (Castells, 2010b). Nations with greater access to ICT are believed to have a greater chance to capitalize on the potential benefits of the knowledge-based economy (Castells, 1999b; Cuban, 1993) while poorer nations risk being left in the dark. Castells (2000) also warns of poor countries falling below the "Third World" to the *"Fourth World"* category,

mainly poor African countries, that are excluded from development and therefore from the global network. Accordingly, there seems to be a digital 'deficiency' in developing nations, which can be remedied by the richer nations through expertise and financial assistance delivered through aid agencies and the private sector aiming to bridging the digital gap between developed and developing nations.

"OTHERS" IN NATIONAL REFORM INITIATIVES

The involvement of developed countries, aid agencies, and the private sector in development and reform projects in developing countries has been debated. The United Nations adopted the UN Millennium Development Goals in which the organization stressed upon building global partnership in order to tackle the development problems in developing countries especially through building public-private partnership in order to make available the benefits of ICT for developing countries (United Nations, 2005). Public-private partnership was further promoted in Jordan at the World Economic Forum meeting in 2003 (Abuhmaid, 2011; McKinsey & Company, 2005; World Economic Forum, 2004).

Over the last six decades, large international private companies from developed countries often access local markets through local private affiliates or under aid proposed to economically poorer nations. A growing number of large international enterprises have established development or aid affiliates, which gives them greater access to new markets in developing countries (e.g. Cisco Systems has established *Cisco Institute* and Intel has established *Intel Education Initiative*). The new trend of involving affiliates might project a new strategy in expanding businesses and influences under the umbrella of aid and development proposed to developing countries.

The scarcity of resources available for costly education reform in Jordan often pressures successive governments to seek external assistance and foreign funds. Financial assistance and expertise are increasingly sought through building partnerships between public education and the private sector. However, the limited capacity of the local private sector in developing countries, such as Jordan, in terms of resources and expertise, pressures education systems to expand partnership to involve the international private sector. Partnership with international private sector and aid organizations provided critically needed assistance and funding for the Jordanian education system in order to undertake large-scale reform. Nevertheless, this involvement has impacted the overall integration of ICT within the educational system of Jordan. Moreover, the involvement of international aid agencies itself has also shifted over time as they have become more directly involved in national initiatives. According to Abuhmaid (2009), earlier involvement of foreign aid in national projects took the form of fund delivered to the governments while in recent days the involvement can be found in all stages of the reform; from planning to implementation. The agreement between the World Bank and the government of Jordan required the Ministry of Education to establish a Development and Coordination Unit (DCU) in order to coordinate and oversee the implementation of the Education Reform for the Knowledge Economy (ERfKE). The Unit acted on behalf of the Ministry with loaners and donors and was demanded to send progress reports to the Bank on a half-yearly basis. However, the Unit was understaffed which caused its role to be confined to working within the Ministry of Education and coordinating reports and correspondence between the Ministry and the World Bank. Thus, the Unit's role became more superficial as it did not have the time or resources to examine the accuracy and credibility of reports.

ICT training for teachers and the development of e-curricula showcase the pervasiveness of international partners' involvement in ERfKE. The Jordanian Ministry of Education adopted four main professional training courses for ICT, namely, ICDL, Intel, World Links and iEARN, which are all international courses. In addition, e-curricula were developed by the local private sector in cooperation with foreign corporations. For instance, the E-math content was developed by Rubicon, a local company in partnership with Cisco Learning Institute, California, and sponsored by Cisco Systems under the supervision of the Jordan Ministry of Education. On one hand, Cisco Systems was motivated by an opportunity to develop innovative and globally usable e-content trailed in real school contexts (McKinsey & Company, 2005). In addition, Cisco Systems had its own investment strategies with a focus on ICT in education which supported its long-term commercial interests. On the other hand, Rubicon was motivated by resource transferred from global partners as well as the potential to export the developed e-Curricula to regional or global education systems.

During the implementation of the ERfKE, two main issues arose as a result of the involvement of the private sector: firstly, it was reported that private companies did not comply with deadlines and agreements with the Ministry of Education for developing e-contents, which caused delay during the implantation stage causing disrupt to the initial plans. Secondly, dispute emerged after the Ministry made the e-content available for teachers and students through its electronic portal (http://www.elearning.jo/eduwave/elearningme.aspx) vis-à-vis the copyright of the e-contents and which party was responsible for upgrading and updating the materials when needed in the future. Such issues might be overlooked during the initial stages of the reform but they became serious during the implementation stage, causing delay and disruption.

COMPROMISING THE REFORM

It might be inevitable for the Jordanian education system to seek financial and expertise assistance from international partners in order to undertake major reform projects, however, this partnership should be approached with caution. Although Jordan is considered a small country, it has the potential to serve as a springboard for replicating its experiences to other Arab-speaking countries in the region, which together form a population of more than 325 million. This was an explicit factor that encouraged international investment (e.g. USAID and Middle East Partnership Initiative) in the country and probably decided large global corporations to join the ERfKE project (McKinsey & Company, 2005). The involvement of international partners in such projects can have certain effects during planning and implementation.

As the Ministry accepted partnership with various partners within ERfKE and the JEI, it had to be conscious of participating partners' timelines, agendas, and their desire to focus on some aspects of the reform rather than others during planning and implementation. In the beginning, the Jordanian Ministry of Education had to negotiate the timeline of the ERfKE with the World Bank as the major partner in the project. Since the World Bank did not agree on the 10-year plan proposed by the Ministry for the project, it was separated into two phases of five years for each stage (Abuhmaid, 2009). Furthermore, the involvement of other partners lessened the control of the Ministry of Education has over the flow of funds to sustain all stages and aspects of the reform. The Ministry did not have full control over the conditions in which these partners became involved in the project, especially when these partners were involved in the project under the umbrella of 'aid'. For instance, laptops distributed to teachers were donations. Therefore, when most of the laptops broke down only one year later, they were simply withdrawn from schools without replacement (Abuhmaid, 2009).

Additionally, the involvement of international partners seemed to steer the reform in certain directions according to the interests of key players. It seemed that the education system faced a dilemma: while it had to maintain its focus on the payoff of ICT integration across the system, it had to be other-conscious during both planning and implementation stages. Often, this consciousness took the form of a) overemphasizing or highlighting success stories during the digitization process, or b) by manipulating some achievements in order to meet the expectations of fund partners to keep them supportive to the reform. For example, it is worth mentioning that ERfKE (Educational Reform for the Knowledge Economy) is an English acronym despite the fact that the reform project was designed for Jordan; an Arabic speaking country. In addition, the Jordan Education Initiative has an English website without an Arabic version (www.jei.org.jo, accessed on October 22, 2011) despite the fact that the website contains documents and resources which target Arabic speaking teachers. Providing resources and backup to teachers in a foreign language can do little to the majority of teachers and can give an indication of the real intended audiences. This also became clear when a senior official in the Ministry requested changes to be made to figures of a statistical report regarding the quantity of computers in schools, because the true figures fall short of meeting the expectations of reform partners.

There are two main areas where international and private partners can be found more involved in ERfKE and the JEI: the e-contents and ICT professional development. The two issues are discussed next.

E-Contents

As noted above, it became evident that the agendas of external partners could impact education intervention in a way might serve their short or long term interest. This was seen in the extraordinary fast pace at which the development of certain e-content was progressing, which left all other tracks (e.g. training and infrastructure) lagging far behind. The e-math content was created by Cisco Learning Institute and Rubicon, a Jordanian local private company, and was sponsored by Cisco Systems. However, this investment was aligned with Cisco Systems' long-term commercial interest (McKinsey & Company, 2005) which was motivated by the opportunity to develop e-content to be useable and trialed within a real school context. In this way, other education systems, especially those of other Arab countries, might then be convinced to adopt the developed 'product' as it would have been already trialed in a similar education system.

Furthermore, after the development of the e-math contents, the private company which developed the materials became engaged in a fierce legal dispute with the Ministry of Education over the copyright issue. However, there was an initial agreement that enabled the private company to retain the copyright outside Jordan while the Ministry of Education reserved the copyright within the country (Abuhmaid, 2009). At the same time, other subjects did not receive the same attention and therefore they were significantly slower in their progress, especially civics and geography (World Economic Forum, 2004). Understandably, mathematics has a relatively universal nature with minimal cultural and local impact on localized curricula, and therefore, it is more easily transferred from one educational context to another. Likewise, English as a Foreign Language e-contents might be easily transferred from one context to another. On the other hand, transferring civics and geography from one particular context to another can be difficult as they have more to deal with the local and cultural contexts.

ICT Training Courses

Several ICT training courses were adopted for teacher professional development by the Ministry of Education. However, the main courses adopted by ERfKE were ICDL, World Links, Intel Teach to the Future, and iEARN (even it was discarded in early stages during implementation). These courses played an important role in training teachers on ICT at two levels: ICT use level and the pedagogical use of ICT level. The two levels improved teachers' attitudes and utilization of ICT. However, it is also clear that all these international courses are provided by either profitable companies, or by politically driven organizations. For instance, iEARN is part of the Building Respect through Internet Dialogue and Global Education (BRIDGE) which aims at bridging the cultural divide between the USA and Islamic countries (BRIDGE, 2004) and funded by the US Department of State. Jordan is considered as a moderate country in the Middle East region with strong ties with the West, where international companies and NGOs might consider a place to expand in the regional market. Therefore, after establishing roots in Jordan they might expand to other more conservative countries in the region. For instance, World Links subsequently extended its mission to include Syria, Yemen and Palestine through its office in Jordan.

THE DECISION FOR EDUCATION REFORM

Theoretically, "the purpose of educational change presumably is to help schools accomplish their goals more effectively by replacing some structures, programs and/or practices with better ones" (Fullan & Stiegelbauer, 1991, p.15). Usually, education reform is sought due to dissatisfaction with the status quo (Niederhauser et al., 1999; Shuldam, 2004), inconsistency, or intolerability in our current situation (Fullan & Stiegelbauer, 1996). According to Ely (1999), education reform is sought when we feel that something is not right, others are moving ahead, or we are standing still, and therefore we act in order to improve our situation. Therefore, the *what* and *how* questions must be the core of any educational change (Fullan et al., 1991). Castells (Cited in: Ogilvy, 1998) stresses that action for change has to be driven by knowledge, for which research is a tool that ensures making informed decisions instead of relying only on either theory or practical experiences in order to achieve goals.

Experiences generated in particular educational contexts are culturally and contextually sensitive, so, replicating experiences does not guarantee their success in the new context (Dimmock, 2000). The uniqueness of each educational system makes its experiences and possibilities also unique; thus, the term 'best practice' should be strictly limited to the context where it is generated. This might draw into question the procedure of diffusing ERfKE through the Discovery Schools initiative. Habitually, the Jordanian education system starts new initiatives by implementing them in a few selected schools before they are rolled out to other schools. For the JEI, 30 schools were initially selected in order to pilot ideas and new technologies. Subsequently, the Discovery Schools expanded to become 100 all of which are located in Amman, the capital of Jordan, and these schools had long history of pioneering reform projects and initiatives. The schools were mainly located in the vicinity of the Ministry of Education and Queen Rania Center, which provided exceptional advantages for these schools through acquiring resources and expertise needed for the implementation of ICT at the school level. Therefore, the procedure of rolling out experiences and practices from these schools to other schools countrywide should not expect similar results considering the high percentage of disadvantaged and remote schools across the country.

Rigor research should guide development and education reform. Research in the Middle East and North Africa (MENA) region counts for one-tenth of one percent (0.01%) of the world's research and development spending; less than any other region in the world excluding sub-Saharan Africa (Akkari, 2004). At the same time, Arab countries

spend more than five percent of their Gross National Product (GNP) on education which is the highest percentage among all countries (Akkari, 2004). Nonetheless, this spending has not created satisfactory education systems in the region by international standards (Billeh, 2002). Therefore, rigor and contextual research is crucially needed in order to guide spending on education and to evaluate the effectiveness of efforts aiming to improve the education system. In Jordan, the Ministry of Education has pointed to its limited capacity to analyze and make use of data for decision-making (Ministry of Education, 2004). Thus, the evaluation of educational initiatives is often conducted by international organizations or private companies relying on experts from other parts of the world mainly Westerners. Despite the great value of such research conducted by seasoned Western scholars (Kozma *et al.*, 2006; Kozma, 2006), there might be a concern of it as an outsider's point of view.

The reliance on foreign aid to undertake reform usually pushes the education system to go in certain paths. For instance, the system might be lured or pressured to draw on particular experiences as 'best practices.' While benefiting from the experiences of others in planning for national reforms is essential, merely replicating these experiences may reflect uncertainty and unclear vision of the local initiatives. According to Maddux et al. (2001), when we are not clear about what is our decision then we might:

1. Rely on experts to tell us what to do;
2. Use what is currently popular;
3. Simply continue doing what we have always done in the past; or
4. Rely on trial and error.

Ironically, the four strategies are often practiced by education systems in developing countries. In Jordan, planing for the knowledge-based economy resulted in the launch of e-strategy in 2000. However, according to the World Bank (2005), the e-strategy drew on data from other countries mainly from the USA and Europe. Therefore, the e-strategy was weak in implementation (i.e. monitoring and evaluation) resulting in missing its objectives. Accordingly, in 2004 the e-strategy was modified to become more realistic by identifying achievable goals; subsequently, the initial goals were lowered substantially (Billeh, 2002; World Bank, 2005).

Education systems should clearly define their own standards for ICT-related initiatives in order to meet clear and well-defined educational goals (Billeh, 2002). While adopting internationally developed ICT professional development courses can be justified in many ways, the local educational authority should develop national standards for local integration (European SchoolNet, 2005). ICT related projects in Jordan were marked by substantial participation of international partners despite the absence of detailed standards to guide the reform and make it coherent. In the training track within the ERfKE, standards for ICT training courses were not well-defined, nor was there sufficient coordination between the various courses, resulting in competition for allocation of resources and accreditation. Thus, the competitiveness and lack of coordination added more pressure on teachers who were undertaking the courses and compromised the outcomes their outcomes (Abuhmaid, 2009).

Clearly, drawing upon international best practices and experiences can enrich the Jordanian educational system's integration of ICT. However, the absence of clear national standards defined by the Jordanian education system was supplemented by the heavy reliance on each program to have its own standards which resulted in fragmentation and competitiveness within the reform. Furthermore, there was no careful selection from the various training programs as the educational system welcomed all ICT training courses as long as they comply with *general* guidelines. In earlier research study, Omar, an official from the Ministry of Education in charge of ICT training programs explained the strategy for selecting international training courses "The Ministry of Education opened its doors for international courses [like] highway, all courses are welcomed as long as they can secure fund and get the approval from us [the Ministry] as we ensure their sensitivity to the local culture and values" (Abuhmaid, 2009, p.167).

CENTRALIZATION AND ICT INTEGRATION

The educational system of Jordan is centralized. All regulations, mandates, and interventions originated in the Ministry of Education before they are diffused across the system through the regional directorates of education. The ERfKE project further illustrated this mechanism of decision-making and diffusion of innovations.

Clearly, the process in which an intervention is disseminated across centralized systems may affect the essence of the intervention. As the decision seeps from the upper level where the initiative was originated, it has to go through several levels of the bureaucratic system before reaching classrooms. Furthermore, the implementation might be lengthy and the core of the initiative might be modified. During this process, attitudes, experiences, resources and knowledge at each level of the education system might modify the core of the intervention. For instance, in an earlier study, Abuhmaid (2009) pointed to a principal at one school who refused to accept new computers at her school in order to avoid being responsible for them, while some directors at the regional level were not convinced with the effectiveness of ICT in teaching and learning. Certainly, such attitudes and decisions at the directorate and school levels would limit teachers' and students' access at that school and thus impact the overall implementation of ICT across the education system.

The process of diffusing an innovation across a multi-layered organization, such as the Jordanian educational system, can have impact on the integrity of the innovation itself. This is in part due to the involvement of human resources at each of the several levels of the system, and the long chain created between decision-making and implementation, which may modify and misshape the essence and contents of the original courses. Understandably, the longer the chain between decision-making and implementation the more vulnerable to modifications the reform project becomes (Castells & Himanen, 2002). This might also support Ely's (1999) claim that the closer the leadership to the user the better for implementing new innovations.

The centralized nature of the Jordanian education system can be spotted in two issues within the ERfKE and JEI initiatives: Cascading ICT training courses across the system and the top-down mentality in diffusing innovations.

Cascading ICT Training

Due to the highly centralized nature of the education system of Jordanian, ICT training courses were disseminated through cascading. That is, a core team from the Ministry of Education trains core teams from the regional directorates of education who train mentors and teachers trainers in their directorates who then train teachers in the field (Abuhmaid, 2009). Clearly, this model of diffusion can substantially modify the essence of the original course. According to Navarro and Verdisco (2000) this approach in training teachers usually produces "less-than-convincing results in practice" (p.4). Furthermore, the cascading model presumes that one-size-fits-all regardless of teachers' and schools' individual and unique needs, an approach which is also largely discredited in a complex context such as that of education.

Top-Down Reform

Top-down mechanism of ICT integration is mandated by central authority and diffused across an educational system. It has been argued that this

mechanism can be necessary in order to create a favorable environment for ICT within a given educational context (Pedrelli et al., 2001). However, the model has also been received with skepticism. The complexity of educational contexts can limit the effectiveness of top-down mechanisms in diffusing innovations. According to Tyack and Cuban (1995), top-down regulations can, at best, create some necessary but not sufficient conditions which attract interested teachers and curious students. In addition, Fullan (1993) asserts that what really matters for educational change cannot be mandated because it requires complex skills, creative thinking and committed action. Gilmore (1995), also stressed that top-down educational interventions are generally under-resourced, badly-understood, or simply unpopular with teachers, all of which naturally affect the quality of the intervention itself.

Within the educational context, the top-down mentality may achieve little success as education reform has to involve teachers who are the primary agents of school change (Gillingham & Topper, 1999; Sarbib, 2002). Although teachers have little choice over whether or not to use ICT, they retain a great deal of the more fundamental role of deciding how and when to use them in the classroom (Somekh & Davis, 1997).

Moreover, another concern associated with top-down reform is that schools' and teachers' practices can absorb changes and buffer them when they are mandated by "outsiders". Teachers and schools can twist reforms and weave some of the elements into their old practices, which is a typical response from institutions to large-scale educational reforms. Thus, changes can be made to the surface structures while at the same time changing little at the core (Elmore, 1996). Therefore, external changes seemed at best to affect teachers' use of materials but would not result in changes in practices or beliefs (Fullan, 2000).

An alternative model is cited in the literature for educational reform emphasizing the bottom-up approach in education reform aided by top-down support, which is increasingly a popular approach

(TeleLearning, 1999). According to Means, et al. (1993), this model is in line with the site-based management model which gives more power, authority, and accountability to teachers by involving them in the reform. This model may enhance teachers' understanding of the reform, and their willingness to implement an innovation to which they have contributed.

ICT AND THE CAPACITY OF THE SYSTEM

Successful implementation of innovations requires clear and realistic objectives in terms of time, resources and support (Fullan, 1982). Neglecting the inbuilt capabilities and limitations within a particular context might leave educational interventions meaningless or burdensome as they might not be executed as intended in the first place. The Jordanian education system was overstretched by the fast pace and magnitude of the educational interventions which were funded and largely overseen by external partners (Abuhmaid, 2009). That is, the Ministry of Education found it difficult to simultaneously maintain efforts in all aspects of reform projects (e.g. training, infrastructure, and digitization). Therefore, efforts and resources were often redirected to tracks of the reform where the demand was most pressing, leaving other tracks exposed and unguided. There were unrealistic or unclear objectives for the adoption of ICT by the Jordanian education system which often resulted in ad hoc actions (Abuhmaid, 2009; McKinsey & Company, 2005). For instance, in the beginning there was remarkable emphasis on developing e-contents which required the allocation of disproportionate resources. However, when the e-contents for some subjects became available on the Ministry's online portal (EduWave), the Ministry realized that teachers were not adequately prepared to use them and infrastructure across the education system was inadequate. At that point, the training track was accelerated and new ICT train-

ing courses were rushed into the scene. However, the Electronic Training department was already overwhelmed by the massive task of providing all teachers with basic ICT training through the ICDL course. Thereafter, when the e-content became available online, the system realized that even though the vast majority of teachers had undertaken the ICDL course, they did not know how to use ICT in teaching and learning. Accordingly, other training courses were adopted such as the Intel Teach to the Future, the World Links, and CADER programs in order to train teachers on how to use ICT into teaching subjects. In addition, mentors were mobilized to train teachers resulting in diminishing their crucial role in the follow-up and support for teachers in classrooms. Furthermore, another shift of focus happened yet again when many mentors were redirected to support the department of curricula in the Ministry of Education in order to assist in authoring new curricula for ICT (Abuhmaid, 2009). Ad hoc responses in education reforms might point to a failure in the initial place to acknowledge and appreciate the organization's inherent capacity to undergo such manoeuvre. One aspect of the impact of inbuilt capacity of the Jordanian education system while implementing a large-scale reform projects was the inability to maintain extensive efforts over an extended period of time. For instance, during the first year of piloting the E-math, mentors' visits and support to schools and teachers were remarkable, however, that was not feasible due to mentors' loads and shortage in numbers, as it will be discussed next.

Furthermore, the education system was struggling to meet the deadlines set out for ICT integration. The launch of ERfKE was delayed by one year, which was due to the built-in capacity of the Ministry of Education. In addition, infrastructure improvement did not meet expectations (Abuhmaid, 2009; McKinsey & Company, 2005) due to bureaucracies and the limited capacity of the system.

Follow-Up and Ongoing Support

The literature stressed on the crucial role for the follow-up in the adoption of ICT by teachers (Anderson, 1997; Bradshaw, 2002; Fiszer, 2004; Lewis, 1998). For instance, each mentor was responsible for 120-130 schools making him/her extremely overloaded and reducing the role of mentoring to superficial one. In addition, mentors were often removed from their mentoring role in order to reinforce other fields within the education system (e.g. training and authoring), which deprived teachers of crucial support when they needed it the most: during ICT utilization in classrooms. In another sign of overload placed on mentors, they used to visit schools daily or four to five times a week during the first year of implementing ERfKE. However, this level of follow-up took place only in the Discovery Schools and during the first year of implementing the E-math. Surprisingly, mentors' visits to schools declined drastically after the first year of implementation. During the second and the third year, mentors' visits to schools, even to the Discovery Schools, occurred once or twice a year (Abuhmaid, 2009) because they were carrying out other responsibilities.

In the Jordanian education system, the regional directorates disseminate and oversee the implementation of decisions and policy statements made at Ministry level. Mentors in the regional directorates are responsible for supporting, monitoring and reporting teachers' and schools' performance. Most importantly, mentors are the main part of the education system of Jordan that provides teachers with follow-up support during their teaching. Nevertheless, Abuhmaid (2009) revealed that mentoring departments were markedly under-staffed and were unable to carry out their crucial role during the implementation of ERfKE and JEI.

Maintenance and Technical Support

Continuous maintenance, replacement and upgrade are essential companions to any reform involving ICT. Technical assistance is a key factor for the success of innovations and can be a significant predictor of teachers' use of ICT (Fullan, 1982; Plomp et al., 1996). Byrom (2001) found a significant positive correlation between the technical assistance provided and ICT integration, i.e. schools that receive more technical support than others, are more likely to adopt ICT.

Obtaining support was lengthy, time consuming, and services did not reach schools at times when they were needed; even machines that were still under warranty had to go through certain bureaucratic channels to be fixed. Teachers complained about the deficiency in providing maintenance and technical support. For instance, a mathematics teacher who was keen to use computer in his teaching especially that his subject was fully digitized and its e-content was available on the Ministry's e-portal, the teacher complained that he was using the computer in his teaching until it needed to be repaired. The teacher went through a lengthy process through the directorate of education for more than 45 days and it was still not repaired. When the teacher insisted on the directorate to get the computer repaired he was told to get it fixed on his own. Another teacher confirmed that saying: "It has been almost a year since I handed the laptop to them [the directorate]" in order to get it repaired [showing me the receipt report]. Furthermore, a principal mentioned that "we have to get them [laptops] repaired through the directorate of education and this process takes too much time."

Furthermore, mentors and other official referred to slow and time consuming processes for maintenance and technical assistance. A mentor indicated that "despite computers are in satisfying numbers in some schools, the process of mainte-nance is slow." However, the head of Computers and Networks Department puts this issue into perspective saying that his department was not able to cope with pressure and demand from 160 schools with only 3 or 4 technicians. He also in-dicated that in order to reach schools and provide them with services on site, it might take a week or more to find transportation to reach schools due to bureaucracy and shortage of resources.

Clearly, directorates of education were work-ing with limited capacity within a bureaucratic system, and this directly influenced the quality of service provided to schools, with delays in providing technical support to schools due to staff shortage and bureaucratic decision-making.

IMPLEMENTION OF REFORM

The ERfKE project combined four components of which Component 2 aimed to *transform educa-tion programs and practices to achieve learning outcomes relevant to the knowledge economy* (Ministry of Education, 2004). This component had three main sub-components:

- Prepare curriculum and assessments for the knowledge economy;
- Provide professional development for the Ministry of Education personnel; and
- Provide required resources to support ef-fective learning.

The project shows sound and comprehensive planning for reforming the Jordanian education system for the knowledge-based economy. The education system successfully generated inter-national support for the project in the World Economic Forum held in Jordan in June 2003. Therefore, ICT integration was remarkably ac-celerated across the education system through assistance from international partners. Neverthe-less, after the implementation of Phase I of the project between 2003 and 2008, and despite some

improvements, achievements seemed to be modest compared to the ambitious plans and expectations.

Earlier studies indicated that the outcomes of the ERfKE and JEI do not align with the vision originally adopted (Abuhmaid, 2009; Kozma, 2006). The mismatch between planning and implementation was identified as a major threat to educational interventions (Fullan, 2005; Ful-lan & Stiegelbauer, 1991; Rogers, 2003). Fullan and Stiegelbauer (1991) stressed that the failure of educational change to achieve its objectives may be related just as much to the fact that it was never implemented in practice. For instance, in cooperation with Menhaj Technologies, a private local company, the Ministry of Education devel-oped e-contents for students in the last two years of science stream called *"I Love Physics."* The materials were distributed to schools on CDs. Although a great deal of resources and efforts were spent on developing the materials, the CD was not utilized by the vast majority of physics teachers (Abuhmaid, 2009). In addition, the slow internet connection provided to schools severely impacted the value and utilization of online e-contents made available for teachers and students on the Ministry's e-Portal. That is, teachers and students had to spend excessive time in order to use the materials due to the slow connection.

Furthermore, Fullan (2000) argued that the successes of change after 3, 5, or 8 years can be misleading, that is they may remain not institution-alized and they can be "easily undone by a change in leadership or direction" (p.20). For instance, in earlier study, the researcher found that changing a principal at a particular school resulted in drastic decrease in ICT utilization in the school due to the principal's attitude towards ICT (Abuhmaid, 2009). Therefore, reform continues to be shaped and influenced by its implementers and its suc-cess remains vulnerable during implementation (Abuhmaid, 2010). Thus, although it is important to adopt initiatives in order to improve education through ICT, the actual implementation and con-tinuation stages are the key stages of the reform when change takes place.

CONCLUSION

This chapter discussed issues influence the integrity of ICT integration within education systems where external partners play a key role in national reform projects in Jordan. The discussion made it clear that while seeking external partnership might become inevitable to the Jordanian education system due to resources and expertise restrains, coordination of that involvement becomes paramount. The integrity and success of the reform project might dependent to a large extent on coordinating the involvement of various stakeholders. Such coordination might play a major role in maintaining the wholeness of the reform projects and save them from being fragmented due to the wide range of partners involved. By defining clear objectives and standards, the education system of Jordan can improve coordination between stakeholders and minimize their competitiveness knowing what each partner is expected to fulfill as part of the reform project. Change and reform should not be driven by marketing principles. Thus, education systems have to adopt and implement effective reform initiatives to deal with *real* educational problems rather than perceived or exaggerated crises promoted by vendors or profitable organizations.

REFERENCES

Abuhmaid, A. (2009). *ICT integration across education systems: The experience of Jordan in educational reform*. Saarbrücken, Germany: VDM Verlag Dr. Müller.

Abuhmaid, A. (2010). *Centralization and reform: Information technologies in large-scale education reform*. Paper presented at the E-learning Excellence in the Middle East 2010: Bringing Global Quality to a Local Context, Dubai, UAE.

Abuhmaid, A. (2011). Embracing ICT by the Jordanian education system. In Albadri, F., & Abdullah, S. (Eds.), *Cases on ICT acceptance, investment and organization: Cultural practices and values in the Arab world*. Hershey, PA: IGI Global. doi:10.4018/978-1-60960-048-8.ch003

Akkari, A. (2004). Education in the Middle East and North Africa: The current situation and future challenges. *International Education Journal, 5*(2), 144–153.

Anderson, S. E. (1997). Understanding teacher change: Revisiting the concerns based adoption model. *Curriculum Inquiry, 27*(3), 331–367. doi:10.1111/0362-6784.00057

Appleby, R. (2005). *The spatiality of English language teaching, gender and context*. Unpublished doctoral dissertation, University of Technology, Sydney, Sydney.

Billeh, V. (2002). Educational reform in the Arab region. *Newsletter of the Economic Research Forum, for the Arab Countries, Iran and Turkey, 9*(2).

Bradshaw, L. K. (2002). Technology for teaching and learning: Strategies for staff development and follow-up support. *Journal of Technology and Teacher Education, 10*(1), 131–150.

BRIDGE. (2004). *Building respect through internet dialogue and global education [BRIDGE]*. Retrieved from rom http://us.iearn.org/collaborate/programs/bridge/index.php (August, 8 2006)

Byrom, E. (2001). *Factors influencing the effective use of technology for teaching and learning*. Retrieved from http://www.serve.org/seir-tec/publications/lessons.pdf

Castells, M. (1999a). Flows, networks, and identities: A critical theory of the informational society. In Castells, M., Flecha, R., Freire, P., Giroux, H. A., Macedo, D., & Willis, P. (Eds.), *Critical education in the new information age*. New York, NY: Rowman & Littlefield Publishers, Inc.

Castells, M. (1999b). *Information technology, globalization and social development.* Geneva, Switzerland: United Nations.

Castells, M. (2010a). *The information age economy, society and culture: End of millennium* (2nd ed., *Vol. III*). West Sussex, UK: Wiley-Blackwell.

Castells, M. (2010b). *The information age: Economy, society and culture: The rise of the network society* (2nd ed., *Vol. I*). West Sussex, UK: Wiley-Blackwell.

Castells, M., & Himanen, P. (2002). *The information society and the welfare state: The Finnish model.* Oxford, UK: Oxford University Press. doi:10.1093/acprof:oso/9780199256990.001.0001

Cuban, L. (1993). Computers meet classroom: Classroom wins. *Teachers College Record, 95*(2).

Delvin, J. C. (2010). *Challenges of economic development in the Middle East and North Africa region* (*Vol. 8*). New Jersey World Scientific Publishing.

Dimmock, C. (2000). *Designing the learning-centred school: A cross-cultural perspective.* New York, NY: Falmer Press.

Elmore, R. F. (1996). Getting to scale with good educational practice. *Harvard Educational Review, 66*(1), 1–26.

Ely, D. P. (1999). Conditions that facilitate the implementation of educational technology innovations. *Educational Technology, 39*(6), 23–27.

European SchoolNet. (2005). *Assessment schemes for teachers' ICT competence- A policy analysis.*

Fiszer, E. P. (2004). *How teachers learn best: An ongoing professional development model.* Maryland: Scarecrow Education.

Fullan, M. (1982). *The meaning of educational change.* Ontario, Canada: The Ontario Institute for Studies in Education.

Fullan, M. (1993). *Change forces: Probing the depths of educational reform.* London, UK: The Falmer Press.

Fullan, M. (2005). *The new meaning of educational change* (3rd ed.). New York, NY: Routledge Falmer.

Fullan, M., & Stiegelbauer, S. (1991). *The new meaning of educational change.* New York, NY: Teachers College Press.

Fullan, M., & Stiegelbauer, S. (1996). *The new meaning of educational change* (2nd ed.). New York, NY: Teachers College Press.

Gillingham, M. G., & Topper, A. (1999). Technology in teacher preparation: Preparing teachers for the future. *Journal of Technology and Teacher Education, 7*(4), 303–321.

Gilmore, A. M. (1995). Turning teachers on to computers: Evaluation of a teacher development program. *Journal of Research on Computing in Education, 27*(3).

Hawkridge, D. (1989). Machine-mediated learning in third-world schools. *Machine-Mediated Learning, 3*, 319–328.

Kozma, R. (2006). *Contributions of technology and teacher training to education reform: Evaluation of the world links Arab region in Jordan.* Retrieved from http://www.wlar.org/pdfs/WLAR_Jordan_Evaluation.pdf

Leithwood, K., Jantzi, D., & Mascall, B. (2002). A framework for research on large-scale reform. *Journal of Educational Change, 3*, 7–33. doi:10.1023/A:1016527421742

Lewis, A. C. (1998). A new consensus emerges on the characteristics of good professional development. In Tovey, R. (Ed.), *Harvard Education Letter Focus series 4: Professional development* (pp. 12–16). Cambridge, MA: Gutman Library.

Logan, R. K. (1995). *The fifth language: Learning a living in the computer age.* Toronto, Canada: Stoddart Publishing Co. Limited.

MacDonald, J. (2008). *Blended learning and online tutoring: Planning learner support and activity design.* Hampshire, UK: Gower Publishing Limited.

Maddux, C. D., Johnson, D. L., & Willis, T. W. (2001). *Educational computing: Learning with tomorrow's technologies* (3rd ed.). Boston, MA: Allan and Bacon.

McKinsey & Company. (2005). *Building effective public-private partnerships: Lessons learned from the Jordan Education Initiative.* Retrieved August 22, 2007, from http://www.jei.org.jo/KnowledgeCenterfiles/McKinsey%20Final%20Report_May%2005.pdf

Means, B. (1994). Technology and education reform: The reality behind the promise. In Means, B. (Ed.), *Introduction: Using technology to advance educational goals.* John Wiley & Sons.

Means, B., Blando, J., Olson, K., Middleton, T., Morocco, C. C., Remz, A. R., & Zorfass, J. (1993). *Using technology to support education reform.* U.S. Department of Education and Office of Educational Research and Improvement. Retrieved from from http://www.ed.gov/ZipDocs/TechReforms.zip

Ministry of Education. (2004, 8-11 September 2004). *The development of education: National report of the Hashemite Kingdom of Jordan.* Paper presented at the International Conference on Education, Geneva, 8-11 September 2004, Geneva.

Navarro, J. C., & Verdisco, A. (2000). *Teacher training in Latin America: Innovations and trends.* Washington, DC: World Bank, Inter-American Development Bank. Retrieved from http://www.iadb.org/sds/doc/EDU-114E.pdf

Niederhauser, D. S., Salem, D. J., & Fields, M. (1999). Exploring teaching, learning, and instructional reform in an introductory technology course. *Journal of Technology and Teacher Education, 7*(2), 153–172.

Pedrelli, M., & Emilia, R. (2001). *Developing countries and the ICT revolution.* Luxembourg: European Parliament Directorate General for Research.

Plomp, T., Anderson, R., & Kontogiannopoulou-Polydorides, G. (1996). *Cross national policies and practices on computers in education.* Dordrecht, The Netherlands: Kluwer Academic Publishers. doi:10.1007/978-0-585-32767-9

Reeves, T. C. (1998). *The impact of media and technology in schools.* A research report prepared for the Bertelsmann Foundation. The University of Georgia. Retrieved from http://www.athensacademy.org/instruct/media_tech/reeves0.html

Rogers, E. M. (2003). *Diffusion of innovations* (5th ed.). New York, NY: Free Press.

Sarbib, L. (2002). *Building knowledge societies in the Middle East and North Africa.* Retrieved August 20, 2004, from http://www.worldbank.org/k4dmarseille

Shuldam, M. (2004). Superintendent conception of instructional conditions that impact teacher technology integration. *Journal of Research on Technology in Education, 36*(4), 319–344.

Somekh, B., & Davis, N. (Eds.). (1997). *Using information technology effectively in teaching and learning.* London, UK: Routledge.

Subhi, T. (1999). Attitudes toward computers of gifted students and their teachers. *High Ability Studies, 10*(1), 69–84. doi:10.1080/1359813990100106

TeleLearning. (1999). *Working group on professional development: In-service teachers professional development models in the use of information and communication technologies.* Retrieved from http://www.tact.fse.ulaval.ca/ang/html/pdmodels.html

Tyack, D. B., & Cuban, L. (1995). *Tinkering toward Utopia: A century of public school reform.* Cambridge, MA: Harvard University Press.

United Nations. (2005). *UN millennium development goals.* Retrieved 25 May, 2007, from http://www.un.org/millenniumgoals

Wagner, D. A., Day, B., James, T., Kozma, R. B., Miller, J., & Unwin, T. (2005). *Monitoring and evaluation of ICT in education projects: A handbook for developing countries.* Washington, DC: The International Bank for Reconstruction and Development / The World Bank. Retrieved from http://www.infodev.org/en/Document.9.aspx

World Bank. (2005). *Monitoring and evaluation toolkit for e-strategies results.* Washington, DC: Global Information and Communication Technologies Department, World Bank.

World Economic Forum. (2004). *Jordan education initiative.* Retrieved from http://www.moict.gov.jo/moict/downloads/JEI_Track_Update_Document.pdf

ADDITIONAL READING

Al-Sa'd, A. (2007). *Evaluation of students' attitudes towards vocational education in Jordan.* Lärarutbildningen, Sweden: Malmohogskola.

Bannayan, H. (2007, October). *Jordan education initiative.* Paper presented at the MIT LINC Conference: Technology-Enabled Education: A Catalyst for Positive Change, Amman.

El-Berr, S. (2004). *Non-German donor activities in education in Jordan Center for Development Research, University of Bonn.* Retrieved January 11, 2005, from http://www.zef.de/fileadmin/webfiles/downloads/projects/el-mikawy/jordan_non-german-donor.pdf

El-Berr, S., & El-Mikawy, N. (2004). *Regional perspectives on education reform in the Arab countries: ZEF.* Retrieved January 11, 2005, from http://www.zef.de/fileadmin/webfiles/downloads/projects/el-mikawy/study_regional_perspectives.pdf

Emaduldeen, M. M. (2007). The role of the Jordanian educational system in the development towards the knowledge economy. *Risalat Al Muallim, 43*(1), 12–21.

Escobar, A. (2004). Development, violence and the new imperial order. *Development, 47*(1), 15–21. doi:10.1057/palgrave.development.1100014

Fullan, M. (2000). The three stories of education reform. *Phi Delta Kappa International, 81*(8), 581–584.

Gavlak, D. (2007, July 27). Jordan appeals for help in dealing with Iraqi refugees. *Washington Post,* p. A16.

Hasan, O. (2000). Improving the quality of learning: Global education as a vehicle for school reform. *Theory into Practice, 39*(2), 97–103. doi:10.1207/s15430421tip3902_6

Hepp, P., Hinostroza, E., Laval, E., & Rehbein, L. (2004). *Technology in schools: Education, ICT and the knowledge society.* Retrieved June 18, 2006, from http://www-wds.worldbank.org/external/default/main?pagePK=64193027&piPK=64187937&theSitePK=523679&menuPK=64187510&searchMenuPK=64187283&theSitePK=523679&entityID=000160016_20050110162933&searchMenuPK=64187283&theSitePK=523679

Hill, P. W., & Crevola, C. A. (1999). The role of standards of educational reform for the 21st century. In Marsh, D. D. (Ed.), *Preparing our schools for the 21st century* (pp. 117–142). Alexandria, VA: Association for Supervision and Curriculum Development.

Holland, R. (2002). *Federal law will require research-based programs* (pp. 1–3). School Reform News.

Jaradat, E. (1992). The philosophy of educational development in Jordan. *Risalat Al Muallim, 33*(3), 5–62.

Moore, P. (2004). *Doing business in the Middle East: Politics and economic crisis in Jordan and Kuwait.* Cambridge, UK: Cambridge University Press. doi:10.1017/CBO9780511492242

Sahlberg, P. (2006). Education reform for raising economic competitiveness. *Journal of Educational Change, 7*, 259–287. doi:10.1007/s10833-005-4884-6

Seijaparova, D., & Pellekaan, J. W. H. (2004). *Jordan: An evaluation of World Bank assistance for poverty reduction, health and education.* Washington, DC: The World Bank Operations Evaluation Department, World Bank.

Servon, L. J. (2002). *Bridging the digital divide, technology, community, and public policy.* Oxford, UK: Blackwell Publishing. doi:10.1002/9780470773529

Talal, A. B. (1998, September). *Teacher education and school reform in a changing world.* Paper presented at The 43rd World Assembly, International Council of Education for Teaching, Amman.

Tawalbeh, M. (2001). The policy and management of information technology in Jordanian schools. *British Journal of Educational Technology, 32*(2), 133–140. doi:10.1111/1467-8535.00184

Todaro, M. (1985). *Economic development in the third world* (3rd ed.). New York, NY: Longman.

KEY TERMS AND DEFINITIONS

Cascading ICT Training: Training which follow the pattern of training small group and each one in the group trains other groups until training reaches classroom teachers.

Education Reform: An attempt to improve the performance of a given education system.

ERfKE: An acronym stands for Education Reform for the Knowledge Economy. A project adopted by the Jordanian education system in 2003.

JEI: An acronym stands for Jordan Education Initiative. An initiative adopted by the Ministry of Education in Jordan aiming to accelerate ICT diffusion within schools country wide through piloting new ideas and disseminating them to other schools.

Jordan: Officially known as "The Hashemite Kingdom of Jordan." A small developing country located in the Middle East.

Knowledge-Based Economy: An economy that has knowledge and information as paramount to its structure and development.

Ministry of Education: The central education authority in Jordan where all education policies and statement are originated and distributed across the system through regional directorates of education.

Chapter 10
ICT in Arab Education:
Issues and Challenges

Saba Fatma
Manipal University, UAE

ABSTRACT

Developing countries are facing many challenges today, such as globalization and the information and communication technologies revolution, as governments and societies are coping with change. Technology adoption in the classroom setting, as well as in other formats of education across the world in the past several years, has resulted in the realization that the benefits accrued from these technologies are not mainly related to getting access to new technology, but to integrating technology in the holistic framework of curriculum, teacher competencies, institutional readiness, and long term financing. Arab governments have rapidly established a great number of schools and universities in recent years. Most programs focus largely on the technology itself, placing very little emphasis on the practical implications of the use of ICTs to meet broad educational objectives. Also, amidst the emerging digital divide, it is important to note the prevailing gaps between countries within the Arab world. There are marked variances between countries in their efforts to adopt ICT tools and grow their networked economies. The chapter focuses on knowledge society and education and ICT challenges faced by Arab countries.

INTRODUCTION

ICTs stand for Information and Communication Technologies and are defined as a diverse set of technological tools and resources used to communicate and to create, disseminate, store, and manage information. These technologies are inclusive of computer, internet and broadcast technologies like television, radio and telephony. There has been a lot of focus on the use of comput-

ers to increase the efficiency and effectiveness of education at every level and in non- formal and formal settings. But the older technologies like television and radio have longer and richer history as instructional tools than newer and faster developing technologies like computers and the internet. For example, television and radio has been used as instructional tool for delivery of education in the open and distant learning mode in both developed and developing countries for

DOI: 10.4018/978-1-4666-1984-5.ch010

the past 60 years rather than print and electronic media which are the cheapest and more accessible in the present times. Although the internet and computers is proliferating the world over, in the developing world their use is still in its infancy due to limited infrastructure and attendant high cost of access. In many countries a mix of technologies are used for delivery of education for example, the Kothmale Community Radio Internet uses both radio broadcasts and computer and Internet technologies to facilitate the sharing of information and to provide educational opportunities for rural community in Sri Lanka. The Open University of the United Kingdom (UKOU) which was established in 1969 (the first educational institution in the world wholly devoted to delivery of education only through open and distance learning mode) still relies heavily on print based materials supplemented by radio and television and very recently online programming. Similar to this, the Indira Gandhi National Open University in India combines the use of print, recorded audio and video, broadcast radio and television, and audio conferencing.

Although most commonly associated with higher education and corporate training, e-learning is increasingly gaining acceptance at all levels of education through the use of information network —the Internet, an intranet (LAN) or extranet (WAN)—whether wholly or in part, for course delivery, interaction and facilitation. Another term that is gaining importance is Blended Learning. This refers to learning models that combine traditional classroom practices with e-learning solutions. An example of this could be that students in a traditional classroom can be assigned print and online materials, are subscribed to class email list and have online mentoring by their teachers through chat. Conversely, complete web based programs can be enhanced by periodic face to face interaction.

Education is increasingly becoming a defining element in the knowledge society. Education along with ICT, information, knowledge and innovation are now seen as the foundations of the new global knowledge economy. Over the past twenty years, globalization and technological changes have worked in tandem to create a new global economy powered by technology, fueled by information and driven by knowledge. Consequently this new global economy has serious implications for the nature and purpose of educational institutions.

However the existence of the digital divide, which is the gap between those who have access to and control of technology and those who do not, means that introduction and integration of ICT's in various levels of education and various modes of education will be the most challenging. Failure to meet the challenge would further widen the knowledge gap and result in deeper social and economic inequalities. In order to improve access to education and quality of education, creative and innovative applications of ICT in educational technologies could be used to accelerate education reform process.

The explosion of Internet in 1990's and also the simultaneous use and large scale proliferation of low cost computing devices and diffusion of computers throughout society resulted in ICT and education wave. Most countries focused on building policies and projects around technology driven education designed to prepare students for information age. However, most initial programs focused on the narrow objective of ICT literacy, focusing mainly on technology itself rather than incorporation of ICT to fulfill broader educational objectives. Most programs of this nature, which were often initiated in an attempt to address issues related to the 'digital divide', did not take a holistic approach to ICT, failing to link the educational goal of expanded ICT use to associated reforms of the curriculum, student assessment system, pedagogical approaches in the classroom, and teacher training. Technological use in education is limited by more stress on acquisition of latest technology rather than application and integration of technology. Although such attempts may give success for short term, the real use of application of ICT in education needs to have a holistic approach for any long term gain.

INFORMATION TECHNOLOGY AND EDUCATION

Changes in established patterns of life and necessary expertise are taking place as a consequence of globalization, ICT technologies and emergence of knowledge economy. Newer information technologies and business processes are transforming business practices. Training has become an indispensable part of adaptation and change (Summers, 2004). Information and communication technology has become an important part in most organizations and businesses (Zhang and Aikman 2007). Several researchers have concluded that ICT will be an important part of future education (Bransford, Brown &Cocking, 2000, Grimus, 2000, Yelland 2001).

Research studies in ICT and education have stressed the role of ICT in education should be comprehensive and holistic. Researchers like O'Hara (2007) proposed that changes in education away from the industrial age in which they were founded, should address mission, curriculum content, pedagogy and modes of inquiry. Several studies have concluded that modern technology has major role to play in education. Means of teaching and learning in the classroom can be improved by modern technology (Lebebvre, Deaudelin & Loiselle, 2006).New technologies can provide new opportunities for communication and curriculum thereby influencing the way teaching is done (Dawes, 2001, Schoepp 2005). Use of digital technology can help in knowledge dissemination and also help in reduction of direct instruction (Iding, Crosby& Speitel, 2002, Shamantha, Pressini & Meymaris, 2004, Romeo, 2006). Technology can help students complete learning tasks better (Grabe &Grabe, 2007).

Across the world there is a digital divide which separates those with competencies and skills to benefit from computer use to those without it. Since the year 2000 and with the rapid proliferation and use of internet the world has become increasingly interconnected and digital and the skills required

from students in industrial economy have begun to shift to skills required in knowledge economy. This is mainly about finding creative solutions to newer changing set of problems. The spread of ICT in education across the world especially in the developing countries is slower. There have been a number of factors impeding the wholesale uptake of ICT in education across all sectors. These have included such factors as a lack of funding to support the purchase of the technology, a lack of training among established teaching practitioners, a lack of motivation and need among teachers to adopt ICT as teaching tools.

In several Arab states there is a rapid introduction of internet access devices and a surge in mobile phone usage. Furthermore, businesses and educational sector are readily accepting newer technologies. Examples of these include the pioneering Tejari e-marketplace to support multinationals and corporations in streamlining business and trading functions. Similarly, governments of Arab states are moving towards

E-governance in terms of online operations, migration of major government activities like customs, procurement and citizen management capabilities to electronic platforms. In educational sector also usage of online methods along with traditional techniques are now being used. Although for past several years courses were framed around textbooks and academicians have propagated the use of lectures, tutorials as well as presentations designed to consolidate and rehearse the content, contemporary setting now promotes curriculum which highlights competency and performance. Curriculums are starting to emphasize more on how to use information rather than what the information is.

The move to competency and performance-based curricula are well supported and encouraged by emerging instructional technologies. Students using ICTs for learning purposes become immersed in the process of learning and as more and more students use computers as information sources and cognitive tools, learning capabilities of students are enhanced by influence of technology (Reeves & Jonassen, 1996). The role of teacher is now changing, providing more opportunities for the instructor to offer better learning to students and increased opportunities for others like workplace mentors, trainers and specialists to participate in the process. It is only through support of ICT technologies that an expanded pool of teachers with varying roles is able to encourage and support learners in a variety of flexible settings. New ICT applications are being incorporated at a rapid pace in education. And within this changed pool of teachers will come changed responsibilities and skill sets for future teaching involving high levels of ICT and the need for more facilitative than didactic teaching roles.

Another area of concern is the funding of ICT in educational sector. The main pillars of knowledge economy are the following:

1. Educated and skilled population
2. Economic and institutional regime that encourages use of knowledge and entrepreneurship
3. Information and communication infrastructure to support technology diffusion

In the education sector major changes are taking place in the Arab world. One notable change is the funding pattern. The changes in funding pattern taking place in Arab world are as follows:

1. Reduction in public allocations
2. Encouragement of private sector especially in higher education
3. Decreasing financial services for education

In this, the major emerging factor is the private sector becoming an alternative to higher education funding. Many private and semi-private universities have come up all through the Arab world without sufficient planning, infrastructure and qualified personnel. The model of western world for private universities was not emulated but these universities were encouraged to solve social problems rather than with an end objective to improve quality of education and research activities.

The region, as a whole, has made progress in the access to and use of ICT. However, teledensity levels remain below 10% in most countries. The penetration of personal computers is considered to be the main cause of the gap in ICT markets. The Arab region, with 5% of world population, represents less than 1% of the world internet population (Dutta, 2003).

ICT AND EDUCATION IN THE ARAB WORLD

Any change in the region can only be done through regional integration especially in the field of education, new technological opportunities such as open universities and virtual universities show a lot of promise. The notable joint programs in education are the Arab League Education, Science and Cultural Organization and Kuwait based Arab Open University.

In the Arab world there is huge illiteracy, notably among women. This can be attributed to the following:

1. Less emphasis on early childhood education
2. Lack of alternative modes of learning
3. Selective exclusion of girls in basic and higher education
4. Non continuation of education due to family pressures or other factors

The quality of Arab education is not high. This can be mainly attributed to:

1. Low preference given to technical education, science and engineering
2. Neglect of mother tongue as required for growth of innovation and creativity

3. Restriction of freedom, lack of qualified teachers, poor content and pedagogy as well as evaluation which hamper quality education

Especially in higher education many franchisee organizations of western universities based on the same model as parent universities have come up in several Arab states.

The information and communication technology (ICT) sector has become the hallmark of all knowledge economies with the aim of sustainable social and economic development. Across the world the digital divide i.e. difference between connected and unconnected population is the main focus of ICT strategies of governments. Effective development and usage of ICT technologies can have far reaching consequences for education growth.ICT incorporation in development of hinges articulates on three main axes:

1. ICT Environment
2. ICT Readiness
3. ICT Usage

ICT Environment

Environment is mainly concerned with conducive setting for ICT development. This mainly involves an analysis of regulation, government support, IT skills access to population, cost, funding and leadership.

The following cases make an interesting study.

Jordan

The government of Jordan with the aim of becoming a regional and international force in ICT and to realize the full potential of ICT in the region embarked upon the REACH initiative in 1999. The Information Technology Association of Jordan (INTAJ) represents and promotes domestic software and IT services industry in the global market.

At the local, national and regional level cooperation was embarked for:

1. Support for schemes involving technology incubation and encouragement to start-ups in this field
2. Setting up of information and telecommunication centers
3. Setting network of partner institutions

With an IT agenda for the region, United Nations Development Program has initiated a project called Information and Communication Technology for Development in the Arab Region (ICTDAR). The aim of ICTDAR is the propagation and proliferation of IT especially among less developed areas, growth of IT education, promotion of ICT in small and medium enterprises and formation of a number of bilateral and multilateral joint ventures and encouraging small and medium enterprises to improve their IT systems and promoting e-government initiatives in the Arab region.

In the area of telecommunication systems, which are a backbone of ICT technologies, major improvements are required. Mobile phones proliferation is more than landline. This has resulted mainly because of liberalization of mobile markets and monopolization of fixed line telephony in most of Arab states. Mobile penetration is growing at a high rate.

Egypt

The government declared ICT a national priority in Sep 1999. The first implication for this was the creation of separate ministry for Information and Communication Technology in October 1999. The major milestone of this was a three year plan for growth of ICT sector and proliferation of IT technologies to education and business sector. This would facilitate long term growth of the economy. The initiatives are enumerated below:

1. The Computer for Every Home initiative is to provide end-users with PCs at affordable prices. The number of PCs sold reached 48,000 (November 2003). PC penetration remains low at 2.3%.

2. The Free Internet Initiative main focus is to increase the number of Internet users from 1 million in January 2002 to 2.5 million in November 2003 through 940,000 connected households. (El-Berr & El-Mikawy, 2004).

3. The Nile Technology University is a non-profit university specializing in information technology. Nile Tech puts strong emphasis on applied research and development, as well as on graduating the middle managers and future entrepreneurs of Egypt.

4. The Information Technology Institute (ITI) was established by IDSC to provide specialized software development programs for new graduates and training programs and IT courses for the Egyptian ministries, and local decision support centers. ITI also provides IT training materials in Arabic to promote local language content.

5. The Smart Schools Network aims to introduce IT education in schools. The network aims to enhance public and private sector partnership to promote computer usage in schools.

6. The Global Campus Initiative which was launched in 1997 by the Regional Information Technology and Software Engineering Centre (RITSEC), focuses on distance learning tools by promoting a global e-learning community. It involves many e-learning programs and services. It provides many executive courses jointly with World Bank Institute through its Global Distance Learning Center (GDLC).

7. The ICT Clubs model is a public-private sector initiative to bring affordable internet access across the country. The model has been proposed by Ministry of education with the purpose to connect all schools to the internet. A large number of such centers are based in villages and deprived areas. Users are provided basic training as well as guidance by instructors. All the equipment and software necessary for the club is provided by the government. It has also provided employment opportunities to graduates who join the Training of Trainers program.

8. The Egyptian Universities Network focuses on exchange of data between universities through inter university collaboration.

9. Small and Medium Enterprise Businesses is supported by Microsoft Egypt to promote the SME industry with a special focus on empowering women. The project was created by RITSEC, in partnership with the government of Egypt. The project has a special focus on empowering unemployed women through IT skills training and qualifications thus creating job opportunities for women in the SME industry. The aim is to empower SME businesses through the use of ICT to enhance productivity, market share and open international business avenues. The project focuses on IT training programs for small and medium enterprises which encourage young people to set up their own businesses.

ICT Readiness

It involves the access to technology, skills required to use it as well as desire for usage. Positive environment encourages opportunities which can be capitalized by governments, businesses and individuals.

The main elements of ICT readiness are:

*   **ICT infrastructure:** Syria, Egypt and Oman have less than 50 residential lines per 1000 households. Egypt, Jordan and Morocco have the highest bandwidth per account in the Arab region (Dutta, 2003).

*   **PC acquisition and connection charges:** The import duties and taxes are highest on

PCs in the countries Egypt, Morocco, Syria and Jordan in the Arab region. Internet penetration continues to increase as costs are lowered.

The region suffers from a large public sector, over-regulation, bureaucracy, and control of information. However, there are important differences within the region. Jordan and the U.A.E. are somewhat on the forefront, and some countries like Egypt have already used e-governance to promote transparency and availability of information. The MENA countries' readiness for the knowledge economy indicates that the MENA countries' overall knowledge economy position is not in line with their level of economic development.

The major obstacle in readiness is government support at grassroots level as well as lack of inter-departmental coordination within the government.

- **Usage:** It involves proliferation of IT use in businesses and also involves the promotion of e-government usage such that citizens and businesses are benefited by the use of technology which increases speed, access and transparency. It also extends to promotion of usage among household with the aim to increase information and access to knowledge

The usage of ICT can only be widespread if trained professionals are available. These professionals should not only be proficient in ICT usage but professionals are also required for training initiatives by governments. This can only be done through alignment with universities. In most Arab countries the following initiatives are required:

1. Collaboration with universities
2. Funding for universities
3. Promotion of degree programs in ICT
4. Setting up of training institutes

5. Development of ICT eco system
6. Promotion of e –learning
7. Promotion of IT skills for all students
8. Collaboration with world renowned universities in education

The following countries are initiating the programs:

Egypt

The government initiated a program for the training of 5000 professionals a year. The ministry of communications and information technology concentrates on development of manpower equipped to deal with ICT challenges. A large number of information technology institutes are planned to open throughout the country.

Jordan

Similarly in Jordan under the REACH initiative, training programs and universities encouragement is being initiated. In Jordan, IT Community Centers Initiatives was launched in 1999 to promote the use of internet by disadvantaged communities. Sixty such centers have been developed in a phased approach. Many world renowned IT firms are choosing Arab countries as their regional headquarters.

Since online Arabic content is in nascent stage, this has deterred the spread of ICT in Arab world. Microsoft Middle East has developed BBC Arabic to widen the user base. However much is needed to be done in terms of online Arabic software development and usage. This is the cornerstone of all education i.e. the development and integration of local language online. Development of Arabic software industry not only adds value to industrial activity but could be a source of employment activity also.

ECONOMIC, INSTITUTIONAL, AND INNOVATIVE PARTNERSHIPS

Knowledge economies are always based on the pillars of science and technology. Research and development in Arab countries is not high, especially in fields of science, engineering and technology. R&D institutions are plagued by regulations, bureaucracy and red tape, lack of funding and support from government as well as incentives for collaboration with the industry. Private sector cooperation and contribution is the key source of development. Collaboration with global research centers and universities as well as removal of restrictions on import of technologies promotes sustainable development of ICT growth.

The GDNet MENA Regional Window is a part of the GDNet (Global Development Network). The main aim of GDNet is to create a network of researchers and organizations from MENA through knowledge databank, access to research and dissemination of knowledge. This is one of the pioneering and innovative initiatives which has promotion of ICT in Arab education as one of the major end objectives.

SOLUTIONS AND RECOMMENDATIONS

One major inherent difficulty in use of ICT in education is the comprehensive nature of technology which can be used in many ways and at the same time can pose many challenges. Although the obvious advantages of use of ICT in education are to act as important driver of educational reforms, act as a lever for organizational change, as a vehicle to introduce new teaching and learning practices and as an enabler for educational reforms. ICT's can facilitate various education delivery models, professional development programs for teachers, education data collection and processing in a much faster and easier way. National research education networks can form a building block linking research activities, researchers and projects which can help governments identify focus areas facilitated by ICT enabled services. A major role can also be played by ICT is by making systems more efficient and transparent which in turn can help in anti corruption efforts in education sector.

Emerging ICT tools may also be a new opportunity provider for basic literacy programs where technology facilitation can encourage and supplement formal teaching methods for greater access. Changes in technology are faster than education changes which means that technology life cycles are shorter than education reforms life cycle. This poses many challenges as pace of reforms in education should be faster to keep pace with new and emergent technology as it may be possible that reforms may be dependent on technology (hardware, software, and training) which is obsolete or no longer available. This is a major challenge in developing countries in the Arab world which have to keep pace of technological innovation with institutional innovation.

While education driven by technology is becoming more and more learner centric it cannot replace the major role played by teachers in education and learning process. In fact the newer modes of education using ICT only supplement the process of learning rather than replace the role of teacher. This realization is already there in the western world that enabling technologies are as important as the teachers who facilitate them. Global experience highlights than learning process can be facilitated by using technology as a tool rather than an end in itself.

ICT introduction is usually associated with equity issues. The general belief is that uses of ICT can further marginalize group which are usually excluded from existing educational environments. Especially in the Arab countries this group could include women, special needs students, ethnic minorities, students in remote areas and very low income communities. However ICT use can facilitate the inclusion of these marginalized groups which can get access to education through use of internet and other telecommunication medium resulting in more involvement and empowerment. This can mainly be achieved through government support and encouragement.

The catalogue of ICT technologies is not limited to Internet, computers or laptops but with a host of other options which can be used by Arab countries to improve quality and access of education. These include tools like mobile phones, interactive whiteboards, IP TV, tablet devices like iPad and other scientific equipments used for learning including traditional technologies like radio and television and newer devices like gaming consoles etc.

The diffusion of ICT in education affects the learning process in terms of mode of education, delivery of courses and learning processes but is also related to the overall system of education which for example may be inclusive of monitoring teacher attendance, payment of salaries, student's database as well as school database. ICT uses should have a more system wide application and approach rather through the narrow approach of limiting its use only to learning process. This has wider implication for the whole education system of a country and requires policy initiatives and encouragement at government level. This might also involve changes in regulations, funding of ICT initiatives and monitoring of ICT systems implementation and usage. It requires integrative approach not an isolated one.

Proper utilization of ICT in education presents a huge opportunity to Arab World which can help in sustainable development and empowerment of communities, help them to occupy important position in the world's geo-informatics landscape. It can also help in providing access to education for programs related to adult literacy, primary education as well as tertiary and higher education. This can help to bridge the digital divide between countries in the Arab world and within the countries. Growth of Arab world is also dependent on regional cooperation between countries in reference to information exchange,

research collaboration and faculty exchange and infrastructure collaboration. All this is easily facilitated by the use of appropriate information and communication technologies. This would help the Arab countries integrate efforts towards building knowledge economies enabled by ICT. Arab States need to achieve the balance required to include traditional economy, knowledge economy, and building a strong industry for Arabic content in order to build the society of information and knowledge.

CONCLUSION

Worldwide there has been a lot of focus on the use of computers to increase the efficiency and effectiveness of education at every level and in both non-formal and formal settings. This involves a mix of old and new technologies inclusive of internet and computers as well as radio, television and telephony. A notable development is the increasing use of e-learning which is gaining acceptance in all levels of education through the use of information technology. The major problems facing the Arab world are limited infrastructure and attendant high cost of access. Also the existence of digital divide which is the gap between those who have access to and control of technology and those who do not, is the most challenging aspect of introduction and integration of education at all levels of education and all modes of education.

In order to improve access to education and quality of education innovative and creative applications of ICT in education setting should be used to initiate education reforms. There are many factors which impede the uptake of ICT in education in Arab world which include lack of funding to support purchase of technology, lack of training among educational workforce and lack of integration of technology to the larger ecosystem of education. Governments are increasingly reducing public allocations and encouraging private sector in education. Private sector is becoming an alternative to higher education funding. Many private and semi-private universities have come up all across Middle East. However they are plagued by insufficient infrastructure, poor planning and lack of trained personnel.

Any change in the region can only be done through regional integration especially in the field of education. New technological opportunities such as open universities and virtual universities show a lot of promise. In the Arab world there is huge illiteracy notably among women and also the quality of Arab education is not high. This is mainly because of low preference given to technical education, science and engineering and neglect of mother tongue.

Development of Arabic software would add value to industrial activity as well could be a source of employment. National research education networks can form a building block linking research activities, researchers and projects which can help governments identify focus areas facilitated by ICT enabled services. Emerging ICT tools may also be a new opportunity provider for basic literacy programs where technology facilitation can encourage and supplement formal teaching methods for greater access.

Proper utilization of ICT in education presents a huge opportunity to Arab World which can help in sustainable development and empowerment of communities and thus help them to occupy important position in the world's geo-informatics landscape and an important position in the knowledge economies in the world.

REFERENCES

Bransford, B. A., & Cocking, R. R. (2000). *How people learn: Brain, mind, experience & school* (2nd ed.). Washington, DC: National Academy Press.

Dawes, L. (2001). What stops teachers using new technology? In Leask, M. (Ed.), *Issues in teaching using ICT* (pp. 61–79). London, UK: Routledge.

Dutta, S. (2003). Challenges for information and communication technology development in the Arab world. In Cornelius, P., & Schwab, K. (Eds.), *Arab world competitiveness report 2002-2003* (p. 197). New York, NY: Oxford University Press.

El Berr, S., & El Mikawy, N. (2004). *Regional perspectives on educational reforms in the Arab countries*. Retrieved August 8, 2011, from http://www.zef.de/fileadmin/webfiles/downloads/projects/el-mikawy/study_regional_perspectives.pdf

Grabe, M., & Grabe, C. (2007). *Integrating technology for meaningful learning* (5th ed.). Boston, MA: Houghton Mifflin.

Grimus, M. (2000). *ICT and multimedia in primary school*. Paper presented at the 16th Conference on Educational Uses of Information and Communication Technologies, Beijing, China.

Iding, M., Crosby, M. E., & Speitel, T. (2002). Teachers and technology: Beliefs and practices. *International Journal of Instructional Media*, *29*(2), 153–171.

Lebebvre, S., Deaudelin, D., & Loiselle, J. (2006, 27-30 November). *ICT implementation stages of primary school teachers: The practices and conceptions of teaching and learning*. Paper presented at the Australian Association for Research in Education, National Conference, Adelaide, Australia

O'Hara, M. (2007). Strangers in a strange land: Knowing, learning and education for the global knowledge society. *Futures*, *39*(8), 930–941. doi:10.1016/j.futures.2007.03.006

Reeves, T. C., & Oh, E. J. (2007). Generation differences and educational technology research. In Spector, J. M., Merrill, M. D., van Merriënboer, J. J. G., & Driscoll, M. (Eds.), *Handbook of research on educational communications and technology* (pp. 295–303). Mahwah, NJ: Lawrence Erlbaum Associates.

Romeo, G. (2006). Engage, empower, enable: Developing a shared vision of technology in education. In Khine, M. S. (Ed.), *Engaged learning and emerging technologies*. The Netherlands: Springer Science. doi:10.1007/1-4020-3669-8_8

Schoepp, K. (2005). Barriers to technology integration in a technology rich environment. *Learning and Teaching in Higher Education: Gulf Perspectives*, *2*(1), 1–24.

Shamantha, J. H., Pressini, D., & Meymaris, K. (2004). Technology supported mathematics activities situated within an effective learning environment theoretical framework. *Contemporary Issues in Technology & Teacher Education*, *3*(4), 362–381.

Summers, G. J. (2004). Today's business simulation industry. *Simulation & Gaming*, *35*(2), 208–241. doi:10.1177/1046878104263546

Yelland, N. (2001). *Teaching and learning with information and communication technologies (ICT) for numeracy in the early childhood and primary years of schooling*. Australia: Department of Education, Training and Youth Affairs.

Zhang, P., & Aikman, S. (2007). Attitudes in ICT acceptance and use. In Jacko, J. (Ed.), *Human-computer interaction* (pp. 1021–1130). Berlin, Germany: Springer-Verlag.

ADDITIONAL READING

Andrews, R., & Haythornthwaite, C. (Eds.). (2007). *The SAGE handbook of e-learning research*. London, UK: SAGE Publications.

Coiro, J., & Dobler, E. (2007). Exploring the online reading comprehension strategies used by sixth-grade skilled readers to search for and locate information on the Internet. *Reading Research Quarterly*, *42*(2), 214–257. doi:10.1598/RRQ.42.2.2

Cuban, L. (2001). *Oversold and underused: Computers in the classroom*. Cambridge, MA: Harvard University Press.

El-Sanabary, N. (1992). *Education in the Arab Gulf states and the Arab world: An annotated bibliography*. New York, NY: Routledge.

Selwyn, N. (2010). *Schools and schooling in the digital age: A critical analysis*. London, EnglanddUK: Routledge.

KEY TERMS AND DEFINITIONS

Digital Divide: Digital divide is the disparity between the "haves" and the "have-nots" in the technology revolution.

E Learning: Electronic learning (e-Learning) is computer and network enabled education system. It is inclusive of web based learning, computer based learning and digital collaboration.

GDNet: The Global Development Network (GDNet) is the biggest network of scientific organizations in the development field. It combines 4000 organizations, 8000 scientists and 15000 papers in its knowledge base. It gives a centralized access to huge amounts of data used in developmental studies and policy framework.

ICT: Information and communication technology is a wide term that encompasses communication devices or applications inclusive of television, radio, mobile phones, computer and network hardware and software, satellite systems as well as services and applications associated with them like video conferencing and distance learning.

REACH: The REACH Initiative, Jordan's first national information technology strategy, was launched in 1999. The strategy included a five-year detailed action plan to develop the information technology industry in Jordan.

Virtual University: It characterizes an organization that provides education and learning opportunity through architected web-portal on the Internet.

Chapter 11
Information Systems in UAE Education Sector:
Security, Cultural, and Ethical Issues

Abbas Naser
Ministry of Education, Bahrain

Reem Jaber
Al Ain Primary School, UAE

Ibtisam Jaber
Hafsa School, Oman

Khalidah Saeed
Cognition Education, UAE

ABSTRACT

This chapter demonstrates some of the most important issues pertaining to information systems, such as security, ethics, and culture in the Arab education sector. Despite the fact that there is an evident shortage of references on this important topic in the Arab region context, the authors managed to gather sufficient information to develop a reasonable insight that has led to suggesting recommendations for improvement in future studies. They demonstrate how the concerned issues are managed in the Arab region, with specific interest and focus at the UAE context. Ethics in information systems are very important, especially as information systems are global by nature; its impact cannot be limited. The UAE is part of the GCC countries, which represent the richest Arab countries, yet ethics are highly regarded. The second part of the chapter discusses information systems security issue related and the third is focused on the cultural issues. Although, separated for the purpose of research, cultural and ethical issues are inter-related and are very important, because both directly reflect the society's morals, traditions, language, customs, et cetera.

INTRODUCTION

In the technology and information era, increasing numbers of people are using computers that are connected through networks for communication between users. Unfortunately, the use of computers has caused new problems involving hardware theft and infringement of software copyright laws. Computer technology largely influences the development of any country and has many positive benefits presented in the use of both software and hardware. However, there are some negative aspects which may occur as a result of these benefits. The infringement of copyright laws,

DOI: 10.4018/978-1-4666-1984-5.ch011

the unlawful acquisition of private information, disputes over software patents, and the spread of electronic viruses across networks, are parts of those negative aspects.

There are so many definitions of information system. According to Wikipedia, Information System is any combination of Information Technology and people's activities that support operations management and decision making are related to the interaction by people, processes, data and technology. It is also a form of a communication system in which data is presented and processed as a form of social memory. The value of information professional systems stems from a breadth of knowledge and skills. Another definition of IS, given in an encyclopedia describes it as a system consisting of the network of all communication channels used within an organization. We may have so many other definitions, but the main components of IS are there.

Information systems have so many aspects. Security, Culture and Ethics which have become very important issues we deal with in IS. In this paper, we will try to cover the basic concerns related to each of these issues. Our focus will be on the Arab world in general and the United Arab Emirates specifically.

Educational Information System

Any educational organization or school nowadays is using information systems to do its work and develop education all over the world. (Ala M. & Rima Sh., 2008) "Hence, Telem and Avidov (1994) define a School Information System (SIS) as a specialized Management Information System (MIS) that "matches the structure, management tasks, instructional process and special needs of the school". On the other hand, Information Technology in Education Management can bring a number of the benefits to a large number of stakeholders (administrators, teachers, students and parents) in educational institutions. These benefits include but not limited to: improving information

quality, saving time and efforts and improving control and utilization of school resources (Barta et al., 1991). In addition, the use of Information Technology in Education Management (ITEM) could facilitate the activities related to school management, student registration, and fee collection, reporting and timetabling (Friedman, 1994). Furthermore, school administration can use ITEM in all steps of the decision-making process to improve productivity (efficiency and effectiveness), labor quality and organizational structure (Barta et al., 1991; Oostheok, 1989; Visscher, 1988, 1991, 1996)." In addition, there are many types of educational information technology which can be used in educational organizations to enhance the learning as well as the teaching processes and facilitate them. However, we can mention here some of these technologies like the internet which is the most important instrument which is used to open the door of educational technology for other technologies types. Furthermore, there are some web sites which serve as resources of educational information, for example, Electronic Resources Portal (ERP) for education, Wiki and some social networks, such as Facebook and Twitter. On the other hand, there are some other types of educational technologies that can play an effective role in delivering information in successful educational organizations. They vary in their designs, purposes and the way of managing each one for instance, the Electronic learning, Discussion board, Blogs and Smart boards. So, over these varied types of technology and expanding number of users, there should be frameworks to manage them. In information sectors, these frameworks are information ethics. In this case, there is a need to identify them and discuss their characteristics.

Information Ethics

Information ethics have developed recently, encompassing areas such as computer ethics and global information ethics. It deals with the moral conduct of information-users based on their responsibility and their accountability. Furthermore, a system of laws classifies the most important and significant ethical standards, and provides an appropriate mechanism for holding people, organizations or any unethical activities of the government. IT mostly creates ethical problems, like infringement of others' privacy, and these ethical problems produce unexpected dynamics. At the same time, increasing processing power, storage capacities, and networking capabilities in IT can greatly extend the reach of individual actions and magnify their impact. As a result, information technology may present new temptations with the potential to make huge and disastrous impacts (Laudon and Laudon, 1996).

Information technology involves the conflict between observing others' privacy, and the simultaneous pursuit of the individual freedom and autonomy. Privacy is the moral right of the individuals to be left alone and in charge of the information they let others know about them. However, governments, private organizations, or individuals are interested in learning individuals' personal information, new information technologies pose problems for the protection of intellectual property (Branscomb, 1995).

On the other hand, intellectual property includes all the tangible and intangible products of the human mind. There are three forms of intellectual property protection: patents, copyrights, and trade secrets. Patents protect inventions in machine processes, including underlying principles behind patented inventions. Copyrights protect the expression of ideas but not the underlying idea itself. Trade secrets protect any intellectual product, such as formulas, product ideas, and methods of doing business, computer programs and database compilations (Chien-Pen Ch. & Joseph C., 1999). However, to avoid and protect other's right to privacy, everyone who deals with information system and technology has to learn all the laws about protective intellectual products. In order to deal with information ethics there are some characteristics one could use to recognize them; next section gives some characterization.

Characteristics of Information Ethics

Information ethics is a very important concept that needs care and attention whenever working with information systems. In other words, we assume that information ethics in the future should be a discipline that carries out functions. It has several characteristics that could make it clearly appear for everyone. Hoeunng and Soeongjinis (2004) have found some of these characteristics and mentioned in these points:

- Information ethics should be preventive to give us the amount of support to consider the development of information and technology which produces types of ethical problems.
- It is prescriptive ethics which make out all fundamentals of information society behaviors.
- Transformation ethics is another feature of information ethics. It should focus on the necessity of human experience and the variation of the system and policy.
- Information ethics must consist of global and local disciplines. So, it must be described as universally global ethics.
- It must promote behavior as a sense of responsibility, considering the possibility of an action according to the view of the means and a method, while comparing a purpose to incidental result. It is responsibility ethics.
- Information ethics must establish and apply various ethical theories that are useful in solving ethical problems in both direct and indirect ways.

However, there is an importance to identify the reasons behind existence of these ethics of information. Information ethics format to reach specific goals in any society of information. We need to clarify them and know their principles.

Goals and Basic Principles of Information Ethics

In information society, the education related to information ethics sites has four goals according to description of Hoeung Ki. and Soeongjin Ahn. (2004), They are: First, respect for others must be cultivated. Second, although sharing beneficial information but other people's intellectual property right must not be infringed. Third, various forms of information will be used productively. Fourth, telecommunications and the Internet will be used for acceptable time periods so that it does not harm actual life.

Furthermore, Severson, 2000, presented that there are four basic principles of information ethics. Firstly there is the respect of the intellectual property, which stands on the basis of a cultural conviction that original work remains the property of its owner. Secondly, there is the respect of privacy, which we have to deal with actively with more specific information. Thirdly, there is a proper mark, which related to show sellers and inform customers about goods and services. This is when ethics teaches us the ethical root of the responsibility. Fourthly, there is the prohibition of mischief, which means to refrain from damaging other people, directly or indirectly. However, this could encourage us to develop as well improving our ethics of information systems to save our information either from computer crime or piracies (hacking). It should be understood that hacking is a criminal offence, hurting other people also; methods for protecting an individual's computer system should be taught.

The chapter aims to identify the information systems and their ethics issue in the educational organizations of the UAE. In the other words, we could start with a brief description of the system of education in UAE.

UAE Education System

The Educational System structure in the UAE consists of primary and secondary schools. At six years of age, a student starts at a primary public school. The student spends five years at the first unit (levels 1-5), four years at cycle 2 (levels 6-9) and three years at a secondary school (levels 10-12). The structure and characteristics of the primary public schools in seven Emirates of the UAE is similar. The Ministry of Education (MOE) is committed to invest in technology, to improve schools infrastructure and devolve some of its authority to the nine Educational zones (Abu Dhabi educational zone, Al Ain Educational zone, Al-Gharbia Educational zone, Dubai Educational zone, Sharjah Educational zone, Ajman Educational zone, Ras-Al-Khaimah Educational zone, Al-Fujira Educational zone and Um Al- Quwain Educational zone) in line with its decentralization policy (MOE, 2011).

The UAE is a real example of the great country which trusts on what can recognize and achieve in order to develop successful information systems in its Educational organizations. In order to find a healthy information society in its Educational organizations, it must be built a clear and strong basic to protect its organizations and their participants by putting the information ethics in hands of their users.

Information System Ethics of Educational Organization in the UAE

School information systems in the UAE can be considered as an early sporadic experience rather than a planned diffusion of Information and Communication Technologies (ICT) and Information Systems (IS). In fact, many threats exist today in many forms including unacceptable acts performed by people (including cyber criminals of diverse type). Abu Dhabi Education Council (ADEC) established Information Security Policies to clearly articulate what business rules will follow to improve the information security posture as it relates to the protection of its people and information in a safe, practical and cost-effective manner. It provides guidance and direction to develop operational procedures that achieve the ADEC Management's goals and requirement for the protection of ADEC information assets (ADEC, 2009). It describes many sectors and issues which should be included in any educational organization in the country and has arrangements of the participants' rights and duties.

Through these policies which were identified by ADEC, we can figure out the information ethics of the Educational organization of the UAE. In fact, there are ethics arranged to protect information against misuse and harm.

However, there are different types of technologies used in Educational organizations of the UAE. Instances of these types of technologies are Emails, Voicemails, Internet, Mobiles and laptops. On the other hand, these technologies are used by administrators, students, teachers and other workers of these organizations in order to discuss the information ethics of information and technology in Educational organizations of the UAE, we have to clarify each technology with its ethics as following according to ADEC (2009):

First: Email Rules of Ethics

These rules give the users of all Educational organizations a method for using emails ethically.

- Outbound emails must have a disclaimer.
- Using email facilities for business transactions or educational purposes. Emails can be legally binding.
- Creating or sending unsolicited, unwanted, irrelevant or inappropriate messages and chain letters is prohibited.

- Opening unknown or suspicious attachments or clicking on links in emails from unknown senders is prohibited.
- Emails are owned and monitored by ADEC.
- Providing an ADEC email address to mailing lists, blogs, forums etc or to subscribing to Internet sites that are not related to ADEC is prohibited.
- Outbound emails must be encrypted.

Second: Internet Rules of Ethics

The ethics in using Internet of any educational organizations arranged as following:

- Viewing or downloading inappropriate material (offensive, sexual images, jokes and comments, or any other comments that would be expected to offend someone based on their physical or mental disability, age, religion, marital status, sexual orientation, political beliefs, national origin) is prohibited.
- Internet Usage is monitored by ADEC's IT department.
- Using the Internet to attempt unauthorized access to other computers, information or services is prohibited.
- Downloading or copying of copyrighted material, including software, books, articles, and photographs etc, which are not licensed for the use by ADEC is prohibited.
- Undertaking any activity that may introduce viruses or other malicious software on ADEC's network is prohibited.

Third: Voicemail Rules of Ethics

It contains two rules of ethics to be considered:

- Staff must only leave messages that contain no sensitive information.

- The owner of voicemail box must regularly check incoming messages and delete messages already listened to as soon as possible.

Fourth: Mobile Rules of Ethics

Using mobiles technology to exchange or deliver information. Some information of these organizations could be filled under the following rules of ethics:

- Lost or stolen devices must be reported immediately.
- Mobile Devices must be encrypted (depends on sensitivity).
- Lockout settings must be enabled in order to loc devices when not in use.
- A password settings must be in compliance with password polices.
- Timeout and lockout settings must be appropriate.

Fifth: Laptop Use Rules of Ethics

Educational organizations of the UAE supplement the laptops as one of information technology for their participants. The following points identified the laptop use rules of ethics:

- Laptops must not operate without a firewall.
- Laptops must have up to date antivirus software installed.
- Passwords settings will be in compliance with password policies.
- Information residing on laptop must be encrypted at all the time.
- Modifications to security settings (port, firewall, antivirus etc…) are prohibited.
- Timeout and lockout settings will be appropriate.

Sixth: Publicly Rules of Ethics

There is one rule of ethics which can be mentioned on this technology related to ADEC\s classifications:

- Care must be taken to protect the integrity of electronically published information. Formal authorization must be obtained before any information is made publicly available in order to ensure it is accurate and complies with quality standards.

Whenever, all stakeholders in any Educational organization follow those rules and take them as important ethics in all information societies they deal with the privacy right and intellectual property will be protected. However, ADEC put good disciplines in order to find a protected information system which can help all stakeholders in any educational organizations in the country.

In order to ensure that all stakeholders have access to the information at any given point of time and they use it ethically, ADEC established Access control. It talks about how users access management, what are the user's access rights and users identifications and authentication. In addition, how different technologies in educational organizations should be managed, procedures of access, and ways of connecting and maintaining (ADEC, 2004).

Information Systems and Security Issues

One of the most crucial factors which strongly affects the success and progress of information systems are the security issues related to them. Generally, security refers to the absence of risks and dangers. Similarly, information systems security means preventing unauthorized recipients from accessing information which can lead to its destruction or alteration. So, information systems security can be defined as the protection of information from various, different threats. To achieve this, we have to preserve the characteristics of confidentiality, integrity and availability. Consequently, this will assist in the continuous operation of the organization's services and its ability to keep up with the daily usual business. Tomas Olovsson defines a secure system as one which offers people enough trust allowing them to use it with sensitive information.

The Significance of Information System Security

The world of information technology is going through numerous, endless changes everyday which by no doubt enhances the use of IS, but it also brings other various kinds of threats. These threats call for more attention on security by all participants whether they were governments, organizations or individuals.

As a result of the increased use of the internet and the way it dominates even our daily simple life, we notice that it gradually replaces the stand-alone systems in closed networks. (The OECD Council 2002). Recently, participants have become more and more interconnected and these connections go far beyond national borders. In addition, the Internet has developed so much to offer support to critical infrastructures such as energy, transportation and finance and it plays a vital role in how organizations do business, how governments provide services to citizens and enterprises and how individuals communicate and exchange information. The nature and type of technologies that make up the communications and information infrastructure have also changed dramatically. The number and nature of infrastructure access devices have doubled to include fixed, wireless and mobile devices and a growing percentage of access is through connections which are always on. Therefore, the nature, volume and sensitivity of information that is exchanged have expanded considerably.

Social Security Awareness

In order to boost readiness to face to the upcoming security threats, it is very important to raise awareness of certain security issues consistently on both the public and individual levels. Different methods and techniques can be used to raise awareness, such as: websites, press releases, education. Governments other responsible authorities should focus on identifying possible threats and risks and raise awareness of the consequences, in addition to provide suitable safeguards.

As such, parties involved should be fully aware of the Internal and external threats and risks that potentially affect information systems and networks and cause substantial damage as a result of loss of control. The interconnectivity and interdependency to and from others can lead to potential harm.

- Participants should understand the configuration of their systems and that updates are available for them. They must also be aware of where their system stands within networks and what good practices can be implemented to increase security and enhance the needs of others.
- They should make use of adopted safeguards and solutions to deal with repeated threats and vulnerabilities.
- Suitable security goals should be developed to prevent, detect and respond to identified threats and vulnerabilities.
- They should be responsible in a way appropriate to their individual roles.
- They should review their own policies, practices, measures, and procedures regularly and assess whether these are suitable to their current environments

UAE's IS Security Ability

In an article published by WAM, November 11th, 2010, Director General of the UAE's Telecommunications Regulatory Authority (TRA) Mohamed

Nasser Al Ghanim explained that protecting data and information has become a hard task nowadays task because of the highly diversified and developed hacking methods. He added that that they have to keep pace with the fast-paced cyber developments which protect cyber security for governmental departments and private business is a top priority for TRA and that is why the Computer Emergency Response Team (aeCERT) was set up.

The UAE Computer Emergency Response Team (aeCERT)

The UAE Computer Emergency Response Team (aeCERT), introduces a local citizen called SALIM to be the Emirati Cyber first phase of the awareness campaign on how to prevent Internet threats. SALIM will help against cyber threats and guides and supports you towards a safe cyber culture in the UAE.

The aeCERT aims to enhance the cyber security law and assist in the creation of new laws; enhance information security awareness across the UAE; build national expertise in information security, incident management and computer forensics; provide a central trusted point of contact for cyber security incident reporting in the UAE; establish a national center to disseminate information about threats, vulnerabilities, and cyber security incidents; foster the establishment of and provide assistance to sector-based Computer Security Incidents Response Teams (CSIRTs); coordinate with domestic and international CSIRTs and related organizations; and become an active member of recognized security organizations and forums.

Expectations and Recommendations

To start with, individual users need to be aware of possible security risks and the available safeguards for their systems. With this knowledge, they also need to be responsible for maintaining the security of their systems according to their roles. For example, they need to update their systems and software regularly so that known security holes are eliminated from their systems. They also need to understand and implement common security practices, such as, shutting down their computers when leaving the offices and homes, not opening unidentified e-mails, not sharing passwords, introducing anti-virus software and not opening unknown executable files. Individual users need to be instructed and supported by both government and business (suppliers), where appropriate.

Culture and Information System

It is significantly clear that during the past years there has been increasing interest in the influences of cultural differences on the use of technology and information, which in turn had a deep impact on the educational systems everywhere and the international markets which tend to move towards globalism. Many information and technology applications were implemented across the national and cultural boundaries, which during this transfer process caused some problems attributed to the differences between the national cultures of these different organizations.

Definition of Culture

Many articles and books have been written in recent years about the role of "Corporate Culture". Culture is a major factor which directly influences information systems. This is mainly because information systems are context sensitive. In order to make this clear, we must first understand what the word culture means. There are many inter-related definitions for the word culture. The most common to our subject is the following as given in the Wikipedia Dictionary, "The set of shared attitudes, values, goals, and practices that characterizes an institution, organization, or group". Hofstede, (1980), who has done some valuable research on the impact of culture on IS, defines culture as a collective programming of the mind which distinguishes one group from another. He also, later, stated that culture entails mental programming, patterns of thinking and feeling and potential acting (Hofstede, 1991). The word "programming" symbolizes the process which takes place in an organization to grow into a bigger society. Every organization has its own unique culture or value set. Most organizations don't consciously try to create a certain culture. The culture of the organization is typically created unconsciously, based on the values of the top management or the founders of an organization, (Cross Cultural Business Management, P2)

Cultural Issues

Ali & Brooks 2008, say that during the last two decades, 'the practical relevance of researching cultural issues, and especially comparing phenomena across cultures was questioned'. However, the importance of cultural issues is becoming increasingly evident in many applied disciplines including the managing information technology (IT). According to the writers, interest in IS research literature on the impact of cultural differences and on the development and use of information and communications technologies, has been of wide increase. This is mostly because of the interest of many companies to do business on the international level which is highly dominated by the latest communications and information technologies.

The Importance of Culture

It has become clear to the information system researchers how important culture is in designing, managing and developing IS protocols and infrastructure, which in turn encourages them to do extra research and studies on the different cultural phenomena affecting IS and how to make use of that in achieving the targeted goals and improve overall performance. This is highly visible in many different government sectors in the Emirate of Abu Dhabi, where many efforts have

been exerted to improve staff performance and learners achievement using the latest technologies available.

Levels of Culture

According to Ali & Brooks, 2008, IS researchers have studied culture within the IS discipline at different levels, including national, organizational, group (professional or sub-culture) and individual (Subjective Culture). The National Level Culture refers to the culture shared between people in a society or a country. With a culture that people are working in is an organization share, it is called organizational culture. Similarly people working in the same organization and have the same profession or occupation share a professional or occupational culture or sub-culture of a specific interest group. On the other hand, the amount an individual takes from these different cultures which he is part of, is known as individual or subjective culture. These different levels of culture influence an individual's behavior according to the behavior under focus. National cultures have predominant impact on those behaviors that carry a strong social component or have terminal and moral values. Within an organizational context, managerial and work behavior has been influenced by different types of cultures other than national cultures. In addition, behavior is also influenced by different levels of culture, ranging from the national level through organizational levels to the group and other sub-culture levels. These different levels interact and have different influences on individual behavior. These influences vary from one level to the other depending on the situation faced and the values and ethics one has. (p 4 & 5).

The various levels of culture are laterally related (see Figure 1). The levels of culture are not necessarily hierarchical from the more general (national) to the least general (group). For instance, in the case of multinational corporations, organizational culture can span national, professional, and other sub-cultures. Furthermore, groups may include members from several organizations, professions, nations, religions, ethnic backgrounds.

In Figure 1, the area labeled individual represents the subjective culture or the individual level of culture where an individual's culture is the final product of a number of levels of culture. Each individual belongs to a specific national culture. Individuals may also have a religious orientation, a professional degree, belong to a specific ethnic, linguistic group, and so on, which is represented by different sub-culture groups. Individuals may work in an organization, which is represented by organizational culture. Some of these cultures may dominate depending on the situation. The cultures that enfold the individual interact and comprise the individual's unique culture, will eventually affect the individual's subsequent actions and behaviors.

ICT Adaptation in Government Sector

According to Rabaai, 2009", governments are generally enthusiastic about Information and Communication Technology (ICT) adoption, (since these also facilitate digital inclusion in the wider global economy) the phenomenon of globalization means that globally used technologies have not only to be adopted but also adapted into local cultures and to their prevailing norms. This is sometimes problematic, and particularly with technologies such as Enterprise Resource Planning (ERP) systems that embed (Western) assumptions about organizational practices and that impose specific, homogeneous ways of communication through technology there is clear potential for a cultural clash when these do not fit the adopting culture's norms. "As ERP systems diffuse into developing countries, it is essential to be aware of the implications of cultural assumptions embedded in ERP software and those reflected in developing country organizations" (Molla and Loukis, 2005: 3). Avison and Mataurent (2007) for example found that an ERP implementation in China was unsuccessful due to national cultural factors, and other researchers have noted similar issues of culture and business environment affecting implementation success. Across various develop-

Figure 1. Interrelated levels of culture; Source: Adapted from Karahanna et al., 2005

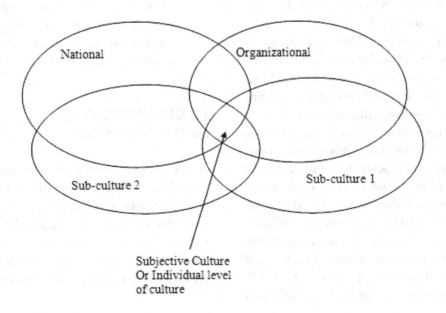

ing countries, Huang and Palvia (2001) identified many factors of national and organisational culture affecting ERP implementation including economic status and growth, infrastructure, government regulation, low IT maturity, small firm size, and lack of process management and BPR experience.

The United Arab Emirates' Culture

The United Arab Emirates is regarded as the highest income Arab country. Relative to its size and oil wealth, the UAE has a small population estimated at 2,624,000 in 1997. The commercial production of oil triggered rapid population growth as a result of improvements in diet, health care, and living standards and the importation on a large scale of mostly male foreign laborers. The latter factor has generated a dependence on expatriate labor and the UAE has become a multiethnic society, and Emirati nationals account for only about 20 percent of the population. About two-thirds of the immigrants are Asians, mainly from India, Pakistan, Iran, Sri Lanka, Bangladesh, and the Philippines. The remainders are Arabs, Europeans, and Americans. The official language is Arabic. Among the immigrant population, English, Hindi, Urdu, Farsi, and Filipino are spoken. English is the language of commerce (Retrieved from the website everyculture.com).

The UAE has made major changes and reforms in both the private and public sectors. "A government without papers", is the logo of the UAE Government. They aim to do all the transactions electronically. This means the implementation of ERP systems (enterprise resource planning) in every organization. By doing this, organizations can benefit a lot, e.g. reducing the costs, organized information and quick access to it anytime and from anywhere. As a result business will develop and performance will improve but the difficulty faced here is the rich multicultural organizations.

It is important that organizations understand their culture and enhance it. This in turn will lead to improved implementation and adaption of Information Systems in those organizations. The UAE culture which highly respects culture and heritage and supports preserving them is one of the first Arab countries heading towards an electronic society,

According to Yeganeh, whenever culture is in agreement with the IT, the following consequences may result:

- It will be clear to us if the implementation of IT will be successfully acceptable
- It provides the pattern for the information usage. In addition, it tells us which information is important, where to take that information from and most importantly to whom we must supply that information.
- It is regarded as an important means of communication, inside and outside of the organization and it also lets us assess how effective was the IT applied to telecommunications.
- By explaining how things are done in an organization, it creates cohesion among its members.
- It allows the creation of a social control in the organization.
- It can help in increasing the internal collaborators of the organization, as it facilitates environmental adaptation and internal integration which in result reduces the anxiety resulting from IT use.

RECOMMENDATIONS AND SOLUTIONS

As we demonstrate the most important issues of IS in the Arab world generally and in the United Arab Emirates specifically, we may have some recommendations and solutions for the better IS society. These recommendations educators can take them into their consideration to enhance and create a better learning environment. The following points would be helpful (there are so many other points which may help in this situation)

1. Educational leaders should make a very clear definition of ethical roles to their staff and demonstrate them throughout the organization.
2. The educational authority should ensure the implementations of security measures in accordance with the procedures of the activities.
3. The higher educational authorities must ensure the development and the documentations of information system security awareness for the staff.
4. The information system security program should be established and monitored for the whole staff in every organization.
5. Educational leaders should be aware of the issues of security, ethics and culture related to information system adopted in their organizations.
6. Educational leaders should Ensure that people who belong to the educational organization are well trained on using the information systems prescribed security restrictions and safeguards before they are initially allowed to access the system.
7. Each user of the information system must sign acknowledgment of responsibility for the security.
8. As educational leaders, we have to develop policies and procedures influencing ethical conduct in the public service.
9. The ethical standards of information system should be clear and demonstrated to the staff of the educational organization.
10. Ethical guidance must be available for your staff at any time.
11. As educational leaders, you should inform your staff of their rights and obligations.
12. Leaders should promote the ethical conducts by presenting themselves as good examples.
13. The higher education must put a strategic plan for the role of information system in education and have a future insight about it.
14. The whole educational staff needs to understand and implement common security practices.
15. More researches should be done on the impact of culture on IT development.
16. The higher education must put a strategic plan for the role of information system in education and have a future insight about it.

CONCLUSION

To conclude with, it has become obviously clear that information systems have grown to be one of the most successful key factors in our educational organizations. The higher authorities should adapt and implement it, and the school leaders should consider its different issues and be aware of its priority.

A successful organizational leader can implement the right system with the right people and consequently becomes fully responsible of encouraging and training his staff on ways to work as one team and use it appropriately. The other important point here, is that the process of implementing or practicing the information system in any educational organization is complex with many different steps and these should be followed in a professional way. An educational leader has peculiar and significant role to play. This includes that certain practices and work effectively. Issues such as ethical, cultural and security are important, and should be considered in our daily practices.

REFERENCES

Abu Dhabi Education Council (ADEC). (2009). *ADEC information security policy document,* (pp. 18-19). Final-Version 3.0 September 2009.

Ala, M., & Shishakly, R. (2008). Assessment of school information system utilization in the UAE primary schools. *Issues in Informing Science and Information Technology, 5.*

Avison, D., & Malaurent, J. (2007). Impact of cultural differences: A case study of ERP introduction in China. *International Journal of Information Management, 27*(5), 368–374. doi:10.1016/j.ijinfomgt.2007.06.004

Barta, B. Z., Telem, M., & Gev, Y. (1991). *Information technology in educational management.* Chapman & Hall.

Beheshti, H. (2006). What managers should know about ERP/ERP II. *Management Research News, 184.*

Branscomb, A. W. (1995). *Who owns information? From privacy to public access.* New York, NY: American Library Association.

Business dictionary. (n.d.). *Information system security: Engineering principles for IT security.* Retrieved from http://csrcinist.gov/publications

Chien-Pen, C., & Josaph, C. (1999). Issues in information ethics and educational policies for coming age. *Journal of Information Technology, 15*(4).

EveryCulture. (n.d.). *Countries and their culture: Culture of the United Arab Emirates.* Retrieved from http://www.everyculture.com/To-Z/United-Arab-Emirates.html

Friedman, E. A. (1994). A management perspective on effective technology integration: Top ten questions for school administration. *T.H.E. Journal, 22*(4), 89–90.

Hoesung, K., & Seongjin, A. (2006). A study on the methodology of information ethics education in Youth. *International Journal of Computer Science and Network Security, 6*(6).

Hofstede, G. (1980). *Culture's consequences: International differences in work-related values.* Beverly Hills, CA: SAGE Publications.

Hofstede, G. (1991). *Cultures and organizations: Software of the mind.* New York, NY: McGraw-Hill.

Huang, Z., & Palvia, P. (2001). ERP implementation issues in advanced and developing countries. *Business Process Management Journal, 7*(3), 276–284. doi:10.1108/14637150110392773

Karahanna, E., Evaristo, J., & Srite, M. (2005). Levels of culture and individual behaviour: An integrative perspective. *Journal of Global Information Management, 13*(2), 1–20. doi:10.4018/jgim.2005040101

Laudon, K. C., & Laudon, J. P. (1996). *Information technology and society* (2nd ed.). Boston, MA: Course Technology, Inc.

Ministry of Education Portal. (2011). *The United Arab Emirates educational system.* Retrieved from www.moe.ae

Molla, A., & Loukis, I. (2005). Success and failure of ERP technology transfer: A framework for analyzing congruence of host and system cultures. *Development Informatics,* working paper no. 24. IDPM, University of Manchester, UK. Retrieved May 13, 2010, from http://www.sed.manchester.ac.uk/idpm/research/publications/wp/di/di_wp24.htm

Myers, M. D., & Tan, F. (2002). Beyond models of national culture in information systems research. *Journal of Global Information Management, 10*(1), 24–32. doi:10.4018/jgim.2002010103

Oosthoek, H. (1989). Higher education and new technology. *Proceedings of the 5th Congress of the European Association for Research and Development in Higher Education (EARDHE) and the Dutch Association for Research and Development in Higher Education* (CRWO), Pergamon Holland, (pp. 367-378).

Rabaai, A. (2009). The impact of organizational culture on ERP systems implementations: Lessons from Jordan. *Proceedings PACIS 2009, Pacific Asia Conference on Information Systems.* Association for Information Systems.

Security Culture. (n.d.). Retrieved from http://security.resist.ca/personal/culture.shtml

Severson, R. (2000). *Fundamentals of information ethics, philosophy and reality* (B.-W. Chu & J.-H. Ryu, Trans.).

Telem, M., & Avidov, O. (1994). Management information system (MIS) impact on the loosely coupled nature of a high school: A case study. *Planning and Changing, 25*(3-4), 192–205.

United States Government Accountability Office. (2005, May). *Emerging cybersecurity issues - Threaten federal information systems - Report to congressional requesters.*

Visscher, A. J. (1988). The computer as an administrative tool: Problems and impact. *Journal of Research on Computing in Education, 21*(1), 28–35.

Visscher, A. J. (1991). Computer-assisted school administration - The Dutch experience. *Journal of Research on Computing in Education, 24*(1), 91–106.

Visscher, A. J. (1996). Information technology in educational management. *International Journal of Educational Research, 25*(4), 291–296. doi:10.1016/S0883-0355(97)89361-5

ADDITIONAL READING

Davison, R., & Martinsons, M. (2003). Guest editorial- Cultural issues and IT management: Past and present. *IEEE Transactions on Engineering Management, 50*(1). doi:10.1109/TEM.2003.808249

Ives, B., & Jarvenpaa, S. L. (1991). Applications of global information technology: Key issues for management. *Management Information Systems Quarterly, 15*(1). doi:10.2307/249433

McCoy, S. (2003). Integrating national cultural into individual IS adoption research: The need for individual level measures. *Proceedings of the Ninth Americas Conference on Information Systems (AMCIS) 2003*, Tampa, Florida, USA (CD Proceedings).

Myers, M. D., & Tan, F. (2002). Beyond models of national culture in information systems research. *Journal of Global Information Management, 10*(1). doi:10.4018/jgim.2002010103

Shore, B., & Venkatachalam, A. R. (1994). Prototyping: A metaphor for cross-cultural transfer and implementation of IS applications. *Information & Management, 27*(3). doi:10.1016/0378-7206(94)90045-0

Tractinsky, N., & Jarvenpaa, S. L. (1995). Information systems design decisions in a global versus domestic context. *Management Information Systems Quarterly, 19*(4). doi:10.2307/249631

KEY TERMS AND DEFINITIONS

Accreditation: The official management decision given by a senior entity official (chairman) to authorise operation of a Government service and to explicitly accept the risk to entity operations, entity assets, or individuals based on the implementation of an agreed-upon set of security controls.

ADEC: Abu Dhabi Educational Council.

ADSIC: Abu Dhabi Systems & Information Centre.

Availability: Ensuring timely and reliable access to and use of Information.

BPR: Business Process Re-engineering.

CERT: Computer Emergency Response Team.

Confidentiality: Preserving authorized restrictions on information access and disclosure, including means for protecting personal privacy and proprietary information.

Control: Means of managing risk, including policies, procedures, guidelines, practices or organizational structures, which can be of administrative, technical, management, or legal nature.

CSIRTs: Computer Security Incidents Response Teams.

ERP: Enterprise Resource Planning.

eSIS: Enterprise Student Information System.

GCC: Gulf Cooperation Council.

Guideline: A description that clarifies what should be done and how, to achieve the objectives set out in policies.

ICT: Information and Communication Technologies.

Information Security: Protection of information and information systems from unauthorized access, use, disclosure, disruption, modification, or destruction in order to provide confidentiality, integrity, and availability.

Information System: A discrete set of information resources organized for the collection, processing, maintenance, use, sharing, dissemination or disposal of information, including manual processes or automated processes. This includes information systems used by an entity either directly or used by another entity, or a contractor under a contract with the entity that:

(i) requires the use of such information systems ; or (ii) requires the use, to significant extent, of such information systems in the performance of a service or the furnishing of a product.

Information Technology: Any equipment or interconnected system or subsystem of equipment that is used in the automatic acquisition, storage, manipulation, management, movement, control, display, switching, interchange, transmission, or reception of data or information.

Information: Any communication or representation of knowledge such as facts, data, or opinions in any medium or form; including textual, numerical, graphic, cartographic, narrative, or audiovisual forms

Integrity: Guarding against improper information modification or destruction, and includes ensuring information non repudiation and authenticity.

IT: Information Technology.

ITEM: Information Technology in Educational Management.

MIS: Management Information System.

Policy: Overall intention and direction as formally expressed by management.

Risk: The level of impact on entity services, assets, or individuals resulting from the potential consequences of a threat and the likelihood of that threat occurring.

SIS: School Information System.

Threat: A potential cause of an unwanted incident, which may result in harm to a system or organization

UAE: United Arab Emirates.

Vulnerability: A weakness of an asset or group of assets that can be exploited by one or more threats.

Chapter 12
Arab Youth and the Internet:
Educational Perspective

Zakieh Ali Al Disi
Al Ain Education Office, UAE

Fayez Ahmad Albadri
Abu Dhabi University, UAE

ABSTRACT

This study investigates the levels and patterns of use of the Internet among secondary school students in Al Ain City, United Arab Emirates, and attempts to assess the levels of parental supervision at home. The prime aim of the study is to determine how widespread the Internet use is among UAE secondary students, and to examine the activities that the students adopt the Internet for. In conclusion, the study explores possible effects that the Internet use may have on the students' social relations and other activities. A survey was designed and adapted to support the investigation, and a questionnaire was distributed to 100 secondary school students (50 boys and 50 girls) in six secondary schools in Al Ain city. The investigation findings revealed that the majority of the respondents use the Internet for communication and leisure rather than for educational purposes, while some respondents affirmed improved general knowledge and academic performances as a result of using the Internet. Whilst acknowledging the Internet potential positive impact on students' educational performance, the study recommends that the use of the Internet should be monitored and guided by school authorities and parents, so as to prevent the misuse of this facility and to direct it towards teaching and learning improvement.

INTRODUCTION

Education and learning are among the most significant of all human activities, and they have always been considered the major capital in generating innovative, productive and sustainable societies. With globalization and the rapidly increasing governing role that information and knowledge occupy in all economies, providing quality education is becoming ever more important. Integrating technology, especially computer-based, in education is considered as a key element to the quality of teaching and learning among most of the education systems around the world. In terms of technology utilization to support education, it has gone through an important shift from using primarily as an instructional delivery medium to an integral part of the learning environment. Informa-

DOI: 10.4018/978-1-4666-1984-5.ch012

tion and Communication Technology (ICT) serves different purposes in schools and educational organizations benefiting from access to a wealth of information and knowledge and enhanced communications through the Internet and other related information technologies (Noeth, Volkov, 2004). Bajcsy (2002) views technology in teaching and learning as an enabler and highlights its role of facilitating and assisting in the authentication and prioritization of Internet material.

Education in most of the Arab countries has witnessed a great advancement in the past few years. Extensive efforts were made to reform Educational systems to overcome the internationally recognized failure. Although Arab governments have generally allocated significant portions of their national income to education, yet, there has been very low return on investment in terms of meaningful educational outcomes. Education systems throughout the region are thought to be hindered by low quality, irrelevancy and inequity (Anda Adams, 2011). In terms of integrating technology in education there has been a great rush to equip schools with proper technology in most of the Arab countries, but the best way of how it should be utilized has not received the adequate attention. Cassidy, Thomas (2004) in a paper titled 'Education in the Arab States: preparing to compete in the Global Economy' concluded "generally, the results of reform have been less dramatic than hoped, and more taxing on the capacitance of education professionals than anticipated. It is one thing to redefine standards, curriculums, and rehab facilities and install computers and computer networks in schools, but it can be quite a matter to change what people do and how they do it. Experience and research tell us that changing people's behavior takes time, sustained effort, and lots of support."

In the United Arab Emirates (UAE), the shortcomings identified in the Education system in 2005, highlighted the poor utilizing of ICT as one of the eleven major problems that contributed to education failure. Later on, the public was notified that AED 46 billion (USD 13 billion) would be spent in the next 10 years on rectifying the problems (Macherson et al, 2007). Although, the educational reform movement in the (UAE) is a relatively recent phenomenon, there was an agreement on the need for large-scale change. The establishment of a reliable technology infrastructure in schools was one of the targets of education directors in the country. Along with the rapid advancement in telecommunication networks in UAE, Abu Dhabi Education Council (ADEC), the director of education in the Emirate of Abu Dhabi, managed to help schools solve issues of the Internet connection to encourage the use of information and communication technology in education, and make the Internet available to teachers as well as students at public schools. This stage of educational reform requires concerted efforts by educators and the students' families to use this resource in the proper way. As the implementation is in its early stages, many questions need to be answered to so as to make it effective and fruitful: How can the internet access in schools help in teaching and learning? What are the possible risks? How can schools minimize misuse? What might be the features of an effective implementation?

Advantages of Internet Use in Teaching and Learning

It is well known that the Internet has broken down barriers of communication and information access all over the world. It is fast, reliable and has a limitless range of facilities, which assist users to access almost infinite amounts of information. It offers the opportunity for access to up- to- date research reports and knowledge databases. Thus, it has become an important component in academic institutions. Globally, the Internet has opened countless new opportunities for students. Actually, it has given a very open approach to education, where students are no longer highly dependent on their teachers, textbooks or school libraries as their only sources of information (Olatokun, 2008).

According to the Pew Internet & American Life Project (2005), Internet use is a staple of college students' educational experience as they use it to communicate with professors and classmates, to do research and to access library materials. For the majority of students, the Internet is a functional tool that has drastically changed the way they interact with others and access information during their studies. Thus, the Internet broadens students' horizons beyond their local boundaries and provides an environment in which its impact may be immeasurable. Several studies have established a high degree of access and use of the Internet among students, and confirmed tangible impact on students' behavior and educational performance

The Internet technologies integration in education relies on several assumptions about learners and the learning process: learning is an active, constructive process; resource-rich contexts can support learning; learning is inherently social; and, learners have diverse learning needs according to Mills& Steven (2006).

Provenzo (1998), cited by Kasowits (2005), listed several advantages of the Internet for instruction, including the following:

- World Wide Web motivates students of various learning styles (e.g., graphics for visual learners and lower reading abilities, sounds for auditory learners)
- E-mail programs allow communication and collaboration between students and subject experts or students in other areas of the country and the world.
- Provides access to world wide range of information from a variety of sources and universities, professional organizations, business, museums, government agencies.
- Presentation of students work on the World Wide Web promotes confidence and a sense of importance that their work will be seen by others.

- Allow for activities that can enhance learning of subject area and knowledge as well as information literacy skills.
- Allows educators and instructional resource creators to gather and present information and communicate ideas during pre-instruction activities and instruction.
- Facilitates teachers' roles as a "guide in the discovery of new knowledge" rather than "dispensers of information".

The Internet obviously adds some real value, to teaching and learning. Some of the appropriate activities of the Internet in education are: communication and collaboration; visualization and animation; providing current data and data Analysis; publishing; and providing research resources (Ebiefung, 2000). On the other hand, the utilization of the Internet into the classroom as a teaching and learning tool is relatively new, thus there is no decisive judgment about its effectiveness. Bekele & Menchaca (2008) reviewed 29 studies that indicated students' grade achievement as the prime measure of effectiveness in Internet Supported Learning environments, in spite of some additionally assessed student motivation, participation and satisfaction. Some 45% of the studies reported positive results, whereas 55% reported no significant differences. Most studies used quantitative design methodologies (Bekele & Menchaca, 2008).

However, there is an agreement that the use of the Internet in the classroom introduces students to the technology that will certainly play a key role in their lives. Another privilege of implementing the Internet as a teaching tool in the classroom is that the students will continue to have the face-to-face communication with their teacher and peers.

Risks, Limitations, and Challenges

In spite of the numerous privileges of the Internet, there are also many drawbacks. A patch of overlapping risks, limitations and challenges accompany the internet use in education, and may serve to hinder its effectiveness. Consequently, it is quite crucial that educational institutions should pay attention to overcome what seem to be obstacles to effective implementation and utilization of Internet-supported education if the student achievement is to be really improved, otherwise the modernization of education will be the ultimate result.

In terms of risks, student's safety, when surfing the NET, is a subject of debate that raised the issue of 'security vs. access' among scholars and practcioners. Although the availability of free information can be considered as an advantage, there is a risk that some valued information can fall into the wrong hands. Some materials available on the Internet may be offensive to students (Li and Chung. 2006; Suhail and Barges, 2006). Although it is possible to create network servers and proxies that block the avenues to these materials, students 'with interest' can still find alternative paths. School children can be improperly exposed to immoral information because there is neither control nor 'checks' on the information available on the NET (Osunade, 2003).

A national survey, conducted by the Annenberg Public Policy Center (1999), in Washington found that the majority of parents in households with computers fear the Internet's influence on their children due to its wide-open nature and interactivity. However, they still believe that their children need the Internet. They cited as benefits the ability to discover useful things and the advantages for schoolwork. Furthermore, there is general agreement among teens and their parents that the Internet can be a useful tool for school (Pew Internet & American Life Project (2004).

While the Internet can be considered a means of facilitating and promoting communication (Huffaker, 2004; Lombardo, Zakus, & Skinner, 2002), it could be well considered as a social barrier (Weber et al., 2005; Ybarra & Mitchell, 2004), that promotes social isolation (Sanders, Field, Diego, & Kaplan, 2000), leading to the loss of

social skills (Maczewski, 2002; Wilhelm, 2002), persisting gender, cultural and social inequalities (DiMaggio et al., 2001; Li & Kirkup, 2007) and associated with addiction behaviors (Li & Chung, 2006; Johansson & Gotestam, 2004), and gambling (Griffiths & Wood, 2000), some consider it as information bliss while others perceive it as a curse that threatens individual liberties and democracy (Maniere de voir, 1996).

Furthermore, additional to various risks, there are certain limitations regarding the use of the Internet in education. Yusuf (2006) listed some of the limitations are as follows:

- **Plagiarism:** Students may copy out others work to be presented as theirs.
- **Instability of information on the internet:** due to the possibility of changing, updating and removing information.
- **Skills needed for web search:** It is difficult to search well, particularly by novice/non-expert users.
- **Reliability of information:** The materials on the Internet are sometimes not regulated or monitored because no quality control is applied.
- **Information bias:** Some information is provided in favor of certain subjects and to the detriment of others.
- **Information distractions:** Students may be distracted to other things which have no relevance to intellectual development.

Education directors as well as schools may face some of the following challenges when implementing the Internet as an educational open resource:

- **Sustainability** (Yuan et al, 2008): this include sustainability of funding as well as production and sharing of internet compatible materials.
- **Intellectual property and copyright issues** (Yuan et al, 2008): providing solutions in obtaining legal access to valuable inter-

net resources as well as obtaining rights for teachers and students to publish work.

- **Quality Assessment and Enhancement** (Yuan et al, 2008): utility and effectiveness of the Internet as an information recourse, technology aid and new methodology should be evaluated and modified on a regular basis regarding its influence on students achievement.
- **Integration with curriculum** (Kasowits (2005): school curricula should be compatible with the use of internet as an educational resource.
- **Preparation of teachers** (Kasowits 2005): teachers should acquire necessary technical competencies to help their students participate in the Internet activities.
- **Ongoing management** (Kasowits 2005): monitoring is a key element to successful implementation for both teachers and students.
- **Policies** (Yuan et al, 2008): Schools should formulate Internet use policies that address curriculum development; financial support; intellectual property; culture of sharing; assessment and authorization; quality assurance; professional development, student support; technical infrastructure/software, security and institutional model.
- **Socio-cultural issues** (Joo, 1999): awareness of the social structures and the school cultures is a key element in effective implementation. An Internet use culture should be created with compliance with ethical, religious, social norms and values.

Taking into consideration the advantages, risks, limitations, and challenges associated with using the Internet for educational purposes, an effective implementation can be achieved by exploiting the opportunities to maximize gain and mitigating risks and managing issues and challenges. Careful planning as well as systematic execution with continuous follow up, evaluation and modifica-

tion should result into the desired improvement of students' performance which is considered the definitive goal of school education.

Internet Use in UAE Schools

UAE is the most wired nation in the Arab World and one of the top nations of the online world. In 2009 UAE scored the 23rd among the world countries regarding the internet penetration rate (Internet World Stats Website). As the rapid increase in telecommunication wiring in the country was timed with the declaration of a radical reform in Education, the Internet utility in education was a logical result. The Internet infrastructure in UAE schools was listed as a priority in the government education funding project and was almost fully deployed in all public schools. The next step and the most important is the establishment of an effective implementation plan that will lead to the required education reform.

Although the use of the Internet was introduced only few years ago in the country as a voluntary practice by some teachers who were either innovative or technology fans, the utilization of this recourse was not satisfactory. The scarcity of research in the area, as it is with other educational aspects, provides little information about these practices. However, a study done by Al-Mekhlafi (2004) regarding the use of the Internet in teaching English as a foreign language in the UAE revealed that in spite of their familiarity with Information Technology and their positive attitudes towards the use of the Internet in their classrooms, the majority of teachers were not in practice doing so. Al-Meklafi recommended that further research is needed to investigate the reasons behind the results of his study. AlGhazo (2006) in a study titled "Quality of Internet Use by Teachers in the United Arab Emirates" concluded that "teachers, have limited access to the Internet in schools, and low skills in using the Internet. In turn, the rate of integrating it in teaching is very low." In her study she identified the positive perceptions that teachers had toward the importance of the Internet. These positive perceptions, as she predicted, would encourage teachers to be more eager to get the proper professional development and willing to utilize the Internet effectively if they were provided with the environment that supports such utilization.

From students' perspective, there was no available published research work concerning the usage of UAE school students of the Internet. In order to compose an approximate image of the situation, a preliminary study was conducted to investigate patterns of Internet use among students, as this would give some indicators about their attitudes to the use of Internet, as well as their usage skills and navigation preferences. The results of this study can be considered as initial findings that can be built on to substantiate in future research in the same area.

INVESTIGATION METHOD

In order to examine and understand selected aspects of school students' usage of the Internet, the research has focused on the following issues:

- The required skills to use the Internet
- The way students use the Internet
- The reasons for which students use the Internet
- The patterns of parental supervision students experience as they use the Internet
- Students' perceptions of the Internet usage effect on students' other activities
- Students' preferred websites when browsing the Internet.

A survey questionnaire was distributed to a total of 100 secondary school students aged 15–18, 50 of them were males and 50 were females. Most of the survey questions were adopted from a similar research conducted by Aslanidou S.& Menexes, G.(2007).

The survey included general questions to indicate the availability of personal computers, frequency of Internet use, average daily time spent on the Internet, places where students learnt Internet browsing and whether they usually browse the Internet alone or in company with others. The survey has also included sets of questions each of which focused on a different issue; the type of parental control on Internet use, the Internet activities practiced by students and the effects of surfing the Internet on some common leisure activities and some other aspects.

Table 1. Place where the student learnt to use of the Internet

Where did you learn to use the Internet?	At home	At an Internet café	At school	At a library	Some- where else
boys	70%	12%	4%	2%	12%
girls	82%	2%	4%	2%	10%

Table 2. Internet use duration

When you started using the Internet?	Less than 1 year	1-2 years	More than 2 years	I don't remember
boys	2%	16%	52%	20%
girls	0%	10%	68%	22%

INVESTIGATION RESULTS

1. General Information: Tables 1-5, and Figures 1, 2, and 3

- 92% of boys and 94% of girls reported that they have their own personal computers at home.

- 90% of boys and 92% of girls reported that the Internet connection was always available to them at home.

- 72% of boys and 52% of girls reported that they can access sometimes the Internet at school.

Figure 1. Internet use duration chart

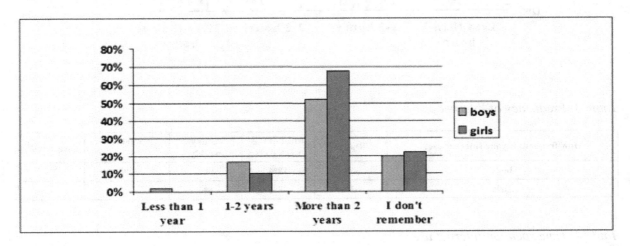

Figure 2. Frequency of Internet use chart

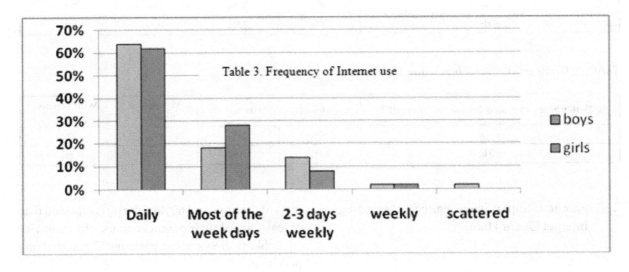

Figure 3. Time spent on Internet use chart

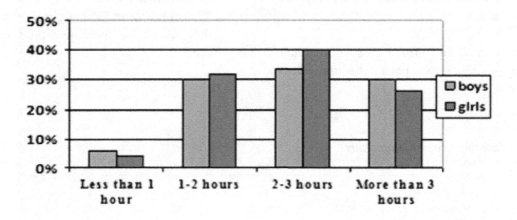

Table 3. Frequency of Internet use

How frequent is your Internet use?	Daily	Most of the week days	2-3 days weekly	weekly	scattered
boys	64%	18%	14%	2%	2%
girls	62%	28%	8%	2%	-

Table 4. Time spent on Internet use

How much time do you spend when you use the Internet?	Less than 1 hour	1-2 hours	2-3 hours	More than 3 hours
boys	6%	30%	34%	30%
girls	4%	32%	40%	26%

Table 5. Companionship when using the Internet

With whom you usually browse the Internet?	Alone	With friends	With sisters/ brothers	With parents
boys	50%	24%	20%	6%
girls	64%	10%	22%	4%

2. Parental Supervision Pattern Regarding Internet Use at Home

80% of the boys and 60% of the girls reported that at least one of their parents can use the Internet.

Table 6 shows some patterns of parental supervision.

Table 6. Patterns of parental

Do your parents permit you to:	Always		Often		Sometimes		Rarely		Never	
	boys	girls	boys	girls	boys	girls	boys	girls	boys	girls
Use the Internet for a long time?	10%	8%	10%	22%	30%	24%	24%	16%	26%	30%
Chat with strangers?	20%	72%	10%	12%	4%	10%	16%	6%	50%	10%
Buy products?	50%	48%	10%	8%	10%	16%	10%	6%	20%	22%
Getting into certain Web-pages?	36%	34%	8%	14%	20%	18%	12%	12%	24%	32%
Play online games?	4%	8%	4%	10%	10%	8%	16%	6%	66%	70%

3. Internet Activities Used by Students (Table 7)
4. The Effect of Using Internet on Studying and Some Other Leisure Activities (Table 8)
5. The Overall Effect of the Internet Use on the Students from their Point of View (Table 9)
6. Websites Frequently Visited (Table 10)

DISCUSSION

According to the study results, some basic findings regarding the Internet uses and practices can be reported as follows:

The majority of the students in the sample (96% of boys, 92% of girls) stated that they had their own computers at home and (90% 0f boys,

Table 7. Internet activities used by students

Do you use the Internet to:	Always		Often		Sometimes		Rarely		Never	
	boys	girls	boys	girls	boys	girls	boys	girls	boys	girls
Search for information for your own use?	44%	48%	20%	30%	20%	16%	8%	6%	8%	-
Search for information related to your homework?	30%	46%	20%	22%	36%	24%	10%	8%	4%	-
Play and download games?	30%	18%	20%	18%	40%	34%	10%	26%	-	4%
Communicate with others?	56%	60%	28%	18%	10%	18%	6%	4%	-	-
Listen and download music?	44%	50%	10%	30%	25%	8%	15%	6%	6%	6%
Watch and download films?	20%	20%	20%	24%	16%	36%	30%	16%	14%	8%
Search for images?	32%	62%	34%	30%	22%	6%	12%	2%	-	-
Buy products?	12%	2%	2%	6%	6%	30%	10%	20%	70%	44%

Table 8. Effects of Internet use

Since you started using the Internet:	Less than before		Just like before		More than before	
	boys	girls	boys	girls	boys	girls
Do you study?	26%	30%	64%	60%	10%	10%
Do you watch TV?	60%	62%	40%	34%	10%	4%
Do you go out?	34%	32%	56%	58%	10%	10%
Do you spend time with your family?	10%	36%	80%	56%	10%	4%
Do you spend time with your friends?	10%	10%	70%	40%	20%	50%

Table 9. Overall effect of Internet use

In your opinion: What is the overall effect of using Internet on...	Positive		Neutral		Negative	
	boys	girls	boys	girls	boys	girls
Your school achievement?	44%	16%	40%	68%	16%	16%
Your general knowledge?	76%	66%	20%	26%	4%	8%
The relationship with your family?	30%	14%	70%	74%	-	12%
You in general?	64%	48%	24%	42%	12%	10%

Table 10. Websites frequently visited

Website	Frequent Users %	
	Boys	Girls
Electronic Mail	50%	54%
Social Network Service (like Facebook)	50%	40%
Internet chat rooms	10%	10%
Games websites	36%	14%
Forums	40%	30%
Educational websites	30%	36%

96% of girls) stated that the Internet access is always available to them at home. More than half of the students (52% of boys, 68%of girls) stated that they started using the Internet more than two years ago. More than 60% of both female and male students mentioned that they use the Internet on a daily basis. Around 65% of the whole total number of students stated that they spend more than two hours surfing the net and more than 30% of them stated that they spend more than 3 hours. Furthermore, 10% stated that they use the Internet for almost the whole day. Those responses give an indicator about the widespread use of Internet in the UAE, especially among young people. It may also give an indicator about the mastery level of those young people. Another fact which evident in Table 5 is that the Internet seems to be considered by students as private space where they can dive alone to attain personal objectives since a considerable percentage of them (50% of boys, 64% of girls) usually surf the net alone.

Regarding the parental supervision on the Internet use shown in Table 6, it appears that there was no conscious control on the Internet use. Although 70% of the boys' fathers and 40% of their mothers know how to use the Internet, most of them didn't have restrictions on the time of use, playing online games or even chatting with strangers. A relatively higher limitation was put only for buying items through the Internet and for browsing certain websites. For girls, with 46% fathers and 46% mothers knowing how to use the Internet, similar findings can be reported except the high percentage of parental restriction on chatting with strangers (72%). This can be traced easily to the prevailing cultural religious norms of the region. This, somewhat, loose parental control calls for more attention to educate parents about the dangers of careless use of the Internet in order to avoid the dire consequences of the persistence of young people, in the use of Internet and communication with non- trustworthy individuals or organizations.

Regarding the Internet related activities, it seems that majority of students used the Internet for communication and entertainment purposes rather than for school homework as indicated in Table 7. Communication came at the top of the list (rating 56% of boys and 60% of girls). Another Internet activity by the students that was relatively high is searching information for their own use, which provides evidence to the positive effect they think Internet use had on their general knowledge as shown in Table 9. Although a considerable percentage of the students (72% of boys, 52% of girls) stated that they can access the Internet at school, it seems that it was not well utilized in the classroom for educational purposes. In fact students mainly surf the Internet at school mainly in IT lessons as a part of the IT curriculum activities. Browsing the Internet in other school subjects is considered a waste of time for almost all teachers. When the Internet is used for instruction, most teachers will spend some minutes streaming a video or displaying an animation or presenting a simulation for a demonstrating purpose. Even with homework assignments, searching the net seemed to be a poorly requested activity especially with boys who a 30% reported that they used the Internet for homework purposes compared with 46% of girls that reported the use of Internet for that purpose. School teachers, in this case, need to be aware of this issue and to devote a part of their homework assignments to internet search in order to save some of the time that students consume in net surfing.

The use of the Internet at home seems to have limited effects on the students other activities as a perception of the students themselves (both boys and girls), as shown in Table 8. The most affected activity was TV watching. A considerable number of the students (around 61%) stated that they watch TV less than before. Most students claimed that the Internet use had not affected studying, but around 30% of them stated that they study less than before. More than half of the students stated that they are still going out as they were before using the Internet, but around third of them stated that they go out less than before. One difference between boys and girls is that 50% of the girls stated that they spend time with friends more than before. This may be related to that most girls tend to use the internet chatting and communicating with their friends.

From students' point of view, using the Internet had positive effects on their general knowledge (76% of girls, 66% of girls). School achievement is positively affected for 44% of boys, and just 16% of girls. 40% of boys and 68% of girls stated that their school achievement was not affected. Most of the students (around 70% of all) believed that their family relationship was not affected. The overall effect was rated positive by 64% of boys and 48% of girls. Negative effects in all had a percentage between 4% and 16%, which means that using the Internet did not do any harm as the students think. Instead, Internet was a means of communication and a resource of information that fulfilled their young age needs and curiosity.

Finally, the top websites frequently visited by students were the electronic mail and the social network services for both boys and girls as shown in Table 10. Educational websites were frequently visited by 30% of boys and 36% of girls. These responses highlight again the deep desire to communicate among youths and add more question marks to what role the Internet use has in the school setting.

CONCLUSION AND RECOMMENDATIONS

- This study, while useful in the absence of other similar studies in the UAE, does not give precise indications about some important aspects like students' efficacy, capability and maturation when dealing with the Internet. It also represents the students' point of view in a simple way with no further investigation for the teachers and parents perceptions. Further studies should be done to cover those aspects as well as other issues related to the youth's use of the Internet. This can be considered very important regarding the global debate about Issues like Internet addiction, social isolation associated with the long time spent in Internet browsing.

- The positive impact of Internet in higher education had been recognized in the UAE; hence its positive impact in schools has to be achieved in a proper way. Education decision makers should pay attention when planning the implementation of free Internet in the schools to ensure adequate finance, upgradable infrastructure, high standards student protection system, proper technical and educational support, adequate authorization and access to trusted educational and technical websites and resources, as well as the adoption of an encouraging staff buy-in reward system.

- Schools seem to be little aware of the impacts of Internet, both positive and negative ones. Their support and control are essential to better utilize the Internet as an open resource and avoid risks related to its openness. Some recommendation are:
  - Teachers should get the proper knowledge and skills needed to use the Internet and its services. Previous research indicated that most teachers cannot navigate the Internet effectively. Good knowledge of the Internet as well as adequate technical skills are important to the teachers to be able to successfully use the Internet for teaching, and to assist students in their classroom activities involving the Internet.
  - Training should be on a continual basis that must be provided to teachers by technical and educational experts

to make sure they are acquiring proper skills and are frequently updated with new Internet recourses and exploitations regarding the educational field.

- Availability and regular maintenance of Internet equipment as well as the needed hardware and software is a key issue.
- Schools should cooperate with Education decision makers in formulating an Internet usage policy that eliminates risks and overcomes limitations and challenges that serve as obstacles to effective implementation. Policies should be authentically built to meet the real needs, avoid the realistic risks, and ensure the convenience and acceptance of the type of use regarding the Emirates context. Policies should not be imported blindly from other environments; if so, proper modification should be made to make it compatible with the socio-cultures and religious norms.
- School leaders should be willing to provide time and money for in-service training, teachers' appreciation, and for the purchasing the needed equipment. They should play a proactive positive role when dealing with problems related to using the Internet as a tool in the school setting.
- School leaders should be able to build a learning community and to create a culture of knowledge sharing that will accelerate the implementation process and bring out the desired success, rather than the widespread knowledge hording culture. Teachers' evaluation should be dedicated to appreciate teacher's collaboration and team work instead of individual practices.

○ Using the Internet as a tool not as a means by itself. The Internet should be a part of an integrated teaching system. That is the only way that the Internet adds value to the learning process.

○ Finally, parents, families and responsible community members and institutions should be allowed to make constructive contribution into this experimental stage to make it reach satisfaction as well as success.

As a conclusion, Education in the UAE is about to enter a new era where technology with its best potential is used as tool to serve the education' goals. With the provision of free Internet access in schools a pause should be made before implementation, to give time for careful planning and school staff preparing. There is no harm in consulting others who have the experience neither in spotting lessons learned in other countries, but at the end the implementation process should be structured to be authentically Emirati.

REFERENCES

Adams, A. (2011).*The role of education in the Arab World revolutions*. The Brookings Institution. Retrieved from http://www.brookings.edu/opinions/2011/0610_arab_world_education_winthrop.aspx

Al-Mekhlafi, A. (2004). The Internet and EFL teaching: The reactions of UAE secondary school English language teachers. *Journal of Language and Learning, 2*(2), 88–113.

Alghazo, I. M. (2006). Quality of Internet use by teachers in United Arab Emirates. *Education, 126*(4), 769–781.

Anderson, J. W. (2000). The information revolution. *The Middle East Journal, 54*(3).

Aslanidou, S., & Menexes, G. (2007). Youth and the Internet: Uses and practices in the home. *Computers & Education, 51*, 1375–1391. doi:10.1016/j.compedu.2007.12.003

Bajcsy, R. (2002). *Technology and learning*. In Visions 2020: Transforming education and training through advanced technologies. Washington, DC: U.S. Department of Commerce. Retrieved from http://www.technology.gov/reports/TechPolicy/2020Visions.pdf

Bekele, T. A., & Menchaca, M. P. (2008). Research on Internet-supported learning: A review. *The Quarterly Review of Distance Education, 9*(4), 373–405.

Chinwe, M. T. N. (2009). *The impact of internet use on teaching, learning and research activities in Nigerian universities.*

Griffiths, M., & Wood, R. (2000). Risk factors in adolescence: The case of gambling, videogame playing, and the Internet. *Journal of Gambling Studies, 16*(2/3), 199–225. doi:10.1023/A:1009433014881

Johansson, A., & Gotestam, G. (2004). Internet addiction: Characteristics of a questionnaire and prevalence in Norwegian youth (12–18 years). *Scandinavian Journal of Psychology, 45*, 223–229. doi:10.1111/j.1467-9450.2004.00398.x

Joo, J.-E. (1999). Cultural issues of the Internet in classrooms. *British Journal of Educational Technology, 30*(3), 245–250. doi:10.1111/1467-8535.00113

Kasowitz, A. S. (2005). *Teaching and learning with the Internet: A guide to building information literacy skills*. Washington, DC: Office of Educational research and Improvement (ED).

Kumar, R. (2006). Internet use by teachers and students in engineering colleges of Punjab, Haryana, and Himachal Pradesh States of India: An analysis. *Electronic Journal of Academic and Special Librarianship, 7*(1).

Lal, V. (2002). *The impact of computer-based technologies in Schools-A preliminary literature review.*

Li, N., & Kirkup, G. (2007). Gender and cultural differences in Internet use: A study in China and the UK. *Computers & Education, 48*(2), 301–317. doi:10.1016/j.compedu.2005.01.007

Li, S. M., & Chung, T.-M. (2006). Internet function and Internet addictive behavior. *Computers in Human Behavior, 22*(6), 1067–1071. doi:10.1016/j.chb.2004.03.030

Ling Zhao, A., Yaobin, L. A., Bin Wang, B., & Wayne Huang, C. (2010). What makes them happy and curious online? An empirical study on high school students' Internet use from a self-determination theory perspective. *Computers & Education, 56*, 346–356. doi:10.1016/j.compedu.2010.08.006

Lombardo, C., Zakus, D., & Skinner, H. (2002). Youth social action: Building a global latticework through information and communication technologies. *Health Promotion International, 17*(4), 363–371. doi:10.1093/heapro/17.4.363

Mills, S. C. (2006). *Using the Internet for active teaching and learning.* Pearson/Merrill/Prentice Hall

Noeth, R. J., & Volkov, B. B. (2004). *Evaluating the effectiveness of technology in our schools.* ACT Policy Report.

Osunade, O. (2003). *An evaluation of the impact of Internet browsing on students' academic performance at the tertiary level of education in Nigeria.* Retrieved on 15 March, 2007, from http://www.rocare.org/smaligrant nigeria2003.pdf

Pew Internet & American Life Project. (2004). *The Internet goes to college: How students are living in the future with today's technology.* Retrieved on May 16, 2008, from http://www.pewinternet.org/pdfs/PIP_College_Report.pdf

Sanders, C., Field, T., Diego, M., & Kaplan, M. (2000). The relationship of Internet use to depression and social isolation among adolescents. *Journal of Adolescence, 35*, 237–239.

Suhail, K., & Barges, Z. (2006). Effects of excessive internet use in undergraduate students in Pakistan. *Cyberpsychology & Behavior, 9*(3), 297–307. doi:10.1089/cpb.2006.9.297

Wilhelm, A. (2002). Wireless youth: Rejuvenating the net. *National Civic Review, 91*(3), 293–302. doi:10.1002/ncr.91308

Ybarra, M., & Mitchell, K. (2004). Youth engaging in online harassment: Associations with caregiver-child relationships, Internet use, and personal characteristics. *Journal of Adolescence, 27*, 319–336. doi:10.1016/j.adolescence.2004.03.007

Yuan, L., MacNeil, S., & Kraan, W. (2008). *Open educational resources – Opportunities and challenges for higher education.* JISC CETIS.

ADDITIONAL READING

Abdulla, R. A. (2007). *The Internet in the Arab World: Egypt and beyond.* New York, NY: Peter Lang International Academic Publishers.

Anderson, J. W. (2000). Producers and Middle East internet technology: Getting beyond "impacts". *The Middle East Journal*, 419–431.

Danet, B. (2001). *Cyberpl@y.* London, UK: Berg.

Dmitri, R., Weiguo, F. J., & Robles, F. (2008). Beyond keywords: Automated question answering on the web. *Communciations of the ACM*, 60-65.

Freestone, O., & Mitchell, V. (2004). Generation Y attitudes towards e-ethics and internet-related misbehaviours. *Journal of Business Ethics*, 121–128. doi:10.1007/s10551-004-1571-0

Gross, E. F. (2004). Adolescent Internet use: What we expect, what teens report. *Journal of Applied Developmental Psychology*, 633–649. doi:10.1016/j.appdev.2004.09.005

Hills, P., & Argyle, M. (2003). Uses of the Internet and their relationships with individual differences in personality. *Computers in Human Behavior*, *19*, 59–70. doi:10.1016/S0747-5632(02)00016-X

Hongladarom, S. (2001). Global culture, local cultures and the Internet: The Thai example. In Ess, C., & Sudweeks, F. (Eds.), *Culture, technology and communication: Towards an intercultural global village* (pp. 307–324). SUNY Press. doi:10.1007/BF01205985

Jukes, I., McCain, T., & Crockett, L. (2010). *Education and the role of the educator in the future.* Retrieved from http://njost.weebly.com/.../kappan_future_educator_article12_2010.pdf

Livingstone, S., & Bovill, M. (2001). *Families, schools and the internet.* London, UK: Media@LSE.

Magoulas, G. D., & Chen, S. Y. (2006). *Advances in Web-based education: Personalized learning environments*. Information Science Publishing.

McMillan, S. J., & Morrison, M. (2006). Coming of age with the Internet: A qualitative online exploration of how the Internet has become an integral part of young people's lives. *New Media & Society*, 73–95. doi:10.1177/1461444806059871

Montgomery, K., Gottlieb-Robles, B., & Larson, G. O. (2004). *Youth as E-citizens: Engaging the digital generation*. Washington, DC: Center for Social Media, American University.

Owen, J., Calnin, G., & Lambert, F. (2002). Evaluation of information technology. In *Evaluation of science and technology education at the dawn of a new millennium*. New York, NY: Kluwar Academic. doi:10.1007/0-306-47560-X_6

Poster, M. (2001). *What's the matter with the Internet?* Minneapolis, MN: University of Minnesota Press.

Prensky, M. (2006). *Don't bother me Mom-I'm learning*. Minneapolis, MN: Paragon House Publishers.

Salum, H. (2002). *The opening media and its threat to the values of the Muslim youth.* 9th International Conference for Muslim Youth, Al Riyadh.

Schofield, J. W., & Davidson, A. L. (2002). *Bringing the internet to school: Lessons from an urban district.* San Francisco, CA: Jossey-Bass.

Selwyn, N. (2011). *Education and technology: Key issues and debates.* London, UK: Continuum.

Shi, J., Chen, Z., & Tian, M. (2011). *Internet self-efficacy, the need for cognition, and sensation seeking as predictors of problematic use of the internet.* Cyberpsychology, Behaviour, and Social Networking.

Zhao, Y., & Frank, K. A. (2003). Factors affecting technology uses in schools: An ecological perspective. *American Educational Research Journal*, 807–840. doi:10.3102/00028312040004807

Zhao, Y., Sheldon, K., & Byers, J. (2002). Conditions for classroom technology innovations. *Teachers College Record*, 482–515. doi:10.1111/1467-9620.00170

KEY TERMS AND DEFINITIONS

Access: A means of approaching, entering, exiting, communicating with, or making use of.

Arab: A member of an Arabic-speaking people.

Education: The knowledge or skill obtained or developed by a learning process.

Internet: Is a worldwide system of computer networks.

Learning: The act, process, or experience of gaining knowledge or skill.

Teaching: The activities of educating or instructing; activities that impart knowledge or skill.

UAE: A federation of seven Arab emirates on the eastern Arabian peninsula.

Youths: People in the time of life between childhood and adulthood.

Chapter 13
ICT Integration in Post-Secondary English Teaching and Learning:
Evidence from Blended Learning Programs in the Arabian Gulf

Christina Gitsaki
Sharjah Higher Colleges of Technology, UAE

Abbad Alabbad
King Saud University, Saudi Arabia

ABSTRACT

The positive effects of computer-assisted language learning (CALL) have been widely acknowledged in the body of literature. While the majority of studies concern the use of CALL in the West, there is a dearth of research on the use of CALL in the Middle East and in particular in the Arabian Gulf where the English language plays a prominent role and being able to speak English is the passport to attending higher education and gaining employment. This chapter documents two case studies in higher education institutions in the Gulf, one in Saudi Arabia and one in the United Arab Emirates. The studies show how the use of CALL positively affected Arab students' language skills and their attitudes towards learning English with technology, paving the way for further research in the Arabian higher education context, where the use of Information and Communication Technology (ICT) for teaching and learning is gaining ground at a fast pace.

INTRODUCTION

Some of the most recent innovations in pedagogical practice are due to the integration of Information and Communication Technologies (ICTs) in the traditional educational context. The ability to display and process text, hypertext, audio, video, pictures, animations, and voice recognition are only some examples of how ICT-based tools and resources can be implemented in language teaching. Computer-assisted language learning (CALL) in classrooms has never been more affordable and versatile than it is today.

DOI: 10.4018/978-1-4666-1984-5.ch013

CALL has made gradual and constant progress since it first began in the 1960s (Levy & Stockwell, 2006). However, conceptually speaking, best practice in CALL is not clear at present, mainly due to the variability that characterises the field and the largely techno-centric approach applied by CALL enthusiasts that seems to overlook aspects of pedagogy and task design principles (Gitsaki, 2012). There is a plethora of views as to what CALL is and how it can be successfully implemented. Furthermore, the process of designing CALL materials has become a complex one as the practice of language teaching is moving away from the didactic, teacher-centered model and more towards communicative and content-based learning with authentic language tasks (Levy & Stockwell, 2006).

In countries where CALL has not yet been widely implemented, there is a problem of how CALL will fit into the paradigm of existing traditional teaching and learning practices. This chapter examines the use of CALL in two Gulf countries, Saudi Arabia (SA) and the United Arab Emirates (UAE). In both these countries there is a well-established tradition of English language learning in schools and at university and the integration of ICT in language courses is gaining ground with significant effects in students' motivation and performance.

BACKGROUND

Impact of ICTs in Second/Foreign Language Learning

The use of computers and the Internet in language teaching has varied throughout the history of CALL because of rapid technological developments. In fact, technology is developing at such a rate that we still cannot predict what the next development of computers and Internet technology is going to be. Consequently, the CALL field requires continuous attention from researchers, who constantly seek to determine how best to implement ICTs in language teaching and learning.

There is an abundance of studies that have investigated the effectiveness of CALL in language teaching and learning (for a review of recent CALL studies see Macaro, Handley, & Walter, 2012). By and large, computers have been shown to be effective in facilitating the teaching and learning of language skills. In writing, most recently, studies have investigated the use of computer-mediated communication (CMC) tools, such as e-mail, chat, discussion forums, wikis, digital story-telling, and blogging, for enhancing L2 students' writing skills (see for example, Fidaoui, Bahous, & Bacha, 2010; Greenfield, 2003; Lin & Wu, 2010; Lund, 2008; Mak & Coniam, 2008, Soares, 2008; Tsou, Wang, & Tzeng, 2006; Zhang, Gao, Ring, & Zhang, 2007). While results vary across the different studies, it was found that using computers for L2 writing can increase the amount of text students write and the discourse features of these texts (Mak & Coniam, 2008).

A number of studies have investigated the impact of ICT-based resources on improving L2 learners' listening skills (see for example, Decker, 2004; LeLoup, Cortland, & Ponterio, 2007; Liu & Chu, 2010; Verdugo & Belmonte, 2007) and have concluded that providing learners with access to multimedia resources enhances their listening abilities and provides them with instances of authentic use of the target language.

In reading comprehension, using computers and Internet technology can offer helpful resources to facilitate the understanding of unknown words. Online dictionaries and glosses, hypermedia and multimedia resources can help learners not only to better understand oral and written conversation, but they are also helpful for better word retention and vocabulary acquisition (Li, 2010; O'Hara & Pritchard, 2008; Peters, 2007; Silverman & Hines, 2009). In addition, Torlakovic and Deugo (2004) found that L2 students improved significantly in grammatical performance and confidence after being exposed to CALL grammar instruction.

Further, their study found that students' control of learning, the immediate feedback provided by the system, and the lack of negative psychological effect that can follow face-to face-negative feedback were all beneficial in language learning with CALL. Other authoring tools and computer programs, such as Hot Potatoes and Quia (Godwin-Jones, 2007) were found to enhance the students' language practice.

Furthermore, CALL can enhance students' non-linguistic skills, such as the acquisition of cultural aspects of the target language and the development of intercultural knowledge which are essential for effective communication. Different studies showed that ICT can make access to authentic learning content more efficient than printed materials, while authentic video can offer L2 learners context-rich cultural and linguistic materials (Herron, Dubreil, Cole & Corrie, 2000; Zhao, 2003). In a study on the effectiveness of video materials Weyers (1999) compared a group of L2 college students, who watched video clips 60 minutes daily for 8 weeks with another group studying the regular curriculum without video materials. Weyers found that the performance of the video group was significantly better than the regular group in listening comprehension and oral production. Similarly, Chang (2007) carried out a comparative study and found that the group that received L2 instruction in the form of culturally rich and popular L2 video talk-shows outperformed the group that received traditional instruction through a textbook. Furthermore, the use of the CALL multimedia materials fostered positive learning attitudes and self-efficacy in students.

In addition to providing access to authentic materials, ICTs can create opportunities for L2 learners to communicate in the target language through various computer and Internet tools (Hanson-Smith, 1999; Warschauer & Kern, 2000). Facebook, e-mail, and Twitter are examples of the various social networking tools that can be used for this objective. Different ICT applications are also capable of providing feedback to the learner. MS Word spell and grammar checkers, automatic speech recognition technology, and students' error tracking analysis via computer programs are examples of the various tools ICT could provide the L2 classroom with to enhance L2 input quality, authenticity of communication and provide useful feedback to the learner.

Finally, among the advantages of using computers in language teaching is the ability to encourage classroom participation and learner autonomy (Sullivan & Pratt, 1996; Warschauer, 1996). Using computer technology in learning offers students the flexibility to complete their assignments outside the classroom (Sagarra & Zapata, 2008), focus better on difficult topics (Adair-Hauck, Willingham-McLain, & Earnest Youngs, 1999; Torlakovic & Deugo, 2004), and encourage negotiation of meaning (Kern, 1996), and independent learning (Murray, 1999; Stepp-Greany, 2002; Warschauer & Meskill, 2000). In a web-based instruction study using BlackBoard, Lee (2005) reported positive results in learner control over the learning process and engaging the students in active learning. Online learning environments are also seen to create a less stressful atmosphere for the L2 learners (Lee, 2002; Magnan, Farrell, Jan, Lee, Tsai, & Worth, 2003).

While the positive effects of ICT on L2 learning have been researched extensively in the context of western education, CALL research in the Middle East is still sparse. The next section provides a short review of CALL-related studies in SA and the UAE, which are the context of the research studies examined in this chapter.

CALL in Gulf Arab Universities

English as a foreign language (EFL) education in both SA and the UAE is characterized by consistent low student performance in standardized international tests such as the International English Language Testing System (IELTS). In 2010, Emirati and Saudi students scored an average 5.1

in the Academic module, below the overall average score of 5.3 for Arabic-speaking test takers and below the international average of 5.9 for that year (IELTS, 2010). In the General Training module, UAE had the lowest overall mean (4.4) compared to all other countries, while the mean performance of Saudi students (4.6) was equally poor (IELTS, 2010). After years of learning English at school, 94% of Emirati students have to take remedial English language courses before starting university (Lewis & Bardsley, 2010). Students' low motivation and teachers' adherence to traditional teacher-centered, textbook-driven, didactic approaches are among the main reasons for the poor performance results (see Gitsaki & Alabbad, 2011; Fields, 2011).

There is a growing realization of the potential value of technology, in the improvement of EFL teaching in the Arab Gulf countries. The studies conducted in the field of CALL in the Gulf are limited and show only a restricted use of computers in general education with hardly any implementation in foreign language teaching and learning. Even in the few well-equipped educational institutions that use CALL resources, there is either limited access to these resources or these resources are used with no adequate pedagogical understanding of CALL implementation (for a review see Alabbad, 2010). There is clearly a need for further investigation of CALL implementation in the educational context in the Arab Gulf countries.

In Saudi Arabia there have been a number of studies on the use of computers for learning English (see for example Abalhassan, 2002; Al-Bureikan, 2008; Aljamhoor, 1999; Al-Juhani, 1991; Al-Kahtani, 2001; Al-Subeai, 2000). With the exception of Al-Bureikan (2008) and Al-Kahtani (2001), the rest of the studies were conducted at schools. The use of CALL in government-funded universities was found to be minimal and superficial, with limited resources and technical support (Al-Kahtani, 2001). Nevertheless, there is growing attention from the government and EFL departments in Saudi Arabia for enhanced technological implementation in learning in general, and EFL in particular (SCITC, 2005).

In the UAE, higher education institutions are equipped with the latest in ICT and faculty are expected to fully integrate technology into their teaching. However, access to technology must be accompanied by research studies into how computer technology is integrated in the classroom and continuous monitoring of its effect on student learning and attitudes towards the use of technology for teaching and learning. The large majority of the publications on the use of ICT in teaching at UAE universities focus primarily on describing how the technology was used rather than on its effects on student learning. For example, of the nine papers included in the September 2011 issue of the UAE Journal of Educational Technology and eLearning, only one (Behl & Devitt, 2011) reported evaluation results. Nevertheless, papers on the use of ICT in higher education that do include a research component (see for example, Behl & Devitt, 2011; Bergh, 2009; Franche, 2009) reported positive results in teaching and learning.

Given the dearth of evidence-based studies on the effectiveness of CALL at post-secondary level English programs in SA and the UAE, the studies reported in this chapter make an important contribution to the field.

THE CASE STUDIES

This chapter reports on two case studies, one in SA and one in the UAE. Both studies investigated the use of ICT in the teaching and learning of English as a foreign language at the post-secondary level. Each case study is described separately in the following sections.

Case Study 1: Saudi Arabia

The study reported here is part of a larger comparative study conducted at a major university in Riyadh, SA. Two intact groups were used in this research: 30 subjects in the treatment group and 36 subjects in the control group. All subjects were male, native Arabs and they were studying a compulsory English as a foreign language course (Eng 101) at their University. They were between 18 and 20 years and they came from similar socioeconomic backgrounds. During the 16-week treatment, each group attended three 50-minute lessons per week. The control group studied Eng 101, using the University mandated textbook, *American Kernel Lessons* (AKL). The treatment group, on the other hand, studied Eng 101 using a CALL courseware designed specifically for this study. The CALL course comprised:

- *A web-based video course, English for All (EFA) (50%);*
- *Three collaborative Web-based projects from Internet English (40%); and*
- *PowerPoint lessons covering grammar topics (10%).*

Data were collected using the Quick Placement Test (QPT) at the start of the treatment study, and the Key English Test (KET), the University Final Examination, an Evaluation Questionnaire, and individual interviews at the end of the treatment. The evaluation questionnaire and the interviews were used only with the treatment group to find out their attitudes towards the CALL course. For a detailed description of the structure of the course and the data collection instruments see Alabbad (2010).

Results

The QPT was used at the start of the study in order to determine the level of English proficiency of all the subjects participating in both groups. The results of the test showed no significant differences in the groups' English level (t (60) =0.097, p=0.923). The Key English Test (KET) took place in the last week of the course. Although neither group studied specific topics related to the KET exam, there was a significant difference between the two groups' performance in this test, with the treatment group (Mean=25.81) outperforming the control group (Mean=16.34). An independent samples t-test showed that the difference in the groups' means was highly significant (t (60)=5.19, p=0.000). The other performance measurement for the two groups was the Final University Examination. The examination took place one week after the end of the course. Both groups performed similarly and an independent samples t-test showed that the difference in the groups' means was not significant (t (58)=0.117, p=0.907). In summary, with regards to language performance, the CALL group outperformed the control group in KET.

The Evaluation Questionnaire comprised thirty-one Likert scale items and seven open-ended questions. Nearly all subjects (96%) agreed that computers and the Internet made learning interesting and they felt that they liked and enjoyed learning English more than before the treatment. Most of the subjects (81%) agreed that because of the CALL course they were thinking seriously of using the Internet to learn English on their own. A further 96% of the subjects evaluated the CALL method as a successful teaching method for learning English, while 88% believed that it helped them achieve good results in learning English. All of the subjects believed that the materials used during the treatment helped them to learn how native speakers of English used the language in real situations. In addition, the majority of the subjects (85%) were satisfied with the assessment method in the course, which included task-based projects and online interactive assignments and found it preferable to the traditional exam-based methods of assessment. The CALL program positively motivated most of the subjects (85%) to devote more effort to learning English.

In the open ended questions of the questionnaire and in the interviews similar issues were mentioned by the students. More than a one quarter of the subjects (27%) commented that the new teaching method had provided them with opportunities for self-learning such as studying at their own pace. One of the subjects pointed out that "This method opens our minds to new styles of learning English" [Student 3, I-2, 42-43].

The majority of the subjects (95%) thought that the computer-based class had been better for their performance, while 69% of the subjects stated that the new teaching method made them enjoy learning. Subject 10, for instance, reported that one of the advantages of using computers and the Internet was that he "[...] could search the Internet in English and learn with fun as well" [Student 10, I-2, 47]. According to the students, the interactive nature of the CALL resources, the colours, animations and other design features of the computer programs facilitated their language learning.

The actual use of real language was also mentioned frequently by many subjects. About 42% reported that they could use the language in real life after learning English with the CALL method. A similar percentage of subjects (38%) also mentioned that the new method enabled them to experience language spoken in simulated authentic situations. Two subjects also mentioned that the new method gave them the opportunity to use the target language more extensively. With regards to the resources, the subjects asserted that they liked the content of the EFA videos because they exemplified the type of English that people normally use. One of the subjects commented that, "The video clips were very enjoyable. The topics of the episodes were very relevant to what I needed to know" [Student 17, I-2, 8-10]. In addition to the video clips, the students also liked the program's focus on reading and the type of texts used for reading. Nearly half of the subjects mentioned the convenience of being able to hear and pronounce the new words, a feature embedded in the EFA program. Similarly, 12% reported that this method enabled them to have more practice in the target language. About one quarter of the subjects (23%) valued the opportunity that the new method gave them to correct their pronunciation

of English words. One of the subjects pointed out that one of the advantages of the CALL method was that it focused on all language skills and not only on grammar, as the traditional method did. Four of the subjects mentioned that the new teaching method gave them self-confidence in learning English.

The active role of the students in the learning process was directly mentioned in 19 out of the 26 interviews conducted. Although the CALL course was the subjects' first experience of group work, their impressions about the collaborative web-based projects were positive. More than one half of the subjects described the collaborative projects as fun. Most of the subjects, in fact, thought that working in groups was more enjoyable than working individually. The small groups enabled the students to interact and cooperate in the classroom tasks and activities more comfortably, as reported by almost one half of the subjects. Subject 20, for instance, stated, "It was easier to learn, ask and discuss [in the small groups] with students who are within the same level. We learnt from each other" [Student 20, I-2, 26-27]. There was also a social benefit from working in groups. The subjects considered strengthening their relations with their classmates as one of the advantages of working in small groups. Not only did collaborative projects have an impact on the subjects' attitudes, but also on their perception of their performance improvement. More than one half believed that the collaborative projects enhanced their language learning results more than the individual mode of learning. Subject 1, for example, reported that "the projects were very useful and enjoyable at the same time. We had to work very hard but in the end we got good results" [Student 1, I-2, 10-12].

The comparative study in SA showed that university students who learned English through CALL not only performed better than students taught using a textbook but they also enjoyed learning English, became more independent and confident learners and developed their intercultural skills.

Case Study 2: UAE

The second case study reported in this chapter is based on a research project carried out in the UAE. The project involved the evaluation of the use of laptops in an intensive EFL course at a higher education institution. The results reported here are a subset of a larger pool of data collected for the project. There were 395 subjects involved in the study (30% male and 70% female). All subjects were native Arabs between 18-20 years of age. The subjects had just completed one academic year during which they were taught English using laptops and CALL materials available online on Blackboard Vista (BBV). Subjects attended 20 hours of English during two 18-week semesters and each subject brought their laptop to their classroom which was equipped with wireless Internet access and a smartboard. The CALL program comprised: various online activities and quizzes for practicing vocabulary, grammar, writing, listening and reading; access to video clips and other internet-based multimedia resources relevant to the lesson topics; electronic copies of worksheets; links to websites that contained authentic material and also ESL practice activities.

Data were collected using an Evaluation Questionnaire which comprised 105 Likert scale items and four open-ended questions. The questionnaire sought to elicit information about the students' use of the laptops as well as their views and attitudes about the use of technology for learning English. For a more detailed description of the larger study see Gitsaki (2012).

Results

Students reported that the laptops were easy to use (87.9%) and that they had enhanced their language learning experience. They used their laptops daily to search for information (58.8%), to access learning materials on BBV (47.6%), to do classwork (56.6%), and write assignments (31.4%). They also used their laptops for fun, such as listening to music (43.9%), watching movies (23.7%), and playing computer games (24.4%). Overall students held positive views about the use of laptops for learning English (86.6%). The majority of the students (83%) reported that they liked using the laptops in class as they made learning more interesting (86.3%) and fun (89.4%). Students thought that even though the laptops had increased their workload (82.1%), using them helped them do their homework faster (85.4%). One of the subjects commented that using the laptops "makes everything easier and faster" (Student 153, Q1). Students also reported that using laptops increased their writing ability (87.9%) and their reading skills (81.7%) and they expected to get better grades as a result of using technology in the classroom (81.8%). As one student commented "I like using the program on my laptop and my English is better than in the past" (Student 56, Q1). Almost three quarters of the students (76.3%) reported that they preferred using laptops instead of textbooks for learning English. Students also reported that using the laptops increased their ability to learn by themselves (87.3%). In the open ended questions several students mentioned the fact that the laptops allowed them to access their learning materials anytime anywhere making it easier for them to "find and organize files" (Student 218, Q1) as well as "…finish the homework and submit it on time" (Student 123, Q1).

In the open questions, students also expressed their desire to do more fun activities as part of their English course such as activities that were creative and involved social networking tools. For example, students wanted to join chat rooms and forums, design websites and post information online, play online games, and create their own podcasts in order to improve their English pronunciation. All of the activities that the students mentioned were aimed at helping them practice English in fun and exciting ways.

DISCUSSION

The results of the two Gulf-based studies reviewed in this chapter show that CALL can increase and enhance the learning experiences of college-level EFL students. Learner-centredness, increased motivation, active learner-engagement, exposure to authentic and culture-rich materials, and real-life language practice opportunities were some of the benefits of the two CALL programs.

According to the literature (Neo, Neo, & Xiao-Lian, 2007; Newby, Stepich, Lehman, & Russell, 2000; Yildirim, 2005) in a student-centred educational model the learner is an active participant in the learning process. Student-centredness and active engagement were evident in the two case studies in that the learners were exposed in a technology-rich learning environment where they had access to a variety of language learning resources and they were encouraged to engage with materials at their own pace leading them to be self-directed and actively involved in the learning process. As one of the students commented:

[the CALL course] gave me the chance to watch and study the learning materials at any time anywhere and repeat them as much as I needed to. The çomputer gave me feedback on my learning. It also gave me a chance for self-learning [Student 3, I-2, 55-57].

In both studies, it was also interesting to observe that the students enjoyed the fact that they were not limited by the boundaries of the classroom. They were engaging with language learning materials outside of classroom hours. One of the advantages of such engagement was that the students realized that language learning could take place without the need for traditional textbooks and teachers. This boosted their confidence in their ability to be in charge of their own learning. In the words of a student: "This [CALL] teaching method gave me confidence in myself to really learn and speak in English" [Student 17, I-2, 3-4]. These

findings are consistent with Son's (2007) study, in which subjects enjoyed the Web-based tasks and viewed the Web as a helpful tool to practise their language skills and support further language learning at home.

Despite the fact that engagement and learning seem to be correlated, there is still little research into the relationship among classroom activities, students' engagement, and their learning outcomes (Fredricks, Blumenfeld, & Paris, 2004). Students in both studies were pleased to report that they thought their language proficiency had improved because of using the CALL resources. In the UAE study, Emirati students reported that their writing, reading and pronunciation skills had improved as a result of the laptop program. In the comparative SA study, the language performance measures provided unquestionable evidence that indeed active learner engagement in a CALL environment can lead to increased language proficiency more than the traditional, teacher-centered, textbook-based, didactic approach. The use of authentic learning materials and online tasks added challenging learning opportunities for the learners whereby they had to search online resources, filter large amounts of information and participate in tasks that entailed authentic language practice. The studies found that students appreciated the authenticity of the learning materials and tasks. As one of the students put it:

I learnt English in this mode as if I was in an English-speaking country, including watching how language is used and pronounced. Video clips were authentic. It can't be compared to the traditional method, which was boring and used only the text book and the board. [Student 7, I-2, 3-6]

This student comment expresses all too well what educators have known for a while: unless we integrate ICT and multimedia resources in the classroom, students will lose interest in what we are trying to teach them. For example, engaging students in traditional written output production of plain text may no longer be the optimum method of helping them to develop their L2 writing skills. As many researchers have indicated (see for instance Iedema, 2003; Kress, 2003; Warschauer, 2008), these days when computers and multimedia are common, students have moved beyond traditional writing practices and have developed more sophisticated, creative and multimodal ways of communicating meaning in writing. In order to foster these skills in the classroom, the adoption of technology is necessary. Otherwise, what students are doing in class will have no connection to their experiences outside the classroom.

Undoubtedly, students' language achievement is affected by their attitudes towards learning (Dörnyei, 2003; Masgoret & Gardner, 2003). As a result of the intensive use of technology in the two studies reviewed in this chapter, students developed a positive attitude towards learning, perceived their engagement in language learning activities in and out of the classroom as fun and enjoyable, and ultimately improved their English language skills. This is also consistent with earlier studies on the relationship between students' attitudes and their achievement in the Arabian Gulf context (Al-Bassam, 1987; Alfallaj, 1995).

CONCLUSION

The two case studies examined in this chapter demonstrate how the use of technology holds a promising future for language learning in the Arabian Gulf region. The large-scale implementation of ICT for language learning, though currently limited to institutions that are well-equipped in terms of infrastructure and techno-literate human capital, is gaining ground at a fast pace not only because of the technology being readily available and affordable these days but also due to the expectations of 21st century students who are adept to digital media.

Even though the two studies employed different CALL resources, it was encouraging to see that students responded to the two language learning programs with similar degrees of enthusiasm and active engagement. This was mainly due to the fact that both programs included a range of authentic multimodal resources and meaningful real life language practice opportunities, and allowed students to access the resources in and out of the classroom and learn at their own pace. The message from the two case studies is clear: ICT integration in language learning is imperative not only because it can positively enhance students' attitudes towards learning but also because it can improve their language skills.

REFERENCES

Abalhassan, K. M. I. (2002). *English as a foreign language instruction with CALL multimedia in Saudi Arabian private schools: A multi-case and multi-site study of CALL instruction.* Unpublished Ph.D. Indiana University of Pennsylvania, USA.

Abraham, L. B. (2008). Computer-mediated glosses in second language reading comprehension and vocabulary learning: A meta-analysis. *Computer Assisted Language Learning, 21*(3), 199–226. doi:10.1080/09588220802090246

Adair-Hauck, B., Willingham-McLain, L., & Earnest Youngs, B. E. (1999). Evaluating the integration of technology and language learning. *CALICO Journal, 17,* 269–306.

Al-Bassam, M. M. (1987). *The relationship of attitudinal and motivational factors to achievement in learning English as a second language by Saudi female students.* Unpublished Ph.D. University of Florida, USA.

Al-Bureikan, A. (2008). *The effectiveness of CALL in the EFL Saudi female students' listening and speaking skills at the College of Health Sciences, Onaizah.* Unpublished Ph.D. King Saud University, Saudi Arabia.

Al-Juhani, S. O. (1991). *The effectiveness of computer-assisted instruction in teaching English as a foreign language in Saudi secondary school.* Unpublished Ph.D. University of Denver, USA

Al-Subeai, W. (2000). *The effectiveness of CALL on improving vocabulary learning and reading comprehension among EFL Saudi students of the secondary commercial in Riyadh.* Unpublished Master's Dissertation, King Saud University, Saudi Arabia.

Alabbad, A. (2010). *Introducing constructivism and computer-assisted language learning (CALL) into traditional EFL programs in Saudi Arabia.* Unpublished Ph.D. The University of Queensland, Australia.

Alfallaj, F. S. (1995). *The effect of students' attitudes on performance in English language course at the College of Technology, Buraydah, Saudi Arabia.* Unpublished Thesis. University of Toledo, USA.

Aljamhoor, A. (1999). The effectiveness of using computers to teaching EFL in secondary school students: An experimental study. In *Proceedings of the Symposium on Educational Technology and Information*, Bahrain University. Riyadh, Saudi Arabia: King Saud University Press.

AlKahtani, S. (2001). *Computer-assisted language learning in EFL instruction at selected Saudi Arabian universities: Profiles of faculty.* Unpublished Ph.D. Indiana University of Pennsylvania, USA.

Behl, D., & Devitt, P. (2011). Virtual international experiences: Testing the boundaries of student global learning. *UAE Journal of Educational Technology and eLearning, 2*, 13-20.

Bergh, J. (2009). An examination of faculty use of Blackboard Vista and Web 2.0 tools to determine strategies for faculty training. *UAE Journal of Educational Technology and eLearning, 1*. Retrieved 14th January, 2011, from http://ejournal.hct.ac.ae/issues/2009-issue/faculty-use-blackboard-vista-web2-tools

Chang, L. L. (2007). The effects of using CALL on advanced Chinese foreign language learners. *CALICO Journal, 24*(2), 331–353.

Decker, M. A. (2004). Incorporating guided self-study listening into the language curriculum. *Language Teaching, 28*(6), 5–9.

Dörnyei, Z. N. (2003). Attitudes, orientations, and motivations in language learning: Advances in theory, research, and applications. *Language Learning, 53*(S1), 3–32. doi:10.1111/1467-9922.53222

Fidaoui, D., Bahous, R., & Bacha, N. (2010). CALL in Lebanese elementary ESL writing classrooms. *Computer Assisted Language Learning, 23*(2), 151–168. doi:10.1080/09588221003666248

Fields, M. (2011). Learner motivation and strategy use among university students in the United Arab Emirates. In Gitsaki, C. (Ed.), *Teaching and learning in the Arab world* (pp. 29–48). Bern, Switzerland: Peter Lang.

Franche, G. (2009). Technology supports learning at the higher colleges of technology. *UAE Journal of Educational Technology and eLearning, 1*. Retrieved on 14th January, 2011, from http://ejournal.hct.ac.ae/issues/2009-issue/technology-supports-learning

Fredricks, J. A., Blumenfeld, P. C., & Paris, A. H. (2004). School engagement: Potential of the concept, state of the evidence. *Review of Educational Research, 74*(1), 59–109. doi:10.3102/00346543074001059

Gitsaki, C. (2012). Teachers' and students' attitudes and perceptions towards the use of laptops for teaching and learning English: A case study. In Gitsaki, C., & Baldauf, R. B. Jr., (Eds.), *The future of applied linguistics: Local and global perspectives* (pp. 122–138). Newcastle, UK: Cambridge Scholars Publishing.

Gitsaki, C., & Alabbad, A. (2011). Attitudes toward learning English: A case study of university students in Saudi Arabia. In Gitsaki, C. (Ed.), *Teaching and learning in the Arab world* (pp. 3–28). Bern, Switzerland: Peter Lang.

Gitsaki, C., & Taylor, R. (2000). *Internet English: WWW-based communication activities. Student book.* Oxford, UK: Oxford University Press.

Godwin-Jones, R. (2007). Emerging technologies: Tools and trends in self-paced language instruction. *Language Learning & Technology, 11*(2), 10–17.

Greenfield, R. (2003). Collaborative e-mail exchange for teaching secondary ESL: A case study in Hong Kong. *Language Learning & Technology, 7*(1), 46–70.

Hanson-Smith, E. (1999, March/April). CALL environments: The quiet revolution. *ESL Magazine*, 8-12.

Herron, C., Dubreil, S., Cole, S., & Corrie, C. (2000). Using instructional video to teach culture to beginning foreign language students. *CALICO Journal, 17*(3), 395–427.

Iedema, R. (2003). Multimodality, resemiotisation: Extending the analysis of discourse as multisemiotic practice. *Visual Communication, 2*, 29–57. doi:10.1177/1470357203002001751

IELTS. (2010). *Analysis of data.* Retrieved on 14th January, 2011, from http://www.ielts.org/researchers/analysis_of_test_data.aspx

Kern, R. (1996). Computer-mediated communication: Using e-mail exchanges to explore personal histories in two cultures. In M. Warschauer (Ed.), *Telecollaboration in foreign language learning: Proceedings of the Hawai'i Symposium* (pp. 105-109). Honolulu, HI: University of Hawaii, Second Language Teaching & Curriculum Center.

Kress, G. (2003). *Literacy in the new media age.* London, UK: Routledge. doi:10.4324/9780203164754

Lee, L. (2002). Enhancing learners' communication skills through synchronous electronic interaction and task-based instruction. *Foreign Language Annals, 35*(1), 16–24. doi:10.1111/j.1944-9720.2002.tb01829.x

Lee, L. (2005). Using web-based instruction to promote active learning: Learners' perspectives. *CALICO Journal, 23*(1), 139–156.

LeLoup, J. W., Cortland, S., & Ponterio, R. (2007). On the Net listening: You've got to be carefully taught. *Language Learning & Technology, 11*(1), 4–15.

Levy, M., & Stockwell, G. (2006). *CALL dimensions.* Mahwah, NJ: Lawrence Erlbaum Associates.

Lewis, K., & Bardsley, D. (2010, February 23). University remedial English to end. *The National.* Retrieved 22nd September, 2010, from http://www.thenational.ae/apps/pbcs.dll/article?AID=/20100223/NATIONAL/702229804&SearchID=73393762668150

Li, J. (2010). Learning vocabulary via computer-assisted scaffolding for text processing. *Computer Assisted Language Learning, 23*(2), 253–275. doi:10.1080/09588221.2010.483678

Lin, J. M.-C., & Wu, Y.-J. (2010). Netbooks in sixth-grade English language classrooms. *Australasian Journal of Educational Technology, 26*(7), 1062–1074.

Liu, T. Y., & Chu, Y. L. (2010). Using ubiquitous games in an English listening and speaking course: Impact on learning outcomes and motivation. *Computers & Education*, *55*(2), 630–643. doi:10.1016/j.compedu.2010.02.023

Lund, A. (2008). A collective approach to language production. *ReCALL*, *20*(1), 35–54. doi:10.1017/S0958344008000414

Macaro, E., Handley, Z., & Walter, C. (2012). A systematic review of CALL in English as a second language: Focus on primary and secondary education. *Language Teaching*, *45*(1), 1–43. doi:10.1017/S0261444811000395

Magnan, S., Farrell, M., Jan, M., Lee, J., Tsai, C.-P., & Worth, R. (2003). Wireless communication: Bringing the digital world into the language classroom. In Lomicka, L., & Cooke-Plagwitz, J. (Eds.), *Teaching with technology*. Boston, MA: Thomson & Heinle.

Mak, B., & Coniam, D. (2008). Using Wikis to enhance and develop writing skills among secondary school students in Hong Kong. *System*, *36*(3), 437–455. doi:10.1016/j.system.2008.02.004

Masgoret, A.-M., & Gardner, R. C. (2003). Attitudes, motivation, and second language learning: A meta-analysis of studies conducted by Gardner and associates. *Language Learning*, *53*, 123–163. doi:10.1111/1467-9922.00212

Murray, G. L. (1999). Autonomy and language learning in a simulated environment. *System*, *27*(3), 295–308. doi:10.1016/S0346-251X(99)00026-3

Neo, M., Neo, T.-K., & Xiao-Lian, G. T. (2007). A constructivist approach to learning an interactive multimedia course: Malaysian students' perspectives. *Australasian Journal of Educational Technology*, *23*(4), 470–489.

Newby, T. J., Stepich, D. A., Lehman, J. D., & Russell, J. D. (2000). *Instructional technology for teaching and learning: Designing instruction, integrating computers, and using media* (2nd ed.). New Jersey: Merrill/Prentice Hall.

O'Hara, S., & Pritchard, R. (2008). Hypermedia authoring as a vehicle for vocabulary development in middle school English as a second language classrooms. *The Clearing House: A Journal of Educational Strategies. Issues and Ideas*, *82*(2), 60–65.

O'Neill, R., Kingsbury, R., Yeadon, T., & Cornelius, E. T. (1978). *American kernel lessons: Intermediate*. White Plains, NY: Longman.

Peters, E. (2007). Manipulating L2 learners' online dictionary use and its effect on L2 word retention. *Language Learning & Technology*, *11*(2), 36–58.

Sagarra, N., & Zapata, G. (2008). Blending classroom instruction with online homework: A study of student perceptions of computer-assisted L2 learning. *ReCALL*, *20*(2), 208–224. doi:10.1017/S0958344008000621

SCITC. (2005). *Information and telecommunication technology in Saudi Arabia*. Paper presented at the World Summit on the Information Society, Tunis.

Silverman, R., & Hines, S. (2009). The effects of multimedia-enhanced instruction on the vocabulary of English-language learners and non-English language learners in pre-kindergarten through second grade. *Journal of Educational Psychology*, *101*(2), 305–314. doi:10.1037/a0014217

Soares, D. (2008). Understanding class blogs as a tool for language development. *Language Teaching Research*, *12*(4), 517–533. doi:10.1177/1362168808097165

Son, J.-B. (2007). Learner experiences in Web-based language learning. *Computer Assisted Language Learning, 20*(1), 21–36. doi:10.1080/09588220601118495

Stepp-Greany, J. (2002). Student perceptions on language learning in a technological environment: Implications for the new millennium. *Language Learning & Technology, 6*(1), 165–180.

Sullivan, N., & Pratt, E. (1996). A comparative study of two ESL writing environments: A computer-assisted classroom and a traditional oral classroom. *System, 29*(4), 491–501. doi:10.1016/S0346-251X(96)00044-9

Torlakovic, E., & Deugo, D. (2004). Application of a CALL system in the acquisition of adverbs in English. *Computer Assisted Language Learning, 17*(2), 203–235. doi:10.1080/0958822042000334244

Tsou, W., Wang, W., & Tzeng, Y. (2006). Applying a multimedia storytelling Website in foreign language learning. *Computers & Education, 47*(1), 17–28. doi:10.1016/j.compedu.2004.08.013

Verdugo, D. R., & Belmonte, I. A. (2007). Using digital stories to improve listening comprehension with Spanish young learners of English. *Language Learning & Technology, 11*(1), 87–101.

Warschauer, M. (1996). Comparing face-to-face and electronic communication in the second language classroom. *CALICO Journal, 13*, 7–26.

Warschauer, M. (2008). Laptops and literacy: A multi-site case study. *Pedagogies: An International Journal, 3*, 52–67.

Warschauer, M., & Kern, R. (2000). *Network-based language teaching: Concepts and practice.* Cambridge, UK: Cambridge University Press.

Warschauer, M., & Meskill, C. (2000). Technology and second language learning. In Rosentha, J. (Ed.), *Handbook of undergraduate second language education* (pp. 303–318). Mahwah, NJ: Lawrence Erlbaum.

Weyers, J. (1999). The effect of authentic video on communicative competence. *Modern Language Journal, 83*(3), 339–353. doi:10.1111/0026-7902.00026

Yildirim, Z. (2005). Hypermedia as a cognitive tool: Student teachers' experiences in learning by doing. *Journal of Educational Technology & Society, 8*(2), 107–118.

Zhang, T., Gao, T., Ring, G., & Zhang, W. (2007). Using online discussion forums to assist a traditional English class. *International Journal on E-Learning, 6*(4), 623–643.

Zhao, Y. (2003). *What should teachers know about technology: Perspectives and practices.* Greenwich, CT: Information Age Publishing.

ADDITIONAL READING

Al-Shehri, S., & Gitsaki, C. (2010). Online reading: The impact of integrated and split-attention formats on L2 students' cognitive load. *ReCALL, 22*(3), 356–375. doi:10.1017/S0958344010000212

Alabbad, A., Gitsaki, C., & White, P. (2010). CALL course design for second language learning: A case study of Arab EFL learners. In Pullen, D. L., Gitsaki, C., & Baguley, M. (Eds.), *Technoliteracy, discourse and social practice: Frameworks and applications in the digital age.* Hershey, PA: IGI Global.

Chambers, A. (2005). Integrating corpus consultation in language studies. *Language Learning & Technology, 9*(2), 111–125.

Chang, W.-L., & Sun, Y.-C. (2009). Scaffolding and web concordancers as support for language learning. *Computer Assisted Language Learning, 22*(4), 283–302. doi:10.1080/09588220903184518

Chapelle, C. (2001). *Computer applications in second language acquisition: Foundations for teaching, testing and research*. Cambridge, UK: Cambridge University Press.

Chapelle, C. (2003). *English language learning and technology: Lectures on teaching and research in the age of information and communication*. Amsterdam, The Netherlands: John Benjamins.

Chapelle, C., & Douglas, D. (2006). *Assessing language through computer technology*. Cambridge, UK: Cambridge University Press. doi:10.1017/CBO9780511733116

Dooey, P. (2008). Language testing and technology: Problems of transition to a new era. *ReCALL, 20*(1), 21–34. doi:10.1017/S0958344008000311

Felix, U. (2008). The unreasonable effectiveness of CALL: What have we learned in two decades of research? *ReCALL, 20*(2), 141–161. doi:10.1017/S0958344008000323

Gánem-Gutiérrez, G. A. (2009). Repetition, use of L1 and reading aloud as mediational mechanism during collaborative activity at the computer. *Computer Assisted Language Learning, 22*(4), 323–348. doi:10.1080/09588220903184757

Heift, T., & Schulze, M. (2007). *Errors and intelligence in computer-assisted language learning: Parsers and pedagogues*. Routledge.

Hubbard, P. (2009). *Computer assisted language learning: Critical concepts in linguistics*. London, UK: Routledge.

Kárpáti, A. (2009). Web 2 technologies for Net native language learners: A "social CALL". *ReCALL, 21*(2), 139–156. doi:10.1017/S0958344009000160

Kukulska-Hulme, A. (2009). Will mobile learning change language learning? *ReCALL, 21*(2), 157–165. doi:10.1017/S0958344009000202

Lenders, O. (2008). Electronic glossing - Is it worth the effort? *Computer Assisted Language Learning, 21*(5), 457–481. doi:10.1080/09588220802447933

Neri, A., Cucchiarini, C., & Strik, H. (2008). The effectiveness of computer-based speech corrective feedback for improving segmental quality in L2 Dutch. *ReCALL, 20*(2), 225–243. doi:10.1017/S0958344008000724

Oxford, R., & Oxford, J. (2009). *Second language teaching and learning in the Net Generation. Hawai'i*. National Foreign Language Resource Center University of Hawai'i at Manoa.

Peterson, M. (2009). Learner interaction in synchronous CMC: A sociocultural perspective. *Computer Assisted Language Learning, 22*(4), 303–321. doi:10.1080/09588220903184690

Skehan, P. (2003). Focus on form, tasks, and technology. *Computer Assisted Language Learning, 16*(5), 391–411. doi:10.1076/call.16.5.391.29489

Taylor, R., & Gitsaki, C. (2003). Teaching WELL in a computerless classroom. *Computer Assisted Language Learning, 16*(4), 275–294. doi:10.1076/call.16.4.275.23412

Vandewaetere, M., & Desmet, P. (2009). Introducing psychometrical validation of questionnaires in CALL research: The case of measuring attitude towards CALL. *Computer Assisted Language Learning, 22*(4), 349–380. doi:10.1080/09588220903186547

Xu, J. (2010). Using multimedia vocabulary annotations in L2 reading and listening activities. *CALICO, 27*(2), 311–327.

Yilmaz, Y., & Granena, G. (2010). The effects of task type in synchronous computer-mediated communication. *ReCALL, 22*(1), 20–38. doi:10.1017/S0958344009990176

KEY TERMS AND DEFINITIONS

Authentic Tasks/Activities: A learning task that resembles a task performed in a non-educational setting and that requires students to apply a broad range of knowledge and skills.

Collaborative Learning/ Cooperative Learning: The learning state where two or more students work together in small groups to learn through different activities such as solving problems, discussing issues or questions, or working together in a task-based project.

Computer Assisted Language Learning (CALL): the use of computer technology in language learning and teaching.

Information and Communication Technology (ICT): The use of digital technologies and resources such as web materials (both authentic and ELT materials), electronic dictionaries, software, interactive web-based programs, and computer-mediated communication applications that can be employed in language teaching.

Online Resources: The use of web-based resources for learning.

Student-Centered Classroom: The student is seen to be an active participant in the learning process. The students play an important role in determining their goals and objectives and observing their progress in learning.

Teacher-Centered Classroom: The teaching methodology whereby the students' role is mainly to receive the information delivered to them by the instructors.

Traditional Education Context: Traditional education contexts are teacher-centered and promote a 'passive learning' style: where the teacher is the only source of knowledge.

Chapter 14
Enhancing Education in the UAE through Blended Learning

Rana M. Tamim
Zayed University, UAE

ABSTRACT

The advent of technology has changed the landscape in post-secondary academic institutions and technology-enhanced university courses are becoming the norm. While Distance Education was previously restricted to traditional correspondence having limited options for student interaction with the instructor and no interaction with other learners, technology's progression changed the context drastically. One of the emerging delivery modes is blended learning which combines the advantages of technology enhanced face-to-face instruction and electronic supported learning. The chapter offers a general overview of the influence of technological development on the post-secondary Distance Education sector and presents the advantages of the blended learning approach. Insights are offered from a UAE e-learning University case study while discussing implications for university professors and faculty members pertinent to instructional design and course delivery.

INTRODUCTION

Research is not needed to demonstrate that the advent of technology has changed the landscape in post-secondary academic institutions. At the present time, technology-enhanced university courses (in-class and/or out-of-class) are becoming the norm. Computer technology tools are used for presentation, content organization and delivery, knowledge search and retrieval, collaborative activities and knowledge building, in addition to synchronous and asynchronous communication.

This is true for universities around the world, and the United Arab Emirates (UAE) is no exception.

One of the main sectors that have been highly influenced by the advent of computer technology and Internet throughout the world is Distance Education (DE). Prior to the technological innovation boom and the widespread use of the World Wide Web, DE was mainly limited to correspondence between the student and the professor through regular mail. Students received course content and submitted assignments by mail while having limited interaction with the instructor and almost

DOI: 10.4018/978-1-4666-1984-5.ch014

no interaction with other students. Technology's progression changed the DE context drastically, and educational institutions are increasingly taking advantage of developments in computer and communication technologies leading to a variety of modes through which learning is provided. One of the most prominent emerging delivery modes is blended learning which combines the advantages of technology enhanced face-to-face instruction and electronic supported learning. Within such contexts, three major forms of interaction (student-instructor, student-student, and student-content) are highly important for effective learning to occur (Moore, 1989; Moore & Kearsley, 2005).

This chapter offers a general overview of the influence of technological development on the post-secondary DE educational sector around the world and the UAE, including its influence on the advent of blended learning. The chapter will also draw on research findings pertaining to ensuring the successful support of the three forms of interactivity in course design. Finally, the chapter will highlight how blended learning can support the successful transformation of the Arab educational systems from the current traditional status to more vibrant and innovative ones by offering insights from a case study of an e-learning university in the UAE.

Technology and Education

The level to which computer technology has permeated our lives is undeniable. Whether a believer in its advantages or not, one has to admit that it is a central part of the daily life in the 21st century. The pervasiveness of computer technologies, including information and communication technologies, has reached a level at which it is almost impossible to find a household or an institution that is computer and Internet free.

The profusion of computer technology has not always been the case nor has it been a predictable progression of events during the earlier years of development in the computer technology arena.

Although not fully supported by documented evidence, it is alleged that in 1943 Thomas Watson, the chairman of IBM said: "I think there is a world market for maybe five computers" ("Thomas J. Watson", 2008) reflecting the overall perception about the future of computers at that time. Nevertheless, the advent of technology and its forward march has been so steady and quick it led Bill Gates to claim that: "If GM had kept up with technology like the computer industry has, we would all be driving $25 cars that got 1000 MPG" (Bill Gates quotes, 2008).

It is not surprising that the education sector experienced the ripples of the computer technology wave since its early days. Ever since the late 1970's when microcomputers became available and Apple II microcomputers succeeded in accessing schools (Alessi & Trollip, 2000) the computer technology march into the classroom has grown stronger by the day. The list of terms emerging due to the development of learning technologies is growing by the day and it includes computer-assisted instruction, computer-based instruction, intelligent tutoring systems, videoconferencing, interactive multi-media, web-based instruction, e-learning, assistive technology; audio-visual instruction; computer-mediated communication; virtual-classrooms; virtual universities; and blended learning.

Throughout the years, many researchers have argued that computer technology will help change the teachers' role from the sage on the stage to the guide on the side while supporting meaningful and active learning (Jacobson, 1998). Higher achievement, increased motivation, enhanced self-confidence, greater student satisfaction, and more effective support for special needs students are only some of the desired and promised benefits. Other advantages include improved presentation of course content, improved learning outcomes, increased access to information, easier and faster communication, enhanced problem solving skills, and active involvement of students in knowledge construction. While it is not fully clear how and under what circumstances technology works best, overall research findings indicate that technology does have a positive impact on students' performance in most educational contexts (Tamim, Bernard, Borokhovski, Abrami, & Schmid, 2011).

Distance Education and Interactivity

Overall, no empirical research is needed to support the statement that one of the areas most influenced by the progressive development in the technological arena is the DE field. While it has not been highly popular or valued in earlier times, DE has started gaining worldwide attention especially with research that indicates its success and efficiency.

DE is believed by many researchers, academicians, and policy makers to offer numerous advantages including accessibility, cost-effectiveness, and the opportunity for learning anytime anywhere. An influential meta-analysis conducted by the systematic reviews team at the *Centre for the Study of Learning and Performance* (CSLP) at Concordia University synthesized findings from 232 studies published between the years 1985 to 2002 and addressing how DE compares to classroom instruction (Bernard, Abrami, Lou, Borokhovski, Wade, Wozney, et al., 2004). In total, the meta-analysis included 599 effect sizes focusing on students' achievement, attitude towards instruction, and retention. Findings indicated that DE and classroom instruction are similar with regards to the three different outcome measures with a wide variability in effect size. Results also revealed that asynchronous DE courses were correlated with more positive achievement and satisfaction results. However, DE fell short with regards to attrition, where findings revealed that classroom instruction resulted in higher retention rates. More importantly, the results revealed that pedagogy accounted for a larger percentage of variance as compared with media study features thus highlighting the importance of instructional

design in the success of both DE and classroom instruction.

From a theoretical perspective, Moore distinguished three important types of interaction that are important in distance or online education: *student-instructor, student-student, and student-content* (Moore, 1989). *Student-instructor interaction* addresses mainly the communication between the learner and the instructor in which the instructor tries "to stimulate or at least maintain the student's interest in what is to be taught, to motivate the student to learn, to enhance and maintain the learner's interest, including self-direction and self-motivation" (Moore, 1989, p. 2).

On the other hand, *student-student interaction* refers to various forms of interaction among learners including general communication or more focused group work (Moore, 1989). It is easy to understand why such interaction was almost absent in previous forms of correspondence DE and how technological advancements have helped in rendering such a form of interaction possible, convenient and easy.

Finally, *student-content* interaction refers to the learners' interaction with the content matter in order to construct meaning, enable knowledge building and transfer, and support problem solving (Moore, 1989). While this form of interaction must have been at the core of correspondence DE, technological advancement has been able to move it to a higher level.

A more recent meta-analysis by the CSLP systematic reviews team investigated the relationship between the three types of interaction and students' achievement (Bernard, Abrami, Borokhovski, Wade, Tamim, Surkes, et al., 2009). The meta-analysis synthesized effect sizes from 74 empirical studies with findings indicating that more interactive setups, whether *student-student, student-instructor, or student-content*, are more favorable for students' achievement in comparison with less interactive treatments. The overall weighted average effect size for achievement was

0.38 in favor of the more interactive treatments over the less interactive ones. Such an effect size indicates that the mean in an experimental condition would be at the 65th percentile in comparison to that of the control group. In simpler words, this means that the average student in a course where interactivity is higher will achieve 15 percentile points higher than the average student in the lower interactivity group.

Distance Education: From Correspondence to Blended Learning

Nasser and Abouchedid (2000) argue that the strongest development of the 21st century is the evolution of DE's role as a method to meet the needs of the global and exponentially growing information economy. This is reflected in the ongoing increase in the number of universities offering DE in its different formats around the world. According to Moore and Kearsley (2005), one of the most prominent cases is China's DE system that is supported by an overall organizational structure. This has enabled China to establish a variety of Radio and TV Universities in addition to more than 60 ministry authorized dual mode universities. Another leading country in the area of DE is Australia with its pioneering initiatives and experiments such as the University of Queensland. Other successful programs around the world include the United Kingdom's Open University, Korea's National Open University, University of South Africa, Turkey's Anadoul University, India's Indira Gandhi National Open University, Pakistan's AllamaIqbal Open University, Thailand's Sukhothai Thammathirat Open University, Universiti Sains Malaysia, The FernUniversitat in Germany, and Athabasca University in Canada (Moore & Kearsley, 2005).

In the Arab world and the Gulf Cooperation Council (GCC) region, the educational sector has witnessed an impressive growth, particularly at the University level, where Saudi Arabia has the highest number of newly established universities followed by the United Arab Emirates (Mukerji & Jammel, 2008). Al-Harithi (2005) stresses that although DE has a relatively short history in this region, it has started to gain the attention and respect it deserves. Examples of DE and blended learning universities include the Virtual Arab University, the Syrian Virtual University, the Arab Open University, and Al-Quds Open University (Lasser, 2006).

Prior to gaining a worldwide standing, DE moved through various stages of development and maturity where Moore and Kearsley (2005) highlight five main generations of DE. According to Moore and Kearsley, the first generation provided the basis for individualized distance instruction and was represented as correspondence/home/independent study. This form of DE was only possible in the early 1880's due to the development of the cheap and reliable postal services as a result of the proliferation of the railway networks. Correspondence education in this form was implemented in different countries including USA, Great Britain, Germany, and France.

Moore and Kearsley note that the second generation of DE owes its commencement to the advent of broadcasting technologies, namely the radio in the 1920's and the television in the late 1920's and early 1930's. While this form of DE still had minimal interaction between the students and the teachers, it differed drastically from the previous one due to the added visual dimension in the presentation of information. Both the first and second generations involved numerous but sporadic experimentations rather than nationwide systematic initiatives.

The third generation of DE made use of audio, video, and face-to-face tutorials in the late 1960's and early 1970's resulting in the establishment of Open Universities. During this time, DE also witnessed the emergence of the systems approach and the involvement of course teams in the design and delivery of instruction with an industrial approach. Within this context, the most successful initiatives were the University of Wisconsin's Articulated Instructional Media Project and Great Britain's Open University.

With the progression of technological innovations, and with the success of audio and video conferencing technologies in the 1970's and 1980's, DE moved to a new era that Moore and Kearsley consider as the fourth generation. With such conferencing technologies that enable group involvement, DE became more appealing to a wider group of educators and policy makers than previous forms of DE. For the first time, DE allowed for real-time interaction not only between the student and the instructor but also among students themselves. This form of DE was most successful in corporate training, but it was also experimented with in other academic sectors such as universities and schools.

The most influential technology that resulted in drastic changes in the quality and delivery mode of DE, and consequently to an explosion in its popularity, was the Internet leading to Web-based delivery of courses and programs. In 1992, the Web hosted around fifty pages, whereas there were at least one billion Web pages in the year 2000 (Maddux, 2001). As of 9th of July 2001, and according to the WorldWideWebSize website which keeps daily records of the growth of the World Wide Web, the Indexed Web contains at least 19.89 billion pages. This proliferation of the World Wide Web resulted in new forms of DE delivery and allowed for the emergence of a variety of single mode, pure electronic modes, and new combinations of program and course delivery, while allowing for the application of constructivist collaborative strategies through the use of text, audio, and video on single unified platforms.

Blended Learning: What and Why?

Similar to many terms in the field, blended learning has a variety of definitions, with the consensus focusing on the combined use of face-to-face and DE delivery systems while making use of techno-logical and online tools to maximize on the benefits of in-class and online instruction (Osguthorpe & Graham, 2003). Colis and Moonen (2001) define blended learning as a hybrid of face-to-face and online learning where the online component of instruction becomes a natural extension of the traditional in-class constituent. Considering the issue from a course design perspective, a blended course may fall at any point in a continuum between full face-to-face in-class delivery and full online instruction (Rovai & Jordan, 2004).

Osguthorpe and Graham (2003) argue that each of the two forms of instruction has its own advantages which blended-learning can make use of while overcoming the weaknesses of DE. They stress that from one perspective, face-to-face allows for positive and active student-student and student-instructor interaction without offering any flexibility regarding time and place. On the other hand, blended learning provides the flexibility featured in DE programs while enabling students to interact with other students and the instructors through the use of the physical face-to-face component as well as the utilized technological platforms. This ability to facilitate and enable communication, discourse, and interactivity is key to minimizing the sense of social isolation that is known to be DE's weakest aspect.

Rovai and Jordan (2004) stress that blended learning allows educators and instructional designers to focus more on learning production rather than instruction delivery; reaching out to students with the help of distance education technologies, and most importantly working on positively establishing a sense of community among the students. Rovai and Jordan's research findings indicated that blended courses resulted in significantly higher measures of connectedness between students and with the instructors than both traditional face-to-face and full online courses. Moreover, the findings suggest that the blended courses also result in higher student performance.

With all the above, it is no surprise that Garrison and Kanuka (2004) advocate blended learning's transformative potential and ability to redefine higher education institutions allowing them to be more learner centered and capable of delivering richer learning experiences.

Distance Education and Blended Learning in the Arab World

As noted earlier, the educational sector in the Arab world has been moving through some major reforms and developments including the higher acceptance and awareness to DE as reflected by the number of listed universities. However, the progress and advancement of DE were not very fast in this region due to a variety of reasons. Nasser and Abouchedid (2000) highlight that perceptions regarding DE and e-learning in the Arab World are generally negative. Similarly, Ibrahim, Rwegasira, and Taher (2007) argue that two of the main challenges facing the progression of DE in Arab countries include the social skepticism towards DE delivery and the lack of formal recognition and accreditation for most of the DE programs. Ibrahim and her colleagues also note that the current DE programs suffer from the use of traditional DE instructional media that does not support interactivity. Moreover, most currently available course content is in the form of printed material designed and developed by faculty members with traditional face-to-face university experience and no qualifications or training in DE design and delivery.

In spite of the negative attitudes and available challenges facing successful DE implementation in the Arab world, the awareness to the need for a different form of higher education delivery is becoming more evident. A major reason is the fact that the Arab States are facing an increased need for the establishment of higher education institutions whose financial implications are very demanding and not easy to meet by many of the Arab governments (Ibrahim, Rwegasira, & Taher, 2007).

With this in mind, blended learning presents a very viable and strong alternative that can provide students with the potential of life-long learning while offering advantages of both face-to-face in-class instruction and online DE delivery modes. With its face-to-face component, blended learning can minimize the students' feeling of isolation. This is of high importance and relevance in a region where e-learning is still in its infancy and awareness to its viability and strengths is catching up, and it may consequently address part of the social skepticism towards full online learning. The in-class component also allows for a smoother student transition to the self-regulated more autonomous forms of DE learning. Further and above, the blended learning mode is more capable of meeting accreditation criteria in the region thus allowing for formal recognition of programs offered with such an approach.

In the United Arab Emirates, Hamdan Bin Mohammed e-University (HBMeU) is a new academic institution that is using blended learning for the delivery of its programs to meet the needs of the fast growing society of the UAE. In the following sections, we discuss how the technological advancements are utilized to offer student-centered programs while catering for learners' needs and ensuring successful student-instructor, student-student, and student-content interaction.

Hamdan Bin Mohammed e-University

HBMeU was originally established as the e-Total Quality Management College (eTQM) in September 2002. In 2009, the College evolved into an e-Learning University and was subsequently renamed as Hamdan Bin Mohammed e-University (HBMeU). The delivery model implemented by HBMeU is a blended technology enhanced approach that makes use of a combination of face-to-face, online, and self-paced learning to deliver its accredited graduate and undergraduate programs as presented in Figure 1. The advanced

Figure 1. HBMeU blended learning approach

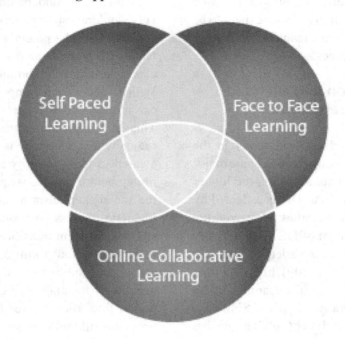

Virtual Learning Environment that is used to support this blended delivery form makes use of the MOODLE Learning Management System (LMS) and WIMBA Virtual Classroom with Figures 2 and 3 providing a snapshot of each platform.

The face-to-face component depends on pre-scheduled physical in-class sessions during which students meet their professors and colleagues. These encounters enable students to become acquainted with their instructors and with each other, thus allowing for the establishment of a sense of community. This is believed to be instrumental in minimizing the students' feeling of isolation during synchronous and asynchronous online sessions, and in ensuring that the students interact more effectively throughout the course. The online constituent depends on a combination of synchronous and asynchronous sessions and interactions. During the pre-scheduled synchronous meetings, students log onto a virtual classroom (WIMBA) to meet with the professor. As for the asynchronous communication, it is enabled with the help of the MOODLE Learning Manage-

ment System where students can access a variety of resources, and participate in a series of activities such as discussion forums and blogs. Finally, the self-study element includes guided periods of personal study that are enhanced by asynchronous or synchronous communication with the instructors as needed.

From the technological perspective, the MOODLE platform provides a safe and user-friendly environment for students where they can download course materials and documents, hand in assignments, consult and download resources, participate in online discussions, and communicate with the professors and other learners in an asynchronous fashion. The platform goes beyond what a regular emailing system can allow for, and offers a particular level of flexibility and interaction that supports collaborative learning. In combination with the various tools available on MOODLE, students have access to study books and digitized material through each course portal which they can make use of based on their own needs and time availability.

Figure 2. A snapshot of the MOODLE learning management system

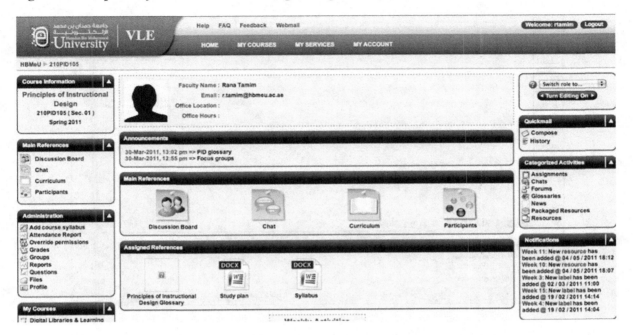

The WIMBA virtual classroom allows for the delivery of online synchronous sessions that are scheduled and planned for ahead of time. Faculty members and students can work on shared PowerPoint presentations, present information on the Electronic Whiteboard, send messages, browse the web, conduct chats and even share their desktops with each other. The platform also allows for scheduling virtual synchronous meetings between the students and the professors or for study group purposes as deemed necessary.

Interactivity and Blended Learning at HBMeU

Due to the importance of the three forms of interaction (student-instructor, student-student, and student-content) for the success of online and DE courses, it becomes imperative for course designers and instructors to ensure that the three are enabled appropriately. While the advanced VLE system allows for supporting all forms of interactivity, the achievement of successful interactions is only possible with the use of appropriate and adequate pedagogies. Through the MOODLE platform, the instructors can make use of numerous tools such as mailing options, note posting opportunities, file and document uploading and sharing, and most importantly the discussions boards and forums where learners may share their opinions with their instructors and with each other and receive feedback pertaining to different topics and issues relevant to the course at hand. Similarly, the WIMBA Virtual Classroom possesses particular affordances that may be used to support and enhance interactivity. Communication over the WIMBA platform includes chatting, two-way audio, and two-way video capabilities, while allowing professors to present material, and lead discussions for the successful creation of a meaningful learning experience, in addition to the ability to assign students to work in groups in separate breakout rooms.

Although the technology has the potential, it is not a magic wand, rather it is merely a tool that the instructor can use as he/she wishes. With all

Figure 3. A snapshot of the WIMBA virtual classroom

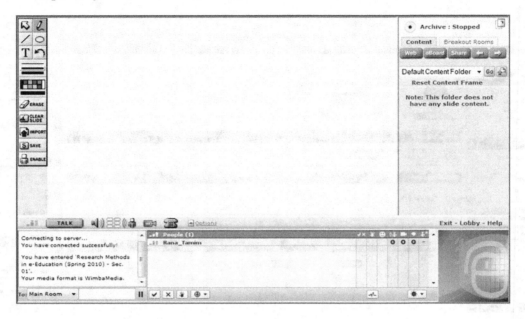

its affordances, the MOODLE can be rendered a simple online digital library where instructors can upload material for their students, or a plain emailing system for regular communication between individuals signed in the same course. Similarly, the WIMBA platform can be reduced to a simple presentation tool that emulates a chalkboard for instructors to show their power point presentations on. Unfortunately, many new comers to the e-learning arena fall into the trap of replicating in-class techniques and strategies of content delivery through the online portals and platforms thus diminishing the return on investment and the expected added value of the blended learning mode.

In light of evidence-based research findings, and with instructional design principles in mind, instructors can harness the power of technology and utilize it for the advancement of the learning experience. While designing the different physical and online sessions and the various synchronous and asynchronous activities, it is advisable that instructors keep the learner centered principles advocated by the American Psychological As-

sociation (APA) in 1997. The principles emphasize the psychological factors under the learner's control and consist of: cognitive and meta-cognitive factors; motivational and affective factors; developmental and social factors, and individual differences (APA, 1997). McCombs (2000) and McCombs and Vakili (2005) stress that learner-centered principles present an appropriate framework for utilizing technological tools for the development of successful learning environments. In addition, Laurillard (2002) emphasizes the importance of the APA principles especially since the effectiveness of computer technology is affected by various factors including instructional design, nature of the learning task, and learner characteristics.

Besides implementing the basic premises of successful teaching such as offering clear objectives and guidance, prompt and constructive feedback, and varying the teaching strategies and approaches to cater for individual differences, instructors need to minimize lecturing and allow for active student participation. Nevertheless, it is important to stress that while increasing the amount of interaction is beneficial for learning and satisfaction, the quality of such interactions is of higher importance, especially in terms of cognitive engagement and meaningfulness (Tamim, Bernard, Borokhovski, & Abrami, 2011).

It is interesting to know that although the UAE students do not have a long experience with online learning, they are highly aware of the importance of such interactions. When asked about the most memorable and meaningful experiences in their blended learning courses, HBMeU students agreed that these were situations where they worked on collaborative projects in synchronous and asynchronous online modes, and when they were empowered and given the chance to be in control (Tamim, 2010). Students also believe that the technology use with a student-centered approach is allowing for the emergence of leadership consensus among their groups (Senteni & Tamim, 2011). In a particular research addressing HBMeU's female students' perceptions about the blended learning delivery mode, participants noted the it is allowing them to develop a variety of skills such as time management, decision making skills, ability to take initiatives, online communication and collaborative skills, sharing ideas, and self-confidence (Tamim & Senteni, 2011). More importantly participants noted that the process is allowing them to become better self-regulators and is enhancing their critical thinking skills.

Implications for Practitioners

It is obvious that blended learning has the potential to enhance academic institutions' ability to meet the needs of the fast growing and vibrant communities in the Arab Region. While HBMeU's experience may not be easy to replicate completely with other universities due to major differences in the vision and mission of each institution, it is very easy to draw implications and make use of the lessons learned. It is understandable that not all universities are supportive of a full shift to an online delivery mode; however, it is undeni-

able that the majority strives to make use of the technological advancements. As such, how can traditional face-to-face universities make use of the blended learning mode? While administrative support is highly important, the most important variable remains the professor whose innovativeness and commitment is the key to the success of any instructional approach.

With regards to making use of the blended learning approach for the enhancement of the learning process, the first suggestion for faculty members is to make use of already available Learning Management Systems at their universities. In situations where this is not the case, interested faculty members can make use of available free online resources. While MOODLE is a free source e-learning software platform, it needs a level of technical expertise to help in its operation and hosting. Examples of free, simple, and easy course management systems include myicourse (http://www.myicourse.com/welcome) and rcampus (http://www.rcampus.com/). In addition, instructors may opt to use wiki and blog spaces to create their own personal online course. Examples of wiki platforms include wikispaces (http://www.wikispaces.com/) and wikidot (http://www.wikidot.com/). Alternately, instructors may decide to make use of social communication network websites such as FaceBook for the educational communication and collaboration purposes.

The above also applies with regards to the WIMBA Virtual Classroom. While traditional universities may not allow for the flexibility of replacing a face-to-face session with an online one, faculty members can enhance the overall learning experience with numerous activities. Examples include online lectures or presentations by guest lecturers from around the world or the use of virtual classrooms to support students' in their group projects. While WIMBA is not an open source, there is no shortage in similar platforms on the net such as the WIZIQ classroom (http://www.wiziq.com/). Professors may also want to make use of the Skype communication tool (http://

www.skype.com/) that includes advanced communication features such as file and desktop sharing. Other strong and powerful software and websites that faculty members may use innovatively in their teaching include GoogleApps (http://www.google.com/apps/intl/en/edu/), DabbleBoard (http://www.dabbleboard.com/), and definitely the popular YouTube (http://www.youtube.com/).

There is no shortage in online resources and definitely no specific recipe or template that dictates how and when each tool is to be used, however, what research indicates is that making use of technological advancements to design instruction with student-centered principles in mind, while catering for meaningful and successful interaction, will provide students with a more enhanced learning experience.

CONCLUSION

This chapter has offered an overview of the progressive development of DE around the world and in the Arab region in light of the technological innovations and profusion. Attention was given to the establishment of blended learning as an acceptable and popular delivery mode of instruction that has the potential of enhancing the educational systems in the Arab countries. HBMeU offers an example of how blended learning may be used to address social skepticism towards DE and the lack of formal acceptance of pure online delivery modes. More importantly, it enables the provision of learner-centered environments that are capable for catering for learners' needs while enhancing the different forms of interaction needed for the success of DE programs.

It is important to keep in mind that the road is still long before blended learning is fully established in the region. There is the need for in-depth research to provide an adequate understanding of the current status, the challenges, the strong points, and the best ways forward. There is also a substantive demand for government policies to support the establishment of the field and raise awareness to the viability and effectiveness of the blended delivery mode. Nevertheless, and in the meantime, it is important to make use of the tools available at hand to enrich our students' learning experience, especially that the technological advancement is annulling any excuse of inaccessibility or unavailability of resources.

REFERENCES

Al-Harithi, A. S. (2005). Distance higher education experiences of Arab Gulf students in the United States: A cultural perspective. *International Review of Research in Open and Distance Learning*, *6*(3), 1–14.

Alessi, S. M., & Trollip, S. R. (2000). *Multimedia for learning: Methods and development* (3rd ed.). New York, NY: Allyn & Bacon.

APA. (1997). *Learner-centered psychology principles: A framework for school redesign and reform*. Retrieved 25 March, 2005, from http://www.apa.org/ed/lcp.html

Bernard, R. M., Abrami, P. C., Borokhovski, E., Wade, A. C., Tamim, R. M., & Surkes, M. A. (2009). A meta-analysis of three types of interaction treatments in distance education. *Review of Educational Research*, *79*(3), 1243–1289. doi:10.3102/0034654309333844

Bernard, R. M., Abrami, P. C., Lou, Y., Borokhovski, E., Wade, A., & Wozney, L. (2004). How does distance education compare with classroom instruction? A meta-analysis of the empirical literature. *Review of Educational Research*, *74*(3), 379–439. doi:10.3102/00346543074003379

Bill Gates quotes. (2008). Retrieved November 10, 2008, from http://thinkexist.com/ quotation/ if_gm_had_kept_up_with_technology_like_ the/188702.html

Colis, B., & Moonen, J. (2001). *Flexible learning in a digital world: Experiences and expectations.* London, UK: Kogan-Page.

Garrison, D. R., & Kanuka, H. (2004). Blended learning: Uncovering its transformative potential in higher education. *The Internet and Higher Education, 7,* 95–105. doi:10.1016/j.iheduc.2004.02.001

Ibrahim, M., Rwegasira, K. S. P., & Taher, A. (2007). Institutional factors affecting students' intentions to withdraw from distance learning programs in the Kingdom of Saudi Arabia: The case of the Arab Open University (AOU). *Online Journal of Distance Learning Administration, 5*(1).

Jacobson, M. (1998). *Adoption patterns of faculty who integrate computer technology for teaching and learning in higher education.* Retrieved 15 March, 2005, from http://www.ucalgary.ca/~dmjacobs/phd/phd-results.html

Lasser, W. (2006). Virtual universities for African and Arab countries. *Turkish Online Journal of Distance Education, 7*(4), 147–160.

Laurillard, D. (2002). *Rethinking university teaching: A framework for the effective use of educational technology* (2nd ed.). London, UK: Routledge. doi:10.4324/9780203304846

Maddux, C. D. (2001). *Educational computing: learning with tomorrow's technologies.* Needham Heights, MA: Allyn & Bacon.

McCombs, B. L. (2000). *Assessing the role of educational technology in the teaching and learning process: A learner-centered perspective.* Retrieved September, 2005, from http://www.ed.gov/rschstat/eval/tech/techconf00/mccombs_paper.html

McCombs, B. L., & Vakili, D. (2005). A learner-centered framework for E-learning. *Teachers College Record, 107*(8), 1582–1600. doi:10.1111/j.1467-9620.2005.00534.x

Moore, M. (1989). Three types of interaction. *American Journal of Distance Education, 3*(2), 19–24. doi:10.1080/08923648909526659

Moore, M. G., & Kearsley, G. P. (2005). *Distance education: A systems view.* Belmont, CA: Wadsworth.

Mukerji, S., & Jammel, N. K. (2008). Perspectives and strategies towards collaboration in higher education in the GCC Arab States of the Gulf. *Asian Journal of Distance Education, 6*(1), 76–86.

Nasser, R., & Abouchedid, K. (2000). Attitudes and concerns towards distance education: The case of Lebanon. *Journal of Distance Learning Administration, 3*(4), 1–10.

Osguthorpe, R. T., & Graham, C. (2003). Blended learning environments: Definitions and directions. *The Quarterly Review of Distance Education, 4*(3), 227–233.

Rovai, A. P., & Jordan, H. M. (2004). Blended learning and sense of community: A comparative analysis with traditional and fully online graduate courses. *International Review of Research in Open and Distance Learning, 5*(2).

Senteni, A., & Tamim, R. M. (2011, June). *Online collaboration empowering minds for the future.* Paper presented at the World Conference on Educational Multimedia, Hypermedia & Telecommunications, Lisbon.

Tamim, R. M. (2010, March). *Learner-centered use of a virtual classroom in the United Arab Emirates.* Paper presented at the Higher Education in the Gulf: Research Insights in Learning and Teaching Symposium, Dubai.

Tamim, R. M., Bernard, R. M., Borokhovski, E., & Abrami, P. C. (2011). The value of interaction treatments in distance and online learning. In Cooper, J., & Robinson, P. (Eds.), *Small group learning in higher education: Research and practice.* Oklahoma City, OK: New Forums Press.

Tamim, R. M., Bernard, R. M., Borokhovski, E., Abrami, P. C., & Schmid, R. F. (2011). What forty years of research says about the impact of technology on learning: A second-order meta-analysis and validation study. *Review of Educational Research, 81*(3), 4–28. doi:10.3102/0034654310393361

Tamim, R. M., & Senteni, A. (2011, May). *Empowering female learners through blended learning in the UAE.* Paper presented at the Annual Conference of the Comparative and International Education Society Montreal.

Wikipedia. The free encyclopedia. (2008). *Thomas J. Watson.* Retrieved December 12, 2008, from http://en.wikipedia.org/wiki/Thomas_J._Watson

WorldWideWebSize. (2011). Retrieved July 9th, 2011, from http://www.worldwidewebsize.com/

ADDITIONAL READING

Alsunbul, A. (2002). Issues relating to distance education in the Arab world. *Convergence, 35*(1), 59–80.

Anderson, T. (2003). Modes of interaction in distance education: Recent developments and research questions. In Moore, M. G., & Anderson, W. G. (Eds.), *Handbook of distance education.* Mahwah, NJ: Lawrence Erlbaum associates.

Anderson, T. (Ed.). (2008). *The theory and practice of online learning.* Edmenton, Canada: Athabasca University Press.

Bates, T. (1997). The impact of technological change on open and distance learning. *Distance Education, 18*(1), 93–109. doi:10.1080/0158791970180108

Bernard, R. M., De Rubalcava, B., & St. Pierre, D. (2000). Collaborative online distance learning: Issues for future practice and research. *Distance Education, 21*(2), 260–277. doi:10.1080/0158791000210205

Carliner, S. (2004). *An overview of online learning* (2nd ed.). Amherst, MA: HRD Press.

Dreyfus, H. (2001). How far is distance from education. *Bulletin of Science, Technology & Society, 21*(3), 165–174. doi:10.1177/027046760102100302

Garrison, D. R., & Vaughan, N. D. (2008). *Blended learning in higher education: Framework, principles, and guidelines.* San Francisco, CA: Jossey-Bass.

Gunawardena, C. N., & McIsaac, M. S. (2004). Distance education. In Jonassen, D. (Ed.), *Handbook of research on educational communications and technology.* New York, NY: Simon &Shuster Macmillan.

Holmberg, B. (2003). A theory of distance education based on empathy. In Moore, M., & Kearsley, G. P. (Eds.), *Handbook of distance education* (pp. 79–86). Mahwah, NJ: Lawrence Erlbaum Associates.

Mohamed, A. (2005). Distance higher education in the Arab region: The need for quality assurance frameworks. *Online Journal of Distance Learning Administration, 8*(1).

Naidu, S. (2003). Designing instruction for e-learning environments. In Moore, M. G., & Anderson, W. G. (Eds.), *Handbook of distance education.* Mahwah, NJ: Lawrence Erlbaum Associates.

Saba, F. (2003). Distance education theory, methodology, and epistemology: A pragmatic paradigm. In Moore, M. G., & Anderson, W. G. (Eds.), *Handbook of distance education.* Mahwah, NJ: Lawrence Erlbaum Associates.

Shearer, R. (2003). Instructional design in distance education: An overview. In Moore, M. G., & Anderson, W. G. (Eds.), *Handbook of distance education.* Mahwah, NJ: Lawrence Erlbaum associates.

Simonson, M., Smaldino, S., Albright, M., & Zvacek, S. (2003). *Teaching and learning at a distance: Foundations of distance education.* Upper Saddle River, N.J.: Merrill Prentice Hall.

UNESCO. (2002). *Open and distance learning: Trends, policy and strategy consderations.*

Veletsianos, G. (Ed.). (2010). *Emerging technologies in distance education.* Edmenton, Canada: Athabasca University Press.

Weller, M., Pegler, C., & Mason, R. (2005). Students' experience of component versus integrated virtual environments. *Journal of Computer Assisted Learning, 21*, 253–259. doi:10.1111/j.1365-2729.2005.00132.x

Yacci, M. (2000). Interactivity demystified: A structural definition for distance education and intelligent CBT. *Educational Technology, 39*(4), 5–16.

KEY TERMS AND DEFINITIONS

Asynchronous Communication: Is any technology-supported communication that is occurring in a different-time and different-place mode between two or more individuals.

Blended Learning: Any instructional delivery mode that makes use of a variety of learning environments and approaches, especially a combination of face-to-face instructional strategies and electronic supported learning.

Distance Education: A form of education that depends on delivering instruction to students who are separated from the instructor by geographical location and time and who are not bound by the traditional face-to-face in-class instruction.

Learning Management System: Any software that enables the management, delivery and sharing of course material between the instructor and the students. In more advanced and elaborate learning management systems, both synchronous and asynchronous communications are enabled.

Student-Content Interaction: Refers to the learners' interaction with the content and subject matter in order to construct meaning, enable knowledge building and transfer, and support problem solving.

Student-Instructor Interaction: Encompasses all forms of communication and interaction taking place between the learner and the instructor within the context of any form of instruction, be it face-to-face, distance, or blended in form.

Student-Student Interaction: Encompasses all forms of communication ad interaction taking place between the learners and their fellow colleagues within the context of any form of instruction, be it face-to-face, distance, or blended in form.

Synchronous Communication: Is any technology supported communication that is occurring in real-time between two or more individuals, be it through audio, video, chat, or a combination of these options.

Virtual Classroom: Online spaces that allow teachers to offer live instruction with the help of a shared whiteboard and real-time audio interaction with the students.

Chapter 15
Meaningful Learning from Sustained Online Communication:
A Reflection with a Group of Adults

Salam Abdallah
Abu Dhabi University, UAE

Fayez Ahmad Albadri
Abu Dhabi University, UAE

ABSTRACT

This case study discusses a model of evaluating a group of adult students learning resulting from using an online social constructivist tool. The study is based on using a discussion board for sharing and co-constructing knowledge. Learning through social interactions and critical thinking is increasingly considered an essential teaching approach and especially for adult students. This approach promotes active learning and leads to better understanding of the subject matter. Online interaction evidently promotes critical thinking, problem solving, and knowledge construction. The literature provides a large set of approaches for evaluating discussion boards. However, their uses are not easily adoptable by faculty who are primarily interested in measuring the quality of online discussion. The authors contend that faculty should not adhere to a single measure but rather to be experiential and to develop their own models of evaluation of the students' online learning experience. This case study discusses our own model for understanding the students' learning experience and the authors' approach to assess an individual's level of engagement in critical thinking. The study contributes to the body of knowledge on adopting e-learning technologies at institutions in the Arab World for teaching adult students.

INTRODUCTION

Wurm (2005) argues that bulk of adult education research has focused on self-directed learning, critical reflection, experiential learning, distance learning, and learning how to learn. Knowles who developed the andragogy theory argued that adults learn differently from children because the learning process of adults is different as adults are more self-directed, autonomous i.e more responsible for their learning and take decisions more than children (Simith, 2002). This could be linked t

DOI: 10.4018/978-1-4666-1984-5.ch015

that fact that adults accumulate experience over the years and they become conscious and aware of what is relevant and useful to them. In this theory, teachers take on a facilitating role and intervene only when necessary. Based on the concept behind andragogy, adults need opportunities to construct their relevant knowledge and to collaborate with others to simulate life experiences.

To motivate adult learners they need to be engaged in activities to make them think, reflect and express their experiences and views. Andragogy may be enforced using social constructivism activities such as using online discussion boards. Discussion boards have the potential to promote deep thinking and can also lead into random chat leading to surface learning and adding little to their learning experience (Knowlton, 2001).

Social constructivism is about knowledge construction that is co-constructed through social interaction (Simpson, 2002). The basis of its philosophy is that students' learning is strengthened by applying prior knowledge and principles to a new environment resulting in construction of new knowledge (Beaumie, 2001).

Nevertheless, engaging students through online discussion boards does not automatically guarantee meaningful learning, warranting the need for suitable assessment tools to measure students learning and performance. The question is "how to evaluate students learning through the examination of the knowledge constructed by them to ensure that learning is occurring?"

EVALUATING LEARNING ONLINE DISCUSSION BOARDS

The extant literature on analyzing online learning using discussion boards is quite extensive. Nevertheless, most of the assessment approaches discussed in the literature rely on examining the students' postings seeking indicators related to various knowledge elements. These indicators are used by educators to evaluate learning that occurred during knowledge construction and sharing using online discussions. The analyzing approach can be either approached quantitatively or qualitatively. Probably the most cited approach is the 'community of inquiry model' developed by Garrision et. al. (2000), who proposed three fundamental categories related to; cognitive presence, social presence and teaching presence. The cognitive presence category is the relevant category in this study, which includes triggering events, exploration, integration and solution. The dimension of the cognitive presence encapsulates a range of cognitive processes encountered by users when engaged in online discussions forums. The Interaction Analysis Model (Gunawardena, Lowe, & Andeson, 1997) another common model of five phases that is used as an analysis protocol to ascertain and measure the meaningful learning occurring online. Table (1) draws a comparison between the most common approaches that are used to evaluate online learning using discussions boards and specifically the cognitive processes that may occur in that environment. Bloom's Taxonomy of Education Objectives (1956) has also been used by educators and was found useful to evaluate students' contribution in online discussions (Meyer, 2004). From the comparison of the common approaches, it is clear that the models have much in common as well as differences.

Unlike other categories of learning, adult learning requires a type of engagement that can facilitate deep thinking. Table (2) shown below, distinguishes between surface and in-depth cognitive processes (Henri, 1992), considering that faculty are usually interested in instilling deep learning processes to their students.

The use of these models for learning assessment and analysis relies on the coder reading of each posting and mapping the statement to the most applicable category although the statement

Table 1. Various common approaches used to evaluate online discussions

Garrision et. al. (2000)	Gunawardena, Lowe, & Andeson, 1997	Bullen (1998)	Henri (1992):
cognitive presence, social presence and teaching presence	Sharing/Comparing Discovery Negotiation of meaning Testing/Modification -Agreement and applications of newly constructed meaning.	Clarification, assessing evidence, making and judging inferences, using appropriate strategies and tactics.	Elementary clarification, in-depth clarification, inference, judgment, strategies,
Brookfield (1987)	Norris and Ennis (1989)	Newman, Webb & Cochrane (1995):	Bloom (1956)
Trigger event, appraisal, exploration, Developing alternatives, integration	Elementary clarification, Basic support, inference, advanced clarification, strategies and tactics.	clarification, in-depth clarification, inference, judgment, strategy formation,	Knowledge Comprehension Application Analysis Synthesis Evaluation

may have be mapped to multiple categories. The end result of analysis is a range of statements grouped under different categories.

These models offer their own unique strengths and weaknesses and they vary in complexity and ease of use by educators. As a general rule, the use of multiple approaches is encouraged to illuminate the various aspects of learning using online discussion. Furthermore, faculty are encouraged to experiment and develop their own assessment models that are appropriate to the situation on hand considering the complexity and level of the taught course and the learners attributes and familiarity with online learning. Researchers can also have a major contribution by continuously exploring effective models to develop reliable frameworks that can help explain what goes in online interactions and how this could be translated into meaningful measure of students learning and education performance.

This chapter is mainly concerned with the challenge of analyzing and assessing adults learning in online discussion boards and learning forums. It discusses a model that was developed and tested by the authors to determine the value of the online discussion boards when a group of MBA students were engaged in such environment.

METHODOLOGY

This is an exploratory qualitative case study using rich data for analysis. The purpose of the study is to understand whether students are gaining merely surface learning or deep learning that can motivate them to become self-learners and critical thinkers.

The case study method belongs to qualitative research methods (Yin, 1994), aiming to gain insights rather than gather statistically significant evidence. Qualitative research method refers to the strategy for data collection and analysis. Theories developed using qualitative approaches are more representative of the real world because they generate 'rich' data collected from the words, actions, and symbols (explicit and tacit knowledge) of people. Rich or qualitative data are the results of meaning allocated by people to events and objects. Interpretation of qualitative data is subjective because researchers' presuppositions or pre-understandings affect the interpretation of data (Lopez and Willis, 2004); therefore, the findings are the researchers' perspective to the interpretation of the students' statements.

The rich data was generated from the content of online discussions contributed by two groups of MBA graduate students attending a course in e-Business. Not all discussion threads were included for analysis. The criteria for selection of

Table 2. Comparison between surface and in-depth cognitive processes

Henri's (1992) analytical model: Processing information.	
Surface processing	In-depth processing
Repeating the information contained in the statement of the problem without making inferences or offering an interpretation	Linking facts, ideas and notions in order to interpret, infer, propose and judge
Repeating what has been said without adding any new elements	Offering new elements of information
Stating that one shares the ideas or opinions stated, without taking these further or adding any personal comments	Generating new data from information collected by the use of hypotheses and inferences
Proposing solutions without offering explanation	Proposing one or more solutions with short–, medium–, or long–term justification
Making judgments without offering justification	Setting out advantages and disadvantages of a situation or solution
Asking questions which invite information not relevant to the problem or not adding to the understanding of it	Providing proof or supporting examples Making judgments supported by justification
Offering several solutions without suggesting which is most appropriate	Perceiving the problem within a larger perspective
Perceiving the situation in a fragmentary or short short–term manner	Developing intervention strategies within a wider framework

the discussion threads were based on discussions that were sustained over a long period of time and which engaged a large number of students.

The online activity component of the MBA E-Business subject required each student to raise one critical thinking question and to answer at least 9 questions. As the online component of the course was intended to complement the in-class lectures and activities, the topics of the critical thinking questions had to be related to the theme of topics discussed in the face-to-face class environment.

The rich data from the discussion threads was converted into a text file consisting of over 70 pages. The text file was later exported into NVivo qualitative analysis software for analysis.

The analysis proceeded with no fixed set of categories, rather categories emerged using the constant comparative method to code the data into categories. Each statement was taken separately and allocated a representative category and the categories were then used to understand and explain students' interaction using discussion boards.

FINDINGS AND DISCUSSIONS

The interpretative analysis of the students' co-constructed content using the discussion boards provided us with information on the level of interaction or the level of learning that may lead to useful knowledge construction. Four categories related to cognitive processes emerged from the analysis namely, observation, insight, deliberations and learning from others. As mentioned earlier the discussion is initiated by someone who raised a critical thinking question followed by answers and further questioning.

The category 'Observation' is probably the first process that students engage in during an online discussion. Students were extensively engaged in observation, due to searching for information or trying to understand or read other students' postings that may reflect ways of thinking and opinions. This gave students the opportunity to progressively learn by observation. Through the process of observation students were triggering ideas/questions to initiate the discussions. The following is one of the statements from one of the discussion threads, illustrating a question being raised by a student to initiate a discussion:

As we knew that, it is not always having E-Business for making profit, sometimes you should give a service to the social or our community, and facilitate people to make their life happier, rather than making profit.

In Addition, all of us we know about spinsterhood as social issue these days, not only in UAE but also in all the Islamic world.

In the above excerpts, the student had made observations related to a social issue and the capability of electronic commerce to address this situation. Under this category, the student would likely engage in recognizing or triggering a certain problem or idea and recalling information gained during the face-to-face sessions on the value of EC or comprehending a certain knowledge which may have assisted him/her in recognizing the problem.

Raising questions would usually engage students in answering and raising further questions or concerns related to the topic. The next category that has emerged is 'Insights'. Gaining insights on certain issues is a higher level of thinking than mere observation. In observation, students are engaged in noticing or becoming aware of information without gaining a deep, clear picture or gaining insights. Some of the students' comments show that students engaged in deep perception, such as providing elaboration or giving clarification. Students prior to their posting may be engaged in further searching for information to get insights on the issue raised, an example from a student's statement is shown below:

Marriage sites on the Internet may help acquaintance between the parties, particularly in conservative communities, but its role in marriage does not measure up to the role of matchmaker or the traditional marriages characterized by the availability of credibility and seriousness.

The marriage through a matchmaker (khatabah) or through a referral from a family member or family friend, have elements of stability and continuity, since the specifications (qualities), manners, origin, and traditions are known to the parties in advance, unlike via the Internet. The marriage in this case is subject to formal measures, far from sound fundamentals required for the marriage.

The above statement is made by the same student who is attempting to provide his colleagues with further insights on the issue by sharing his knowledge and understanding. The student here is not providing an observation but rather he is giving a focused understanding and elaborating on the issue of concern.

The value of the discussion stems from the students ability to engage in act of 'deliberation'. This is probably the highest level of cognitive process used by students. The act of deliberation is different from gaining insights. The act of deliberation requires more analytical skills and students attempt to bring together fragments of knowledge together in order to develop a holistic understanding and to try to understand the purpose or deep meaning of things. Students under this category may engage in different cognitive processes such as thinking deeply, reflecting, analyzing, comparing, abstracting, constructing, organizing ideas and thinking, innovative thinking, predicting outcomes, solving problems, making choice, and taking group decisions. Also, because content is always accessible, students were prompted to reassess and edit or clarify their contributions. In addition, students may be involved in applying certain knowledge to different contexts, including their own lives clearly manifested in the following excerpt from one of the students:

The first impression from meeting the person is also very important moment, these thing can't be done through the internet. you may send a picture, a voice, a words, describing your feelings, but you can't sent your actual feelings.

I know allot of cases that are married because of the internet, they knew each other from chatting and forums. but they were surprised after marriage, because it was build on wrong basis, and something is missing between them.

The student in the above statement has clearly gone through deep thinking about the topic and attempted to link his understanding to other fragments of knowledge such as the limitation of computer communication. In the next statement the student had reflected on his past experience in relation to the topic of discussion in order to defend one side of the argument.

Most of the students' contribution focused on arguing either for or against the topic by organizing their ideas in a sequence to formulate and put forward their opinion or to raise further critical questions such as this student:

but how can they ensure the truthfulness of the information posted, and how can they validate claims of the proposed person?

In the above statement, the student had reflected on the trustworthiness of communicating information through the internet. Trustworthiness of electronic commerce was discussed in the face-to-face environment and was transferred from business to a social context by the student. These types of cognitive processes represent a clear sign of the students' engagement in act of deliberation.

The last type of cognitive processes that student were engaged in is to 'learn from others'. Learning from others is a process that rarely appears as a category of cognitive processes, but in fact from our observation it could be the most critical important factor of creating a rich learning environment, where students can learn from each other. The ability of learning from each other can be an important driving force for sustaining the discussion over a long period of time with meaningful learning outcome. This process is different from the other cognitive categories that were mentioned earlier. Here students engage in active thinking in order to extract a certain behavior, skill or a practical lesson exhibited by their colleagues. Students would then use the acquired lesson, skill or behavior elsewhere either in the discussion forum or utilized in their daily lives. This category is an intrinsic behavior that is difficult to determine its occurrences unless students specifically specify the value of their online interaction on their cognitive or learning skills. However, we can assume that sustained communication over a long period of time allows students an opportunity to extract various positive behaviors and lessons. In-addition, postings that contain social remarks may indicate that students are learning form others, and compelled them to give social remarks such as "I like your comments", "your are always a positive man", "I do respect everyone replies and suggestions", It is a good discussion and feedback", "I'd like to thank you for your posting your comments and opinion" and "I agree with your idea". Such comments may arise if students feel that they are gaining something of value from their colleagues' contributions. We can argue that a discussion that does not offer students something useful would be most likely considered as being dull and not worthy of their participation.

Figure 1 illustrates the four derived categories and their interaction with each other, also Table (3) summaries the derived assessment dimensions.

CONCLUSION

The literature offers a large range of approaches for analyzing the value gained from using discussion boards. From our experience the usage of such dis-

Figure 1. Interacting cognitive dimensions for assessing learning and knowledge construction using discussion boards

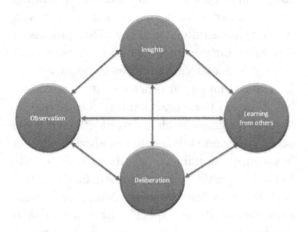

cussion boards is not easy and does not always fit the faculty environment. This study indicates that online interaction depends on several interacting cognitive activities, which can be used by faculty to assess and to enhance the students' critical thinking using online discussion boards. The four dimensions (Observation, Insights, Deliberation, Learning form others), are used as indicators of the quality of learning and knowledge construction by the students. The argument being enforced in this paper is that a good discussion should lead to a more meaningful knowledge and consequently to a more significant learning experience. This study contributes to improve the understanding of the effectiveness of online knowledge construction and may be used as a guide for assessing its

quality. The derived four categories is a reflection of the learning experiences and strategies gained by students.

The model still requires further development and validation and specifically on how we can determine if students are learning from each other. However, faculty are encouraged to use variety of critical thinking analysis frameworks and to attempt to derive their own that is more applicable to their context and needs. The process of developing own framework allows faculty to gain deep understanding on the learning and cognitive processes that can occur using discussion boards.

REFERENCES

Beaumie, K. (2001). Social constructivism. In M. Orey (Ed.), Emerging perspectives on learning, teaching, and technology. Retrieved from http://www.coe.uga.edu/epltt/SocialConstructivism.htm

Brookfield, S. D. (1987). *Developing critical thinkers*. San Francisco, CA: Jossey-Bass.

Bullen, M. (1998). Participation and critical thinking in online university distance education. *Journal of Distance Education, 13*(2), 1–32.

Clulow, V., & Brace-Govan, J. (2001). *Learning through bulletin board discussion: A preliminary case analysis of the cognitive dimension*. Paper presented at the Moving Online Conference II, September 2-4, 2001, Gold Coast, Australia.

Garrison, R., Anderson, T., & Archer, W. (2000). Critical inquiry in text-based environment: Computer conferencing in higher education. *The Internet and Higher Education, 2*(2-3), 87–105. doi:10.1016/S1096-7516(00)00016-6

Table 3. Categories of cognitive processes

Category	Description
Observation	Students are engaged in noticing or becoming aware of information
Insight	Deep perception on a certain issue
Deliberation	Use of analytical skills, thinking deeply and related information
Learning from others	Extract behavior, skills and lessons from others

Gunawardena, C. N., Lowe, C. A., & Anderson, T. (1997). Analysis of global online debate and the development an interaction analysis model of examining social construction of knowledge in computer conferencing. *Journal of Educational Computing Research*, *17*(4), 397–431. doi:10.2190/7MQV-X9UJ-C7Q3-NRAG

Henri, F. (1992). Computer conferencing and content analysis. In Kaye, A. R. (Ed.), *Collaborative learning through computer conferencing: The Najaden papers* (pp. 115–136). Berlin, Germany: Springer-Verlag. doi:10.1007/978-3-642-77684-7_8

Knowlton, D. S. (2001). *Promoting durable knowledge construction through online discussion*. Mid-South Instructional Technology Conference.

Lopez, A. K., & Willis, G. D. (2004). Descriptive versus interpretive phenomenology: Their contribution to nursing knowledge. *Qualitative Health Research*, *14*(5), 726–735. doi:10.1177/1049732304263638

Meyer, K. A. (2004). Evaluating online discussions: Four different frame of analysis. *Journal of Asynchronous Learning Networks*, *8*(2), 101–114.

Newman, D. R., Webb, B., & Cochrane, C. (1995). A content analysis method to measure critical thinking in face-to-face and computer supported group learning. *Interpersonal Computing and Technology*, *3*(2), 56–77.

Norris, S. P., & Ennis, R. (1989). Evaluating critical thinking. In Schwartz, R. J., & Perkins, D. N. (Eds.), *The practitioners' guide to teaching thinking series*. Pacific Grove, CA: Midwest Publications.

Simpson, T. L. (2002). Dare I oppose constructivist theory. *The Educational Forum*, •••, 347–354. doi:10.1080/00131720208984854

Wurm, K. B. (2005). Andragogy in Survey Education. *Surveying and Land Information Science*, *65*(3), 159–163.

Yin, R. (1984). *Case study research: Design and methods*. Beverly Hills, CA: Sage Publications.

ADDITIONAL READING

Akyol, Z., & Garrison, D. R. (2011). Understanding cognitive presence in an online and blended community of inquiry: Assessing outcomes and processes for deep approaches to learning. *British Journal of Educational Technology*, *42*(2), 233–250. doi:10.1111/j.1467-8535.2009.01029.x

Anderson, T., Rourke, L., Garrison, D. R., & Archer, W. (2001). Assessing teaching presence in a computer conferencing context. *Journal of Asynchronous Learning Networks*, *5*(2), 1–17.

Bates, A. W. (1997). The impact of technological change on open and distance learning. *Distance Education*, *18*(1), 93–109. doi:10.1080/0158791970180108

Beaumie, K. (2001). Social constructivism. In M. Orey (Ed.), *Emerging perspectives on learning, teaching, and technology*. Retrieved from http://www.coe.uga.edu/epltt/SocialConstructivism.htm

Buraphadeja, V., & Dawson, K. (2008). Content analysis in computer-mediated communication: Analyzing models for assessing critical thinking through the lens of social constructivism. *American Journal of Distance Education*, *22*(3), 1–28. doi:10.1080/08923640802224568

Coats, H., James, R., & Baldwin, G. (2005). A critical examination of the effects of learning management systems on university teaching and learning. *Tertiary Education and Management*, *11*, 19–36. doi:10.1080/13583883.2005.9967137

Coffey, A., & Atkinson, P. (1996). *Making sense of qualitative data*. USA: Sage.

Conner, M. L. (1997-2004). Andragogy and pedagogy. *Ageless Learner*. Retrieved from http://agelesslearner.com/intros/andragogy.html

Fichter, D. (2005). The many forms of e-collaboration: Blogs, wikis, portals, groupware, discussion boards, and instant messaging. *Online*, *29*(4), 48–50.

Garrison, D. R. (2003). Cognitive presence for effective asynchronous online learning: The role of reflective inquiry, self-direction and meta-cognition. In Bourne, J., & Moore, J. C. (Eds.), *Elements of quality online education: Practice and direction, Sloan C Series* (*Vol. 4*). Needham, MA: The Sloan Consortium.

Garrison, D. R., Anderson, T., & Archer, W. (2000). Critical inquiry in a text-based environment: Computer conferencing in higher education. *The Internet and Higher Education*, *2*(2), 87–105. doi:10.1016/S1096-7516(00)00016-6

Godwin-Jones, R. (2003). Emerging technologies: Blogs and wikis: Environments for on-line collaboration. *Language Learning & Technology*, *7*(2), 12–16.

Harvard, B., Du, J., & Olinzock, A. (2005). Deep learning: The knowledge, methods, and cognition process in instructor-led online discussion. *Quarterly Review of Distance Education*, *6*(2), 125–135.

Kanuka, H., & Garrison, D. R. (2004). Cognitive presence in online learning. *Journal of Computing in Higher Education*, *15*(2), 30–49. doi:10.1007/BF02940928

Meyer, K. (2004). Evaluating online discussions: Four difference frames of analysis. *Journal of Asynchronous Learning Networks*, *8*(2), 101–114.

Schrire, S. (2006). Knowledge building in asynchronous discussion groups: Going beyond quantitative analysis. *Computers & Education*, *46*(1), 49–70. doi:10.1016/j.compedu.2005.04.006

KEY TERMS AND DEFINITIONS

Andragogy: The learning approach of adults, where they learn more when they have control over learning and require less focus on the teacher.

Bloom's Taxonomy: Classification of learning objectives used to design curricula and examinations.

Cognitive Presence: A process of constructing meaning through sustained online communication.

Critical Reflection: An analysis process that requires a person to engage in questioning past experiences within a broad perspective.

Discussion Boards: An asynchronous digital communication tool that allows one individual to post a comment or respond to other members comments and questions.

Experiential Learning: Learning through experience and reflection on doing.

Learning How to Learn: Building skills and strategies that can be used to help learners learn more effective and become lifelong learners.

Meaningful Learning: refers to deep understanding of a concept and to have the ability to relate that learning to other fragments of knowledge.

Self-Directed Learning: People who take self initiative in learning resulting in learning more, better, and deeper.

Significant Learning: A cognitive taxonomy used by teachers as a framework for formulating course objectives and to evaluate students learning.

Chapter 16
E–Learning Status and Quality in Context of Arab Universities:
Challenges and Threats

Nasim Matar
Zarqa University, Jordan

ABSTRACT

This chapter discusses the status and quality of e-learning in Arab Universities located in the Middle East. The first objective of the study was to provide an analytical overview of the use of e-learning and the quality of electronic courses and learning objects in these universities to fill the gap in the literature in this particular topic regarding the Middle East region, and also to draw into different solutions and recommendations in order to make a successful match that could result in a better adoption and serving of the e-learning technology. The study was based on two different approaches that included a survey to navigate the official websites of universities in the region plus a survey into e-learning courses to obtain the current stand of e-learning quality in the region. The results of each approach have been analyzed, and the outcomes and recommendations were presented to be used for future adoption and other related studies.

INTRODUCTION

Research in the topic of "e-learning status in Arab countries" provides useful information that is indicative of the general status of ICT infrastructure and e-learning deficiencies in the Arab countries.

This study employs comprehensive survey tools to accurately define the status of adopting e-learning, e-courses and learning objects that can help in defining the status of e-learning in particular. The survey study was initiated based on content analysis methodology (Krippendorff, 2004); to provide different questions that could assist in answering the main research question, i.e., the current status of e-learning, e-courses and learning objects in the Middle Eastern universities. The results of the survey study are believed to assist in filling the gap in literature. It is also at that stage of the research to gain insight knowledge of the situation on the ground.

DOI: 10.4018/978-1-4666-1984-5.ch016

METHODOLOGY

The approach used was based on content analysis methodology (Krippendorff, 2004) for defining both the e-learning status and "e-courses and learning objects" quality and uses two surveys.

The first survey was conducted by navigating 172 official universities' web sites across the Middle East. Content analysis methodology is based on defining criteria for analyzing the content. Therefore, two criteria have been defined and employed to collect information pertinent to the each of the visited web sites. The criteria in concerned with the following:

1.   Availability of e-learning portal through the universities web site.
2.   Accessibility of the e-learning portal through the internet.

The study also adopts a set of analysis targets that are associated with the survey data. The targets are:

- Identifying the adoption of e-learning services in the region.
- Defining the e-learning adoption percent in terms of public and private universities.
- Defining the adoption level of e-learning based on the classification of the region countries as (Gulf and Non-Gulf).
- Defining the e-learning adoption level based on region classification and university type.
- Defining the e-learning adoption level based on e-learning type and region classification.
- Defining LMS adoption level with respect to each country in the region.

Following the definition of the above criteria and targets, lists of universities were obtained from the Ministry of Higher Education in each country surveyed. Each university's web site was

visited and data was gathered and categorized with respect to each country and stored in MS Excel Spreadsheet. The data was analyzed using both Microsoft Excel and SPSS (Statistical Package for the Social Sciences) (Elliot, A.C., 2007). Excel was used for generating percentages and charts, while SPSS was used for generating cross tabulation to display the joint distribution of variables in a contingency table in a matrix format.

The second survey was conducted by navigating 9 e-learning portals with a total of 268 e-courses. Two-parts criteria were defined for this study and that were used in assessing each visited e-learning portal:

1.   Availability of e-learning courses within the portal.
2.   Availability of different electronic modules within the course, such as:
     ◦   Chat
     ◦   Forum
     ◦   Assignment
     ◦   Assessment
     ◦   External Resources
     ◦   HTML Pages
     ◦   PowerPoint Slides
     ◦   Files (PDF, Word, Excel etc.)
     ◦   Interactive files or applications (Flash, Java Applet, JavaScript etc.)
     ◦   Video Files (original or embedded)

For defining the quality of e-learning courses within the Middle East region, the following analysis targets were defined for the survey data:

- What are the percentages of the different electronic modules within the courses?
- What are the predominant electronic modules used in constructing e-courses in the region?

After the definition of the criteria and targets, nine universities' e-learning portals were visited and the data was gathered and categorized with respect to each university in Excel spreadsheet. The data was analyzed using Microsoft Excel, and percentages and charts were generated. The information obtained was considered vital and complemented the outputs defined in the questionnaire study, in order to make better judgments for solutions and future recommendations.

STUDY OUTCOMES

This section presents the compendiums of the surveys outcomes. The results have been summarized into facts about the Middle East region.

First Survey's Outcomes (E-Learning Status)

1. General E-Learning Status in the Middle East Countries

The survey study included most universities in the region with a total of 172 universities. The study revealed that 41.3% of Arab universities have adopted e-learning within their educational curriculums. This percentage represents a total of 71 universities in the region.

2. E-Learning Status in Terms of University Type

Further analysis of the data using SPSS cross-tabulation reveals the status of e-learning in terms of university types (governmental/private) that adopted e-learning in the region as shown in Table 1 and 2.

By breaking down the data further, it was possible to determine what percentage of universities using LMS were government run, and what percentage were in private hands with respect to each surveyed country, this is depicted in the Figure 1.

3. E-Learning Status in Terms of Region (Gulf and Non-Gulf) Adoption Levels

In this part, a cross-tabulation analysis was performed between Gulf countries (Saudi Arabia,

Table 1. E-learning adoption according to university type (governmental/private)

E-Learning * University Type Cross-tabulation			University Type		Total
			Governmental	Private	
E-Learning	yes	Count	42	29	71
		% within e-learning	59.2	40.8	100.0
		% within university type	51.9	31.9	41.3
		% of total	24.4	16.9	41.3
	no	Count	39	62	101
		% within e-learning	38.6	61.4	100.0
		% within university type	48.1	68.1	58.7
		% of total	22.7	36.0	58.7
Total		Count	81	91	172
		% within e-learning	47.1	52.9	100.0
		% within university type	100.0	100.0	100.0
		% of total	47.1	52.9	100.0

Oman, Qatar, Bahrain, Yemen, UAE) and Non-Gulf Countries (Jordan, Egypt, Palestine, Syria, Lebanon) (Table 3).

The chart represents the percentage of e-learning adoption with respect to each country in comparison with total e-learning adoption in the region (Figure 2).

4. E-Learning Status in Terms of Region and University Type

Table 5 shows the e-learning adoption percentage with respect to each region (Gulf and Non-Gulf) and University (governmental and private) type.

Categorizing the data according to each country in the region gave an overview of adoption levels according to the number of universities using e-learning, and those levels are represented in percentage format (Figure 3).

5. E-Learning Status in Terms of Region and Type of E-learning

Table 7 shows the adoption percentage of e-learning based on the region and type of e-learning. The type of e-learning in this study was classified based on two options (Blended e-learning, Fully Online e-learning).

The survey has also showed that out of the total of 71 universities providing e-learning in the region, 13 also run 20% of their programs online. Figure 4 shows the number of universities running online programs in each country.

6. E-Learning Status in Terms of LMS Adoption and Countries

In terms of e-learning management systems used, it was revealed that there are three preferable types of software used for providing the management of learning and the learners. These software applications are Moodle, Blackboard and WebCT (Matar, Hunaiti et al., 2007a). Table 8 shows how many universities in each country have chosen a particular type of LMS.

According to this table, 44% of the region's universities are using licensed programs while 41% use open-source programs and 14% remain undefined.

Second Survey's Outcomes (E-Courses and Learning Objects Quality)

The survey study has included in its scope 268 electronic courses in nine different universities in

Table 2. Chi- square test for e-learning adoption according to university type (governmental/private)

Chi-Square Tests					
	Value	**Df**	**Asymp. Sig. (2-sided)**	**Exact Sig. (2-sided)**	**Exact Sig. (1-sided)**
Pearson Chi-Square	7.060(b)	1	.008		
Continuity Correction (a)	6.260	1	.012		
Likelihood Ratio	7.096	1	.008		
Fisher's Exact Test				.009	.006
Linear-by-Linear Association	7.019	1	.008		
N of Valid Cases	172				
a Computed only for a 2x2 table					
b 0 cells (.0%) have expected count less than 5. The minimum expected count is 33.44.					

Figure 1. Percentage of governmental versus private adoption for e-learning in each country

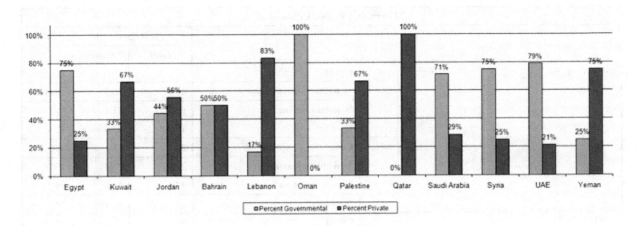

the region. 166 courses were found to be empty, just reserving a name for the course. This reduces the nmber of valid electronic courses to (102) that contained materials and modules. The results of the survey are shown in Table 9.

DISCUSSION OF RESULTS

Based on the results presented above, this section provides a discussion for each point in each survey study. The discussion will follow the order presented in the results section.

Discussion of First Survey towards Defining E-Learning Status

1. General E-Learning Status in the Middle East Countries

Regarding the status of e-learning in the Middle East region, this study found that 41.3% of the investigated universities, which correspond to 71 universities out of the 172 universities, adopted e-learning, which is considered relatively low, compared with the European Union countries with 75% of their universities adopting e-learning (LTAC Project Group, 2009). Although there are

several possible explanations for this result,, it is thought that the main reason suggests that it is a consequence of deficiencies in ICT infrastructure in the Middle East region. Another reason that was stated by the UNDP and Mohamad Bin Rashid Al-Maktoum Foundation Report (2009), is that in spite of some initiatives by some Arab countries to utilize ICT in the various stages of education, these efforts, although important they remain inadequate and are evidently short of what is required or possible (Arab Knowledge Report, 2009). This research study has revealed this low adoption percentage as it was not investigated in the literature of Arab countries in the region. The findings of this study have important implications for future practices and considerations, either by this research study or by different researchers, educational establishments, and public sector invading the Middle East market of e-learning.

2. E-Learning Status in Terms of University Type

It is apparent from Table 1 that the e-learning percentage for governmental universities (59.2%) is higher than that for private universities (40.8%) in the region. Also, if compared with the total number of 172 universities in the region, 24.4% are

Table 3. E-learning adoption according to region classification (Gulf/non-Gulf)

E-Learning * Region Cross-tabulation				Region		Total
				Gulf	Non-Gulf	
E-Learning	yes	Count		31	40	71
		% within e-learning		43.7	56.3	100.0
		% within region		52.5	35.4	41.3
		% of total		18.0	23.3	41.3
	no	Count		28	73	101
		% within e-learning		27.7	72.3	100.0
		% within region		47.5	64.6	58.7
		% of total		16.3	42.4	58.7
Total		Count		59	113	172
		% within e-learning		34.3%	65.7	100.0
		% within region		100.0%	100.0	100.0
		% of total		34.3%	65.7	100.0

governmental and 16.9% for private universities. This variance in percentages can be pinned down to many factors that were outlined by previous studies (Shehabat & Mahdi, 2009; Moussa & Moussa, 2009; Arab Knowledge Report, 2009). These include the following:

1. Since most of the governmental universities are supported by ministries of higher education, they receive financial support and are allocated yearly budget from the government.

2. Most of the financial aid from supporting countries to the Middle East is spent on the governmental bodies and establishments.

3. Governmental universities have more students, which results in having more budgets to support such educational and technological trends.

4. Governmental universities have established a name and a presence since they were the first

Table.4. Chi-square test for e-learning adoption by region classification (Gulf/non-Gulf)

Chi-Square Tests					
	Value	df	Asymp. Sig. (2-sided)	Exact Sig. (2-sided)	Exact Sig. (1-sided)
Pearson Chi-Square	4.700(b)	1	.030		
Continuity Correction(a)	4.019	1	.045		
Likelihood Ratio	4.672	1	.031		
Fisher's Exact Test				.035	.023
Linear-by-Linear Association	4.673	1	.031		
N of Valid Cases	172				
a Computed only for a 2x2 table					
b 0 cells (.0%) have expected count less than 5. The minimum expected count is 24.35.					

Figure 2. E-learning adoption percentage in countries located in Middle East region

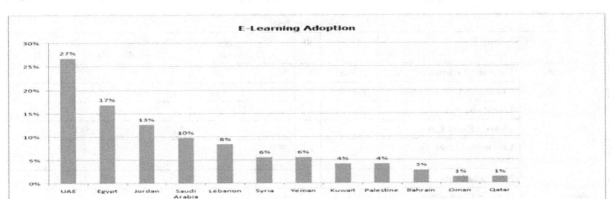

Table 5. E-learning adoption according to university type and region classification

E-Learning * REGION * University Type Cross-tabulation				Gulf	Non-Gulf	Total
University Type				**Gulf**	**Non-Gulf**	**Total**
Governmental	E-Learning	Yes	Count	21	21	42
			% within e-learning	50.0	50.0	100.0
			% within region	51.2	52.5	51.9
			% of total	25.9	25.9	51.9
		No	Count	20	19	39
			% within e-learning	51.3	48.7	100.0
			% within region	48.8	47.5	48.1
			% of total	24.7	23.5	48.1
	Total		Count	41	40	81
			% within e-learning	50.6	49.4	100.0
			% within region	100.0	100.0	100.0
			% of total	50.6	49.4	100.0
Private	E-Learning	Yes	Count	10	19	29
			within e-learning	34.5	65.5	100.0
			within region	55.6	26.0	31.9
			of total	11.0	20.9	31.9
		No	Count	8	54	62
			within e-learning	12.9	87.1	100.0
			within region	44.4	74.0	68.1
			of total	8.8	59.3	68.1
	Total		Count	18	73	91
			% within e-learning	19.8	80.2	100.0
			% within region	100.0	100.0	100.0
			% of total	19.8	80.2	100.0

Table 6. Chi-square for e-learning adoption according to university type and region classification

Chi-Square Tests						
University Type		Value	df	Asymp. Sig. (2-sidedd)	Exact Sig. (2-sided)	Exact Sig. (1-sided)
Governmental	Pearson Chi-Square	.013(b)	1	.908		
	Continuity Correction(a)	.000	1	1.000		
	Likelihood Ratio	.013	1	.908		
	Fisher's Exact Test				1.000	.543
	Linear-by-Linear Association	.013	1	.909		
	N of Valid Cases	81				
Private	Pearson Chi-Square	5.799(c)	1	.016		
	Continuity Correction(a)	4.518	1	.034		
	Likelihood Ratio	5.470	1	.019		
	Fisher's Exact Test				.024	.019
	Linear-by-Linear Association	5.735	1	.017		
	N of Valid Cases	91				
a Computed only for a 2x2 table						
b 0 cells (.0%) have expected count less than 5. The minimum expected count is 19.26.						
c 0 cells (.0%) have expected count less than 5. The minimum expected count is 5.74.						

universities in the region, which promotes more cooperation and sharing knowledge and expertise with foreign universities.

5. Private universities are concentrating their financial efforts on expanding their facilities, preparation of laboratories, and marketing to attract larger numbers of students rather than implementing a supplementary educational technology.

In terms of differences between countries in the region, Bahrain and Jordan are the only two coun-

Figure 3. Percentage of universities using e-learning in each country

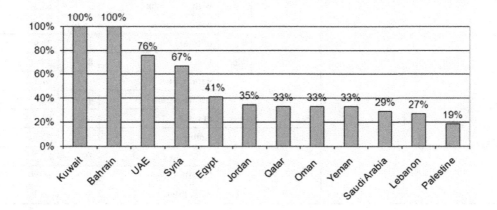

Table 7. E-learning adoption according to university type and region classification

E-Learning * Region * Type of E-Learning Cross-tabulation					
Methods of Delivery			**Region**		
Type of E-Learning			**Gulf**	**Non-Gulf**	**Total**
Blended	E-Learning	Count	29	28	57
		% within e-learning	50.90	49.10	100.00
		% within region	100.00	100.00	100.00
		% of total	50.90	49.10	100.00
Online	E-Learning	Count	2	9	11
		% within e-learning	18.20	81.80	100.00
		% within region	100.00	100.00	100.00
		% of total	18.20	81.80	100.00

tries that showed equal and moderate differences between the percentile level of governmental and private universities, which might be an indication of a shortage of governmental support or a powerful investment in the private sector. A detailed research study for those two countries is needed to clarify the true stand of governmental support or large private investment.

In terms of association, a chi-square test was performed to test the null hypothesis of no association between e-learning availability and type of universities in the region. An association between e-learning availability and type of universities was found, $\chi 2$ (1, N =172) =7.060, p =0.008. Examination of the cell frequencies showed that about 59.2% (42 out of 71) of universities type were governmental with support of e-learning, while 38.6% (39 out of 101) of universities did not show support for e-learning. In terms of private universities the results were 40.8% (29 out of 71) adopted e-learning while 61.4% (62 out of 101) did not.

Figure 4. Number of universities running online programs in each country

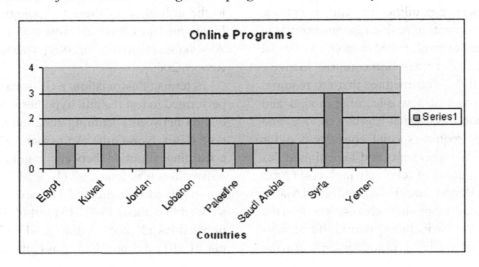

Table 8. Universities and LMS

Country	Moodle	WebCT	Blackboard	Not Defined
Egypt	12	×	×	×
Kuwait	1	×	1	×
Jordan	3	×	4	2
Bahrain	1	1	×	×
Lebanon	2	2	1	3
Oman	×	×	×	×
Palestine	3	×	×	×
Qatar	×	×	1	×
Saudi Arabia	3	4	×	×
Syria	×	×	×	4
UAE	1	14	4	×
Yemen	4	×	×	×

3. Learning Status in Terms of Region (Gulf & Non-Gulf) Adoption Levels

Table 3 in the results section shows that Non-Gulf countries have a higher current adoption level with 56.3%, compared to 43.7% for Gulf countries. Commenting on the previous percentages would be deceiving as we can also see that the Gulf countries have a larger adoption percentile within their region (52.5%) than the Non-Gulf countries (35.4%). Thus we conclude that the Gulf countries are keener on implementing e-learning technologies and services. This can be linked to the financial capabilities the Gulf countries, whose governments have financial and economic prosperity due to the oil-based economy. Financial prosperity enables many Gulf countries to invest in modern ICT infrastructures that are required for the adoption of new e-learning models and solutions, considering that learning services and technologies require special consideration for many physical equipments and logical modules that are considered of relatively high cost (Arab Knowledge Report, 2009). UAE and Saudi Arabia have the largest adoption level of e-learning in the Middle East region including both Gulf and Non-Gulf countries, while Egypt and Jordan lead in the

Non-Gulf region. The results of this study are in synch with the findings that have been provided by the report of Interuniversity Research Centre on Science and Technology initiated by CIRST (Gentzoglanis, A., 2007), which is Canada's main interdisciplinary cluster of researchers studying the historical, social, political, philosophical and economic dimensions of science and technology. The case of Egypt and Jordan having a better stance among Non-Gulf countries come from the fact that they have institutionalized ICT through policy formulation, infrastructure, institution building and the enactment of laws and regulations related to the utilization of these technologies, as was highlighted in UNDP & Mohamad Bin Rashid Al Maktoum Foundation, 2009 (Arab Knowledge Report, 2009).

In terms of association, a chi-square test was performed to test the null hypothesis of no association between e-learning adoption and region type (Gulf, Non-Gulf). An association between e-learning adoption between region type and universities was found, $\chi^2 (1, N =172) = 4.700$, $p = .030$. Examination of the cell frequencies showed that about 43.7% (31 out of 71) of Gulf universities adopted e-learning, while 27.7% (28 out of 101) did not. For Non-Gulf universities

Table 9. Survey results towards defining e-learning quality

	Electronic Module	Percent	Rank
1	Interactive Material	4	1
2	Video/Audio	5	2
3	External Resources	8	3
4	Chat Modules	17	4
5	Forum	17	4
6	HTML	18	5
7	Assessment	25	6
8	PowerPoint	69	7
9	Assignment	84	8
10	Files	100	9

the results were 56.3% (40 out of 71) adopted e-learning while 72.3% (73 out of 101) did not.

4. E-Learning Status in Terms of (Region and University Type)

Table 5 shows no significant difference between governmental adoption of e-learning in both Gulf and Non-Gulf countries. In terms of private universities, the results are going in favor of Gulf countries with (55.6%) that can be also be pinned to the economical prosperity that those countries are enjoying (Arab Knowledge Report, 2009). Another factor is that many private universities in the Gulf region benefit from indirect financial support from governmental agencies through facilitating big loans from banks with a large amount of flexibility in the repayments plan and with a small fraction of interest. Such scenario are rarely evident in nNon-Gulf countries, where the capital for establishing such universities is mainly sourced from medium size companies, banks and individuals, that are faced by many restrictions and obstacles on loan repayment plans and with a high interest fraction (Gentzoglanis.A, 2007).

In terms of association, a chi-square test was performed to test the null hypothesis of no association between e-learning adoption and region type (Gulf, Non-Gulf). "An association between e-learning adoption between region type (Gulf and Non-Gulf) and Governmental universities was not found, $\chi^2 (1, N =81) = .013, p = .908$. Examination of the cell frequencies showed that about 50.0% (21 out of 42) of Gulf governmental universities adopted e-learning, while 51.3% (20 out of 39) did not. Also in terms of Non-Gulf governmental universities the results were 50.0% (21 out of 42) adopted e-learning while 48.7% (19 out of 39) did not. In terms of private universities, an association between e-learning adoption between region type (Gulf and Non-Gulf) and private universities was found, $\chi^2 (1, N =91) = 5.799, p = .016$. Examination of the cell frequencies showed that about 34.5% (10 out of 29) of Gulf private universities adopted e-learning, while 12.9% (8 out of 62) have not. Also in terms of Non-Gulf private universities the results were 65.5% (19 out of 29) adopted e-learning while 87.1% (54 out of 62) did not.

5. E-Learning Status in Terms of Region and Type of E-Learning

Data in Table 7 indicate no significant difference between Gulf and Non-Gulf countries in terms of blended e-learning type of delivery, while a big difference is shown in the online type of e-learning with a percent of 81.8% for Non-Gulf countries and 18.2% for Gulf countries. The big difference in percentage can be attributed to the financial and economical burdens that Non-Gulf countries suffer from. With the high population growth in the region, and the increase in the numbers of students attending university education, the Non-Gulf universities started accepting the idea of online education as a practical solution and viable substitute for the traditional one. The adoption ratio for online learning is still minimal with 6% out of 172 Arab universities and 15% out of 71 Gulf universities adopting e-learning in the region. These results add another dimension for defining the responses towards different challenges that each region (Gulf and Non-Gulf) faces in providing higher education. Gulf private universities are keener in providing e-learning for their students regarding the total cost of ownership, while Non-Gulf universities are becoming keener in adopting online delivery modes of learning to cut the cost of operations and to be able to extract more students. The biggest challenge faced today by the online method of learning in this region is the educational-policy hostility (Abouchedid & Eid, 2004). Most countries in the region have not yet recognized and accredited online degrees. In fact, there appears to be an on-going effort by authorities to discourage students from enrolling in online degree programs offered by many European, Australian and North American universities (Mohamed, A., 2005). The first Arab Online University (AOU) was established in Kuwait in the year 2000. Being the pioneer, it was greeted with scorn in many countries. It was only after it had proven itself that it started gaining acceptance. Nevertheless, AOU was successful to convince some of the region's countries such as Kuwait, Jordan, Bahrain, Saudi Arabia and Lebanon to accredit its degrees (UNESCO Regional Bureau, 2009). The huge step taken by Arab Open University has paved the way for other universities to follow. Nowadays the number of universities accepting a blend of traditional and online learning is on the rise. The Al-Baath University, the University of Aleppo and the University of Damascus in Syria; the University of Science and Technology in Yemen; and the Al-Quds Open University in Palestine have all taken to online education. The future outlook is positive in that the coming few years we will witness an an increasing acceptance of the new learning models, which is expected to translate into more, countries and universities accrediting e-learning degrees (UNESCO Regional Bureau, 2009). In terms of association a chi-square test that was performed to test the null hypothesis of no association between e-learning adoption and region type (Gulf, Non-Gulf), an association between e-learning adoption between region type

universities was found, $\chi2$ (1, N =172) = 4.700, p = .030. The examination of the cell frequencies showed that about 18.0% (31 out of 172) of Gulf universities adopted e-learning, while 16.3% (28 out of 172) did not. However, Non-Gulf universities results indicated that 16.9% (29 out of 172) adopted e-learning while 36.0% (62 out of 172) did not.

6. E-Learning Status in Terms of LMS Adoption and Countries

It is apparent from Table 8 that (44%) universities in the region are in favor of using licensed online learning programs. Whilst universities in the Gulf region preference is for programs such as WebCT and Blackboard, Non-Gulf countries are in favor of using open source such as Moodle. These varied preferences could also be due to financial and economical challenges and differences in the region. Licensed programs bring different challenges in terms of demanding hardware specification, and the necessity for other software specifications, which in turn requires more focus on specification and licensing. Usually, such demands translate into accumulative high budget for acquiring such software programs. In the case of open source programs such as Moodle,, less restrictions are applied with no financial demand associate with it at all. However, for the preferable end user support for licensed applications and installation, the availability of training services are what makes such applications a first choice for many Gulf universities that can handle such expensive products and services (Matar & Hunaiti et al., 2007a). Table 10 summarizes all the derived facts that have been presented in this section.

Discussion of 2nd Survey to Define "E-Courses & Learning Objects" Quality

In this section, the results that have been presented in the previous section that are related to "e-courses and learning objects" quality will be discussed with respect to their presence in the results section. They will be presented with respect to questions associated with each result for simplicity of discussion.

Defining the Quality of Electronic Courses: The presented outputs in the previous results section are based on all nine universities that have been included in the survey study; the discussion will be based on having the same presented results plus eliminating one online university of the study in order to have more representative results, since the percent of online university education in the region is minimal compared with the traditional universities.

Q1. What is the ratio of chat modules defined in the surveyed sample? The Chat module utilization is considered minimal within the participated universities with a percent of 17%. This percent would drop to 10% if one online university were removed from the group of study. Chat module is considered time consuming by the instructors, especially as it is not usually associated with recognition or financial reward. Thus majority of the instructors are not in favor of adding

additional burden on their busy schedule of lecturing and research.

Q2. What is the ratio of forums defined in the surveyed sample? The forum module utilization is also considered minimal within the participated universities with a ratio of 17%. This ratio would drop to 5% if one online university were removed from the group of study. Forum module is an important module for collaborative learning and discussion. Having this module as part of courses is also considered time consuming by instructors, as they have to keep control on the participants' submission and make correction or put further clarification and discussion.

Q3. What is the ratio of assignment modules defined in the surveyed sample? The ratio of the assignments module is a high 84%. However, if one online university were to be removed from the study the rate would drop to 47%, which is still considered relatively high compared with the previous results of the discussed modules. The reason for this high result could be due to the nature of this module, which is used mainly for informing students of the required assignments,

Table 10. Middle East region facts

Fact	Result	Percent
3. E-learning adoption in the Middle East is low.	Adoption percent	41.3%
4. Governmental universities are keener to adopt e-learning when compared to private universities.	Government	59.2%
	Private	40.8%
5. Governmental Gulf universities are having the same adoption level towards e-learning, while private Gulf universities exceed Non-Gulf ones.	(Government) Gulf = Non-Gulf	
	(Private) Gulf > Non-Gulf	
• Blended e-learning mode of delivery is equal in both Gulf and Non-Gulf, while online is more utilized in Non-Gulf countries.	(Blended) Gulf = Non-Gulf	
	Non-Gulf Private	81.8%
	Gulf Private	18.2%
• Gulf universities are in favor of licensed e-learning programs, while Non-Gulf are in favor of open source.	Gulf	44%
	Non-Gulf	41%

and which will be sent out electronically or physically to the instructor. Also, no additional skills are required from the instructor other than posting a file or announcements.

Q4. What is the ratio of assessment modules defined in the surveyed sample? The Assessment modules had a ratio of 25%, which can drop to 11% should we opt to remove one major online university. This ratio is considered low, and it has not been utilized properly in the electronic courses due to the following factors:

○ The additional skills that were needed to be acquired by instructors to make such assessments.

○ The time consumption of making such assessments.

○ The validity of such assessments in online environment.

Thus, generally, instructors are in a favor of assessing the students using traditional methods.

Q5. What is the ratio of external resources defined in the surveyed sample? External resources have scored 8%, which can be reduced to 5% if one major online university is eliminated.. In both cases, the ratios are dismally low, considering that the Internet is very rich with resources that can be used to support the educational process. The reasons for this low ratio could be related to the following factors:

○ It is time consuming to check for external resources that fit the syllabus or learning objective of the course (Antoniou & Harmelen, 2004).

○ Many external resources will not give the exact learning objective for the topic or issues being taught, as they have not been prepared for such purposes (Taibi, Gentile & Seta, 2005).

○ Many external resources will carry copyright issues (Web-Based Education Commission, 2000).

○ Some external resources will require specific software in order to be used (Collis & Strijker, 2004).

○ Many external resources will need additional skills in order to incorporate them into the course material (Collis & Strijker, 2004).

So as long as these factors exist, the use of external resources will be minimal.

Q6. What is the ratio of HTML pages defined in the surveyed sample? Posting HTML pages has a ratio of 18%, that can be dropped to 10% should one major online university is eliminated. In the previous discussion table (Table 9), it was seen that most of the universities give courses on constructing HTML pages, but this practice is not necessarily fruitful, as many MS Office applications are capable of producing HTML pages with little effort by the user.. The case for learning HTML is weakened since the same files that produces HTML format can be posted as is in any LMS/LCMS? HTML is considered appropriate within LMS/LCMS if it will have some scripting languages that produce interactivity in term of calculations or simulations, so the practice of giving HTML courses without supporting them with proper knowledge of interactivity and multimedia have proven to be a total waste of time in such solutions, and are not to be considered in future.

Q7. What is the ratio of PowerPoint Slides defined in the surveyed sample? The percent of 69% for using PowerPoint files for presentation is considered high. In case one major online university is to be eliminated of this study the ratio would drop to 44%. Using PowerPoint slides proves to be indeed a favorite option by the instructors in the Middle East region, not only because they are easy to use but also because files are mad readily prepared and available by many publishers and they are packed into what is called instructor pack for the course that they are teaching. However, many instructors restrain from using such methods of educational delivery, as they feel that they have a better interaction with the class by using the traditional classroom board or by posting their own manuals or notes. Instructors who have the time, determination and experience to transform those files into PowerPoint format are doing such initiations, while many instructors are posting information on the board or referring to them in the section or chapter book.

Q8. What is the ratio of "other files" defined in the surveyed sample? Posting different files has the highest score of 100% for files of different type such as (Word, PDF, Excel, TXT, Images, Zip), although if one major online university is to be eliminated the score would drop to 63%, which is still considered relatively high in comparison with the previous modules. This process is considered easy to achieve by instructors, and it will save them a lot of time and efforts for distributing various physical contents, either as syllabus, examples, news, reports, journals and so forth. A score of 63% is so vital, as it conveys that even if simple tasks are to be presented by instructors that do not require any sophisticated skills, there will be a resistance towards this technology and 37% of instructors would reject any solution provided by this technology. This percent is to be used by this study, and a further research would be appropriate to prove such findings.

Q9. What are the scores of interactive material defined in the surveyed sample? Interactive materials are the most appreciated learning objects by most of the learners and instructors. These types of materials are also the most demanding in terms of technology and experience. The study showed that 4% of courses have used different interactive materials. Again, by eliminating one major

online university the score would drop to 2%. This result is not surprising, as the previously discussion table (Table 9), showed that most of the universities in the region are not investing much in giving proper courses for creating such materials. Not to put the blame on the universities only, it is believed that giving such sophisticated courses for instructors of non-technical background will raise the resistance to a surprising level (Thompson & Lamshed, 2006). Further research would be appropriate to define the exact resistance percentage based on the course created outcome.

Q10. What are the scores of video/audio files defined in the surveyed sample? Using video and audio files is generally appreciated by many students. The study showed a low score of 5% that could drop to 4% should one of the major university's' eliminated from the sample.

Using video/audio files as part of the course proves to be cumbersome in many cases due to the following factors (Bates, 2005):

- ◦ The required equipments to produce and edit video/audio files.
- ◦ The required knowledge to create or embed video/audio files.
- ◦ Copyright issues towards using outside resource video/audio files.
- ◦ Inappropriate learning objective posted by many video/audio files.

SUMMARY

Most of the studies into e-learning adoption in the Arab region are ascribed to the ICT deficiency in the region. However, the findings of our investigation provide an insight to the current situation in the region, as it highlights strengths and pinpoints persisting gaps and weaknesses. A key result from this research study shows that Middle East governmental and private universities have equal levels of e-learning adoption, while the results are in favor of the private sector in Gulf universities. It was also evident that the Gulf universities rely on licensed programs, while the Non-Gulf universities tend to rely on open source applications. The Gulf countries are expanding their campuses and building new universities to absorb the increasing demand of students attending higher education with the region's high rate of population increase, while the Non-Gulf universities are relying on providing online e-learning delivery mode, to cope with the increasing demand towards students in the region. In most of the mentioned cases the variation between Gulf and Non-Gulf countries in the region are due to financial and economical availability and investments. The current e-learning status has not been treated as sufficient input for this study, another inputs are need that are related to the quality of e-learning courses and services that are provided by the universities that adopted e-learning in the region. The quality of e-learning services, the role players' attitude towards e-learning and the quality of e-courses should be treated as a main concern in the Middle East region. The results showed serious deficiencies in the implementation and quality towards e-learning in the region. Most of the concerns are related to inexperienced approach towards that field of educational technology, the negative approach by universities policy board for implementing e-learning, lack of support and appropriate training towards this technology, lack of motivation from instructors' side in learning this new educational technology and lack of collaborative efforts between universities to share experiences and resources. The previous section of the chapter presented much useful information regarding the quality of e-learning in terms of defining the specific obstacles and barriers facing e-learning technology and evaluating instructors/learners attitude towards the current e-learning

implementation and services. Different inputs have been highlighted as point to be used and considered towards providing any direct solutions and recommendations in the future towards better adoption of e-learning services and technology in the region.

REFERENCES

Abouchedid, K., & Eid, G. (2004). E-learning challenges in the Arab world: Revelation from a case study profile. *Quality Assurance in Education, 12*(1), 15–27. doi:10.1108/09684880410517405

Antoniou, G., & van Harmelen, F. (2004). *A Semantic Web primer*. Cambridge, MA: The MIT Press.

Collis, B., & Strijker, A. (2004). Technology and human issues in reusing learning objects. *Journal of Interactive Media in Education, 2004*. Retrieved May 27, 2008, from http://www.jime.open.ac.uk/2004/4

Elliot, A. C. (2007). *Statistical analysis: Quick reference guidebook with SPSS examples*. London, UK: Sage Publications.

Gentzoglanis, A. (2007). *International competitiveness in the telecommunications and ICT sectors: A cross-country comparison*. Montreal, Canada: Centre Interuniversitaire de recherché sur la science et la technologie (CIRST).

Krippendorff, K. (2004). Reliability in content analysis. *Journal of Human Communication Research, 30*(3), 441–433.

LTAC Project Group. (2009). *Student induction to e-learning (SIEL)*. IMS Global Learning Consortium. Retrieved November 2, 2009, from http://www.imsglobal.org/siel.cfm

Matar, N., Hunaiti, Z., Huneiti, Z., & Al-Naafa, M. (2007). E-learning status in Arab counties. *Proceeding of the International Conference on Information Society (i-Society 2007),* Merriville, Indiana, USA, 7–11 October 2007.

Mohamed, A. (2005). Distance higher education in the Arab region: The need for quality assurance frameworks. *Online Journal of Distance Learning Administration, 3*(1).

Moussa, N., & Moussa, S. (2009). Quality assurance of e-learning in developing countries. *Nonlinear Analysis: Theory, Methods & Applications, 71*(12), 32–34.

Report, A. K. (2009). *Towards productive intercommunication for knowledge.* Mohammed Bin Rashid Al-Maktoum Foundation & United Nations Development Program. Retrieved December 4, 2009, from http://www.arabstrategyforum.org/asf2009en/attachments/144_programme-english.pdf

Shehabat, I., & Mahdi, S. (2009). E-learning and its impact to the educational system in the Arab world. *IEEE Computer Society- International Conference on Information Management and Engineering* (pp. 220-225).

Taibi, D., Gentile, M., & Seta, L. (2005). A semantic search engine for learning resource. *Recent Research Development in Learning Technologies-FORMATEX.* Retrieved July 18, 2008, from www.formatex.org/micte2005/349.pdf

Thompson, L., & Lamshed, R. (2006). *E-learning within the building and construction and allied trades.* Australia: Australian Government-Department of Education, Science and Training.

UNESCO Regional Bureau. (2009). *A decade of higher education in the Arab states: Achievements & challenges.* Beirut, Lebanon: UNESCO Regional Bureau for Education in the Arab States.

Web-Based Education Commission. (2000). The power of the internet for learning: Moving from promise to practice. Final report of the Web-Based Education Commission to the President and Congress of the United States, Washington, D.C. Retrieved April 3, 2006, from http://www.ed.gov/offices/AC/WBEC/FinalReport/WBECReport.pdf

KEY TERMS AND DEFINITIONS

Course Management System: A web based learning system, that is used to manage the courses and content to be delivered for students and it provide different functionalities such as assessment and administration.

E-Ticket Unified E-Learning System: It is an online system for providing flexibility towards unified online learning systems between different universities.

Infrastructure: Represents the Hardware and Software needed for any solution to operate successfully.

Interactive: Refers to the capability of a computer environment to respond to user activity by providing feedback.

Learning Management System: Web based learning system that administrates the online learning environment and manage students and courses and it adds different activities and functionality similar to Course Management Systems.

Learning Objects: Refers to any components, lessons, modules, courses, or programs that are individually-structured for use or reference in online learning systems.

Multimedia Technologies: A number of different media-based technologies provide delivery services for online learning.

Online Learning: Educational technology using computer-mediated communication facilities that generally arise from the use of Internet and Web technology.

Chapter 17
Enhancing e-Learning Environment with Embedded Recommender Systems

Mohamed S. El Sayed
Canadian International College (CIC), Egypt

Mona Nasr
Helwan University, Egypt

Torky I. Sultan
Helwan University, Egypt

ABSTRACT

A recommender system in an e-learning context is a software agent that tries to "intelligently" recommend actions to a learner based on the actions of previous learners. These recommendation systems have been tried in e-commerce to entice purchasing of goods, but haven't been tried in e-learning. The majority of current web-based learning systems are closed learning environments where courses and learning materials are fixed, and the only dynamic aspect is the organization of the material that can be adapted to allow a relatively individualized learning environment. The proposed framework for building automatic recommendations in e-learning platforms is composed of two modules: an off-line module which preprocesses data to build learner and content models, and an online module which uses these models on-the-fly to recognize the students' needs and goals, and predict a recommendation list.

Recommended learning objects are obtained by using a range of recommendation strategies based mainly on content based filtering and collaborative filtering approaches, each applied separately or in combination.

INTRODUCTION

In this chapter we describe an automatic personalization framework for Virtual Learning Environment (VLE) aiming to provide online automatic recommendations for learners. A recommender system in e-learning context is a software agent that tries to "intelligently" recommend actions to a learner based on two ways. First, the user preferences which gathered while user registers in the system. Second, the tutor recommendations in different forms like links, PDFs etc. These recom-

DOI: 10.4018/978-1-4666-1984-5.ch017

mendation systems have been tried in e-commerce to entice purchasing of goods, but haven't been tried in e-learning yet practically.

The majority of current web-based learning systems are closed learning environments where courses and learning materials are fixed and the only dynamic aspect is the organization of the material that can be adapted to allow a relatively individualized learning environment. The proposed framework for building automatic recommendations in e-learning platforms is composed of two modules: a module which preprocesses data to build learner and content models, and a module which uses these collected data on-the-fly to recognize the user preferences during registration process, and tutor's recommendations and predict a recommendation list.

Recommended learning objects are obtained by using a range of recommendation strategies based mainly on similarity of users preferences and courses categorization also the tutor's recommendation for these courses and collaborative filtering approach, each applied separately or in combination.

By collecting the recommendation according to the user preferences and matching it with courses we can generate a recommendation list that can be displayed to the user as a related topics or courses. Also tutor's recommendation will be displayed for the users when they browse the courses contents for the first time, and by this the achieved target is obtained to minimize the time that users take to find a suitable course.

Research in e-learning has gained increasing attention thanks to the recent explosive use of the Internet. However, Web-based learning environments are becoming very popular. In a virtual classroom, educators provide resources such as text, multimedia and simulations, and moderate and animate discussions. Remote learners are encouraged to peruse the resources and participate in activities.

E-LEARNING SYSTEMS

Distance learning is a general term used to refer to a form of learning in which the instructor and student are separated by space or time where the gap between the two is bridged through the use of online technologies.

E-Learning is used interchangeably in a wide variety of contexts. In distance education Universities like Open University, it is defined as a planned teaching/learning experience that uses a wide spectrum of technologies mainly Internet to reach learners at a distance (Jonathan, 2004). Lately in most Universities, E-Learning is used to define a specific mode to attend a course or programs of study where the students rarely, if ever, attend face-to-face or for on-campus access to educational facilities, because they study on-line.

E-Learning Provider Categories

There are thousands of E-Learning sites on the internet and they fall into two basic categories.

- **Service providers:** Partner with businesses and provide an environment where users can find an array of training-related resources.
- **Content providers:** Develop and sell custom-designed training courses in response to specific information the customer provides.

E-LEARNING SOLUTION SOFTWARE

The E-Learning Solution Software combines both service providers and content providers, but it is much more. It is a concept that places learning and development at the core of organizational sustainability and competitiveness and thus addresses the classic division between the training and development function and the operational (business) function of organizations. It is an organizing and integrating mechanism designed to capture the richness of information available within the 'knowledge economy', to facilitate individuals and organizations to use that information, share it, process it, identify its relevance and if necessary store it.

The E-Learning Solution Software concept generates a series of metaphors for learning and development. These recognize that individuals will apply learning if the process and outcomes are relevant and captures and invites immediate learning preferences.

We posit that an overly optimistic view of eLearning might be more prevalent than expected and needs to be addressed by researchers and educators. Our opinion is supported by some who similarly recognize that eLearning is a popular movement not without limitations, and that greater consideration and reflection upon pedagogical issues is necessary (Fox, 2003)(Conacannon, 2005).

We agree with other academics in recognizing that Distance-Learning ≠ eLearning (Guri-Rosenblit, 2005). In lack of a widely accepted definition of eLearning, we feel it important to emphasize a clear distinction between distance learning, multimedia supported learning, and technological intelligent agents [TIA]. From our perspective, distance learning implies eLearning, potentially uses multimedia technologies in additional to other resources, although this is not necessary and could possibly be revolutionized by TIA.

E-Learning Objectives

Before implementing E-Learning, organizations need to set common goals or objectives include the following:

- **To reduce learning costs:** as a small business owner, you know that online transactions cost a fraction as much those requiring paper or staff. It's the same with E-Learning.
- **To reduce the time required for effective learning:** E-Learning is sometimes called "just-in-time" learning. Such learning enables employees to take what they have just learned from their computer screens and apply it to the tasks at hand.
- **To motivate employees:** E-Learning is considered an effective way to keep up with new technology, to generate new ideas, and to keep your workforce fresh and inspired.
- **To improve flexibility of course delivery:** Most of smaller businesses do not have the staff to manage their training and development initiatives. E-Learning technologies can overcome these administrative restrictions.
- **To expand the capabilities of the business:** Small organizations need to get more out of their high-potential employees. E-Learning helps employers take these employees to a higher level of contribution.

Learning Management System

The LMS/CMS is an e-learning platform which is considered as an important part of e-learning solutions from the university's viewpoint. Anyway, LMS is software that automates the administration of training events.

All LMSs Manage the login of registered users, manage courses catalogs, track learner activities and results, and provide reports to management (Ellis, 2009).

The market of LMS is increasing very fast; some of LMSs are commercial software like WebCT (http://www.webct.com), while others are open sources like MOODLE.

APPROACHES AND METHODOLOGIES

Computer-Based Learning

Computer Based Learning, sometimes abbreviated to CBL, refers to the use of computers as a key component of the educational environment. While this can refer to the use of computers in a classroom, the term more broadly refers to a structured environment in which computers are used for teaching purposes. The concept is generally seen as being distinct from the use of computers in ways where learning is at least a peripheral element of the experience (e.g. computer games and web browsing) (Whyte, 1989).

Computer-Based Training

Computer-based training (CBT) services are where a student learns by executing special training programs on a computer relating to their occupation. CBT is especially effective for training people to use computer applications because the CBT program can be integrated with the applications so that students can practice using the application as they learn. Historically, CBT's growth has been hampered by the enormous resources required: human resources to create a CBT program, and hardware resources needed to run it.

Web-Based Training

Web-based training (WBT) is a type of training that is similar to CBT; however, it is delivered over the Internet using a web browser. Web-based training frequently includes interactive methods, such as bulletin boards, mail, chat rooms, instant messaging, videoconferencing, and discussion threads. Web based training is usually a self-paced learning medium though some systems allow for online testing and evaluation at specific times. (http://en.wikipedia.org/wiki/Elearning).

RECOMMENDER SYSTEMS

Recommender systems have become a popular technique and strategy for helping users to select desirable products or services. Most researches in this area focused on applying the method to help the customers in Business-to-Customer (B2C) electronic commerce (e-commerce) but in E-Learning systems not applied yet.

Concepts

The recommender systems compare the collected data to similar and not similar data collected from others and calculate a list of recommended items for the user. (Montaner, June 2003) provide the first overview of recommender systems, from an intelligent agent's perspective. Adomavicius (June 2005) provides a new overview of recommender systems. Herlocker (January 2004) provides an overview of evaluation techniques for recommender systems.

RECOMMENDER SYSTEMS/ RECOMMENDATION ENGINES

Recommender Systems or recommendation engines form or work from a specific type of information filtering system technique that attempts to recommend information items (films, television, video on demand, music, books, news, images, web pages) that are likely to be of interest to the user. Typically, a recommender system compares a user profile to some reference characteristics, and seeks to predict the 'rating' that a user would give to an item they had not yet considered.

These characteristics may be from the information item (the content-based approach) or the user's social environment (the collaborative filtering approach).

THE SUITABILITY OF RECOMMENDER SYSTEMS APPROACHES

Actually, Recommender Systems are consisting of approaches; every approach has its advantages/disadvantages. However, there are many systems used Hybrid Recommender System (HRS), which combines two or more recommendation techniques to gain better performance. According to Burke (2002) the best known recommender system approaches are as follows:

Content-Based System (CBS)

In this type, the objects are selected by having correlation between the content of the objects and the user's preferences. Examples: Infofilter and InfoFinder (http://infofinder.cgiar.org). In the case of LMS, CBS can be used within LMS to recommend objects learning, as a primer approach by detecting similarities between the current course attributes (keywords, abstract …etc.) and the other courses.

Collaborative Filtering Systems (CFS)

It recommends courses or items to a member, based on similar members' preferences, and on the opinions of other members with similar tastes. It employs statistical techniques to find a set of members known as neighbors to the target member(Shi, 2004). CFS has some methods to calculate the likeliness from the rating matrix whose entry $v_{u,i}$ represents the rating member u gave to course c.

In order to estimate similarity between customers, various metrics have been proposed. One of them, for example, is the Pearson correlation (Resnick, 1994). Results obtained range from -1 for negative correlation to $+1$ for perfect positive correlation.

$$Corr(m, u) = \frac{\sum_{j \in J} (v_{m,j} - \bar{v}_m)(v_{u,j} - \bar{v}_u)}{\sqrt{\sum_{j \in J} (v_{m,j} - \bar{v}_m)^2 \sum_{j \in J} (v_{u,j} - \bar{v}_u)^2}}$$

(1)

stand for the correlation between members m and u, where J is the set of courses rated by both members c and u, $v_{L,j}$ is the rating member L gave to product j and v_L is the average rating of member L for the courses that belong to J, for L $\in$ {m, u}.

The weighted sum equation below can then be used to predict the rating of a member m on a course j. The resulting predictions are sorted and those with highest values are considered for recommendation purposes

$$P_{m,j} = \bar{v}_m + \frac{\sum_{u \in U} corr(m, u)(v_{u,j} - \bar{v}_u)}{\sum_{u \in U} |corr(m, u)|},$$

(2)

where U is the set of all the members who have supplied a rating for course j.

Demographic-Based System (DBS)

It uses "prior knowledge on demographic information about the members and their opinions for the recommended items as basis for recommendations"(Olsson, 2003). It aims to categorize the member based on personal explicit attributes and make recommendations based on demographic group that a member belongs to, such as (income, age, learning level, or geographical region), or a combination of these clusters/groups.

Examples: Grundy, a book recommender system, where people's descriptions of themselves were used to build a user model and then predict characteristics of books that they would enjoy and the free e-mail suppliers put advertisements based on the user demographic information, such as RS used in Hotmail and Yahoo. The DBS could be used in the process of recommending learning objects as a complementary approach.

Rule- Based Filtering (RBF)

It is filtering information according to set of rules expressing the information filtering policy (Terveen, 2001). These rules may be part of the user or the system profile contents and it may refer to various attributes of the data items. In general, this system used with:

- **Censorship:** RBF is useful in the protection domain e.g. the protection of kids from accessing some materials, e.g. Cyberpatrol. com and Cybersitter.com.
- **Spam Filtering:** RBF is useful to be used against the Spam e-mails, e.g. Spam Assassin (spamassassin.apache.org/) and MailEssentials (www.gfi.com).

Hybrid Recommender System (HRS)

"HRS combines two or more recommendation techniques to gain better performance with fewer of the drawbacks of any individual one" (Robin, 2002).

Another Recommendation Process

Another idea of the Recommendation process based on two way of recommendation:

Recommending using the course creator additions in table (recommends):

- The recommendation here is free added by the course creator of any type (papers, PDFs, URLs … etc), recommendation appear to the user when he/she view the course as a list.
- Recommending according to saved prefers list in table (prefer_recommeds).

Algorithm for second type recommendation is matching the member prefers which he/she select from database table named (prefer_recommends) when he /she register at first time which stored in the database table named (member_prefer) with the course keyword that selected from database table named (prefer_recommends) by the course creator previously when he/she creates a course and recommend it to the new visitors.

Let's suppose that we have a courses array named CorAry and a members array called MemAry. We need to match the field named fixrecid in table member_prefer with table course_prefer and get the results. If they are equal then we recommend the course to the member.

THE SYSTEM FRAMEWORK COMPOSED OF THE FOLLOWING MODULES

Registration Module

This module used by visitors to register in the system in order to use its resources and get its benefits.

The registration form is suitable and can be extended to gain more fields according to the organization that uses the system. The required fields in this form is the username and password which will be used to login to the system.

The form is validated using AJAX programming, to ensure that the entered data is true and suitable to be used.

Administrator Module

This module used by the administrator of the system, administrator is responsible for creating new users, classify users and recover lost passwords.

Administrator area is restricted for the administrator only and it is protected by a username and password.

Instructors Module

This module used by instructors of the system or course creators, they can use it to create courses categories, courses and lectures. Also, they can attach files to the lecture using a special file uploader.

During the course creation instructors can add some recommendation for the students to allow them review more resources related to this course.

Students Module

This module used by the students who can view the categories and its courses. Also, students can access the uploaded files which are attached in each lecture.

Statistics Module

This module shows the statistics of the site by numbers, it display the number of registered users and number of the courses in the system in order to give a full view of the system.

Calendar Module

This module shows the current and the future events that can be created by the instructors to the students.

Visitor Counter Module

This module displays the visitor numbers of the site. Each visit counted and displayed on the site home page without login to the system.

DATAFLOW AND DATABASE

In this section we will review the database formation and its tables that will hold the system data. This database was created using MYSQL database server which is a free online server based on Apache server and has a control panel called phpmyadmin (see Figure 1).

Accessing the system steps:

- Visitors will register in the site using the registration form.
- He/she can access the courses and review its details by category.

Figure 1. The framework database

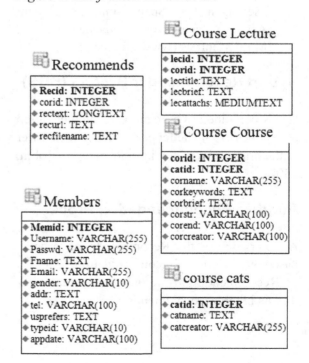

- Each category or course has its brief and creator name at the bottom of it.

In this section we will discuss the coding of the system, the system is based on the file named index.php and all the other interfaces are generated by the http requests through the user interaction.

For the database communication there is a file named biclass.php which responsible for the connecting to database and make all related database issues like add, edit and delete records from it.

System interface is controlled by the cascade style sheet named style.css and stored on the site main folder.

RECOMMENDING SYSTEM IDEA AND CODING

In order to evaluate the usefulness of different recommender algorithms that will be used to build the recommender system and then applying it in E-Learning field. We need to examine them to the matching process. While we recognize that recommendation accuracy alone does not guarantee users a satisfying experience, we focus on user preferences and courses keywords for evaluation of recommender system performance in this framework. It is possible to simulate, to a satisfying degree, the reaction of different variants of the recommender algorithms and thus create the proposed recommender algorithm.

Last decade, Recommendation Systems (RSs) have been widely implemented and accepted in many sectors of Internet. We are familiar with recommendations of products (e.g., books, music, movies) and of services (e.g., restaurants, hotels, web sites), likewise "recommendation is not a new phenomenon arising from the digital era, but an existing social behavior in real life" (Tseng, 2002). In everyday life, we rely on recommendations from others where a lot of information is available electronically; moreover, the World Wide Web (WWW) is still growing faster; as a result, the users suffer from the "Information Overload" problem, when searching on internet.

Generally, the aim of RSs in web applications, is presenting interest information that fits the users tastes and preferences with little effort. In contrast, sometimes RSs are used to hide special information, and specifically, the aim of RSs in e-learning applications (e.g., Learning Management Systems (LMS)) is listing "the closest available learning objects to what the instructor describes as the module's content" (Calvo, 2003).

TECHNICAL VIEW

A prerequisite of the entire experimental evaluation process is deciding which courses will be recommended to the user that we want to show. The choice of data sets, experimental setup, and evaluation metrics all depend on which specific recommender task we select (Jonathan, 2004).

First and foremost are the end users (students), who should be provided with recommended items that relate to their preferences. However, recommender systems can also be designed, tweaked, or tuned to serve other goals.

In this section we describe three types of recommendation that used in this framework. The first type is the recommending courses according to the user preference. This will be done when a new visitor register in the system, where his preferences are collected and saved in the users table in order to be used as a key to detect what user preferences and then make the recommendation process which appear as list to the visitor.

We collect the new user preferences as an array of objects, in the same time we collect the courses keywords that stored in the database and then by applying the matching algorithm of the recommendation process to them, we finally get a list of recommender objects that displayed to the new user.

Second type is the recommending courses according to the course keywords which were entered by the course creator and the other courses keywords which represent as a field in the database. After collecting the keywords of the course which viewed by the user and the saved courses in the database, we match them with the other courses keywords and then output the recommended courses to the user.

Finally, the third type of recommendation is the instructor recommendation. The "instructor recommendations" are the resources which the instructor put them in his course as recommended resources. They could be internal resources (courses from the same LMS) or external resources. However, the algorithm shows the resources to allow then to be added to the recommendation list.

Mechanism

The system code works based on PHP as the script language and MYSQL as the database server for the system. This code is embedded inside the E-Learning system and it works at the background to make the recommendation process.

In this recommendation process we use a self constructed algorithm based on matching items together and get the matched items. The algorithm is extracted from a review of other algorithms like Brute Force algorithm and Knuth-Morris-Pratt algorithm (Charra,1997).

Brute Force Algorithm

Main Features

- No preprocessing phase;
- Constant extra space needed;
- Always shifts the window by exactly 1 position to the right;
- Comparisons can be done in any order;
- Searching phase in O(mn) time complexity;
- 2n expected text characters comparisons.

Description

Brute force algorithm consists in checking, at all positions in the text between 0 and n-m, whether an occurrence of the pattern starts there or not. Then, after each attempt, it shifts the pattern by exactly one position to the right.

Brute force algorithm requires no preprocessing phase, and a constant extra space in addition to the pattern and the text. During the searching phase the text character comparisons can be done in any order. The time complexity of this searching phase is O(mn) (when searching for am-1b in an for instance). The expected number of text character comparisons is 2n.

The C Code

```
void BF(char *x, int m, char *y, int
n) {
  int i, j;
  /* Searching */
  for (j = 0; j <= n - m; ++j) {
    for (i = 0; i < m && x[i] ==
y[i + j]; ++i);
    if (i >= m)
      OUTPUT(j);
  }}
```

Knuth-Morris-Pratt Algorithm

Main Features

- Performs the comparisons from left to right;
- Preprocessing phase in O(m) space and time complexity;
- Searching phase in O(n+m) time complexity (independent from the alphabet size);
- Delay bounded by log(m) where is the golden ratio ().

Description

The design of the Knuth-Morris-Pratt algorithm follows a tight analysis of the Morris and Pratt algorithm. Let us look more closely at the Morris-Pratt algorithm. It is possible to improve the length of the shifts.

Consider an attempt at a left position j, that is when the window is positioned on the text factor y[j.. j+m-1]. Assume that the first mismatch occurs between x[i] and y[i+j] with 0 < i < m. Then, x[0.. i-1] = y[j.. i+j-1] =u and a = x[i] y[i+j]=b.

When shifting, it is reasonable to expect that a prefix [v]of the pattern matches some suffix of the portion u of the text. Moreover, if we want to avoid another immediate mismatch, the character following the prefix v in the pattern must be different from [a]. The longest such prefix v is called the tagged border of u (it occurs at both ends of u followed by different characters in x).

This introduces the notation: let kmpNext[i] be the length of the longest border of x[0.. i-1] followed by a character c different from x[i] and -1 if no such tagged border exits, for 0 < i m. Then, after a shift, the comparisons can resume between characters x[kmpNext[i]] and y[i+j] without missing any occurrence of x in y, and avoiding a backtrack on the text as shown in Figure 2. The value of kmpNext[0] is set to -1.

The table kmpNext can be computed in O(m) space and time before the searching phase, applying the same searching algorithm to the pattern itself, as if x=y.

The searching phase can be performed in O(m+n) time. The Knuth-Morris-Pratt algorithm performs at most 2n-1 text character comparisons during the searching phase. The delay (maximal number of comparisons for a single text character) is bounded by log(m) where is the golden ratio ().

The C Code

```c
void preKmp(char *x, int m, int
kmpNext[]) {
    int i, j;
    i = 0;
    j = kmpNext[0] = -1;
    while (i < m) {
        while (j > -1 && x[i] != x[j])
            j = kmpNext[j];
        i++;
        j++;
        if (x[i] == x[j])
            kmpNext[i] = kmpNext[j];
        else
            kmpNext[i] = j;
    }
}
void KMP(char *x, int m, char *y, int
n) {
    int i, j, kmpNext[XSIZE];
    /* Preprocessing */
    preKmp(x, m, kmpNext);
    /* Searching */
    i = j = 0;
    while (j < n) {
```

Figure 2. Shift in the Knuth-Morris-Pratt algorithm (v border of u and c b)

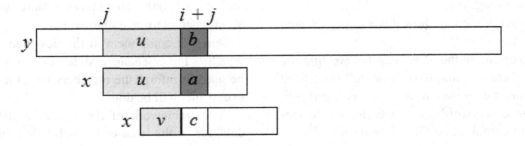

```
    while (i > -1 && x[i] != y[j])
        i = kmpNext[i];
    i++;
    j++;
    if (i >= m) {
        OUTPUT(j - i);
        i = kmpNext[i];
    }
    }
}
```

The Proposed Algorithm

The algorithm used in this framework is:

```
function getMatch(){
$Result = array();
for($i=0;$i<count($MemAry);$i++){
    for($j=0;$j<count($CorAry);$j++)
{
        if($MemAry['fixrecid']
[$i]==$CorAry['fixrecid'][$j]){
            array_
push($Result,$CorAry['corid'][$j];
}
}
}
return $Result;
}
```

We have in this framework database a field in the "users table" that holds the user preferences and another field in "courses table" that holds the course keywords. The code will split these values down to an array of [ids], these [ids] will be used during the matching process that will be done by the system engine.

The script view for how it works is presented in Box 1.

As appears in the code snapshot we split the user preferences that have been collected from user when he registered in the system, and split the courses keywords then matching the two arrays and output the result for the user.

In case of the instructor recommendations, the system allow to the instructor to add what he want of recommendation objects. These objects are stored in the database in order to show them to the user who previews the course.

The instructor has ability to add PDF files to the course when he creates it. The user can download this file to view what instructor wants to show.

THE FRAMEWORK DESIGN

In this section we will feed the E-learning system with data and test the recommendation system and how it works for members of the system. The E-Learning framework composed of courses categories and courses that will be viewed by the instructors. Each instructor can create his own category and add courses to it also other instructors can add courses in this category. The owner can manage his category.

The framework was designed to test applying recommendation system in the E-Learning systems and check the usability of recommendation systems in this field. So, the E-learning system is a mini-system designed for this purpose only and it can be expanded as it is an open source system.

The usage of the system is so easy, categories are listed then visitor can navigate to courses through the categories. Visitor can view the lectures of each course.

Also, we add ability to attach files to the lectures of the course with a nice view to make it user friendly by using the AJAX technique which allow adding a pre-loader when attaching the file.

Courses and categories can be managed by their owners only. This makes it more secure to all instructors to save their works.

Another component in the designed system which is the calendar module, this module can be used to inform the members with the future events that will be done.

The framework of the system based on a database in the back-end which holds the data;

Box 1.

```
// User preference keys
$Usrpref_keys = explode("*",$MemAry['prefer']);
$CorsPref_keys = explode("*",$rowCorOne['corkeywords']);
// Collect All courses for recommender
$rsAllCor = $Obj->Select($cortable,"*","",'corid','ASC');
$rowAllCor = $Obj->Row_Rs($rsAllCor);
$totalAllCors = $Obj->getTotalRows($rsAllCor);
Then,
if($totalAllCors>0){//check on courses presence
    do{
// $Usrpref_keys is the preferences of the users
// Recommender By User preferences and named See Also on website
$AllCorsPref_keys = explode("*",$rowAllCor['corkeywords']);
$StopLoop = false;          // to stop loop in first value founded
for($i=1;$i<count($AllCorsPref_keys);$i++){       // Loop on All Keys for cur-
rent course
if($AllCorsPref_keys[$i]!=""){           // to sure that key is not empty
if(in_array($AllCorsPref_keys[$i],$Usrpref_keys) and $StopLoop==false){
if($rowAllCor['corid'] != $rowCorOne['corid']){      // to don't select itself
array_push($Recom, $rowAllCor['corid']);        // push course ID
array_push($RecomTitle, $rowAllCor['corname']);     // push course title
$StopLoop = true;                                   // stop the loop
}}}}
// $CorsPref_keys is the preferences of the current course
// Recommender By Related courses in key preferences
if($id != ""){
    $StopLoop2 = false;      // to stop loop in first value founded
    for($i=1;$i<count($AllCorsPref_keys);$i++){
    if($AllCorsPref_keys[$i] != ""){ // to sure that key is not empty
    if(in_array($AllCorsPref_keys[$i],$CorsPref_keys) and $StopLoop2==false){
if($rowAllCor['corid'] != $rowCorOne['corid']){      // to don't select itself
array_push($Recom_bycor, $rowAllCor['corid']);
array_push($RecomTitle_bycor, $rowAllCor['corname']);
$StopLoop2 = true;      // stop the loop
}}}}}
}while($rowAllCor = $Obj->Row_Rs($rsAllCor));
}
```

here we will review how the data will be feed in the tables:

Categories are stored in a table named course_cats, the fields for this table are catid, catname and catcreator. These fields are for category ID, category name and category creator, instructor can create any number of categories and then add his courses in this category.

To add a category, members must create an account and login to the system and then click on courses link in the menu and then click on create new category as in Figure 3.

After clicking on the create category button a form for new category will appear, this form contain a field for the new category name as in Figure 4 which can be filled by the instructor.

As appears in the figure, the category name is the only field that the instructor can deals with it. The other fields are hidden due to managerial reasons. catid will be added automatically according to incremental counter in the table of the categories and the owner field (catcreator) will be filled automatically be the session name of the instructor.

Also, there is ability to edit or delete the category and its courses and lectures.

Courses in the system are stored in a table called course, the fields for this table are corid, catid, corname, corkeywords, corbrief, corstr, corend and corcreator. These fields are for course id, category id, course name, course keywords, course brief, course start date, course end date and course creator.

Here we will not use the course start date and end date because we need to see the recommendation system results only and check its results. Also, we ignore the enrollment in the courses and make it available for all members who create an account in the system.

Rollover again, instructor can add the course by enters the category and then he will find create new course, edit category, delete category and my courses buttons as appears in Figure 5.

Figure 3. Create new category

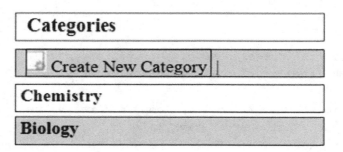

Figure 4. Add new category

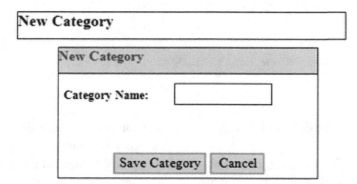

As appear in the figure, by clicking the create new course link it will lead us to the create course form as in Figure 6.

The course title is used to add the course title or name and course description will hold the description of the course. For the course keywords the instructor will select suitable keywords for this course and then marks it.

The courses keywords can be increased by the admin of the system according to requirements for the courses.

Also, we support the system with an edit and delete forms for the courses that have been created. In case of delete the course its related lectures will be deleted.

Inside each course there is ability to add lectures and recommendation links that can be

Figure 5. Category view

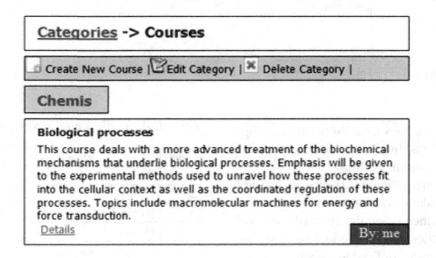

Figure 6. Add new course

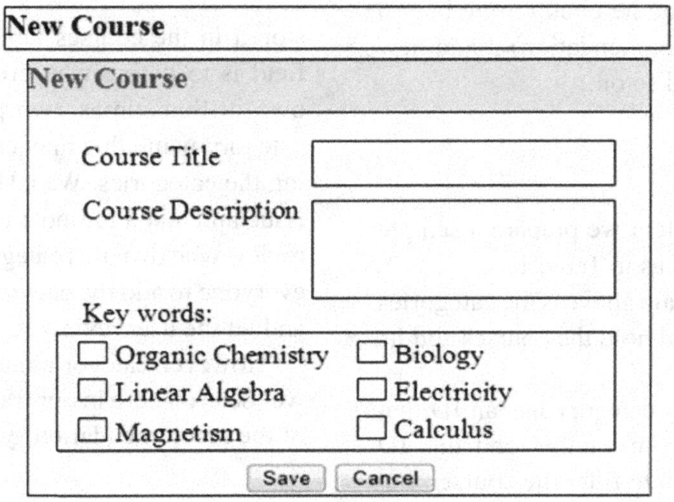

Figure 7. Inside a course

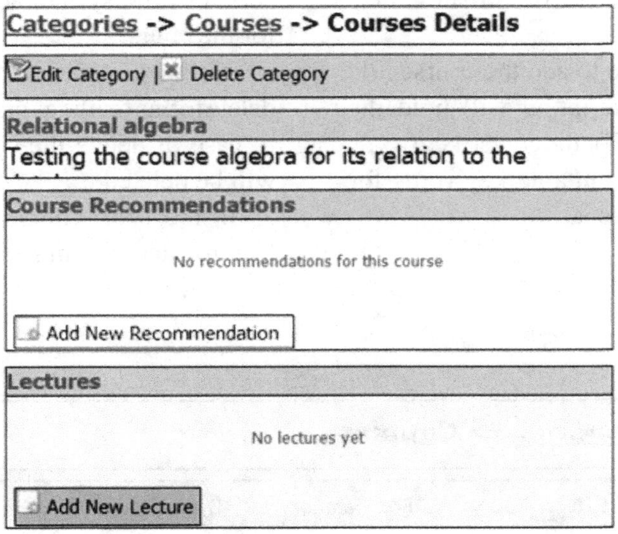

Categories -> Courses -> **Courses Details**

Edit Category | ✕ Delete Category

Relational algebra

Testing the course algebra for its relation to the

Course Recommendations

No recommendations for this course

Add New Recommendation

Lectures

No lectures yet

Add New Lecture

recommended for the viewer of the course. Figure 7 shows the adding of the course resources (lectures and recommendation).

As appears in the Figure (7) instructor can add new recommendations and also new lectures. For the new recommendation the allowed types are links or PDF files and for the lecture there is a lecture title, lecture brief and lecture attachments for more resources purpose.

The instructor can use this form to add any number of recommendations and any number of lectures, thus every time he click on the button add new (lecture / recommendation) it add new one and goes down and so on.

Data Sample

In order to test the system we prepare a sample data to feed the system as in Table 1.

This data as we explain above is the categories stored in the system and hold the courses and its resources.

As we see that each category has an ID that distinguish category from another and this ID used through the system to filter the courses that

Table 1. A sample data for categories

catid	Catname	Catcreator
1	Chemistry	As
2	Biology	as
3	Mathematics	as
4	Physics	ms
5	Biological Engineering	ms
6	Chemical Engineering	ms
7	Computer Science	as

stored in the courses table. Also the catcreator field is to define who create this category and own it. Sometimes, two people have the same category name this may cause conflict on viewing the categories. We take in consideration this issue and add a red note under each category to review who own this category. This trick to allow everyone to add the category he wants to name it and let the user review it.

However, categories names or title is not what we focus on here in our framework, but the using of the recommendation system.

RECOMMENDATION RESULTS

In this section, the results are collected by some steps to get the recommendation list that can be ready to be shown as a list.

When user registers in the system, we collect interests that he prefers by allowing him to select from a list of keywords. When he views a course in the system, the system makes the process and then gets the result recommendation list and shows it to him in three categories. First category is the recommendation according to the related courses to what he views. The second is the recommendation according to what he prefers or what he selects in his profile to view. Finally, recommendations created by the instructors.

The recommendation box will appear at the right down side of the main menu as a pink box and divided into three parts which acts as the recommendation categories as shown in Figure 8.

As appear in Figure 8 a list of recommendation courses in three categories as described.

Each line in the recommendation box is a link to the course in the first and second sections. When member click this line or course it goes to its details and he can review the details of this course. If there is a recommendation for the course the member goes to it, it will be listed too in the same way.

For the third section of recommendation box, the instructor recommendation area which named (add by teacher) will be a description for the recommendation and a link to outside resource of the system or a PDF file that can user download it to review. This feature allows the instructors to add what they see that will help the members to gain more information about the course.

In some cases, two or more courses may be like in their recommendation list, this may occur when they are related to each others in somewhat like a chain or something like that. The recommendation results appear to help the members not to be a heavy duty on him.

Figure 8. Recommendation box

RECOMMENDATIONS
See Also,
structure and reactivity of organic molecules
Introduction to organic chemistry
intermediate course
introduction experimental chemistry
principles of Inorganic Chemistry
Related course
structure and reactivity of organic molecules
Introduction to organic chemistry
intermediate course
Biological Chemistry
Molecular Biology
Molecular Principles of Biomaterials
Added by teacher
Check my vote
Link
this is a test recomed
File
sdfcsf
File

In instructor recommendation area, instructor can add what appears as recommended resources even a video, a slideshow or a PDF file as a resource for a course.

CONCLUSION AND FUTURE WORK

In this chapter we try to enhance e-Learning Environment with Embedded Recommender System that can be applied. More specifically, we have investigated the task of item recommendation, where interesting and relevant items are retrieved and recommended to the user, based on a variety of information sources about and characteristics of the user and the items. The proposed recommendation algorithm based on matching the user preferences and the courses keywords.

In deciding which tasks to tackle it is essential to profile the users: what do they want, how and what are they currently using the system for? We believe that focusing on real-world tasks in research can drive successful innovation, but only if the tasks under investigation are also desired by the users.

For future work; Additional modules can be added like audio/video modules, chat module and forum module in order to support more facilities for the students that make the learning process more easy and useful.

REFERENCES

Adomavicius, G., & Tuzhilin, A. (2005, June). Toward the next generation of recommender systems: A survey of the state-of-the-art and possible extensions. *IEEE Transactions on Knowledge and Data Engineering, 17*(6), 734–749. doi:10.1109/TKDE.2005.99

Black Board Learning System. (n.d.). *Website.* Retrieved from http://www.webct.com

Burke, R. (2002). Hybrid recommender systems: Survey and experiments- Customer model. *Customer-Adapted Interaction, 4*(12), 331–370. doi:10.1023/A:1021240730564

Calvo, R. (2003). User scenarios for the design and implementation of LMS. In *Proceedings of the AIED 2003 Workshop, Towards Intelligent Learning Management Systems,* (pp. 14-22).

Charras, C. (1997). *Exact string matching algorithms.* France: Thierry Lecroq, Laboratoire d'Informatique de Rouen, Université de Rouen, Faculté des Sciences et des Techniques, Mont-Saint-Aignan Cedex.

Conacannon, F., Flynn, A., & Campbell, M. (2005). What campus-based students think about the quality and benefits of e-learning. *British Journal of Educational Technology, 36*(3), 501–512. doi:10.1111/j.1467-8535.2005.00482.x

Elkhalifa, L. (2004). *InfoFilter: Complex pattern specification and detection over text streams.* Master's Thesis, Faculty of the Graduate School, USA. Retrieved from http://itlab.uta.edu/ITLABWEB/Students/ sharma/theses/Laali.pdf

Ellis, R. K. (2009). *Field guide to learning management systems.* ASTD Learning Circuits.

Fox, S., & Mackeogh, K. (2003). Can elearning promote higher-order learning without tutor overload? *Open Learning, 18*(2), 121. doi:10.1080/02680510307410

Guri-Rosenblit, S. (2005). Distance education and e-learning: Not the same thing. *Higher Education, 49*(4), 467–493. doi:10.1007/s10734-004-0040-0

Herlocker, J. L., Konstan, J. A., Terveen, L. G., & Riedl, J. T. (2004, January). Evaluating collaborative filtering recommender systems. *ACM Transactions on Information Systems, 22*(1), 5–53. doi:10.1145/963770.963772

Montaner, M., Lopez, B., & de la Rosa, J. L. (2003, June). A taxonomy of recommender agents on the internet. *Artificial Intelligence Review, 19*(4), 285–330. doi:10.1023/A:1022850703159

Moore, M. G., & Kearsley, G. (2005). *Distance education: A systems view* (2nd ed.). Belmont, CA: Wadsworth.

Olsson, T. (2003). *Bootstrapping and decentralizing recommender systems.* Licentiate Theses 2003-006, Department of Information Technology. Retrieved from www.it.uu.se/research/reports/lic/2003-006/2003-006.pdf

Resnick, P., Iacovou, N., Sushak, M., Bergstrom, P., & Riedl, J. (1994). Grouplens: An open architecture for collaborative filtering of netnews. *Proceedings of Computer Supported Collaborative Work Conference (CSCW)*, (pp. 175–186). Chapel Hill, NC.

Robin, D., & Burke, R. (2002). Hybrid recommender systems: Survey and experiments. *User Modeling and User-Adapted Interaction, 12*(4), 331–370. doi:10.1023/A:1021240730564

Shih, Y. (2004). *Extending traditional collaborative filtering with attributes extraction to recommend new products*. Master's Thesis, Department of Business Administration, National Sun Yat-sen University. Retrieved from http://thesis.lib.ncu.edu.tw/ETD-db/ ETD-search/View_etd?URN=91421019

Terveen, L., & Hill, W. (2001). Beyond recommender system: Helping people help each other. In Carroll, J. (Ed.), *Human-computer interaction in the new millennium* (pp. 487–509). ACM Press.

Tseng, C. (2002). *Cluster-based collaborative filtering recommendation approach*. Master's Thesis, Information Management Department, National Sun Yat-sen University. Retrieved from etd.lib.nsysu.edu.tw/ETD-db/ETD-search/getfile?URN=etd-0812103-164119&filename=etd-0812103-164119.pdf

Whyte, C. B. (1989). Student affairs-The future. *Journal of College Student Development, 30*, 86–89.

Wikipedia. (n.d.). *E-learning*. Retrieved from http://en.wikipedia.org/wiki/Elearning

ADDITIONAL READING

Agrawal, R., Imielinski, T., & Swami, A. (1993) Mining association rules between sets of items in large databases. In *Proceedings of the ACM SIGMOD International Conference on Management of Data* (ACM SIGMOD'93), Washington, (pp. 207-216).

Agrawal, R., & Srikant, R. (1994). Fast algorithms for mining association rules. *Proceedings of the 20th International Conference on Very Large Databases*, Santiago, Chile.

Albano, G., Gaeta, M., & Ritrovato, P. (2007). IWT: An innovative solution for AGS e-learning model. *International Journal of Knowledge and Learning, 3*(2-3), 2007.

Chakrabarti, S., van den Berg, M., & Dom, B. (1999). Focused crawling: A new approach to topic specific web resources discovery. In *Proceedings of the 8th ACM International World Wide Web Conference (WWW8)*, 1999.

Cooley, R., Mobasher, B., & Srivastava, J. (1999). Data preparation for mining world wide web browsing patterns. *Knowledge and Information Systems, 1*(1), 5–32.

De Rosis, F., De Carolis, B., & Pizzutilo, S. (1993). User tailored hypermedia explanations. *INTERCHI'93 Conference Proceedings: Conference on Human Factors in Computing Systems, INTERACT'93 and CHI'93*, Amsterdam, The Netherlands, (pp. 169-170).

Debevc, M., Meyer, B., & Svecko, R. (1997). An adaptive short list for documents on the world wide web. In *Proceedings of ACM International Conference on Intelligent User Interface* (IUI 1997), (pp. 209-211). Orlando, FL.

Diligenti, M., Coetzee, F., Lawrence, S., Giles, C. L., & Gori, M. (2000). Focused crawling using context graphs. In *Proceedings of the 26th International Conference on Very Large Databases (VLDB 2000), Cairo*, (pp. 527-534). Morgan Kauffmann Publishers.

Foss, A., Wang, W., & Zaiane, O. R. (2001). A non-parametric approach to web log analysis. In *Web Mining Workshop in Conjunction with the SIAM International Conference on Data Mining*, (pp. 41–50). Chicago, IL, USA, April 2001.

McCalla, G. (2000). The fragmentation of culture, learning, teaching and technology: Implications for the artificial Intelligence in education research agenda in 2010. *International Journal of Artificial Intelligence in Education, 11*(2), 177–196.

McNee, S. M., Albert, I., Cosley, D., Gopalkrishnan, P., Lam, S. K., & Rashid, A. M. … Riedl, J. (2002) On the recommending of citations for research papers. In *Proceedings of ACM International Conference on Computer Supported Collaborative Work* (CSCW'02), (pp. 116-125).

Menczer, F., Pant, G., Srinivasan, P., & Ruiz, M. E. (2001) Evaluating topic-driven web crawlers. In *Proceedings of the 24th International ACM SIGIR Conference on Research and Development in Information Retrieval* (SIGIR '01). September 2001, New Orleans, U.S.A.

Meteren, R. V., & Someren, M. V. (2000). *Using content-based filtering for recommendation*. MLnet / ECML2000 Workshop, May, Barcelona, Spain.

Munzner, T., & Burchard, P. (1995). Visualizing the structure of the world-wide web in 3d hyperbolic space. In *Proceedings of VRML '95*, 1995.

Paepcke, A., Garcia-Molina, H., Rodriguez-Mula, G., & Cho, J. (2000). Beyond document similarity: Understanding value-based search and browsing technologies. *SIGMOD Record, 29*(1), 80–92. doi:10.1145/344788.344828

Pazzani, M., & Billsus, D. (1997). Learning and revising user profiles: The identification of interesting web sites. *Machine Learning, 27*, 313–331. doi:10.1023/A:1007369909943

Popescul, A., Flake, G. W., Lawrence, S., Ungar, L. H., & Giles, C. L. (2000) Clustering and identifying temporal trends in document databases. In *Proceedings of IEEE International Conference on Advances in Digital Libraries (ADL 2000), Washington*, (pp. 173-182).

Sarwar, B. M., Konstan, J., Borchers, A., Herlocker, G., Miller, B., & Riedl, J. (1998). Using filtering agents to improve prediction quality in the grouplens research collaborative filtering systems. *Proceedings of the ACM Conference on Computer Supported Cooperative Work*, Seattle, Washington.

Shahabi, C., Zarkesh, A. M., Adibi, J., & Shah, V. (1997). *Knowledge discovery from user's webpage navigation*. Paper presented at the 7th IEEE International Conference on Research Issues in Data Engineering, April 7-8, Birmingham, UK.

Spiliopoulou, M., Faulstich, L. C., & Winkler, K. (1999). *A data miner analyzing the navigational behaviour of web users*. In Workshop on Machine Learning in User Modeling of the ACAI'99, Creta, Greece, July 1999.

Weber, G., & Brusilovsky, P. (2001). ELM-ART: An adaptive versatile system for web-based instruction. *International Journal of Artificial Intelligence in Education, 12*, 1–35.

Woodruff, A., Gossweiler, R., Pitkow, J., Chi, E., & Card, S. K. (2000) Enhancing a digital book with a reading recommender. In Proceedings of ACM CHI 2000, (pp. 153-160).

Yan, T., Jacobsen, M., Garcia-Molina, H., & Dayal, U. (1996). From user access patterns to dynamic hypertext linking. *Proceedings of the 5th INTERNATIONAL World Wide Web Conference*, Paris, France.

Zaiane, O. R. (2002). *Building a recommender agent for e-learning systems.* Paper presented at the 7th International Conference on Computers in Education, December 3-6, Auckland, New Zealand.

KEY TERMS AND DEFINITIONS

CBL: Computer Based Learning.

CBT: Computer-Based Training.

CMS: Content Management System.

LMS: Learning Management System.

MOODLE: An open source E-Learning solution used by most universities.

Php: Preprocessor hypertext language.

TIA: Technological Intelligent Agents.

VLE: Virtual Learning Environment.

WBT: Web-Based Training.

WebCT: A ready-made E-Learning solution with an online subscription.

Chapter 18
Adaptive E–Learning System Based on Semantic Search and Recommendation in the Arab World

Khaled M. Fouad
Taif University, Kingdom of Saudi Arabia

Nagdy M. Nagdy
Al-Baha Private College of Science, Kingdom of Saudi Arabia

Hany M. Harb
Hal-Azhar University, Egypt

ABSTRACT

The success of any e-learning system depends on the retrieval of relevant learning contents according to the requirement of the learner (user). This leads to the development of the adaptive e-learning system to provide learning materials considering the requirements and understanding capability of the learner. This chapter aims to propose the system of personalized semantic search and recommendation of learning contents on the e-learning Web-based systems. Semantic and personalized search of learning contents is based on expansion the query keywords by using of the semantic relations and reasoning mechanism in the ontology. Personalized recommendation of learning objects is based on the learner profile ontology to guide what learning contents a learner should study. For the Arab world, to achieve the learning for all goals and meet the learner's requirements, it must build more inclusive, including the personalization services, and has semantic learning content in the learning systems. The authors' proposed system is efficient, more effective, and more learner-friendly in the Arab sector because it responds to every learner and his needs individually with a timely and precise adaptation of learning materials.

DOI: 10.4018/978-1-4666-1984-5.ch018

INTRODUCTION

When an E-learning system to be delivered contains learning materials covering different levels of learning, the level of learner (user) is taken into consideration to provide the learner with the learning materials that suit his/her level and his/her fields of interest (Alian & AL-Akhras, 2010). Adaptation is needed as some learning resources may not be in a format that is acceptable for different learners' needs and that fit the capabilities of different mobile devices, additionally content adaptation is needed to provide learners with appropriate courses view. To this end, E-learning systems should employ some sort of Adaptation. Adaptation in the context of this work means that the same learning materials are represented differently to individual learners based on their interest which is determined based on their previous learning behavior.

Ontology (Fayed & Sameh, 2006) comprises a set of knowledge terms, including the vocabulary, the semantic interconnections, and some simple rules of inference and logic for some particular topic. Ontologies applied to the Web are creating the Semantic Web. Ontologies (Thomas & Juan, 2010) facilitate knowledge sharing and reuse, i.e. a common understanding of various contents that reaches across people and applications. Using ontology in learning environments aims to provide mechanisms to enhance the process of searching and finding learning resources. And, they have the capability to organize and display information that makes it easier for learners to draw connections, for instance, by visualizing relationships among concepts and ideas.

The behavior of an adaptive system (Christoph, 2005) varies according to the data from the learner model and the learner profile. Without knowing anything about the learner, a system would perform in exactly the same way for all learners. It was described the application of learner models as follows:

"Users are different: they have different background, different knowledge about a subject, different preferences, goals and interests. To individualize, personalize or customize actions a user model is needed that allows for selection of individualized responses to the user." (Christoph, 2005).

Personalized information retrieval (Daoud, Tamine, & Mohand, 2009) has become a promising area for disambiguating the web search and therefore improving retrieval effectiveness by modeling the user profile by his interests and preferences. Personalizing the search for needed information in an E-learning environment (Zhuhadar & Nasraoui, 2008) based on context requires intelligent methods for representing and matching both the learning resources and the variety of learning contexts. On the one hand, semantic web technologies can provide a representation of the learning content (lectures). On the other hand, the semantics of the learner interests or profiles can form a good representation of the learning context that promises to enhance the results of retrieval via personalization. The key knowledge in any personalization strategy for E-learning is an accurate learner model.

In existing recommender systems (Lu, 2004), the systems can be broadly categorized into content-based and collaborative. Content-based recommender systems provide recommendations to a user by automatically matching his preferences with content. In content-based systems, contents are described by a common set of attributes. User preferences are predicted by analyzing the relationship between the content ratings and the corresponding content attributes. A central problem in content-based recommender systems is the need to identify a sufficiently large set of key attributes. Collaborative recommender systems estimate a user's preferences for a content based on the overlap between his preference ratings for the content and those of other users. The main difference between collaborative and content-based recommender systems is that the collaborative systems track past actions of a group of users to make a recommendation for individual members of the group.

Learner model (Baishuang & Wei, 2009; Li, et al., 2008) can be collected by two ways: explicit and implicit collection. Explicit collection is predefined or feedback by learner's ratings through an interface. There are roughly two kinds of automatic way to capture a learner's interest implicitly: behavior-based and history-based. The behavior-based research proves that the time spent on a page, the amount of scrolling on a page and the combination of them has a strong positive relationship with learner interests. Browsing histories capture the relationship between learner's interests and his click history in which sufficient contextual information is already hidden in the web log.

From a developmental perspective (Amr, 2011; Hegazy & Radwan, 2010), the Arab world learning has the potential to play a significant role in accelerating the development process because its population is young. For the Arab world to achieve the learning for all goals and meet the learner's requirements, it must build more inclusive, including the personalization services, and has semantic learning content in the learning systems. In order to invest in this large and young source of human capital, the Arab world is striving to improve education at different levels by using the personalized and semantic learning environments.

This chapter aims to propose the adaptive E-learning system that performs the personalized semantic search and recommendation of learning objects on the learning Web-based environments. Semantic and personalized search of learning contents is based on introducing ontology into query expansion and makes good use of semantic relations of concepts in ontology to expand query keywords and to make the retrieval results for learning objects more accuracy and comprehensive. Personalized recommendation of learning objects is based on learner behavior during is

working and learner profile ontology to guide what learning contents a learner should study, i.e. what learning objects should have according to learner behavior and interests. The main goal of this proposed system is to construct effective and efficient an E-learning environment, which adapts itself to individual learners in the Arab world to enable the learner to search in the learning contents more accurate and recommend him what contents, should have according to learner behavior and interests.

The chapter is organized as follows: Section 2 discusses related works. Section 3 describes the domain ontology. We describe the proposed framework in section 4. The Suggestions and recommendations is described in section 5.

RELATED WORKS

Personalized search (Gauch, Speretta, & Pretschner 2007) is addressed by a number of systems. Persona (Tanudjaja & Mui, 2002) uses explicit relevant feedback to update user profiles that are represented by means of weighted open directory project taxonomy (Open Directory Project, 2012). These profiles are used to filter search results as found in PersonalizedGoogle or the outride Personalized Search System (Pitkow, Schütze, & Cass, 2002). Persival (McKeown, Elhadad, & Hatzivassiloglou, 2003) re-ranks the search results of queries for medical articles profiles keywords, associated concepts, and weights generated from an electronic patient record. In (Liu, Yu, & Meng, 2002), it was filtered search results on the grounds of user profiles obtained from earlier queries. These profiles consist of a set of categories, and weighted terms associated with each category. In their work on personalizing search results, (Sugiyama, et al. 2004) distinguish between long-term and short-term interests. While aiming at personalization in a broader sense, (Mu, Chen, Li, & Jiang, 2009) use click-through data to increase the performance of search results.

Nowadays (Duong, Uddin, Li, & Jo, 2009), personalization systems are developed by considering ontology to reduce the limitation of traditional information retrieval such as information overload or cold start problem. So considering ontology to build an accurate profile brings some extra benefit in user modeling. A user profile can be presented as a weighted concept hierarchy for searching and browsing in the web. User profile can be own created by user with his/her personal information and interest or it can be a reference one. However, profile can be created by manually entering the user's information or automatically by watching the use's activities.

In (Jin, Ning, Jia, Wu, & Lu, 2008), it was proposed a novel approach which enables intelligent semantic web search for best satisfying users search intensions. The approach combines the user's subjective weighting importance over multiple search properties together with fuzziness to represent search requirements. A special ranking mechanism based on the above weighed fuzzy query is also presented. The ranking method considers not only fuzzy predicates in the query, but also the user's personalized interests or preferences. Therefore, the search results shall be properly ordered in terms of their "degree of relevance" with respect to the query request. In addition, the ranking method is general and unique rather than arbitrary. To verify its effectiveness, we evaluate the approach over real world data from CiteSeer metadata (http://citeseer.ist.psu.edu/oai.html) which covers literatures in the field of computer science and computer technology.

MedSearch is a complete retrieval system for medical literature (Hliaoutakis, Varelas, & Petrakis, 2006). It supports retrieval by SSRM (Semantic Similarity Retrieval Model), a novel information retrieval method which is capable for associating documents containing semantically similar (but not necessarily lexically similar) terms. SSRM suggests discovering semantically similar terms in documents and queries using term taxonomies (ontologies) and by associating such terms using semantic similarity methods. SSRM demonstrated very promising performance achieving significantly better precision and recall than Vector Space Model (VSM) for retrievals on Medline.

Authors in (Nasraoui & Zhuhadar, 2010) proposed and evaluated an architecture that can provide, manage, and collect data that permits high levels of adaptability and relevance to the learner's profile, in addition, the proposed system used clustering techniques to divide the documents into an optimal categorization that is not influenced by the hand-made taxonomy of the colleges and course titles. To achieve this objective, an approach for personalized search was implemented that took advantage of the semantic Web standards to represent the content and the user profiles.

Personalized recommendation (Yu & Liu, 2010) is a widely used application of Web personalized services which alleviate the burden of information overload by collecting information which meets user's needs. An essential of Web recommendation is how to build user profile, which involves the information and preference of user and has great impact on the performance of Web personalized recommendation. For example, if a user profile provides information that can not represent user's recent interests; an e-Commerce system is unable to accurately recommend specific goods to the user.

Recommendation strategies (Wang, Tsai, Lee, & Chiu, 2007) can be divided roughly into three types, i.e. the content-based, the collaborative-based and the hybrid methods. The idea behind the content-based method is that if a user liked an object in the past, he/she would probably like other similar objects in the future. This method obtains learning objects' features and compares them with users' profiles to predict their preferences. Typically a collaborative-based method recommends learning objects to a user based on the preferences of his/her neighbors by using a nearest-neighbor algorithm. On the other hand, a hybrid method, attempting to combine the former two techniques to eliminate drawbacks of each, usually applies a user's profile and descriptions of learning objects to find users who have similar interests, and then uses collaborative filtering to make better predictions. For the time being, to combine the content-based and the collaborative-based method is usually considered to be a better methodology for the recommendation mechanisms.

The article (Yang, et al., 2010) described the relevant technologies of personalized recommendation that is based on the domain ontology, for the intermediary in domain ontology, to construct user interest ontology modeling user interest, at last, recommendation based on KNNs algorithm. Systems take full account of the semantic factor, carry out excavation by ontology, and recommend resources to the user by domain ontology

In this paper (Wu, Chen, & Chen, 2001), authors defined user interests and behaviors based on the documents read by the user. A method for mining such user interests and behaviors is then presented. In this way, each user is associated' with a set of interests and behaviors, which is stored in the user profile. In addition, they defined six types of user profiles and a distance measure to classify users into clusters, and three kinds of recommendation services using the clustered results are realized. Based on ontology (Mu, et al., 2009), the method of document feature extraction and user interest model were improved. Two personalized recommendation models were proposed for different scenes. In order to get the user's real and original interest and provide efficiently personalized information services, ontology concepts were introduced, and then, the methods of web pages features extraction and user interest model were improved.

It was proposed (Yu, Nakamura, Jang, Kajita, & Mase, 2007) an ontology-based approach for semantic recommendation to realize context-awareness in learning content provisioning. Authors aimed to make recommendation by exploiting knowledge about the learner (user context), knowledge about the content, and knowledge

about the learning domain. The recommendation approach is characterized with semantic relevance calculation, recommendation refining, learning path generation, and recommendation augmentation. The knowledge modeling and the whole recommendation process are performed based on ontology. In the current system, we mainly consider two kinds of the most important contexts in learning, i.e., the learner's prior knowledge and his learning goal.

THE DOMAIN ONTOLOGY

The main reason for ontology (Using, et al., 2010) is to enable communication between computer systems in a way that is independent of the individual system technologies, information architectures and application domain. Ontology includes rich relationships between terms and each specific knowledge domain and organization will structure its own ontology which will be organized into mapped ontology. The domain of our learning content and the ontology we have developed within proposed system is that of computer science. The ontology covers topics like artificial intelligence, communications; computational theory, computer graphics, data structures, database, programming, etc. It is used mainly to index the relevant learning objects and to facilitate semantic search and re-usability of learning objects.

Ontology engineering is a subfield of knowledge engineering that studies the methods and methodologies for building ontologies. It researches the ontology development process, the ontology life cycle, the methods and methodologies for building ontologies, and the tools suite and languages that support them. Knowledge Engineering field usually uses the IEEE 1074-2006 standard (IEEE Standard, 1997) as reference criteria. The IEEE 1074-2006 is a standard for developing a software project life cycle processes. It describes the software development process, the activities to be carried out, and the techniques

Figure 1. Main steps of the ontology development

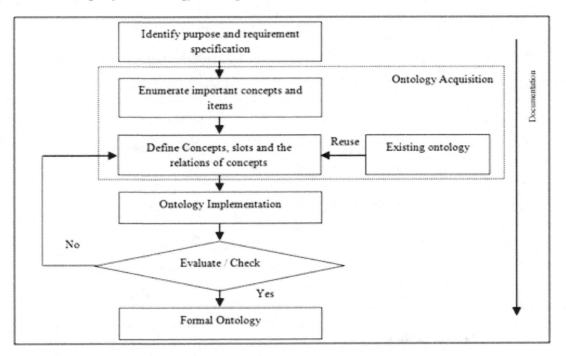

that can be used for developing software. It was proposed (Hong-yan, Jian-liang, Mo-ji, & Jing, 2009) a knowledge engineering approach to build domain ontology. Figure 1 shows main steps of the ontology development process.

Identifying the purpose and the requirement specification concerns to clearly identify the ontology purpose, scope and its intended use, which is the competence of the ontology. Ontology acquisition is to capture the domain concepts based on the ontology competence. The relevant domain entities (e.g. concepts, relations, slots, and role) should be identified and organized into hierarchy structure. This phase involves three steps as follows: first, enumerate important concepts and terms in this domain; second, define concepts, properties and relations of concepts, and organize them into hierarchy structure; third, consider reusing existing ontology. Ontology implementation aims to explicitly represent the conceptualization captured in a formal language. Evaluation/Check means that the ontology must

be evaluated to check whether it satisfies the specification requirements. Documentation means that all the ontology development must be documented, including purposes, requirements, textual descriptions of the conceptualization, and the formal ontology.

We use protégée (Noy, et al., 2001; Hogeboom, Lin, Esmahi, & Yang, 2005) as our ontology tool which generates the OWL (Bechhofer, et al., 2009) the ontology language. Since protégée is an open source ontology editor, developed by Stanford Center for Biomedical Informatics Research and coded by JAVA. Protégé interface style is similar to Windows applications' general style, so it is easy to learn and use. Figure 2 shows visual representation of the part of our domain ontology.

THE PROPOSED FRAMEWORK

In our proposed approach, personalized search of learning objects in E-learning is based on a

Figure 2. Part of the domain ontology

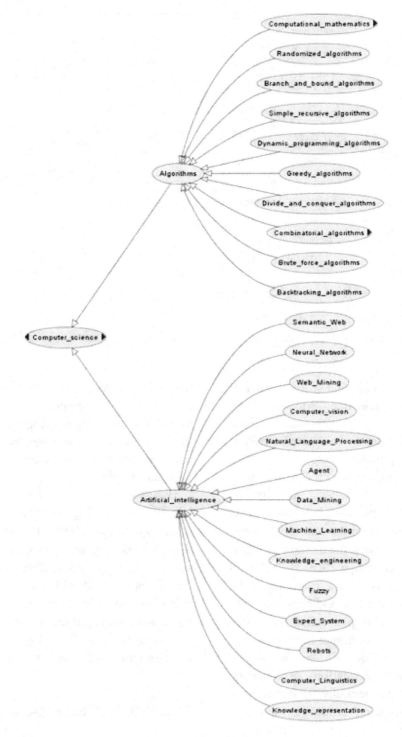

comparison of the learner profile and the learning object (resource) metadata (Biletskiy, Baghi, Keleberda, Fleming, & 2009; Keleberda, Lesna, Makovetskiy, & Terziyan, 2004). Because such an approach needs to present both the learner profile and the learning object description as certain data structures, it requires the development of ontological models (Zhang, Song, & Song, 2007; Gauch, et al., 2007) of the learner and learning object. The proposed approach has two aspects, first for personalized search of learning objects is generally described in (Biletskiy, et al., 2009; Keleberda, Repka, & Biletskiy, 2006), second for personalized recommendation suitable learning objects is proposed in (Wang, et al., 2007; Tsai, Chiu, Lee, & Wang, 2006).

Our proposed system constructs effective and efficient an E-learning environment, which adapts itself to individual learners in the Arab world (Shehabat & Mahdi, 2008) to enable the learner to search in the learning contents more accurate and recommend him what contents, should have according to learner behavior and interests.

The key idea of the Semantic Web is to have data defined and linked in such a way that its meaning is explicitly interpretable by software processes rather than just being implicitly interpretable by humans. The Semantic Web can represent knowledge, including defining ontologies as metadata of resources. Ontologies are used to describe the semantics of information exchange.

The present research will describe details of building the learner and learning object ontological models to perform personalizes search in learning objects and recommendation suitable learning objects to learners. In order to implement the proposed personalized search of learning objects

according to the created ontological models of the learner and learning object, some IMS Learner Information Package Specification corresponding to some IEEE LOM standard (Learning Technology Standards Committee, 2002) have been chosen, and the criteria to estimate conformity of LOM to the learner personal profile with the coefficients of importance. Adaptive recommendation model for retrieving and recommending to a learner the suitable learning objects uses specific ontology to infer what learning object a learner should study and what learning objects a system should look for automatically. Similar learning objects retrieved are recommended to a learner according to the result of a ranking mechanism. This ranking mechanism not only uses a learner's preference but also adjusts periodically the ratios of two weights to achieve adaptive personalized optimal recommendation. The proposed system architecture is shown in the Figure 3.

The abbreviation of Figure 4 found in the Table1.

SHAREABLE LEARNING OBJECTS (SLO) CREATION

As mentioned in (Singh, Bernard, & Gardeler, 2004), authors have determined that the reusable learning objects are a reusable chunk of content with the following two fundamental properties: first is instructionally sound content with focused learning objectives. Second property is the facility that allows the learner to practice, learn, and receive assessment. Also they define the sharable learning objects as a reusable LO with the additional interoperability property that is the

Table 1. Abbreviation of Figure 4

LO	Learning Object	LP	Learner Profile
SLO	Sharable Learning Objects	DO	Domain Ontology
LOM	Learning Object Metadata	LOR	Learning Object Repository

Figure 3. Architecture of proposed system

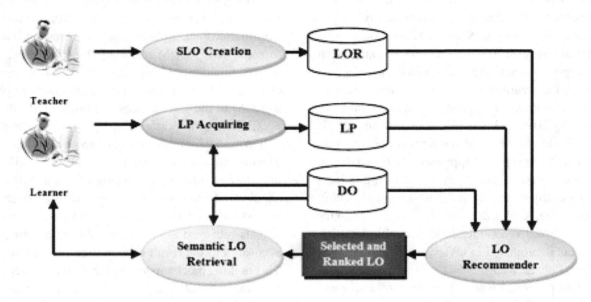

Figure 4. Steps to create RLO

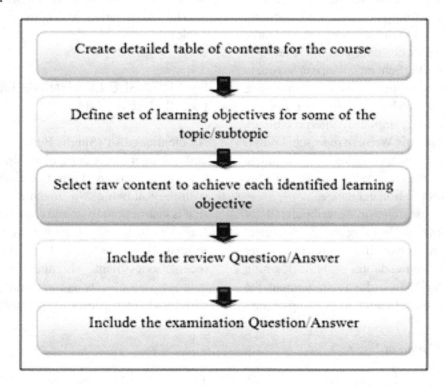

metadata or keywords that describe the object's attributes and mechanisms for communicating with any E-learning system.

Creating the Reusable Learning Objects (RLO)

The aim of this methodology is to select and extract as much of the existing raw content into RLO. The methodology is an iterative five step process to select appropriate content for the RLO with opportunities to refine and re-structure as the extraction is taking place. The steps are shown in Figure 4.

Creating the Sharable Learning Objects (SLO)

In order to create SLO from RLO, the metadata must be added. The metadata will describe its properties which can be used to determine how should interact with LO. The metadata is also used to facilitate discovery of the SLO when it is stored in digital repository. IMS Learner Information Package Specification corresponding to some IEEE LOM (Learning Technology Standards Committee, 2002) standard has been chosen. The IEEE LOM standard specification specifies a standard for learning object metadata. It specifies a conceptual data schema that defines the structure of a metadata instance for a learning object. The IEEE LOM specification consists of nine categories, which includes 60 data elements. Table 2 shows the main categories of IEEE LOM.

Although the lack of clarity in the IEEE LOM standard makes its value spaces hard to interpret, most metadata editors today continue to use that standard without seeking to explain the meaning of each space (Morgado, Peñalvo, Ruiz, Rego, & Moreira, 2008). We set out to address this issue to enable suitable learning objects management data to be introduced into learning environments by devising a set of definitions to clarify the

content of each value space in the LOM "5. Educational" metadata category as shown in Table 3.

To design the metadata schema, we have followed the IEEE LOM standard as shown in the Table 2. We have identified a subset of metadata from the IEEE LOM specification, which are relevant for finding the suitability of a document to a particular e-learner and can automatically be extracted from learning materials. Even though we would like to include many of the attributes from the IEEE LOM that are important from instructional design perspective, currently our system deals with a small subset of the IEEE LOM attributes from general, technical, educational and classification category. We have added a few more additional attributes, which are not there in the IEEE LOM, but seem to be useful for the learning management and retrieval systems. The LOM (Mohan & Brooks, 2003) Standard uses nine categories of XML data elements to describe a learning object. It is intended that LOM metadata will simplify the discovery, management, and exchange of learning objects over the Web. XML is used to markup the structure of a learning object in a machine readable way.

The Schema of Learning Objects

A learning object can be defined as "any digital resource that can be reused to support learning" (Abad, 2008). Learning objects (LO) is a relatively recent trend in Web-based courseware authoring (Mavrommatis, 2008). They are based on the idea that an instructor creates small learning components that can be combined and reused in different contexts. Learning Objects Metadata (LOM) is the information used to describe a LO. Recent work (Learning Technology Standards Committee, 2002) provides standardization of LO metadata: the LOM framework is already part of the Sharable Content Object Reference Model (Dodds, 2001) and all this effort, despite of some criticism, is expected to speed up the creation of learning objects repositories, that is large pools

Table 2. The main categories of IEEE LOM (Learning Technology Standards Committee, 2002)

Category Name	Category Fields	Explanation
General	Identifier, Catalog, Entry, Title, Language, Description, Keyword, Coverage, Structure, Aggregation Level	General information that describes the learning object as a whole.
Life Cycle	Version, Status, Contribute, Role, Entity, Date	History and current state of the learning object and those entities that have affected the learning object during its evolution.
Meta-Metadata	Identifier, Catalog, Entry, Contribute, Role, Entity, Date, Metadata Schema, Language	Metadata record itself (rather than the learning object that the record describes). This category describes how the metadata instance can be identified, who created the metadata instance, how, when, and with what references.
Technical	Format, Size, Location, Requirement, Composite, Type, Name, Minimum Version, Maximum Version, Installation Remarks, Other Platform Requirements, Duration	Technical requirements and characteristics of the learning object.
Educational	Interactivity Type, Learning Resource Type, Interactivity Level, Semantic Density, Intended End User Role, Context, Typical Age Range, Difficulty, Typical Learning Time, Description, Language,	Key educational or pedagogic characteristics of the learning object.
Rights	Cost, Copyright and Other Restrictions, Description	Intellectual property rights and conditions of use for the learning object.
Relation	Kind, Resource, Identifier, Catalog, Entry, Description	Relationship between learning objects. To define multiple relationships, there may be multiple instances of this category. If there is more than one target-learning object, then each target shall have a new relationship instance.
Annotation	Entity, Date, Description	Provides comments on the educational use of the learning object, and information on when and by whom the comments were created. This category enables educators to share their assessments of learning objects, suggestions for use, etc.
Classification	Purpose, Path, Source,, Id, Entry, Description, Keyword	It describes where the learning object falls within a particular classification system.

containing retrievable LO and metadata indexes based on the standard (Neven & Duval, 2002). Figure 6 shows the part of schema for learning objects. Figure 5 shows the part of DTD of the XML file of learning objects

The Schema of Learning Objects Metadata

Using a unique XML schema will not significantly harm the interoperability of the E-learning system. We choose the tags from the standard schema, so every tag in our schema is still meaningful to others. A third-party search engine that can handle the XML metadata documents conforming to the standard schema could also handle ours. Figure 6 shows the part of schema for learning objects metadata. Figure 7 shows the part of DTD of the XML file of learning objects metadata.

Learning objects repository (LOR) stores both LO's and their metadata, both by storing them physically together or by presenting a combined repository to the outside world, while the metadata and LO are actually stored separately. A LOR allows registered or unregistered learners to search and retrieve LO's from the repository. Searching for LO is based on criteria that relate to LOM data elements. A LOR typically supports simple and advanced queries, as well as browsing through the material by subject or discipline. In a simple

Table 3. The values space in the LOM educational metadata category

Category Field	Value	Value Explanation
Interactivity Type: Predominant mode of learning supported by this learning object	Active	LOs which have a high interactivity level (learners interact with many activities which promotes high cognitive levels, like taking decisions, design projects, etc.
	Expositive	LOs featuring a very low interactivity level, with students receiving information yet remaining unable to interact with the content.
	Mixed	LOs which have combined interactivity. Learners have the possibility to interact with sophisticated documents with multiple links.
Learning Resource Type	Exercise, Simulation, Questionnaire, Diagram, Figure, Graph, Index, Slide, Table, Narrative text, Exam, Experiment, Problem statement, Self assessment, Lecture	Specific kind of learning object. The most dominant kind shall be first.
Interactivity Level: The degree of interactivity characterizing this learning object. Interactivity in this context refers to the degree to which the learner can influence the aspect or behavior of the learning object.	Very Low	LOs which have an expositive interactivity level. Learners receive information and don't have interactivity possibilities.
	Low	LOs with an expositive interactivity level – minimal student participation (web pages with few links)
	Medium	LO content designed to promote smooth learning and application of knowledge
	High	LOs related with high interactivity type of activities.
	Very High	LOs related with very high interactivity type of activities which promotes users' productive activities e.g. take decisions, open answers, etc.
Semantic Density: The degree of conciseness of a learning object. The semantic density of a learning object may be estimated in terms of its size, span, or in the case of self-timed resources such as audio or video duration.	Very Low	The LO contents information are not concise and are highly irrelevant
	Low	The LO contents information is low concise and low relevant
	Medium	The LO contents information is medium concise and not very relevant.
	High	The LO contents information is high concise e.g. an image together with a brief text.
	Very High	The LOs contents are extremely concise, and very relevant e.g. a symbolic representation.
Intended End User Role		Principal user(s) for which this learning object was designed, most dominant first.
Context	Higher education, School, Training, Other.	The principal environment within which the learning and use of this learning object is intended to take place.
Typical Age Range		Age of the typical intended user.
Difficulty: How hard it is to work with or through this learning object for the typical intended target audience.	Very Easy	Basic, concrete, LO is easily recognized by users.
	Easy	Information is easily associated with previous knowledge
	Medium	It is possible to apply and understand the LO contents without difficulties.
	Difficult	Complex. The LO is directed to high cognitive levels.
	Very Difficult	The LO contains very complex information which requires applying high cognitive levels.

query, keywords given by the learner are matched against the text in a number (or all) of the metadata elements. An advanced query allows a learner to specify values for specific metadata elements (e.g. 'easy' or 'medium' for 'Difficulty level'), and sometimes also to rely on logical combinations of search criteria. Browsing typically allows the end learner to descend in a tree

Figure 5. Part of DTD of the XML file of learning objects

```
<?xml version="1.0" encoding="UTF-8"?>
<!--DTD generated by XML Spy v4.2 U (http://www.xmlspy.com)-->
<!ELEMENT Ba_ LOContext (LOContextID, LOContext, Dy_LOM_Education*)>
<!ELEMENT Ba_ LODifficulty (LODifficultyID, LODifficulty, Dy_LOM_Education*)>
<!ELEMENT Ba_ LOIntEndUserRoleID (LOIntEndUserRoleID, LOIntEndUserRole, Dy_LOM_Education*)>
<!ELEMENT Ba_ LOIntLevel (LOIntLevelID, LOIntLevel, Dy_LOM_Education*)>
<!ELEMENT Ba_ LOIntType (LOIntTypeID, LOIntType, Dy_LOM_Education*)>
<!ELEMENT Ba_ LOLRType (LOLRTypeID, LOLRType, Dy_LOM_Education*)>
<!ELEMENT Ba_ LOLanguage (LOLanguageID, LOLanguage, Dy_LOData*)>
<!ELEMENT Ba_ LOSemDensity (LOSemDensityID, LOSemDensity, Dy_LOM_Education*)>
<!ELEMENT Ba_ LOType (LOTypeID, LOType, Dy_LOData*)>
<!ELEMENT Ba_CourseData (CourseID, CourseNO, DomainID, CourseTitle, CourseObjective,
CourseSkills, CourseRequired, CourseLang, CourseDesigner, CourseDesDate, Dy_LOData*)>
<!ELEMENT Ba_DomainData (DomainID, DomainTitle, SpecMajorID, Ba_CourseData*)>
<!ELEMENT Ba_GenMajorData (GenMajorID, GenMajorTitle, Ba_SpecMajorData*)>
<!ELEMENT Ba_SpecMajorData (SpecMajorID, GenMajorID, SpecMajorTitle, Ba_DomainData*)>
<!ELEMENT LOMDataGenID (#PCDATA)>
<!ELEMENT LOMDataGeneralID (#PCDATA)>
<!ELEMENT LOMDataTechnicalID (#PCDATA)>
<!ELEMENT LOMDataEducatID (#PCDATA)>
<!ELEMENT LOMDataRelationID (#PCDATA)>
<!ELEMENT LOMDataClassificationID (#PCDATA)>
<!ELEMENT EdID (#PCDATA)>
<!ELEMENT InteractivityType (#PCDATA)>
<!ELEMENT InteractivityLevel (#PCDATA)>
<!ELEMENT SemanticDensity (#PCDATA)>
<!ELEMENT LearningResType (#PCDATA)>
<!ELEMENT DifficultyLevel (#PCDATA)>
<!ELEMENT IntEndUserRole (#PCDATA)>
<!ELEMENT ContextLevel (#PCDATA)>
<!ELEMENT TypicalAgeRange (#PCDATA)>
<!ELEMENT GenID (#PCDATA)>
<!ELEMENT Identifier (#PCDATA)>
<!ELEMENT Title (#PCDATA)>
<!ELEMENT Language (#PCDATA)>
<!ELEMENT Description (#PCDATA)>
<!ELEMENT Keyword (#PCDATA)>
<!ELEMENT RelID (#PCDATA)>
<!ELEMENT Kind (#PCDATA)>
<!ELEMENT Resource (#PCDATA)>
```

Figure 6. Part of schema for learning objects metadata

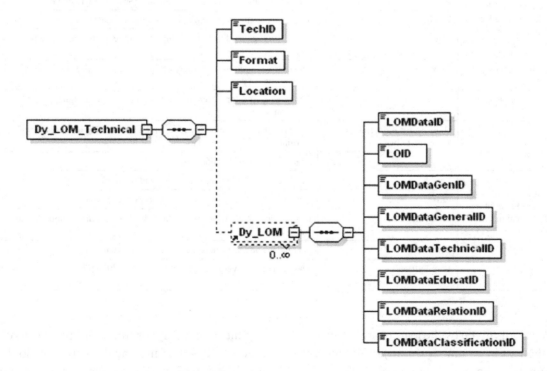

Figure 7. Part of DTD of the XML file of learning objects metadata

```
<?xml version="1.0" encoding="UTF-8"?>
<!--DTD generated by XML Spy v4.2 U (http://www.xmlspy.com)-->
<!ELEMENT Ba_ LOContext (LOContextID, LOContext, Dy_LOM_Education*)>
<!ELEMENT Ba_ LODifficulty (LODifficultyID, LODifficulty, Dy_LOM_Education*)>
<!ELEMENT Ba_ LOIntEndUserRoleID (LOIntEndUserRoleID, LOIntEndUserRole, Dy_LOM_Education*)>
<!ELEMENT Ba_ LOIntLevel (LOIntLevelID, LOIntLevel, Dy_LOM_Education*)>
<!ELEMENT Ba_ LOIntType (LOIntTypeID, LOIntType, Dy_LOM_Education*)>
<!ELEMENT Ba_ LOLRType (LOLRTypeID, LOLRType, Dy_LOM_Education*)>
<!ELEMENT CourseTitle (#PCDATA)>
<!ELEMENT CourseObjective (#PCDATA)>
<!ELEMENT CourseSkills (#PCDATA)>
<!ELEMENT CourseRequired (#PCDATA)>
<!ELEMENT CourseLang (#PCDATA)>
<!ELEMENT CourseDesigner (#PCDATA)>
<!ELEMENT CourseDesDate (#PCDATA)>
<!ELEMENT DomainID (#PCDATA)>
<!ELEMENT DomainTitle (#PCDATA)>
<!ELEMENT SpecMajorID (#PCDATA)>
<!ELEMENT GenMajorID (#PCDATA)>
<!ELEMENT GenMajorTitle (#PCDATA)>
<!ELEMENT SpecMajorID (#PCDATA)>
<!ELEMENT GenMajorID (#PCDATA)>
<!ELEMENT SpecMajorTitle (#PCDATA)>
<!ELEMENT LOID (#PCDATA)>
<!ELEMENT CourseID (#PCDATA)>
<!ELEMENT LOTitle (#PCDATA)>
<!ELEMENT LOTypeID (#PCDATA)>
<!ELEMENT LODesc (#PCDATA)>
<!ELEMENT LOLanguageID (#PCDATA)>
```

of disciplines and sub-disciplines to get an impression of the objects available in different domains. In (Neven & Duval, 2002) authors summarized the different LOR's they studied, with a comparative analysis of their features and characteristics.

LEARNER PROFILE (LP) ACQUIRING

An extensive learner profile must contain information about the learner's domain knowledge, the learner's progress, preferences, goals, interests and other information about the learner, which is important for the used systems. Learner profiles can be classified according to the nature and form of information contained in the models. Considering the subject domain, the information stored in a learner profile can be divided into two major groups: domain specific information and domain independent information.

There are five popular and useful features when is viewing the learner as an individual, these are: the learner's knowledge, interests, goals,

background, and individual traits (Brusilovsky & Millán, 2007). The learner knowledge of the subject is being taught or the domain represented in hyperspace appears to be the most important learner feature. Learner interests (Harb & Fouad, 2010) always constituted the most important (and typically the only) part of the learner profile in adaptive information retrieval and filtering systems that dealt with large volumes of information. The learner's goal or task represents the immediate purpose for a learner's work within an adaptive system. Depending on the kind of system, it can be the goal of the work (in application systems), an immediate information need (in information access systems), or a learning goal (in educational systems). In all of these cases, the goal is an answer to the question "What does the learner actually want to achieve?". The learner's background is a common name for a set of features related to the learner's previous experience outside the core domain of a specific Web system (for example, the core domain of a city guide is a specific city and its objects of interest; the core domain for a hospital information system is a specific hospital, its objects and procedures). The learner's individual traits are the aggregate name for learner features that together define a learner as an individual. By cognitive style, researchers typically mean an individually preferred and habitual approach to organizing and representing information. Learning styles are typically defined as the way people prefer to learn (Brusilovsky & Millán, 2007).

Figure 8 shows the part of schema of learner log that can be used to deduce the learner profile.

Figure 9 shows the part of schema of the learner profile.

Figure 10 shows the part of DTD of the XML file of learner profile.

Learner Interests Acquiring

In our proposed system (Harb & Fouad, 2010; Fouad, Harb, & Nagdy, 2011), learner interest model's knowledge expression uses the thought,

which is based on the space vector model's expression method and the domain ontology. This method acquires learner's interest was shown in (Harb & Fouad, 2010; Fouad, et al., 2011). Figure 11 shows certain steps to acquire learner interest.

The Vector Space Model (Baishuang & Wei, 2009; Pan, Zhang, Wang, Wu, & Wei, 2007; Pan, Zhang, Wang, & Wu, 2007) is adapted in our proposed system to achieve effective representations of documents. Each document is identified by n-dimensional feature vector where each dimension corresponds to a distinct term. Each term in a given document vector has an associated weight. The weight is a function of the term frequency, collection frequency and normalization factors. Different weighting approaches may be applied by varying this function. Hence, a document j is represented by the document vector dj:

$$d_j = (w_{1j}, w_{2j}, ..., w_{nj})$$

Figure 8. Part of schema of user (learner) log

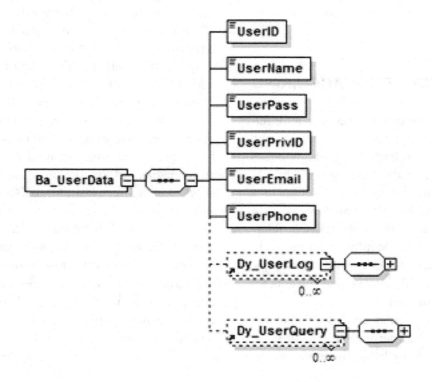

Figure 9. Part of schema of the learner profile

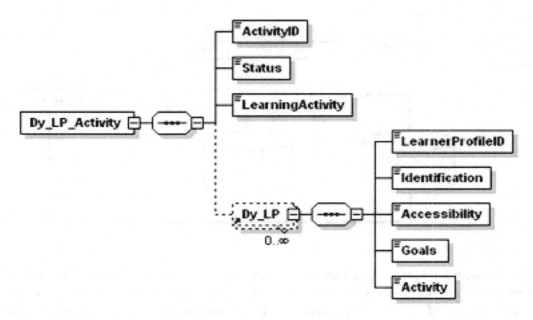

Where, w_{kj} is the weight of the kth term in the document j.

The term frequency reflects the importance of term k within a particular document j. The weighting factor may be global or local. The global weighting factor clarifies the importance of a term k within the entire collection of documents, whereas a local weighting factor considers the given document only.

The document keywords were extracted by using a term-frequency-inverse-document-frequency (tf-idf) calculation (Pan, et al., 2007; Pan, et al., 2007), which is a well-established technique in information retrieval. The weight of term k in document j is represented as:

$$w_{kj} = tf_{kj} \times \left(\log_2^n - \log_2^{df_k} + 1\right)$$

Figure 10. Part of DTD of XML for the learner profile

```
<?xml version="1.0" encoding="UTF-8"?>
<!--DTD generated by XML Spy v4.2 U (http://www.xmlspy.com)-->
<!ELEMENT Ba_UserData (UserID, UserName, UserPass, UserPrivID, UserEmail, UserPhone, Dy_UserLog*, Dy_UserQuery*)>
<!ELEMENT Ba_UserPrivilege (PrivID, PrivTitle, Ba_UserData*)>
<!ELEMENT Dy_LP (LearnerProfileID, Identification, Accessibility, Goals, Activity)>
<!ELEMENT Dy_LP_Accessibility (AccessID, Eligibility, Dy_LP*)>
<!ELEMENT Dy_LP_Activity (ActivityID, Status, LearningActivity, Dy_LP*)>
<!ELEMENT Dy_LP_Goal (GoalID, Refrence, Priority, Status, Dy_LP*)>
<!ELEMENT UserID (#PCDATA)>
<!ELEMENT UserName (#PCDATA)>
<!ELEMENT UserPass (#PCDATA)>
<!ELEMENT UserPrivID (#PCDATA)>
<!ELEMENT UserEmail (#PCDATA)>
<!ELEMENT UserPhone (#PCDATA)>
<!ELEMENT PrivID (#PCDATA)>
<!ELEMENT PrivTitle (#PCDATA)>
<!ELEMENT LearnerProfileID (#PCDATA)>
<!ELEMENT Identification (#PCDATA)>
<!ELEMENT Accessibility (#PCDATA)>
<!ELEMENT Goals (#PCDATA)>
<!ELEMENT Activity (#PCDATA)>
<!ELEMENT AccessID (#PCDATA)>
<!ELEMENT Eligibility (#PCDATA)>
```

Figure 11. Steps to acquire learner interest

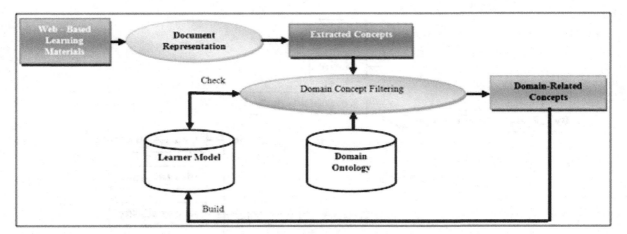

Where: tfkj = the term k frequency in document j, dfk = number of documents in which term k occurs, n = total number of documents in collection. Table 4 shows the term frequency in different documents in the domain of computer science.

The main purpose of this step is to extract interested items in the web page, then get term frequency that reflects the importance of term. Finally get the weight of terms in the selected page. The output of this step is the weight of terms in selected page that can be used to build learner interest profile. Table 5 shows a sample of the weighted terms in the documents; that found in Table 4.

This process discovers concepts which represent the learner's interests. These concepts and items are compared to the domain ontology to check the relevant items to the learner profile. The most relevant ones update the learner profile. The items relevance is based on ontology-based semantic similarity where browsed items by a learner on the web are compared to the items from a domain ontology and learner profile. The importance is combined with the semantic similarity to obtain a level of relevance. The page items are processed to identify domain-related words to be added to the learner profile. A bag of browsed items is obtained via a simple word indexing of

the page visited by the learner. We filter out irrelevant words using the list of items extracted from domain ontology. Once domain-related items are identified, we evaluate their relevance to learner's interests.

The selected method was used in (Reformat & Koosha, 2009; Rodrıguez & Egenhofer, 2003; Cai, Lu & Gu, 2010) to compute semantic similarity function (S) based on a domain ontology. The similarity is estimated for each pair of items where one item is taken from a learner profile, while the other one from a set of browsed items.

The functions Sw is the similarity between synonym sets, Su is the similarity between features, and Sn is the similarity between semantic neighborhoods between entity classes a of ontology p and b of ontology q, and w_w, w_u, and w_n are the respective weights of the similarity of each specification component.

$$S(a^p, b^q) = w_w \times S_w(a^p, b^q) \\ + w_u \times S_u(a^p, b^q) \\ + w_n \times S_n(a^p, b^q)$$

For w_w; w_u; $w_n \geq 0$:

Weights assigned to Sw, Su, and Sn depends on the characteristics of the ontologies. The simi-

Table 4. Sample of the documents with their representation

DOC/items	Computer science	AI	Programming	Software eng.	Networks	LAN	WAN	Computer Arch.	Processors	Parallel processing
Doc1	20	25	20	15	10	0	0	5	0	0
Doc 2	15	15	25	15	5	0	0	0	0	0
Doc 3	0	5	25	10	25	10	15	5	0	0
Doc 4	0	5	25	10	20	5	15	5	0	0
Doc 5	0	0	5	0	10	0	0	5	20	20
Doc 6	0	0	0	5	20	0	0	0	25	30
Doc 7	0	0	5	0	0	0	0	5	20	10
Doc 8	0	0	0	5	0	0	0	10	25	5
Doc 9	15	5	30	30	0	0	0	5	0	0
Doc 10	5	0	25	25	0	0	0	0	0	0
Doc 11	10	0	0	0	10	0	0	25	10	30
Doc 12	10	0	0	0	10	0	0	30	10	25
Doc 13	20	25	5	0	10	0	0	5	0	0
Doc 14	15	15	5	0	5	0	0	0	0	0
Doc 15	0	30	20	15	25	0	5	0	0	0
Doc 16	0	25	25	15	20	0	0	0	0	0

larity measures (Saruladha, Aghila, & Raj, 2010) are defined in terms of a matching process (Open Directory Project, 2012; Using, Ahmad, & Taib, 2010) as in Equation 1:

$$S(a,b) = \frac{|A \cap B|}{|A \cap B| + \alpha(a,b)|A/B| + (1-\alpha(a,b))|B/A|} \quad (1)$$

where A and B are description sets of classes a and b, i.e., synonym sets, sets of distinguishing features and a set of classes in semantic neighborhood; $(A \cap B)$ and (A/B) represent intersection and difference respectively, $|\,|$ is the cardinality of a set; and α is a function that defines relative importance of non-common characteristics. A set of browsed items that are similar to items from the learner profile is considered as a set of items that can be added to this profile.

Learner Interest Ontology Construction Using Domain Ontology

We construct learner interest ontology by domain ontology, through the mapping of learner's interest information and the concept in domain ontology; convert the contents of the learner's interest into the form of ontology concept, and using these ontology concepts to construct learner interest ontology. At last, carry out the learner pattern recognition by the constructed learner interest ontology. The details of the method are found in (Yang, Sun, Li, & Cai, 2010).

The learner ontology (Yang, et al., 2010; Wei, Huang, & Tan, 2009) is the specifications of the conceptualization of learner information, which defines the various terms relationship related to the learner concept, and gives the semantics of the term. Learner interest ontology mainly describes the interests of the learner and displays the different attributes and relationships of the learner

Table 5. Sample of the weighted terms in the documents

DOC/items	computer Science	AI	programming	Software Engineering	Network	LAN	WAN	Computer Architecture	Processors	Parallel Processing
Doc1	0.40	0.46	0.28	0.25	0.14	0.00	0.00	0.09	0.00	0.00
Doc2	0.30	0.27	0.35	0.25	0.07	0.00	0.00	0.00	0.00	0.00
Doc3	0.00	0.09	0.35	0.17	0.35	0.40	0.51	0.09	0.00	0.00
Doc4	0.00	0.09	0.35	0.16	0.28	0.20	0.51	0.00	0.00	0.00
Doc5	0.00	0.00	0.07	0.00	0.14	0.00	0.00	0.09	0.48	0.48
Doc6	0.00	0.00	0.00	0.08	0.28	0.00	0.00	0.00	0.60	0.72
Doc7	0.00	0.00	0.07	0.00	0.00	0.00	0.00	0.09	0.48	0.24
Doc8	0.00	0.00	0.00	0.08	0.00	0.00	0.00	0.18	0.60	0.12
Doc9	0.20	0.09	0.42	0.50	0.00	0.00	0.00	0.09	0.00	0.00
Doc10	0.10	0.00	0.35	0.41	0.00	0.00	0.00	0.00	0.00	0.00
Doc11	0.20	0.00	0.00	0.00	0.14	0.00	0.00	0.45	0.24	0.72
Doc12	0.20	0.00	0.00	0.00	0.14	0.00	0.00	0.54	0.24	0.60
Doc13	0.40	0.45	0.07	0.00	0.14	0.00	0.00	0.09	0.00	0.00
Doc14	0.30	0.27	0.07	0.00	0.07	0.00	0.00	0.00	0.00	0.00
Doc15	0.00	0.54	0.28	0.25	0.35	0.00	0.17	0.00	0.00	0.00
Doc16	0.00	0.45	0.35	0.25	0.28	0.00	0.00	0.00	0.00	0.00

interests. The Figure 12 shows the procedures to model the learner interest ontology.

Learner's interests are described in semantic level through the ontology concept set. It is based on the relations of concept in the ontology, and collects together the topics that learners are interested in by the related weights. In the interaction process with system and the learner, the learner's interest will change and adjust, that is, weights of the original interest ontology node will gradually decay, weights of the original interest ontology node will gradually increase, and therefore, there must be incremental updates of learner interest.

LEARNING OBJECTS RECOMMENDATION

Using Learner Behavior

Once the learner started the navigation of the system, previous visits to each Learning Object that belongs to the course currently navigated are taken into account. All visits data to each Learning Object are saved in the system database. As shown in Figure 10, the design of the learner log XML that saves all actions in which the learner system store the behavior of the learners. Equation 2 illustrates weight of Learning Object i LO_i ().This description was the theoretical and technical aspects that were taken into consideration in

Figure 12. The learner interest ontology construction

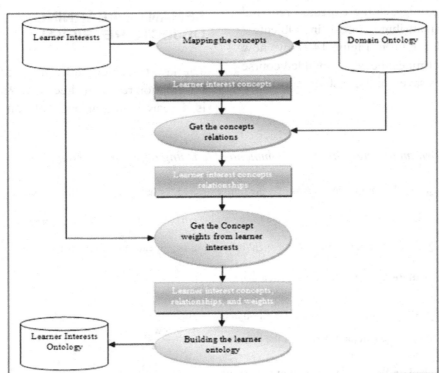

the design process of a web-based adaptive E-learning environment (Alian & AL-Akhras, 2010).

$$W_{LO_i} = \frac{\sum t_s}{t_e \times n_{visit}} \qquad (2)$$

Where, W_{LO_i}: The weight for the learning object LO_i, t_s: The time that the learner spent in learning LO_i in each previous visits, t_e: The time expected for learning LO_i, n_{visit}: Number of previous visits.

The next algorithm in Figure 13 shows how the system determines the recommended learning object in the course. Future recommendations for the learner depends on information like the time that learner actually spent studying a learning object which is a main factor in calculating the weights of a learning object and the weight of courses. Another factor in calculating the weight of the learning object is the expected required time which is an attribute in Learning Objects.

The next algorithm in Figure 14 shows how the system determines the recommended course from all courses saved in the system repository.

Using Learner Profile Ontology

The recommendation algorithm (Yang, et al., 2010) is based on the collection and analysis of learner information, learning the learner's interests. Thus it recommends the information of learner needs and interests to the learner. The algorithm for recommending learning objects based on the learner interests ontology is shown in Figure 15.

The algorithm first set up correspondence between items in two set accordance with similarity, then calculate the similarity of user score item set: the similarity of user score item set is equal to the similarity of their elements on the weighted average. Because the score between the elements of the item set are equal, so all the weights take the same, then the similarity of the items set is equal to arithmetic average of the similarity of their item pair.

SEMANTIC LEARNING OBJECTS RETRIEVAL

The key to achieve efficient and user-friendly information retrieval (Lee, Tsai, & Wang, 2008) is a search mechanism that can guarantee to

Figure 13. Algorithm to determine the recommended learning object in the course

Input: n_{visit}: number of previous visits, t_e: the time expected for learning LO_i, n: the number of learning objects.
Output: The largest weight of the learning object to be considered the recommended learning object.
Procedure:
Calculate $\sum t_s$: total time that the learner spent in learning LO_i in each previous visit.
Do While $i <= n$

    Calculate W_{LO_i}: the weight for each $LO_i = \frac{\sum t_s}{t_e \times n_{visit}}$.

EndDo

Calculate $\sum W_{LO_i}$: the overall weight for all objects.

Calculate W_{LOdef}: the default weight of the learning objects $= \frac{\sum W_{LO_i}}{n}$
Do While $i <= n$

    Calculate W_{new_i}: new weight of the learning object $= \frac{W_{LO_i}}{W_{LOdef}}$

EndDo
Get the recommended LO_i that has the largest W_{new_i}.

Figure 14. Algorithm to determine the recommended course

Input: n_{visit}: number of previous visits, t_e: the time expected for learning LO_i, n :the number of learning objects, n_{Course} the number of the courses in the repository.
Output: The largest weight of the C to be considered the recommended course.
Procedure:
Calculate $\sum t_s$: total time that the learner spent in learning LO_i in each previous visit.
Do While $j <= n_{Course}$
    Do While $i <= n$
        Calculate W_{LO_i} : the weight for each $LO_i = \frac{\sum t_s}{t_e \times n_{visit}}$.
    EndDo
    Calculate $\sum W_{LO_i}$: the overall weight for all objects in the course that is considered as W_{C_j} : the weight of the course.
    Calculate W_{LOdef} : the default weight of the learning object $= \frac{\sum W_{LO_i}}{n}$
EndDo
Calculate W_{Cdef} : the default weight of the course $= \frac{\sum W_{C_j}}{n_{Course}}$
Do While $j <= n_{Course}$
    Calculate W_{Cnew_j} : new weight of the course $= \frac{W_{C_j}}{W_{Cdef}}$
EndDo
Get the recommended C_j that has the largest W_{Cnew_j}

Figure 15. Algorithm for recommending learning objects based on the learner interests ontology

Input: O_L : Learner interests ontology, O_D : Domain ontology
Output: Recommended Learning Objects .
Procedure:
// calculation of user interest ontology similarity.
1. **Calculate** the similarity of concepts in the domain ontology included by user interests ontology by using *Path Length Approaches* by this equation: $Sim(C_1, C_2) = \frac{2 \times N_3}{N_1 + N_2 + 2 \times N_3}$
   Where: N_1 and N_2 is the path length from C_1 and C_2 to their nearest public ancestors node C_3, N_3 is the path length from C_3 to root node.

// The mean value that is the similarity of interests ontology A, and B.
2. **Calculate** the mean value by the this equation: $Sim(B, A) = \frac{\sum_{i=1}^{m} \sum_{j=1}^{n} sim(B_i, A_j)}{m \times n}$

// The similarity between scoring items
3. **Calculate** similarity between score items by this equation:
   $Sim(i, j) = \frac{\sum_{u \in U_{ij}} (R_{ui} - \overline{R_i})(R_{uj} - \overline{R_j})}{\sqrt{\sum_{u \in U_{ij}} (R_{ui} - \overline{R_i})^2 \times \sum_{u \in U_{ij}} (R_{uj} - \overline{R_j})^2}}$

// Generate recommended set
4. **Calculate** score P_{ui} of target that can achieved from the score that the nearest neighbor set V evaluate item i, the equation is as follows:
   $P_{ui} = \overline{R_i} + \frac{\sum_{v \in V} sim(i, v) \times (R_{uv} - \overline{R_v})}{\sum_{v \in V} (|sim(i, v)|)}$
   Where : R_i : is the average score of user i, $sim(i, v)$ is the similarity of the user i and user v, $\overline{R_v}$ is the average score of user.

minimize the delivery of irrelevant information (high precision) and relevant information not being ignored (high recall). Traditional solutions generally employ keyword-based searches, such as the vector space model. The documents retrieved are those containing user-specified keywords. However, there may be many documents convey desirable semantic information without containing these keywords, and these documents are not retrieved. This problem is generally eased using query expansion algorithms, in which additional search terms are added to the original query based on the statistical co-occurrence of terms.

Problems related to precision can be reduced by indexing documents in terms of their context and meaning rather than keywords only. However, this requires a method of mapping the context and their possible meanings and the creation of a meaning-based indexed database. Additionally, the document analysis is time consuming. We use the ontological semantic query expansion approach (Wang, Qin, & Shao, 2009) to make good use of semantic relations of concepts in ontology to expand query keywords and to make the retrieval results more accuracy and comprehensive.

The algorithm of semantic retrieval of learning objects is shown in Figure 16. The algorithm expands the query keywords by using of the semantic relations and reasoning mechanism in ontology. It employs query expansion handle algorithm to extract the synonym relation, father relation, son relation and brother relation in ontology and generate pre-expansion words. It computes the relativity between expansion words and query words and puts the high relativity words as expansion words. In the end, it puts the N expansion words into original query and generates new query expression sentence and submits to retrieval module.

Figure 16. Algorithm for semantic retrieval of the learning objects

Input: Learner Query keywords (Q).
Output: QS that has query keywords set that contains Query keywords (Q_{or}) in addition to Expanded keywords (Q_{Ex}).
Procedure:
1. Tokenize the Learner Query.
2. Remove Stop Words.
3. Get The Stem Words to each term.
4. Get the original query key words (Q_{or}) and add it to the query set (QS).
5. **Do While** $i <= n$ // where n is the number of items in (Q_{or})

    Search W_i in the domain ontology.
    If W_i is root node in the ontology then
        Find the *Hyponyms* (Sons) and Find *synset* (brother) respectively, GoTo step6.
        Add to Q_{Ex}.
    ElseIf W_i is not root node, and not Leaf in the ontology then
        Find the *Hyponyms* (Sons) . Find *Hypernyms* (Parents), and Find *synset* (brother) respectively, GoTo step6.
        Add to Q_{Ex}.
    ElseIf W_i is Leaf in the ontology then
        Find *Hypernyms* (Parents), and Find *synset* (brother) respectively, GoTo step6.
        Add to Q_{Ex}.
    EndIf
  EndDo
6. **Compute** the similarity between concepts, put N pre-expansion words that has high relativity as expansion words Q_{Ex}, turn to step4
7. **Add** Q_{Ex} to QS where QS = Q_{or} ∪ Q_{Ex}

SUGGESTIONS AND RECOMMENDATIONS

In order to achieve personalization and improve the precision and recall of learning resources retrieval, we need a good annotation of the extracted learning objects and using similarity assessment algorithm for the use of semantic web technology in semantic search to fetch more relevant learning content to the learner.

We suggest using our results of learner profile ontology and semantic web to personalize the semantic search of learning objects by building a semantic inference engine to determine relationship between user queries and learning object metadata to retrieve learning objects semantically.

We recommend using fuzzy clustering technique that allows an entity to belong to more than one cluster with different degrees of accuracy. While hard clustering assigns each entity exactly to one of the clusters. Fuzzy clustering is suitable for constructing the learner profiles representations such as (learner ontology). Such representation of learner profiles is useful because some information is not forced to fully belong to any one of the learner profiles. Fuzzy clustering methods may allow some information to belong to several learner profiles simultaneously with different degrees of accuracy.

Semantic and personalized learning used in building adaptive E-learning system in the Arab region is a newly introduced concept. Additionally our system inserts the semantics and personalization to the search and recommendation processes in the learning environments. So our system makes the learning services become attractive and useful to learners and teachers in the Arab regions.

CONCLUSION

The current chapter aims to describe the learner model based on semantic web to be built in the learning system, and use the model to realize personalized E-learning. The advantages of the system were: first the system can provide the semantic and adaptive learning content that is based on the learner's interest, its behavior, and the semantic web. This system can support the self-directed learning and collaborative Learning.

This method uses the learner behavior in weblog and ontology-based semantic similarity to compare items browsed by a learner on the web with the items from a domain ontology and learner profile to acquire learner interests and build the learner ontology.

We used semantic based approach to extract the recommended learning objects that is based on the learner behavior and learner profile ontology. We also introduced semantic retrieval of learning objects by expanding the query keywords by using of the semantic relations and reasoning mechanism in ontology.

Current work showed that the semantic web technologies can be used to achieve the personalization and improve the precision and recall of learning resources semantic retrieval in learning systems.

Our proposed system aims to construct effective and efficient an E-learning environment, which adapts itself to individual learners in the Arab world. By using the semantic and personalized learning, the Arab world learning systems achieve the learning for all goals and meet the learner's requirements, because the proposed system include the personalization services, and has semantic learning content in the learning systems.

REFERENCES

Abad, C. (2008). *Learning through creating learning objects experiences with a class project in a distributed systems course*. ITiCSE'08, June 30–July 2, 2008, Madrid, Spain, 2008. ACM. 978-1-60558-115-6/08/06.

Alian, M., & AL-Akhras, M. (2010). *AdaLearn: An adaptive e-learning environment*. ISWSA'10, June 14–16, ACM. 978-1-4503-0475

Amr, M. (2011). Teacher education for inclusive education in the Arab world: The case of Jordan. *Prospects, 41*, 399–413. Springer. DOI: 10.1007/s11125-011-9203-9

Baishuang, Q., & Wei, Z. (2009). *Student model in adaptive learning system based on Semantic Web*. In First International Workshop on Education Technology and Computer Science. DOI 10.1109/ETCS.2009.466

Bechhofer, S., Harmelen, F., Hendler, J., Horrocks, I., McGuinness, D., Patel-Schneider, P., & Stein, L. (2009). *OWL Web ontology language reference*. Document Status Update, 12 November 2009. Retrieved From http://www.w3.org/TR/owl-ref/

Biletskiy, Y., Baghi, H., Keleberda, I., & Fleming, M. (2009). An adjustable personalization of search and delivery of learning objects to learners. *Expert Systems with Applications, 36*, 9113–9120. doi:10.1016/j.eswa.2008.12.038

Brusilovsky, P., & Millán, E. (2007). *User models for adaptive hypermedia and adaptive educational systems. The Adaptive Web, LNCS 4321* (pp. 3–53). Berlin, Germany: Springer-Verlag.

Cai, S., Lu, Z., & Gu, J. (2010). An effective measure of semantic similarity. In *Advances in Wireless Networks and Information Systems, LNEE 72* (pp. 9–17). Berlin, Germany: Springer-Verlag. doi:10.1007/978-3-642-14350-2_2

Christoph, F. (2005). User modeling and user profiling in adaptive e-learning systems. Master's Thesis at Graz University of Technology.

Daoud, M., Tamine, L., & Mohand, B. (2009). A session based personalized search using an ontological user profile. *SAC, 09*(March), 8–12.

Dodds, P. (2001). *Sharable content object reference model*. Retrieved from http://www.adlnet.org/

Duong, T., Uddin, M., Li, D., & Jo, G. (2009). A collaborative ontology-based user profiles system. In Nguyen, N. T., Kowalczyk, R., & Chen, S.-M. (Eds.), *ICCCI 2009, LNAI 5796* (pp. 540–552). Berlin, Germany: Springer-Verlag.

Fayed, G., & Sameh, D. (2006). E-learning model based on Semantic Web technology. *International Journal of Computing &Information Sciences, 4*(2), 63–71.

Fouad, K., Harb, H., & Nagdy, N. (2011). *Semantic Web supporting adaptive e-learning to build and represent learner model*. The Second International Conference of E-learning and Distance Education - eLi 2011.

Gauch, G., Speretta, M., & Pretschner, A. (2007). *Ontology-based user profiles for personalized search*. Springer, US.

Harb, H., & Fouad, K. (2010). *Semantic Web based Approach to learn and update learner profile in adaptive e-learning*. Al-Azhar Engineering Eleventh International Conference, December 23-26.

Hegazy, A., & Radwan, N. (2010). *Investigating learner perceptions, preferences and adaptation of e-learning services in Egypt*. 2010 International Conference on Education and Management Technology (ICEMT 2010). 978-1-4244-8618-2/10

Hliaoutakis, A., Varelas, G., & Petrakis, E. (2006). MedSearch: A retrieval system for medical information based on semantic similarity. In Gonzalo, J. (Eds.), *ECDL 2006, LNCS 4172* (pp. 512–515). Berlin, Germany: Springer-Verlag. doi:10.1007/11863878_56

Hogeboom, M., Lin, F., Esmahi, L., & Yang, C. (2005). Constructing knowledge bases for e-learning using Protégé 2000 and Web services. *Proceedings of the 19th International Conference on Advanced Information Networking and Applications* (AINA'05), 1550-445X/05, IEEE.

Hong-Yan, Y., Jian-liang, X., Mo-Ji, W., & Jing, W. (2009). *Development of domain ontology for e-learning course* (p. 09). IEEE.

IEEE. (1997). *Standard for developing software life cycle processes.* New York, NY: IEEE Computer Society.

Jin, H., Ning, X., Jia, W., Wu, H., & Lu, G. (2008). Combining weights with fuzziness for intelligent semantic web search. *Knowledge-Based Systems, 21*, 655–665. doi:10.1016/j.knosys.2008.03.040

Keleberda, I., Lesna, N., Makovetskiy, S., & Ter-ziyan, V. (2004). Personalized distance learning based on multiagent ontological system. *Proceedings of the IEEE International Conference on Advanced Learning Technologies* (ICALT'04). ISBN: 0-7695-2181-9/04

Keleberda, I., Repka, V., & Biletskiy, Y. (2006). *Building learner's ontologies to assist personalized search of learning objects.* ICEC'06, August 14–16, 2006, Fredericton, Canada, ACM.

Learning Technology Standards Committee. (2002). *Draft standard for learning object metadata* (LOM). IEEE P1484.12.1. IEEE Learning Technology Standards Committee. Retrieved from http://ltsc.ieee.org/wg12/files/LOM_1484_12_1_v1_Final_Draft.pdf

Lee, M., Tsai, K., & Wang, T. (2008). A practical ontology query expansion algorithm for semantic-aware learning objects retrieval. *Computers & Education, 50*, 1240–1257. doi:10.1016/j.compedu.2006.12.007

Li, F., Li, Y., Wu, Y., Zhou, K., Li, Z., & Wang, X. (2008). *Discovery of a user interests on the internet.* 2008 IEEE/WIC/ACM International Conference on Web Intelligence and Intelligent Agent Technology, DOI 10.1109/WIIAT.2008.18

Liu, F., Yu, C., & Meng, W. (2002). Personalized web search by mapping user queries to categories. *CIKM '02 Proceedings of the Eleventh International Conference on Information and Knowledge Management* (pp. 558-565). ACM.

Lu, J. (2004). A personalized e-learning material recommender system. *Proceedings of the 2nd International Conference on Information Technology for Application* (ICITA 2004).

Mavrommatis, G. (2008). Learning objects and objectives towards automatic learning construction. *European Journal of Operational Research, 187*, 1449–1458. doi:10.1016/j.ejor.2006.09.024

McKeown, K., Elhadad, N., & Hatzivassiloglou, V. (2003). Leveraging a common representation for personalized search and summarization in a medical digital library. In *Proceedings of the 3rd ACM/IEEE-CS Joint Conference on Digital Libraries* 2003 (pp. 159-170).

Mohan, P., & Brooks, C. (2003). *Learning objects on the Semantic Web.* The 3rd IEEE International Conference on Advanced Learning Technologies (ICALT'03). ISBN 0-7695-1967-9/03

Morgado, E., Peñalvo, F., Ruiz, A., Rego, H., & Moreira, T. (2008). *Learning objects for elearning systems. WSKS 2008, CCIS 19* (pp. 153–162). Berlin, Germany: Springer-Verlag.

Mu, X., Chen, Y., Li, N., & Jiang, J. (2009). *Modeling of personalized recommendation system based on ontology* (p. 09).

Nasraoui, O., & Zhuhadar, L. (2010). *Improving recall and precision of a personalized semantic search engine for e-learning.* 2010 Fourth International Conference on Digital Society. ISBN: 978-0-7695-3953-9/10

Neven, N., & Duval, N. (2002). *Reusable learning objects: A survey of LOM-based repositories.* Multimedia'02, December 1-6, 2002, Juan-les-Pins, France, ACM. DOI 1-58113-620-X/02/0012

Noy, N., Sintek, M., Decker, S., Crubézy, M., Fergerson, R., & Musen, M. (2001). *Creating Semantic Web contents with Protégé-2000*. IEEE Intelligent Systems. ISSN: 1094-7167/01

Open Directory Project (ODP). (n.d.). Retrieved from http://dmoz.org

Pan, J., Zhang, B., Wang, S., & Wu, G. (2007). *A personalized semantic search method for intelligent e-learning*. 2007 International Conference on Intelligent Pervasive Computing. DOI 10.1109/IPC.2007.48

Pan, J., Zhang, B., Wang, S., Wu, G., & Wei, D. (2007). *Ontology based user profiling in personalized information service agent*. Seventh International Conference on Computer and Information Technology. ISBN 0-7695-2983-6/07

Pitkow, J., Schütze, H., & Cass, T. (2002). Personalized search. *Communications of the ACM, 45*(9), 50–55. doi:10.1145/567498.567526

Reformat, M., & Koosha, S. (2009). *Updating user profile using ontology-based semantic similarity*. FUZZ_IEEE 2009, Korea, August 20-24. 978-1-4244-3597-5

Rodrıguez, M., & Egenhofer, M. (2003). Determining semantic similarity among entity classes from different ontologies. *IEEE Transactions on Knowledge and Data Engineering, 15*(2). ISSN: 1041-4347/03

Saruladha, K., Aghila, G., & Raj, S. (2010). *A survey of semantic similarity methods for ontology based information retrieval*. 2010 Second International Conference on Machine Learning and Computing. ISBN 978-0-7695-3977-5/10

Shehabat, I., & Mahdi, S. (2008). *E-learning and its impact to the educational system in the Arab world*. 2009 International Conference on Information Management and Engineering. ISBN 978-0-7695-3595-1/09

Singh, R., Bernard, M., & Gardeler, R. (2004). Creating sharable learning objects from existing digital course content. *WCAE '04 Proceedings of the 2004 Workshop on Computer Architecture Education*. ACM.

Sugiyama, K., Hatano, K., & Yoshikawa, M. (2004). Adaptive web search based on user profile constructed without any effort from users. In *Proceedings 13th International Conference on World Wide Web 2004*, (pp. 675-684). ACM.

Tanudjaja, F., & Mui, L. (2002). A contextualized and personalized web search. *Proceedings of the 35th Hawaii International Conference on System Sciences.*

Thomas, Z., & Juan, V. (2010). *Towards an ontology for the description of learning resources on disaster risk reduction*. WSKS 2010, Part I, CCIS 111 (pp. 60–74). Berlin, Germany: Springer-Verlag.

Tsai, K., Chiu, T., Lee, M., & Wang, T. (2006). A learning objects recommendation model based on the preference and ontological approaches. *Proceedings of the Sixth International Conference on Advanced Learning Technologies* (ICALT'06). ISBN: 0-7695-2632-2/06

Using, S., Ahmad, R., & Taib, S. (2010). *Ontology of programming resources for semantic searching of programming related materials on the Web*. ISBN: 978-1-4244-6716-7110

Wang, H., Qin, J., & Shao, H. (2009). *Expansion model of semantic query based on ontology*. Second Pacific-Asia Conference Web Mining and Web-based Application, WMWA '09. DOI: 10.1109/WMWA.2009.31

Wang, T., Tsai, K., Lee, M., & Chiu, T. (2007). Personalized learning objects recommendation based on the semantic-aware discovery and the learner preference pattern. *Journal of Educational Technology & Society, 10*(3), 84–105.

Wei, C., Huang, C., & Tan, H. (2009). *A personalized model for ontology-driven user profiles mining.* 2009 International Symposium on Intelligent Ubiquitous Computing and Education. ISBN 978-0-7695-3619-4/09

Wu, Y., Chen, Y., & Chen, A. (2001). *Enabling personalized recommendation on the Web based on user interests and behaviors* (p. 01).

Yang, Q., Sun, J., Li, Y., & Cai, K. (2010). *Domain ontology-based personalized recommendation research.* 978-1-4244-5824-0

Yu, J., & Liu, F. (2010). *A short-term user interest model for personalized recommendation.* 978-1-4244-5265-1/10

Yu, Z., Nakamura, Y., Jang, S., Kajita, S., & Mase, K. (2007). *Ontology-based semantic recommendation for context-aware e-learning. UIC 2007, LNCS 4611* (pp. 898–907). Berlin, Germany: Springer-Verlag.

Zhang, H., Song, Y., & Song, H. (2007). Construction of ontology-based user model for Web personalization. In Conati, C., McCoy, K., & Paliouras, G. (Eds.), *UM 2007, LNAI 4511* (pp. 67–76). Berlin, Germany: Springer-Verlag. doi:10.1007/978-3-540-73078-1_10

Zhuhadar, L., & Nasraoui, O. (2008). *Personalized cluster-based semantically enriched web search for e-learning. ONISW'08, October 30, 2008.* Napa Valley, California, USA: ACM.

ADDITIONAL READING

Baldoni, M., Baroglio, C., Patti, V., & Torasso, L. (2004). *Reasoning about learning object metadata for adapting SCORM courseware.* Paper presented at the EAW'04.

Carmagnola, F., Cena, F., Gena, C., & Torre, I. (2005). A multidimensional approach for the semantic representation of taxonomies and rules in adaptive hypermedia systems. In *Proceedings of the PerSWeb'05 Workshop* (UM 2005).

Fok, A. W. P. (2006). PEOnto – Integration of multiple ontologies for personalized learning. In Uskov, V. (Ed.), *Proceedings of Web-Based Education.*

Glavinic, V., Stankov, S., Zelic, M., & Rosic, M. (2008). Intelligent tutoring in the Semantic Web and Web 2.0 environments. *World Summit on the Knowledge Society, 2,* 172–177.

Graf, S., & Kinshuk. (2007). *Considering cognitive traits and learning styles to open Web-based learning to a larger student community.* Paper presented at the International Conference on Information and Communication Technology and Accessibility.

Hammoud, H. (2005). *Illiteracy in the Arab world.* Paper commissioned for the EFA Global Monitoring Report 2006, Literacy for Life. Retrieved from http://unesdoc.unesco.org/images/0014/001462/146282e.pdf

Jim, E. G., & Gordon, I. M. (Eds.). (1994). *Student modelling: The key to individualized knowledge based instruction.* Springer-Verlag.

Looi, C. K., McCalla, G., Bredeweg, B., & Breuker, J. (Eds.). (2005). Artificial intelligence in education: Supporting learning through intelligent and socially informed technology. *Proceedings of AI-ED2005,* Amsterdam, The Netherlands: IOS Press.

Murray, T., Blessing, S., & Ainsworth, S. (Eds.). (2003). *Authoring tools for advanced technology learning environments: Toward cost-effective adaptive, interactive and intelligent educational software.* Dordrecht, Netherlands: Kluwer.

Nash, S. S. (2005). Learning objects, learning object repositories, and learning theory: Preliminary best practices for online courses. *Interdisciplinary Journal of Knowledge and Learning Objects, 1*, 217–228.

Rugh, W. A. (2002). Education in Saudi Arabia: Choices and constraints. *Middle East Policy, 9*(2), 40–55. doi:10.1111/1475-4967.00056

Rumetshofer, H., & Wo, W. (2003). XML-based adaptation framework for psychological-driven e-learning systems. *Journal of Educational Technology & Society, 6*(4), 18–29.

Shahabi, C., & Chen, Y. (2003). Web information personalization: Challenges and approaches. In *Proceedings of the 3nd International Workshop on Databases in Networked Information Systems* (DNIS 2003), Aizu-Wakamatsu, Japan (pp. 5-15).

Sheth, A., Ramakrishnan, C., & Thomas, C. (2005). Semantics for the Semantic Web: The implicit, the formal and the powerful. *International Journal on Semantic Web and Information Systems, 1*(1), 1–18. doi:10.4018/jswis.2005010101

Stojanovic, L., Staab, S., & Studer, R. (2001, October 23-27). eLearning based on the Semantic Web. In W. A. Lawrence-Fowler & J. Hasebrook (Eds.), *Proceedings of WebNet 2001—World Conference on the WWW and Internet*, Orlando, Florida (pp.1174-1183). AACE.

Towle, B., & Quinn, C. (2000). *Knowledge-based recommender systems using explicit user models* (Tech. Rep. WS-00-04, 74-77). Paper presented at the AAAI Workshop.

Türksoy, H. (2007). *Ontology based activity and learning object sharing system*. Unpublished Master's thesis, Ankara, Turkey: Hacettepe University.

Wenying, G., & Deren, C. (2006). Semantic approach for e-learning system. In *Proceedings of First International Multi-Symposiums on Computer and Computational Sciences* (IMSCCS 2006), (Vol. 2, pp.442-446). Hangzhou, Zhejiang, China.

Yahya, Y., & Yusoff, M. (2008). Towards a comprehensive learning object metadata: Incorporation of context to stipulate meaningful learning and enhance learning object reusability. *Interdisciplinary Journal of E-Learning and Learning Objects, 4*, 13–48.

Zhiping, L., Tianwei, X., & Yu, S. (2008). A Web-based personalized intelligent tutoring system. *2008 International Conference on Computer Science and Software Engineering CSSE*, (Vol. 5, pp. 446-449).

KEY TERMS AND DEFINITIONS

Adaptive Learning: Provides the content and services to meet individual or group learning needs with improved learning achievement and efficiency. Adaptive learning uses prior successes and measures learner progress to identify and provide future targeted learning strategies.

Electronic Learning (E-Learning): All types of technology-enhanced learning, where technology is used to support the learning process.

Learner Model: The representation of the system's beliefs about the user. The model of the learner is based on this information and is therefore only a small part of the real user. Nevertheless, the learner model must represent the needed characteristics of the learner regarding the context of the application.

Learner Profile: Collection of personal information. The information is stored without adding further description or interpreting this information. Learner profiles represent cognitive skills, intellectual abilities, and intentions, learning styles, preferences and interactions with the system. These properties are stored after assigning them values. These values may be final or change over time.

Learning Object: A chunk of elements that can be independently drawn into a momentary assembly to create an instructional expectation. These chunks can be reused, re-created and maintained, re-organized and stuck together.

Metadata: Data on data. Semantic Web metadata are data on Web resources and are often called semantic annotations, since they rely on ontologies and aim at representing underlying meaning of these resources or additional information about these resources (even not included in the resource itself).

Ontology: Ontology is an explicit specification of a shared conceptualization for a domain of interest. Although in theory, an ontology can be specified in different languages (either formal or natural), the utility of the Semantic Web relates primarily to formal ontologies which are machine-interpretable.

OWL (Ontology Web Language): Ontology representation language recommended by W3C, and intended for publishing and sharing ontologies in the Web. It comprises three layers: OWL Lite, OWL DL, and OWL Full.

Personalization: Algorithms and techniques that tailor content to individual learners.

Semantic Web: A vision of the future where information is automatically exchanged and acted upon on our behalf by the Web itself by virtue of formatting to make it readily "understandable" by computers.

Web-Based Learning: A learning using web-based technologies as a principal means of interaction with learners.

XML: eXtensible Markup Language; meta-language for creating markup languages.

Chapter 19
Wiki–Based Training for the Development EFL Prospective Teachers in Egypt

Manal Mohammed Khodary
Suez Canal University, Egypt

ABSTRACT

This chapter provides a description of how wikis can be used to develop the writing performance of English as a Foreign Language (EFL) prospective teachers. Wiki has gained popularity as a frequent topic of discussion at the field of education. It has been used to provide a collaborative environment which encourages its users to engage effectively in the writing process and to develop their writing performance. This chapter involves an introduction to the importance of developing writing performance among prospective EFL teachers and a description of how new technologies based on the Internet have given new approaches for designing courses in writing. This chapter also provides background information including: the definition of wiki, characteristics of wiki, educational uses of wikis, historical development of wikis and previous studies related to the application of wikis in classrooms. Moreover, this chapter provides an illustration of the author's experience with using wikis to develop prospective EFL teachers' writing performance. It concludes with recommendations on effective use of wikis for educational purposes.

INTRODUCTION

Writing is often referred to as verbal literacy (Huffaker, 2004b). Verbal literacy remains paramount for success throughout life – from the beginnings of education to the future employment of adults. Writing provides the foundation of education and the basic requirements for all academic disciplines (Herffernan, Linclon & Atwrill, 2001). It is worth mentioning that writing plays an important role in EFL prospective teachers' personal and professional lives. According to Haneline and Aiex (1997) the possession of writing skills can open up real possibilities in EFL prospective teachers' professional and personal lives. Therefore, the

DOI: 10.4018/978-1-4666-1984-5.ch019

development of writing performance is of vital importance for EFL prospective teachers.

The advent of new technologies has opened up new approaches for designing courses in writing (Kroutl–Helal, 2007). Technology has added a new type of literacy which is referred to as digital fluency (Huffaker, 2004b). Digital fluency will be another prerequisite for sociability, lifelong learning and employment opportunities (Resnick, 2002). New technologies could empower students when they are used appropriately. They could also provide some pedagogical suggestions for the effective use of computer in the foreign language classroom (Warschauer, Turbee & Roberts, 1996).

With the emergence of the Internet, computer technology has extended its potential and possibilities in assisting language learning. Web resources could bring about beneficial results for learning which could not be accomplished alone. Huffaker (2004a) stressed that "the Internet continues to generate new applications that not only foster individual expression, but also cohesive community development" (p. 1). Besides, educators attempted to improve students' independent use of the Internet as well as students' Internet-based communication and interaction skills (Peng, Tsai & Wu, 2006).

BACKGROUND

Wiki is a major component of Web 2.0 and is regarded as "a web communication and collaboration tool that can be used to engage students in learning with others within a collaborative environment" (Parker & Chao, 2007, p. 57). It can accumulate users' opinions, and cultivate active on-line communities on the web (Wang, Lu, Yang, Hu, Chiou, Chiang, et.al., 2005). A wiki is characterized by ease of use and rapidity of deployment, making possible powerful information sharing and supporting collaborative activities and improving student interaction (Boulos, Maramba, & Wheeler, 2006).

According to Arreguin (2004) wikis could offer "unique collaborative opportunities for education combining freely accessible information, rapid feedback, simplified HTML, and access by multiple editors, wikis are being rapidly adopted as an innovative way of constructing knowledge" (p.1). Besides, Solvie (2008) stressed that wikis "are quick user-friendly web pages that allow users to create, edit, and save text collaboratively" (p.59).

Bergin (2002) wrote about the advantages of having a wiki for each of his courses and noted that wikis enabled him to communicate more easily and asynchronously with students on course topics. The students also used it to communicate with him and each other. It was also used to quickly dispel misconceptions and correct errors made in class. Prensky (2004) suggested that wiki functionality should be an integral part of the new generation of teaching software. Bruns and Humphrey (2005) noted that a wiki could encourage and enable learning in ways that many other web-based tools fail to do. Moreover, wikis could assist interactive collaboration among students (Beldarrain, 2006).

Characteristics of Wiki

Duff, Peter and Bruns (2006), Grant (2006) and Duffy (2008) revealed that a wiki has the following characteristics:

- It is essentially a database for creating, browsing and searching through information.
- It can be personal but usually open to collaboration as it can allow an individual user to edit her / his work and it can also allow multiple contributors to edit their own work and the work of others.
- It does not need detailed technical knowledge of HTML on the part of the user as it is easy to create and update individual pages and the entire wiki as well.
- It supports easy addition of hyperlinks, provides every content page with its dedi-

cated discussion page, allows for user authentication and different access levels, informs users when a particular page has been edited, and allows easy viewing of all contributions by an individual user.

- It can record each change that occurs over time, so that at any point a page can be compared and reverted to any of its previous versions.

Educational Uses of Wikis

The following section highlights how wikis can be used in education for the purpose of collaboration, facilitation of work, audience extension, knowledge building, reflection and effective writing as indicated by (Goodwin-Jones, 2003; Bristow,2005; Connell, 2005; Edington, Funk, Thorpe & Warrington, 2005; Dearstyne, 2007; Solvie,2008).

- Wikis can be used as social networking spaces for communication, sharing information in the form of reviews, reports and note-taking.
- Students can use a wiki to develop research projects. Student groups can edit each other's work as they complete a class project.
- Wikis can be used as repositories for document collection. Teachers can upload interactive lessons which take place in class and add online resources. They can also upload information and links related to topics for research. Besides, teachers can upload homework assignments, reading assignment and project guidelines.
- Wikis can encourage multiple modalities as they can incorporate graphics, audio, video and animation that allow learners to express themselves and communicate the meaning that may not be fully expressed in the text format.

- Students can use wikis to add summaries of their thoughts from the prescribed readings.
- Wikis can be used for course evaluation, course administration and timetabling. Students can add their comments on a course they have received.
- Teachers can use wikis in distance learning to publish course resources as syllabus and handouts. Students can edit and comment on them easily.
- Wikis can be used to map concepts. They are effective for brainstorming on a given topic and to edit it to produce a linked network of resources.
- Teachers can use wikis to introduce a presentation instead of conventional software as power point. Students can directly comment on the presentation while it occurs.
- Wikis can be utilized by teachers to share reflections and thoughts regarding teaching practices.
- Wikis can be used by groups to collaborate on a document by sending it on to each member of the group in turn; emailing a file which each person edits on their computer and the edits are to be coordinated so that everyone's work is equally represented.
- A wiki can be used as a message board and serves as a collaboration tool in organizing the network of a group. Users can use a wiki as an alternative to e-mail by adding messages to a central location-the wiki document. The sequenced messages on the wiki provide a record of the group's thinking.
- A wiki can be used as an electronic portfolio (e-portfolio). In the creation of an e-portfolio, text may provide an introduction to the work presented. Documents and other artifacts can be uploaded to the wiki page. Users of the wiki could provide feedback on the organization and or the contents of the e-portfolio.

Historical Development of Wikis

Wikis are newcomers to the Internet and they have been successfully used in education as viable tools for teaching and learning as early as 1999 (Guzdial, 1999). The term 'wiki' was taken from the Hawaiin language where 'wiki wiki' means 'quick' to represent that a wiki web site could be quickly created for a collaborative team (Lamb & Johnson, 2007). Ward Cunningham created and conceptualized the first wiki in 1995 and used it as a composition system, a discussion medium and a collaborative tool. Cunningham and Leuf (2001) described a Wiki as "a freely expandable collection of interlinked web pages, a hypertext system for storing and modifying information - a database, where each page is easily edited by any user with a forms - capable Web browser client" (p.14).

The use of wikis for educational and other applications is starting to penetrate all the academic fields (Schwartz, Clark, Cossarin & Rudolph, 2004). According to Lamb (2004) "wikis are already making their mark in higher education and are being applied to just about any task imaginable. They are popping up like mushrooms, as wikis will, at colleges and universities around the world sometimes in impromptu ways and more often with thoughtful intent" (p.36).

Wikis use is growing in popularity since they allow their users to create and change content more easily and quickly than with traditional websites. All one needs to edit a wiki is a computer with Internet connection and web browser. Users working on their first wiki can easily create and publish a basic page. This ease of editing means that the teachers and students can quickly learn and start expanding any page or site. Those pages can be used for discussion, posting assignments, and various collaborative projects. Besides, wiki technology makes it very easy to work on a collaborative document, track work in progress and see how much each individual in a group has contributed to the assignment (Ebersbach, Glaser & Heigle, 2006). Therefore, wikis are gaining ground in higher education (Choy & Ng, 2007). It is difficult to estimate the number of wikis currently used in university settings, and the range of ways in which they are being used (Schwartz, et. al., 2004).

Wikipedia, The Free Encyclopedia, is the most popular and well known wiki since it has been successfully used and edited by millions. Wikipedia is considered an online encyclopedia created by users from all over the world. It is a valuable tool for group writing assignments which involve referencing, translating, or copy editing. Anyone can add entries to Wikipedia and anyone can change or add to existing entries (Farmer, 2004). There are number of wiki tool providers on the web where teachers and students can create their own wikis for free, such as Wikispaces. Other examples of public wikis are Wikevent which is a worldwide calendar of public events, such as lectures, classes and sporting events and Wiktionary which is a collaborative project to produce a free dictionary with definitions, pronunciations, synonyms, antonyms and translations.

Previous Studies Related to the Application of Wikis in Classrooms

Rick, Carroll, Holloway-Attaway and Walker (2002) conducted a research to study the effect of using two sections of an English composition class, taught by the same instructor. In the first section, the instructor used CoWeb, a wiki-based tool, to complete various assignments. In the second section, the same instructor conducted the same activities, but worked in a discussion on line environment. The results showed that the CoWeb section outperformed the second section in each rating category.

Augar, Raitman and Zhou (2004) carried out a study about using wikis in Deakin University in Australia in order to explore new ways to help students know one another in their online learning groups. The results showed that the wiki proved to be useful for online collaboration. The number of pages increased each day. Times of editing also increased every day with over 2000 wiki edits in total.

Augar, Raitman and Zhou (2005) conducted a study about employing wikis for online collaboration. The results of this study revealed that the majority of the students noted that the use of wiki increased their comprehension of material and they stressed that working with wiki was enjoyable. They also concluded that 73% of students found the wiki software is easy to use.

Byron (2005) investigated the uses of wikis in his distance learning symbolic logic class. The participants were required to summarize various assigned readings and post them on the wiki. They were also allowed to edit collaboratively those postings to develop accuracy and completeness. The results of this study revealed the usefulness of using wikis as collaborative learning tools.

In a study conducted by Engstrom and Jewtt (2005), students were organized into groups of four to six students to make the wiki web pages manageable. The results showed that the participated students expressed satisfaction with their learning and indicated that they had the most positive experience. The participated teachers also pointed out that their technology knowledge and skills improved after the project and that most students became independent about their learning.

Forte and Bruckman (2006) conducted a study to investigate how to design wiki publishing tools and curricula to support learning among students. The results revealed that collaborative publishing on a wiki offered a model for creating authentic classroom writing activities.

Richardson (2006) conducted a study about using wikis as a web tool implemented for use in classrooms. This study revealed that wikis facilitated a collaboration environment, which provided the students opportunities to learn how to work with each others, create knowledge and operate in

a world that values group effort. The results of the study showed that the students learned from each others' work and from the process of working on their group assignments because a wiki is an open editing and collaborative writing environment.

Cobb (2007) conducted a study to investigate the use of wikis to encourage active learning and collaborative problem-solving in legal education. This study discussed a legal research and writing class in which students used wikis to collaboratively gather information. The results revealed the usefulness of using wikis in active learning and collaborative problem-solving.

Lundin (2008) conducted a study about the use of wikis in first year composition classes. This study assumed that wikis can challenge a number of traditional pedagogical assumptions about the teaching of writing. These assumptions were organized in four categories of interest to composition studies. These categories were new media composition, collaborative writing, critical interaction and online authority. The results showed that wikis were effective in helping facilitate improvement in composition classes.

Mak and Coniam (2008) designed a study to investigate authentic writing through the use of wikis by secondary school students in Hong Kong. The researchers used wikis as a collaborative writing platform to produce. Over a period of two months, the participated students designed and put together, through a series of successive drafts, a description of their secondary school. The students' final draft was a printed brochure of their 'new' school. The results showed the usefulness of using wikis in teaching writing to students at the Secondary Stage.

Solvie (2008) conducted a study to examine the use of a wiki in a teacher education reading methods course. The results indicated the benefits of using wikis as tools to support students' construction of knowledge. The results also revealed the importance of scaffolding students' wiki work in constructivist settings.

The Author's Experience with Using Wikis to Develop Prospective EFL Teachers' Writing Performance

The researcher conducted a study which aimed at investigating the effect of using wikis to develop prospective EFL teachers' writing performance. The participants were fourth year prospective EFL teachers at Suez Faculty of Education in Egypt. The participants were all females and their ages ranged from 20 to 21 years old. All the participants were proficient in using computer as all of them obtained the International Computer Driving License (ICDL) before conducting the experiment. All of them had no experience with writing by using wikis before conducting the experiment. The participants were randomly chosen and assigned into two groups, an experimental group of (30 students) and a control group of (30 students). The experimental group and the control group used a computer word program to write their essays. Both groups were pre-tested by using the Writing Performance Test (WPT) for equivalence in their writing performance. Difference between the mean scores of the experimental group and control group on the pre-WPT was calculated by using the t-test. The results of the pre-WPT revealed that the experimental group and the control group were equivalent in their writing performance before conducting the experiment. These findings are provided in Table 1.

The researcher taught essay writing to the experimental group and the control group. The experimental group was trained throughout all the sessions of the wiki-based program, while the control group did not receive similar program as the researcher taught them the same essay topics and encouraged them to write their essays by using word program on computer. The experiment lasted for five weeks, eight hours per week conducted over two days. The experimental group and the control group were post-tested by using the WPT. Differences between the mean scores

Table 1. The t-value of the difference in the mean scores between the experimental group and the control group on the pre-WPT

Group	N	Mean	SD	DF	T	Sig.
Experimental	30	38.60	5.30	58	0.455	0.651
Control	30	38.03	4.27			

of the pre- and post-WPT were calculated by using the t-test.

The results showed that statistically significant differences were found between the mean scores of the experimental group and the control group on the post-WPT in favor of the experimental group. The results also revealed that there were statistically significant differences in the mean scores of the experimental group between the pre- and post-WPT in favor of the post-WPT. These results revealed the usefulness of using wikis in developing prospective EFL teachers' writing performance. Majority of the experimental group indicated that they enjoyed working with wikis. They asserted that the training program based on using wikis was effective in helping them develop their writing performance. The results of this study are provided in Table 2 and Table 3.

How the Author Applied the Wiki-Based Program

The researcher designed a program which was based on using wikis in the writing classrooms to train the experimental group on using wikis when they write essays. The researcher assessed the validity of the program by submitting it to a panel of prominent, Professors of Curriculum and TEFL at some Faculties of Education in Egypt, who asserted the validity of the program. She also developed a list of six persuasive essay topics to be given to the experimental group and the control group. These topics were chosen from the essay course provided to fourth year prospec-

Table 2. The t-value of the difference in the mean scores between the experimental group and the control group on the post-WPT

Group	N	Mean	SD	DF	T	Sig.
Experimental	30	79.86	7.16	58	26.908	0.000
Control	30	38.23	4.52			

tive EFL teachers at Suez Faculty of Education. To ensure the validity of these topics, the same panel of Professors was consulted. They indicated the validity of the persuasive essay topics for the present study.

The researcher divided the 30 students of the experimental group into six groups with 5 students in each group as it would be easier for the students to collaborate in small groups. Each group was responsible for writing a persuasive essay which was selected by the group from a list of persuasive essay topics. The process writing approach was used for writing the essays since the editing functions of wikis make them a practical tool for the students to practice drafting, revising and editing. The researcher distributed roles among the members of each group as follows: a leader who was responsible for posting and editing of the written products, encouragers who should encourage group members to contribute, elaborators who were responsible for explaining important and unclear points and recorders who were responsible for recording the assignments done by the group. Besides, the researcher encouraged the students in each group to exchange roles throughout the program sessions.

The first session included training the experimental group on the pre-writing stage in which the researcher discussed with the experimental group topics which are related to wikis characteristics, uses and benefits. The experimental group was also trained on how to write a wiki page, edit an existing page on a wiki and view previous pages edited on a wiki. Then, the researcher divided the experimental group into six groups with five students in each group, provided the groups with a list of persuasive essay topics and asked each group to choose a topic to write on. The students in each group were encouraged to brainstorm and generate ideas exploring the pros and cons of the concerned topic. After that, the researcher asked each group to record together the information that they brainstormed on charts. By the end of this session, every student in the experimental group was provided with an assessment sheet on this session.

The second session involved training the experimental group on the drafting stage in which the researcher created a wiki for the experiment on Wikispaces. Wikispaces (www.wikispaces.com) was chosen to be the wiki environment in the present study due to the fact that they were free and were easy to use. The wiki created by the researcher contained six pages, one page for each group. The students in each group allocated their own page on the wiki. The researcher encouraged the students in each group to organize the charts they created in the pre-writing stage. They were

Table 3. The t-value of the difference in the mean scores of the experimental group between the pre- and post-WPT

Group	N	Mean	SD	DF	T	Sig.
Pre- experimental	30	38.60	5.30	26	25.481	0.000
Post- experimental	30	79.86	7.16			

also encouraged to write their drafts on their wiki pages. Each group was asked to read the drafts of other groups on the wiki pages. By the end of this session, the researcher provided every student in the experimental group with an assessment sheet on this session.

The third session included training the experimental group on the revising stage in which the researcher held a meeting with each group to explain how to organize ideas into coherent paragraphs, write topic sentences and arrange statements for emotional appeal by using strong and exact words. The students in each group were consequently encouraged to go back to their group page on the wiki and to revise the draft of their group page. Then, the students in each group were asked to look at their own written work on the wiki pages critically considering audience questions and comments. The students in each group were also encouraged to read each other's drafts on the wiki pages and to suggest improvements. By the end of this session, every student in the experimental group was provided with an assessment sheet on this session.

The fourth session included training the experimental group on the editing stage in which the researcher held a meeting with each group to review their written product and to indicate the common mistakes in their writing. The students in their groups were encouraged to look at their wiki pages to scan their writing to check spelling, grammar and sentence structure to modify and rearrange ideas. The researcher helped the students evaluate whether the content style and goals had been achieved. She also provided them with mini-lessons based on their errors in specific areas such as punctuation, spelling and grammar. Then, the students were encouraged to reduce the texts and edit them after concentrating on the most important information. By the end of this session, the researcher provided every student in the experimental group with an assessment sheet on this session.

The fifth session involved training the experimental group on the publishing stage in which the students in each group were asked to publish their own final copy of writing on their wiki page. Then, the researcher encouraged the students in all groups to read each other's essays and to write responses to the published written essays. By the end of this session, the researcher provided every student in the experimental group with an assessment sheet on this session.

By the end of the training sessions, the researcher post-tested the experimental group and the control group by using the WPT. The researcher compared and analyzed the data obtained from the pre- and post-WPT.

RECOMMENDATIONS

In the light of the outcome of the investigation and a clear evidence of improved learning accomplished by the groups which have used wikis to develop their writing performance, this study concludes with the following recommendations:

- Training programs should be offered to EFL teachers to provide them with the necessary skills for using and utilizing wikis in teaching writing.
- Published materials about using wikis in writing should be available to teachers and students.
- Curriculum designers, teacher-trainers and textbook writers should adopt educational strategies that incorporate using wikis in teaching writing to EFL learners at all Stages.

CONCLUSION

It can be concluded from this overview that wikis are effective in developing the writing performance of their users. They can provide a collaborative environment which can encourage their users to engage effectively in the writing process and thus they can develop their writing performance. The editing functions of wikis make them an ideal tool for the writers to practice drafting, reviewing and editing.

Wikis can also support peer review and reflections. They can enable their users to effectively participate and contribute in writing their essays as they allow them to publish content with ease. The easy editing process of wikis can help their users participate in collaborative work. Therefore, they can easily share and exchange ideas to develop their writing performance.

Wikis proved to be ideal for collaborative writing assignments as they can help writers to review rough drafts, post comments, and publish a final essay. This reveals that wikis can enhance writers to collaborate with each other as well as learn from each others' work and helped them develop their writing performance. Besides, wikis can provide a flexible user friendly atmosphere for collaboration, knowledge creation and interaction in writing classrooms.

REFERENCES

Arreguin, C. (2004). Wikis. In B. Hoffman (Ed.), *Encyclopedia of educational technology*. Retrieved May 11, 2008, from http://coe.sdsu.edu/eet/articles/wikis/start.html

Augar, N., Raitman, R., & Zhou, W. (2004). *Teaching and learning online with wikis*. Retrieved March 15, 2008, from http://www.ascilite.org.au/conferences/perth04/procs/augar.html

Bergin, J. (2002). *Teaching on the wiki web*. Paper presented in the 7th Annual Conference on Innovation and Technology in Computer Science Education. New York, NY: ACM Press.

Boulous, M., Maramba, I., & Wheeler, S. (2006). Wikis, blogs and podcasts: A new generation of web-based tools for virtual collaborative clinical practice and education. *BMC Medical Education, 6*(41). Retrieved March 15, 2008, from http://www.biomedcentral.com/content/pdf/1472-6920-6-41.pdf

Bristow, R. (2005). Beyond email: Wikis, blogs and other strange beasts. *Ariadne, 42*. Retrieved May 25, 2008, from http://www.ariadne.ac.uk/issue42/beyond-email-rpt/intro.html

Bruns, A., & Humphreys, S. (2005). *Wikis in teaching and assessment - The M/Cyclopedia project*. Paper presented at The 2005 International Symposium on Wikis, October 16-18, San Diego, CA, U.S.A. Retrieved October 1, 2008, from http://snurb.info/files/wikis%20in %20 Teaching %20 and %20 assessment.pdf

Byron, M. (2005). Teaching with tiki. *Teaching Philosophy, 28*(2), 108–113.

Cassell, J. (2004). Towards a model of technology and literacy development: Story listening systems. *Journal of Applied Developmental Psychology, 25*, 75–105. doi:10.1016/j.appdev.2003.11.003

Choy, S., & Ng, K. (2007). Implementing software for supplementing online. *Australasian Journal of Educational Technology, 23*(2), 209–226.

Cobb, T. (2007). Public interest research, collaboration, and the promise of wikis perspectives. *Teaching Legal Research and Writing, 16*, 1–11.

Connell, S. (2005). *Comparing blogs, wikis, and discussion boards as collaborative learning tools*. Retrieved May 11, 2008, from http://soo2sone.com/PDFs/plan_ConnellED690.pdf

Cunningham, W., & Leuf, B. (2001). *The wiki way: Quick collaboration on the web*. Addison-Wesley: Longman Publishing Company, Inc.

Dearstyne, B. (2007). Blogs, smashups, and wikis oh my! *Information Management Journal, 41*(4), 24–33.

Duff, P., Peter, A., & Bruns, A. (2006). The use of blogs, wikis and RSS in education: A conversation of possibilities. In *Proceedings Online Learning and Teaching Conference* 2006, Brisbane. Retrieved April 15, 2008, from http://eprints.qut.edu.au

Duffy, P. (2008). Engaging the YouTube Google eyed generation: Strategies for using web 2.0 in teaching and learning. *The Electronic Journal of e-Learning, 6*(2), 119-130.

Ebersbach, A., Glaser, M., & Heigl, R. (2006). *Wiki: Web collaboration.* New York, NY: Springer.

Edington, J., Funk, J., Thorpe, R., & Warrington, J. (2005). *Professional applications of wikis and weblogs. Open source development and documentation project.* Retrieved October 25, 2008, from http://osddp.org/files/issues/WPWikisBlogs.7.pdf

Engstrom, M., & Jewett, D. (2005). Collaborative learning the wiki way. *TechTrends: Linking Research and Practice to Improve Learning, 49*(6), 12–16.

Farmer, S. (2004). *The wide world of wiki: Choosing a wiki for an element of a fully online undergraduate course.* Retrieved March 25, 2008, from http://radio.weblogs.com/0120501/2004/06/10.html

Forte, A., & Bruckman, A. (2006). From Wikipedia to the classroom: Exploring online publication and learning. *The Proceedings of the 7th International Conference on Learning Sciences,* Bloomington, Indiana, June 27-July 1, (pp. 182-188). Retrieved May 11, 2008, from http://www.static.cc.gatech.edu/~asb/papers/forte- brunckman-iclso6.pdf

Goodwin-Jones, R. (2003). Blogs and wikis: Environments for on-line collaboration. *Language Learning and Teaching, 7,* 12–16.

Grant, L. (2006). *Using wikis in schools: A case study.* Retrieved October 15, 2008, from http://www.futurelabe.org.uk/research/tm

Guzdial, M. (1999). *Teacher and student authoring on the web for shifting agency.* Retrieved January 25, 2008, from http://coweb.cc.gatech.edu.8888/csl/uploads/24/default.html

Haneline, D., & Aiex, N. (1997). *Asking the right question: Reading assignments and work for writing.* ERIC Clearinghouse on Reading English and Communication, Digest # 122.

Heffernan, J., Linclon, J., & Atwrill, J. (2001). *Writing a college handbook* (5th ed.). New York: WW. Norton and Company Ltd.

Huffaker, D. (2004a). *The educated blogger: Using weblogs to promote literacy in the classroom.* Paper presented at the International Conference of Educational Multimedia in Quebec City, Canada.

Kroutl-Helal, A. (2007). *Creating online collaborative models for ESL writing exercises.* Retrieved December 15, 2008, from http: //www.eadtu.nl/conference-2007/default.html

Lamb, A., & Johnson, L. (2007). An information skills workout: Wikis and collaborative writing. *Teacher Librarian, 34*(5), 57–59.

Lamb, B. (2004). Wide open spaces: Wikis ready or not. *EDUCAUSE Review, 39*(5), 36–48.

Lundin, R. (2008). Teaching with wikis: Toward a new worked pedagogy. *Computers and Composition, 25*(4), 432–448. doi:10.1016/j.compcom.2008.06.001

Mak, B., & Coniam, D. (2008). Using wikis to enhance and develop writing skills among secondary school students in Hong Kong. *System, 36*(3), 437–455. doi:10.1016/j.system.2008.02.004

Parker, K., & Chao, J. (2007). Wiki as a teaching tool. *Interdisciplinary Journal of Knowledge and Learning Objects, 3,* 57–72.

Peng, H., Tsai, C., & Wu, Y. (2006). University students' self-efficacy and their attitudes toward the Internet: The role of students perceptions of the Internet. *Educational Studies, 32*(1), 73–86. doi:10.1080/03055690500416025

Prensky, M. (2004). Proposal for educational software development sites: An open source tool to create the learning software we need. *Horizon, 12*, 41–44. doi:10.1108/10748120410699585

Resnick, M. (2002). Rethinking learning in the digital age. In G. Kirkman (Ed.), *The global information technology report: Readiness for the networked world* (pp. 32-37). Oxford, UK: Oxford University Press. Richardson, W. (2006). *Blogs, wikis, pod casts and other powerful web tools for classrooms*. Thousand Oaks, CA: Corwin Press.

Rick, J., Guzdial, M., Holloway-Attaway, K. C., & Walker, B. (2002). Collaborative learning at low Cost: Co Web use in English composition. *Proceedings of Computer Support for Collaborative Learning Conference,* Boulder, Co, USA: January 7-11, (pp. 435-442). Retrieved October 25, 2008, from http://coweb.co.gatech.edu.8888/csl/uploads/24/CoWebInEnglish

Schwartz, L., Clark, S., Cossarin, M., & Rudolph, J. (2004). Educational wikis: Features and selection criteria. *The International Review of Research in Open and Distance Learning, 5*(1). Retrieved May 25, 2008, from http://www.irrodl.org/index.php/irrodl/article/view /163/244

Solvie, P. (2008). Use of the wiki: Encouraging pre service teachers' construction of knowledge in reading methods courses. *Journal of Literacy and Technology, 9*(2), 57–87.

Wang, H., Lu, C., Yang, J., Hu, H., Chiou, G., Chiang, Y., et al. (2005). An empirical exploration of using wiki in an English as a Second Language course. *Fifth IEEE International Conference on Advanced Learning Technologies,* (pp. 155-157).

Warschauer, M., Turbee, L., & Roberts, B. (1996). Computer learning networks and student empowerment. *System, 24*(1), 1–14. doi:10.1016/0346-251X(95)00049-P

ADDITIONAL READING

Andrus, D. (2005). The wiki and the blog: Toward a complex adaptive intelligence community. *Studies in Intelligence, 49*(3).

Beldarrain, Y. (2006). Distance education trends: Integrating new technologies to foster student interaction and collaboration. *Distance Education, 27*(2), 139–153. doi:10.1080/01587910600789498

Biesenbach-Lucas, S., & Weasenforth, D. (2001). E-mail and word processing in the ESL classroom: How the medium affects the message. *Language Learning & Technology, 5*(1), 135–165.

Bold, M. (2006). Use of wikis in graduate course work. *Journal of Interactive Learning Research, 17*(1), 5–14.

Bowers, M., Woo, K., Roberts, M., & Watters, P. (2006). *Wiki pedagogy - A tale of two wikis.* Paper presented at the 7th International Conference on Information Technology Based Higher Education and Training, Sydney, Australia.

Cassell, J. (2004). Towards a model of technology and literacy development: Story listening systems. *Journal of Applied Developmental Psychology, 25*, 75–105. doi:10.1016/j.appdev.2003.11.003

Chang, M. (2004). I've gathered a basket of communication and collaboration tools. *Computers in Libraries, 24*(8), 6–9.

Chang, Y., & Schauert, D. (2005). *The design for a collaborative system of English as foreign language composition writing of senior high school students in Taiwan*. Paper presented in the 5th IEEE International Conference on Advanced Learning Technologies. Retrieved October 13, 2008, from http://www.computer.org/portal/web/cdsl/doi/10.1109/ICALT.2005.261

Chao, J. (2007). *Student project collaboration using wikis*. Paper presented in the 20th Conference on Software Engineering Education and Training (CSEE&T2007), Dublin, Ireland, July 3-5.

Dean, P., Stahl, M., Sylwester, D., & Pear, J. (2001). Effectiveness of combined delivery modalities for distance learning and resident learning. *Quarterly Review of Distance Education, 2*(3), 247–254.

DeGuia, M. (2004). Differentiating the learning environment. In B. Hoffman (Ed.), *Encyclopedia of educational technology*. Retrieved May 25, 2008, from http://coe.sdsu.edu/eet/articles/differentlearningenv/start.htm

DeLacey, B., & Leonard, D. (2002). Case study on technology and distance in education at the Harvard Business School. *Journal of Educational Technology & Society, 5*(2), 13–28.

Desilets, A., Gonzalez, L., Paquet, S., & Stojanovic, M. (2006). Translation the wiki way. *Proceedings of symposium on wikis*, (pp. 19-31). CAN Press. Retrieved May 15, 2008, from http://www.wikisym.org/ws2006/proceedings/plg.pdf

Dickey, M. (2004). The impact of weblogs (blogs) on student perceptions of isolation and alienation in a web based distance-learning environment. *Open Learning, 19*(3), 279–291. doi:10.1080/0268051042000280138

Farabaugh, R. (2007). The isle is full of noises: Using wiki software to establish a discourse community in a Shakespeare classroom. *Language Awareness, 16*(1), 41–56. doi:10.2167/la428.0

Flavin, S. (2001). *E-learning advantages in a tough economy*. Retrieved March 11, 2008, from http://www.babsoninsight.com/contentmgr/showdetails.php/id/217

Fleck, A. (1999). We think he means … Creating working definitions through small group discussion. *Teaching English in the Two-Year College, 27*, 228–231.

Fountain, R. (2005). *Wiki pedagogy*. Retrieved May 15, 2008, from http://www.profetic.org:16080/dossiers/rubrique.php3?id_rubrique=11068-

Gabrilovich, E., & Markovitch, S. (2006). Overcoming the brittleness bottleneck using Wikipedia: Enhancing text categorization with encyclopedic knowledge. *Proceedings of the 21st National Conference on Artificial Intelligence* (AAAI-06), (pp. 1301-1306). Retrieved March 23, 2008, from http://www.cs.technion.ac.il/~gabr/papers/wiki-aaai06.pdf

Goosik, K. (1999). *The process approach to teaching writing*. Retrieved May 11, 2008, from http://www.Dartmouth.edu/compose/ tutor/ pedagogy/ process.html

Hyland, K. (2003). *Second language writing*. Cambridge, UK: Cambridge University Press. doi:10.1017/CBO9780511667251

Jara, M., & Mohamad, F. (2007). *Pedagogical templates for e-learning*. Occasional papers in work-based learning 2, Institute of Education, University of London. Retrieved November 15, 2008, from http://www.wlecentre.ac.uk/cms/files/occasionalpapers/wle_op2.pdf

Jewitt, C. (2005). Multimodality, reading, and writing for the 21st century. *Discourse: Studies in the Cultural Politics of Education, 26*(3), 315–331. doi:10.1080/01596300500200011

Johnson, H. (1996). Survey review: Process writing in course books. *ELT Journal, 50*(4), 374–378.

Kasper, L., & Petrello, B. (1996). Responding to ESL student writing: The value of a nonjudgmental approach. *Communication Review*, *14*, 5–22.

Ketih, M. (2006). Wikis and student writing. *Teacher Librarian*, *34*(2), 70–72.

Kress, G. (2003). *Literacy in the new media age*. London, UK: Routledge. doi:10.4324/9780203164754

Lim, C. (2002). Trends in online learning and their implications for school. *Educational Technology*, *42*(6), 43–48.

Liou, H. (1997). The impact of WWW texts on EFL learning. *Computer Assisted Language Learning*, *10*(5), 455–478. doi:10.1080/0958822970100505

Luce-Kapler, R. (2007). Radical change and wikis: Teaching new literacies. *Journal of Adolescent & Adult Literacy*, *51*(3), 214–223. doi:10.1598/JAAL.51.3.2

Oshima, A., & Hogue, A. (2007). *Introduction to academic writing* (3rd ed.). White Plains, NY: Peason Education.

Raygan, R., & Green, D. (2002). *Internet collaboration: Twiki*. Columbia, SC: Proceedings for the IEEE Southeastcon.

Rossett, A. (2002). *The ASTD e-learning handbook*. McGraw-Hill.

Sands, P. (2002). Inside, outside, upside, downside: Strategies for connecting online and face to face instruction in hybrid courses. *Teaching with Technology Today, 8*(6).

Soonpaa, N. (2007). *Product vs. process approach to teaching legal writing*. Paper presented at the Conference on the Pedagogy of Legal Writing for Academics in Africa, March 14-17, Texas Tech University, School of Law.

Tonkin, E. (2005). *Making the case for a Wiki*. Retrieved March 11, 2008, from http:///www.ariadne.ac.uk/issue42/tonkin/intro.html

Ward, J., & LaBranche, G. (2003). Blended learning: The convergence of e-learning and meetings. *Franchising World*, *35*(4), 22–23.

Wei, C., Maust, B., Barrick, J., Cuddihy, E., & Spyridakis, J. (2005). Wikis for supporting distributed collaborative writing. *Proceedings for the Third International Conference on Information Technology and Applications.*

Yarrow, F., & Topping, K. (2001). Collaborative writing: The effects of metacognitive prompting and structured peer interaction. *The British Journal of Educational Psychology*, *71*, 261–282. doi:10.1348/000709901158514

Young, J. (2002). Hybrid teaching seeks to end the divide between traditional and online instruction. *The Chronicle of Higher Education*, A33.

KEY TERMS AND DEFINITIONS

Blog: It is an online collection of personal commentaries. It can be used as an online journal that an individual can continuously update with her or his own words, ideas and thoughts through software that enables her / him to easily do so.

Digital Literacy: The ability to use digital technology, communication tools or networks to read and interpret media, to reproduce data and images through digital manipulation, and to locate, evaluate, use, create information and apply new knowledge gained from digital environments.

Discussion Board: It is also known by various other names such as: discussion forum, discussion group, message board, and online forum. It refers to any online "bulletin board" where a user can leave and expect to see responses to messages she / he has left.

English as a Foreign Language: It refers to English for use in a non-English-speaking region, by people whose first language is not English. It is also used to describe English language learning in countries where English is not an official first language.

Wiki: A web based tool which can be used by users to collaboratively create, edit and publish written products.

Writing Performance: It is the production of a writer's ideas on a certain topic in a written form with clear organization of ideas, adequate and relevant content taking the audience into consideration and demonstrating appropriate mechanics.

Writing Apprehension: It is a condition that writers have when they write and sometimes leads them to avoid writing.

Chapter 20
Online Learning Communities in UAE Schools:
Opportunities and Challenges

Alia Fares
Al Foah Primary School, UAE

ABSTRACT

The emergence of the Internet in a time when the world was struggling to cope with new information systems and technologies has put additional burdens on businesses, individuals, and societies, not only to adapt to new ways but also to creatively explore feasible applications and opportunities to drive improvements in all walks of life. This has translated into a multitude of tangible and intangible improvements and has generally improved decision making as a direct result of improved data storages, faster data processing, and retrieval. For educators, the Internet has provided excellent opportunities to improve the processes of online collaborative learning to complement conventional classes as well as reaping the benefits from information and knowledge bases that are relatively easy to access and are ready to share by both educators and students alike. This chapter explores the opportunities and challenges associated with using Internet Online Learning Communities to complement and aid conventional classes and enhance learning outcomes in UAE schools. The study describes the use of online forums to support English language classes in Al Foah Primary School, weighing its pros and cons and identifying lessons learned.

INTRODUCTION

The maturity and affordability of information technology hardware and software over the past decade, coupled with major breakthroughs in the communication side of technology have led to a general trend of merging both information technol-

ogy and communication technology disciplines, since the software had always the control over the utility of the hardware. This is described as 'the infrastructure that operates the technology of information' and has proven to be popular and capable of serving a wider audience at the same time. Initially, the audience was comprised of organizations and universities exchanging information that transformed the basic level of ordinary

DOI: 10.4018/978-1-4666-1984-5.ch020

people from not only seeking information, but also contributing in its evolution.

The term Information and Communication Technology (ICT) has started to find its way in academic research and the literature as a more representative term to describe new technology applications that make use of Information Technology (IT) and Communication Technology (CT) components. Typically, new applications, systems and business solutions would be a combination of software, hardware and networks including the internet.

Analog cellular or mobile phones when introduced represented a breakthrough in the communication industry by providing the convenience to users to connect from anywhere via phone calls and text messages. Driven by rapid change and demand, the manufacturers of these industries understood the impact of the Internet and met the demands of both: the revolution of technology and the change in the public needs and requirements to turn ordinary mobile phones into smart ones that merged the internet with its applications into all aspects. The advent in the digital technology and the applications of the Internet have both contributed to a shift succeeded to redefine the design and function of cellular phones to become conveniently small, mobile computers and computers communication devices that laid the foundation for social networking connectivity and virtual communities' models where the users are online and reachable.

Internet generation (Web2.0) paved the way for new networking models using Wikis, Blogs, Chat rooms and discussion forums that has found great appeal and acceptance among the younger generations as alternative models to physical interaction and socializing. Today youngsters use of Web2.0 social networking applications to locate friends and peers of similar interests, needs, goals or even issues and problems beyond the usual limitations, thereby changing the way people interact with each other -- dissolving any kind of social, cultural or physical boundaries.

This explains the exponentially increasing number of subscribers to social network sites, such as, Facebook, Twitter, Google and Wikis, LinkedIn, blogs, journals all of which can be accessed through a personal computer, a laptop or a mobile phone where these social networks act as a medium for people to discuss an issue or a topic. These varied methods of communication between members have changed and influenced the way they document and connect their daily lives.

The past decade has not only witnessed unprecedented changes of socialization and interaction patterns among youngsters, but also the introduction of new applications that have enhanced and improved productivity, thereby making social networks enjoyable, attractive and addictive, as well as models used by businesses and education entities. Using social networks for educational purposes was introduced long before the appearance of the Internet by means of connecting personal computers on a local or wide area networks.

As a practical observation, it is only normal nowadays to expect the majority of UAE students to bring along with them to school, college or university one or more smart phones or technology devices such as blackberries or iPhones, laptops, tablets or hand-held devices. Such devices have huge capabilities in terms of access to information and to download thousands of free or (affordable) applications over the Internet. Practical observation also indicates that the majority of students regularly and frequently access their preferred networks and chatting forums, including, but not limited to: Facebook, iTunes, YouTube, Skype, or Twitter, many times daily thereby making the learning experience more appealing, more enjoyable and enhancing of ordinary school subjects.

The chapter reflects on the experience of using online technology by creating a mobile learning community for a grade nine students in a UAE elementary school. The main trigger to consider the creation of an online community was that accessing the Internet using different technological devices (mobiles, laptops, tablets etc) by students seemed to be consuming a great deal of students' time.

This has prompted the author of this chapter, who is a language teacher of grade nine students to explore the feasibility of creating an online community forum to aid her teaching. The required forum should give students the facility for participation in useful and enjoyable discussions and debates and by initiating and sharing thoughts, ideas and knowledge and elaboration of concepts and applications related to learning material that were discussed in the class room.

Although the chapter is a reflection of a personal experience and an exhibition of a real application of an online learning community that was created to enhance her students learning outcomes, it is meant to be viewed as an example of numerous attempts by Arab educators' and organization to utilize technologies to improve learning and education.

Since the early days of the Internet along with the revolution of information and communication technology introducing, new applications for the business organizations, educators had an invested interest to benefit from such technologies and strived to combine and integrate education on the internet and technology. These attempts have gone a long way from simple, primitive websites about and for education to the more complex online learning forums and learning management systems, such as, getting accredited university degrees online that were for educators and people within education. The internet then played an important part in education on so many levels and forms, and Online learning community is one of these forms and it is the subject of discussion in this chapter.

The focus of this chapter is on the approach that was employed to create and utilize an online learning community for Grade 9, English language class, and the reasons that motivated its need and the main challenges that were encountered in throughout this venture.

BACKGROUND

E-learning as a part of online learning communities has been around for years is presented as a new approach to Knowledge Management (KM). In his paper, the synergies are shown as using e-learning as a tool to help internalize tacit knowledge; using e-learning as a way to acquire knowledge; and applying e-learning to promote knowledge sharing. E-learning in this regard can be seen to be part of organizational learning in which Knowledge Management plays a key role in the knowledge acquisition, sharing, and application phases as well.

Studies related the importance of developing a knowledge community through e-learning as a critical element in implementing Knowledge Management Policy. It is argued that E-learning, should help nurture a learning organization and foster a corporate culture based on knowledge sharing.

Further, it was observed that the complementary roles of Knowledge Management and e-learning through the following critical success factors for knowledge community-based e-learning: participation of key personnel in the development of a knowledge strategy; procedural design needs to complement current work and help to establish a loop of knowledge sharing; learner-focused technology; knowledge community involvement to complement company business goals; new business strategies and marketing; establishment of a culture of learning; providing concrete rewards for goal achievement; providing ample learning time and space within the company; and establishing mutual trust between members of a team. Taken together, a culture of knowledge sharing combined with or enhanced by e-learning will develop.

Research has also looked at the influence of culture on e-learning and Knowledge Management; including learners' acceptance of e-learning. Aside from the implementation of the educational model to address the learner's needs and educational objectives, the success of e-learning is thought to be determined by instructor characteristics, teaching materials, perceived usefulness, playfulness, and perceived ease of use. These characteristics seem to be consistent with the research on e-learning in different countries. Other studies explores culture relating to e-learning, concluding that attention to the cultural needs of users is crucial for e-learning success. Moreover, he argues that a failure to recognize cultural learning differences will lessen the effectiveness of e-learning.

Learning Communities

Before going into details about online learning communities and how they are used to support conventional instructor-led classes, it is worthwhile noting that an online learning community is derived from a broader trend of using the Internet in education, which is considered by many as equivalent to e-learning and/or blended learning. The author's choice of 'Online Learning Communities' (OLC) specifically to be the theme of this research and a subject of this chapter is primarily linked to the conviction that technology applications hold a huge potential for a better education and improved learning performance outcomes.

The author's use of the Internet to aid her as a teacher of English language classes has extended over four years, and the initially simple online forum that was used has evolved over the years into sophisticated Online Learning Communities that comprise a variety of components including, forums, email groups and recently, blogs.

Although, this initiative has proven to be a major undertaking in terms of efforts and resources, the author's choice to take up the challenge was justified by the anticipated gains to education and learning to both teachers and students alike.

In addition to its positive impact to achieving learning goals and objectives, the 'Online Learning Communities' have evidently helped the teacher with following up on students issues and progress, attaining students feedback, planning for learning materials as well as focusing on students' real and actual learning needs.

The online forums were particularly effective in building communication channels that were used by the teacher to reach out to students in order to encourage, motivate or even provoke them toward learning English in a user-friendly environment, and were useful for students' interactions and discussions among themselves and with the teacher.

Most of grade nine students who have taken part in this initiative were considered expert Internet users, capable of Internet surfing, website browsing, using search engines, emails, and are familiar with popular social network sites.

Students' evident capabilities and interest in the Internet and the fact that students spend long hours on the Internet on daily basis, have prompted the teacher to question why not to use the potential of students' interest, easy access and frequent use of the Internet to serve and improve education. The driving proposition suggested as a rationale 'knowledge creation, sharing and utilization can be more effectively accomplished if done in friendly, enjoyable environment" This is about making the learning process more fun and appealing to students, by using the Internet with all its glamorous interface and multimedia as the main platform for the delivery of knowledge and he achievement of learning objectives.

Another important factor that played an important role in the success of the 'Online Learning Community' was the constant and easy access that the teach had to the Internet: initially, through the use of the mobile phone, then smart devices, such as, I-phone and blackberry, and most recently, the I-Pad, which has virtually replaced the laptop. Interestingly, the use of 'Online Learning Communities' has not only helped in improving students' learning performance in the taught subject 'English Language' but also has contributed indirectly to sharpen students' computer knowledge and competencies and improving their performance in 'Computer' and 'Internet' subjects. Apart from the realization of educational and learning gains, the teacher has observed major improvements in student's communication and presentation skills.

The Online Learning Experience

According to Wikipedia, the free encyclopedia, an Online Learning Community (OLC) is a common place on the Internet that addresses the learning needs of its members through proactive and collaborative partnerships. Through social networking and computer-mediated communication, people work as a community to achieve a shared learning objective. Learning objectives may be proposed by an instructor or may arise out of discussions between participants that reflect personal interests. In an online community, people communicate via textual discussion, audio, video, or other Internet-supported devices. Blogs blend personal journaling with social networking to create environments with opportunities for reflection.

Although there are various definitions for the term 'Online Learning Community' highlighting technological, social or educational aspects, for the purpose of the of this chapter, Wikipedia's provided definition is the most suitable definition because it is comprehensive in outlining the objectives, components and the environment without indulging in the technical aspects.

This 'Online Learning Community' definition was used conveniently by the teacher in building the framework and developing the approach to guide the implementation of this ambitions project.

The four main aspects of 'Online Learning Communities' derived from its definition include; 1) having a place on the internet 2) the learners' needs 3) the collaborative relationship of teachers and students, and finally 4) the usage of computing and technology to reach the shared goal of more effective constant learning. These four aspects correspond to the main components of any 'Online Learning Community' and require adequate attention to ensure its success. For instance, to create such a community it is essential to ensure a fast and reliable Internet access. Slow or unreliable access to the Internet can be a major obstacle to accomplishing the sought online collaboration by members of the community.

The creation of an 'Online Learning Community' also requires a web page, a domain or a space whether it is paid [reserving or renting a space for a monthly or annually subscription or fees] or a free one [such as personal spaces that can be used as learning communities provided by sites like MySpace and Face book]. The choice of the domain is subject to a suitability assessment that includes the domain (name),, location and storage capacity considering the anticipated users (students and teachers) and the nature and frequency of use by members of the community.

The author's experience in creating an 'Online Learning Community' to support the English Language class has made use of both options: the paid sites and the free sites. The initial online forum that was developed has used a paid web site that was nominated by the IT function of the school.. Students were assigned a local company for digital solutions to reserve a domain name that represented the school, created a forum with many sections, and were fully responsible for technical support [including backups, updates and upgrades]. With the limited starting 2000Mb capacity of the website and a bandwidth of 40000 monthly MB, it was quite costly at the time, but functionally, it was satisfactory. At a later stage the author has tested a free private Blog site by students as a forum for discussions and learning activities and a basis for the Online Learning Community. The feedback by the majority of students was very positive, highlighting its powerful features, friendly interface, easy of use and managing dashboard. As this was considered as a pilot to check the suitability of this forum to the objectives and how students perceive it, the outcome has justified endorsing it as the official 'Online learning Community' forum to complement the physical class.

A review of the use of this forum four years down the track, indicate that despite faced obstacles, by large the intended goals were accomplished. However, it was evident the level of interaction and engagement by the teachers was limited compared to that of the ninth grade students possibly due teachers' feeling of unease with new technology and/or their lack of computer/internet competencies. Overall, the blog has proven to be very useful and the forum has evolved as an important component of the English Language classes, and was very popular by many students, encouraging other teachers to consider creating similar online learning forums to serve other classes and students. The perceived success has also encouraged school administration to look out for suitable online learning management systems that has similar features and that can serve all teachers and students.

Addressing the Learning Needs

It is known that there are individual differences between students reflecting their capabilities, personalities and background, and also, it has been established that learners have different learning needs –or, in other words-- the students differ in their learning styles. Therefore, it is only logical and smart that teachers try to understand these differences and strive to address the needs of individual students.

From this perspective, the Online Learning Community subject of this discussion has helped and revealed some of the needs that were invisible to the teacher in the classroom. Observing students interaction among themselves has helped the teacher in identifying strengths, weaknesses and issues as well students' differences and potentials.

The written tests that students are subjected to are not good measure of learning a language, where there is the need to consider many skills and competencies, such as, listening, reading, speaking and writing.

The 'Online Learning Communities' forum has proven useful in that regard as it allowed the teacher to refer low achieving students to engage in extra online activities that would otherwise consume too much time on the expense of other students in class. With the help of a follow-up plan to make the most of these activities and make sure that they achieved their purpose, showed some improvement in these students' written examinations, which can be partly attributed to the Online Learning Community.

The Online Learning Community gave this category of students what is needed of space and time to participate and to shine --even though they struggled at the beginning with using the site-- but the desire was there, and it was enough to push them forward. The feedback from the students, especially the bright ones, was used by the teacher as indicators and guiding signs through planning. The feedback from low achievers was used by the teacher to indicate how the teacher performance is perceived by those students and many decisions were taken based upon this feedback. Decisions regarding best strategy to address students' personal needs from the curriculum regarding low achievers who need special help and regarding high achieving students with a need for a change and who are constantly hungered for something new and challenging,

OLC as Proactive and Collaborative Partnerships

Both, the teachers/instructors and the students, who are members of this learning forum and who are actively involved in the discussion, debates and interaction, creating, processing and sharing knowledge are in fact in a partnership-relationship more than the ordinary learning process directed from the teacher in class to the students. This partnership-relationship, which indicates equality in roles played by both parties, serves them equally. This equation, for the teacher, helps he/she make sure that his/her learning objectives with the students have been satisfactorily achieved, and for the students, to have successfully learned the required knowledge and associated skill.

The two words: proactive and collaborative describe exactly the nature of interaction between teachers and students in the 'Online Learning Community' OLC forum. The forum turned out to be a convenient and suitable platform to measure how much knowledge students acquire in the class time and if whether the planned learning objectives of the relevant class have been accomplished.. The forum provides the teacher with indicators of the adequacy level of skills and/or knowledge attained by students in order to resort to a suitable technique or by taking suitable corrective actions, or to define additional help that may be needed to overcome difficulties that students may be facing in understanding, appreciating or applying the knowledge points.

By frequently analyzing students' online contribution, interactions, and assessing their progress and performance, the teacher was able to understand the issues and to decide the most suitable action to address these issues and reflect appropriate actions on daily, weekly and semester planning.

The teacher has often sneaked homework without them being conscious about it because they mainly see what I ask them to do as something fun to do, and not as boring homework.

Another positive gain from the using the 'Online Learning Community' is the fact that students and teachers are kept connected together and some kind of bonding has grown between the members of the forum and that has reflected a growing improvement of the class relationships between the students themselves.

OLC Main Challenges

Having discussed some of the positive gains that have culminated from using the Online Learning Communities forum to support traditional classes and enhance students learning and performance, it is important however to highlight that the venture was not problem-free. In fact major challenges one of the main challenges was to gain management and school administration sponsorship and financial support, which included deploying hardware and network infrastructure within the school, as well as investing in fast high-band Internet connection and web-development and support.

Another important challenge was related to some parents' resistance to have their children participate in this unconventional method as they were not able to fully understand the purpose behind the 'Online Learning Community'. Some parents did not only believe in playing by the book in that students should be taught in traditional classroom style, from text book, but also had a negative view to the Internet and associated it with time wasting. Fortunately, some of these parents were more positive after exerted efforts by the teacher to explain the education value of the experience and that it would complement rather than replace the traditional class.

An important internal challenge was related to individual differences that students have demonstrated in coping with using technology, let alone, learning English remotely or through an online community.

CONCLUSION

The experience of creating and using an 'Online Learning Communities' forum to enable students to learn from each other through a community of interest was successful. The sense of individuality of learning that the learning community provided for students cannot be overestimated and justifies the exerted efforts and committed resources. The progress in students' performance and achievement in addition to some social skills was visible. The online community has also enhanced student-to-student or peer-to-peer interaction.

I conclude this chapter with this statement "Communication with my students is the winning prize of the online learning community."

REFERENCES

Altahuser, R., & Matuga, J. M. (1998). *On the pedagogy of electronic instruction. Electronic Collaborators: Learner-Centered Technologies for Literacy.* Apprenticeship, and Discourse.

Baker, P., & Moss, K. (1996). Building learning communities through guided participation. *Primary Voices, 4*(2), 2–6.

Bauman, M. (1997). *Online learning communities.* Paper presented at the Teaching in the Community Colleges Online Conference.

Carnoy, M. (2005). ICT in education: Possibilities and challenges. Universitat Oberta de Catalunya, 2005.

Cherifi, H., Zain, M. J., & El-Qawasmeh, E. (2011). *Digital information and communication technology and its applications, part 2.* DICTAP 2011.

Cragg, P. B., & Zinateli, N. (1995). The evolution of information systems in small firms. *Information & Management, 29,* 1–8. doi:10.1016/0378-7206(95)00012-L

Davis, G. B., Lee, A. S., Nickles, K. R., Chatterjee, S., Hartung, R., & Wu, Y. (1992). Diagnosis of an information system failure–A framework and interpretive process. *Information & Management, 23,* 293–318. doi:10.1016/0378-7206(92)90059-O

Ewusi-Mensah, K., & Przasnyski, Z. H. (1991). On information systems project abandonment: An exploratory study of organizational practices. *Management Information Systems Quarterly, 15*(1), 67–86. doi:10.2307/249437

Haythornthwaite, C., Kazmer, M., Robins, J., & Shoemaker, S. (2000). *Making connections: Community among computer-supported distance learners.* Paper presented at the ALISE 2000, San Antonio, TX.

Hill, J. R., & Raven, A. (2000). *Creating and implementing web-based instruction environments for community building.* Paper presented at the AECT, Denver.

IDE. (2000). An emerging set of guiding principles and practices for the design and development of distance education. *IDE: Innovations in Distance Education.* Retrieved March 9, 1999, from http://www.outreach.psu.edu/de/ide/guiding_principles/

Johnson, D. W., & Johnson, R. T. (1996). Cooperation and the use of technology. In Jonassen, D. H. (Ed.), *Handbook of research for educational communications and technology.* New York, NY: Macmillan Library Reference.

Kim, A. J. (2000). *Community building on the Web.* Berkeley, CA: Peachpit Press.

Lederer, A. L., & Nath, R. (1991). Managing organizational issues in information systems development. *Journal of Systems Management,* November, 23-39.

Sharma, M. (2008). *Elgg social networking.* Birmingham, UK: Packt Publishing Ltd.

Spraul, V. A. (2005). *Computer science made simple.* New York, NY: Broadway Books.

Stevenson, D. (1997). *The independent ICT in schools commission – Information and communication technology in UK schools, an independent enquiry.* London, UK.

Wenger, E. (1998). *Communities of practice: Learning, meaning, and identity.* Cambridge, UK: Cambridge University Press.

Wilson, B., & Ryder, M. (1996). *Dynamic learning communities: An alternative to designed instructional systems*. (ED397847).

Yaverbaum, G. J., & Ocker, R. J. (1998). *Problem-solving in the virtual classroom: A study of student perceptions related to collaborative learning techniques*. WebNet 1998 World Conference of the WWW, Internet and Intranet, Orlando, FL.

KEY TERMS AND DEFINITIONS

Blogs: A blog or a weblog is, literally, a "log" on the Web. A blog is a diary-style site, in which the author called the "blogger" writes content that is displayed in reverse chronological order.

Technorati, a blog search engine, tracks more than 50 million blogs.

FTP (File Transfer Protocol): Allows user to move a file from one computer to another on the internet.

Telnet: Allows user to log in to another computer somewhere on the internet.

Usenet News: Allows group of users to exchange their views, ideas and information.

Web 2.0: The term Web 2.0, coined by O'Reilly media in 2004, isn't a technology update to the Internet, but rather refers to the so-called second generation of web-based services that encourages reader-participation.

Chapter 21
A Low–Cost Learning Object Repository for Egyptian Teachers

Alaa Sadik
South Valley University, Egypt

ABSTRACT

Within the last five years, governments and education authorities worldwide have developed and implemented approaches to facilitate access to a wide range of quality digital resources and reduce the costs of production. This chapter reports on a study which invited school teachers and university academics in Egypt, as a developing and Arabic-speaking country, to cooperate in establishing a learning object repository to store, locate, and share quality learning objects for class teaching and e-learning programs. The proposed solution is originally a vendor hosted web-based groupware, file management, and sharing system that meets the basic criteria of instructional learning object repositories called eStudio. Motivators and inhibitors to using the repository, factors that determine locating, using, and sharing learning objects within the repository and their qualities are assessed to help in developing repositories that demonstrate an understanding of the existing needs and the work practices of Egyptian teachers and other user groups.

INTRODUCTION

The main problems that have been facing education authorities in developing countries are over-crowded classrooms, test-driven curriculum focusing on rote memorization of unimportant material, lack of equipment, and a shortage of financial resources (Jarrar and Massialas, 1992; Tawila et al., 2000). In Egypt, there is currently a strong emphasis on systemic reform in educa-tion at all levels. This development is encouraging stakeholders to collaborate in supporting the achievement of high standards in the schools. Like many education authorities around the world, the Ministry of Education (MOE) has seized on technology as a way to better prepare students and help teachers in achieving their objectives. A special unit within the MOE, called the Technology Development Center, was formed to coordinate the MOE's effort to infuse technology into schools (Warschauer, 2004). According to MOE, infusion of technology implies development in

DOI: 10.4018/978-1-4666-1984-5.ch021

improving the performance of students, arranging of information, and increasing the capacities of information exchange.

As a result, teachers face the need to improve learning by providing new means for presenting curriculum materials, illustrate concepts that are less easily explained through traditional media, support new types of learning opportunities, and provide enrichment activities for students whether it is in a classroom or through e-learning environments. One of these new means is learning objects.

Learning objects differ from conventional learning materials in that they use a variety of media sources including text, graphics, audio, and video (Muirhead and Haughey, 2005). Learning objects are essentially the digital resources (e.g., audio, photos, graphics, animations, video, Word/PDF documents, HTML pages, Java applets, and interactive exercises) that are designed to generate and support learning activities and enrich learners' experiences (Richards, et al., 2002).

Within the last five years, institutions and academics have developed approaches to facilitate access to a wide range of learning objects to support teaching across the curriculum. Suthers (2000) believes that this interest is motivated in large part by the desire to be able to find and reuse the work of others. Institutions (such as Institute of Electrical and Electronics Engineers or IEEE) have developed standards for learning object packaging.

Although learning objects could be reused in many instructional contexts, much of this investment is used for specific audiences and remains unknown beyond the immediate developers and consumers (Richards, et al., 2002). Wiley (2002) indicates that learning objects are generally deliverable over the Internet, meaning that teachers can access and use them anywhere and simultaneously (as opposed to traditional media, such as maps or videotapes, which can only exist in one place at a time). Moreover, teachers can collaborate on and benefit immediately from new versions. LORs provide faculty, teachers, curriculum developers, and students with easy access to a large storehouse of learning objects that can be shared and used within and across universities and schools (SREB, 2005).

According to JORUM (2004), it could be argued that a repository, at its core, is only a database of objects, with import and export interfaces. However, there is a distinction to be made in LORs between the database (that holds the metadata and objects) and the tools that are used to interact with this database (by searching, downloading, importing, etc.). A review of existing learning object repositories reveals that a repository is essentially a file storage system that has a form of control over the quality of the files (learning objects) to classify and store them using metadata, a searchable database to categorise and locate learning objects, an easy-to-use mechanism for uploading, updating, retrieving, and exchanging learning objects and an appropriate technical infrastructure, including software (e.g., database, and security system) and hardware (e.g., server and telecommunication capabilities).

PROBLEM OF THE STUDY

Internet databases and search approaches widely used on the Web are proving inadequate for the location of high quality resources appropriate to specific learning contexts, levels, and styles (Richards, McGreal and Friesen, 2002). Research indicates many barriers to the selection of quality online resources that could be avoided through systems that easily encourage teachers to locate, store, share, and manage materials themselves. At the same time, although administrators and teachers are often concerned with the effort, time, and costs required to create and use quality learning materials, there is a lot of duplication in teachers' production of digital learning materials which could be reduced if they work together.

Although LORs are a worldwide phenomenon that have received significant funding and many countries are moving rapidly in repository research and development, particularly the United States, Canada, and Australia, they are still a new technology whose worth has yet to be proven, particularly for those in developing countries.

In Egypt, like many other developing countries, no attention is paid to help teachers store, access, and share quality digital learning objects so that they can be reused. Therefore, the need is emphasised to help Egyptian teachers to establish an easy-to-use, accessible, and low-cost repository of learning objects and evaluate its effectiveness. This system should be appropriate for teachers' needs and skills.

OBJECTIVE OF THE STUDY

This study aims to, firstly, provide an accessible on-line LOR to store and share accurate and high-quality learning objects appropriate for the Egyptian curriculum and teachers and evaluate its effectiveness. According to Wiley (2003), the various approaches to LORs attempt to meet two objectives: to reduce the overall costs of digital resources by reusing and sharing them, and to obtain better learning resources (Wiley, 2003). Using this repository, teachers can develop and store a significant number of meta-tagged, high-quality, classified, and relevant learning objects that would be immediately and easily used by teachers in classrooms or e-learning projects all across the country. Secondly, this study aims to investigate the type of learning objects teachers use and the circumstances surrounding their use, along with the factors that are likely to motivate and inhibit the use of the proposed repository.

QUESTIONS OF THE STUDY

Based on the above objectives, this study seeks to answer the following questions:

1. What are the features of the repository that facilitate locating and sharing learning objects?
2. What are the factors that determine locating and using learning objects within the repository?
3. What are the factors that motivate the sharing of learning objects within the repository?
4. What is the quality of learning objects located and shared within the repository, as ranked by teachers and according to evaluation criteria?

METHODOLOGY

Participants

The general population of this study is public school and university teachers, who range widely in terms of their knowledge and use of computers and the Internet for teaching purposes. Invitation letters and email messages were sent to 34 schools located at different areas, and 130 university academic staff at three universities in Egypt inviting them to participate in the repository project at two levels of involvement; user and advisor. The teachers and faculty from different subject areas were asked to visit the repository Web site and register with their names and e-mail addresses.

None of the participants were required to have experience with learning objects or online resources. Participation in the study was voluntary and they were guaranteed confidentiality of responses. The only criterion for selection was that they indicated an interest in using learning objects for instruction. In February 2006, an e-mail message was sent to 72 teachers and faculty confirming that they have been accepted as members in the project.

Procedures of Implementation

A three-stage methodology was adopted in this study. The first stage was one of orientation and discussion to identify issues and teachers' needs, the second stage was implementing the repository in reality, and the third stage was to consolidate participants' perceptions and examine their online activities throughout the repository.

At the beginning of the study, workshops were held with local participants and remote schools. Presentations about the concept of learning objects, classifying and using learning objects, the applicability of learning objects to current teaching contexts and LORs, and their advantages were provided. In addition, more detailed information about the design and use of the proposed repository was handled and an open discussion forum was established. The workshops emphasised the importance of co-operation among teachers for the success of the project.

The purpose of the implementation is to supply information on how the repository functions in reality and its effectiveness in achieving its objectives. In addition, evaluation focused on teachers' behaviours during and at the end of the implementation and their perceptions toward the functionality of the repository. Repository technology also allowed the present study to investigate the extent to which teachers participated in the repository by uploading, downloading, searching, and sharing learning objects, the quality of objects, and the reality of collaboration among participants. Issues arising from the implementation stage were explored further through quantitative and qualitative methods, using the instruments below.

Description of the Repository

To offer an LOR for Egyptian teachers, therefore, there is a need to install and run a commercial LOR system or develop an LOR system. However, a review of the literature and LOR systems indicated that the majority of LOR systems available were developed for large organisations or higher education levels and need advanced and expensive technical requirements which are not usually available at school-level in Egypt. In addition, many appropriate LORs are found based on project-based funding and their sustainability is not guaranteed.

Also, although new programming tools (like .NET and SQL Server) and networking solutions make web-based and database development easier than ever and allow full control over the LOR, designing and implementing a project of this magnitude requires much effort, needs an appropriate technical infrastructure, and needs trained staff to ensure security and maintain the system, all of which represent significant costs.

However, within the last five years, web-based groupware file storage and document management services have grown rapidly. Currently, the number of groupware file storage and management service providers is estimated at more than ten (for example, FilesAnywhere, Xdrive, TeamSpace, Same-Page, etc.). Many of these services have been reviewed and tested for the purposes of this study based on the above description and features of LORs (accessibility, ease of use, metadata support, search techniques, file sharing, user management, collaboration support etc.), and in light of the current objectives and needs. These services have varied in their features and costs. Therefore, the proposed solution in this study is to subscribe to a commercial online file storage and management service that provides access to an online database where a groupware can store, access, and share files.

One of these services that was found to be appropriate for the purposes of this study, and also met the above needs and criteria, is Same-Page eStudio (www.same-page.com). eStudio is a web-based collaborative system for project and document management and sharing that facilitates workflow and communication between workgroups and does not require an IT department to maintain. One of the main features of eStudio is called WorkSpace (Figure 1). WorkSpace is an online file sharing tool that allows users to upload, download, review, comment on, describe, and share files and URLs that are stored on eStudio projects. WorkSpace is ideal for teams of users, from 2 up to 500 users, who need from 500MB to 120GB of combined file space.

Files in the WorkSpace are organised by a Windows Explorer type tree folder system. Each folder (and any folders inside a folder) can be restricted so that only specified users can access and modify the contents of a folder. The WorkSpace is navigated by the clicking on buttons and directories. The buttons enable the user to do many common tasks, such as adding a file/folder, changing a file/folder options, delete a file/folder, and edit file/folder proprieties. In addition, one of the most useful features of the system is the inclusion of an efficient and easy-to-use search function for locating objects.

Metadata can be attached to each file allowing others to review, comment on, approve or disapprove files. If Users that review and approve a file post a comment, the comment is displayed under the file and a new link labeled "Reply" is added. "Reply" is used for encouraging further dialogue about that Comment. If a user wants to Comment about another aspect of the file, they can start a

Figure 1. eStudio WorkSpace for file management and sharing

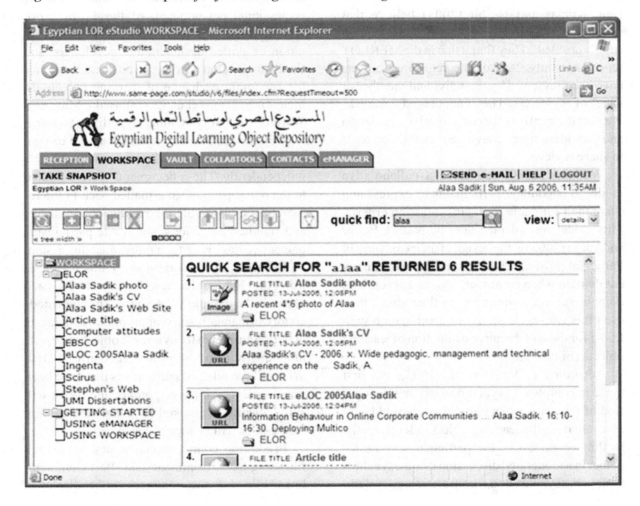

"New Comment". When all the users that have been asked to review it have approved the file, it will automatically be marked as "Final" and the file icon color will change to Green.

The e-Studio administrator has full control over eStudio for things such as creating, editing, and deleting user groups, monitoring users' logs, and controlling user access to files. Therefore, Same-page eStudio service is chosen to establish and implement a learning object repository for Egyptian teachers and evaluate its effectiveness. The repository address is: http://www.freewebs.com/edlor.

Procedures of Evaluation of Learning Objects

Han, Kumar and Nesbit (2003) believe that evaluation of learning objects usually faces a supply problem. They found that in the MERLOT repository, only 28% of the registered objects have been reviewed by an individual member or panel of reviewers. They encouraged establishing social incentives for collaborative evaluation and providing more convenient evaluation tools to share reviews.

Williams (2000) suggested a collaborative model to encourage participants to express and share their rationale for their evaluation criteria. This model was adapted later by Nesbit, Belfer and Vargo (2002) in the design of their Convergent Participation Model, which could apply to a different domain when combined with an appropriate, domain-specific instrument. In their study, they used this two-cycle model in combination with LORI for the collaborative evaluation of learning objects (Figure 2).

According to Vargo et al. (2003), the first cycle is completed asynchronously within a period of few days when participants would begin by evaluating the learning object independently. In the second cycle, the participants come together in a moderated discussion using a synchronous or asynchronous conferencing system.

During the discussion, participants adjust their individual evaluation in response to the arguments presented by others. At the end of the discussion, the moderator seeks consent of the participants to publish a team review synthesized from the mean ratings and aggregated comments. According to Krauss and Ally (2005), this model would be valuable for the participants as they would be able to learn more about the process of selecting and using learning objects by being exposed to the rationales of others.

Nesbit, Belfer and Vargo (2002) identified many reasons for developing this evaluation approach: to help individual users in searching for and selecting objects, to provide guidance on how best to use an object, to drive the practices of designers and developers, to contribute to the professional development of those who work with learning objects, to promote social recognition of skilled designers and developers, and finally to develop a workable business model for the economic exchange of learning objects. In their study, Vargo et al. (2003) used a Microsoft Word document containing hyperlinks to learning objects and LORI, with data capture using a Microsoft Excel spread-sheet to assess objects independently. These documents were e-mailed to the participants, then e-mailed back to the researchers to assemble the results, obtain means and standard deviations, and invite participants one or two days later for a moderated discussion.

However, in the current study this was done using the 'Request Review' link attached to each object in the eStudio WorkSpace. The team moderator can manually select appropriate participants or define an eTeam to review the object or objects individually using an online version of LORI. When all the selected participants that have been asked to review it have approved the file, it will automatically be marked as 'Final' and the file icon colour will change to green.

In addition, comments can be attached to each file using 'New Comment' and 'Post Comment' links, allowing the comment to be displayed

Figure 2. Convergent participation with LORI (Nesbit, Belfer, and Vargo, 2002)

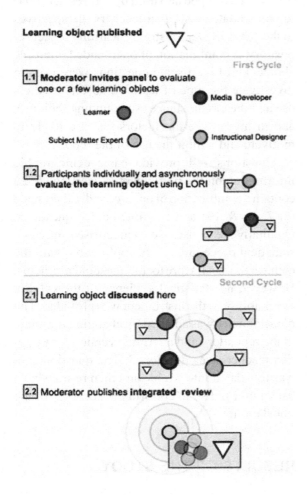

under the object and a new link labelled 'Reply' to be added. Other participants are asked to review comments attached to each file and click on 'Reply' link to commence or continue a threaded asynchronous dialogue about that comment. In addition, 'Continue Thread' is used if a participant wants to add another comment related to that subject. 'New Comment' link is used again if a participant wants to comment about another aspect of the object not mentioned in the thread or compare and discuss their evaluations. Lastly, team members can edit their ratings and comments

during the session based on others' comments and discussions.

When the collaborative evaluation session is completed, the moderator posts a final aggregated comment and checks the 'Sign Out' box which means that other participants will not be able to modify this object or delete it in the future. Moreover, the moderator could mark an object as 'Approved and Final' if he/she does not need other users to review or add their comments.

Learning Objects Instruments

1. Learning Objects Review Instrument (LORI)

The need to establish a learning object repository requires criteria to help teachers submit and assess learning objects. These criteria are essential to ensure the quality of resources and maintain the repository. Vargo et al. (2003) developed a Learning Object Review Instrument (LORI 1.3) to evaluate learning objects. The LORI 1.3 uses ten measures to examine learning objects: (1) Presentation: aesthetics; (2) Presentation: design for learning; (3) Accuracy of content; (4) Support for learning goals; (5) Motivation; (6) Interaction: usability; (7) Interaction: feedback and adaptation; (8) Reusability; (9) Metadata and interoperability compliance; and (10) Accessibility.

A descriptive rubric is provided for each level, each measure is weighted equally and rated using a Likert-style five-point response scale, and the items are scored by the following key: Perfect=5, Strong=4, Moderate=3, Weak=2, and Absent=1. Using a two-phase evaluation approach, a participant can first use LORI to rate and comment on the quality of a learning object individually, and then collaborate with a team of evaluators, who have their individual reviews, to create and publish a collaborative LORI review.

A formative reliability analysis revealed that when the ratings of 10 evaluators were averaged, three items showed reliability above .90, three items showed reliability between .80 and .90, two items showed reliability between .70 and .80, and the reliability of two items could not be measured. Vargo et al. (2003) found that learning objects that were evaluated collaboratively led to greater inter-rater reliability as opposed to ones evaluated individually. Vargo et al. (2003) provided evidence that LORI can be used to reliably assess some aspects of learning objects, and that using a collaborative assessment process can improve inter-rater reliability.

Consequently, LORI 1.3 was developed to LORI 1.5 (Nesbit et al., 2003). LORI 1.5 is the result of a revision process that used findings from the reliability study to simplify rubrics and improve the reliability of all items. LORI 1.5 uses only 9 items, with short descriptive rubrics associated to each item and Likert-style five-point response scale, and the items are scored from low (1) to high (5). If an item is judged not relevant to the learning object, or if the reviewer does not feel qualified to judge that criterion, then the reviewer may opt out of the item by selecting 'not applicable'.

Although other approaches were suggested to help reviewers assess learning objects submitted by faculty (for example, Merlot and the CLOE), they adopted criteria and standards based on those developed by Vargo et al. (2003). LORI 1.5 is used in this study to help participants and the researcher to assess the quality of learning objects posted and shared by participants through the repository. To make LORI 1.5 available to the intended users, the instruments were translated into Arabic and then re-translated back into English to confirm the accuracy of the translation.

2. Design and Functionality of the Repository Evaluation Questionnaire (DFREQ)

A principal aim of this study is to investigate participants' perspectives to the design and functionality of the proposed learning object repository.

An online questionnaire adapted for this purpose was first developed and used by Woo et al. (2004) to consolidate Australian teachers' perspectives to the 'COLIS Demonstrator' learning object repository. A combination of open-ended, multiple choice, and Likert scale questions were used to investigate the type of learning objects teachers use and the circumstances surrounding their use, and to investigate the factors that are likely to motivate and inhibit the use of the repository.

Questions 1–4 provide basic demographic information on the participants. Questions 5–26 contain a combination of open-ended, Likert scale (6, 7, 15 & 19) and multiple-choice questions. Qualitative responses were categorised and basic statistical procedures were applied to obtain the count or the mean score for the questionnaire items. However, no statistical evidence of the validity or reliability of the instrument was provided. The questionnaire was adapted by changing the name of the repository and an Arabic version for Egyptian teachers was developed. The questionnaire was translated into Arabic and then re-translated back into English to confirm the accuracy of the translation.

RESULTS OF THE STUDY

The results are organised so it directly addresses the research questions.

Question 1: What are the features of the repository that facilitate locating and sharing learning objects?

Participants' responses to open-ended questions revealed that they found the ease of use (32%) and well-designed navigation hierarchy of the WorkSpace (29%), which organises and stores files by a Windows Explorer type-tree folder system are the most useful features of the repository that motivate them to locate objects. In addition, participants favour the potentional file management system (23%), allowing them to upload, download, copy, delete, rename, and edit learning objects easily, powerful search function, allowing them to easily locate suitable resources, ease of access anytime and anywhere (19%), compatibility with Web browsers (17%), user-friendly interface design (12%), and the potential user management services, which allow them to register quickly and easily, track others' activities, and receive notifications (9%).

In terms of cooperation and the sharing of learning objects, participants believe that the effective collaborative review functions are the most useful feature that allows them to ensure the quality of learning objects and use others' learning resources (40%). In addition, they indicated that the inclusion of easy-to-use asynchronous and synchronous interaction tools, called "CollabTools", (25%), the standard description system or metadata associated with each object (21%) and the clear indication of user rights (15%) are major factors that encourage them to share learning objects within the repository.

Question 2: What are the factors that determine the locating and using of learning objects within the repository?

To answer this question, participants were asked to indicate factors that they would take into consideration when they make decisions about searching, inclusion, and use of a particular learning object. The mean ranking is calculated on a five-point Likert scale, where 5 denotes 'Strongly Agree' and 1 denotes 'Strongly Disagree'. Responses of 'Not Applicable' and 'Strongly Disagree' are collapsed into a single category (Strongly Disagree) in the analysis of the results.

Based on participants' perspectives in the evaluation questionnaire, the majority of participants indicated that keywords, subject matter and learning objectives are the most important criteria that influence their decisions when they search for learning objects within the repository.

These three types of criteria listed in Table 1, in descending order of preference, scored a mean of 4.00 or above, indicating a strong preference of this type of criteria.

In addition, participants were asked to rank and identify the various information (metadata) they would take into consideration when they make decisions about the suitability of a particular learning object to their teaching context or choices between similar objects. Participants suggested that they would request information relating to the audiences, the teaching and learning objectives for which it was developed, a review provided by peers, and the technical requirements and instructions for using the object.

Table 2 shows the preferred information used for the selection of learning objects in descending order of preference. The first two types of information listed in the Table scored a mean above 4.00, indicating a strong preference for this type of information. However, life history of the object and a review provided by a curriculum authority did not score highly compared to other information participants would seek when choosing learning objects.

More specifically, when participants were asked to rank three technical factors that may influence their use of an object, they indicated that poor access to the technology required to use the learning object is the most important factor they consider when choosing an object, followed by the students' ability to access the object. However, a lack of confidence in their own technical skills was the factor least likely to influence their decisions, as shown below (Table 3).

Responses to open-ended questions concerning circumstances surrounding and affecting the inclusion and use of learning objects reported pedagogical circumstances and technical circumstances. The most cited circumstances, in descending order of preference, are quality of the content (53%), relevancy of the learning objectives (49%), ease of use (42%), ease of modification to specific group of learners (42%), clarity of the lan-

Table 1. Preferred search criteria (N=65)

Search criteria	SA & A	Mean	StdDev
Keyword	43	4.45	0.49
Subject	39	4.13	0.64
Outcomes/ Competencies	37	4.00	0.83
Media type	34	3.82	1.02
Sector	33	3.73	1.29
Syllabus requirements	31	3.65	0.77
Creator(s)	27	2.43	0.89
Institution of Creator(s)	24	2.38	0.79
State/ Country	23	2.24	0.97

guage (31%), interactivity of the object (23%), identification of pre-requisites (19%), availability of hardware and software (16%), and user-friendliness (13%).

Question 3: What are the factors that motivate the sharing of learning objects within the repository?

The findings from the questionnaire revealed that the motivation to share learning objects with other users is dampened by a number of factors. The majority of participants believe that recognition is the most important issue that encourages them to share their learning objects. In addition,

participants indicated that they would be inclined to share their objects if they knew more information about how copyright and intellectual property issues affected their rights.

However, misuse of learning objects by other teachers or uncertainty about their applicability to others' teaching contexts are not significant factors that affect the culture of sharing. The minority of participants strongly agreed or agreed that they would be inclined to share only if they can receive payment for the use of objects they have created (Table 4).

Question 4: What is the quality of the learning objects located and shared within the repository, as ranked by teachers and according to evaluation criteria?

In evaluating learning objects using the Convergent Participation Model with LORI, each participant was first asked to review, rate and comment on at least three learning objects individually using the LORI scoring sheet. These objects should be uploaded by other participants, not by the evaluator him/herself. Results are presented as a set of averaged ratings, one per item, and summarized as a final average covering the

Table 2. Information used for the selection of learning objects (N=65)

Useful information	SA & A	Mean	StdDev
1. The student group for which it was developed (e.g., age, expertise, special needs).	48	4.19	0.84
2. The specific teaching aims and learning outcomes for which it was developed.	47	4.12	0.73
3. A review provided by my teaching peers.	40	3.92	0.71
4. Technical information such as hardware and software requirements, file size, download times.	39	3.86	1.11
5. The teaching and learning context associated with its use (e.g., its role, pre-requisite knowledge required, supporting materials).	39	3.81	1.07
6. A record of previous uses of the learning object.	33	3.74	0.77
7. Technical instructions for students on how to use the learning object (if applicable).	29	3.64	1.17
8. The life history of the object-details of creation, publication and last modification.	28	3.44	1.29
9. A review provided by a curriculum/syllabus authority.	25	3.15	0.88

Table 3. Technical issues considered in the selection of learning objects (N=65)

Technical information	SA & A	Mean	StdDev
1. Poor access to the technology required to use learning object.	49	4.38	1.14
2. Uncertainty about my students' access to reliable technology.	39	3.88	1.23
3. A lack of confidence in my own technical skills associated with using the required technology (e.g. classroom, lecture theatre).	30	3.42	1.03

nine items used in the evaluation of 61 different objects by 25 evaluators (Table 5).

Overall, the quantitative analysis of the LORI scoring sheets show that the learning objects stored within the repository are highly rated by participants. Participants' responses based on the LORI rating criteria indicate that objects rated perfect in the categories of motivation, interaction usability, and accessibility. It also rated strong in content quality, learning goal alignment, presentation design and reusability. However, feedback and adaptation and standards compliance received the lowest scores.

For example, in terms of motivation, participants' comments concluded that objects have many features that attract learners (such as inclusion of multimedia elements, interactivity, and reality) and minimizes teacher intervention mean learn-

ers are likely to show an interest in learning with the objects.

In terms of interaction usability, participants found that most learning objects show clear user-interface and effective navigations (e.g., clear indicators and back and forward buttons) that provide accessibility to all the learning object parts and help learners to interact with the object. In addition, the design of learning objects took into account the differences in users' hardware and software, allowing objects to be accessible without troubleshooting.

The majority of participants believe that most learning objects have accurate and well-presented content and appropriate learning goals for the intended learners. However, participants agreed that the majority of learning objects do not have the ability to deliver instruction or learning activities

Table 4. Factors determine sharing of learning objects (N=65)

Factors of sharing	SA & A	Mean	StdDev
1. I would be inclined to share if the user of my object acknowledges me as the object's author.	44	4.13	0.81
2. My uncertainty of how copyright, intellectual property and user rights will affect me as a creator makes me reluctant to share my learning objects.	39	3.88	0.89
3. I would not be inclined to share my learning objects if I have to undertake processes of copyright clearance by myself.	37	3.22	1.13
4. I would not share Learning objects if it meant I was given the responsibility for their maintenance and update.	34	3.17	1.03
5. I would not share learning objects I have created because of uncertainty about their quality in relation to content, technical or other factors.	29	2.76	0.92
6. I would not share learning objects I have created because of my uncertainty about their applicability to other teaching contexts.	26	2.66	0.84
7. I would not share my learning objects because of the potential misuse by other teachers.	28	2.66	0.88
8. I would be inclined to share only if I can receive payment for the use of an object I have created.	22	2.15	0.73

Table 5. Ratings of learning objects (N=28)

Item	1	2	3	4	5	Mean of rating	StdDev
1. Content quality				√		4.13	1.20
2. Learning goal alignment				√		4.32	0.86
3. Feedback and adaptation			√			3.25	0.93
4. Motivation					√	4.61	0.94
5. Presentation design				√		3.99	0.86
6. Interaction usability					√	4.27	1.25
7. Accessibility					√	4.76	1.17
8. Reusability				√		3.86	0.79
9. Standards compliance			√			3.43	0.86
Final Score				√		4.07	0.92

according to learners' needs or inputs. In addition, participants indicated that insufficient educational metadata is provided to describe learning objects to help them search and use learning objects appropriately.

DISCUSSION

Although the proposed repository is initially a web-based groupware for project management and file sharing that facilitates interaction between users and allows them to upload, download, review, share, and comment on files that are stored on the server, this system is found to be ideal for a team of teachers and satisfactory in terms of the locating and sharing of learning objects. The above findings highlight eleven key features that facilitate the manipulating and sharing of learning objects within the repository. The system provides easy-to-use components, simple navigation hierarchy, efficient file management system, powerful search facility, flexible access to learning objects, simple user-interface design, efficient user management service, collaborative review and comment tools, integrated interaction tools, easy-to-use meta-tagging tools, and clear user rights.

According to Woo et al. (2004), these features are the most important qualities for such a system to populate it and unite a community of users and should be used to guide the appropriate creation or establishment of repositories. In other words, a repository as a place to store learning objects is not enough. The system should be searchable and collaborative and support an efficient approach for meta-tagging, rights clearing, reviewing, evaluating, and sharing resources.

In terms of locating and using learning objects within the repository, it is noticed that participants usually prefer keyword and subject matter description, specified by the object creator or a reviewer, as the most important criteria when searching and choosing between learning objects, the same way that they search for traditional resources. In addition, participants indicated a strong need for pedagogical information related to the learners for which the object is developed and its teaching and learning objectives.

However, less attention is paid to other pedagogical and technical information (e.g., educational context, life history, media type, etc.). This issue emphasizes the importance of re-defining pedagogical metadata criteria that should be associated within the learning object, which remains an issue for further consideration (Muirhead and

Haughey, 2005), and highlights the need to encourage teachers to pay more attention to these types of specifications to help them find and use resources appropriately.

In terms of the sharing of learning objects, overall, participants declared positive attitudes toward the exchanging of learning objects. At the beginning of the implementation, teachers did not visualize how learning objects developed by them would be helpful to others. However, it is found that acknowledgement of a participant as an author of his/her object or the feeling of being a sender or an author is a greater incentive for sharing than other factors.

In addition, it is visible that the willingness of teachers to exchange learning objects improved as they developed personal communication with other participants of the same grades or subjects during collaborative evaluation sessions. For example, some teachers had a problem with finding Arabic-written objects that are suitable for their students. But the presence in asynchronous collaborative evaluation sessions made them come up with some solutions to help their colleagues.

Lastly, as the ultimate purpose of establishing the repository is to provide better access to quality resources to support learning outcomes, participants' perspectives to the quality and usefulness of learning objects is taken into account. Individual (peer-review) and group-based (collaborative) evaluations of learning objects provided important data related to the quality of the learning objects. Evaluation data shows that the repository facilitates access to quality learning objects created by participants from a wide range of sources. Without this quality, participants would find public search engines and web directories much better than the repository.

These objects are considered to be attractive, interactive, accessible and accurate, which are a key factor in resource efficiency and engaging the learner with materials (Thomas and Horne, 2004). According to Gosper et al. (2003), efficiency factors are the most influential factors to influence

teachers' re-use of learning objects. In particular, teachers are likely to use the objects because they are relevant to students and the requirements of the curriculum.

CONCLUSION

The proposed repository is a vendor hosted, web-based groupware, file management and sharing system that does not require a technical team to run and maintain the system. This repository is found to meet the basic criteria of instructional LORs and help Egyptian teachers to store, meta-tag, find, share, and assure the quality of learning objects in a collaborative environment. This system would be openly available on the web and accessible to any number of teachers. Although new programming tools and servers make web-based and database development easier than ever, designing a project of this magnitude still required much effort, particularly in a developing community of teachers.

While the proposed repository has accomplished the goals for which it was established, a learning object requires more than having access and the skills to use it. It requires commitment from teachers and administrators to maximise the efficiency and understanding of teachers' instructional and cultural needs in order to promote sharing with others.

Lastly, it will be important to discover factors influencing the actual level of use of the repository and to seek to implement strategies to maximise this level of use. As more and more objects are added to the repository, it is hoped that the repository will grow and support the culture of sharing and re-using of learning objects in the community of Egyptian teachers. At this stage, it will be possible to tackle evidence-based research to assess the value and return-on-investment of learning object repositories.

REFERENCES

Gosper, M., Woo, K., Gibbs, D., Hand, T., Kerr, S., & Rich, D. (2003). *The selection and use of learning objects for teaching: Users perspectives. Interaction of IT systems & repositories project report*. Macquarie University & Open Training and Education Network.

Jarrar, A., & Massialas, G. (1992). Arab Republic of Egypt. In Cookson, J., Peter, W., Sadovnik, A., & Semel, S. (Eds.), *International handbook of educational reform* (pp. 149–167). New York, NY: Greenwood Press.

JORUM. (2004). *The JISC online repository for learning and teaching materials: JORUM scoping and technical appraisal study*. JORUM and the JISC Information Environment. Retrieved April 6, 2006, from http://www.jorum.ac.uk

Muirhead, B., & Haughey, M. (2005). *An assessment of the learning objects, models and frameworks developed by The Learning Federation Schools Online Curriculum Content Initiative Australia*. Adelaide, Australia: The Le@rning Federation.

Nesbit, J., Belfer, K., & Leacock, T. (2003). *Learning object review instrument (LORI 1.5): User manual, e-learning research and assessment network*.

Nesbit, J. C., Belfer, K., & Vargo, J. (2002). A convergent participation model for evaluation of LOs. *Canadian Journal of Learning and Technology, 28*(3), 105–120.

Richards, G., McGreal, R., & Friesen, N. (2002). *Learning object repository technologies for tele-learning: The evolution of POOL and CanCore*. InSITE-Where Parallels Intersect. Retrieved December 22, 2005, from http://www.informingscience.org

Richards, G., McGreal, R., Hatala, M., & Friesen, N. (2002). The evolution of learning object repository: Technologies: Portals for On-line objects for learning. *Journal of Distance Education, 17*(3), 67–79.

SREB. (2005). *Principles of effective learning objects guidelines for development and use of learning objects for the SCORE Initiative of the Southern Regional Education Board*. Atlanta, GA: Southern Regional Education Board (SREB).

Suthers, D. (2000). Using learning object metadata in a database of primary and secondary school resources. *Proceedings of the International Conference on Computers in Education*, November 21-24, Taipei, Taiwan.

Tawila, S., Lloyd, B., Bensch, S., & Wassef, H. (2000). *The school environment in Egypt: A situational analysis of public preparatory schools*. Cairo, Egypt: Population Council.

Thomas, G., & Horne, M. (2004). *Using ICT to share the tools of the teaching trade: A report on open source teaching. British Educational Communications and Technology Agency*. Coventry, UK: BECTA.

Vargo, J., Nesbit, J. C., Belfer, K., & Archambault, A. (2003). Learning object evaluation: Computer mediated collaboration and inter-rater reliability. *International Journal of Computers and Applications, 25*(3), 198–205.

Warschauer, M. (2004). *The rhetoric and reality of aid: Promoting educational technology in Egypt.*

Wiley, D. (2000). Connecting learning objects to instructional design theory: A definition, a metaphor, and a taxonomy. In D. Wiley (Ed.), *The instructional use of learning objects*. Retrieved November 21, 2005, from http://reusability.org/read/chapters/wiley.doc

Wiley, D. (2003). *Learning objects: Difficulties and opportunities*. Retrieved March 13, 2006, from http://wiley.ed.usu.edu/docs/lo_do.pdf

Woo, K., Gosper, M., Gibbs, D., Hand, T., Kerr, S., & Rich, D. (2004). *User perspectives on learning object systems*. The Tenth Australian World Wide Web Conference, SeaWorld Nara Resort, Gold Coast, 3-7 July.

ADDITIONAL READING

Gruber, T. (1995). Toward principles for the design of ontologies used for knowledge sharing. *International Journal of Human-Computer Studies, 43*(5/6), 907–928. doi:10.1006/ijhc.1995.1081

Harman, K., & Koohang, A. (2005). Discussion board: A learning object. *Interdisciplinary Journal of Knowledge and Learning Objects, 1,* 67-77. Retrieved from http://www.ijklo.org/Volume1/v1p067-077Harman.pdf

Jackson, C., & Mogg, R. (2007). The information literacy resource bank: Re-purposing the wheel. *Journal of Information Literacy, 1*(1), 49–53.

Keown, R. (2007). Learning objects. *Distance Learning, 4*(4), 73–77.

Li, Q. (2004). Knowledge building community: Keys for using online forums. *TechTrends: Linking Research & Practice to Improve Learning, 48*(4), 24-28, 70.

Nesbit, J. C., Belfer, K., & Vargo, J. (2002). A convergent participation model for evaluation of LOs. *Canadian Journal of Learning and Technology, 28*(3), 105–120.

Wiley, D. A., & Edwards, E. K. (2002). Online self-organizing social systems: The decentralized future of online learning. *Quarterly Review of Distance Education, 3*(1), 33–46.

KEY TERMS AND DEFINITIONS

Accessibility: Is a general term used to describe the degree to which a product, device, service, or environment is available to as many people as possible. Accessibility can be viewed as the ability to access and benefit from some system or entity.

Content Quality: Refers to the usefulness, relevance, clarity, accuracy, influence, engagement, completeness, voice, style, and usability of materials used in teaching and learning.

Cost-Effectiveness Analysis (CEA): Is a form of economic analysis that compares the relative costs and outcomes (effects) of two or more courses of action.

Intellectual Property: Is any innovation, commercial or artistic, or any unique name, symbol, logo or design used commercially.

Learning Object Repository: Is a kind of digital library that enables educators and students to upload, share, manage and use educational resources.

Learning Objects: Are the digital resources (e.g., audio, photos, graphics, animations, video, Word/PDF documents, HTML pages, Java applets, and interactive exercises) that are designed to generate and support learning activities and enrich learners' experiences (Richards, et al., 2002).

Media: Are the storage and transmission channels or tools used to store and deliver information or data. Text, image, audio, and video are different types of media used in teaching and learning.

Reusability: In multimedia and learning objects, reusability refers to the ability to re-use the learning objects again and again by teachers and students with the possibility to modify or adapt the content.

Chapter 22
Teaching Enterprise Information Systems in the United Arab Emirates

Tony Jewels
American University in the Emirates, UAE

ABSTRACT

Although the notion of an enterprise information system (EIS) has been around now for several decades, there appears still to be a general lack of understanding within various sections of higher education over the true nature of these systems and subsequently how they should be presented to students. Although the topic itself is currently a hot one, with potential employers around the globe eagerly seeking new graduates versed in various aspects of EIS, this apparent lack of understanding has the potential to translate into courses or curricula that may not provide the most appropriate graduate skill sets. This chapter discusses how one university in the United Arab Emirates is addressing this issue by providing a curriculum and courses that set out to develop local graduates that will be highly valued by organisations seeking to extract full value from their own EIS's.

INTRODUCTION

The terms Enterprise Information System (EIS), Enterprise System (ES), Enterprise Wide System (EWS) and Enterprise Resource Planning (ERP) have at various times, been used synonymously to describe a similar phenomenon. These systems have become the de facto standard for large and medium organisations to run their major functional and process operations, being described by Kumar & Van Hillegersberg, (2000) as merely the price of entry for running a business.

Aloini, Dulmin, & Mininno, (2007) describe an ERP implementation not merely as just another computer project, but as a strategic tool which must be approached as such, (p559). ERP systems are, in effect, information systems that enable organisations to make decisions from the

DOI: 10.4018/978-1-4666-1984-5.ch022

principle perspective of the enterprise, rather than from a principle perspective of a single or group of departments belonging to that organisation. Evans, (1997) once defined them as systems having *one* database, one application, and one user interface for the entire enterprise. He went on to say that where once disparate systems ruled manufacturing, distribution, finance and sales, it is a tool that takes information from every function, assisting employees and manager's plan, monitor and control the entire business. The term Enterprise Information Systems (EIS) will be predominantly used in this chapter, as it describes best what the author believes represents the raison d'être of this phenomenon — a system designed to enable information to flow throughout an enterprise.

There remains some debate throughout academia as to whether the subject of enterprise systems is best delivered by business colleges adopting an information technology perspective or information technology colleges adopting a business perspective. Indeed, within the United Arab Emirates (UAE) of the two principle national universities, one delivers the topic through its Faculty of Business & Economics within a management information systems degree while the other delivers it through its College of Information Technology within an enterprise computing major of an information technology degree. Teaching enterprise systems does require that elements of both business and information technology be addressed, so it is reasonable to expect that any business or information technology college would be capable of delivering their own particular version of an EIS curriculum. Implementations of various types of enterprise system often requires significant alterations in the way that things are done and as such may cause major changes in employees' work lives, (Bala, 2008). They have been described by Stewart, Milford, Jewels, Hunter, & Hunter, (2000, p967) as technology diffusions through social systems, and as such are always likely to be significant interventions in organisational life, (Stewart, 2001). The teach-

ing of any type of modern information system, and particularly for enterprise systems, a social psychology perspective needs also to be added to the technology and business perspectives. It is however how these three perspectives interact with each other that is likely to provide the most useful outcomes for EIS students. This chapter will describe how one university in the UAE has developed its courses and curriculum to prepare its graduates to contribute within enterprise computing environments.

A STRATEGIC PERSPECTIVE

In an era of economic rationality, few universities, if any, throughout the world have been able to avoid the reality of addressing the issue of matching economic imperatives with academic initiatives. As such, academic faculty may not always be able to provide what they consider to be ideal curriculums because of limited budgets or conflicting demands for resource funding. Initiatives that are undertaken with the best of intentions by those charged with the responsibility of creating ideal curricula that best meet the needs of the student, industry and society generally, often find that practical considerations and administrative constraints will force changes to their original plans. If, for example, a new curriculum requires that a topic be covered that is outside the scope of any existing faculty member it is an economically attractive option to modify the ideal curriculum by replacing that topic with something that an existing faculty is an expert in. At any given time therefore any curriculum may not always represent the ideal but more one that reflects the constraints of the presenting organisation. As Maslow, (1965) once pointed out, for a man with a hammer every problem is a nail.

The whole concept of an enterprise system, which needs to be at the heart of teaching EIS is, in practice, alien to many higher education institutions. Seldom, do individual universities, colleges or faculties collaborate openly with each other to offer an enterprise (university or educational system) solution. As an example, in 2005, academics from the Australian university where the author had worked at that time, a key note paper entitled 'ICT & Curriculum Design to Bridge the Gap between Industry and Academia' was published. Ironically, even though the topic directly related to ICT, there was absolutely no-one involved from its own IT faculty.

An enterprise solution to the problem of limited resources would be to look beyond the boundaries of a single or group of departments belonging to an organisation (as described in the introductory paragraph). In reality, in order for themselves to adopt enterprise solution principles into practice, universities might have to more seriously look at curricula solutions involving more than a single college or faculty, and administrators might more seriously look at providing courses from more than one university. This after all is the very essence of an enterprise system and would move presenting organisations from a 'talk the talk' to a 'walk the talk' situation.

Universities throughout the world have long embraced a concept of 'shared governance' when responding to the economic, social and technological forces that are now challenging the very nature of what we have traditionally considered the role of 'higher education' institutions. Individual university's choices of how curricula is constructed, the topics taught, the quality of teaching, infrastructures and administrative frameworks and a myriad of other management decisions, are already partially the product of some form of external overseeing, possibly having no academic or pedagogical base. In a period of unprecedented rates of change and subsequent changing expectations, successful universities are likely to be the ones that can respond and react most appropriately to such external demands. The balancing act of interpreting inputs from industry and government (as two of the main external overseers) with the realities of modern academia would seem to be

of critical importance in creating curricula and courses that are able to produce industry savvy graduates.

The practical reality of curriculum design must therefore be considered a function of academic, industry and social (through government) perspectives. A recently introduced Enterprise Computing major in the Bachelor of IT degree of one of the UAE's national university's has been carefully constructed using input from a variety of external sources as well as the internal expertise from existing faculty members. Currently the topic is available only at an undergraduate level at both the Dubai and Abu Dhabi campuses of its IT College though it is also currently designing a post-graduate Master's degree in the same subject area.

With a Master's degree specialisation in Enterprise Wide Systems, the Dubai campus convenor of the course has previously taught Enterprise Information Systems courses at both undergraduate and postgraduate levels within the UAE. His long industry experience with integrated information systems together with an academic background in Enterprise Computing has been used to flesh out an existing, carefully designed curriculum.

The Abu Dhabi campus convenor has taught Information Systems, Operations Management, and Enterprise Systems at the undergraduate and master levels for over twenty years in seven countries. He has developed, modified, and adapted courses over the years, as information systems and the instruction of information systems have evolved, and these programs are included in the Enterprise Computing program.

TECHNOLOGY, BUSINESS, AND SOCIAL PSYCHOLOGY

It was earlier stated that EIS posits at the nexus between technology, business and social psychology. Just what the most appropriate mix might be is likely to depend on the type of work that any graduating student is likely to be involved in, but it is obvious that for enterprise system specialists in particular there is a very real need to be conversant with all three areas.

An additional set of individual skills likely to contribute to any type of IT project success has been identified by Jewels & Ford, (2006). Their taxonomy included what they identified as specific work related skills and traits and those which they classified as adding value to the individual in every type of environment. They included interpersonal as well as personal characteristics while providing what they found to be the most desired values of a project team member, according to other project team members.

This taxonomy indicates that simply providing work environment specific skills, i.e. graduates who have high levels of subject application knowledge, is not enough. Work ready IT graduates must also have other qualities in order for them to effectively contribute to an organisation's goals. Although qualities cannot always be taught specifically, they can be embedded into the structures and pedagogies within existing subject matter courses. Overall, these conclusions confirm the earlier study by Lee, Trauth, & Farwell, (1995) who suggested that industry will demand a cadre of IS professionals with knowledge and skills in technology, business operations, management and interpersonal skills to effectively lead organiza-

tional integration and process engineering activities, (p314). Further, Barnett, (2007) contributes to this position when he states, "*In the contemporary world, as well as it being a means of acquiring high-level knowledge, understanding and skills, higher education should foster the development of human qualities and dispositions, of certain modes of being, appropriate to the twenty-first century*", (p29).

Technology

It might be reasonably assumed that any College of Information Technology version of an EIS program might be heavily biased towards the technology component, yet as with the Australian IT faculty from which the Dubai convenor originally came from, there is actually a surfeit of technology in the UAE curriculum. The changing nature of industry demands for IT graduates has been documented by Zweig et al., (2006) and generally forecasted a positive future for IT. Although this report in MISQ Executive suggested that the desired IT skill mix was shifting from technical to project management and business skills and that technical skills were increasingly being obtained from specialist third party providers with increased levels of external sourcing, a technical foundation was still considered as important.

Table 1. Taxonomy of desired personal qualities in project team members, (Jewels & Ford, 2006)

Area / Characteristics		Environment specific *examples*	Ubiquitous *examples*
Personal	skills	*application area skills*	*self-management*
	traits	*business aware*	*has a sense of humor*
Interpersonal	skills	*ability to supervise staff*	*good communication skills*
	traits	*thinks win-win*	*cooperative*
Values		*hard working*	*trustworthy*

The traditional technical skills such as programming, that were once taught by most IT Colleges, may no longer be the most appropriate technical skills for all modern IT graduates. However, an understanding of architectures, database design, systems analysis and the logic of programming are still necessary building blocks for developing all the various types of professional IT graduate, be it computer science, management information systems, network security or enterprise computing. The absence or downplaying of such technical skills in an enterprise systems environment might always result in less than optimal outcomes, or in cases such as the recent Queensland Health Department/payroll system fiasco an almost complete system failure, (Auditor-General of Queensland, 2010). In this particular case the practices and processes that are embedded within modern IT development projects, such as parallel testing and prototyping were almost totally absent, eventually leading to irretrievable system recovery. It is somewhat ironic that over a decade earlier the same SAP R/3 system when it was being introduced into Queensland Government was identified as being more of a 'technology swap' which had involved too much emphasis on its technology components, (Timbrell & Chan, 2003). It would seem then that an appropriate amount of emphasis on technology, not too much and not too little, is still vitally important for contributing to enterprise systems success.

Business

As business environments become increasingly competitive, I.S. professionals faced with more stringent pressures for resource allocation must search for more cost-effective ways to apply computer technologies to solve business problems and they must demonstrate to upper management that information technology investments will provide commensurate returns. According to Bancroft, Seip, & Sprengel, (1998) not only are the key benefits from ERP systems that of increased functionality and process improvement, but they provide more overall cost effective management of all IT resources. While once IT professionals might justifiably have been accused of adopting a '*build it, and they will come*' mentality, in today's highly competitive business environments there is now seldom the opportunity to provide IT centric applications in the hope that they may somehow be of business value. The alignment of IT with business objectives is of critical importance in an era where mutual respect must exist between business and IT functions. Enterprise solutions dull the distinction between these once two disparate functional areas and enterprise computing graduates must thus feel comfortable being in the area in which either business or IT graduates once dominated.

It might also be reasonably assumed that business graduates rather than IT graduates might be in a better position to appreciate the business aspects of EIS. There is some evidence to suggest that some of these required fundamental business perspectives are not only missing in many IT students but also missing in business students. Brady, Monk, & Wagner, (2001) raised a poignant issue when describing Brady's earlier failures teaching ERP students. Brady states that his own students initially viewed his SAP R/3 classes as merely tedious date-entry exercises and it was not until he addressed his faulty assumptions that this approach was corrected.

1. We assumed that all of our students understood how businesses and functional areas operate; in fact, many of our undergraduate students did not yet have a good grasp of how profit-making organizations operate.
2. We assumed that all of our students understood the problems inherent in unintegrated systems; in fact even most of our advanced undergraduate and MBA students did not truly grasp what goes on in real companies where people from different functional areas must work together to achieve company goals.

3. *We assumed that all of our students under-stood how an information system should help business managers make decisions; in fact some of our students did not understand this well.* (Brady et al., 2001, pvii)

As part of the 2011 Pacific Asia Conference on Information Systems (PACIS) a 'Teaching ERP' workshop attracted faculty from the whole Australasian region. The overwhelming message to emerge from this workshop was that regardless of whether EIS was being taught by a business or an IT college, most undergraduate students appeared to struggle with some of the business concepts that were fundamental in understanding and applying enterprise solutions. While ERP terms such as 'deeming' may be unfamiliar to many, simple terms such as 'accounts receivable', 'accounts payable' and 'sales credits' also needed to be explained to many undergraduate students before actual transaction processing in an ERP application would make sense.

Current undergraduates may not in fact have all the prior knowledge necessary, indicating to curriculum designers that these types of funda-mental business principles need to be specifically included in a prerequisite course if students are to make sense of any EIS application course.

Social Psychology

A wide body of evidence exists to indicate that organisational or corporate culture is critical to the success of most, if not all ERP implementations, with Markus, (1983) suggesting that no-one knows how many computer-based applications designed at great cost of time and money, are abandoned or expensively overhauled because they were un-enthusiastically received by their intended users. Research suggests that the most critical problems in implementing most information systems are not technical, but related to organizational and managerial issues. Thee full potential of IT can only be realized if an implementation is accompa-

nied with appropriate changes to the organization, business processes and human resource practices, (Jurison, 2002).

Many factors can produce user resistance to I.T. implementations and two different kinds of resistance can occur when IT conflicts with an organization's culture ...

- Implementation failure through an under-mining of the analysis and design process, leading to an underutilization of the system once implemented, or a sabotaging of the implemented system.
- Adaption of the IT during implementation or use so that any conflict with the existing culture is diminished. (Cooper, 1994)

Understanding why counter-implementation tactics might occur, and what to do about it, is a key factor in any information system implementa-tion but absolutely critical in large ERP systems. Conner & Prahalad, (1996) have suggested that for many firms, an ERP system is critical to ongoing operations of the company while possibly also representing their largest IT investment.

Enterprise information systems might be de-scribed merely as 'agents of change' for organisa-tions developing systems and business processes for the purpose of generating and maintaining com-petitive advantages in a marketplace. To harvest the potential benefits of an EIS implementation, organisations should still be prepared to generate incremental improvements but must also embrace the concept of radical redesign, more commonly known as business process re-engineering, (Ham-mer, 1990).

Sustained competitive advantages can thus bet-ter be realised by engaging in both incremental and radical innovative practices. While incremental improvements are likely to evolve from organi-sations that recognise continual improvement as a core component of their own quality assurance (QA) system, radical innovations are more likely to happen when certain cultural values are present within the organisation. Stewart et al's., (2000) description of an ERP system as '*technology diffusion through a social system*' highlights the social aspects that are inherent within such systems. It indicates why social psychology from the individual, group and organisational perspectives is an important component in understanding how to successfully manage enterprise systems.

TOPICS IN AN ENTERPRISE COMPUTING CURRICULUM

Once the idea that enterprise computing comprises of technology, business and social psychology concepts has been established, it becomes obvious that the topic cannot easily be taught by any one specialist section of a college, be they business or IT focused. The range of skills required to effectively provide work ready graduates for an enterprise computing environment would normally be beyond the teaching scope of one faculty member or even one group of faculty within any specialised area within a college. Although it is always possible to provide single courses that merely provide an overview, or sampling of an enterprise systems environment, to provide an effective enterprise computing specialisation degree it would normally be necessary for presenting organizations to 'walk the talk' by providing an enterprise solution themselves. This effectively means that unless a specialist enterprise computing department has already been established for the purpose, resources for teaching an enterprise computing curriculum should be drawn from multiple sources within existing specialist areas. It is entirely possible that these specialist skills may need to be drawn from beyond the presenting organisation's own faculty if they do not already exist internally.

Enterprise information systems normally involve a range of enterprise resource planning (ERP) functional applications that may include:

- Supply chain management (SCM),
- Customer relationship management (CRM) and
- Human resource management (HRM)

The successful implementation and ongoing maintenance of these systems demand specialist knowledge of project management (PM) practices and processes and the concept of having a system that enables information to be distributed throughout an enterprise requires an understanding of knowledge management (KM) principles.

The implementation of an EIS solution should always be looked upon not as the final step of an organization's information systems development but merely the starting point of a new one. In today's fast paced business environment, creativity and innovation is a prerequisite for success; perhaps even for survival, and is why creativity and innovation are now moving to the top of the agenda for organizations around the world, (Creativity Australia, 2010). In environments where rewards have been traditionally given for the absence of failure rather than for an acknowledgement of success, the concept of risk taking is both difficult to appreciate and difficult to explain to individuals who have developed in risk averse or risk neutral cultures. Conserving resources by avoiding risks that might result in failure has been described by Duvall, (1999) as 'playing not to lose' rather than 'playing to win'. Fisher Jr, (1997) suggests that this type of working culture can program learned helplessness and a sense of non-responsibility into workers, where obedience takes precedence over initiative, and discipline takes priority over risk taking. Cultures such as these are seldom hotbeds of innovation. An understanding of the principles of innovation, creativity and entrepreneurship within an enterprise systems environment is therefore essential in understanding why many such applications ultimately never achieve their potential benefits for an organisation.

Enterprise information systems might be described merely as 'agents of change' for organisations developing systems and business processes for the purpose of generating and maintaining competitive advantages in a marketplace. Enterprise systems by themselves do not provide the benefits expected of such applications, so knowledge of business process re-engineering (BPR) practices is essential in achieving organisational benefits. Joseph Schumpeter, (1975) once used the term '*creative destruction*' to describe processes in which old ways of doing things are endogenously destroyed and replaced by new ways. BPR provides a means of implementing new business ideas that may evolve from within an innovative cultural environment which is allowed to be creative. A full understanding of how an organisation's business processes actually works is a prerequisite to understanding how they could be altered.

There has been a trend, supported by ERP suppliers, implementation partners and clients that 'vanilla' implementations, i.e. installations that are of a standard configuration, are more likely to be successful than highly modified ones which are difficult to maintain and update with new software versions. After all, ERP systems such as SAP R/3 have always promised 'best of breed' solutions embedded within their processes, so it is alluring for an ERP client to infer that their state of the art ERP solution simply requires no further examination. However, we contend that the decision to modify away from vanilla should ultimately rest with the ERP client and that a means of modifying should still be available as an option. For example the teaching of ABAP/4 (for SAP) or C/AL (for Microsoft Dynamics NAV) would appear to be a worthwhile option in developing work ready graduates for an enterprise computing environment.

Much of an enterprise solution relies on links with external sources. E-business applications look inward from outside the organization (seeking to connect an outside entity with the enterprise's information), whereas ERP is now being forced to look outward from within the organization. The term 'inside out, outside in' is often used to demonstrate the now almost arbitrary relationship between enterprise systems and e-business. In terms of extended supply chains for example an enterprise solution must be fundamentally linked to an e-business platform, making the topic of e-business in an enterprise computing environment a virtual necessity.

Different types of enterprise solution require different types of systems architectures. Whereas a small EIS application such as MYOB may operate quite successfully on a LAN, larger systems may require various types of client server solutions that could extend to cloud computing environments. An understanding of the various types of systems architectures, their limitations and strengths and their appropriateness for various types of enterprise application would appear to be fully justifiable for providing well rounded enterprise computing graduates.

The topics that have been discussed in this section comprise a mix of technical, business and social psychology issues that are all believed necessary in developing the modern EIS professional. This section has related primarily to the types of courses and content that we believe should contribute to a comprehensive enterprise computing degree. The following section will concentrate on a pedagogy that might provide students with the skills to apply this content knowledge in a real-world environment.

Pedagogical Perspectives

It is fortunate (from an enterprise perspective) that the university responsible for delivering this curriculum has already identified six learning outcomes (L.O.) that they feel are essential to assure students' future success. These L.O.'s are embedded within all courses delivered by all colleges within the university and are:

- **Language:** Graduates will be able to communicate effectively in English and Modern Standard Arabic, using the academic and professional conventions of these languages appropriately.
- **Information Technology:** Graduates will be able to effectively understand, use, and evaluate technology both ethically and securely in an evolving global society.
- **Critical Thinking and Quantitative Reasoning:** Graduates will be able to demonstrate competence in understanding, evaluating, and using both qualitative and quantitative information to explore issues, solve problems, and develop informed opinions.
- **Information Literacy:** Graduates will be able to find, evaluate and use appropriate information from multiple sources to respond to a variety of needs.
- **Global Awareness:** Graduates will be able to understand and value their own and other cultures, perceiving and reacting to differences from an informed and socially responsible point of view.
- **Leadership:** Graduates will be able to undertake leadership roles and responsibilities, interacting effectively with others to accomplish shared goals.

Additionally, each college has a list of major learning objectives (MALO) that extend the enterprise LO's into specific subject areas. The combination of these enterprise LO's and MALO's are used to map the desired outcomes from students in each of the courses within the enterprise computing curriculum.

In what Prosser & Trigwell, (1999, p3), refer to as "some of the most exciting and relevant research to have been reported on learning in higher education in the past 20 years", they describe work originally undertaken by Marton & Saljö, (1976) and expanded on by Biggs, (1987); Marton, Hounsell, & Entwistle, (1997); Ramsden, (1992) which describes students as approaching their learning in two qualitatively different ways. The approach used by students to 'understand ideas and seek meanings' is referred to as a 'deep approach' and is contrasted with an approach where students see tasks as external impositions with a 'focus being on the words, the text or the formulae without reflection on purpose or strategy' referred to as a 'surface approach'.

The principle goal within the enterprise computing curriculum is in preparing students to contribute to enterprise systems success for their eventual employers. The objectives of this curriculum demand an understanding of ideas and meanings rather than merely learning traditional techniques used in enterprise systems. An approach to teaching recognising and encouraging a 'deep approach' rather than the alternative 'surface approach' to learning is therefore used. In research conducted by Hicks, (1996), it was claimed that *"experiential learning, action learning and action research are built on the recognition that learning by experiencing and reflecting on that experience can be most effective in helping students and practitioners acquire professional knowledge and skills"*. Using this approach helps individuals become reflective practitioners who take responsibility for their own learning and performance over a lifetime. The curriculum has been carefully crafted to provide this very type of experience and reflection.

Too often, management approaches developed for an industrial era are still being taught and applied within our new information or knowledge era environment. Managers have been traditionally described as either being 'managers of things' or 'managers of people', yet modern knowledge intensive enterprise systems environments have created the need for yet a third type of manager, which Glen, (2006) has referred to as 'managers of abstraction'. *"Where most managers are focussed on ends, these managers are responsible for particular features of the means to those ends."* The curriculum sets out to develop graduates who not only understand the 'managers of abstraction' concept but who are able to eventually apply these principles in their own work environments.

There is a growing recognition that EIS projects do not normally fail because of a lack of adequate technology; it is the so-called 'soft skills' that contribute most to the success of such projects. Acknowledging this reality, we believe that soft skills in team members are vital, and hence there is strong emphasis on communication and teamwork.

From our earlier literature review relating to EIS implementation success, four general non-technical themes have emerged.

It is neither the purpose nor intention of this chapter to discuss the finer details of all the various courses within this Enterprise Computing curriculum, yet it is appropriate to discuss from a pedagogical perspective the model that is used in one of its courses to help provide students with the appropriate practical EIS skills that will be of value to future employers.

The objectives of the enterprise computing courses being taught clearly demand an understanding of ideas and meanings rather than merely learning the techniques used to achieve success in EIS. In their study of the use of case studies, Rees & Porter, (2002), list nine potential benefits of using a case method.

1. The development of diagnostic skills
2. Subject and functional integration
3. Deep vs surface learning
4. The involvement and motivation of students
5. The effective use of class time
6. Development of team learning
7. The analysis of group discussion processes
8. Repeat use
9. Review of policy and practice.

Case method teaching can, according to Mostert & Sudzina, (1996), describe real-world problems that are too complex to approach experimentally (Glaser & Strauss, 1967; Lincoln & Guba, 1985; Patton, 1980). They list a number of arguments for the use of cases that include:

- Cases investigate phenomena in a real-life context.
- Cases are appropriate where the boundaries between the phenomenon and the setting, as in classroom instruction, are not clearly evident
- Cases use multiple sources of evidence to describe the phenomenon under investigation.

According to Barnes, Christensen, & Hansen, (1994, p285), "Effective cases portray real people in moments of decision, faced with a need to take action and accept its consequences", and they suggest that as a "second-best" alternative to apprenticeship good cases permit a "long look over the shoulder of a practitioner at work", (p287).

These types of benefit were believed to be ideally matched to the goals and objectives set for the programme so a decision was subsequently taken to use a case method approach whenever appropriate.

Table 2. Non-technical issues relating to EIS success

Theme	Research
Organisational Culture	(Barney, 1986; Kilmann, Saxton, & Serpa, 1986; Srivardhana & Pawlowski, 2007; Stewart et al., 2000)
Risk Orientation	(Aloini et al., 2007; Lee-Mortimer, 1995; Scott & Vessey, 2002; Sumner, 2000)
Leadership	(Bass, 1995; Kampmeier, 1998; Ke & Wei, 2005)
User Involvement & Empowerment	(Berger & Beynon-Davies, 2005; Jewels & Berger, 2005; Morgan, 1997)

An example of how cases are actually used is demonstrated in a course that is simply entitled 'Enterprise Systems'. In order to illustrate the difficulties and dangers of implementing an ERP system the classic 'FoxMeyer Drugs' Bankruptcy: Was it a Failure of ERP?' case study (Scott, 1999) is used. This case study describes how the US's 4th largest pharmaceutical company was driven to bankruptcy through mismanagement of an SAP implementation in the mid 1990's. Students are required to interpret and describe the main issues that are evident from this case but are not initially required to make recommendations on how to address each of the issues.

When the issues relating to FoxMeyer have been clearly established, a framework that can be used to provide a better understanding of how an enterprise can prepare itself for ERP implementations is introduced. An Americas Conference on Information Systems (AMCIS) presentation entitled 'Organizational Readiness for ERP Implementation', (Stewart et al., 2000) which articulates what cultural values are thought to be important for increasing ERP project success is introduced. This case discusses issues such as risk orientation, leadership qualities and user involvement, providing a foundation for analysing pre-implementation whether an ERP project is likely to be successful. Students are required to discuss what organisation culture issues might influence ERP project success, and how might these issues be addressed?

To illustrate how the correct application of these issues can lead to success, a case study entitled 'Nibco's Big Bang', (Brown & Vessey, 2001) is introduced. This case describes how an organisation successfully implemented an ERP system, even using a 'big bang' approach where all modules go live across the whole organisation at the same time, by applying the techniques discussed in the two previous studies. Students are then required to combine the three cases to explain why the Nibco implementation was successful and to describe what sort of things Nibco

did to increase the chances of project success that organisations such as FoxMeyer failed to properly address?

Tacitly embedded within these three case studies are concepts that become apparent only after the cases have been discussed in detail. Each of the case studies had as Lawrence cited in Erskine, Leenders, & Mauffette-Leenders, (1981, p11)) describes it, 'pulled apart the complex situations' and 'kept class discussion grounded upon stubborn facts faced in real life situations' but in the subsequent stage of 'putting it together again before the situations can be understood', additional factors become obvious to students. The need to be innovative is not always recognised as a key factor in ERP success. Indeed, Davenport, (2000) has stated that the common views of ERP systems are that they are like cement ... highly flexible in the beginning, but rigid later. However, innovation (or the ability to be innovative) plays an important role in the development of both new business product and processes, which is at the heart of ERP success. The relationship between organisational risk orientation and innovative behaviour normally becomes clearly apparent to students using this pedagogical approach. Local cultural issues relating to risk orientations and leadership approaches are often vigorously discussed.

However, the obvious need for specialised enterprise computing project management skills usually becomes apparent only to those students who have already completed the project management course. This indicates that the curriculum for best affect must be delivered in a particular sequence rather than simply as a group of disparate courses. The issue of pre-requisite courses is thus critical to achieving the objectives of the enterprise computing programme.

CONCLUSION

This enterprise computing programme has been developed with a clear goal of providing UAE students with the skills and knowledge which will enable them to graduate as work-ready contributors in enterprise computing environments. The comprehensiveness of the enterprise computing topics covered will hopefully allow graduates to contribute to organisational effectiveness in a number of areas, but their education will continue in their eventual workplaces. It is not unusual for an enterprise computing professional to eventually specialise in one particular area, so by providing graduates with a comprehensive knowledge base graduates might be better positioned to select which area that they eventually want to specialise in. However, such specialisations should never form the basis of new functional areas. After all, the true nature of an enterprise computing solution is that there should be only one joint application with a common purpose of increasing organisational effectiveness and efficiency for the enterprise. In providing a curriculum that follows this enterprise wide philosophy it is hoped that as a presenting organisation we are ourselves 'walking the talk'.

REFERENCES

Aloini, D., Dulmin, R., & Mininno, V. (2007). Risk management in ERP project introduction: Review of the literature. *Information & Management, 44*(6), 547–567. doi:10.1016/j.im.2007.05.004

Auditor-General of Queensland. (2010). *Information systems governance and control, including the Queensland Health Implementation of Continuity Project. The State of Queensland.* Queensland Audit Office.

Bala, H. K. (2008). *Nothing endures but change: Understanding employees' responses to enterprise systems implementation and business process change.* Unpublished DBA thesis, University of Arkansas, Fayetteville.

Bancroft, N. H., Seip, H., & Sprengel, A. (1998). *Implementing SAP R/3* (2nd ed.). USA: Manning Publications.

Barnes, L. B., Christensen, C. R., & Hansen, A. J. (1994). *Teaching and the case method: Text cases and readings* (3rd ed.). USA: Harvard Business School Press.

Barnett, R. (2007). Assessment in higher education: An impossible mission. In Boud, D., & Falchikov, N. (Eds.), *Rethinking assessment in higher education.* Chippenham, UK: Routledge.

Barney, J. B. (1986). Organizational culture - Can it be a source of sustained competitive advantage. *Academy of Management Review, 11*(3), 656–665.

Bass, B. M. (1995). Transformational leadership - Looking at other possible antecedents and consequences - Comment. *Journal of Management Inquiry, 4*(3), 293–297. doi:10.1177/105649269543010

Berger, H., & Beynon-Davies, P. (2005, 22nd-24th March). *Cultural issues impacting on a UK government IS project that is adopting a RAD-type development approach.* Paper presented at the UK Academy for Information Systems, Newcastle, UK.

Biggs, J. B. (1987). *Student approaches to learning and studying.* Hawthorne, Australia: Australian Council for Educational Research.

Brady, J., Monk, E., & Wagner, B. (2001). *Concepts in enterprise resource planning.* Canada: Course Technology.

Brown, C. V., & Vessey, I. (2001). Nibco's big bang. *Communications of the AIS, 5.*

Conner, K., & Prahalad, L. (1996). A resource-based theory of the firm: Knowledge versus opportunism. *Organization Science, 7*(5), 477–501. doi:10.1287/orsc.7.5.477

Cooper, R. (1994). The inertial impact of culture on IT implementation. *Information & Management, 27*(1), 17–31. doi:10.1016/0378-7206(94)90099-X

Creativity Australia. (2010, 4 February). *The importance of innovation in business*. Retrieved 28 September, 2010, from http://creativityaustralia.blogspot.com/2010/02/importance-of-innovation-in-business.html

Davenport, T. H. (2000). *Mission critical: Realizing the benefits of enterprise systems*. Boston, MA: Harvard Business School Press.

Duvall, C. K. (1999). Developing individual freedom to act: Empowerment in the knowledge organization. *Participation and Empowerment, 7*(8), 204–212. doi:10.1108/14634449910303603

Erskine, J. A., Leenders, M. R., & Mauffette-Leenders, L. A. (1981). *Teaching with cases*. London, Canada: University of Western Ontario.

Evans, M. (1997). *Enterprise resource planning for manufacturers*. Retrieved 29 October, 2008, from http://www.ovum.com/news/erp/erppwp.html

Fisher, J. R. Jr. (1997). A culture of contribution. *Executive Excellence, 14*(1), 16.

Glaser, B. G., & Strauss, A. L. (1967). *Teaching and the case method*. Boston, MA: Harvard Business School.

Glen, P. (2006). What kind of manager are you, anyway? (Reading 2). In Richardson, G. L., & Butler, C. W. (Eds.), *Readings in information technology project management*. Boston, MA: Thomson Course Technology.

Hammer, M. (1990). *Reengineering work: Don't automate, obliterate. Harvard Business Review*. July-August.

Hicks, R. E. (1996). Experiential learning in a postgraduate project management programme. *Education + Training, 38*(3), 28-38.

Jewels, T., & Berger, H. (2005, November 30 - December 2). *The effect of organisational culture on knowledge sharing: A comparison of European, United States and Australian behaviour.* Paper presented at the Australasian Conference on Information Systems, Sydney NSW.

Jewels, T., & Ford, M. (2006). The development of a taxonomy of desired personal qualities for IT project team members and its use in an educational setting. *Journal of Information Technology Education, 5*, 285–298.

Jurison, J. (2002). Integrating project management and change management in an IS curriculum. *Communications of the Association for Information Systems, 8*, 26–40.

Kampmeier, C. (1998). Organizational culture and leadership. *Journal of Management Consulting, 10*(2).

Ke, W., & Wei, K. K. (2005, 7-10 July). *Organizational culture and leadership in ERP implementation.* Paper presented at the Pacific Asia Conference on Information Systems, Bangkok, Thailand.

Kilmann, R. H., Saxton, M. J., & Serpa, R. (1986). Issues in understanding and changing culture. *California Management Review, 28*, 87–94.

Kumar, K., & Van Hillegersberg, J. (2000). ERP experiences and evolution. *Communications of the ACM, 43*, 23–26.

Lee, D. M. S., Trauth, E. M., & Farwell, D. (1995). Critical skills and knowledge requirements of IS professionals: A joint academic/industry investigation. *Management Information Systems Quarterly*, (September): 313–340. doi:10.2307/249598

Lee-Mortimer, A. (1995). Managing innovation and risk. *World Class Design to Manufacture, 2*(5), 38–42. doi:10.1108/09642369310095210

Lincoln, Y. L., & Guba, E. G. (1985). *Naturalistic inquiry*. Beverly Hill, CA: Sage.

Markus, L. (1983). Power, politics and MIS implementation. *Communications of the ACM, 26*(6), 430–444. doi:10.1145/358141.358148

Marton, F., Hounsell, D., & Entwistle, N. J. (Eds.). (1997). *The experience of learning: Implications for teaching and studying in higher education* (2nd ed.). Edinburgh, UK: Scottish Academic Press.

Marton, F., & Saljö, R. (1976). On qualiatative differences in learning: 1.Outcome and process. *The British Journal of Educational Psychology, 46*, 4–11. doi:10.1111/j.2044-8279.1976.tb02980.x

Maslow, A. H. (1965). *Eupsychian management*. Homewood, IL: Irwin-Dorsey.

Morgan, G. (1997). *Images of organisation* (2nd ed.). Thousand Oaks, CA: Sage Publications.

Mostert, M. P., & Sudzina, M. R. (1996, February). *Undergraduate case method teaching: Pedagogical assumptions vs the real world*. Paper presented at the Annual Meeting of the Association of Teacher Educators, St Louis MO.

Patton, M. Q. (1980). *Qualitative evaluation methods*. Newbury Park, CA: Sage Publications.

Prosser, M., & Trigwell, K. (1999). *Understanding learning and teaching: The experience in higher education*. Bury St Edmunds: Open University Press.

Ramsden, P. (1992). *Learning to teach in higher education*. Chatham, UK: Routledge. doi:10.4324/9780203413937

Rees, W. D., & Porter, C. (2002). The use of case studies in management training and development part 1. *Industrial and Commercial Training, 34*(1), 5–8. doi:10.1108/00197850210414026

Schumpeter, J. A. (1975). *Capitalism, socialism and democracy* [orig. pub. 1942]. New York, NY: Harper and Row.

Scott, J. E. (1999, August 13-15). *The FoxMeyer Drugs' bankruptcy: Was it a failure of ERP?* Paper presented at the 5th Americas Conference on Information Systems, Milwaukee, WI.

Scott, J. E., & Vessey, I. (2002). Managing risks in enterprise systems implementations. *Communications of the ACM, 45*(4), 74–81. doi:10.1145/505248.505249

Srivardhana, T., & Pawlowski, S. D. (2007). ERP systems as an enabler of sustained business process innovation: A knowledge-based view. *The Journal of Strategic Information Systems, 16*(1), 51–69. doi:10.1016/j.jsis.2007.01.003

Stewart, G. (2001, 4th-7th December). *Factors constraining the exploitation of enterprise systems: A research program*. Paper presented at the Australasian Conference on Information Systems, Coffs Harbour, NSW.

Stewart, G., Milford, M., Jewels, T., Hunter, T., & Hunter, B. (2000, Aug 10-13). *Organisational readiness for ERP implementation*. Paper presented at the AMCIS 2000, Long Beach, CA.

Sumner, M. (2000). Risk factors in enterprise-wide/ ERP projects. *Journal of Information Technology, 15*(4), 317–327. doi:10.1080/02683960010009079

Timbrell, G., & Chan, T. (2003, 26-28 November). *Investigating enterprise systems issues using a modified Delphi method and exploratory factor analysis*. Paper presented at the 14th ACIS, Perth WA.

Zweig, P., Kaiser, K. M., Beath, C. M., Bullen, C., Gallagher, K. P., & Goles, T. (2006). The information technology workforce: Trends and Implications 2005-2008. *MIS Quarterly Executive, 5*(2), 101–108.

ADDITIONAL READING

Ahmed, Z., Zbib, I., Arokiasamy, S., Ramayah, T., & Chiun, L. M. (2006). Resistance to change and ERP implementation success: The moderating role of change management initiatives. *Asian Academy of Management Journal, 11*(2), 1–17.

Al-Mudimigh, A., Zairi, M., & Mashari, M. A. (2002). ERP software implementation: An integrative framework. *European Journal of Information Systems, 10*(4), 216–226. doi:10.1057/palgrave.ejis.3000406

Alshawi, S., & Themistocleous, M., & Almadani. (2004). Integrating diverse ERP systems: A case study. *Journal of Enterprise Information Systems, 17*(6), 454–462.

Arlbjørn, J. S., Freytag, P. V., & de Haas, H. (2011). Service supply chain management: A survey of lean application in the municipal sector. *International Journal of Physical Distribution & Logistics Management, 41*(3), 277–295. doi:10.1108/09600031111123796

Bennis, W., & Townsend, R. (1995). *Reinventing leadership*. London, UK: Piatkus.

Bingi, P., Sharma, M. K., & Godla, J. (1999). Critical issues affecting an ERP implementation. *Information Systems Management, 16*(3), 7–14. doi:10.1201/1078/43197.16.3.19990601/31310.2

Brown, C., & Vessey, I. (1999, December 13-15). *ERP implementation practices: Toward a contingency framework*. Paper presented at the International Conference on Information Systems, Charlotte, NC.

Buonanno, G., Faverio, P., Pigni, F., Ravarini, A., Sciuto, D., & Tagliavini, M. (2005). Factors affecting ERP system adoption: A comparative analysis between SMEs and large companies. *Journal of Enterprise Information Management, 18*(4), 384–426. doi:10.1108/17410390510609572

Davenport, T., & Brooks, J. (2004). Enterprise systems and the supply chain. *Enterprise Information Management, 17*(1).

de Jong, J., & Den Hartog, D. (2007). How leaders influence employees' innovative behaviour. *European Journal of Innovation Management, 10*(1), 41–64. doi:10.1108/14601060710720546

Esteves, J. (2009). A benefits realisation roadmap framework for ERP usage in small and medium-sized enterprises. *Journal of Enterprise Information Management, 22*(1/2), 25–35. doi:10.1108/17410390910922804

Herbert, I. (2009). Business transformation through empowerment and the implications for management control systems. *Journal of Human Resource Costing & Accounting, 13*(3), 221–244. doi:10.1108/14013380910995511

Ho, C.-F., Wu, W.-H., & Tai, Y.-M. (2004). Strategies for the adaptation of ERP systems. *Industrial Management & Data Systems, 104*(3), 234–251. doi:10.1108/02635570410525780

Jewels, T., Al-Rawshdi, A., Abusharekh, R. N., & Shamisi, A. S. (2011). Organisational culture and its effects on innovation within ERP systems. In de Pablos Heredero, C. (Ed.), *Open innovation at firms and public administrations: Technologies for value creation*. Hershey, PA: IGI Global.

Jewels, T., & Ford, M. (2007). Factors influencing knowledge sharing in IT projects. *e-Service Journal, 5*(Fall).

Kreiser, P. M., Marino, L. D., Dickson, P., & Weaver, K. M. (2010). Cultural influences on entrepreneurial orientation: The impact of national culture on risk taking and proactiveness in SMEs. *Entrepreneurship: Theory and Practice, 34*(5), 959–984. doi:10.1111/j.1540-6520.2010.00396.x

McGaughey, R. E., & Gunasekaran, A. (2007). Enterprise resource planning (ERP): Past, present and future. *International Journal of Enterprise Information Systems*, *3*(3). doi:10.4018/jeis.2007070102

Mehrjerdi, Y. Z. (2010). Enterprise resource planning: risk and benefit analysis. *Business Strategy Series*, *11*(5), 308–324. doi:10.1108/17515631011080722

Mohammed, U. K., White, G. R. T., & Prabhakar, G. P. (2008). Culture and conflict management style of international project managers. *International Journal of Business and Management*, *3*(5), 3–11.

Morabito, V., Themistocleous, M., & Serrano, A. (2010). A survey on integrated IS and competitive advantage. *Journal of Enterprise Information Management*, *23*(2), 201–214. doi:10.1108/17410391011019778

Poba-Nzaou, P., Raymond, L., & Fabi, B. (2008). Adoption and risk of ERP systems in manufacturing SMEs: A positivist case study. *Business Process Management Journal*, *14*(4), 530–550. doi:10.1108/14637150810888064

Sia, K. S., & Neo, B. S. (2008). Business process reengineering, empowerment and work monitoring: An empirical analysis through the Panopticon. *Business Process Management Journal*, *14*(5), 609–628. doi:10.1108/14637150810903020

Srivardhana, T., & Pawlowski, S. D. (2007). ERP systems as an enabler of sustained business process innovation: A knowledge-based view. *The Journal of Strategic Information Systems*, *16*(1), 51–69. doi:10.1016/j.jsis.2007.01.003

Sumner, M. (2009). How alignment strategies influence ERP project success. *Enterprise Information Systems*, *3*(4), 425–448. doi:10.1080/17517570903045617

Warren, L., & Fuller, T. (2009). Contrasting approaches to preparedness: A reflection on two case studies. *International Journal of Enterprise Information Systems*, *5*(3), 60–71. doi:10.4018/jeis.2009070105

KEY TERMS AND DEFINITIONS

EIS Teaching: At the nexus between technology, business and social psychology.

Enterprise Information System (EIS): A system designed to enable information to flow throughout an enterprise.

Implementation of EIS Solution: Considered not as the final step of an organization's information systems development but merely the starting point of a new one.

Managers of Abstraction: Where most managers are focused on ends, these managers are responsible for particular features of the means to those ends.

Practical Reality of Curriculum Design: A function of academic, industry and social (through government) perspectives.

Sustained Competitive Advantages: Better realised by engaging in both incremental and radical innovative practices.

Technology Diffusions through Social Systems: Implementations of various types of enterprise system often requires significant alterations in the way that things are done and as such may cause major changes in employees' work lives.

Technology Swap: Adopting only the technology components of a new enterprise system within changing any of the business processes that should accompany it.

Vanilla Implementations: ERP systems that that are of a standard configuration.

338

Compilation of References

(2011). Information Technology Association- int@j. (2007). National ICT strategy of Jordan 2007. Amman, Jordan: Author.

Abad, C. (2008). Learning through creating learning objects experiences with a class project in a distributed systems course. ITiCSE'08, June 30–July 2, 2008, Madrid, Spain, 2008. ACM. 978-1-60558-115-6/08/06.

Abalhassan, K. M. I. (2002). English as a foreign language instruction with CALL multimedia in Saudi Arabian private schools: A multi-case and multi-site study of CALL instruction. Unpublished Ph.D. Indiana University of Pennsylvania.

Abdelbaqi, W., & Abdelaziz, W. (2011, February). Governance in e-learning. Paper presented at 2nd International Conference on e-Learning and Distance Learning, Riyadh, Saudi Arabia.

Abdelghaffar, H., & AbdelAzim, R. H. (2010). Significant factors influencing ERP implementaion in large organizations: Evidence from Egypt. European, Mediterranean & Middle Eastern Conference On Information systems. Abu Dhabi, UAE.

Abdelraheem, A. (2006, November). The implementation of e-learning in the Arab universities: Challenges and opportunities. Paper presented at DLI 2006, Tokyo, Japan.

Abouchedid, K., & Eid, G. (2004). E-learning challenges in the Arab world: Revelation from a case study profile. Quality Assurance in Education, 12(1), 15–27. doi:10.1108/09684880410517405

Abraham, L. B. (2008). Computer-mediated glosses in second language reading comprehension and vocabulary learning: A meta-analysis. Computer Assisted Language Learning, 21(3), 199–226. doi:10.1080/09588220802090246

Abu Dhabi Education Council (ADEC). (2009). ADEC information security policy document, (pp. 18-19). Final-Version 3.0 September 2009.

Abu Dhabi Education Council (ADEC). (2009). Enterprise school information system eSIS. Official Documents.

Abu Dhabi Education Council. (2009). Strategic plan for P-12 education. Retrieved from http://www.adec.ac.ae/ADEC%20Shared%20Documents/attachments/Public%20schools/Strategic%20Plans/P12-Summary-June-2009-D.pdf

Abu-Duhou, I. (1999). School-based management. Fundamental of Education Planning, 62. Paris, France: UNESCO.

Abuhmaid, A. (2010). Centralization and reform: Information technologies in large-scale education reform. Paper presented at the E-learning Excellence in the Middle East 2010: Bringing Global Quality to a Local Context, Dubai, UAE.

Abuhmaid, A. (2009). ICT integration across education systems: The experience of Jordan in educational reform. Saarbrücken, Germany: VDM Verlag Dr. Müller.

Abuhmaid, A. (2011). Embracing ICT by the Jordanian education system. In Albadri, F., & Abdullah, S. (Eds.), Cases on ICT acceptance, investment and organization: Cultural practices and values in the Arab world. Hershey, PA: IGI Global. doi:10.4018/978-1-60960-048-8.ch003

Abu-Samaha, A. M., & Shishakly, R. (2008). Assessment of school information system utilization in the UAE primary schools. Issues in Informing Science and Information Technology, 5, 525–542.

Adair-Hauck, B., Willingham-McLain, L., & Earnest Youngs, B. E. (1999). Evaluating the integration of technology and language learning. *CALICO Journal, 17*, 269–306.

Adams, A. (2011). *The role of education in the Arab World revolutions*. The Brookings Institution. Retrieved from http://www.brookings.edu/opinions/2011/0610_arab_world_education_winthrop.aspx

ADEC. (2011, June 27). *AL Khaili: 400 public & private schools have benefitted from eSIS*. Retrieved December 13, 2011, from http://www.adec.ac.ae/English/Pages/NewsDisplay.aspx?ItemID=395

Adomavicius, G., & Tuzhilin, A. (2005, June). Toward the next generation of recommender systems: A survey of the state-of-the-art and possible extensions. *IEEE Transactions on Knowledge and Data Engineering, 17*(6), 734–749. doi:10.1109/TKDE.2005.99

Ahmed, T. (2011, February). *Evaluating e-learning effectiveness in higher-education institutions at developing countries: An empirical study and proposed model*. Paper presented at 2nd International Conference on e-Learning and Distance Learning, Riyadh, Saudi Arabia.

Akinyemi, A. (2002). E-learning: A reality in Sultan Qaboos University. In G. Richards (Ed.), *Proceedings of World Conference on E-Learning in Corporate, Government, Healthcare, and Higher Education 2002* (pp. 1113-1115). Chesapeake, VA: AACE.

Akkari, A. (2004). Education in the Middle East and North Africa: The current situation and future challenges. *International Education Journal, 5*(2), 144–153.

Akken. (2008). *Application price and online e-works*. Retrieved April 14, 2012, from http://www.akken.com/pricing.php

Al Khayyat, I., & Al Musawi, A. (2004, April). *E-connect, electronic linking among higher education institutions in the Gulf cooperation council states*. Paper presented at 2nd Meeting on Implementing Higher Council's Decisions in HE Field, Riyadh, Saudi Arabia.

Al Musawi, A. (2010, April). *E-training and its HRD applications in education sector of the GCC countries* (Invited Paper). Paper presented at 1st Symposium on ICT Applications in Education and Training Proceedings, King Saud University, Riyadh.

Al Musawi, A., & Abelraheem, A. (2004a). E-learning at Sultan Qaboos University: Status and future. *British Journal of Educational Technology, 35*(3), 363–367. doi:10.1111/j.0007-1013.2004.00394.x

Al Musawi, A., & Abelraheem, A. (2004b). The effect of using on-line instruction on Sultan Qaboos University Students' achievement and their attitudes towards it. *Education Journal, 18*(70), 11–26.

Al Senaidi, S. (2009). *An investigation of factors affecting Omani faculty members' adoption of information and computing technology*. Unpublished doctoral dissertation, University of North Texas, USA.

Ala, M., & Shishakly, R. (2008). Assessment of school information system utilization in the UAE primary schools. *Issues in Informing Science and Information Technology, 5*.

Alabbad, A. (2010). *Introducing constructivism and computer-assisted language learning (CALL) into traditional EFL programs in Saudi Arabia. Unpublished Ph.D.* Australia: The University of Queensland.

Al-Bassam, M. M. (1987). *The relationship of attitudinal and motivational factors to achievement in learning English as a second language by Saudi female students. Unpublished Ph.D.* USA: University of Florida.

Al-Bureikan, A. (2008). *The effectiveness of CALL in the EFL Saudi female students' listening and speaking skills at the College of Health Sciences, Onaizah. Unpublished Ph.D.* Saudi Arabia: King Saud University.

Aldojan, M. (2007). *An exploratory study about internet use among education faculty members in Jordanian public universities*. Unpublished doctoral dissertation, Ohio University, USA.

Alebaikan, R. (2011, February). *A blended learning framework for Saudi higher education*. Paper presented at 2nd International Conference on e-Learning and Distance Learning, Riyadh, Saudi Arabia.

Alessi, S. M., & Trollip, S. R. (2000). *Multimedia for learning: Methods and development* (3rd ed.). New York, NY: Allyn & Bacon.

Alfallaj, F. S. (1995). *The effect of students' attitudes on performance in English language course at the College of Technology, Buraydah, Saudi Arabia.* Unpublished Thesis, University of Toledo, USA.

Al-Gattoufi, S., Al-Naabi, S., & Gattoufi, B. (2007). Readiness for shifting from a traditional higher education learning system to an e-learning system: A case study from the Sultanate of Oman. *Journal of College Teaching and Learning, 4*(11), 55–60.

Alghazo, I. M. (2006). Quality of Internet use by teachers in United Arab Emirates. *Education, 126*(4), 769–781.

Al-Harithi, A. S. (2005). Distance higher education experiences of Arab Gulf students in the United States: A cultural perspective. *International Review of Research in Open and Distance Learning, 6*(3), 1–14.

Alherbish, J. (2005, November). *GOTEVT e-learning initiative.* Paper presented at 4th e-Merging e-Learning Conference, Abu Dhabi, United Arab Emirates.

Alian, M., & AL-Akhras, M. (2010). *AdaLearn: An adaptive e-learning environment.* ISWSA'10, June 14–16, ACM. 978-1-4503-0475

Aljamhoor, A. (1999). The effectiveness of using computers to teaching EFL in secondary school students: An experimental study. In *Proceedings of the Symposium on Educational Technology and Information,* Bahrain University. Riyadh, Saudi Arabia: King Saud University Press.

Al-Jarf, R. S. (2005). *Using three online course management systems in EFL instruction.* The Annual Meeting of the Asia Association of Computer Assisted Language Learning (AsiaCALL). Geongju, South Korea: Sorabol College.

Al-Jazeera. (2007). *Al-Jazeera TV Viewer Demographic.* Retrieved November 27, 2007, from http://www.allied-media.com/aljazeera/JAZdemog.html

Al-Juhani, S. O. (1991). *The effectiveness of computer-assisted instruction in teaching English as a foreign language in Saudi secondary school. Unpublished Ph.D.* USA: University of Denver.

AlKahtani, S. (2001). *Computer-assisted language learning in EFL instruction at selected Saudi Arabian universities: Profiles of faculty. Unpublished Ph.D.* USA: Indiana University of Pennsylvania.

Ally, M. (2011, February). *Best practices and standards for e-learning.* Paper presented at 2nd International Conference on e-Learning and Distance Learning, Riyadh, Saudi Arabia.

Al-Mekhlafi, A. (2004). The Internet and EFL teaching: The reaction of UAE secondary school English language teachers. *Journal of Language and Learning, 2*(2), 88–113.

Almekhlafi, A. G. (2006a). Effectiveness of interactive multimedia environment on language acquisition skills of 6th grade students in the United Arab Emirates. *International Journal of Instructional Media, 33*(4), 427–441.

Almekhlafi, A. G. (2006b). The effect of computer assisted language learning (CALL) on United Arab Emirates English as a foreign language (EFL) school students achievement and attitude. *Journal of Interactive Learning Research, 17*(2), 121–142.

Almekhlafi, A. G., & Almeqdadi, F. A. (2010). Teachers' perceptions of technology integration in the United Arab Emirates school classrooms. *Journal of Educational Technology & Society, 13*(1), 165–175.

Aloini, D., Dulmin, R., & Mininno, V. (2007). Risk management in ERP project introduction: Review of the literature. *Information & Management, 44*(6), 547–567. doi:10.1016/j.im.2007.05.004

Alsalloum, O. (2011, February). *E-learning and UN award: King Saud University case study.* Paper presented at 2nd International Conference on e-Learning and Distance Learning, Riyadh, Saudi Arabia.

Alsofyani, M., Aris, B., & Alshareef, M. (2011, February). *A blended online training model for TPACK development in Saudi higher education institutions.* Paper presented at 2nd International Conference on e-Learning and Distance Learning, Riyadh, Saudi Arabia.

Al-Subeai, W. (2000). *The effectiveness of CALL on improving vocabulary learning and reading comprehension among EFL Saudi students of the secondary commercial in Riyadh.* Unpublished Master's Dissertation, King Saud University, Saudi Arabia.

Altahuser, R., & Matuga, J. M. (1998). *On the pedagogy of electronic instruction. Electronic Collaborators: Learner-Centered Technologies for Literacy.* Apprenticeship, and Discourse.

Al-Washahi, M. (2007). *The perceived effectiveness and impact of educational technology faculty development activities in the College of Education at Sultan Qaboos University.* Unpublished doctoral dissertation, Ohio University, USA.

Alzind, W. (2011, February). *Distance learning programs evaluation.* Paper presented at 2nd International Conference on e-Learning and Distance Learning, Riyadh, Saudi Arabia.

Amer, T., & Al Musawi, A. (2009). *Ethical standards for the use of computers and the Internet by faculty members in the Arab World. International Council on Education for Teaching (ICET) World Assembly 2009.* Oman: Sultan Qaboos University.

Amr, M. (2011). Teacher education for inclusive education in the Arab world: The case of Jordan. *Prospects, 41*, 399–413. Springer. DOI: 10.1007/s11125-011-9203-9

Anderson, J. W. (2000). The information revolution. *The Middle East Journal, 54*(3).

Anderson, S. E. (1997). Understanding teacher change: Revisiting the concerns based adoption model. *Curriculum Inquiry, 27*(3), 331–367. doi:10.1111/0362-6784.00057

Antoniou, G., & van Harmelen, F. (2004). *A Semantic Web primer.* Cambridge, MA: The MIT Press.

APA. (1997). *Learner-centered psychology principles: A framework for school redesign and reform.*

Appleby, R. (2005). *The spatiality of English language teaching, gender and context.* Unpublished doctoral dissertation, University of Technology, Sydney, Sydney.

Arreguin, C. (2004). Wikis. In B. Hoffman (Ed.), *Encyclopedia of educational technology.* Retrieved May 11, 2008, from http://coe.sdsu.edu/eet/articles/wikis/start.html

Aslanidou, S., & Menexes, G. (2007). Youth and the Internet: Uses and practices in the home. *Computers & Education, 51*, 1375–1391. doi:10.1016/j.compedu.2007.12.003

Astiz, M. F., Wiseman, A. W., & Baker, D. P. (2002). Schooling towards decentralization: Consequences of globalization for curricular control in national education systems. *Comparative Education Review, 1*(1), 66–86. doi:10.1086/324050

Auditor-General of Queensland. (2010). *Information systems governance and control, including the Queensland Health Implementation of Continuity Project. The State of Queensland.* Queensland Audit Office.

Augar, N., Raitman, R., & Zhou, W. (2004). *Teaching and learning online with wikis.* Retrieved March 15, 2008, from http://www.ascilite.org.au/conferences/perth04/procs/augar.html

Avison, D., & Malaurent, J. (2007). Impact of cultural differences: A case study of ERP introduction in China. *International Journal of Information Management, 27*(5), 368–374. doi:10.1016/j.ijinfomgt.2007.06.004

Bahrani, T. (2011). Speaking fluency: Technology in EFL context or social interaction in ESL context? *Studies in Literature and Language, 2*(2), 162–168.

Baishuang, Q., & Wei, Z. (2009). *Student model in adaptive learning system based on Semantic Web.* In First International Workshop on Education Technology and Computer Science. DOI 10.1109/ETCS.2009.466

Bajcsy, R. (2002). *Technology and learning.* In Visions 2020: Transforming education and training through advanced technologies. Washington, DC: U.S. Department of Commerce. Retrieved from http://www.technology.gov/reports/TechPolicy/2020Visions.pdf

Bakerman, M. (2002, October). *Children with learning difficulties at future school.* Paper presented at KSU's Future School Seminar, Riyadh, Saudi Arabia. eLabs-eLearning and Business Solutions (2006). *Towards an Arabic elearning strategy: Future prospect, eLabs Portal.* Retrieved August 11, 2011, from http://www.elabs.org.eg/index.html

Baker, P., & Moss, K. (1996). Building learning communities through guided participation. *Primary Voices, 4*(2), 2–6.

Bala, H. K. (2008). *Nothing endures but change: Understanding employees' responses to enterprise systems implementation and business process change.* Unpublished DBA thesis, University of Arkansas, Fayetteville.

Baldwin, T. T., & Ford, J. K. (1988). Transfer of training: A review and directions for future research. *Personnel Psychology, 41,* 63–105. doi:10.1111/j.1744-6570.1988.tb00632.x

Balooshi, A. A. (2010, March 15). *News catalog: ERM in institutions.* Retrieved December 13, 2011, from http://www.adec.ac.ae/NewsCatalog/Forms/DispForm.aspx?ID=115

Bancroft, N. H., Seip, H., & Sprengel, A. (1998). *Implementing SAP R/3* (2nd ed.). USA: Manning Publications.

Barnes, L. B., Christensen, C. R., & Hansen, A. J. (1994). *Teaching and the case method: Text cases and readings* (3rd ed.). USA: Harvard Business School Press.

Barnett, R. (2007). Assessment in higher education: An impossible mission. In Boud, D., & Falchikov, N. (Eds.), *Rethinking assessment in higher education.* Chippenham, UK: Routledge.

Barney, J. B. (1986). Organizational culture - Can it be a source of sustained competitive advantage. *Academy of Management Review, 11*(3), 656–665.

Barta, B. Z., Telem, M., & Gev, Y. (1991). *Information technology in educational management.* Chapman & Hall.

Bass, B. M. (1995). Transformational leadership - Looking at other possible antecedents and consequences - Comment. *Journal of Management Inquiry, 4*(3), 293–297. doi:10.1177/105649269543010

Bauman, M. (1997). *Online learning communities.* Paper presented at the Teaching in the Community Colleges Online Conference.

Beaumie, K. (2001). Social constructivism. In M. Orey (Ed.), Emerging perspectives on learning, teaching, and technology. Retrieved from http://www.coe.uga.edu/epltt/SocialConstructivism.htm

Bechhofer, S., Harmelen, F., Hendler, J., Horrocks, I., McGuinness, D., Patel-Schneider, P., & Stein, L. (2009). *OWL Web ontology language reference.* Document Status Update, 12 November 2009. Retrieved From http://www.w3.org/TR/owl-ref/

Beheshti, H. (2006). What managers should know about ERP/ERP II. *Management Research News, 184.*

Behl, D., & Devitt, P. (2011). Virtual international experiences: Testing the boundaries of student global learning. *UAE Journal of Educational Technology and eLearning, 2,* 13-20.

Behrman, J. R., Deolakira, A. B., & Soon, L. Y. (2002). *Conceptual issue in the role of education decentralization in promoting effective schooling in Asian developing countries.* ERD working paper series No 22. Economic and Research Department.

Bekele, T. A., & Menchaca, M. P. (2008). Research on Internet-supported learning: A review. *The Quarterly Review of Distance Education, 9*(4), 373–405.

Bennett, F. (1999). *Computers as tutors: Solving the crisis in education. Publishers Middle East Educator, 11.* Sarasota, FL: Faben Inc.

Berger, H., & Beynon-Davies, P. (2005, 22nd-24th March). *Cultural issues impacting on a UK government IS project that is adopting a RAD-type development approach.* Paper presented at the UK Academy for Information Systems, Newcastle, UK.

Bergh, J. (2009). An examination of faculty use of Blackboard Vista and Web 2.0 tools to determine strategies for faculty training. *UAE Journal of Educational Technology and eLearning, 1.* Retrieved 14th January, 2011, from http://ejournal.hct.ac.ae/issues/2009-issue/faculty-use-blackboard-vista-web2-tools

Bergin, J. (2002). *Teaching on the wiki web.* Paper presented in the 7th Annual Conference on Innovation and Technology in Computer Science Education. New York, NY: ACM Press.

Bernard, R. M., Abrami, P. C., Borokhovski, E., Wade, A. C., Tamim, R. M., & Surkes, M. A. (2009). A meta-analysis of three types of interaction treatments in distance education. *Review of Educational Research, 79*(3), 1243–1289. doi:10.3102/0034654309333844

Bernard, R. M., Abrami, P. C., Lou, Y., Borokhovski, E., Wade, A., & Wozney, L. (2004). How does distance education compare with classroom instruction? A meta-analysis of the empirical literature. *Review of Educational Research, 74*(3), 379–439. doi:10.3102/00346543074003379

Bernard, R. M., De Rubalcava, B., & St. Pierre, D. (2000). Collaborative online distance learning: Issues for future practice and research. *Distance Education, 21*(2), 260–277. doi:10.1080/0158791000210205

Biggs, J. B. (1987). *Student approaches to learning and studying*. Hawthorne, Australia: Australian Council for Educational Research.

Biletskiy, Y., Baghi, H., Keleberda, I., & Fleming, M. (2009). An adjustable personalization of search and delivery of learning objects to learners. *Expert Systems with Applications, 36*, 9113–9120. doi:10.1016/j.eswa.2008.12.038

Bill Gates quotes. (2008). Retrieved November 10, 2008, from http://thinkexist.com/ quotation/if_gm_had_kept_up_with_technology_like_the/188702.html

Billeh, V. (2002). Educational reform in the Arab region. *Newsletter of the Economic Research Forum, for the Arab Countries, Iran and Turkey, 9*(2).

Bingi, P., Sharma, M. K., & Godla, J. K. (1999). Critical issues affecting an ERP implementation. *Information Systems Management, 99*(16).

Black Board Learning System. (n.d.). *Website*. Retrieved from http://www.webct.com

Blanchard, P. N. (2008). *Training delivery method-organization levels: Advantages, manager, model, type, company, disadvantages, workplace, business*. Retrieved at http://www.refernceforbusiness.com/management/Tr-Z/Training-Delivery-Methods

Blitzblau, R., & Hanson, M. (2001). Transforming Georgetown through technology. *EDUCAUSE Quarterly, 2*.

Boulous, M., Maramba, I., & Wheeler, S. (2006). Wikis, blogs and podcasts: A new generation of web-based tools for virtual collaborative clinical practice and education. *BMC Medical Education, 6*(41). Retrieved March 15, 2008, from http://www.biomedcentral.com/content/pdf/1472-6920-6-41.pdf

Bradshaw, L. K. (2002). Technology for teaching and learning: Strategies for staff development and follow-up support. *Journal of Technology and Teacher Education, 10*(1), 131–150.

Brady, J., Monk, E., & Wagner, B. (2001). *Concepts in enterprise resource planning*. Canada: Course Technology.

Branscomb, A. W. (1995). *Who owns information? From privacy to public access*. New York, NY: American Library Association.

Bransford, B. A., & Cocking, R. R. (2000). *How people learn: Brain, mind, experience & school* (2nd ed.). Washington, DC: National Academy Press.

Breuleux, A. (2001). Imagining the present, interpreting the possible, cultivating the future: Technology and the renewal of teaching and learning. *Education Canada, 41*(3), 1–8.

BRIDGE. (2004). *Building respect through internet dialogue and global education [BRIDGE]*. Retrieved from rom http://us.iearn.org/collaborate/programs/bridge/index.php (August, 8 2006)

Brinkerhof, J. (2006). Effects of long-duration, professional development academy on technological skills, computer self-efficacy, and technology integration beliefs and practices. *Journal of Research on Technology in Education, 39*(1), 22–44.

Bristow, R. (2005). Beyond email: Wikis, blogs and other strange beasts. *Ariadne, 42*. Retrieved May 25, 2008, from http://www.ariadne.ac.uk/issue42/beyond-email-rpt/intro.html

Britain, S., & Liber, O. (1999). *A framework for pedagogical evaluation of virtual learning environments*. Bangor, ME: JISC Technology Applications Programme.

Brookfield, S. D. (1987). *Developing critical thinkers*. San Francisco, CA: Jossey-Bass.

Brown, C. V., & Vessey, I. (2001). Nibco's big bang. *Communications of the AIS, 5*.

Brunello, P. (2010). ICT for education projects: a look from behind the scenes. *Information Technology for Development, 16*(3), 232–239. doi:10.1080/02681102.2010.497275

Bruns, A., & Humphreys, S. (2005). *Wikis in teaching and assessment - The M/Cyclopedia project.* Paper presented at The 2005 International Symposium on Wikis, October 16-18, San Diego, CA, U.S.A. Retrieved October 1, 2008, from http://snurb.info/files/wikis%20in %20 Teaching %20 and %20 assessment.pdf

Brusilovsky, P., & Millán, E. (2007). *User models for adaptive hypermedia and adaptive educational systems. The Adaptive Web, LNCS 4321* (pp. 3–53). Berlin, Germany: Springer-Verlag.

Bullen, M. (1998). Participation and critical thinking in online university distance education. *Journal of Distance Education, 13*(2), 1–32.

Burke, R. (2002). Hybrid recommender systems: Survey and experiments- Customer model. *Customer-Adapted Interaction, 4*(12), 331–370. doi:10.1023/A:1021240730564

Business dictionary. (n.d.). *Information system security: Engineering principles for IT security.* Retrieved from http://csrcinist.gov/publications

Byrom, E. (2001). *Factors influencing the effective use of technology for teaching and learning.* Retrieved from http://www.serve.org/seir-tec/publications/lessons.pdf

Byron, M. (2005). Teaching with tiki. *Teaching Philosophy, 28*(2), 108–113.

Cai, S., Lu, Z., & Gu, J. (2010). An effective measure of semantic similarity. In *Advances in Wireless Networks and Information Systems, LNEE 72* (pp. 9–17). Berlin, Germany: Springer-Verlag. doi:10.1007/978-3-642-14350-2_2

Calvo, R. (2003). User scenarios for the design and implementation of LMS. In *Proceedings of the AIED 2003 Workshop, Towards Intelligent Learning Management Systems,* (pp. 14-22).

Carman, J. M. (2002). Blended learning design: Five key ingredients. *Knowledge Net.* Retrieved from http://www.agilantlearning.com/pdf/Blended%20Learning%20Design.pdf

Carnoy, M. (2005). ICT in education: Possibilities and challenges. Universitat Oberta de Catalunya, 2005.

Cassell, J. (2004). Towards a model of technology and literacy development: Story listening systems. *Journal of Applied Developmental Psychology, 25,* 75–105. doi:10.1016/j.appdev.2003.11.003

Castells, M. (1999a). Flows, networks, and identities: A critical theory of the informational society. In Castells, M., Flecha, R., Freire, P., Giroux, H. A., Macedo, D., & Willis, P. (Eds.), *Critical education in the new information age.* New York, NY: Rowman & Littlefield Publishers, Inc.

Castells, M. (1999b). *Information technology, globalization and social development.* Geneva, Switzerland: United Nations.

Castells, M. (2010a). *The information age economy, society and culture: End of millennium* (2nd ed., *Vol. III*). West Sussex, UK: Wiley-Blackwell.

Castells, M., & Himanen, P. (2002). *The information society and the welfare state: The Finnish model.* Oxford, UK: Oxford University Press. doi:10.1093/acprof:oso/9780199256990.001.0001

Central Intelligence Agency. (2010). *CIA- The world factbook.* Retrieved September 12, 2011, from https://www.cia.gov/library/publications

Chang, L. L. (2007). The effects of using CALL on advanced Chinese foreign language learners. *CALICO Journal, 24*(2), 331–353.

Charras, C. (1997). *Exact string matching algorithms.* France: Thierry Lecroq, Laboratoire d'Informatique de Rouen, Université de Rouen, Faculté des Sciences et des Techniques, Mont-Saint-Aignan Cedex.

Cherifi, H., Zain, M. J., & El-Qawasmeh, E. (2011). *Digital information and communication technology and its applications, part 2.* DICTAP 2011.

Chien-Pen, C., & Josaph, C. (1999). Issues in information ethics and educational policies for coming age. *Journal of Information Technology, 15*(4).

Chinwe, M. T. N. (2009). *The impact of internet use on teaching, learning and research activities in Nigerian universities.*

Choy, S., & Ng, K. (2007). Implementing software for supplementing online. *Australasian Journal of Educational Technology, 23*(2), 209–226.

Christoph, F. (2005). User modeling and user profiling in adaptive e-learning systems. Master's Thesis at Graz University of Technology.

Clancy, D. (2009). *Property registration authority.* Retrieved April 13, 2012, from www.eregistration.ie/termsAndConditions.aspx

Clark, R. E. (1983). Reconsidering research on learning from media. *Review of Educational Research, 53*(4), 445–449.

Clark, R. E. (1994). Media will never influence learning. *Educational Technology Research and Development, 42*(2), 21–29. doi:10.1007/BF02299088

Clulow, V., & Brace-Govan, J. (2001). *Learning through bulletin board discussion: A preliminary case analysis of the cognitive dimension.* Paper presented at the Moving Online Conference II, September 2-4, 2001, Gold Coast, Australia.

Cobb, T. (2007). Public interest research, collaboration, and the promise of wikis perspectives. *Teaching Legal Research and Writing, 16*, 1–11.

Colis, B., & Moonen, J. (2001). *Flexible learning in a digital world: Experiences and expectations.* London, UK: Kogan-Page.

Collins, A., & Halverson, R. (2009). *Rethinking education in the age of technology.* New York, NY: Teachers College Press.

Collis, B., & Strijker, A. (2004). Technology and human issues in reusing learning objects. *Journal of Interactive Media in Education, 2004.* Retrieved May 27, 2008, from http://www.jime.open.ac.uk/2004/4

Computer Quotes. (2008). Retrieved December 22, 2008, from http://www.gdargaud.net/Humor/QuotesComputer.html

Computer-assisted instruction. (2008). In *CSharpOnline.NET.* Retrieved December 10, 2008, from http://en.csharp-online.net/Glossary: Definition_-_Computer-Assisted_Instruction

Conacannon, F., Flynn, A., & Campbell, M. (2005). What campus-based students think about the quality and benefits of e-learning. *British Journal of Educational Technology, 36*(3), 501–512. doi:10.1111/j.1467-8535.2005.00482.x

Connell, S. (2005). *Comparing blogs, wikis, and discussion boards as collaborative learning tools.* Retrieved May 11, 2008, from http://soo2sone.com/PDFs/plan_ConnellED690.pdf

Conner, K., & Prahalad, L. (1996). A resource-based theory of the firm: Knowledge versus opportunism. *Organization Science, 7*(5), 477–501. doi:10.1287/orsc.7.5.477

Cooper, R. (1994). The inertial impact of culture on IT implementation. *Information & Management, 27*(1), 17–31. doi:10.1016/0378-7206(94)90099-X

Cornelius, E. T. (2007). *Seven steps in the ERP process: An overview of the higher ed ERP journey.* Retrieved December 13, 2011, from www.collegiateproject.com

Cragg, P. B., & Zinateli, N. (1995). The evolution of information systems in small firms. *Information & Management, 29*, 1–8. doi:10.1016/0378-7206(95)00012-L

Creativity Australia. (2010, 4 February). *The importance of innovation in business.* Retrieved 28 September, 2010, from http://creativityaustralia.blogspot.com/2010/02/importance-of-innovation-in-business.html

Cuban, L. (1993). Computers meet classroom: Classroom wins. *Teachers College Record, 95*(2).

Cuban, L., Kirkpatrick, H., & Peck, C. (2001). High access and low use of technologies in high school classrooms: Explaining an apparent paradox. *American Educational Research Journal, 38*, 813–834. doi:10.3102/00028312038004813

Cunningham, W., & Leuf, B. (2001). *The wiki way: Quick collaboration on the web.* Addison-Wesley: Longman Publishing Company, Inc.

Cunnington, U., & Andersson, S. (1999). *Teachers, pupils and the internet.* Nelson Thomas.

Daoud, M., Tamine, L., & Mohand, B. (2009). A session based personalized search using an ontological user profile. [Honolulu, Hawaii, USA. ACM.]. *SAC, 09*(March), 8–12.

Davenport, T. H. (2000). *Mission critical: Realizing the benefits of enterprise systems.* Boston, MA: Harvard Business School Press.

Davis, G. B., Lee, A. S., Nickles, K. R., Chatterjee, S., Hartung, R., & Wu, Y. (1992). Diagnosis of an information system failure–A framework and interpretive process. *Information & Management, 23,* 293–318. doi:10.1016/0378-7206(92)90059-O

Dawes, L. (2001). What stops teachers using new technology? In Leask, M. (Ed.), *Issues in teaching using ICT* (pp. 61–79). London, UK: Routledge.

De, P. K., Ahmad, S., & Somashekar, M. A. (2004). *Impedements to technology transfer and technology absorption in United Arab Emirates.* Paper presented at the International Association for Management of Technology, Washington.

Dearstyne, B. (2007). Blogs, smashups, and wikis oh my! *Information Management Journal, 41*(4), 24–33.

DeBell, M., & Chapman, C. (2006). *Computer and internet use by students in 2003.* National Center for Education Statistics.

Decker, M. A. (2004). Incorporating guided self-study listening into the language curriculum. *Language Teaching, 28*(6), 5–9.

Deetz, S., Sarah, J. T., & Simpson, J. L. (2000). *Leading organization through transition.* Thousand Oaks, CA: Sage Publication Inc.

Delahoussaye, M., Ellis, K., & Bolch, M. (2002, August). Measuring corporate smarts. *Training Magazine,* 20-35.

Delvin, J. C. (2010). *Challenges of economic development in the Middle East and North Africa region (Vol. 8).* New Jersey World Scientific Publishing.

Dewald, N. H. (2003). Pedagogy and andragogy. In Dupuis, A. E. (Ed.), *Developing web-based instruction: Planning, designing, managing, and evaluating results* (pp. 47–68). London, UK: Facet.

Dimmock, C. (2000). *Designing the learning-centred school: A cross-cultural perspective.* New York, NY: Falmer Press.

Dodds, P. (2001). *Sharable content object reference model.* Retrieved from http://www.adlnet.org/

Dörnyei, Z. N. (2003). Attitudes, orientations, and motivations in language learning: Advances in theory, research, and applications. *Language Learning, 53*(S1), 3–32. doi:10.1111/1467-9922.53222

Duff, P., Peter, A., & Bruns, A. (2006). The use of blogs, wikis and RSS in education: A conversation of possibilities. In *Proceedings Online Learning and Teaching Conference* 2006, Brisbane. Retrieved April 15, 2008, from http://eprints.qut.edu.au

Duffy, P. (2008). Engaging the YouTube Google eyed generation: Strategies for using web 2.0 in teaching and learning. *The Electronic Journal of e-Learning, 6*(2), 119-130.

Duong, T., Uddin, M., Li, D., & Jo, G. (2009). A collaborative ontology-based user profiles system. In Nguyen, N. T., Kowalczyk, R., & Chen, S.-M. (Eds.), *ICCCI 2009, LNAI 5796* (pp. 540–552). Berlin, Germany: Springer-Verlag.

Dutta, S. (2003). Challenges for information and communication technology development in the Arab world. In Cornelius, P., & Schwab, K. (Eds.), *Arab world competitiveness report 2002-2003* (p. 197). New York, NY: Oxford University Press.

Dutta, S., & Mia, I. (2011). *The global information technology report 2010-2011.* INSEAD.

Duvall, C. K. (1999). Developing individual freedom to act: Empowerment in the knowledge organization. *Participation and Empowerment, 7*(8), 204–212. doi:10.1108/14634449910303603

Dwyer, D., Ringstaff, C., & Sandholtz, J. (1991). Changes in teachers' beliefs and practices in technology-rich classrooms. *Educational Leadership, 48*(8).

Ebersbach, A., Glaser, M., & Heigl, R. (2006). *Wiki: Web collaboration.* New York, NY: Springer.

Economy Watch. (2009). *E-business strategy.* Retrieved April 13, 2012 from http://www.economywatch.com/business/e-business-strategy.html

Edington, J., Funk, J., Thorpe, R., & Warrington, J. (2005). *Professional applications of wikis and weblogs. Open source development and documentation project.* Retrieved October 25, 2008, from http://osddp.org/files/issues/WPWikisBlogs.7.pdf

Education Vision 2020. (2000). *Pillars, strategic objectives, projects and implementation programs for UAE education development.*

El Berr, S., & El Mikawy, N. (2004). *Regional perspectives on educational reforms in the Arab countries.* Retrieved August 8, 2011, from http://www.zef.de/fileadmin/webfiles/downloads/projects/el-mikawy/study_regional_perspectives.pdf

Elameer, A., Idrus, R., & Jasim, F. (2011, February). *ICT capacity building plan for The University of Mustansiriyah, Iraq Blended learning project.* Paper presented at 2nd International Conference on e-Learning and Distance Learning, Riyadh, Saudi Arabia. ESCWA- Economic and Social Commission For Western Asia. (2007). *National profile of the information society in Palestine.* New York, NY: United Nations.

Elkhalifa, L. (2004). *InfoFilter: Complex pattern specification and detection over text streams.* Master's Thesis, Faculty of the Graduate School, USA. Retrieved from http://itlab.uta.edu/ITLABWEB/Students/ sharma/theses/Laali.pdf

Elliot, A. C. (2007). *Statistical analysis: Quick reference guidebook with SPSS examples.* London, UK: Sage Publications.

Ellis, R. K. (2009). *Field guide to learning management systems.* ASTD Learning Circuits.

Elmore, R. F. (1996). Getting to scale with good educational practice. *Harvard Educational Review, 66*(1), 1–26.

Elnaggar, A. (2008). Towards gender equal access to ICT. *Information Technology for Development, 14*(4), 280–293. doi:10.1002/itdj.20100

Ely, D. P. (1999). Conditions that facilitate the implementation of educational technology innovations. *Educational Technology, 39*(6), 23–27.

Engstrom, M., & Jewett, D. (2005). Collaborative learning the wiki way. *TechTrends: Linking Research and Practice to Improve Learning, 49*(6), 12–16.

Ennew, C. T., & Fernandez-Young, A. (2005). Weapons of mass instruction? The rhetoric and reality of online learning. *Marketing Intelligence & Planning, 24*(2), 148–157. doi:10.1108/02634500610654008

Erskine, J. A., Leenders, M. R., & Mauffette-Leenders, L. A. (1981). *Teaching with cases.* London, Canada: University of Western Ontario.

Ethridge, R. R., Hadden, C. M., & Smith, M. P. (2000). Building a personalized education portal: Get a behind-the-scenes look at LSU's award-winning system. *Educause Quaterly, 23*(3).

European SchoolNet. (2005). *Assessment schemes for teachers' ICT competence- A policy analysis.*

Evans, M. (1997). *Enterprise resource planning for manufacturers.* Retrieved 29 October, 2008, from http://www.ovum.com/news/erp/erppwp.html

EveryCulture. (n.d.). *Countries and their culture: Culture of the United Arab Emirates.* Retrieved from http://www.everyculture.com/To-Z/United-Arab-Emirates.html

Ewusi-Mensah, K., & Przasnyski, Z. H. (1991). On information systems project abandonment: An exploratory study of organizational practices. *Management Information Systems Quarterly, 15*(1), 67–86. doi:10.2307/249437

Farhat, N. (2008). *The impact of technology on teaching and learning in high schools in the United Arab Emirates.* University of Leicester Doctor of Education.

Farlex Free Dictionary. (2012). *Admission.* Retrieved April 14, 2012, from http://www.thefreedictionary.com/admission

Farmer, S. (2004). *The wide world of wiki: Choosing a wiki for an element of a fully online undergraduate course.* Retrieved March 25, 2008, from http://radio.weblogs.com/0120501/2004/06/10.html

Fawaz, K. A., Salti, Z. A., & Eldabi, T. (2008). *Critical success factors in ERP implementation: A review.* European and Mediterranean Conference on Information Systems, Dubai.

Fayed, G., & Sameh, D. (2006). E-learning model based on Semantic Web technology. *International Journal of Computing & Information Sciences, 4*(2), 63–71.

Ferrell, G. (2003). *Enterprise systems in universities: Panacea or can of worms?* Northumbia University, JISC info Net Publication. Retrieved from http://www.jiscinfonet.ac.uk/InfoKits/infokit-related-files/erp-in-univs.pdf

Fidaoui, D., Bahous, R., & Bacha, N. (2010). CALL in Lebanese elementary ESL writing classrooms. *Computer Assisted Language Learning*, *23*(2), 151–168. doi:10.1080/09588221003666248

Fields, M. (2011). Learner motivation and strategy use among university students in the United Arab Emirates. In Gitsaki, C. (Ed.), *Teaching and learning in the Arab world* (pp. 29–48). Bern, Switzerland: Peter Lang.

Fisher, J. R. Jr. (1997). A culture of contribution. *Executive Excellence*, *14*(1), 16.

Fiszer, E. P. (2004). *How teachers learn best: An ongoing professional development model*. Maryland: Scarecrow Education.

Forawi, S., & Wonderwell, S. (2003). Examining electronic portfolio reflective narratives. *Proceedings of Society of Information Technology and Teacher Education*, Albuquerque, New Mexico, (pp. 2101- 2117).

Forawi, S., Almekhlafi, A., & Almekhlafy, M. (2011-in press). Development and validation of electronic portfolios: The UAE pre-service teachers' experiences. *US-China Education Review Journal*.

Forte, A., & Bruckman, A. (2006). From Wikipedia to the classroom: Exploring online publication and learning. *The Proceedings of the 7th International Conference on Learning Sciences*, Bloomington, Indiana, June 27-July 1, (pp. 182-188). Retrieved May 11, 2008, from http://www.static.cc.gatech.edu/~asb/papers/forte- brunckman-iclso6.pdf

Fouad, K., Harb, H., & Nagdy, N. (2011). *Semantic Web supporting adaptive e-learning to build and represent learner model*. The Second International Conference of E-learning and Distance Education - eLi 2011.

Fox, R., & Pearson, J. (2008). Reviewing ICT research publications in Hong Kong post-secondary education. In Kwan, R., Fox, R., Tsang, P., & Chan, F. T. (Eds.), *Enhancing learning through technology*. Singapore: World Scientific Publishing Co. Pte. Ltd. doi:10.1142/9789812799456_0011

Fox, S., & Mackeogh, K. (2003). Can elearning promote higher-order learning without tutor overload? *Open Learning*, *18*(2), 121. doi:10.1080/02680510307410

Franche, G. (2009). Technology supports learning at the higher colleges of technology. *UAE Journal of Educational Technology and eLearning, 1*. Retrieved on 14th January, 2011, from http://ejournal.hct.ac.ae/issues/2009-issue/technology-supports-learning

Fredricks, J. A., Blumenfeld, P. C., & Paris, A. H. (2004). School engagement: Potential of the concept, state of the evidence. *Review of Educational Research*, *74*(1), 59–109. doi:10.3102/00346543074001059

Friedman, E. A. (1994). A management perspective on effective technology integration: Top ten questions for school administration. *T.H.E. Journal*, *22*(4), 89–90.

Fullan, M. (1982). *The meaning of educational change*. Ontario, Canada: The Ontario Institute for Studies in Education.

Fullan, M. (1993). *Change forces: Probing the depths of educational reform*. London, UK: The Falmer Press.

Fullan, M. (2005). *The new meaning of educational change* (3rd ed.). New York, NY: Routledge Falmer.

Fullan, M., & Stiegelbauer, S. (1991). *The new meaning of educational change*. New York, NY: Teachers College Press.

Fung, A. C. W. (1995). Managing change in ITEM. In Barta, B., Telem, M., & Gev, Y. (Eds.), *Information technology in educational management* (pp. 37–45). London, UK: Chapman and Hall.

Gaad, E., Arif, M., & Scott, F. (2006). Systems analysis of the UAE education system. *International Journal of Educational Management*, *20*(4), 291–303. doi:10.1108/09513540610665405

Garrison, D. R., & Kanuka, H. (2004). Blended learning: Uncovering its transformative potential in higher education. *The Internet and Higher Education*, *7*, 95–105. doi:10.1016/j.iheduc.2004.02.001

Garrison, R., Anderson, T., & Archer, W. (2000). Critical inquiry in text-based environment: Computer conferencing in higher education. *The Internet and Higher Education*, *2*(2-3), 87–105. doi:10.1016/S1096-7516(00)00016-6

Gaska, C. L. (2003). CRM hits the campus. *University Business, 6*(11).

Gauch, G., Speretta, M., & Pretschner, A. (2007). *Ontology-based user profiles for personalized search.* Springer, US.

Gentzoglanis, A. (2007). *International competitiveness in the telecommunications and ICT sectors: A cross-country comparison.* Montreal, Canada: Centre Interuniversitaire de recherché sur la science et la technologie (CIRST).

Germov, J. (2009). *Second opinion: An introduction to health sociology* (4th ed.). Oxford, UK: Oxford University Press.

Gillingham, M. G., & Topper, A. (1999). Technology in teacher preparation: Preparing teachers for the future. *Journal of Technology and Teacher Education, 7*(4), 303–321.

Gilmore, A. M. (1995). Turning teachers on to computers: Evaluation of a teacher development program. *Journal of Research on Computing in Education, 27*(3).

Gitsaki, C. (2012). Teachers' and students' attitudes and perceptions towards the use of laptops for teaching and learning English: A case study. In Gitsaki, C., & Baldauf, R. B. Jr., (Eds.), *The future of applied linguistics: Local and global perspectives* (pp. 122–138). Newcastle, UK: Cambridge Scholars Publishing.

Gitsaki, C., & Alabbad, A. (2011). Attitudes toward learning English: A case study of university students in Saudi Arabia. In Gitsaki, C. (Ed.), *Teaching and learning in the Arab world* (pp. 3–28). Bern, Switzerland: Peter Lang.

Gitsaki, C., & Taylor, R. (2000). *Internet English: WWW-based communication activities. Student book.* Oxford, UK: Oxford University Press.

Glaser, B. G., & Strauss, A. L. (1967). *Teaching and the case method.* Boston, MA: Harvard Business School.

Glass, G. V. (2009). *The realities of K-12 virtual education.* Boulder, CO: Education and the Public Interest Center & Education Policy Research Unit. http://www.cscanada.net/index.php/sll/article/download/1758/2092

Glen, P. (2006). What kind of manager are you, anyway? (Reading 2). In Richardson, G. L., & Butler, C. W. (Eds.), *Readings in information technology project management.* Boston, MA: Thomson Course Technology.

Godwin-Jones, R. (2007). Emerging technologies: Tools and trends in self-paced language instruction. *Language Learning & Technology, 11*(2), 10–17.

Goodwin-Jones, R. (2003). Blogs and wikis: Environments for on-line collaboration. *Language Learning and Teaching, 7*, 12–16.

Gosper, M., Woo, K., Gibbs, D., Hand, T., Kerr, S., & Rich, D. (2003). *The selection and use of learning objects for teaching: Users perspectives. Interaction of IT systems & repositories project report.* Macquarie University & Open Training and Education Network.

Grabe, M., & Grabe, C. (2007). *Integrating technology for meaningful learning* (5th ed.). Boston, MA: Houghton Mifflin.

Grabowski, B. L. (2004). Generative learning contributions to the design of instruction and learning. In Jonassen, D. (Ed.), *Handbook of research on educational communications and technology.* New York, NY: Simon &Shuster Macmillan.

Grant, L. (2006). *Using wikis in schools: A case study.* Retrieved October 15, 2008, from http://www.futurelabe. org.uk/research/tm

Greenfield, R. (2003). Collaborative e-mail exchange for teaching secondary ESL: A case study in Hong Kong. *Language Learning & Technology, 7*(1), 46–70.

Griffiths, J. R., Johnson, F., & Hartely, R. J. (2007). Satisfaction as a measure of system performance. *Journal of Librarianship and Information Science, 39*(3), 142–152. doi:10.1177/0961000607080417

Griffiths, M., & Wood, R. (2000). Risk factors in adolescence: The case of gambling, videogame playing, and the Internet. *Journal of Gambling Studies, 16*(2/3), 199–225. doi:10.1023/A:1009433014881

Grimus, M. (2000). *ICT and multimedia in primary school.* Paper presented at the 16th Conference on Educational Uses of Information and Communication Technologies, Beijing, China.

Griswold, W. (2008). *Cultures and societies in a changing world* (3rd ed.). California: Pine Forge Press.

Guessoum, N. (2006). Online learning in the Arab world. *E-Learn, 10*. Retrieved August 11, 2011, from http://dl.acm.org/citation.cfm?id=1190058&CFID=35185063&CFTOKEN=66842558

Gunawardena, C. N., Lowe, C. A., & Anderson, T. (1997). Analysis of global online debate and the development an interaction analysis model of examining social construction of knowledge in computer conferencing. *Journal of Educational Computing Research, 17*(4), 397–431. doi:10.2190/7MQV-X9UJ-C7Q3-NRAG

Gunawardena, C. N., & McIsaac, M. S. (2004). Distance education. In Jonassen, D. (Ed.), *Handbook of research on educational communications and technology*. New York, NY: Simon &Shuster Macmillan.

Guri-Rosenblit, S. (2005). Distance education and e-learning: Not the same thing. *Higher Education, 49*(4), 467–493. doi:10.1007/s10734-004-0040-0

Guzdial, M. (1999). *Teacher and student authoring on the web for shifting agency*. Retrieved January 25, 2008, from http://coweb.cc.gatech.edu.8888/csl/uploads/24/default.html

Haddara, Z. (2004, Sept.). *Launching the national e-strategy*. Paper presented at The Arab Technology for Development Conference, Beirut, Lebanon.

Haikal, S. (2002, October). *Education and upbringing of the individual in a balanced context between his society and interaction with other communities' cultures: Conceptual analytical study*. Paper presented at KSU's Future School Seminar, Riyadh, Saudi Arabia. ictQatar- Supreme Council of Information and Communication Technology. (2010). *Annual report 2010*. ictQatar, Doha, Qatar.

Hall, A. (2009). *Designing online learning environments for local contexts, as exemplified in the Sultanate of Oman*. Unpublished EdD dissertation, University of Wollongong, Australia. Retrieved August 11, 2011, from http://ro.uow.edu.au/theses/272

Hammad, S., Al-Ayyoub, A., & Sarie, T. (2004). *Combining existing e-learning components: Towards an IVLE: The Medforist knowledge base*. Europe Aid Cooperation Office. Retrieved from http://medforist.grenoble-em.com/Contenus/Conference%20Amman%20EBEL%2005/pdf/15.pdf

Hammer, M. (1990). *Reengineering work: Don't automate, obliterate. Harvard Business Review*. July-August.

Haneline, D., & Aiex, N. (1997). *Asking the right question: Reading assignments and work for writing*. ERIC Clearinghouse on Reading English and Communication, Digest # 122.

Hanna, B. E., & de Nooy, J. (2003). A funny thing happened on the way to the forum: Electronic discussion and foreign language learning. [from http://llt.msu.edu]. *Language Learning & Technology, 7*(1), 71–85. Retrieved September 15, 2010

Hanson, E. M. (1998). Strategies of educational decentralization: Key questions and core issues. *Journal of Educational Administration, 36*(2), 111–128. doi:10.1108/09578239810204345

Hanson-Smith, E. (1999, March/April). CALL environments: The quiet revolution. *ESL Magazine*, 8-12.

Harb, H., & Fouad, K. (2010). *Semantic Web based Approach to learn and update learner profile in adaptive e-learning*. Al-Azhar Engineering Eleventh International Conference, December 23-26.

Hawkridge, D. (1989). Machine-mediated learning in third-world schools. *Machine-Mediated Learning, 3*, 319–328.

Haythornthwaite, C., Kazmer, M., Robins, J., & Shoemaker, S. (2000). *Making connections: Community among computer-supported distance learners*. Paper presented at the ALISE 2000, San Antonio, TX.

Heffernan, J., Linclon, J., & Atwrill, J. (2001). *Writing a college handbook* (5th ed.). New York: WW. Norton and Company Ltd.

Hegazy, A., & Radwan, N. (2010). *Investigating learner perceptions, preferences and adaptation of e-learning services in Egypt*. 2010 International Conference on Education and Management Technology (ICEMT 2010). 978-1-4244-8618-2/10

Heinrich, E., Bhattacharya, M., & Rayudu, R. (2007). Preparation of lifelong learning using e-portfolios. *European Journal of Engineering Education, 32*(6), 653–663. doi:10.1080/03043790701520602

Held, D., McGrew, A., Goldblatt, D., & Perraton, J. (1999). *Global transformations*. Stanford, CA: Stanford University Press.

Henri, F. (1992). Computer conferencing and content analysis. In Kaye, A. R. (Ed.), *Collaborative learning through computer conferencing: The Najaden papers* (pp. 115–136). Berlin, Germany: Springer-Verlag. doi:10.1007/978-3-642-77684-7_8

Herlocker, J. L., Konstan, J. A., Terveen, L. G., & Riedl, J. T. (2004, January). Evaluating collaborative filtering recommender systems. *ACM Transactions on Information Systems*, *22*(1), 5–53. doi:10.1145/963770.963772

Herron, C., Dubreil, S., Cole, S., & Corrie, C. (2000). Using instructional video to teach culture to beginning foreign language students. *CALICO Journal*, *17*(3), 395–427.

Hicks, R. E. (1996). Experiential learning in a postgraduate project management programme. *Education + Training*, *38*(3), 28-38.

Hill, J. R., & Raven, A. (2000). *Creating and implementing web-based instruction environments for community building*. Paper presented at the AECT, Denver.

Hliaoutakis, A., Varelas, G., & Petrakis, E. (2006). MedSearch: A retrieval system for medical information based on semantic similarity. In Gonzalo, J. (Eds.), *ECDL 2006, LNCS 4172* (pp. 512–515). Berlin, Germany: Springer-Verlag. doi:10.1007/11863878_56

Hoesung, K., & Seongjin, A. (2006). A study on the methodology of information ethics education in Youth. *International Journal of Computer Science and Network Security*, *6*(6).

Hofer, B. K., & Pintrich, P. R. (1997). Development of epistemological theories: Beliefs about knowledge and knowing and their relation to knowing. *Review of Educational Research*, *67*(1), 88–140.

Hofstede, G. (1980). *Culture's consequences: International differences in work-related values*. Beverly Hills, CA: SAGE Publications.

Hofstede, G. (1991). *Cultures and organizations: Software of the mind*. New York, NY: McGraw-Hill.

Hofstetter, J. S., & Corsten, D. (2001). *Collaborative new product development - First insights*. Presented at the First International ECR Research Symposium, November 1, 2001, Cambridge.

Hogeboom, M., Lin, F., Esmahi, L., & Yang, C. (2005). Constructing knowledge bases for e-learning using Protégé 2000 and Web services. *Proceedings of the 19th International Conference on Advanced Information Networking and Applications* (AINA'05), 1550-445X/05, IEEE.

Hong-Yan, Y., Jian-liang, X., Mo-Ji, W., & Jing, W. (2009). *Development of domain ontology for e-learning course* (p. 09). IEEE.

Huang, Z., & Palvia, P. (2001). ERP implementation issues in advanced and developing countries. *Business Process Management Journal*, *7*(3), 276–284. doi:10.1108/14637150110392773

Huffaker, D. (2004a). *The educated blogger: Using weblogs to promote literacy in the classroom*. Paper presented at the International Conference of Educational Multimedia in Quebec City, Canada.

Hwang, W.-Y., Shadiev, R., & Huang, S.-M. (2011, May). A study of multimedia web annotation system and its effect on the EFL writing and speaking performance of junior high school students. *ReCALL*, *23*(2), 160–180. doi:10.1017/S0958344011000061

Ibrahim, M., Rwegasira, K. S. P., & Taher, A. (2007). Institutional factors affecting students' intentions to withdraw from distance learning programs in the Kingdom of Saudi Arabia: The case of the Arab Open University (AOU). *Online Journal of Distance Learning Administration*, *5*(1).

IDE. (2000). An emerging set of guiding principles and practices for the design and development of distance education. *IDE: Innovations in Distance Education*. Retrieved March 9, 1999, from http://www.outreach.psu.edu/de/ide/guiding_principles/

Iding, M., Crosby, M. E., & Speitel, T. (2002). Teachers and technology: Beliefs and practices. *International Journal of Instructional Media*, *29*(2), 153–171.

Iedema, R. (2003). Multimodality, resemiotisation: Extending the analysis of discourse as multisemiotic practice. *Visual Communication*, *2*, 29–57. doi:10.1177/1470357203002001751

IEEE. (1997). *Standard for developing software life cycle processes*. New York, NY: IEEE Computer Society.

IELTS. (2010). *Analysis of data*. Retrieved on 14th January, 2011, from http://www.ielts.org/researchers/analysis_of_test_data.aspx

Iheanacho, C. (1997). *Effects of two multimedia computer-assisted language learning programs on vocabulary acquisition of intermediate level ESL students*. (Ph.D) Dissertation: The Virginia Polytechnic Institute and State University. Retrieved from http://scholar.lib.vt.edu/theses/availablended learninge/etd-11397-193839/unrestricted/Clems.pdf

Information Technology Authority- e-Oman. (2010). *Annual report 2010*. Muscat, Oman: Author.

Interact, U. A. E. (2008). *International Association of Universities UNESCO*. Retrieved 12 April, 2012, from http://www.uaeinteract.com/education

Interactive Education. (2007). Retrieved 12 April, 2012 from http://ict-solutions-provider.blogspot.com

Internet World Stats. (2011). *World internet users and population stats*. Retrieved 12 July, 2011, from http://www.internetworldstats.com/stats.htm

Izquierdo, L. O., & Manuel, J. (2007). Information technology and communications (ICT) in academic management of the educational process in higher education. *Pedagogical University Magazine, 12*(1).

Jacobson, M. (1998). *Adoption patterns of faculty who integrate computer technology for teaching and learning in higher education*. Retrieved 15 March, 2005, from http://www.ucalgary.ca/~dmjacobs/phd/phd-results.html

Janmaat, J. G. (2008). Nation building, democratization and globalization as competing priorities in Ukraine's education system. *Nationalities Papers, 36*(1), 1–23. doi:10.1080/00905990701848317

Jarrar, A., & Massialas, G. (1992). Arab Republic of Egypt. In Cookson, J., Peter, W., Sadovnik, A., & Semel, S. (Eds.), *International handbook of educational reform* (pp. 149–167). New York, NY: Greenwood Press.

Jelassi, T., & Enders, A. (2008). *Strategies for e-business: Creating value through electronic and mobile commerce* (2nd ed.). Prentice Hall.

Jewels, T., & Berger, H. (2005, November 30 - December 2). *The effect of organisational culture on knowledge sharing: A comparison of European, United States and Australian behaviour.* Paper presented at the Australasian Conference on Information Systems, Sydney NSW.

Jewels, T., & Ford, M. (2006). The development of a taxonomy of desired personal qualities for IT project team members and its use in an educational setting. *Journal of Information Technology Education, 5*, 285–298.

Jin, H., Ning, X., Jia, W., Wu, H., & Lu, G. (2008). Combining weights with fuzziness for intelligent semantic web search. *Knowledge-Based Systems, 21*, 655–665. doi:10.1016/j.knosys.2008.03.040

Johansson, A., & Gotestam, G. (2004). Internet addiction: Characteristics of a questionnaire and prevalence in Norwegian youth (12–18 years). *Scandinavian Journal of Psychology, 45*, 223–229. doi:10.1111/j.1467-9450.2004.00398.x

Johnson, D. W., & Johnson, R. T. (1996). Cooperation and the use of technology. In Jonassen, D. H. (Ed.), *Handbook of research for educational communications and technology*. New York, NY: Macmillan Library Reference.

Jonassen, D., & Reeves, T. C. (1996). Learning with technology: Using computers as cognitive tools. In Jonassen, D. (Ed.), *Handbook of research for educational communications and technology*. McMillan.

Joo, J.-E. (1999). Cultural issues of the Internet in classrooms. *British Journal of Educational Technology, 30*(3), 245–250. doi:10.1111/1467-8535.00113

JORUM. (2004). *The JISC online repository for [learning and teaching] materials: JORUM scoping and technical appraisal study*. JORUM and the JISC Information Environment. Retrieved April 6, 2006, from http://www.jorum.ac.uk

Junaidu, S., & AlGhamdi, J. (2004). Comparative analysis of face-to-face and online course offerings: King Fahd University of Petroleum and Minerals experience. *International Journal of Instructional Technology, 1*(4), Retrieved August 11, 2011, from http://www.itdl.org/Journal/Apr_04/article03.htm

Jurison, J. (2002). Integrating project management and change management in an IS curriculum. *Communications of the Association for Information Systems, 8*, 26–40.

KAACI- King Abdullah Arabic Content Initiative. (2011). *About the initiative.* Retrieved August 11, 2011, from http://www.econtent.org.sa/AboutInitiative/Pages/AboutInitiative.aspx

Kaaki, S. (2002, October). *Future school management.* Paper presented at KSU's Future School Seminar, Riyadh, Saudi Arabia.

Kalay, Y. E. (2004). Virtual learning environments. *ICT Supported Learning in Architecture and Civil Engineering, 9*, 195–207.

Kampmeier, C. (1998). Organizational culture and leadership. *Journal of Management Consulting, 10*(2).

Karahanna, E., Evaristo, J., & Srite, M. (2005). Levels of culture and individual behaviour: An integrative perspective. *Journal of Global Information Management, 13*(2), 1–20. doi:10.4018/jgim.2005040101

Karake-Shalhoub, Z. (2003). *Profile of the information society in the United Arab Emirates.* ESCWA.

Kasowitz, A. S. (2005). *Teaching and learning with the Internet: A guide to building information literacy skills.* Washington, DC: Office of Educational research and Improvement (ED).

Ke, W., & Wei, K. K. (2005, 7-10 July). *Organizational culture and leadership in ERP implementation.* Paper presented at the Pacific Asia Conference on Information Systems, Bangkok, Thailand.

Keivani, R., Parsa, A., & Younis, B. (2003). Development of the ICT sector and urban competitiveness: The case of Dubai. *Journal of Urban Technology, 10*(2), 19–46. doi:10.1080/1063073032000139688

Keleberda, I., Lesna, N., Makovetskiy, S., & Terziyan, V. (2004). Personalized distance learning based on multiagent ontological system. *Proceedings of the IEEE International Conference on Advanced Learning Technologies (ICALT'04).* ISBN: 0-7695-2181-9/04

Keleberda, I., Repka, V., & Biletskiy, Y. (2006). *Building learner's ontologies to assist personalized search of learning objects.* ICEC'06, August 14–16, 2006, Fredericton, Canada, ACM.

Kern, R. (1996). Computer-mediated communication: Using e-mail exchanges to explore personal histories in two cultures. In M. Warschauer (Ed.), *Telecollaboration in foreign language learning: Proceedings of the Hawai'i Symposium* (pp. 105-109). Honolulu, HI: University of Hawaii, Second Language Teaching & Curriculum Center.

Khan, B. (2003). National virtual education plan: Enhancing education through e-learning in developing countries. *Educomm Asia, 9*(1), 2–5.

Kilmann, R. H., Saxton, M. J., & Serpa, R. (1986). Issues in understanding and changing culture. *California Management Review, 28*, 87–94.

Kim, A. J. (2000). *Community building on the Web.* Berkeley, CA: Peachpit Press.

Kimble, C. (1999). *The impact of technology on learning: Making sense of the research.* Retrieved 25 March, 2005, from http://www.mcrel.org/PDF/PolicyBriefs/5983PI_PBImpactTechnology.pdf

King, P. (2002). *The promise and performance of enterprise systems in higher education.* Respondent Summary. ECAR Respondent Summary.

KISR- Kuwait Institute of Scientific Research. (2005). *State of Kuwait working paper to the World Summit on Information Society.* Retrieved August 11, 2011, from http://www.kisr.edu.kw/webpages/summit/summit.htm#A.%20%20Kuwaits%20Vision%20towards%20the%20Development%20of%20an%20Information%20Society

Klopfer, E., Osterweil, S., Groff, J., & Haas, J. (2009). *Using technology of today in the classroom of today.* The Education Arcade Massachusetts Institute of Technology.

Knowlton, D. S. (2001). *Promoting durable knowledge construction through online discussion.* Mid-South Instructional Technology Conference.

KOB- Kingdom of Bahrain. (2007). *E-government strategy: Summary.* Retrieved August 11, 2011, from http://www.ega.gov.bh/downloads/resources/Strategy-English.pdf

Koh, S., Simpson, M., Padmore, J., Dimitriadis, N., & Misopoulos, F. (2006). An exploratory study of enterprise resource planning adoption in Greek companies. *Industrial Management & Data Systems, 106*(7). doi:10.1108/02635570610688913

Kohut, A., Wike, R., & Horowitz, J. M. (2007). *World publics welcome global trade - But not immigration.* Washington, DC: Pew Research Center.

Komilian, K. (1997). The challenges of globalization. *Journal of Futures Markets, 1*.

Kozma, R. (2006). *Contributions of technology and teacher training to education reform: Evaluation of the world links Arab region in Jordan.* Retrieved from http://www.wlar.org/pdfs/WLAR_Jordan_Evaluation.pdf

Kozma, R. (1991). Learning with media. *Review of Educational Research, 61*(2), 179–221.

Kozma, R. (1994). Will media influence learning: Reframing the debate. *Educational Technology Research and Development, 42*(2), 7–19. doi:10.1007/BF02299087

Kress, G. (2003). *Literacy in the new media age.* London, UK: Routledge. doi:10.4324/9780203164754

Krippendorff, K. (2004). Reliability in content analysis. *Journal of Human Communication Research, 30*(3), 441–433.

Kroutl-Helal, A. (2007). *Creating online collaborative models for ESL writing exercises.* Retrieved December 15, 2008, from http: //www.eadtu.nl/conference-2007/default.html

Kuiper, R. (2005). *ICT and culture.* Retrieved from http://www.cs.ru.nl/mtl/scripties/2005/ReinoutKuiperScriptie.pdf

Kumar, R. (2006). Internet use by teachers and students in engineering colleges of Punjab, Haryana, and Himachal Pradesh States of India: An analysis. *Electronic Journal of Academic and Special Librarianship, 7*(1).

Kumar, K., & Van Hillegersberg, J. (2000). ERP experiences and evolution. *Communications of the ACM, 43*, 23–26.

Kumar, S., & Maija, T. (2008). *Integrating ICT into language learning and teaching: Guide for institution.* New Delhi, India: ODLAC Press.

Laaser, W. (2006). Virtual universities for African and Arab countries. *Turkish Online Journal of Distance Education (TOJDE), 7*(4).

Lal, V. (2002). *The impact of computer-based technologies in Schools-A preliminary literature review.*

Lamb, A., & Johnson, L. (2007). An information skills workout: Wikis and collaborative writing. *Teacher Librarian, 34*(5), 57–59.

Lamb, B. (2004). Wide open spaces: Wikis ready or not. *EDUCAUSE Review, 39*(5), 36–48.

Lam, Y., & Lawrence, G. (2002). Teacher-student role redefinition during a computer-based second language project: Are computers catalysts for empowering change? *Computer Assisted Language Learning, 15*(3), 295–315. doi:10.1076/call.15.3.295.8185

Lasser, W. (2006). Virtual universities for African and Arab countries. *Turkish Online Journal of Distance Education, 7*(4), 147–160.

Laudon, C. K., & Laudon, J. P. (2010). *Management information systems: Managing the digital firm* (11th ed.). Pearson.

Laudon, K. C., & Laudon, J. P. (1996). *Information technology and society* (2nd ed.). Boston, MA: Course Technology, Inc.

Laurillard, D. (2002). *Rethinking university teaching: A framework for the effective use of educational technology* (2nd ed.). London, UK: Routledge. doi:10.4324/9780203304846

Learning Technology Standards Committee. (2002). *Draft standard for learning object metadata* (LOM). IEEE P1484.12.1. IEEE Learning Technology Standards Committee. Retrieved from http://ltsc.ieee.org/wg12/files/LOM_1484_12_1_v1_Final_Draft.pdf

Lebebvre, S., Deaudelin, D., & Loiselle, J. (2006, 27-30 November). *ICT implementation stages of primary school teachers: The practices and conceptions of teaching and learning.* Paper presented at the Australian Association for Research in Education, National Conference, Adelaide, Australia

Lederer, A. L., & Nath, R. (1991). Managing organizational issues in information systems development. *Journal of Systems Management*, November, 23-39.

Lee, D. M. S., Trauth, E. M., & Farwell, D. (1995). Critical skills and knowledge requirements of IS professionals: A joint academic/industry investigation. *Management Information Systems Quarterly*, (September): 313–340. doi:10.2307/249598

Lee, L. (2002). Enhancing learners' communication skills through synchronous electronic interaction and task-based instruction. *Foreign Language Annals*, *35*(1), 16–24. doi:10.1111/j.1944-9720.2002.tb01829.x

Lee, L. (2005). Using web-based instruction to promote active learning: Learners' perspectives. *CALICO Journal*, *23*(1), 139–156.

Lee, M., Tsai, K., & Wang, T. (2008). A practical ontology query expansion algorithm for semantic-aware learning objects retrieval. [Elsevier Ltd.]. *Computers & Education*, *50*, 1240–1257. doi:10.1016/j.compedu.2006.12.007

Lee-Mortimer, A. (1995). Managing innovation and risk. *World Class Design to Manufacture*, *2*(5), 38–42. doi:10.1108/09642369310095210

Leithwood, K., Jantzi, D., & Mascall, B. (2002). A framework for research on large-scale reform. *Journal of Educational Change*, *3*, 7–33. doi:10.1023/A:1016527421742

LeLoup, J. W., Cortland, S., & Ponterio, R. (2007). On the Net listening: You've got to be carefully taught. *Language Learning & Technology*, *11*(1), 4–15.

Levy, M., & Stockwell, G. (2006). *CALL dimensions.* Mahwah, NJ: Lawrence Erlbaum Associates.

Lewis, K., & Bardsley, D. (2010, February 23). University remedial English to end. *The National*. Retrieved 22nd September, 2010, from http://www.thenational.ae/apps/pbcs.dll/article?AID=/20100223/NATIONAL/7022298 04&SearchID=73393762668150

Lewis, A. C. (1998). A new consensus emerges on the characteristics of good professional development. In Tovey, R. (Ed.), *Harvard Education Letter Focus series 4: Professional development* (pp. 12–16). Cambridge, MA: Gutman Library.

Li, F., Li, Y., Wu, Y., Zhou, K., Li, Z., & Wang, X. (2008). *Discovery of a user interests on the internet.* 2008 IEEE/WIC/ACM International Conference on Web Intelligence and Intelligent Agent Technology, DOI 10.1109/WIIAT.2008.18

Li, J. (2010). Learning vocabulary via computer-assisted scaffolding for text processing. *Computer Assisted Language Learning*, *23*(2), 253–275. doi:10.1080/0958822 1.2010.483678

Li, N., & Kirkup, G. (2007). Gender and cultural differences in Internet use: A study in China and the UK. *Computers & Education*, *48*(2), 301–317. doi:10.1016/j.compedu.2005.01.007

Lincoln, Y. L., & Guba, E. G. (1985). *Naturalistic inquiry.* Beverly Hill, CA: Sage.

Ling Zhao, A., Yaobin, L. A., Bin Wang, B., & Wayne Huang, C. (2010). What makes them happy and curious online? An empirical study on high school students' Internet use from a self-determination theory perspective. *Computers & Education*, *56*, 346–356. doi:10.1016/j.compedu.2010.08.006

Lin, J. M.-C., & Wu, Y.-J. (2010). Netbooks in sixth-grade English language classrooms. *Australasian Journal of Educational Technology*, *26*(7), 1062–1074.

Li, S. M., & Chung, T.-M. (2006). Internet function and Internet addictive behavior. *Computers in Human Behavior*, *22*(6), 1067–1071. doi:10.1016/j.chb.2004.03.030

Little, M. C., Wheater, S. M., Ingham, D. B., Snow, C. R., Whitfield, H., & Shrivastava, S. K. (1996). *The university student registration system. A case study in building a high-availability distributed application using general purpose components.* Department of Computing Science, Newcastle University.

Liu, F., Yu, C., & Meng, W. (2002). Personalized web search by mapping user queries to categories. *CIKM '02 Proceedings of the Eleventh International Conference on Information and Knowledge Management* (pp. 558-565). ACM.

Liu, T. Y., & Chu, Y. L. (2010). Using ubiquitous games in an English listening and speaking course: Impact on learning outcomes and motivation. *Computers & Education, 55*(2), 630–643. doi:10.1016/j.compedu.2010.02.023

Logan, R. K. (1995). *The fifth language: Learning a living in the computer age.* Toronto, Canada: Stoddart Publishing Co. Limited.

Lombardo, C., Zakus, D., & Skinner, H. (2002). Youth social action: Building a global latticework through information and communication technologies. *Health Promotion International, 17*(4), 363–371. doi:10.1093/heapro/17.4.363

Lopez, A. K., & Willis, G. D. (2004). Descriptive versus interpretive phenomenology: Their contribution to nursing knowledge. *Qualitative Health Research, 14*(5), 726–735. doi:10.1177/1049732304263638

LTAC Project Group. (2009). *Student induction to e-learning (SIEL).* IMS Global Learning Consortium. Retrieved November 2, 2009, from http://www.imsglobal.org/siel.cfm

Lu, J. (2004). A personalized e-learning material recommender system. *Proceedings of the 2nd International Conference on Information Technology for Application* (ICITA 2004).

Lund, A. (2008). A collective approach to language production. *ReCALL, 20*(1), 35–54. doi:10.1017/S0958344008000414

Lundin, R. (2008). Teaching with wikis: Toward a new worked pedagogy. *Computers and Composition, 25*(4), 432–448. doi:10.1016/j.compcom.2008.06.001

Macaro, E., Handley, Z., & Walter, C. (2012). A systematic review of CALL in English as a second language: Focus on primary and secondary education. *Language Teaching, 45*(1), 1–43. doi:10.1017/S0261444811000395

MacDonald, J. (2008). *Blended learning and online tutoring: Planning learner support and activity design.* Hampshire, UK: Gower Publishing Limited.

Maddux, C. D. (2001). *Educational computing: learning with tomorrow's technologies.* Needham Heights, MA: Allyn & Bacon.

Maddux, C. D., Johnson, D. L., & Willis, T. W. (2001). *Educational computing: Learning with tomorrow's technologies* (3rd ed.). Boston, MA: Allan and Bacon.

Magnan, S., Farrell, M., Jan, M., Lee, J., Tsai, C.-P., & Worth, R. (2003). Wireless communication: Bringing the digital world into the language classroom. In Lomicka, L., & Cooke-Plagwitz, J. (Eds.), *Teaching with technology.* Boston, MA: Thomson & Heinle.

Mak, B., & Coniam, D. (2008). Using wikis to enhance and develop writing skills among secondary school students in Hong Kong. *System, 36*(3), 437–455. doi:10.1016/j.system.2008.02.004

Markus, L. (1983). Power, politics and MIS implementation. *Communications of the ACM, 26*(6), 430–444. doi:10.1145/358141.358148

Martin, A. (2003). Towards e-literacy. In Martin, A., & Rader, H. (Eds.), *Information and IT literacy: Enabling learning in the 21st century* (pp. 3–23). London, UK: Facet.

Marton, F., Hounsell, D., & Entwistle, N. J. (Eds.). (1997). *The experience of learning: Implications for teaching and studying in higher education* (2nd ed.). Edinburgh, UK: Scottish Academic Press.

Marton, F., & Saljö, R. (1976). On qualiatative differences in learning: 1.Outcome and process. *The British Journal of Educational Psychology, 46*, 4–11. doi:10.1111/j.2044-8279.1976.tb02980.x

Masgoret, A.-M., & Gardner, R. C. (2003). Attitudes, motivation, and second language learning: A meta-analysis of studies conducted by Gardner and associates. *Language Learning, 53*, 123–163. doi:10.1111/1467-9922.00212

Maslow, A. H. (1965). *Eupsychian management.* Homewood, IL: Irwin-Dorsey.

Matar, N., Hunaiti, Z., Huneiti, Z., & Al-Naafa, M. (2007). E-learning status in Arab counties. *Proceeding of the International Conference on Information Society (i-Society 2007),* Merriville, Indiana, USA, 7–11 October 2007.

Mavrommatis, G. (2008). Learning objects and objectives towards automatic learning construction. *European Journal of Operational Research, 187*, 1449–1458. doi:10.1016/j.ejor.2006.09.024

McCombs, B. L. (2000). *Assessing the role of educational technology in the teaching and learning process: A learner-centered perspective.* Retrieved September, 2005, from http://www.ed.gov/rschstat/eval/tech/techconf00/mccombs_paper.html

McCombs, B. L., & Vakili, D. (2005). A learner-centered framework for E-learning. *Teachers College Record, 107*(8), 1582–1600. doi:10.1111/j.1467-9620.2005.00534.x

MCIT- Ministry of Communication and Information Technology. (2010). *Yearbook 2010, MCIT- Arab Republic of Egypt.* Retrieved August 11, 2011, from http://www.mcit.gov.eg/Upcont/Documents/MCITYearbook2010.pdf

McKeown, K., Elhadad, N., & Hatzivassiloglou, V. (2003). Leveraging a common representation for personalized search and summarization in a medical digital library. In *Proceedings of the 3 rd ACM/IEEE-CS Joint Conference on Digital Libraries* 2003 (pp. 159-170).

McKinsey & Company. (2005). *Building effective public-private partnerships: Lessons learned from the Jordan Education Initiative.* Retrieved August 22, 2007, from http://www.jei.org.jo/KnowledgeCenterfiles/McKinsey%20Final%20Report_May%2005.pdf

Means, B. (1997). *Critical issue: Using technology to enhance engaged learning for at-risk students.* Retrieved on 21 November, 1999, from www.ncrel.org/sdrs/areas/issues/students/atrisk/400

Means, B., Blando, J., Olson, K., Middleton, T., Morocco, C. C., Remz, A. R., & Zorfass, J. (1993). *Using technology to support education reform.* U.S. Department of Education and Office of Educational Research and Improvement. Retrieved from from http://www.ed.gov/ZipDocs/TechReforms.zip

Means, B. (1994). Technology and education reform: The reality behind the promise. In Means, B. (Ed.), *Introduction: Using technology to advance educational goals.* John Wiley & Sons.

Meyer, K. A. (2004). Evaluating online discussions: Four different frame of analysis. *Journal of Asynchronous Learning Networks, 8*(2), 101–114.

Milligan, C. (1998). *The role of VLEs in the online delivery of staff development. JTAP Report 573 Riccarton.* Edinburgh: Heriot-Watt University.

Mills, S. C. (2006). *Using the Internet for active teaching and learning.* Pearson/Merrill/Prentice Hall

Ministry of Education Portal. (2011). *The United Arab Emirates educational system.* Retrieved from www.moe.ae

Ministry of Education. (1998). *The development of the education system in The United Arab Emirates* (pp. 33–40).

Ministry of Education. (2004, 8-11 September 2004). *The development of education: National report of the Hashemite Kingdom of Jordan.* Paper presented at the International Conference on Education, Geneva, 8-11 September 2004, Geneva.

Ministry of Education. (2005). *Research and development document / IT and MIS department.*

Ministry of Education. (2009). *Students and schools numbers/ academic year 2008-2009.* Official document.

Ministry of Education. (2010). *The strategic vision 2010.* Official Documents, the Ministry of Education in United Arab Emirates.

Mohamed, A. (2005). Distance higher education in the Arab region: The need for quality assurance frameworks. *Online Journal of Distance Learning Administration, 3*(1).

Mohan, P., & Brooks, C. (2003). *Learning objects on the Semantic Web.* The 3rd IEEE International Conference on Advanced Learning Technologies (ICALT'03). ISBN 0-7695-1967-9/03

Molla, A., & Loukis, I. (2005). Success and failure of ERP technology transfer: A framework for analyzing congruence of host and system cultures. *Development Informatics,* working paper no. 24. IDPM, University of Manchester, UK. Retrieved May 13, 2010, from http://www.sed.manchester.ac.uk/idpm/research/publications/wp/di/di_wp24.htm

Montaner, M., Lopez, B., & de la Rosa, J. L. (2003, June). A taxonomy of recommender agents on the internet. *Artificial Intelligence Review, 19*(4), 285–330. doi:10.1023/A:1022850703159

Moore, M. (1989). Three types of interaction. *American Journal of Distance Education, 3*(2), 19–24. doi:10.1080/08923648909526659

Moore, M. G., & Kearsley, G. P. (2005). *Distance education: A systems view.* Belmont, CA: Wadsworth.

Morgado, E., Peñalvo, F., Ruiz, A., Rego, H., & Moreira, T. (2008). *Learning objects for elearning systems. WSKS 2008, CCIS 19* (pp. 153–162). Berlin, Germany: Springer-Verlag.

Morgan, G. (1997). *Images of organisation* (2nd ed.). Thousand Oaks, CA: Sage Publications.

Morris, M. (2005, October). *Organisation, social change and the United Arab Emirates.* Paper presented at the Social Change in the 21st Century Conference, Queensland.

Mostert, M. P., & Sudzina, M. R. (1996, February). *Undergraduate case method teaching: Pedagogical assumptions vs the real world.* Paper presented at the Annual Meeting of the Association of Teacher Educators, St Louis MO.

Moussa, N., & Moussa, S. (2009). Quality assurance of e-learning in developing countries. *Nonlinear Analysis: Theory. Methods & Applications, 71*(12), 32–34.

Muirhead, B., & Haughey, M. (2005). *An assessment of the learning objects, models and frameworks developed by The Learning Federation Schools Online Curriculum Content Initiative Australia.* Adelaide, Australia: The Le@rning Federation.

Muir-Herzig, R. M. (2004). Technology and its impact in the classroom. *Computers & Education, 42*, 111–131. doi:10.1016/S0360-1315(03)00067-8

Mukerji, S., & Jammel, N. K. (2008). Perspectives and strategies towards collaboration in higher education in the GCC Arab States of the Gulf. *Asian Journal of Distance Education, 6*(1), 76–86.

Multimedia in Education - European Parliament STOA. (1997). *The transition from primary school to secondary school.*

Murphy, E. (2009). Theorizing ICTs in the Arab World: Informational capitalism and the public sphere. *International Studies Quarterly, 53*(4), 1131–1153. doi:10.1111/j.1468-2478.2009.00571.x

Murphy, E. (2006). Agency and space: the political impact of information technologies in the Gulf Arab states. *Third World Quarterly, 27*(6), 1059–1083. doi:10.1080/01436590600850376

Murray, G. L. (1999). Autonomy and language learning in a simulated environment. *System, 27*(3), 295–308. doi:10.1016/S0346-251X(99)00026-3

Mu, X., Chen, Y., Li, N., & Jiang, J. (2009). *Modeling of personalized recommendation system based on ontology* (p. 09).

Myers, M. D., & Tan, F. (2002). Beyond models of national culture in information systems research. *Journal of Global Information Management, 10*(1), 24–32. doi:10.4018/jgim.2002010103

Nagel, C., & Staeheli, L. (2010). ICT and geographies of British Arab and Arab American activism. *Global Networks, 10*(2), 262–281. doi:10.1111/j.1471-0374.2010.00285.x

Naidu, S. (2003). Designing instruction for e-learning environments. In Moore, M. G., & Anderson, W. G. (Eds.), *Handbook of distance education.* Mahwah, NJ: Lawrence Erlbaum associates.

Naqvi, S. (2005). Impact of WebCT on learning: An Oman experience. *International Journal of Education and Development using Information and Communication Technology, 2*(4), 18-27.

Naqvi, S. (2008). WebCT and learning (an Oman experience). *International Journal of Computer Science, 35*(4), 4–11.

Nasraoui, O., & Zhuhadar, L. (2010). *Improving recall and precision of a personalized semantic search engine for e-learning.* 2010 Fourth International Conference on Digital Society. ISBN: 978-0-7695-3953-9/10

Nasser, R., & Abouchedid, K. (2000). Attitudes and concerns towards distance education: The case of Lebanon. *Journal of Distance Learning Administration, 3*(4), 1–10.

Navarro, J. C., & Verdisco, A. (2000). *Teacher training in Latin America: Innovations and trends*. Washington, DC: World Bank, Inter-American Development Bank. Retrieved from http://www.iadb.org/sds/doc/EDU-114E.pdf

Neo, M., Neo, T.-K., & Xiao-Lian, G. T. (2007). A constructivist approach to learning an interactive multimedia course: Malaysian students' perspectives. *Australasian Journal of Educational Technology, 23*(4), 470–489.

Nesbit, J., Belfer, K., & Leacock, T. (2003). *Learning object review instrument (LORI 1.5): User manual, e-learning research and assessment network*.

Nesbit, J. C., Belfer, K., & Vargo, J. (2002). A convergent participation model for evaluation of LOs. *Canadian Journal of Learning and Technology, 28*(3), 105–120.

Neven, N., & Duval, N. (2002). *Reusable learning objects: A survey of LOM-based repositories*. Multimedia'02, December 1-6, 2002, Juan-les-Pins, France, ACM. DOI 1-58113-620-X/02/0012

Newby, T. J., Stepich, D. A., Lehman, J. D., & Russell, J. D. (2000). *Instructional technology for teaching and learning: Designing instruction, integrating computers, and using media* (2nd ed.). New Jersey: Merrill/Prentice Hall.

Newman, D. R., Webb, B., & Cochrane, C. (1995). A content analysis method to measure critical thinking in face-to-face and computer supported group learning. *Interpersonal Computing and Technology, 3*(2), 56–77.

Niederhauser, D. S., Salem, D. J., & Fields, M. (1999). Exploring teaching, learning, and instructional reform in an introductory technology course. *Journal of Technology and Teacher Education, 7*(2), 153–172.

Noeth, R. J., & Volkov, B. B. (2004). *Evaluating the effectiveness of technology in our schools*. ACT Policy Report.

Nolan, C. J. P., & Lambert, M. (2001). Information system for leading and managing schools: Changing the paradigm. In Nolan, C. J. P., Fung, A. C. W., & Brown, M. A. (Eds.), *Pathways to institutional improvement with information technology in educational management*. London, UK: Kluwer. doi:10.1007/0-306-47006-3_7

Norris, S. P., & Ennis, R. (1989). Evaluating critical thinking. In Schwartz, R. J., & Perkins, D. N. (Eds.), *The practitioners' guide to teaching thinking series*. Pacific Grove, CA: Midwest Publications.

Noy, N., Sintek, M., Decker, S., Crubézy, M., Fergerson, R., & Musen, M. (2001). *Creating Semantic Web contents with Protégé-2000*. IEEE Intelligent Systems. ISSN: 1094-7167/01

O'Brien, J. A., & Marakas, G. M. (2009). *Management information systems* (9th ed.). Mac Graw-Hill.

O'Hara, M. (2007). Strangers in a strange land: Knowing, learning and education for the global knowledge society. *Futures, 39*(8), 930–941. doi:10.1016/j.futures.2007.03.006

O'Hara, S., & Pritchard, R. (2008). Hypermedia authoring as a vehicle for vocabulary development in middle school English as a second language classrooms. *The Clearing House: A Journal of Educational Strategies. Issues and Ideas, 82*(2), 60–65.

O'Mahony, C. D., Wild, P., Selwood, I. D., Kraidej, L., & Reyes, M. G. (1997). Evaluation strategy for ITEM quality. In Fung, A. C. W. (Ed.), *Information technology in educational management for the school of the future*. Kluwer Academic Publisher.

O'Neill, R., Kingsbury, R., Yeadon, T., & Cornelius, E. T. (1978). *American kernel lessons: Intermediate*. White Plains, NY: Longman.

Oblinger, D. G., & Oblinger, J. L. (Eds.). (2005). *Educating the net generation*. EDUCAUSE.

Oliver, O. (2011, February). *Achieving quality in technology-supported learning: The challenges for e-learning and distance education*. Paper presented at 2nd International Conference on e-Learning and Distance Learning, Riyadh, Saudi Arabia.

Olsson, T. (2003). *Bootstrapping and decentralizing recommender systems*. Licentiate Theses 2003-006, Department of Information Technology. Retrieved from www.it.uu.se/research/reports/lic/2003-006/2003-006.pdf

Oosthoek, H. (1989). Higher education and new technology. *Proceedings of the 5th Congress of the European Association for Research and Development in Higher Education (EARDHE) and the Dutch Association for Research and Development in Higher Education* (CRWO), Pergamon Holland, (pp. 367-378).

Open Directory Project (ODP). (n.d.). Retrieved from http://dmoz.org

Osguthorpe, R. T., & Graham, C. (2003). Blended learning environments: Definitions and directions. *The Quarterly Review of Distance Education, 4*(3), 227–233.

Osunade, O. (2003). *An evaluation of the impact of Internet browsing on students' academic performance at the tertiary level of education in Nigeria.* Retrieved on 15 March, 2007, from http://www.rocare.org/smaligrant nigeria2003.pdf

Pan, J., Zhang, B., Wang, S., & Wu, G. (2007). *A personalized semantic search method for intelligent e-learning.* 2007 International Conference on Intelligent Pervasive Computing. DOI 10.1109/IPC.2007.48

Pan, J., Zhang, B., Wang, S., Wu, G., & Wei, D. (2007). *Ontology based user profiling in personalized information service agent.* Seventh International Conference on Computer and Information Technology. ISBN 0-7695-2983-6/07

Paqueo, V., & Lammert, J. (2000). *Decentralization and school-based management resource kit.* World Bank.

Parker, K., & Chao, J. (2007). Wiki as a teaching tool. *Interdisciplinary Journal of Knowledge and Learning Objects, 3,* 57–72.

Parth, F. R., & Gumz, J. (2003). *Getting your ERP implementation back on track.*

Patton, M. Q. (1980). *Qualitative evaluation methods.* Newbury Park, CA: Sage Publications.

Pedrelli, M., & Emilia, R. (2001). *Developing countries and the ICT revolution.* Luxembourg: European Parliament Directorate General for Research.

Peng, H., Tsai, C., & Wu, Y. (2006). University students' self-efficacy and their attitudes toward the Internet: The role of students perceptions of the Internet. *Educational Studies, 32*(1), 73–86. doi:10.1080/03055690500416025

Peters, E. (2007). Manipulating L2 learners' online dictionary use and its effect on L2 word retention. *Language Learning & Technology, 11*(2), 36–58.

Pew Internet & American Life Project. (2004). *The Internet goes to college: How students are living in the future with today's technology.* Retrieved on May 16, 2008, from http://www.pewinternet.org/pdfs/PIP_College_Report.pdf

Pitkow, J., Schütze, H., & Cass, T. (2002). Personalized search. *Communications of the ACM, 45*(9), 50–55. doi:10.1145/567498.567526

Plante, J., & Beattie, J. (2004). *Connectivity and ICT integration in Canadian elementary and secondary schools: First results from the information and communications technologies in schools survey.* Retrieved September 19, 2006, from http://www.statscan.ca/english/freepub/81-004-XIE/200409/ict.htm

Plomp, T., Anderson, R., & Kontogiannopoulou-Polydorides, G. (1996). *Cross national policies and practices on computers in education.* Dordrecht, The Netherlands: Kluwer Academic Publishers. doi:10.1007/978-0-585-32767-9

Porcaro, D., & Al Musawi, A. (in press). CSCL in higher education in Oman. [EQ]. *EDUCAUSE Quarterly.*

Prensky, M. (2004). Proposal for educational software development sites: An open source tool to create the learning software we need. *Horizon, 12,* 41–44. doi:10.1108/10748120410699585

Prosser, M., & Trigwell, K. (1999). *Understanding learning and teaching: The experience in higher education.* Bury St Edmunds: Open University Press.

Purnell, L. D., & Paulanka, B. J. (2005). *Guide to culturally competent health care.* Philadelphia, PA: F.A. Davis.

QOU- Al Quds Open University. (2007, November). *The future of e-training technologies at Al-Quds Open University.* Paper presented at 13th International Conference on Technology Supported Learning and Training- Online Educa Berlin, Berlin, Germany.

Rabaai, A. (2009). The impact of organizational culture on ERP systems implementations: Lessons from Jordan. *Proceedings PACIS 2009, Pacific Asia Conference on Information Systems.* Association for Information Systems.

Ramsden, P. (1992). *Learning to teach in higher education.* Chatham, UK: Routledge. doi:10.4324/9780203413937

Razmi, J., Sangari, M. S., & Ghodsi, R. (2009, November). Developing a practical framework for ERP Readiness assessment using fuzzy analytic network process. *Advances in Engineering Software.*

Re.ViCa. (2011). *Researching virtual initiatives in education*. The European Commission. Retrieved August 11, 2011, from http://www.virtualcampuses.eu/index.php/

Rees, W. D., & Porter, C. (2002). The use of case studies in management training and development part 1. *Industrial and Commercial Training, 34*(1), 5–8. doi:10.1108/00197850210414026

Reeves, T. C. (1998). *The impact of media and technology in schools*. A research report prepared for the Bertelsmann Foundation. The University of Georgia. Retrieved from http://www.athensacademy.org/instruct/media_tech/reeves0.html

Reeves, T. C., & Oh, E. J. (2007). Generation differences and educational technology research. In Spector, J. M., Merrill, M. D., van Merriënboer, J. J. G., & Driscoll, M. (Eds.), *Handbook of research on educational communications and technology* (pp. 295–303). Mahwah, NJ: Lawrence Erlbaum Associates.

Reformat, M., & Koosha, S. (2009). *Updating user profile using ontology-based semantic similarity*. FUZZ_IEEE 2009, Korea, August 20-24. 978-1-4244-3597-5

Report, A. K. (2009). *Towards productive intercommunication for knowledge*. Mohammed Bin Rashid Al-Maktoum Foundation & United Nations Development Program. Retrieved December 4, 2009, from http://www.arabstrategyforum.org/asf2009en/attachments/144_programme-english.pdf

Resnick, M. (2002). Rethinking learning in the digital age. In G. Kirkman (Ed.), *The global information technology report: Readiness for the networked world* (pp. 32-37). Oxford, UK: Oxford University Press. Richardson, W. (2006). *Blogs, wikis, pod casts and other powerful web tools for classrooms*. Thousand Oaks, CA: Corwin Press.

Resnick, P., Iacovou, N., Sushak, M., Bergstrom, P., & Riedl, J. (1994). Grouplens: An open architecture for collaborative filtering of netnews. *Proceedings of Computer Supported Collaborative Work Conference (CSCW)*, (pp. 175–186). Chapel Hill, NC.

Richards, G., McGreal, R., & Friesen, N. (2002). *Learning object repository technologies for telelearning: The evolution of POOL and CanCore*. InSITE-Where Parallels Intersect. Retrieved December 22, 2005, from http://www.informingscience.org

Richards, G., McGreal, R., Hatala, M., & Friesen, N. (2002). The evolution of learning object repository: Technologies: Portals for On-line objects for learning. *Journal of Distance Education, 17*(3), 67–79.

Rick, J., Guzdial, M., Holloway-Attaway, K. C., & Walker, B. (2002). Collaborative learning at low Cost: Co Web use in English composition. *Proceedings of Computer Support for Collaborative Learning Conference*, Boulder, Co, USA: January 7-11, (pp. 435-442). Retrieved October 25, 2008, from http://coweb.co.gatech.edu.8888/csl/uploads/24/CoWebInEnglish

Rideout, V., Roberts, D. F., & Foehr (2005). *Generation M: Media in the lives of 8-18 year-olds*. Washington, DC: Kaiser Family Foundation.

Rideout, V. J., Vandewater, E., & Wartella, E. A. (2003). *Zero to six: Electronic media in the lives of infants, toddlers and preschoolers*. Kaiser Family Foundation.

Robin, D., & Burke, R. (2002). Hybrid recommender systems: Survey and experiments. *User Modeling and User-Adapted Interaction, 12*(4), 331–370. doi:10.1023/A:1021240730564

Rodrıguez, M., & Egenhofer, M. (2003). Determining semantic similarity among entity classes from different ontologies. *IEEE Transactions on Knowledge and Data Engineering, 15*(2). ISSN: 1041-4347/03

Rogers, E. M. (2003). *Diffusion of innovations* (5th ed.). New York, NY: Free Press.

Romeo, G. (2006). Engage, empower, enable: Developing a shared vision of technology in education. In Khine, M. S. (Ed.), *Engaged learning and emerging technologies*. The Netherlands: Springer Science. doi:10.1007/1-4020-3669-8_8

Romiszowski, A., & Mason, R. (2004). Computer-mediated communication. In Jonassen, D. (Ed.), *Handbook of research on educational communications and technology*. New York, NY: Simon & Shuster Macmillan.

Rovai, A. P., & Jordan, H. M. (2004). Blended learning and sense of community: A comparative analysis with traditional and fully online graduate courses. *International Review of Research in Open and Distance Learning, 5*(2).

Sagarra, N., & Zapata, G. (2008). Blending classroom instruction with online homework: A study of student perceptions of computer-assisted L2 learning. *ReCALL, 20*(2), 208–224. doi:10.1017/S0958344008000621

Said, K. (2007). Arab states strive to bridge the digital divide with the developed world. *Al-Arabiya for Journalism.* Retrieved August 11, 2011, from http://www.al-arabeya.net/index.asp?serial=&f=3392581820

Sanders, C., Field, T., Diego, M., & Kaplan, M. (2000). The relationship of Internet use to depression and social isolation among adolescents. *Journal of Adolescence, 35,* 237–239.

Sarbib, L. (2002). *Building knowledge societies in the Middle East and North Africa.* Retrieved August 20, 2004, from http://www.worldbank.org/k4dmarseille

Saruladha, K., Aghila, G., & Raj, S. (2010). *A survey of semantic similarity methods for ontology based information retrieval.* 2010 Second International Conference on Machine Learning and Computing. ISBN 978-0-7695-3977-5/10

Savage, T. M., & Vogel, K. E. (1996). Multimedia. *College Teaching, 44*(4), 127–132. doi:10.1080/87567555.1996.9932339

Schenker, J. D. (2007). *The effectiveness of technology use in statistics instruction in higher education: A meta-analysis using heirarchical linear modeling.* Ohio: Kent State University.

Schmid, R. F., Bernard, R. M., Borokhovski, E., Tamim, R. M., Abrami, P. C., & Wade, A. (2009). Technology's effect on achievement in higher education: A stage I meta-analysis of classroom applications. *Journal of Computing in Higher Education, 21,* 95–109. doi:10.1007/s12528-009-9021-8

Schoepp, K. (2005). Barriers to technology integration in a technology rich environment. *Learning and Teaching in Higher Education: Gulf Perspectives, 2*(1), 1–24.

Schumpeter, J. A. (1975). *Capitalism, socialism and democracy* [orig. pub. 1942]. New York, NY: Harper and Row.

Schwartz, L., Clark, S., Cossarin, M., & Rudolph, J. (2004). Educational wikis: Features and selection criteria. *The International Review of Research in Open and Distance Learning, 5*(1). Retrieved May 25, 2008, from http://www.irrodl.org/index.php/irrodl/article/view /163/244

SCITC. (2005). *Information and telecommunication technology in Saudi Arabia.* Paper presented at the World Summit on the Information Society, Tunis.

Scott, J. E. (1999, August 13-15). *The FoxMeyer Drugs' bankruptcy: Was it a failure of ERP?* Paper presented at the 5th Americas Conference on Information Systems, Milwaukee, WI.

Scott, J. E., & Vessey, I. (2002). Managing risks in enterprise systems implementations. *Communications of the ACM, 45*(4), 74–81. doi:10.1145/505248.505249

Security Culture. (n.d.). Retrieved from http://security.resist.ca/personal/culture.shtml

Seethamraju, R., & Seethamraju, J. (2008). *Adoption of ERPs in a medium-sized-enterprise-A case study.* The 19th Australian Conference on Information Systems. Sydney.

Senteni, A., & Tamim, R. M. (2011, June). *Online collaboration empowering minds for the future.* Paper presented at the World Conference on Educational Multimedia, Hypermedia & Telecommunications, Lisbon.

Severson, R. (2000). *Fundamentals of information ethics, philosophy and reality* (B.-W. Chu & J.-H. Ryu, Trans.).

Shaheen, S. (2011, February*). Intellectual copyright in an e-learning environment: Towards open textbooks initiative in the Egyptian universities.* Paper presented at 2nd International Conference on e-Learning and Distance Learning, Riyadh, Saudi Arabia.

Shamantha, J. H., Pressini, D., & Meymaris, K. (2004). Technology supported mathematics activities situated within an effective learning environment theoretical framework. *Contemporary Issues in Technology & Teacher Education, 3*(4), 362–381.

Shana, Z. (2009). Learning with technology: Using discussion forums to augment a traditional-style class. *Journal of Educational Technology & Society, 12*(3), 214–228. Retrieved from http://www.ifets.info/journals/12_3/19.pdf

Sharma, M. (2008). *Elgg social networking.* Birmingham, UK: Packt Publishing Ltd.

Shaw, E. (2002). Education and technological capability building in the Gulf. *International Journal of Technology and Design Education, 12,* 77–91. doi:10.1023/A:1013002828605

Shehabat, I., & Mahdi, S. (2008). *E-learning and its impact to the educational system in the Arab world.* 2009 International Conference on Information Management and Engineering. ISBN 978-0-7695-3595-1/09

Shih, Y. (2004). *Extending traditional collaborative filtering with attributes extraction to recommend new products.* Master's Thesis, Department of Business Administration, National Sun Yat-sen University. Retrieved from http://thesis.lib.ncu.edu.tw/ETD-db/ ETD-search/ View_etd?URN=91421019

Shihab, M. (2001). Economic development in the UAE. In Al Abed, I., & Hellyer, P. (Eds.), *United Arab Emirates: A new perspective.* London, UK: Trident Publishing.

Shishakly, R. (2006). *Information technology in education management: Zayed School Information System (ZSIS) implementation model: United Arab Emirates.* Unpublished doctoral dissertation, University of Manchester, Manchester.

Shishakly, R. (2008). Assessment of school information system utilisation in UAE primary school. *Journal of Informing Science and Information Technology, 5*(1), 525–542.

Shuldam, M. (2004). Superintendent conception of instructional conditions that impact teacher technology integration. *Journal of Research on Technology in Education, 36*(4), 319–344.

Silverman, R., & Hines, S. (2009). The effects of multimedia-enhanced instruction on the vocabulary of English-language learners and non-English language learners in pre-kindergarten through second grade. *Journal of Educational Psychology, 101*(2), 305–314. doi:10.1037/a0014217

Simpson, T. L. (2002). Dare I oppose constructivist theory. *The Educational Forum, •••,* 347–354. doi:10.1080/00131720208984854

Singh, H., & Reed, C. (2001). *A white paper: Achieving success with blended learning.* Retrieved from http://www.chriscollieassociates.com/BlendedLearning.pdf

Singh, R., Bernard, M., & Gardeler, R. (2004). Creating sharable learning objects from existing digital course content. *WCAE '04 Proceedings of the 2004 Workshop on Computer Architecture Education.* ACM.

Soares, D. (2008). Understanding class blogs as a tool for language development. *Language Teaching Research, 12*(4), 517–533. doi:10.1177/1362168808097165

Solvie, P. (2008). Use of the wiki: Encouraging pre service teachers' construction of knowledge in reading methods courses. *Journal of Literacy and Technology, 9*(2), 57–87.

Somekh, B., & Davis, N. (Eds.). (1997). *Using information technology effectively in teaching and learning.* London, UK: Routledge.

Son, J.-B. (2007). Learner experiences in Web-based language learning. *Computer Assisted Language Learning, 20*(1), 21–36. doi:10.1080/09588220601118495

Spector, J. M., Merrill, M. D., Van Merrienboer, J., & Driscoll, M. P. E. (Eds.). (2008). *Handbook of research on educational communications and technology* (3rd ed. ed.). London, UK: Lawrence Erlbaum Associates.

Spraul, V. A. (2005). *Computer science made simple.* New York, NY: Broadway Books.

SREB. (2005). *Principles of effective learning objects guidelines for development and use of learning objects for the SCORE Initiative of the Southern Regional Education Board.* Atlanta, GA: Southern Regional Education Board (SREB).

Srivardhana, T., & Pawlowski, S. D. (2007). ERP systems as an enabler of sustained business process innovation: A knowledge-based view. *The Journal of Strategic Information Systems, 16*(1), 51–69. doi:10.1016/j.jsis.2007.01.003

Ssenyonga, A. B. (2007). Americanization or globalization. *Global Envision.* Retrieved from, http://www.globalenvision.org/library/33/1273/

Stepp-Greany, J. (2002). Student perceptions on language learning in a technological environment: Implications for the new millennium. *Language Learning & Technology, 6*(1), 165–180.

Stevenson, D. (1997). *The independent ICT in schools commission—Information and communication technology in UK schools, an independent enquiry.* London, UK.

Stewart, G. (2001, 4th-7th December). *Factors constraining the exploitation of enterprise systems: A research program.* Paper presented at the Australasian Conference on Information Systems, Coffs Harbour, NSW.

Stewart, G., Milford, M., Jewels, T., Hunter, T., & Hunter, B. (2000, Aug 10-13). *Organisational readiness for ERP implementation.* Paper presented at the AMCIS 2000, Long Beach, CA.

Subhi, T. (1999). Attitudes toward computers of gifted students and their teachers. *High Ability Studies, 10*(1), 69–84. doi:10.1080/1359813990100106

Sugiyama, K., Hatano, K., & Yoshikawa, M. (2004). Adaptive web search based on user profile constructed without any effort from users. In *Proceedings 13th International Conference on World Wide Web 2004*, (pp. 675-684). ACM.

Suhail, K., & Barges, Z. (2006). Effects of excessive internet use in undergraduate students in Pakistan. *Cyberpsychology & Behavior, 9*(3), 297–307. doi:10.1089/cpb.2006.9.297

Sullivan, N., & Pratt, E. (1996). A comparative study of two ESL writing environments: A computer-assisted classroom and a traditional oral classroom. *System, 29*(4), 491–501. doi:10.1016/S0346-251X(96)00044-9

Summers, G. J. (2004). Today's business simulation industry. *Simulation & Gaming, 35*(2), 208–241. doi:10.1177/1046878104263546

Sumner, M. (2000). Risk factors in enterprise-wide/ERP projects. *Journal of Information Technology, 15*(4), 317–327. doi:10.1080/02683960010009079

Suthers, D. (2000). Using learning object meta-data in a database of primary and secondary school resources. *Proceedings of the International Conference on Computers in Education*, November 21-24, Taipei, Taiwan.

SVU- Syrian Virtual University. (2011). *Syrian Virtual University prospectus.* Retrieved August 11, 2011, from http://www.svuonline.org/images/upload/File/Prospectus.pdf

Swartz, D., & Orgill, K. (2001). Higher education ERP: Lessons learned. *Educause Quarterly.*

Taha, A. (2007). Networked e-information services to support the e-learning process at UAE University. *The Electronic Library, 25*(3), 349–362. doi:10.1108/02640470710754850

Taibi, D., Gentile, M., & Seta, L. (2005). A semantic search engine for learning resource. *Recent Research Development in Learning Technologies-FORMATEX.* Retrieved July 18, 2008, from www.formatex.org/micte2005/349.pdf

Tamim, R. M. (2009). *YouTube in learner centered classrooms.* Paper presented at the Designing and Delivering Blended Learning in Second Language Context Symposium.

Tamim, R. M. (2010, March). *Learner-centered use of a virtual classroom in the United Arab Emirates.* Paper presented at the Higher Education in the Gulf: Research Insights in Learning and Teaching Symposium, Dubai.

Tamim, R. M., & Senteni, A. (2011, May). *Empowering female learners through blended learning in the UAE.* Paper presented at the Annual Conference of the Comparative and International Education Society Montreal.

Tamim, R. M., Shaikh, K., & Bethel, E. C. (2007, October). *EDyoutube: Why not.* Paper presented at the AACE E-Learn Conference, Quebec.

Tamim, R. M., Bernard, R. M., Borokhovski, E., & Abrami, P. C. (2011). The value of interaction treatments in distance and online learning. In Cooper, J., & Robinson, P. (Eds.), *Small group learning in higher education: Research and practice.* Oklahoma City, OK: New Forums Press.

Tamim, R. M., Bernard, R. M., Borokhovski, E., Abrami, P. C., & Schmid, R. F. (2011). What forty years of research says about the impact of technology on learning: A second-order meta-analysis and validation study. *Review of Educational Research, 81*(3), 4–28. doi:10.3102/0034654310393361

Tam, M. (2000). Constructivism, instructional design, and technology: Implications for transforming distance learning. *Journal of Educational Technology & Society, 3*(2), 50–60. Retrieved from http://www.ifets.info/journals/3_2/tam.html

Tanudjaja, F., & Mui, L. (2002). A contextualized and personalized web search. *Proceedings of the 35th Hawaii International Conference on System Sciences.*

Tatnall, A. (2001). Information technology in educational management: Synthesis of experience. In Visscher, A., Wild, P., & Fung, A. C. W. (Eds.), *Research and future perspectives on computer-assisted school information systems.* Kluwer Academic Publisher.

Tawila, S., Lloyd, B., Bensch, S., & Wassef, H. (2000). *The school environment in Egypt: A situational analysis of public preparatory schools.* Cairo, Egypt: Population Council.

Telba, E. (2010). *E-learning and potential change and development in the Arab Maghreb countries.* Retrieved August 11, 2011, from http://zawaya.magharebia.com/en_GB/zawaya/opinion/257

TeleLearning. (1999). *Working group on professional development: In-service teachers professional development models in the use of information and communication technologies.* Retrieved from http://www.tact.fse.ulaval.ca/ang/html/pdmodels.html

Telem, M. (1996). Recently MIS implementation in school: A system socio-technical framework. *Computers & Education, 27*(2), 85–93. doi:10.1016/0360-1315(96)00021-8

Telem, M., & Avidov, O. (1994). Management information system (MIS) impact on the loosely coupled nature of a high school: A case study. *Planning and Changing, 25*(3-4), 192–205.

Terveen, L., & Hill, W. (2001). Beyond recommender system: Helping people help each other. In Carroll, J. (Ed.), *Human-computer interaction in the new millennium* (pp. 487–509). ACM Press.

The Emirates Center for Strategic Studies and Research (ECSSR). (2011). *Education in the UAE current status and future developments.* Abu Dhabi, UAE: ECSSR.

The New Media Consortium & Educause Learning Initiative (2004). *The Horizon report.*

The New Media Consortium & Educause Learning Initiative (2005). *The Horizon report.*

The New Media Consortium & Educause Learning Initiative (2006). *The Horizon report.*

The New Media Consortium & Educause Learning Initiative (2007). *The Horizon report.*

The New Media Consortium & Educause Learning Initiative (2008). *The Horizon report.*

The New Media Consortium & Educause Learning Initiative (2009). *The Horizon report.*

The New Media Consortium & Educause Learning Initiative (2010). *The Horizon report.*

The New Media Consortium & Educause Learning Initiative (2011). *The Horizon report.*

Thomas, G., & Horne, M. (2004). *Using ICT to share the tools of the teaching trade: A report on open source teaching. British Educational Communications and Technology Agency.* Coventry, UK: BECTA.

Thomas, Z., & Juan, V. (2010). *Towards an ontology for the description of learning resources on disaster risk reduction. WSKS 2010, Part I, CCIS 111* (pp. 60–74). Berlin, Germany: Springer-Verlag.

Thompson, L., & Lamshed, R. (2006). *E-learning within the building and construction and allied trades.* Australia: Australian Government-Department of Education, Science and Training.

Tikly, L. (2001). Globalisation and education in the postcolonial world: Towards a conceptual framework. *Comparative Education, 37*(2), 151–171. doi:10.1080/03050060124481

Timbrell, G., & Chan, T. (2003, 26-28 November). *Investigating enterprise systems issues using a modified Delphi method and exploratory factor analysis.* Paper presented at the 14th ACIS, Perth WA.

Tobin, K., Tippins, D. J., & Gallard, A. J. (1994). Research on instructional strategies for teaching science. In Gabel, D. L. (Ed.), *Handbook of research on science teaching and learning.* New York, NY: Macmillan Publishing Company.

Torlakovic, E., & Deugo, D. (2004). Application of a CALL system in the acquisition of adverbs in English. *Computer Assisted Language Learning, 17*(2), 203–235. doi:10.1080/0958822042000334244

Training Today. (n.d.). *How-to-choose the most effective training techniques.* Retrieved at Http://training.blr.com/employee-training-resources/

Tsai, K., Chiu, T., Lee, M., & Wang, T. (2006). A learning objects recommendation model based on the preference and ontological approaches. *Proceedings of the Sixth International Conference on Advanced Learning Technologies* (ICALT'06). ISBN: 0-7695-2632-2/06

Tseng, C. (2002). *Cluster-based collaborative filtering recommendation approach.* Master's Thesis, Information Management Department, National Sun Yat-sen University. Retrieved from etd.lib.nsysu.edu.tw/ETD-db/ETD-search/getfile?URN=etd-0812103-164119&filename=etd-0812103-164119.pdf

Tsou, W., Wang, W., & Tzeng, Y. (2006). Applying a multimedia storytelling Website in foreign language learning. *Computers & Education, 47*(1), 17–28. doi:10.1016/j.compedu.2004.08.013

Tubaishat, A., Bhatti, A., & El-Qawasmeh, E. (2006). ICT experiences in two different Middle Eastern universities. *Issues in Informing Science and Information Technology, 3,* 668–678.

Turban, E., King, D., McKay, J., Marshall, P., Lee, J., & Viehland, D. (2008). *Electronic commerce: A managerial perspective* (International Edition). Pearson.

Tyack, D. B., & Cuban, L. (1995). *Tinkering toward Utopia: A century of public school reform.* Cambridge, MA: Harvard University Press.

UAE Dubai Modern Education School. (2002). *Multimedia English lab final report.*

UAE TRA. (2011). *ICT initiatives.* Retrieved August 11, 2011, from http://www.tra.gov.ae/tra_initiatives.php

Umble, E. J., & Umble, M. M. (2002, January). Avoiding ERP implementation failure. *Industrial Management.* http://findarticles.com/p/articles/mi_hb3081/is_1_44/ai_n28902999/

UNDP- United Nation Development Program and MCT-Ministry of Communications and Technology. (2004). *National ICT strategy for socio-economic development in Syria.* Damascus, Syrian Arab Republic.

UNESCO Regional Bureau. (2009). *A decade of higher education in the Arab states: Achievements & challenges.* Beirut, Lebanon: UNESCO Regional Bureau for Education in the Arab States.

UNESCO- United Nations Education, Science, and Culture Organization. (2002). *Open and distance learning: Trends, policy and strategy considerations.* UNESCO, France.

United Nations Development Programme (UNDP). (2008). *Website.* Retrieved April 13, 2012, from http://www.undp.org.ae/

United Nations. (2005). *UN millennium development goals.* Retrieved 25 May, 2007, from http://www.un.org/millenniumgoals

United States Government Accountability Office. (2005, May). *Emerging cybersecurity issues - Threaten federal information systems - Report to congressional requesters.*

USA Today. (2006). *'Google,' 'unibrow' added to dictionary.* Retrieved 25 September, 2006, from http://www.usatoday.com/news/offbeat/2006-07-06-new-words_x.htm

USA Today. (2011). *OMG! Online abbreviations make dictionary.* Retrieved 15 April, 2011, from http://www.usatoday.com/tech/news/2011-03-25-online-dictionary_N.htm

Using, S., Ahmad, R., & Taib, S. (2010). *Ontology of programming resources for semantic searching of programming related materials on the Web.* ISBN: 978-1-4244-6716-7110

Van Dusen, G. (2000). Digital dilemma: Issues of access, cost, and quality in media—enhanced and distance education. *ASHE-ERIC Higher Education Report, 27*(5), 1–120.

VandenBos, G., Knapp, S., & Doe, J. (2001). Role of reference elements in the selection of resources by psychology undergraduates. [from http://jbr.org/articles.html]. *Journal of Bibliographic Research, 5,* 117–123. Retrieved October 13, 2001

Vargas, O. B. (2009). *Online education.* Retrieved April 14, 2012, from http://www.centrorisorse.org/proposed-ict-solution-to-educational-problems.html

Vargo, J., Nesbit, J. C., Belfer, K., & Archambault, A. (2003). Learning object evaluation: Computer mediated collaboration and inter-rater reliability. *International Journal of Computers and Applications, 25*(3), 198–205.

Verdugo, D. R., & Belmonte, I. A. (2007). Using digital stories to improve listening comprehension with Spanish young learners of English. *Language Learning & Technology, 11*(1), 87–101.

Visscher, A. J. (1988). The computer as an administrative tool: Problems and impact. *Journal of Research on Computing in Education, 21*(1), 28–35.

Visscher, A. J. (1991). Computer-assisted school administration - The Dutch experience. *Journal of Research on Computing in Education, 24*(1), 91–106.

Visscher, A. J. (1996). Information technology in educational management. *International Journal of Educational Research, 25*(4), 291–296. doi:10.1016/S0883-0355(97)89361-5

Visscher, A. J., & Bloemen, P. P. M. (2001). School managerial usage of computer-assisted school information systems: A comparison of good practice and bad practice school. In Nolan, P., & Fung, A. (Eds.), *Institutional improvement through information technology in educational management*. London, UK: Kluwer.

Wagner, D. A., Day, B., James, T., Kozma, R. B., Miller, J., & Unwin, T. (2005). *Monitoring and evaluation of ICT in education projects: A handbook for developing countries*. Washington, DC: The International Bank for Reconstruction and Development / The World Bank. Retrieved from http://www.infodev.org/en/Document.9.aspx

Wang, H., Lu, C., Yang, J., Hu, H., Chiou, G., Chiang, Y., et al. (2005). An empirical exploration of using wiki in an English as a Second Language course. *Fifth IEEE International Conference on Advanced Learning Technologies*, (pp. 155-157).

Wang, H., Qin, J., & Shao, H. (2009). *Expansion model of semantic query based on ontology*. Second Pacific-Asia Conference Web Mining and Web-based Application, WMWA '09. DOI: 10.1109/WMWA.2009.31

Wang, T., Tsai, K., Lee, M., & Chiu, T. (2007). Personalized learning objects recommendation based on the semantic-aware discovery and the learner preference pattern. *Journal of Educational Technology & Society, 10*(3), 84–105.

Warschauer, M. (2004). *The rhetoric and reality of aid: Promoting educational technology in Egypt.*

Warschauer, M. (1996). Comparing face-to-face and electronic communication in the second language classroom. *CALICO Journal, 13*, 7–26.

Warschauer, M. (2008). Laptops and literacy: A multisite case study. *Pedagogies: An International Journal, 3*, 52–67.

Warschauer, M., & Kern, R. (2000). *Network-based language teaching: Concepts and practice*. Cambridge, UK: Cambridge University Press.

Warschauer, M., & Meskill, C. (2000). Technology and second language learning. In Rosentha, J. (Ed.), *Handbook of undergraduate second language education* (pp. 303–318). Mahwah, NJ: Lawrence Erlbaum.

Warschauer, M., Turbee, L., & Roberts, B. (1996). Computer learning networks and student empowerment. *System, 24*(1), 1–14. doi:10.1016/0346-251X(95)00049-P

Web-Based Education Commission. (2000). The power of the internet for learning: Moving from promise to practice. Final report of the Web-Based Education Commission to the President and Congress of the United States, Washington, D.C. Retrieved April 3, 2006, from http://www.ed.gov/offices/AC/WBEC/FinalReport/WBECReport.pdf

Webster, L., & Murphy, D. (2008). Enhancing Learning through technology: Challenges and responses. In Kwan, R., Fox, R., Tsang, P., & Chan, F. T. (Eds.), *Enhancing learning through technology*. Singapore: World Scientific Publishing Co. Pte. Ltd. doi:10.1142/9789812799456_0001

Wei, C., Huang, C., & Tan, H. (2009). *A personalized model for ontology-driven user profiles mining*. 2009 International Symposium on Intelligent Ubiquitous Computing and Education. ISBN 978-0-7695-3619-4/09

Wenger, E. (1998). *Communities of practice: Learning, meaning, and identity*. Cambridge, UK: Cambridge University Press.

Weyers, J. (1999). The effect of authentic video on communicative competence. *Modern Language Journal*, *83*(3), 339–353. doi:10.1111/0026-7902.00026

Whyte, C. B. (1989). Student affairs-The future. *Journal of College Student Development*, *30*, 86–89.

Wikipedia. (n.d.). *E-learning*. Retrieved from http://en.wikipedia.org/wiki/Elearning

Wikipedia. The free encyclopedia. (2008). *Thomas J. Watson*. Retrieved December 12, 2008, from http://en.wikipedia.org/wiki/Thomas_J._Watson

Wild, P., & Fung, A. C. W. (1996). Evaluation of ITEM for proactive development. In *Proceedings of the 2ⁿᵈ IFIP International Working Conference on ITEM*, July, 1996, Hong Kong Baptist University, Hong Kong.

Wiley, D. (2000). Connecting learning objects to instructional design theory: A definition, a metaphor, and a taxonomy. In D. Wiley (Ed.), *The instructional use of learning objects*. Retrieved November 21, 2005, from http://reusability.org/read/chapters/wiley.doc

Wiley, D. (2003). *Learning objects: Difficulties and opportunities*. Retrieved March 13, 2006, from http://wiley.ed.usu.edu/docs/lo_do.pdf

Wilhelm, A. (2002). Wireless youth: Rejuvenating the net. *National Civic Review*, *91*(3), 293–302. doi:10.1002/ncr.91308

Wilson, B., & Ryder, M. (1996). *Dynamic learning communities: An alternative to designed instructional systems.* (ED397847).

Winograd, T., & Flores, F. (1986). *Understanding computers and cognition: A new foundation for design*. Norwood, NJ: Ablex Publishing Co.

Woo, K., Gosper, M., Gibbs, D., Hand, T., Kerr, S., & Rich, D. (2004). *User perspectives on learning object systems*. The Tenth Australian World Wide Web Conference, SeaWorld Nara Resort, Gold Coast, 3-7 July.

World Bank. (2005). *Monitoring and evaluation toolkit for e-strategies results*. Washington, DC: Global Information and Communication Technologies Department, World Bank.

World Economic Forum. (2004). *Jordan education initiative*. Retrieved from http://www.moict.gov.jo/moict/downloads/JEI_Track_Update_Document.pdf

WorldWideWebSize. (2011). Retrieved July 9ᵗʰ, 2011, from http://www.worldwidewebsize.com/

Wozney, L., Venkatesh, V., & Abrami, P. (2006). Implementing computer technologies: Teachers' perceptions and practices. *Journal of Technology and Teacher Education*, *14*(1), 173–207.

Wurm, K. B. (2005). Andragogy in Survey Education. *Surveying and Land Information Science*, *65*(3), 159–163.

Wu, Y., Chen, Y., & Chen, A. (2001). *Enabling personalized recommendation on the Web based on user interests and behaviors* (p. 01).

Yang, Q., Sun, J., Li, Y., & Cai, K. (2010). *Domain ontology-based personalized recommendation research*. 978-1-4244-5824-0

Yaverbaum, G. J., & Ocker, R. J. (1998). *Problem-solving in the virtual classroom: A study of student perceptions related to collaborative learning techniques*. WebNet 1998 World Conference of the WWW, Internet and Intranet, Orlando, FL.

Ybarra, M., & Mitchell, K. (2004). Youth engaging in online harassment: Associations with caregiver-child relationships, Internet use, and personal characteristics. *Journal of Adolescence*, *27*, 319–336. doi:10.1016/j.adolescence.2004.03.007

Yelland, N. (2001). *Teaching and learning with information and communication technologies (ICT) for numeracy in the early childhood and primary years of schooling*. Australia: Department of Education, Training and Youth Affairs.

Yildirim, Z. (2005). Hypermedia as a cognitive tool: Student teachers' experiences in learning by doing. *Journal of Educational Technology & Society*, *8*(2), 107–118.

Yin, R. (1984). *Case study research: Design and methods*. Beverly Hills, CA: Sage Publications.

Yu, J., & Liu, F. (2010). *A short-term user interest model for personalized recommendation*. 978-1-4244-5265-1/10

Yuan, L., MacNeil, S., & Kraan, W. (2008). *Open educational resources – Opportunities and challenges for higher education*. JISC CETIS.

Yu, Z., Nakamura, Y., Jang, S., Kajita, S., & Mase, K. (2007). *Ontology-based semantic recommendation for context-aware e-learning. UIC 2007, LNCS 4611* (pp. 898–907). Berlin, Germany: Springer-Verlag.

Zain e-Learning Center. (2011). *Welcome to Zain e-learning center*. Retrieved August 11, 2011, from http://www.elearning.uob.edu.bh/

Zamani, B. E., Reza, A., Isfahani, N., & Shahbaz, S. (2010). Isfahan high schools teachers' utilization of ICT. *British Journal of Educational Technology, 41*(5), 92–95. doi:10.1111/j.1467-8535.2009.01000.x

Zhang, H., Song, Y., & Song, H. (2007). Construction of ontology-based user model for Web personalization. In Conati, C., McCoy, K., & Paliouras, G. (Eds.), *UM 2007, LNAI 4511* (pp. 67–76). Berlin, Germany: Springer-Verlag. doi:10.1007/978-3-540-73078-1_10

Zhang, P., & Aikman, S. (2007). Attitudes in ICT acceptance and use. In Jacko, J. (Ed.), *Human-computer interaction* (pp. 1021–1130). Berlin, Germany: Springer-Verlag.

Zhang, T., Gao, T., Ring, G., & Zhang, W. (2007). Using online discussion forums to assist a traditional English class. *International Journal on E-Learning, 6*(4), 623–643.

Zhao, Y. (2003). *What should teachers know about technology: Perspectives and practices*. Greenwich, CT: Information Age Publishing.

Zhuhadar, L., & Nasraoui, O. (2008). *Personalized cluster-based semantically enriched web search for e-learning. ONISW '08, October 30, 2008*. Napa Valley, California, USA: ACM.

Zornada, L., & Velkavrh, T. B. (2005). *Implementing ERP systems in higher education institutions*. 27th International Conference on Information Technology Interfaces ITI 2005, Cavat, Croatia.

Zweig, P., Kaiser, K. M., Beath, C. M., Bullen, C., Gallagher, K. P., & Goles, T. (2006). The information technology workforce: Trends and Implications 2005-2008. *MIS Quarterly Executive, 5*(2), 101–108.

About the Contributors

Fayez Albadri is a well established academic, educator, consultant and manager for over two decades. He holds a Doctorate in Management from MGSM Macquarie University in Sydney Australia, Master's in Intelligent Information Processing Systems from University of Western Australia in Perth, Graduate Certificate in Computer Instructional Design from Edith Cowan University in Perth, and Bachelor's degree in Engineering from University of Westminster in London, UK. He is recognized as IS&T Specialist and Management Expert for his record in managing IT projects, implementing ERP systems and e-business solutions. Dr. Albadri is a pioneer researcher and academic with important contributions in the areas of educational technology and instructional design, entrepreneurship and e-business, IT strategic planning, project management and risk management. He is renowned for his development of (IPRM) the Integrated Project-Risk Model and the introduction of (IELCM) the Integrated ERP Life-Cycle Management approach. He has also delivered numerous seminars and training workshops to hundreds of academics and professionals in Australia and the Middle East.

Salam Abdallah is an IS&T Academic and Practitioner. Dr. Abdallah has a PhD in Information Systems from Australia and a MSc degree from United Kingdom. He has over 15 years of experience working as an IT consultant before joining United Nations Relief and Works Agency for Palestine refugees overseeing ICT facilities and curriculum development at schools and vocational training centers in UNRWA's entire field of operations. He is a founder member of Special Interest Group of the Association of Information Systems: ICT and Global Development. Dr. Abdallah is also an active researcher in the field of Information Systems and has published articles in local and international conferences and journals. Currently he is an Associate Professor of Management Information Systems at Abu Dhabi University, UAE.

Hadia Abudl Fattah has a B.Sc Degree in Nursing from University of Jordan in 1995, Master's in Leadership in Education from Abu Dhabi University (UAE), 2011 and Master's in Health Management from Red Sea University (Sudan), 2008. Ms. Hadia has been working as a faculty in Fatima College for Health Services (FCHS) in the Nursing Program since 2007. She had a key role in laying down the foundations for the course perspective on health culture and nursing & health promotion, designing a set of course objectives and course outline. As a faculty and course coordinator with specific interest in the cultural aspects of education, participating in the book was an opportunity to discuss ICT application in Arab culture which has also helped to fine tune the course content to suit the UAE community culture, belief, and religion, using the latest updates, regarding the taught subject, and emphasizing the importance of having well educated nurses who are equipped with the latest knowledge and skills to utilize ICT effectively to serve the health service at the highest standards possible.

Souha Adlouni was born in Lebanon in 1967. She received her school education in one of the most reputable schools in Lebanon and graduated from the American University of Beirut (AUB) in 1989 with a Bachelor's Degree in Biology in addition to a Diploma in teaching sciences for Secondary levels. Souha moved to UAE in 1990 after getting married where she gained her experience in the field of education. Throughout her years in education she has moved from an elementary teacher to a secondary teacher then to a lead teacher then academic coordinator and finally as a Senior Campus Coordinator. Ms. Adlouni is currently completing her education at Abu Dhabi University for the Master's degree in Educational Leadership, and she is also a member of ASCD educational organization.

Atef Abuhmaid is an Assistant Professor at the Faculty of Educational Sciences, Middle East University, Jordan. His research interests include ICT in Education Reform, e-learning, ICT teacher professional development, blended-learning, and Multimedia. He is the author of "ICT Integration Across Education Systems." He obtained his PhD degree from the University of Technology, Sydney in 2008 and has taught at several universities in Jordan since then.

Abbad Alabbad completed his B.A. degree at King Saud University in Riyadh, Saudi Arabia and continued his higher education in Morgantown in the United States where he finished his Master's in Linguistics and TESOL in 2001. After he completed his Ph.D. at the University of Queensland, Brisbane, Australia, he returned to King Saud University where he manages the English language program. His main research interests are in the area of Computer-Assisted Language Learning, second language acquisition, and online course design.

Sara Al Ahbabi graduated from UAE University (1999) with a Bachelor's degree in Computer Science. She worked as an IT teacher in cycle (3) government schools for 7 years. She joined ADEC (Abu Dhabi Education Council) in 2007 as ICT Educational Advisor for 5 years. Sara organized and run many workshops related in ICT in education to develop and enhance the level in integrating technology in teaching and learning practices. She gained many educational and technological certificates. Sara has experience in working with networking, creating and designing websites and multimedia productions, and establishing many administrative software among several other programs.

Zakieh Al Disi is a Professional Educator, with over 20 years of experience. She worked as a physics teacher then as an educational supervisor for physics and science teachers in Al Ain UAE. Her expertise in curriculum development has helped her in her role in editing and modifying the physics curricula for the UAE schools. Ms. Al Disi also has good expertise in planning and providing professional development for teachers. Her main research interests are related to technology adoption and utilization in the Arab education sector and effective strategies for the development of Education in the UAE and the Arab world. Zakieh holds a Master's degree of Education in Leadership from Abu Dhabi University/ UAE and a Bachelor's degree of Physics and Chemistry from UAE University.

Samia Al Farra is the chief education officer of Taaleem management group. She was the Principal of Amman Baccalaureate School since 1991, which is the first school to offer the IB system in the region. She also served at Al-Bayan School in Kuwait in a variety of positions for 13 years and ultimately as a director. She has served as a chairwoman on many school committees. She was a member of the

Jordan Ministry of Education Council for 13 years. Samia served as a member of the International Baccalaureate Academic Committee from 1997 - 2003, served on the Head of Schools Committee for six years and was a member of the IB Council of Foundation. In 1995 she was awarded by the ECIS for her role in highlighting and promoting international education. She is the founding member of the Middle East International Baccalaureate Association (MEIBA), which she was president of for seven years. She received her doctorate in Education through Bath University, UK. Samia has been serving as an elected for the IBO's Regional Heads Representatives Committee for Africa/Europe and Middle East for the last three years. She served as a keynote speaker on many international conferences on international education. Samia has also chaired and co-chaired accreditation visits for The Council of International Schools and the New England Association of Schools and Colleges.

Zeinab Al Husari holds BSc. in Medical Physics and MBA degree. Ms. Al Husari is a Health Physicist, currently working at UAE Federal Authority for Nuclear Regulation (FANR). Her previous assignments included work at Sheikh Khalifa Medical City (SKMC) for five years and Abu Dhabi Health Authority (ADHA) for two years as a Quality and Radiation Safety Inspector. Her job duties included the participation in the development of UAE nuclear regulations, maintaining international and local radiation safety standards in governmental and private healthcare sectors, performing Quality Control testing on all medical X-ray modalities in order to license hospitals and clinics and delivering radiation safety awareness presentation to medical staff that deal with radioactive materials and X-ray. Zeinab has also participated in some local educational conferences as a speaker and engaged in academic and professional activities reflecting her special interest in radiation protection education, radiation safety, and quality assurance fields.

Salam Omar Ali graduated from Jordan University, with a Bachelor's degree in English Literature. She received her Master's degree in Educational Leadership from Abu Dhabi University. She has an extensive experience in teaching for almost twenty years. She has a special interest in the development of young minds, through utilizing new technologies in her classes. Observing the fun and the positive learning attitudes her students get when applying some educational online games and other technology resources has prompted Ms. Salam to start her research quest in this area trying to enrich the technology file in education. She conducted several research studies to improve the current situation of integrating technology into teaching and learning to develop student's knowledge and skills in the Middle East.

Bashaer Al Kilani, upon the completion of her BSc. Degree in Computer Science, started her career as a Teaching Assistant in United Arab Emirates University - Computer Science Department - in 1993. She joined the Institute of Applied Technology in 2009 after nearly fifteen years of service to Ministry of Education in UAE. During that period she served as an Information Technology Teacher and Advisor and she was actively involved in training courses on integrating ICT in education and the development of E-learning instructional resources. Ms. Kilani published two papers in the Ministry journals on Video Conferencing in Education and Utilizing Technology in Education that were presented in the Ministry conference for promoted advisors in 2004. She has also served as coordinator for 5 years for the ICDL Certification summer project and worked as in 2006 a member of the Organization Committee for the 3rd Specialized English Language Conference (SELC). Since joining IAT, she has served as an ICT Lead Teacher and Head of the ICT Department in Al Ain Campus and as a member of IAT Quality assurance Council.

Ali Al Musawi has obtained his PhD on learning resources and technology centers in 1995 from Southampton University, UK. He works for the Sultan Qaboos University since 1985. At present, he is an Associate Professor at the Instructional and Learning Technologies Department at the College of Education. He has published several journal research articles, chapters in reviewed books, and papers, and contributed in many conferences, symposia, and workshops. He conducted and compiled several national, regional, and Arab studies and reports. He wrote a book on cooperative learning in 1992, contributed in writing another in 2003; and published a book on learning resources and technology centers in 2004. He also translated, with others, two books on e-learning strategies and instructional multimedia to Arabic in 2005 and 2010. Dr. Musawi has several activities in fields of instructional skills development, study skills, instructional design, and web-based design; his interests include Arabic poetry too.

Zainab Al Yahyaei was born in United Arab Emirates in 1983. She received her school education in a government school in Al Ain City. Ms. Al Yahyaei graduated from Higher Colleges of Technology in Al Ain in 2006 with a Bachelor's Degree in teaching English to young learners with a partnership with Melbourne University in Australia. Since 2006, she had been teaching primary students moving between grade one to grade 5. Zainab is currently completing her education at Abu Dhabi University to get a Master's degree in Educational Leadership.

Mohamed Saied El-Sayed was born in Cairo, Egypt. He received his B.A from Faculty of Science, Helwan University (2000) and High Diploma in Business IT from Helwan University Faculty of Computers and Information (2009). At present he is a Lecturer at Helwan University, SCC center, teaching Java, VB, C++, and Unix shell programming to post-graduate students. He worked also as a Webmaster in Helwan University for 2 years. He worked as a Webmaster and Developer for Ain Shams Dental school, and developed E-Learning and website for it with full support for 3 years, then he worked as Senior Web Developer in Canadian International College for 3 years to date. He is a well established and experienced developer in .NET, Java, Action Script, JavaScript, JQuery, SQL, PHP, and ASP classic, having worked in this field for 10 years.

Alia Fares Al Daheri has taught English for nearly ten years at Al Foah School for Girls in Al-Ain. This has followed her graduation in 2002 with a Bachelor's degree in English and Literature from UAE University. She has also a diploma in Professional Teaching from UAE University 2002 and a Master's degree in Educational Leadership from Abu Dhabi University in 2011. She was one of the pioneers in the area to benefit from using Online Learning Communities (OLC) in teaching English as second language classes and this has proven to be a huge success.

Saba Fatma holds a PhD degree in Business Administration from a reputed university in India. Before joining Manipal University, Dubai, UAE, the author was Assistant Professor in Sam Higginbottom Institute of Agriculture, Science, and Technology, India, teaching postgraduate and undergraduate students. The author has several research papers and popular articles in reputed journals and magazines with vast experience of research and guidance of postgraduate students for dissertation. She has attended several national and international conferences in India and UAE. She was instrumental in organizing Faculty Development Program with Prof. David Langley from University of Minnesota as a resource person.

Khalid Fouad received his Master's degree of Artificial Intelligence and Expert Systems. He is currently a PhD candidate in the faculty of engineering at AlAzhar University in Egypt and at the same time working as Lecturer of Computer Science in Taif University in Kingdom of Saudi Arabia (KSA). He is Assistant Researcher in Central Laboratory of Agriculture Expert Systems (CLAES) in Egypt. His research interests are focused on Semantic Web and Expert Systems.

Christina Gitsaki, UNESCO Chair in Applied Research in Education, Sharjah Higher Colleges of Technology, is currently the Executive Treasurer on the AILA Executive Board and past secretary of the Applied Linguistics Association of Australia (2006-2010). She holds a Ph.D. in Applied Linguistics from the University of Queensland in Brisbane, Australia. She has published extensively in the areas of ESL/EFL and CALL. She has authored Second Language Lexical Acquisition (1999), co-authored a textbook Internet English (2000), and edited Language and Languages: Global and Local Tensions (2007) and Teaching and Learning in the Arab World (2011). Her main research interests include second language acquisition and TESOL, the use of ICTs and the Internet for teaching English, Learning Objects design, and CALL applications. Her research papers have been published in numerous refereed journals and books.

Hany Harb is Professor of Computers and Systems Engineering Department - Faculty of Engineering AlAzhar University. He earned Doctor of philosophy (Ph.D.), Computer Science, Illinois Institute of Technology (IIT), Chicago, Illinois, USA (1986). He is the Chairman of Computers and Systems Engineering department, Chairman of Systems and Networks Unit in Al-Azhar University, and Manager of WEB-Based Tansik program. He has supervised many Master's and Doctoral degrees in the Computer Science and Engineering majors.

Ahmed Ibrahim has a BA in English Language & Literature, Mansoura University, Egypt. He also has Master's in Educational Leadership, Abu Dhabi University, United Arab Emirates. He is a TESOL teacher / coordinator in the UAE where he has taught for 18 years in all levels of education starting from primary to secondary. Currently, he is an English Language Teacher / Coordinator in Al Ain Model School. Mr. Ibrahim has also filled the job of an English Language Advisor for two years in Al Ain Model School. Moreover, he has been Coordinator of the School Improvement Plan (SIP) for 3 years.

Ibtisam Jaber has graduated from Ajman University, UAE in 2007 with a Bachelor's degree in Teaching English as Foreign Language. Since then she worked in the Ministry of Education as an English Language teacher at elementary level. Ibtisam has participated in different workshops, seminars, and conferences including Oman International Conference for English Language 2011 in Sultan Qaboos University. She is currently, enrolled in the Master's of Education degree in Educational Leadership in Abu Dhabi University.

Reem Jaber is from Lebanon. She attended Beirut Arab University and got her Bachelor's degree in Business Administration. She started her professional in Lebanon career as an English teacher at Abey and Kabrchmoun Schools. Ms. Jaber is currently working at Al Sanawbar Private School, UAE as an Administrative Supervisor for elementary classes. Her present duties include coordinating and facilitating activities with teachers and students, and interfaces with students' regarding their children progress, safety, and other issues. She acts as a liaison between parents, teachers, students, and administrators. Ms. Jaber is currently pursuing her Master's of Education in Education Leadership at Abu-Dhabi University.

Tony Jewels is currently an Assistant Professor of Enterprise Computing at Dubai's Zayed University. Previously, he taught Management Information Systems courses at UAE University in Al Ain for 3 years and Information Systems courses at Queensland University of Technology's Faculty of Information Technology for 7 years. Now specialising in project management and enterprise information systems, Dr. Jewels has had an extensive career in industry developing advanced inventory management information systems in Australia and Asia. Dr. Jewels has over 70 peer reviewed publications and has been the recipient of many teaching awards culminating in an Australian national teaching award citation.

Manal Khodary is a Lecturer of Curriculum and TEFL at the Curriculum and Instruction Department at the Faculty of Education in Ismailia, Suez Canal University, Egypt. She received her B.A. degree in English from the Faculty of Arts, South Valley University, Egypt, 1988. She has also received General Diploma in Education from the Faculty of Education, South Valley University, Egypt, 1992, and Private Diploma in Education from the Faculty of Education, South Valley University, Egypt, 1993. She obtained her M.Ed. degree in TEFL from the Faculty of Education, Beni Suef University, Egypt, 2001. She received her Ph. D. degree in TEFL from the Faculty of Humanities, Al Azhar University, Cairo, 2004. Dr. Manal has published many articles in international journals and conferences in the area of TEFL, e-learning, educational technology, and curriculum and instruction. She participated in organizing many conferences and workshops. She is currently supervising many M. Ed. and Ph.D. Theses.

Nasim Matar obtained his PhD in 2010 from the school of Computing and Information Technology at Anglia Ruskin University, United Kingdom. He has published 7 different books in Arabic language covering different aspects of computer science, and he has also participated in writing different chapters for many publishers. His research interests are in the field of adaptive e-learning technology, unified e-learning, e-health, and learning object networks (LON). He is currently working in Jordanian universities as a full time Lecturer for the colleges of Computer Science, Computer Information Systems, Management Information Systems, and Education College. His working and research experience has been specifically oriented towards the Middle East region.

Nagdy Nagdy is Professor of Engineering Applications and Computer Systems, Department of Systems Engineering and Computer Engineering - Faculty of Engineering Al-Azhar University. He is working now in Al-Baha Private College of Science, Kingdom of Saudi Arabia (KSA). He received his PhD in 1986 from West-Germany. He has supervised some Master's and Doctoral degrees in the department of Systems Engineering and Computer and Electrical Engineering.

Abbas Naser has been working as a special needs Specialist in the Ministry of Education – Kingdom of Bahrain, for the past 7 years. He deals with students who have both academic and behavioural difficulties. Abbas has facilitated numerous workshops for teachers and parents how to deal with student with learning difficulties. He has a Bachelor's in Psychology –Special Needs and Master's in Educational Leadership.

Mona Nasr is currently Assistant Professor at Information Systems Department, Faculty of Computers and Information, Helwan University. She was born in Cairo, Egypt. She received B.A. degree in Commerce from Faculty of Commerce, Ain Shams University, Egypt (1992), High diploma in "Computers in Commercial Applications," from Faculty of Commerce, Ain Shams University, Egypt (1997), MSc degree in Information Systems from Faculty of Computers and Information, Helwan University, Egypt (2000), and PhD degree in Information Systems from Faculty of Computers and Information, Helwan University, Egypt (2006) - Dissertation Topic: A Proposed Paradigm for Securing Software Mobile Agent Systems. Dr. Mona has published many articles in international journals and conferences in the area of cloud computing, mobile agents, information security and software engineering, e-learning, conceptual mapping, BI, & GIS. She participated in organizing many conferences and workshops, and she is an active reviewer for numerous international journals. She supervised numerous MSc & PhD theses and has the roles of Vice Executive Manager for Development of Students' Assessment System project for Helwan University (8 Faculties), Manager of Student Assessment & Exams Unit at Faculty of Computers & Information, Board Member of the Egyptian Society for Information Systems and Computers Technology and an active member in several societies such as (IEDRC, IACSIT, MJC, TWOWS/OWSD, CSTA, etc.).

Alaa Sadik received his Ph.D. degree in Educational Technology from the Institute for Learning, the University of Hull, United Kingdom, in 2003. He works as an Associate Professor of Instructional technology at South Valley University, Egypt and currently he works at Sultan Qaboos University, Oman. He is interested in the integration of computer and Internet applications in education to improve teaching and learning particularly in developing countries.

Khalidah Saeed is an experienced educator. She has worked as an English teacher for over ten years in public and private schools in both Yemen and the UAE. She holds a Bachelor's degree of Education in English from Hodeidah Unversity/Yemen. She also holds a certificate of Yemeni Sign Language with some experience in teaching English to Special Needs students. She has recently been working as a translator with Cognition Education in Al Naeem Secondary School/UAE since 2009. Her job as provided her with multiple chances to analyze and compare different educational systems. Ms. Saeed is also a post graduate student preparing for her Masters of Education in Leadership.

Rima Shishakly is a Lecturer at The Management Information Systems Department / University of Sharjah, UAE. Dr. Shishakly attained her PhD in Informatics from the University of Manchester in the United Kingdom. Dr. Shishakly also holds a Bachelor's Degree in Mathematics from the University of Damascus and MBA from the Universite Libres de Bruxelles. Dr. Shishakly's main research interest in the Information Systems filed, in particular the use of Information Technology in Educational Institutes and School Information Systems Implementation Models.

Torky Sultan is a now an Emeritus Professor at Faculty of Computers and Information, University of Helwan, Cairo, Egypt. He supervised research work of many students who were awarded Ph.D. and M.Sc. degrees. He chaired conferences and sessions, and presented papers in many international and local conferences. He held important roles in Canada and Middle East institutions including; Helwan

University (Egypt), Misr University of Science and Technology (Egypt), Laurentian University (Sudbury, Canada), Kuwait University (Kuwait), Al Fateh University (Libya), Technical University of Nova Scotia (Halifax, Canada), and University of Cairo (Egypt).

Rana M Tamim is an Assistant Professor at the College of Education at Zayed University. She has a Ph.D. in Educational Technology from Concordia University with an extensive teaching experience in different countries. Dr. Tamim is a collaborator with the Centre for the Study of Learning and Performance in Montreal, Canada, and is an active participant in national and international meetings with an established publication record. Her research interests include: a) knowledge synthesis through systematic reviews particularly meta-analyses, in addition to knowledge dissemination and mobilization for the purpose of improving practice in educational contexts; b) the impact and role played by computer technology in facilitating learning in general and in science education in particular; c) appropriate pedagogical approaches to the integration of technology in the design of learning environments based on student-centered principles; and d) the impact of instructional design of pre-service and in-service training on teachers' attitudes toward technology integration.

Index